# THE FIRST AFRICANS

Africa has the longest record – some 2.5 million years – of human occupation of any continent on earth. For nearly all of this time, its inhabitants have made tools from stone and have acquired their food from its rich, wild plant and animal resources. Archaeological research in Africa is crucial for understanding the origins of humans and the diversity of hunter–gatherer ways of life. This book provides an up-to-date, comprehensive synthesis of the record left by Africa's earliest hominin inhabitants and hunter–gatherers. It combines the insights of archaeology with those of other disciplines, such as genetics and palaeoenvironmental science. African evidence is critical to important debates, such as the origins of stone tool-making, the emergence of recognisably modern forms of cognition and behaviour, and the expansion of successive hominins from Africa to other parts of the world. Africa's enormous ecological diversity and exceptionally long history also provide an unparalleled opportunity to examine the impact of environment change on human populations. More recently, African foragers have been viewed as archetypes of the hunter–gatherer way of life, a view that is debated in this volume. Also examined is the relevance of African hunter–gatherers for understanding the development and spread of food production and the social and ideological significance of rock art.

Lawrence Barham is professor in the School of Archaeology, Classics and Egyptology at the University of Liverpool. A scholar of the evolution of symbolic behaviours, he is the author of *The Middle Stone Age of Zambia* and coeditor of *Human Roots: Africa and Asia in the Middle Pleistocene*. Prof. Barham serves on the Council of the British Institute in Eastern Africa and is editor of the journal *Before Farming: The Archaeology and Anthropology of Hunter-Gatherers*.

Peter Mitchell is professor of African archaeology in the School of Archaeology at the University of Oxford, and Tutor and Fellow in Archaeology at St Hugh's College, Oxford. With a specialisation in the archaeology of southern African hunter-gatherers, but also much broader interests in African archaeology, he is the author of *The Archaeology of Southern Africa* and *African Connections: Archaeological Perspectives on Africa and the Wider World*. Prof. Mitchell is Hon. Secretary of the British Institute in Eastern Africa, serves on the editorial boards of seven leading journals, and is the immediate past president of the Society of Africanist Archaeologists.

# CAMBRIDGE WORLD ARCHAEOLOGY

SERIES EDITOR

NORMAN YOFFEE, *University of Michigan*

EDITORIAL BOARD

SUSAN ALCOCK, *Brown University*
TOM DILLEHAY, *Vanderbilt University*
STEPHEN SHENNAN, *University College, London*
CARLA SINOPOLI, *University of Michigan*

The Cambridge World Archaeology series is addressed to students and professional archaeologists, and to academics in related disciplines. Most volumes present a survey of the archaeology of a region of the world, providing an up-to-date account of research and integrating recent findings with new concerns of interpretation. While the focus is on a specific region, broader cultural trends are discussed and the implications of regional findings for cross-cultural interpretations are considered. The authors also bring anthropological and historical expertise to bear on archaeological problems and show how both new data and changing intellectual trends in archaeology shape inferences about the past. More recently, the series has expanded to include thematic volumes.

CAMBRIDGE WORLD ARCHAEOLOGY

# THE FIRST AFRICANS

## AFRICAN ARCHAEOLOGY FROM THE EARLIEST TOOL MAKERS TO MOST RECENT FORAGERS

LAWRENCE BARHAM

*University of Liverpool*

PETER MITCHELL

*University of Oxford*

CAMBRIDGE
UNIVERSITY PRESS

CAMBRIDGE UNIVERSITY PRESS
Cambridge, New York, Melbourne, Madrid, Cape Town, Singapore, São Paulo, Delhi

Cambridge University Press
32 Avenue of the Americas, New York, NY 10013-2473, USA

www.cambridge.org
Information on this title:www.cambridge.org/9780521612654

First published 2008

Printed in the United States of America

*A catalog record for this publication is available from the British Library.*

*Library of Congress Cataloging in Publication Data*

Barham, Lawrence.
The First Africans : African archaeology from the earliest toolmakers to
most recent foragers / Lawrence Barham, Peter Mitchell.
   p.   cm. – (Cambridge world archaeology)
Includes bibliographical references and index.
ISBN 978-0-521-84796-4 (hardback) – ISBN 978-0-521-61265-4 (pbk.)
1. Antiquities, Prehistoric – Africa.   2. Prehistoric peoples – Africa.
3. Tools, Prehistoric – Africa.   4. Hunting and gathering societies – Africa.
5. Africa – Antiquities.   I. Mitchell, Peter, 1962–   II. Title.   III. Series.
GN861.B37   2008
960′.1 – dc22        2007035552

ISBN   978-0-521-84796-4 hardback
ISBN   978-0-521-61265-4 paperback

# CONTENTS

# LIST OF FIGURES AND TABLES

FIGURES

TABLES

# ACKNOWLEDGEMENTS

A very large number of people have contributed, some of them perhaps unknowingly, to the production of this book. They include, of course, the many students at the Universities of Bristol, Cape Town, Lampeter, Liverpool, and Oxford with whom we have had the pleasure of discussing and debating some of the ideas discussed here, as well as the various colleagues, local people, and funding bodies whom we thank for having facilitated our own field research in Lesotho, Swaziland, and Zambia. Our professional colleagues in researching the archaeology of the first Africans have continually informed our views, even though they may not always agree with them. With apologies to those whom we may have missed, we should particularly like to thank Alison Brooks, Els Cornelissen, Hilary Deacon, Janette Deacon, Savino di Lernia, Elena Garcea, Anne Haour, Kathy Kuman, Paul Lane, David Lewis-Williams, John Parkington, Karim Sadr, Judy Sealy, Dietrich Stout, Christian Tryon, Lyn Wadley, and Eric Wolff. A special thank you is also due to John Brookfield, Sam Challis, Elena Garcea, John Gowlett, Jessica Pearson, and Brian Stewart for having read and commented on parts of the book, and most particularly to Garth Sampson who read it in its entirety and supplied numerous, valued suggestions for improvement. Our gratitude goes, too, to all those colleagues, many of them already mentioned, who have helped us enormously by kindly providing original illustrations or photographs, or permitting us to reuse previously published figures. All are acknowledged individually in the appropriate captions. Any illustrations that remain unacknowledged are our own.

Funding for the initial bibliographical research for this project was generously provided by the British Academy and it is a pleasure to acknowledge its support, not just for this book but also for the wider cause of African archaeology in Britain. That money allowed Lucy Birkett and Marcelle Olivier to spend many hours tracking down and photocopying references in Oxford's by no means straightforward library system and we are grateful to both of them, as well as to Hannes Schroeder for additional help. Rosie Fletcher provided invaluable and calm help in collating the bibliography under pressure of deadlines. Thanks too to Sam Challis, Sue Grice, Sandra Mather, Andrew Wilson, and Suzanne Yee for producing vital artwork, and the financial help that was provided by the University of Liverpool. Further acknowledgement goes to the organisers and participants in several recent conferences that touched on themes relevant to this book. They are the Association of Southern African Professional Archaeologists (Pretoria 2006), the Middle Stone Age of East Africa and Modern Human Origins conference (Nairobi/Addis Ababa 2005), the Pan-African Association for Prehistory (Gaborone 2005), the Society of Africanist Archaeologists (Bergen 2004 and Calgary 2006), the Southern African Association of Archaeologists (Kimberley 2004), the World Archaeological Congress Inter-Congress (Osaka 2006), and the Paleoanthropology Society meeting (Philadelphia 2007). Funding for our attendance came from the British Academy; Japan's Ministry of Culture and Dr Kazunobu Ikeya; St Hugh's College, Oxford; Oxford University's Lockey Bequest; the School of Archaeology, University of Oxford; and the University of Liverpool.

African archaeology in Britain at least is currently in the process of moving from one generation to another. It is appropriate, therefore, that we applaud the contribution of some of the key figures in the field over the past several decades, notably David Phillipson and our late colleagues Desmond Clark, Ray Inskeep, Pat Carter, and John Wymer.

We should also like to acknowledge the editorial support and professional help of colleagues at Cambridge University Press, particularly Simon Whitmore, who edited the Press's archaeology titles when we began, and Beatrice Rehl, who has seen the book through to its publication.

Finally, an enormous thank you to our respective families – Mary, Gloria, and Chiara – for all their help, support, and critique. We hope it has been worth the effort that we have all put in.

December 1st 2006 and June 1st 2007

THE FIRST AFRICANS

# CHAPTER I

# INTRODUCING THE AFRICAN RECORD

Humans have inhabited Africa longer than anywhere else on Earth (see inset). Their history there reaches back beyond the oldest known stone tools to the point, 6 million to 7 million years ago (mya), when the evolutionary lineage that ultimately produced *Homo sapiens* finally diverged from that leading to other **hominids**. Investigating the human past in Africa is thus crucial to developing an understanding of our origins and history as a species, to answering the question, 'What makes (and made) us human'? Responding to this challenge, archaeologists have learned that Africa was not once, but three times, humanity's continent of origin: first, as members of the **hominin** lineage itself; second, as members of the genus *Homo*, which emerged around 2 mya; and most recently with the evolution of anatomically modern humans and their subsequent expansion beyond Africa within the past 100,000 years.

Moreover, an emerging body of evidence indicates that distinctively modern forms of behaviour, specifically the constitution of individual and community life through the use of material objects charged with symbolism and socially ascribed meanings, also have their roots in Africa. Darwin's (1871:161) guarded prediction that 'it is somewhat more probable that our early progenitors lived on the African continent than elsewhere' has been more than borne out by events. Reviewing and assessing the archaeological and fossil evidence that demonstrates this is one of the principal objectives of this book and, as a result, for detailed descriptions of stone artefact assemblages or individual sites, readers should consult the many references that we provide (see J. D. Clark 1982a, Klein 1999, and, for southern Africa, Mitchell 2002a, 2002b as a start here).

---

A NOTE ON DATING

We express absolute dates in one of three ways, depending upon the time frame in question:

**mya and kya** These abbreviations, referring respectively to 'millions of years ago' and 'thousands of years ago', are used for the periods covered by Chapters 3–8, with the switch between them arbitrarily set at 1 million years ago. Where appropriate, for example in discussing some of the archaeological evidence relating to the Pleistocene/Holocene transition, fractional forms of them may be employed. We thus talk of the 8.2 kya event when referring to a well-known, sudden reversion to cooler conditions about 8200 years ago. The 'years ago' here and wherever else these abbreviations are used are provided by techniques such as potassium-argon, uranium-series, and radiocarbon dating. The radiocarbon determinations employed in Chapters 7 and 8 have not been calibrated.

**bp** This abbreviation, meaning 'before present', is employed in Chapters 9 and 10 and is the conventional way of citing uncalibrated radiocarbon dates. The baseline for reference purposes is A.D. 1950 and a date 'bp' is thus so many thousand uncalibrated radiocarbon years older than that.

**B.C./A.D.** We use the Christian calendar in Chapter 10 when referring to archaeological contexts that can be dated by reference to known historical events, including estimates obtained from oral traditions, or by radiocarbon determinations that have been calibrated to calendar years. Our restriction of the use of calibration to this particular period follows from conventional practice in African archaeology and should make comparison with the wider literature easier. For Chapters 7 and 8, it also reflects continuing difficulties with deriving accurate calibration methods beyond the very end of the Pleistocene.

---

However, to examine only those parts of the African archaeological record that relate to the *evolution* of the current human species would be to fall into the trap created by generations of progressivist, evolutionary thought. Contrary to the beliefs of mid-nineteenth-century archaeologists, archaeology does not unequivocally document 'la loi du progrès de l'humanité' celebrated by de Mortillet (1867) and others. Still less does it do so when that progress is defined by the archaeological record of just one part of the world (Europe and the Near East) or by criteria (technological complexity) linked directly to the political and economic power base of nineteenth- and twentieth-century Euro-American societies (cf. Lewis-Williams 1993). The growth of archaeological research, especially in those parts of the world previously colonised by Europe, has shown instead that the Three Age System (Stone, Bronze, Iron) defined by Thomsen (1836) and reformulated in socio-economic terms by Childe (1934) is far from being the universal standard that was once imagined. No more universal is the well-known band-tribe-chiefdom-state succession of social formations popularised by Service (1962) and Sahlins (1968). Such models nonetheless continue to influence how archaeologists and others structure and understand their views of the past (for an example, see Johnson and Earle 1987, and for an Africanist critique, Stahl 1999). Typically, whereas Africa is emphasised in those earlier parts of world prehistory that are necessarily common to all human beings, it is excluded from consideration once the magic moment is reached at which hominins (in more recent syntheses, anatomically modern humans) expanded into Eurasia.[1] All too often, the result is a history that confers universal validity and value on the past of Euro-American societies alone (Stahl 2005a).

Our own view, not surprisingly, is that African societies followed historical trajectories of their own making, trajectories that are not to be forced into the same mould, or measured by the same yardstick, as those of Europe and the Near East (S. McIntosh 1999). It follows that Africa's past has a distinctive value and interest of its own. Moreover, comparing and contrasting that past with what is known from other parts of the world should be directed to their *mutual* critical illumination. These few sentences thus identify the second of this book's goals, the presentation of a new synthesis of the archaeology of more recent hunter-gatherers on the African continent. Themes arising from this that are of wider comparative interest include, but are not limited to:

- the emergence of more sedentary hunter-gatherer societies that emphasised the harvesting of rich, predictable stands of resources such as fish, shellfish, and cereals and that in some cases (but significantly not in all) successfully experimented with the invention of new technologies, such as ceramics and the domestication of wild animal and plant species;
- the integration of Africa's immensely rich rock art record with other components of the archaeological record, its interpretation using insights provided by ethnographic data, and its generation of hypotheses that help explain the production of rock art in quite different parts of the world;
- the many different kinds of relationships that played out between hunter-gatherers and food-producers (horticulturalists, pastoralists, mixed farmers, European settlers) over the past few thousand years.

This last point serves as a reminder that societies depending upon Africa's rich wild plant and animal resources and practising ways of life intimately bound up with them (spiritually as well as economically) survived to the beginning of the twenty-first century. Because of this and the coincidence that they happened to live on the same continent as that in which 'our' (i.e., everyone's) ancestors evolved, groups like the Ju/'hoansi Bushmen[2] have become archetypes of a hunter-gatherer way of life, familiar from introductory anthropology texts, tourism literature, and popular cinema alike. Joined by other African peoples, such as the Hadzabe of Tanzania and the Mbuti foragers of the Congolese rainforests, they have played crucial roles in archaeologists' generation of hypotheses on topics as diverse as the role of carcass scavenging in early hominin subsistence (O'Connell *et al.* 1988), the ways in which hunter-gatherers structure their use of the landscape and thus create a regional archaeological record (Binford 1980), and the viability of human settlement in tropical rainforests in the absence of agriculture (R. Bailey *et al.* 1989).

Rejecting social evolutionary frameworks that once saw contemporary non-Western peoples as conveniently 'frozen' survivals from earlier evolutionary stages (Stahl 2005a) leaves them instead as products of long and complicated histories of their own making (e.g., Wilmsen 1989). This, in turn, raises serious questions about how archaeologists should employ ethnographic observations of such societies to understand the past. Put simply, can this remain a viable project, or were 'hunter-gatherer' societies so radically transformed by centuries of contact with politically and economically more complex, dominating neighbours as to render such usage vain? Examined further in Chapter 10, this is another comparative theme to which Africa makes a vital contribution.

Moreover, the likelihood that the anthropologically studied sample of hunter-gatherers exhausts all the variability that once existed among such societies is itself challengeable from the African evidence. Many hunter-gatherer groups practising delayed-returns economies may, for example, have become successful agriculturalists or pastoralists (but see Chapters 8 and 9 for further discussion of this). Alternatively, the demographic and territorial expansion of food-producers may have displaced hunter-gatherers from many key environments, East Africa's tropical grasslands being a prime example (Foley 1982; Marean 1997). In both instances, the archaeological record of African hunter-gatherers becomes of more than local significance.

Ours is, of course, not the first attempt to collate and make sense of what, in very broad terms, might be called Africa's palaeolithic archaeology, the material evidence left by those whom we choose to term here 'the first Africans', the continent's past hunter-gatherer and hominin inhabitants. The relevant chapters of the magisterial *Cambridge History of Africa* (J. D. Clark 1982a) still stand as a landmark study, even if it is now somewhat dated. More recently, several authors have surveyed the archaeology of Africa as a whole (Connah 2005; D. Phillipson 2005; Stahl 2005b), or in part (H. J. Deacon and Deacon 1999; Mitchell 2002a). All, however, have had to balance the attention accorded matters palaeolithic with that given to the material record created by herders, farmers, and state-level societies. Even where emphasis has been placed on hunter-gatherer and hominin archaeology, coverage is often partial. Sahnouni's (2005a) extremely welcome French-language overview, for example, provides little coverage of post-Acheulean developments in East Africa, less of West and Central Africa. Klein's (1999) *The Human Career*, on the other hand, while superb in synthesising the fossil and archaeological evidence for human evolution, tends to confine African topics and data to the predictable grand moments discussed earlier: the origins of the hominin line, the genus *Homo* and *H. sapiens*, the initial development of stone tool-making, carnivory, and 'modern behaviour'. Moreover, its chronological remit, at least for Africa, scarcely extends more recently than 40,000 years ago. Willoughby's (2007) synthesis of genetic, archaeological, and fossil data relating to the evolution of modern humans is significantly more up-to-date and detailed, but necessarily confined to only a part of the period that is dealt with here.

There is, then, we feel, room for a book that tries to be geographically inclusive rather than exclusive and for one that avoids arbitrarily dividing the past at the evolution of modern humans, the emergence of 'Later Stone Age' technologies, or the initiation of food-production. Moreover, combining in a continuous narrative the archaeology of earlier hominins with that of more recent hunter-gatherers opens up possibilities for comparison across the entire length and breadth of humanity's presence on the African continent. How though to structure such a book? Reviewing the history of previous research helps answer this question.

## RESEARCH HISTORIES

The history of archaeology in Africa divides into five phases, broadly paralleling those noted elsewhere (Trigger 1989). Each has its own characteristics, but the concerns of one have continued into and helped shape its successors, making the overall effect cumulative rather than revolutionary. Robertshaw (1990a) remains the best overview, amplified by the work of Stahl (1999), Schlanger (2002, 2003, 2005), and others, as well as by a growing recognition of the potential of museum collections and their associated documents (Mitchell 2002b; Milliken 2003). Lack of space prevents us from expanding on such observations to analyse in detail the social, political, and economic forces that have moulded the evolution of palaeoanthropology and hunter-gatherer archaeology in Africa.

Rather, we emphasise the development of those key methodologies, analytical techniques, and classificatory systems that continue to order archaeologists' views of the first Africans.

Whether in myth, in oral histories, or by reference to material objects, African societies have doubtless always preserved and constructed accounts of their pasts. Even when not the work of people practising a hunter-gatherer lifeway, such accounts often refer to hunter-gatherers, for example as aboriginal owners of the land or as inventors of the technologies and social mores seen as crucial to a civilised way of life (Woodburn 1988). Rock paintings and stone tools may thus be acknowledged as the work of earlier inhabitants (Roberts 1984), with most (all?) communities recognising that the present is not the same as the past, however telescoped their understandings of chronology and historical change may be (Suzman 2004). Systematic exploration of ancient landscapes and sedimentary deposits for material evidence of past human societies and a proper recognition of the time depth that this unveils are, however, much more recent phenomena, products of archaeology's early nineteenth-century crystallisation as a scientific discipline.

## *The Antiquarian Phase of African Archaeology*

That crystallisation took place primarily in Europe, but it was informed and shaped by European experience of the rest of the world, including Africa (Gosden 1999). Occasional reports of rock art, stone tool use, or the lifeways of Africa's indigenous inhabitants were succeeded from the mid-1800s by a second phase of more serious research, stimulated in part by the rapidly developing acceptance of the genuineness and deep antiquity of stone artefacts in Europe itself. In colonial South Africa, for example, the emerging Anglophone intellectual community included several individuals who collected stone tools from about 1860, taking advantage of their connections with leading figures in Victorian academic and/or political circles to dispatch them to London for confirmation and publication (Mitchell 2002b; Dubow 2004). By the early 1880s, enough of them had been found to warrant the first attempts at regional synthesis (Gooch 1881), broadly contemporary with the initiation of the collection of stone tools in Egypt (Milliken 2003), Algeria (Gowlett 1990), and French West Africa (de Barros 1990). Matching the pace of European colonisation, work in the Congo Basin began at about the same time (de Maret 1990). The Horn followed a little later (Brandt and Fattovich 1990), as did East Africa (Robertshaw 1990b), where Gregory's (1921) discovery of the Olorgesailie site and Reck's (1914) investigations of fossil mammal assemblages at Olduvai Gorge foreshadowed the region's later significance.

For the most part, this antiquarian phase was undertaken by amateurs, many of them geologists, military men, or colonial administrators, something that continued to hold true in many areas until after the Second World War. Perhaps inevitably, discovery and classification were often practised as ends in themselves, the goal being to define stages of human cultural development that could be readily compared with the 'master sequence' for the Palaeolithic already known from Europe (Daniel 1975). Museums there and in North America sought out African artefacts to illustrate this evolutionary account, and from the early twentieth century, their curators took an active role in this. Miles Burkitt from Cambridge University, Henri Breuil, founder of the influential Francophone journal *L'Anthropologie*, and Oxford's Henry Balfour all paid numerous visits to Africa, for example, using their friendships with locally based researchers and their attendance at conferences to inform themselves, build collections, and report home (e.g., Burkitt 1928). However, with the exceptions of southern Africa and the sophisticated five-year research programme in Algeria of North America's Logan Museum (Sheppard 1990:179–184), professionally trained archaeologists able or willing to conduct fieldwork within Africa remained thin on the ground. The lingering influence of the Piltdown forgery, European prejudice in favour of a European origin for the genus *Homo*, and real difficulties in dating the African record compounded this problem, along with a genuine scarcity of financial resources and the widespread assumption that Africa had always been the helpless recipient of external influences. The true significance of finds like the archaic *H. sapiens* fossil from Broken Hill (Kabwe), Zambia (Woodward 1921), or the Taung child type-specimen of *Australopithecus africanus* (Dart 1925), was therefore missed (Gowlett 1990).

## Africa's 'Three Ages'

Despite this, the 1920s did see determined efforts to establish a more distinctively African past, efforts that help define a third phase in the continent's archaeology. Already at the beginning of the twentieth century, Haddon (1905) had advocated the development of an indigenous terminology, free from assumptions about connections with Europe. This bore fruit when Goodwin and van Riet Lowe (1929) invented their own 'Three Age System' for Africa's hunter-gatherer and hominin past. Eschewing the Eurasian usages 'Lower, Middle, and Upper Palaeolithic', they produced a groundbreaking synthesis of southern African prehistory that employed local 'cultural' names organised under the umbrella terms 'Earlier, Middle, and Later Stone Ages', the latter explicitly linked to surviving hunter-gatherers (the Kalahari Bushmen). As Schlanger (2002) shows, however, this was as much a deliberate act of liberation from European systems of thought (and political control) as a change driven by empirical observations, and its rapid extension north of the Zambezi was not independent of South African political ambitions. Regrettably, however, North Africa and Egypt stayed outside the ambit of the new terminology, retaining Eurasian (often specifically French) terms despite early recognition of the specifically African nature of their own industries (e.g., Reygasse 1922). The result was (and to some degree remains) an unhelpful divide between the archaeologies of supra- and sub-Saharan Africa (Garcea 2005), one founded on little more than the combination of 'scholarly tradition and geographic distance' (Klein 1999:407) with North Africa's close *historical* connections with Europe and the Near East.[3]

A necessary concern of mid-twentieth-century archaeology was the development of sound chronologies within which to locate the material being found. Following European example, river terraces from the Nile to the Vaal were favoured in the search for long stratigraphic sequences, along with the exposures that Louis Leakey (1934) had now begun to explore at Olduvai Gorge. He and Wayland (1929), working in Uganda, were among the first to employ a succession of pluvial (wetter) and interpluvial (drier) climatic phases as a dating tool, a succession thought to

correspond to the glacial/interglacial sequence then known in
Europe. Long influential, this pluvial hypothesis took decades to suc-
cumb to advances in geological understanding (Flint 1959), by which
point the professionalisation of African archaeology had advanced
considerably, through the creation of museums[4] and the appoint-
ment of archaeologists to them, universities, and government depart-
ments. J. Desmond Clark (1990), in what is now Zambia, John
Goodwin and Clarens van Riet Lowe in South Africa (J. Deacon
1990a), and Francis Cabu in the then Belgian Congo (de Maret 1990)
were among this first cohort, but the detailed excavation of former
hominin or hunter-gatherer living sites and the systematic recovery of palaeoenvironmental samples remained the exception rather
than the rule. Moreover, whereas the importance of raw material
choice and manufacturing techniques was increasingly recognised,
explanations of cultural change and variability remained dominated
by notions of diffusion and migration that afforded little room to
these and other factors (Schlanger 2003). Reconstructing cultural-
historical frameworks thus persisted as the key theme of this third
phase of African archaeological research, with different stone tool
industries typically thought of as the product of different peoples or
races; Louis Leakey's (1931) work in Kenya is a classic example of
this approach, which prevailed well into the 1950s through most of
the continent.

## The Expansion of African Archaeology

The Second World War marked an important breakpoint for African
archaeology (Gowlett 1990:24), just as it did for the continent's history as a whole. One important step was the 1947 inaugural meeting
in Nairobi of the Pan-African Congress of Prehistory and Related
Studies, which remains the largest grouping of Africanist archaeologists. Another crucial development was the scientific acceptance
of the authenticity as hominins of not just the Taung child, but
also of the various gracile and robust australopithecines discovered
by Robert Broom in South Africa's Sterkfontein Valley since 1936
(Le Gros Clark 1952). Recognition also spread of the importance
of excavating past occupation floors with minute attention to stratigraphic and contextual detail, especially where organic remains were

well preserved. Excavations at Kalambo Falls (J. D. Clark 1969), Olduvai (M. Leakey 1967), and Isimila (Howell *et al.* 1962) were in the vanguard of this movement. Along with the discovery at Olduvai between 1959 and 1961 of the type-fossils of *Paranthropus boisei* and *Homo habilis*, the result was to make Africa the undisputed international focus for early hominin research. East Africa, in particular, took the lead here, propelled by the applicability of the newly invented potassium-argon dating technique to the volcanic geology of the Rift Valley and by massive injections of funding for work in areas beyond Olduvai, such as the Omo Valley, Lake Turkana, and Ethiopia's Afar depression (Reader 1988). Because it is these areas that provide our chronometric framework, they still eclipse the pioneering work of Ruhlmann, Biberson, Arambourg, and others in Morocco and Algeria (Gowlett 1990), and South Africa's own fossil riches, overshadowed until recently by the country's isolation during the apartheid era and the relative difficulties of excavating and dating the relevant limestone cave deposits (Mitchell 2002a).

The post-1959 explosion of fieldwork in East Africa transformed palaeolithic archaeology as a whole, promoting the development of new dating techniques, the invention of the new science of taphonomy to investigate how archaeological sites form (Behrensmeyer and Hill 1980), multi-disciplinary research projects, problem-oriented research, and innovative ways of understanding the finds that archaeologists make. Experimental reproduction of stone tool technologies and refitting of stone artefacts came to be widely applied, more recently partnered by microwear and residue analyses. Experimental approaches to faunal analyses were also developed, substantially informed by ethnoarchaeological research among groups still pursuing a hunter-gatherer lifeway such as the Ju/'hoansi of the northwest Kalahari Desert or the Hadzabe of northern Tanzania (e.g., Yellen 1977; O'Connell *et al.* 1988). An emphasis on replacing a narrow focus on archaeological sites with a more holistic embrace of ancient landscapes also took hold (Foley 1981), with the work of Glynn Isaac (1989) and his students leading this and many of the other changes we have just noted.

Broadly similar comments apply to the archaeology of more recent hunter-gatherers, an obvious crossover being the avowed emphasis in some 1960s ethnographic studies on using observations from anthropological fieldwork to understand earlier phases of human evolution (R. Lee and DeVore 1968, 1976). Mirroring developments in European and North American archaeologies, stone tool typologies rapidly lost importance as radiocarbon dating became available, while increasing emphasis was placed on situating the archaeological record within an ecological framework (J. D. Clark 1959). Palaeoenvironmental reconstruction, how people adapted to ecological change, and how they organised their exploitation of the landscape were among the questions that dominated hunter-gatherer archaeology from the 1960s into the 1980s, and that remain important today. Models of seasonal mobility (e.g., Parkington 1977), in particular, encouraged the development of regional approaches. So, too, did the impending loss of sites to major dam projects, as in Lower Nubia (Adams 1977), and the new fieldwork opportunities arising from the surge in interest in Africa's past in the immediate post-independence era. Most importantly of all, perhaps, was the archaeological training of a growing number of indigenous African scholars. As a result, and especially in countries such as Ethiopia, Kenya, and Tanzania, many more African archaeologists have been enabled to make significant fieldwork and research contributions of their own.

Thus far, we have avoided discussing rock art, the most visually compelling legacy of the first Africans. Our reason has been that until the 1970s (and, in many cases, much later) its study was conducted along the same typological and cultural-historical terms as Stone Age archaeology generally (Davies 1990). Though the relevance of copying and recording a fast-disappearing heritage was recognised in the nineteenth century, and more accurate quantitative records were undertaken from the 1960s, little substantive progress was possible while interpretation remained locked in an empiricist embrace (Lewis-Williams and Loubser 1986). In southern Africa, this started changing when Patricia Vinnicombe (1976) and David Lewis-Williams (1981) grasped the critical importance of nineteenth- and twentieth-century Bushman ethnography for understanding not only what rock imagery meant, but also how it helped underpin the social relations of hunter-gatherer societies. Three decades of research have amplified and confirmed this perspective, while opening up others that complement the dominant position of a shamanistic model (Lewis-Williams 2003; Lewis-Williams and Pearce 2004). Though such 'insider' viewpoints are not as well developed in other regions (e.g., Tanzania or the Sahara), their relevance in southern Africa extends far beyond rock art alone. This is because Lewis-Williams (1982) was instrumental in precipitating a significant refocusing of effort in hunter-gatherer archaeology as a whole. Workers such as Lyn Wadley (1987) and Aron Mazel (1989) turned to Kalahari ethnography to investigate very different aspects of the past from those emphasised by earlier ecological models – gift-exchange, gender relations, and the socialised organisation of space among them. Though problems persist in operationalising some of their ideas in the archaeological record (Barham 1992), there is little doubt that hunter-gatherer archaeology in southern Africa now partakes of many of the broader concerns of post-processual archaeology as a whole, especially its interests in researching social relations, ideology, and cosmology. Furthermore, and unlike hunter-gatherer archaeologies in most of the rest of Africa, it is also linked to the ethnography of one particular set of contemporary peoples.[5]

## Recent Decades

Here, then, a fifth phase of archaeological research can be defined, one more concerned in Mazel's (1987:519) phrase with 'people-to-people' instead of 'people-to-nature' questions. Because of its parallels with changes in the wider discipline, however, similar concerns have also become part of the archaeological agenda in other areas of the continent (e.g., Kent 1998). Partly taking their lead from global surveys by Wolf (1982) and Headland and Reid (1989), another recent theme is the investigation of the relations between societies organised at different levels of social, economic, and political complexity. The well-known 'Kalahari debate' is just one example (Wilmsen and Denbow 1990). It is partnered by equally celebrated controversies over whether Africa's equatorial rainforests could have supported forager communities before the local emplacement of food-production (cf. Bahuchet *et al.* 1991; R. Bailey *et al.* 1991; Blench 1999a), and over the nature of the relationships between hunter-gatherers, farmers, and pastoralists in East Africa (e.g., Chang 1982). All three areas have seen growing recognition of the complexity of such mosaics, of the active role of hunter-gatherer communities in constructing them, and of the historical contingency of the ethnographic record (C. Kusimba and Kusimba 2005; Reid 2005).

The past twenty years have also demonstrated that African archaeology is crucial to understanding not just the origins of the hominin line and the genus *Homo*, but those of *Homo sapiens* itself. Excavation of anatomically modern human fossils from several parts of the continent gained momentum in the 1960s and 1970s, but attracted widespread attention only when correctly dated and coupled with observations on the DNA of contemporary populations. The launch of the 'Out-of-Africa' hypothesis of modern human origins and its effective supplanting of a multi-regional alternative (Klein 1999) have since placed sub-Saharan Africa at the centre of global research into our species' origins. Accumulating evidence for a comparable antiquity for many crucial behavioural traits has amplified this shift, dethroning claims for an Upper Palaeolithic 'revolution', and with them much of the primacy previously accorded the western Eurasian record (McBrearty and Brooks 2000). Perversely, however, the increasing interest in fieldwork focused on what has historically been termed the Middle Stone Age runs the risk of leaving the archaeology of more recent Later Stone Age hunter-gatherers high and dry (Mitchell 2005a).

Such references testify to just how deeply embodied Goodwin and van Riet Lowe's (1929) terminology remains within archaeological thinking about the African past, despite the fact that independent, radiometric dating methods and the discrediting of diffusion as an explanation for cultural change have removed much of the need for this kind of stadial labelling. Indeed, more than four decades ago, dissatisfaction with the stadial terminology of Earlier, Middle, and Later Stone Ages, its confusion of cultural-stratigraphic (technological) and time-stratigraphic (chronological) implications, and the over-enthusiastic generation and generalisation of cultural names, often on the basis of poorly described or small samples, all marked the 1965 Burg-Wartenstein conference on African prehistory (Bishop and Clark 1967). Accordingly, this attempted to dispense not just with the three 'Ages', but also with the two '**Intermediate Periods**' invented at the 1955 Third Pan-African Congress on Prehistory to accommodate assemblages thought to be transitional between them. Instead, the Burg-Wartenstein participants proposed that *archaeological occurrences* be grouped into temporal and/or spatial *phases* that could themselves be collated into *industries* and *industrial complexes*. Garth Sampson's (1974) synthesis of the Stone Age archaeology of southern and south-central Africa was one of the few efforts made to give life to this new taxonomy, which otherwise fell on fairly deaf ears. One reason, as Parkington (1993) points out, was that none of the new terms was defined in any useful fashion; a second was that although hierarchical frameworks of the kind being proposed might work well in describing geological sequences, they were less well-suited to writing history. Opaque, monolithic boxes of the Burg-Waternstein or Goodwin and van Riet Lowe (1929) Three Age kind inevitably play down the heterogeneity, diversity, and internal contradictions of human societies, encouraging a view of people as little more than 'undifferentiated puppets buffeted around by the elements' (Parkington 1993:96). At best, change occurs because people respond to environmental pressure or to some minimally specified form of intercultural contact. At worst, it just happens: The total neglect in one major synthesis of southern African prehistory of any consideration of how the Middle Stone Age turned into the Later Stone Age and what that might signify is a case in point. The one literally succeeds the other by the turning of a page (cf. Volman 1984; J. Deacon 1984a).

## AN ALTERNATIVE FRAMEWORK

### Modes of Stone Tool Production

As a result, our preference here has been to avoid as much as possible classificatory systems that imply the existence of rigid boundaries or homogenise the experiences of human societies within each Age. Instead, and in keeping with other recent overviews of the African past (D. Phillipson 2005; Willoughby 2007), we describe broad patterns in stone tool making not in terms of successive Ages, but

TABLE 1.1. *Modes of Lithic Technology. (After J. G. D. Clark 1969).*

| Mode 1 | Pebble tool industries using choppers and simple flakes struck off pebbles |
| Mode 2 | Bifacially worked tools (handaxes and cleavers) produced from large flakes or cores |
| Mode 3 | Flake tools produced from prepared cores |
| Mode 4 | Punch-struck blades that may be retouched into various specialised tool types |
| Mode 5 | Microlithic components of composite artefacts, often backed or otherwise retouched |

using the five successive modes proposed by Grahame Clark (1969; see Table 1.1). This simultaneously avoids suggesting that particular kinds of stone tools were necessarily associated with specific, bounded periods of time, while minimising the need to compartmentalise what were probably more gradual, continuous processes of change. Moreover, applying one particular term (for example, Mode 4) to a given industry does not imply that other techniques were not also used, only that this was the defining strategy employed. That the system forms a **homotaxial** sequence of global applicability offers another advantage if one wishes to draw comparisons between African patterns of stone tool use and those found on other continents.

Though we prefer Clark's mode system to any stadial model, we have not followed Inskeep's (1967:571) advice and dispensed entirely with cultural labels to write 'in terms of what is known for particular areas through particular periods of time'. Much as we sympathise with this 'plea for historical narrative' (Parkington 1993:95), an important concern in writing this book has been to offer as detailed an introduction to the subject as possible. Inevitably, therefore, we refer to the names of particular industries, seeing no conflict between doing this when needing to discuss the detailed cultural history of individual regions and our use of the mode system when writing about much higher order entities. We do, however, willingly acknowledge that only rarely (and then mostly in the late **Quaternary**, when spatial and temporal controls are most precise) is there any reason to suspect that the entities defined by archaeologists might even partially coincide with the social groupings observable to anthropologists or experienced by the first Africans themselves.

## The Global Marine Isotope Record as a Chronological Framework

We have, however, chosen to emphasise our difference from many other treatments of the African palaeolithic in one further way, and that is in how we structure our account chronologically (Box: Note on dating. See Page 2). Rejecting the conventions left us by Goodwin and van Riet Lowe (1929), and convinced of the need for a framework that is independent of definitions grounded in the similarities and differences between stone tools or other forms of material culture, we opt for a narrative that is linked to the global signatures of climate change reflected in the marine and terrestrial oxygen isotope records. As discussed in Chapter 2, this is not without problems, for example in securely correlating land-based African palaeoenvironmental evidence with the isotope data recorded in deep-sea cores or icecores. However, its advantages are many. We emphasise just four:

- The changes registered in the oxygen isotope record are global in nature and relate directly to processes of palaeoclimatic change that affected precipitation, temperature, and seasonality patterns across the African continent. They thus provide a framework that can structure and compare observations from many different parts of Africa.
- Such a framework facilitates investigation of one of the key questions that archaeologists and palaeoanthropologists may wish to ask of the African record, namely the consequences of recurrent cycles of climatic and environmental change on the distribution, settlement history, and social and subsistence systems of human populations. Africa, with its enormous ecological diversity and unparalleled duration of human habitation, is ideally suited for such studies.
- The global isotope record encourages comparisons between African (where aridity is a major limiting factor) and higher latitude environments (where cold is more important) or other

drought-affected regions (such as Australia). Such possibilities have already begun to be explored in edited volumes for the **Last Glacial Maximum** (Gamble and Soffer 1990; Soffer and Gamble 1990) and the **Pleistocene/Holocene** transition (Straus *et al.* 1996), but their scope is far from being exhausted. We pick up on them ourselves at several points in our text.

- Using the global isotope record to structure chronology can help expose and critique some of the standard divisions of African prehistory. By drawing together into a single discussion material that is often kept apart within self-contained stadial syntheses, it becomes possible to evaluate evidence and develop explanations outside the constraints imposed by older, lithocentric terminologies; for example, when considering the emergence of recognisably modern forms of behaviour or of tool-kits and lifeways similar to those of ethnographically recorded hunter-gatherers.[6] Moreover, this kind of chronological framework may contribute toward expanding the boundaries of archaeological research and interpretation along the lines set out by Stahl (1999). In particular, and as far as hominin and hunter-gatherer archaeology are concerned, it may help question narratives of progression and inevitability, resituate foragers and other 'non-complex' societies within archaeologies of the more recent past, and emphasise diversity, rather than uniformity, when building models.

We are aware, of course, that basing our chronological narrative on the global record of climate change exposes us to the charge of environmental determinism. Like Gamble (1999), we do not believe that even the earliest hominins were mere automata, blindly responding to ecological pressures. Far from it. They, and much more so, behaviourally modern humans and thus all hunter-gatherers of the past several tens of thousands of years, lived not just in a world 'given' them by their environment, but also in one that they created and recreated through their own actions and those of their fellows. Nevertheless, at the levels of technology and spatiotemporal resolution with which we are dealing, it is our conviction that the chronological framework employed here can help make sense of the available evidence and simultaneously act as a productive research strategy for understanding much (but not all) of the variability in hominin and hunter-gatherer behaviour (cf. Gamble 1986; Kelly 1995). Note, however, the caveat. As outlined by G. Bailey (1983) among others, we believe that the framework needed to recognise, study, and explain processes of change operating over centuries or millennia is different from that used when seeking agency and individual social actors on timescales of decades or less. To do this successfully poses a major methodological challenge, demanding greater engagement with short-lived sites, horizontally rather than vertically oriented excavations, and a willingness and capacity to make sense of small samples (Parkington 1993). For the moment, this is most readily done for the relatively recent past when ethnographic, historical, and linguistic sources can be integrated with the archaeological record to provide fine-grained social data. Archaeologists' ability to identify and analyse quite precise 'moments in time' at even the earliest stages of the archaeological record (Roe 1980), coupled with the insights provided by evolutionary psychology and primate research (e.g., Byrne and Whiten 1988; Whiten 1997), nevertheless also offer scope for making the analysis of older timeframes more individually focused than has often been the case. As attempts continue to pull down the curtain of interpretation between an active, socially created past and a passive one of 'adaptation to the conditions of existence' (Gamble 1999:5), we expect that Africa, with the longest human history of all, will have much to contribute towards reconciling the search for long-term process with the quest for social agency.

## SOURCES AND STRUCTURE

### Other Disciplinary Sources

Archaeology is only one, though by far the most important, of the sources we employ in developing the narrative that follows. A wide range of palaeoenvironmental research provides crucial information on how African environments and climates have changed over time. The fossil record itself, in all its complexity, is also critical and we concur with Foley (2002:18) that over the long stretches of prehistory with which we deal, 'the behavioural and biological are deeply intertwined'. However, for lack of space and (we readily confess) relevant expertise, we avoid detailed description of hominin fossils, just as we leave the elaboration of models of hominin behaviour grounded in evolutionary biology to those better qualified than ourselves (e.g., Foley 1995). The importance of drawing upon such models and expertise is nonetheless a constant feature of much of what follows. So, too, is the rapidly advancing field of molecular genetics, which has already led to massive revisions in understanding the evolutionary relationships of primate taxa and helped demonstrate the recency of *Homo sapiens'* expansion out of Africa. As the analysis of DNA from living populations gathers pace and the study of ancient DNA from archaeological specimens becomes routine, we anticipate major new discoveries in this field, leading to fresh insights into the history, movement, and demography of past populations.

For the much more recent past, historical linguistics provides a further body of evidence, partly through the reconstruction of vocabulary elements in languages that, though now extinct, were ancestral to those spoken today, partly through tracing connections between speakers of one language and those of another via shared vocabulary and/or grammatical structures. Where such work can be convincingly linked to other datasets, especially archaeological ones, it can substantially enhance understandings of past hunter-gatherer societies. Whether languages necessarily change in ways analogous to a family tree model of ancestry and descent is, however, debated, whereas the key assumption of **glottochronology**, namely that languages change at a constant rate, is almost certainly misplaced (Borland 1986).

If historical linguistics can, at best, contribute to understanding the prehistory of the past several thousand years, written documents and oral traditions have relevance to an even smaller fraction of the time span with which this book deals. With virtually no exceptions, written sources relating to African hunter-gatherers are a product of Europe's colonial intrusions south of the Sahara, intrusions that began in the later fifteenth century. Indigenous oral histories sometimes reach back beyond this, but in other cases struggle to exceed one or two hundred years ago. With appropriate cautions, however, such as the competence of European observers in African languages and the degree to which their observations and African oral traditions were designed to serve particular political agendas or justify particular contemporary social arrangements, both kinds of sources have much to offer. This is particularly so, of course, where the focus lies on investigating relations between hunter-gatherer societies and others, be they African farmers and herders or European settlers.

One further source of evidence is crucial – the ethnography of Africa's surviving hunter-gatherer peoples. As the incomparable archive built up by Wilhelm Bleek and Lucy Lloyd from their late-nineteenth-century /Xam Bushman teachers shows (e.g., Hollmann 2005a), much vital information predates the dawn of professional field-based anthropological research. Since taking hold after the Second World War, however, this has been extensive, with Kalahari Bushmen, Hadzabe, Ogiek, and a wide range of tropical forest foragers all subjects of ethnographic study. Surveys by Barnard (1992), Kent (1996), Biesbrouck *et al.* (1999), and others illustrate the diversity of the groups themselves and of the work that has been undertaken in collaboration with them. With both archaeologists and anthropologists increasingly aware of the importance of considering the historical context and origins of ethnographic observations and of avoiding widespread generalisations from a few well-known case studies, it seems likely that relations between the two disciplines will strengthen, rather than diminish, in coming decades.

## SOME CLARIFICATIONS

A few further clarifications are needed. First, we should make clear that our own direct field experience is limited to the south and south-central regions of the continent, specifically Zambia, Swaziland, and Lesotho. Despite this, we have, of necessity and through the kindness of colleagues, travelled extensively elsewhere, visiting many of the archaeological sites of greatest relevance to our narrative, though sadly the Sahara and the Congo Basin still remain unvisited. Moreover, although both native speakers of English, we also read fluently in French, Italian, and Afrikaans. Given that we are writing in English, we emphasise English-language sources in the bibliography, indicating, however, wherever appropriate or helpful, sources in other languages as well. In so doing, we hope to have gone some way toward avoiding a purely Anglophone bias in our outlook and presentation, just as we hope to have navigated successfully between the Scylla of over-generalisation and the Charybdis of too much detail, all the while providing a geographical coverage that is truly continental in its scope.[7]

Secondly, and at the risk of producing an over-weighty bibliography, we have tried to provide readers with access to key primary, as well as secondary, sources. We have, however, confined our referencing to the already published literature or, where truly unavoidable, to graduate theses. Reports from contract archaeology operations are increasingly important as primary sources of data in some regions, notably parts of South Africa, but, like reports made at conferences or personal communications, they are difficult, if not impossible, to obtain or to check. For the same reason, works in press have been avoided and references to web sites kept to the bare minimum that coverage of contemporary events requires. Turning to illustrations, which form such an important part of any archaeological narrative, we have tried, within the limits of the possible, to emphasise sites and artefacts that are less well-known at the expense of those more routinely reproduced in other sources.

Thirdly, we have tried to guide readers through an admittedly long and complex story by providing large numbers of headings and subheadings that we hope will help them identify the sections of greatest interest to them. With the same aim in mind, we have also provided short summaries of the material and topics covered at the end of each substantive chapter (Chapters 3–10).

Finally, as will become obvious, we have opted for slightly different approaches when considering the earlier and later parts of our chosen timeframe. In Chapters 3–6, which deal with the evolution of those attributes central to the human way of life (such as tool-use; bipedalism; meat-eating; extended infancy and child care; the use of fire, language, and symbolic thought), the emphasis is more discursive, though with due attention paid to the citation of key examples. Our reasoning here is that Klein's (1999) *The Human Career* and Lewin and Foley's (2004) *Principles of Human Evolution* provide detailed coverage of the fossil record and the stratigraphic and archaeological detail for individual sites. Rather than repeat such information – though we do, of course, note significant *new* discoveries – our preference has been to explore recent *thinking* about the issues just outlined, making use of newly excavated finds as appropriate. In contrast, and as already noted, Klein's (1999) synthesis effectively stops – as far as Africa is concerned – about 40,000 years ago, and other recent works of synthesis (D. Phillipson 2005; Stahl 2005) provide less detailed coverage of the period since then. Our response to this situation has been to change tack and to combine discussion of broader issues of continental concern with a more thorough, data-intensive survey of African hunter-gatherer archaeology for what is conventionally termed the Later Stone Age. Chapters 7–10 reflect this difference in emphasis.

## The Book's Structure

We turn now to the book's structure. Chapter 2 provides a more extended discussion of the frameworks of understanding on which our narrative depends. For those unfamiliar with African geography, it introduces the continent's physical framework and then looks in detail at the range of evidence available for reconstructing patterns of palaeoenvironmental change. We discuss the global record of climate change as it relates to Africa, drawing particular attention to how repeated arid glacial cycles affected the distributions of plants, animals, and, we argue, hominins. The emphasis here, however, is on the basic mechanisms that produced these changes and on shifts in the duration and strength of climatic cycles since each of the following chapters comes with its own, more detailed, palaeoenvironmental overview. Finally, Chapter 2 introduces and assesses the wide range of techniques that allow this palaeoenvironmental framework and the archaeological record itself to be dated.

The chronological narrative begins in Chapter 3, which places the development of tool-making within the broader sweep of hominin evolution. The likelihood of pre-Oldowan tool-use is discussed in the light of relevant primate evidence, but attention focuses on why stone tool-making appears in the archaeological record 2.6 mya and not before. Bipedalism had evolved by 6 mya, but stone tool technology appeared long after and in concert with the onset of global glacial cycles. An increased reliance on technological solutions to ecologically induced pressures seems to have taken place, with stone tools used to obtain meat and perhaps tubers in the context of more open, seasonal habitats. The anatomical and cognitive abilities needed to make stone flakes are reviewed, and the likely tool-makers identified among several coeval hominin species.

Chapter 4 examines what Foley (2002) terms the second major event of hominin evolution, the radiation of the genus *Homo* 2.3–1.0 mya, and considers associated developments in behaviour and morphology. Recent discoveries and developments in methods of analysis have changed perceptions about the cognitive abilities of the earliest stone tool-makers, showing them to be skilled knappers and users of technology in response to variable local ecological conditions. Local traditions of tool-making soon emerged, analogous to chimpanzee cultures observed today with implications for the transmission of social learning between generations. Increased aridity 1.8–1.6 mya and the spread of more open savanna habitats favoured a long-legged, large-bodied hominin, *Homo erectus*, with the capacity to range long distances. This species provides the first convincing evidence for hominin dispersal beyond Africa, and compelling evidence for the emergence of a human-like life history with an extended period of childhood dependency. The metabolic costs of raising large-bodied, large-brained offspring adapted to drier conditions may have initiated the human pattern of shared parenting. Changes in landscape use, the development of fire, and the significance of increased technological variability, including bone tool use, are among the other themes addressed here.

The onset and establishment of extended glacial cycles 1.0–0.43 mya provide the chronological and thematic boundaries for Chapter 5. This interval, often overlooked because of its limited fossil and archaeological databases, encompasses the development of new strategies of preparing tool blanks and shaping bifaces that foreshadow the emergence of composite tool technology. A speciation event ~0.6 mya is recognised with the evolution of the modern human brain size and the appearance of *Homo heidelbergensis* as a descendant of *H. erectus*. Large-brained, *H. heidelbergensis* emerged at a time of heightened climate instability and we use the 'social brain hypothesis' to assess the evidence for syntactic language evolving with this species and as part of a wider suite of adaptations, including increased group size and technologically enhanced mobility in response to highly variable resource distributions. Social behaviours typical of modern hunter-gatherers, including food sharing, a sexual division of labour, and use of base camps, may have evolved under ecological conditions that placed a premium on behavioural flexibility.

The key feature of Chapter 6 is the development of composite tool technologies in the later mid-Pleistocene ~300 kya, a fundamental innovation on which all subsequent lithic technologies were based. We argue that this represents not just a different way of extracting energy from the environment, but new ways of thinking about raw materials in the creation of tools that are greater than the sum of their working parts. Recent research in East and south-central Africa provides a firm basis for dating the transition from hand-held to composite tools, and reveals the extensive technological variability that accompanied this shift, which preceded the evolution of *Homo sapiens* ~200 kya. The first distinctive regional artefact styles emerged before the appearance of *H. sapiens*, and perhaps, too, the first indirect evidence for symbolic expression. Varying concepts and signals of 'behavioural modernity' are discussed, and we explore the African evidence for regional technological variability during the Last Interglacial 130–115 kya (**Marine Isotope Stage**, or MIS, 5e), when environmental conditions resembled those of today and the archaeological evidence becomes more visible. A subsequent cooling trend in global climate between 115–70 kya (MIS 5d-a) sees the focus of evidence shift to the archaeological record of deep cave sequences in southern Africa where undoubted symbolic behaviours were displayed.

With Chapter 7, spatial and temporal resolution increase once more, this time to examine the archaeological record left by African hunter-gatherers during MIS 4, 3, and 2, a period that encompasses the two maxima of the Last Glaciation. Defining this period as The Big Dry in deference to the impact of glacial-era aridity on much of Africa, we explore the impact of such changes on the distribution and organisation of human populations. This chapter also examines the significance of changes in stoneworking traditions usually captured by the transition (or was it multiple transitions?) from Middle Stone Age/Middle Palaeolithic to Later Stone Age/Upper Palaeolithic toolkits. It asks what provoked the appearance of microlithic (Mode 5) technologies in so many areas of Africa and whether continuities in material culture and the use of space and landscape can now be traced with the more recent past and the ethnographic present. Once again, an attempt is made to place this African evidence within a global perspective, including the emerging body of genetic data that speak to the dispersal of modern humans from Africa into the rest of the world and the strategies people used to cope with largescale climatic change.

Chapter 8 examines one of these climatic changes that had global import, the shift from Pleistocene to Holocene conditions. The period examined (15–8 kya) was a time of massive environmental transformation. We look at the human response to and involvement with those changes, including the innovation of new technologies such as ceramics and further experiments with broader spectrum economies, including animal domestication. Although arguments can be made in some regions for the establishment of ethnographically attested patterns of hunter-gatherer social relations, evidence elsewhere indicates the emergence of hunter-gatherer communities without recent parallels that in some cases developed into, or were replaced by, societies practising a variety of farming strategies. Consistent with our rejection of progressivist models of social evolution, however, we also draw attention to situations, such as those along the lower Nile, where such developments did not proceed in a simple, linear fashion.

With Chapter 9, the focus narrows once more, not just chronologically to emphasise the period from 8000 to around 3000–2000 years ago, but also geographically. The Sahara and areas to its north fall out of the picture as pastoralist and mixed farming economies take hold there. Instead, the emphasis is on the increasingly rich evidence for the lifeways of middle Holocene hunter-gatherer populations south of the Sahara. Questions asked include how far such evidence attests to processes of social and economic intensification and, if so, what these may have signified, how far they shared features in common, and whether they were able to encourage the development or adoption of food-production. This chapter also emphasises Africa's abundant hunter-gatherer rock art, much of which may have been produced during this period. It explores how ethnographic evidence allows this art to be 'read' with great accuracy in some parts of the continent, how it provides a major source of data on past social relations, and how those data can best be integrated with the information obtained from excavation and survey.

Chapter 10 continues many of these themes, but in a world progressively altered by the relationships that have emerged over the past 4000–2000 years in many parts of Africa between hunter-gatherers and the pastoralist, agropastoralist, cultivator, colonial, and neo-colonial societies that first neighboured and now enclose them. One emphasis lies on the diversity of these relationships and the archaeological, historical, and ethnographic evidence for them. A related topic is the degree to which such relationships have so altered ethnographically known hunter-gatherer societies as to render them useless as baselines for understanding earlier foragers, a key implication of the so-called Kalahari debate, but by no means a purely southern African problem. A final theme is the political, economic, and social situation of African foragers today, the challenges that this poses them, and the ways in which these challenges are being met.

Finally, Chapter 11 proceeds from this point to consider the responsibilities of archaeologists to such groups, not least where claims are made, or can be made, for connections between communities in the present and those of the past. In addition, it summarises the key points of the preceding discussion, highlighting those themes that emerge from studying the African record that are of general relevance to palaeolithic archaeology and hunter-gatherer research worldwide. In keeping with previously expressed concerns about traditional 'grand narrative' approaches grounded in social evolutionism (Stahl 1999), the emphasis lies not just on obvious issues, such as hominin origins, but also on those debates from which African data are typically excluded, such as 'complex' hunter-gatherers. We conclude by evaluating the overall quality of the existing African dataset and identifying some of the directions along which future research should move. A Glossary then covers technical terms (marked in bold typeface at their first point of use) that are not otherwise defined in the text.

# CHAPTER 2

# FRAMEWORKS IN SPACE AND TIME

Any account of the past needs a set of guidelines if it is to be understandable. This chapter sketches some of the essential frameworks for our history of the first Africans. We begin with a short survey of Africa's geography as it is today. Following this, we look at the key changes that have taken place in African environments and climate over the past several million years and how it is that we know about them. As we have already remarked, the global sequence of oxygen isotope stages is crucial for understanding these changes and also provides the chronological structure for our narrative. Having discussed palaeoenvironmental change in more detail, we conclude this chapter by considering how we can date the past.

## INTRODUCING AFRICA

### Physical Geography

Africa is among the world's oldest landmasses, having taken on its basic geographical form as the Gondwanaland supercontinent, which broke up 200–100 mya (Fig. 2.1). Surrounded by water on almost all sides (save for the narrow Sinai landbridge to southwestern Asia), Africa currently straddles the Equator to almost equal extents, reaching 36°N and 35°S. Its northern part is, however, substantially larger and more extensive from east-to-west. Because much of the continent consists of shallow basins or plateaux separated by scarcely evident watersheds, topography has relatively little effect on climatic zones and biomes. Important exceptions to this generalisation in the south include the Great Escarpment, which reaches altitudes of 3000 m above sea level in places, and the Cape Fold Mountain Belt. In the west, the Cameroonian highlands have been built up by volcanic activity that first began as Africa separated from South America, but the Atlas Mountains of the Maghreb are much younger, formed at the same time as Europe's Alps. Most striking of all are the mountains flanking the Rift Valley, which began forming over 20 mya and are still affected by seismic and volcanic activity. A deep gash stretching some 5000 km from Botswana to Turkey, the Rift encompasses the Red Sea, splits the volcanic dome of the Ethiopian highlands in two, and continues south in broadly parallel eastern and western sections that reunite in Malawi. The Rift system extends southward into earlier tectonic troughs represented by the Zambezi and Luangwa river valleys (Vail 1969). Its towering peaks include Africa's highest mountain, Kilimanjaro, Mt Kenya, and the Virunga volcanoes. Another range, the Ruwenzori, is a block of ancient crystalline rock pushed upward between the Rift's two branches. As well as highlands, the Rift also boasts massive troughs, including two of Africa's biggest bodies of freshwater, Lakes Malawi and Tanganyika; significantly younger, Lake Victoria to their north occupies a shallow basin between the eastern and western rifts. All three contain an incredible diversity of cichlid fishes, products of adaptive radiation comparable to Darwin's famous Galapagos finches (Barlow 2002).

Beyond the Rift Valley, today's Africa has few major bodies of freshwater, with Lake Chad, in particular, a rapidly diminishing shadow of its former self. However, the continent more than makes up for this with the might of its rivers and the broad extent of many of their floodplains and swamps: the Sudd, the Kafue Flats, the Okavango, and the Inland Niger Delta to name but four. Africa's longest river, the Nile, has two main sources. The longer of these, the White Nile, rises a little upstream of Lake Victoria, joining at Khartoum with the Blue Nile, the headwaters of which lie in the highlands of Ethiopia. Draining an even more extensive area is the Congo, the tributaries of which penetrate much of the equatorial rainforest to feed ultimately into the Atlantic Ocean. So too do the

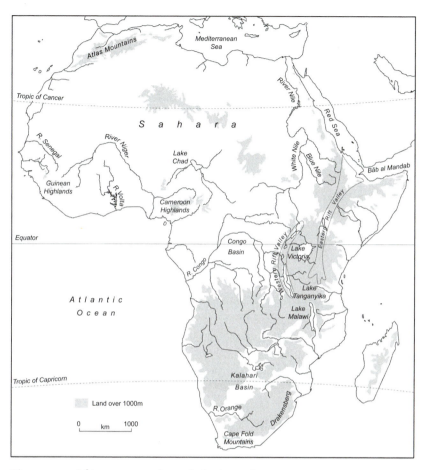

**Figure 2.1.** Africa: topography and physiography.

Niger of West Africa and the much smaller Orange (Gariep) of the far south. The Zambezi, in contrast, which rises close to some of the headwaters of the Congo, flows eastward to empty into the Indian Ocean. One further physical feature is worth noting – the shallow extent of Africa's continental shelf. This is particularly important for our purposes because world sea levels have undergone cyclical rises and falls over the past two million years. Though important along every African coast in changing local ecological conditions, only rarely has this process exposed major areas of land. The Agulhas Shelf off South Africa's southern coastline is the best example to the contrary, adding some 100 km to the continent's southern tip at times of maximum sea level depression (van Andel 1989). The general shallowness of the continental shelf has also meant that rarely, if ever, have the sea-filled gaps between Morocco and Spain (the Strait of Gibraltar), or Djibouti and Yemen (the Bab el-Mandab) been closed (Derricourt 2005). Until the invention of watercraft, then, hominin movements in and out of Africa must always have been via the Isthmus of Suez.

*Climate and Ecology*

Africa is a largely tropical continent, three-quarters of its landmass lying between the Tropic of Cancer and the Tropic of Capricorn. In broad terms, temperatures are thus high throughout the year, though moderated in places by elevation and desert nights. The very few areas of permanent snow and ice are now disappearing rapidly because of global warming, taking with them important ice-core archives of climate change. High temperatures and abundant sunshine mean that Africa also experiences high losses of water through evaporation. Most rainfall is essentially monsoonal in character, high temperatures producing low-pressure areas that draw in humid air from the Atlantic and Indian Oceans. The Inter-Tropical Convergence Zone (ITCZ) marks the boundary between humid air over these oceans and the dry, descending air in the easterlies of continental high-pressure cells. This oscillates north and south throughout the year, currently reaching a latitude of $15°-20°$N in February–August and one of $8°-16°$S the following semester (Adams *et al.* 1996). Rainy seasons of variable length result: single three-month-long seasons near the two Tropics, and two each closer to the Equator, with East Africa experiencing a longer, less variable break between them than is the case in West Africa. Droughts, which are often severe, affect much of non-equatorial Africa, the driest regions being those left largely untouched by the ITCZ. Cold offshore currents along the coasts of Somalia, Morocco, Western Sahara, Mauritania, Angola, and Namibia further exacerbate aridity, though bringing with them highly productive fisheries. Only at the continent's extreme southwestern and northern margins is the influence of the ITCZ replaced by that of onshore-moving mid-latitude depressions.

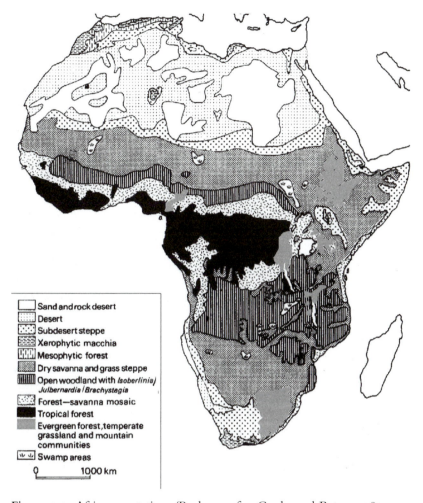

**Figure 2.2.** Africa: vegetation. (Redrawn after Cooke and Butzer 1982: Fig. 1.6.)

The consequence of all this is a largely symmetrical distribution of climatic and ecological zones, separated by generally quite gradual boundaries (Fig. 2.2). The continent's northern littoral experiences a winter-rainfall regime, which supports a scrublike Mediterranean vegetation with pockets of coniferous forest at higher elevations (Fig. 2.3). Alongside more 'obviously' African taxa such as elephant, hartebeest, zebra, and white rhinoceros that probably repeatedly recolonised northernmost Africa across the Sahara during wetter climatic phases only to become extinct later in the Holocene (Klein and

**Figure 2.3.** The Atlas Mountains, Morocco.

**Figure 2.4.** The Sahara Desert, Guilemsi ridge, Mauritania. (Courtesy and copyright Sam Challis.)

Scott 1986), associated mammal species include (or once included) many species typical of Eurasia, such as wild boar (*Sus scrofa*) and aurochs (*Bos primigenius*), supporting the assignment of the Maghreb to the Palaeoarctic faunal region (Dobson 1998). Southward, Mediterranean-like biomes trend into drier, more steppe-like conditions. Farther toward the Equator lies the Sahara, some 19° of latitude across and stretching from the Atlantic to the Red Sea. Rainfall here is low and very erratic, temperatures very high, vegetation sparse (Fig. 2.4). The Nile valley (Fig. 2.5) provides the best known exception to this characterisation, but its greenness depends almost entirely on the supply of water from the Ethiopian highlands, the White Nile providing relatively little input to the annual flood, despite its greater length.[1] Within the desert, however, isolated oases create locally wetter, more moderate conditions, as do mountain massifs like the Ahaggar, Aïr, and Tibesti (Fig. 2.6). Such high-altitude areas still support relict traces of forest and Mediterranean ecologies in the form of olive, myrtle, cypress, baboon (*Papio cynocephalus*), warthog (*Phacochoerus africanus*), and other taxa (Cloudsley-Thompson 1984).

**Figure 2.5.** The Nile Valley, Sudan. (Courtesy and copyright Elena Garcea.)

**Figure 2.6.** The Tadrart Acacus Mountains, Libya. (Courtesy and copyright Elena Garcea.)

**Figure 2.7.** The West African Sahel, Kufan Kanawa, Niger. (Courtesy and copyright Anne Haour.)

Beyond the desert, which consists more of dry, stony plains than of actual dune fields, one enters the first of a series of steppe-like zones that gradually become more wooded on moving south, first becoming savanna and then, below about 11°N, moist woodland. Like the Sahara itself, these zones run almost across the continent. Commonly used terms for them in West Africa are Sahel and Sudan, the latter not to be confused with the modern country of the same name. The Sahel, the 'shore' of the desert in Arabic, is a strip some 400 km wide currently centred on latitude 15°N. It consists principally of grass steppe (Fig. 2.7). Paralleling it to the south, the better-watered Sudanian zone (Fig. 2.8) is a 500 km wide zone of *Acacia*-dominated grasslands, but the term Sahel is often employed with reference to both (Haour 2003). Typical large mammals of these sub-Saharan savannas include Bohor reedbuck (*Redunca redunca*), kob (*Kobus kob*), roan antelope (*Hippotragus equinus*), bushbuck (*Tragelaphus scriptus*), and giraffe (*Giraffa camelopardis*), many of which are also found east and south of the equatorial forests. The Sahel and Sudan themselves continue eastward in the form of drier wooded steppe and subdesert into the Ogaden, Somalia, and northern Kenya.

**Figure 2.8.** The West African Sudan, Mékrou Valley, Niger. (Courtesy and copyright Anne Haour.)

To the north, the highlands of Eritrea and Ethiopia (Fig. 2.9) are Africa's most extensive areas of mountains, their higher reaches covered by montane grasslands and patches of afromontane forest. Similar high-altitude habitats recur farther south on the mountains of East Africa. Endemic to the Ethiopian highlands are species such as gelada baboon (*Theropithecus gelada*) and the highly endangered Ethiopian wolf (*Canis simensis*), whereas regionally distinctive taxa in the more arid areas of northeast Africa include oryx (*Oryx gazella beisa*), gerenuk (*Litocranius walleri*), and Grevy's zebra (*Equus grevyi*).

Banded by a narrow strip of forest-savanna mosaic to their north, Africa's tropical rainforest falls into two distinct regions. The smaller (Fig. 2.10) runs from Sierra Leone in the west to the Ivory Coast in the east, at which point (the Ghana-Bénin Gap) it is largely replaced under current climatic conditions by drier savanna-woodland vegetation. The forest resumes farther east in southern Nigeria, expanding outward beyond southern Cameroon and into the Congo Basin, where it forms the African jungle of the popular imagination

**Figure 2.9.** The Simien Mountains, Ethiopia. (Courtesy and copyright David Phillipson.)

**Figure 2.10.** The West African tropical rain forest, Ghana.

**Figure 2.11.** The equatorial forest of the Congo Basin, Odzala National Park, Republic of Congo. (Courtesy Pierre de Maret and copyright Royal Museum of Central Africa, Tervuren.)

(Fig. 2.11). Incredibly biodiverse, this is more a mosaic of vegetations at different succession stages rather than an undifferentiable mass, part of its variety springing from human impacts like campsite clearance, honey collecting, and concentration of nutrients and useful plants around former habitation locales even before the onset of farming (Ichikawa 1999). Today this is one of Africa's most threatened environments, menaced by rapidly advancing deforestation for the international timber trade, agricultural clearance, and the onset of global warming. Forest elephant (*Loxodonta africana*), chimpanzee (*Pan troglodytes*), bonobo (*P. paniscus*), gorilla (*Gorilla gorilla*), hippopotamus (*Hippopotamus amphibius*), and giant forest hog (*Hylochoerus meinertzhageni*) are among the large mammals found here. A great diversity of monkeys (*Cercopithecus* spp., *Cercocebus* spp., etc.) is also found, with duikers (*Cephalophus* spp.) the most common antelope.

To the south of the equatorial rainforest, the sequence of forest-savanna mosaic, moist woodland savanna and dry woodland savanna repeats itself (Figs. 2.12, 2.13). It is these savannas, above all, the Serengeti-Mara grasslands (Fig. 2.14), that support the greatest

**(a)** **(b)**

**Figure 2.12.** Moist woodland savanna, Zambia.

diversity and density of large mammals in the world and provide one of the continent's best-known images. The precise species found vary from one kind of vegetation to another, but among them we note briefly elephant, giraffe, blue wildebeest (*Connochaetes taurinus*), various kinds of hartebeest (*Alcelaphus* and *Damaliscus* spp.), impala (*Aepcyros melampus*), and an extensive suite of carnivores that includes spotted hyena (*Crocuta crocuta*), leopard (*Panthera pardus*), lion (*Panthera leo*), cheetah (*Acinonyx jubatus*), and wild dog (*Lycaon pictus*).

**Figure 2.13.** Dry woodland savanna, Botswana.

**Figure 2.14.** The Serengeti plains, Tanzania.

The distribution of many of these species extends farther south, where semiarid subdesert vegetation prevails in the Karoo biome of Namibia and South Africa (Fig. 2.15). This is the home, too, of more-arid adapted species such as gemsbok (*Oryx gazella*) and springbok

**Figure 2.15.** The Karoo, South Africa.

**Figure 2.16.** The Namib Desert, Namibia.

(*Antidorcas marsupialis*), both of which also occur in the region's one true desert (the Namib), a narrow coastal strip in Namibia and southern Angola (Fig. 2.16). Distinctively southern African are yet other biomes, the first of them the highland grasslands of South Africa's

**Figure 2.17.** The Fynbos Biome, South Africa.

interior, where dominant **ungulates** once included black wildebeest (*Connochaetes gnou*), red hartebeest (*Alcelaphus buselaphus*), blesbok (*Damaliscus dorcas*), and zebra (*Equus burchelli*). The second comprises the Mediterranean-like climate and vegetation (*fynbos*) of the southern and southwestern Cape, home to one of just six floristic kingdoms on the planet (Fig. 2.17) and smaller associated patches of evergreen forest; though grazers occur, browsing antelope are more typical, among them steenbok (*Raphicerus campestris*), common duiker (*Sylvicapra grimmia*), and the endemic grysbok (*R. melanotis*). Completing the picture, subalpine grassland and, in sheltered areas, afromontane forest occur in the Maloti-Drakensberg Mountains of Lesotho and adjacent parts of South Africa.

## RECONSTRUCTING PAST ENVIRONMENTS

The ecological diversity that exists across Africa today is representative of only the current warm and comparatively wet interglacial in which we live. For the past 3 million years, hominins have adapted to very different conditions in which cooler, drier, and more unstable climates prevailed. Instability and variability in climate have directly affected the distribution of food resources and the availability of surface water. As such, they have been selective forces in human evolution. To assess hominin responses to environmental variability at local and regional scales and over short and long periods requires a high-quality database of well-dated indicators of climate change. Hypotheses about the role of climate change in human evolution are based on a combination of long continuous sedimentary records of global change recovered from deep-sea and polar ice cores with the discontinuous terrestrial deposits offered in lakes, caves, and Rift Valley basins. The combined marine and terrestrial evidence has overturned the once common perception that tropical Africa largely escaped the impacts of glaciation felt at temperate and higher latitudes. We now know that Africa has long experienced dramatic fluctuations in climate linked to the onset of high-latitude glacial cycles that began 3.2–2.6 mya (deMenocal 2004). Declining temperatures led to reduced rainfall, which, in turn, affected the biogeography of the continent and the selection pressures operating on hominins.

Linked to the Earth's orbital variations, large-scale and relatively rapid changes in African climate variability and aridity took place at ∼2.8, 1.7, and 1.0 mya. These dates mark notable intervals in a long-term trend towards increasingly open and more variable habitats. Tectonic uplift has also played a substantial role in altering the distribution of rainfall in eastern Africa, exacerbating orbitally driven periods of aridification in the Pliocene and Pleistocene (Sepulchre *et al.* 2006). Subsequent chapters assess the impact of these events and the underlying rhythm of oscillating dry/wet glacial/interglacial cycles on hominin morphological and behavioural adaptability.

## The Deep-Sea Record

Deep-sea cores provide indirect evidence for the expansion and contraction of polar ice sheets in the form of changing ratios of stable isotopes, principally those of oxygen ($\partial^{18}O/^{16}O$), that reflect changes in temperature and ocean evaporation. As ice sheets build up, evaporated water incorporated into glaciers contains a higher proportion of the lighter isotope $^{16}O$ than the heavier $^{18}O$. The remaining ocean waters are thus enriched in $^{18}O$ and the ratio of the two isotopes is incorporated into the carbonate skeletons of deep-sea foraminifera deposited in marine sediments. Long, continuous marine core records form the basis for reconstructing changes in the periodicity and intensity of glacial/interglacial cycles. The global Marine Isotope Stage (MIS) sequence is used throughout this book with even-numbered stages indicating cold glacials and odd numbers marking warmer interglacials. The marine records show marked shifts in the periodicity of the build-up and melting of glaciers, with the interval from 2.8–1.0 mya characterised by 41,000-year-long glacial cycles. The periodicity shifts again early in the mid-Pleistocene, ∼1.0 mya, with the gradual establishment of a dominant 100,000-year-cycle by ∼600 kya. The 41,000-year-period is linked to variations in the tilt of the Earth's axis of rotation (obliquity), whereas the 100,000-year-cycle reflects the eccentricity of the orbit around the sun. The precession of the seasons in the course of the orbit, which takes place on a 23,000-year cycle, affects the strength of Africa's monsoon system (Weldeab *et al.* 2007). Each of these cyclical orbital variations alters the amount of solar heating (insolation) that drives the global climate system (Imbrie and Imbrie 1980). Deep-sea cores in the North Atlantic also show that much shorter, millennial-scale intervals of cold and warm (stadials and interstadials) occurred in the past 500,000 years (McManus *et al.* 1999). These, too, affected Africa's climate, but their impact on human populations is difficult to detect given current limitations in dating the archaeological record.

The amplitude of oscillation between extremes of cold and warm has also changed with time, becoming more pronounced after 1.0 mya. Pollen and leaf waxes preserved in deep-sea cores adjacent to the African continent also record changes in vegetation, whereas dust levels reflect the impact of variation in ice sheets on terrestrial environments. The primary impact of glacial/interglacial cycles at temperate and high latitudes was one of changing temperatures and ice cover, but in Africa and the tropics, generally, the impact was felt in changes in rainfall. As a general principle, glacials were associated with drier conditions than interglacials, with monsoons waning during cold periods and deserts and semiarid adapted plants and animals expanding at the expense of moisture-loving species. Glacial phase cooling of the land reduced the moisture available for evaporation, an effect enhanced by changes in sea surface temperature. In northern Africa, for example, lower North Atlantic sea surface temperatures reduced the available moisture, whereas the equatorial expansion of the Benguela Current in the southeastern Atlantic reduced rainfall across Central and southern Africa. Weaker monsoonal westerlies had similar impacts across Africa's interior. The combination of reduced rainfall with trade winds that increased because of greater temperature differences between the Poles and the Equator also contributed to desert expansion. Both the Kalahari (the 'Mega-Kalahari') and the Sahara certainly expanded equatorially during more recent glacial cycles (MIS 6–2), and they presumably also did so when similar conditions prevailed during earlier cycles (Thomas and Goudie 1984). Glacial stage aridity thus disrupted the interglacial vegetation zones distributed on either side of the Equator, and during the most recent glacial stage (MIS 2, which peaked at the

Last Glacial Maximum ~20–18 kya) Africa's equatorial rain forests were reduced to isolated patches separated by grassland savanna.

## Terrestrial Records

The marine isotope record of shifting periodicity and amplitude of glacial cycles is also reflected in Arctic and Antarctic ice cores that record changes in oxygen isotopes, other atmospheric gasses, and dust indicative of changes in temperature and effective precipitation. In Antarctica, the Vostok and Dome C ice cores provide climate records that span 420 kya and 800 kya, respectively, with the MIS sequence clearly evident in these deep ice sheets (EPICA 2004). The African terrestrial database also shows the impact of global changes in climate recorded in the oceanic and ice cores, but is less easy to interpret because of its discontinuous deposition. Periods of stable landscape formation interrupted by erosion and coupled with variable rates of sediment deposition create an irregular, but informative record. Proxy measures of habitat variability and climate change come from isotopic signals in soil and cave formations, biological markers such as pollen, phytoliths, and faunal assemblages, and lake deposits that provide a range of temperature and rainfall data (Gasse 2000). To link global climate change with the terrestrial record requires a careful assessment of local and regional processes that control environmental signals. The East African Rift Valley system fortunately offers tectonic basins, such as Turkana and Olorgesailie in Kenya, that not only preserve hominin remains but also contain multiple environmental proxies in relatively well-dated sequences. A comparison of these basin-wide sequences should distinguish between local variations in climate affected by geography and the impact of global events on a regional scale (Behrensmeyer 2006). This kind of multi-basin, multi-proxy approach is restricted in application to East Africa, with the result that this region, with its well-preserved fossil record, is pre-eminent in models of hominin responses to climate change. In South Africa, cave deposits in the Cradle of Humankind provide a less well-dated record of climate and habitat change, but are nonetheless vital for constructing a picture of regional variation related to early hominin evolution. Individual cave sites in southern, central, and northern Africa provide much of the palaeoenvironmental data for later periods in these regions. However, West Africa remains the least well-known area and has poor dating controls, although recent research at the Lake Bosumtwi meteor impact crater in Ghana (Fig. 2.18) promises to provide a high-resolution rainfall record spanning the past 1.1 mya. Changes in the West African monsoonal system should be detectable in these lake sediments and are certainly evident in offshore riverine sediments recovered from a marine core in the Gulf of Guinea. The climate proxy data in the core sequence show a direct link between northern hemisphere glacial and interglacial phases with the respective weakening or strengthening of the West African monsoon during the past 155,000 years (MIS 6 - MIS 1) (Weldeab *et al.* 2007). Farther north, lakes that once existed across the Sahara during wetter interglacial phases often provide multiple proxy data for this vast region, with Lake Chad on its southern margin a remnant of a once much larger body of water. Recent drilling of Lake Malawi, south-central Africa, has, like earlier work at Lake Bosumtwi, begun to produce an unprecedented level of fine-grained data that may span the past 1.5 million years (Scholz *et al.* 2007; Cohen *et al.* 2007). These and other deep lake sequences will help tie the African terrestrial record more closely with the marine and ice core data, as well as illuminating local and regional climate records.

DATING

To bring order to the archaeological and palaeoenvironmental evidence for past human activity in Africa, reliable dating methods are essential. That archaeologists and palaeoanthropologists have paid such attention to deep rock-shelter and cave sequences, or to the long sedimentary sequences exposed by rifting in East Africa, is partly to be explained by the importance still rightly attached to stratigraphy as a fundamental building block of sound chronologies. That other mainstay of nineteenth century archaeology, artefact typology, is no longer as important as it once was, having been dethroned by the invention of a range of dating tools that are independent

**Figure 2.18.** Lake Bosumtwi, Ghana. Like other deep lake basins in tropical Africa, Lake Bosumtwi provides an invaluable long-term record of palaeoclimatic and palaeoenvironmental change. (K. Brooks *et al.* 2004; Peck *et al.* 2004.)

of assumptions about how cultural change has taken place. Where such 'absolute' methods are still difficult to apply, however, typological similarities in artefact style and assemblage composition still aid comparison with better-known, more reliably dated sequences.

A wide range of chronometric methods is now deployed to date Africa's past. At the more recent end of the time frame with which we are concerned, radiocarbon remains fundamental. Providing a sound chronological framework for the past 40,000 years or so, it underpins the chronology employed in Chapters 8–10. However, its use does require some cautions. To begin with, it is clear that fluctuations in the atmospheric production of the $^{14}$C isotope mean that radiocarbon years do not directly equate to calendar years. Tree-ring-based calibration curves extend back into the terminal Pleistocene, beyond which other calibration methods can now be applied using uranium-series-dated stalagmite and coral deposits, which span the period from 12–50 kya (Fairbanks *et al.* 2005). However, it is still highly unusual for archaeologists to employ calibrated radiocarbon determinations in Africa, unless working in situations in which connections with historical data are relevant. Although we think it important for this practice to change, and for archaeologists to move towards exploring cultural and environmental change on a 'real' timescale (cf. Hassan 2002), we have not sought to do this here in order to preserve consistency with general practice. Furthermore, and although the situation is changing, most of the dates delivered thus far by the radiocarbon method are 'conventional' ones that measure the radioactive decay of $^{14}$C atoms, rather than their actual number in a sample. The accelerator mass spectrometer (AMS) technology does do this and is increasingly widely employed. However, it is has not yet supplanted longer-established alternatives, issues of cost being a factor here. One reason for preferring the AMS technique is that it dates very small organic samples that may themselves be of great archaeological interest, for example, ostrich eggshell beads (Robbins 1999) or prehistoric rock paintings (Mazel and Watchman 2003). Often, however, dates are obtained from samples of charcoal (or sometimes bone, shell, or other materials) that are presumed to be correctly associated with the archaeological materials for which an age is being sought: The ease with which materials can be displaced vertically and horizontally through stratigraphic sequences, especially in rock-shelter or cave contexts, means that great attention has still to be paid to context. Sample contamination by (usually) younger material is a further worry, especially as the technique nears its upper limit of viability (cf. Roberts *et al.* 1994). Well-documented fluctuations in atmospheric $^{14}$C production during MIS 3 also make the conversion of radiocarbon determinations into actual ages and their comparison with the results obtained using different dating techniques particularly awkward between 40–30,000 years ago (cf. Conard and Bolus 2003).

A final caution applies not just to the radiocarbon method, but to all other chronometric techniques, given that any 'date' obtained is no more than a mean figure expressed with an error factor. Consider, for example, a radiocarbon 'date' of 1730 ± 40 years before present (defined as A.D. 1950). What this actually signifies is that there is a 68% probability of the sample's correct age falling within 40 years either side of the mean figure quoted, a 95% probability of it falling within twice this, and a 98% probability of it lying within limits of 120 years. These statistical boundaries give a sense of the reliability of dates, but the results are often broad and can obscure short-lived events or processes. A further narrowing of radiocarbon time spans and improved reliability has been achieved in recent years by the application of Bayesian statistics to the interpretation of dating results. The Bayesian method integrates knowledge of the archaeological context of samples, such as stratigraphic order and artefact typology, to refine the likely probability of an age range (Meadows *et al.* 2007). For radiocarbon dating generally, Bayesian modelling is becoming increasingly routine and we expect greater precision to emerge in African contexts, especially from rock-shelter and cave sequences in which well-constrained depositional contexts can be identified and samples carefully selected for dating. For Pleistocene contexts at the margin or beyond the range of radiocarbon dating, Bayesian modelling is being applied successfully to other dating methods discussed subsequently, with notable effectiveness at well-stratified sites such as Border Cave, South Africa (Millard 2006), and Taforalt, Morocco (Bouzouggar *et al.* 2007).

## Potassium-Argon Dating and the East African Record

With this in mind, let us now briefly examine some of the other key dating methods on which the earlier parts of our story depend. In many ways, the most important of these is potassium-argon dating, which, like radiocarbon, uses the principle of radioactive decay (in this case of potassium $^{40}K$ to argon $^{39}Ar$). In this case, it is not the death of an organism that sets the radioactive 'clock' to zero, but the driving off of the sample's original argon gas content as it cools. For the dating method to be reliable, the cooling rock must form an effective trap, in its crystalline structure, which retains any $^{40}Ar$ produced subsequently by the decay of $^{40}K$. The ratio between $^{40}Ar$ and $^{40}K$ is measured using a mass spectrometer, and the ratio is converted into an age based on the known half-life of 1.26 billion years ($1.26 \times 10^9$) for the decay sequence. The extremely long half-life makes this technique more than adequate for covering the 7+ million years of the hominin fossil record. The method is particularly suitable for potassium-rich volcanic rocks, tuffs (ash falls), and lavas, which conveniently form many of the features of the East African landscape. Important sites like Hadar, Olduvai Gorge, and Laetoli are thus among those dated by the technique, which has been amplified since the 1980s by the more accurate argon-argon ($^{39}$Ar/$^{40}$Ar) variant that measures ratios within individual crystals rather than in larger samples that might incorporate fractions with differing histories of cooling. Single-crystal $^{39}$Ar/$^{40}$Ar is now the primary method used, and the age range has been extended to cover more recent periods, including the Holocene, with great precision. As a case in point, the eruption of Vesuvius, which is known to have taken place in A.D. 79, has been dated by argon-argon to 1925 $\pm$ 94 Before Present (BP), a remarkably close result (Renne *et al.* 1997). Also relevant for samples of volcanic origin is fission-track dating, which is based on the fact that spontaneous fission of uranium ($^{238}$U) atoms produces microscopically identifiable tracks in volcanic minerals and glasses. With a half-life of 4.5 billion years, the method is applicable to the entire geological record.

The primary limitation of both techniques is their restriction of application to volcanic deposits, and these occur largely in the tectonically active rift basins of eastern Africa. As a result, these comparatively well-dated sedimentary sequences stretching from Ethiopia to Malawi provide the chronological framework for studying hominin evolution in Africa. Within East Africa, the widespread distribution of some volcanic ash falls creates regional marker horizons that can be identified geochemically and, when dated by argon-argon, they offer a vital means of correlating depositional sequences within and between rift basins. As a case in point, the deep sedimentary deposits around Lake Turkana in northern Kenya (Chapters 3 and 4), contain stratified marker tuffs that can be traced on both sides of the lake and provide a chronology for the important fossil-bearing and archaeological deposits. Some of the Turkana tuffs, notably the KBS tuff dated to 1.8 mya, can also be identified to the north in the Shungura Formation of the lower Omo River of Ethiopia and form the basis of a regional Plio-Pleistocene sequence (Drake *et al.* 1980).

Emerging on the horizon is an expansion of the application of tuff-based correlations to regions outside East Africa. Microscopic particles of volcanic ash known as microtephra or cryptotephra can be carried long distances by upper atmospheric winds and deposited in archaeological sites, in polar ice sheets, and in deep-sea sediments. The potential exists for correlating these various kinds of deposits to build regional tephrochronologies that are independent of radiocarbon and other dating methods, with the added benefit that archaeological records could also be linked to palaeoclimatic data from marine and ice cores. This kind of research is actively underway in Europe in the context of dating Late Upper Palaeolithic population movements (Blockley *et al.* 2006) and its potential is being explored in Morocco and in the Luangwa Valley, Zambia, where visible tephra horizons have not been reported.

## Other Ways of Dating the Early Hominin Record

The still-experimental radiometric technique of cosmogenic nuclide dating has been applied to estimating the time of burial of sediments containing hominin fossils in a South African cave deposit (Sterkfontein) (Partridge *et al.* 2003) and in Mode I artefact-bearing river terraces in Zambia (Luangwa Valley). Burial dating compares the differential decay rates of two isotopes or radionuclides, $^{26}$Al (half-life 0.73 million years) and $^{10}$Be (half-life 1.34 million years), produced in quartz exposed to cosmic rays near the ground surface. The respective radioactive clocks begin ticking with the subsequent burial of quartz at depths sufficient to block further exposure to the cosmic rays (neutrons and muons) that generate $^{26}$Al and $^{10}$Be. Depths of 10 m or more are needed for robust estimates of burial age that are based on the calculation of the original nuclide concentrations before burial and rate of burial combined with the effects of erosion and changes in bulk sediment density in fluvial contexts. The element of uncertainty in these estimated parameters currently limits the reliability of this technique, and in the case of Sterkfontein Cave, the cosmogenic nuclide burial age of ~4 mya for the nearly complete australopithecine fossil known as 'Little Foot' (Member 2) looks highly anomalous when compared with uranium-series (U-Pb) dates (see below) of ~2.2 mya from flowstones bracketing the specimen (R. Walker *et al.* 2006). Cosmogenic nuclide dating has the potential to contribute to chronology building in those large areas of Africa outside the Rift Valley, but it should be used in combination with other techniques, both absolute and relative, to ensure confidence in the results.

Other methods frequently used in conjunction with these techniques do not themselves produce absolute ages, but do reveal distinctive signatures that permit correlation between one sequence and another. Perhaps the best known is palaeomagnetism, which exploits the fact that the Earth's north and south magnetic poles repeatedly switch around. Metallic minerals in sediments and lavas align themselves according to this polarity at the time these rocks form. Analysis can thus determine whether their polarity is 'normal' (i.e., like present) or 'reversed' (when a compass needle would have pointed south, not north). A global master sequence of such changes exists for the past several million years, with potassium-argon and other dating methods anchoring each event's absolute age. Site-specific magnetostratigraphic sequences can be related to this master sequence and in favourable circumstances further correlations can be obtained using still other data. Similarities in the chemical make-up of volcanic ash deposits offer one possibility here, and have been widely used in East Africa. Another comes from biostratigraphy, the recognition that different suites of animal species, or sometimes specific individual taxa, characterise different periods of time: absolute dates of first and last appearances can be estimated by reference to an already dated master sequence, usually that from the East African Rift Valley basins. As an example, the lack of suitably aged volcanic rocks in South Africa makes biostratigraphy and palaeomagnetism particularly helpful for estimating the age of australopithecine-bearing cave deposits that cannot be directly dated by the potassium-argon, argon-argon, or fission-track methods (Partridge 2000). Long-distance biostratigraphic correlations, such as between southern and eastern Africa, necessarily assume some degree of contemporaneity in faunal communities across differing environments. To minimise the inherent circularity of this method of indirect dating, detailed analyses of morphological change within certain taxa can help refine local relative biochronologies, as with the extinct baboons (papionins) found in abundance in the South

African karstic caves (Williams *et al.* 2007). Analysis of cranial features and·changing patterns of sexual dimorphism among the papionins reveals a relative chronological sequence from the Pliocene to Pleistocene that clarifies the likely age of associated australopithecines, as well as providing palaeoecological information.

### Dating the Muddle in Middle

Writing some decades ago, Glynn Isaac (1975) famously referred to the 'muddle in the middle', an apt description of the period between those to which potassium-argon dating and radiocarbon can be readily applied. Happily, this 'middle', which includes key events and processes in the evolution of modern humans (Chapters 5–7), is now shrinking with the extension of argon-argon dating to the Holocene (e.g., Vesuvius) and the effective range of radiocarbon being pushed back to 50 kya. A more dramatic narrowing of the dating gap has taken place since the mid-1970s, with the development of a suite of new techniques with wide archaeological application to artefacts and deposits in caves, rock shelters, and open sites. Most notably, these include electron-spin resonance (ESR), luminescence, and uranium-series dating.[2] ESR and luminescence dating share a common physical process in which the samples accumulate radioactivity over time from their surroundings, with electrons trapped in crystals and held for differing lengths of time depending on the sample type and sources of radiation (Schwarcz 2001). In the case of ESR, the crystalline structure of tooth enamel traps electrons, and, in principle, annual rates of irradiation can be measured in the field. If this has remained constant over time, then the number of trapped electrons directly reflects age since burial. In practice, things are not so simple, and samples may have undergone complex histories of electron loss and acquisition from the environment. Variables such as moisture content, depth of burial, uptake of uranium, and association with a mix of clast sizes all contribute to the uncertainty of ESR results from any particular locality (Schwarcz 2001:42).

With luminescence dating, electrons are trapped in the crystalline structures of siliceous rocks (such as quartz, flint, or chert) and in the laboratory the intensity of the glow released by heating (thermoluminescence, TL) or by exposure to light from a laser or other monochromatic source (optically stimulated luminescence, OSL, and infra-red stimulated luminescence, IRSL) reflects the length of time that the crystal has been storing electron charges. Luminescence dating requires some event that clears the electron traps of stored charges, after which they accumulate again. The accidental burning of siliceous rocks around a hearth is one such zeroing event with obvious archaeological application. TL is typically applied to burnt material and some flint-like materials can, in principle, store trapped charges for millions of years, making this technique of particular interest to archaeologists working with early to middle Pleistocene sites. As with ESR dating, the accuracy of the TL date depends on assessing the sources of radiation that contributed to the accumulated dose in the sample itself, and this can be affected by changes in the water content of the surrounding sediments, the presence of bedrock or other large clasts, and depth of burial. Brief exposure to sunlight can also empty electron traps and re-set the luminescence clock to zero, and the time elapsed is measured by OSL and IRSL methods. Windblown sands are particularly suited to bleaching by sunlight, but water transported grains may also be effectively zeroed under the right conditions of transport. Not every depositional environment will bleach fully background signals, with the resulting risk of overestimating ages of deposits. The innovation of analysing single quartz grains, rather than composite samples, has improved the accuracy of the method by enabling the detection of insufficiently bleached grains (Duller *et al.* 2000). The primary disadvantage of this form of luminescence dating is its relative short time scale, with OSL signals difficult to detect in sediments older than 150 kya as the crystal traps become saturated, especially in environments with high levels of background radiation. This age limitation may be overcome by applying ESR dating to single quartz grains bleached by sunlight (Beerten and Stesmans 2005). This still-experimental method has the potential to date wind-blown sediments up to 2 mya (Beerten and Stesmans 2006), and if its reliability can be demonstrated, it has obvious applications to sites in the Sahara, Namib, the ancient Mega-Kalahari, and semi-arid regions such as the Karoo and the Sahel.

Uranium-series (U-series) dating, like potassium-argon, is based on the process of radioactive decay rather than trapped electrons, and in this method uranium decays to lead through several isotopes with differing half-lives (Schwarcz and Rink 2001). Two long-lived isotopes of uranium ($^{238}$U, $^{235}$U) decay to shorter-lived isotopes, which offer a range of half-lives with which to date the archaeological record. Uranium occurs in solution in water and as it migrates through soil, in streams, or in springs, its daughter isotopes are geochemically separated from the parent U isotopes (Schwarcz 2001:42). Cave and spring deposits derived from the fresh deposition of dissolved calcium carbonate, known generally as speleothem, often contain traces of U but lack the daughter isotopes of thorium-230 and protactinium-231. Once deposited, the U-series sequence of decay begins and the ratio of parent-to-daughter isotopes, combined with known half-lives, provides an accurate measure of time since formation. The increasing use of more precise means of assessing isotope ratios – in particular, thermal ionisation mass spectrometers – has improved the precision of dates to $\pm 1\%$, in contrast to the lower levels of precision associated with luminescence methods ($\sim 10\%$) and ESR, which is the least precise and least accurate in this suite ($\sim 10\% - 20\%$) (Schwarcz 2001:42). Detrital contamination of speleothem, such as windblown dust embedded in flowstone or stalactites, is an important source of inaccuracy in U-series dating, but it can be detected in the laboratory and corrected. The fluidity of flowstone means it may move over rocks and between layers with the result that the dates do not necessarily relate directly to their surrounding archaeological deposits. Careful recording of stratigraphic relationships between samples and archaeological contexts recording is essential. The U-series dating of porous materials such as shell and bone suffers from the movement of uranium in and out of the material over the history of its burial. Assumptions must be made about an early, late, or continuous uptake of U when calculating a bone-based age. Promising improvements in the dating of bone are underway with the use of laser ablation technology to extract minute quantities of bone through a cross-section. This technique measures variation in uranium uptake and ages from the external surface through the cortical bone and has the potential to date directly fossil hominins from otherwise poorly dated contexts (Pike and Pettitt 2003). The nondestructive dating of bone by counting gamma rays emitted by $^{234}$U and $^{236}$U has been attempted on just a few African fossil hominins (Bräuer *et al.* 1997), and the results from this still-experimental technique have been inconsistent when applied elsewhere (Schwarcz and Rink 2001). The age range of U-series dating has, until recently, been limited to <450 kya, but the dating of speleothem bracketing the Sterkfontein hominin 'Little Foot' has shown the potential of the decay sequence of $^{238}$U to an isotope of lead ($^{206}$Pb) to extend more than 2 million years.

The conclusion to draw from this review of dating methods is a positive one, with continual improvements being made in analytical techniques yielding ever more reliable results over a greater time span. Whereas any one technique may produce misleading results and a degree of variation is likely among the estimates that they provide, individually – and, much better, collectively – the ESR, TL, OSL, and U-series methods have revolutionised dating of the last half-million or so years. Applied, for example, to an increasing number of sites in southern Africa, they now offer a robust chronology for sites such as Blombos Cave and Klasies River that are crucial to understanding the antiquity and development of recognisably modern forms of behaviour (e.g., Tribolo *et al.* 2005).

# CHAPTER 3

# FIRST TOOL-USERS AND -MAKERS

It is important to distinguish between the using and making of tools in human evolution as these are conceptually different behaviours, and arguably require different cognitive abilities. Tool-users apply unmodified natural objects to do work. Tool-makers deliberately modify materials, and may make tools for use in making other tools. We know more about stone tool technology simply because stone survives better in the archaeological record, but this dichotomy applies equally to organic materials, with both having the potential to provide information on the extent of learned as opposed to innate behaviours. Examples of the learned ability to use tools occur in just a few non-primate species such as the Californian sea otter, bottlenose dolphin, and Egyptian vulture.[1] Tool-making is even rarer among non-primates, with only the New Caledonian crow observed to shape leaves into a variety of tools for extracting insects from crevices (Hunt *et al.* 2004). The ability of young crows to make leaf tools in captive isolation without input from peers or parents indicates an innate behaviour transmitted genetically rather than socially, though some details of shaping tools may be learned by observation (Kenward *et al.* 2005). The ability of primates, in particular chimpanzees, to use and make tools is now well documented (Whiten *et al.* 1999), and involves a degree of social learning surpassed only by humans. The shared ability of apes and humans both to use and make tools suggests an inheritance from a common ancestor, but in the case of hominins, we developed an absolute dependence on tools for our survival. Why hominins diverged in this significant respect from the apes remains a fundamental question in palaeoanthropology, and one that the African archaeological record can address when placed in an interdisciplinary context.

As consummate tool-users and -makers, we take these capacities for granted, but they appeared relatively late in the 7-million-year span of the hominin record. Africa provides the earliest archaeological evidence for systematic stone tool-making, with artefact assemblages recovered from the Gona region of Ethiopia in deposits radiometrically dated to 2.6–2.5 mya (Semaw *et al.* 2003). The Gona flakes and cores represent a Mode 1 tool-making strategy (see Chapter 1 for Mode definitions), and the first appearance of what is also known as the Oldowan Industry, which encompasses the oldest stone tools in Africa (Leakey 1971) and adjacent regions of Eurasia. It features deliberate flaking of stone to produce sharp cutting, chopping, and scraping edges (Toth 1985), as well as tool use in the form of unmodified hammerstones and stone anvils used for pounding and grinding (Mora and de la Torre 2005). Stone tools continue to be used in one region of highland Ethiopia today, though by a dwindling number of artisans (Brandt 1996). The longevity of stone working reflects the practicality of stone as a raw material, not just for cutting, scraping, chopping, and grinding, but also for drilling and making other tools, both organic and inorganic.

The hominin dependence on technology, which today underpins all our lives, including our relations with other people and the physical environment (Gosden 1994), has an evolutionary history with roots in the Pliocene (5–1.8 mya) of Africa, if not before. The basic questions of when, where, who, how, and why stone toolmaking emerged are the subjects of this chapter. Three related issues are explored: the primate heritage of tool use, the anatomical and cognitive requirements for stone toolmaking, and the adaptive advantages of toolmaking in the context of ecological, dietary, and social changes between 3.0 and 1.6 mya. We conclude with a geographical and chronological overview of the distribution of Mode I technologies across Africa and farther afield in Eurasia, where they reflect the broadening range of toolmaking hominins beyond Africa.

## PRIMATE TOOL-USE

Tool dependency has long been considered a distinctively human trait (Oakley 1956), but decades of systematic observations have shown that some monkeys and all apes sometimes use tools in captivity, but only orangutans and chimpanzees use them regularly in the wild (McGrew 2004b). Gorillas have been observed to use tools in the wild as well (Breuer *et al.* 2005), but do so only rarely and, unlike chimpanzees, in ways not directly linked to food collecting and processing. Other supposedly uniquely human traits have been defined, including the use of tools to make other tools, the construction of tools of multiple parts (composite tool or Mode 3 technology), and the sheer variety of materials used by humans to make tools, including stone, wood, bone, shell, antler, ivory, metal, plastic, and so on. Each of these behaviours appears at differing times and places in the archaeological record, but the capacity for these behaviours may have existed among early hominins, or even the last common ape ancestor (Byrne 2004), their varied expression across time and space reflecting local ecological, social, and demographic factors. A trait list may help us recognise thresholds of behavioural change in later hominin evolution, but is less useful for unravelling the evolution of tool-making itself. To understand this, we turn to tool use among other primates and, in particular, our nearest biological relatives, the chimpanzees. This uniformitarian approach assumes that behaviours common to humans and the great apes, especially chimpanzees, must derive from a last common ancestor that lived 7 million years ago. If this was indeed the case, then we can use contemporary primates as analogues for reconstructing not just the cognitive capacity of early hominins, but also for modelling the ecological and social contexts for the emergence of stone-toolmaking that initiated our own dependence on technology.

Before examining chimpanzee technology, it is worth noting recent field-based observations of tool-use among New World capuchin monkeys (*Cebus* spp.). Capuchins are known for their ability in captivity to use natural objects as tools and to make tools by modifying twigs to probe for food, but they seem to have a limited cognitive capacity to innovate because of a poor understanding of cause and effect (Byrne 1997). This prevailing view has been challenged by observations of the range of tools used and made by wild capuchin groups living in the seasonally dry forests of northeastern Brazil. As well as making probes for insects, honey, and water, these monkeys also use stones as hammers for breaking hard seeds, reducing tubers into edible pieces, pulverising small prey, or processing cactus. They also use stones to dig for tubers and insects (de Moura and Lee 2004), a behaviour that has not been observed among primates other than humans. The innovative use of stone for digging gives these monkeys greater access to seasonally scarce sources of carbohydrates and proteins, an observation of direct relevance for assessing the potential uses of Mode 1 technologies. The digging stones used by capuchins are not modified and technically these monkeys are not stone tool-makers, but they are stone tool-users, and on an almost daily basis. Their apparent reliance on tools, organic and inorganic, to meet basic food needs under stressful conditions provides an analogue for considering the environmental contexts for the emergence of tool use among apes and early hominins in Africa. Also emerging from the study of wild capuchins is evidence for differences in food processing behaviours based on age (experience), sex, and possibly local social traditions (O'Malley and Fedigan 2005). The growing body of data of unexpectedly diverse technical and social behaviours among these New World monkeys suggests that the capacity for tool-use may have existed in a common ancestor of Old and New World monkeys that lived 35 mya. Alternatively, this is an example of independent invention or convergent behavioural evolution unrelated to a shared primate heritage except for a generalised large brain relative to body size.

If there is a deeply rooted anthropoid capacity for tool-use and tool-making, it is expressed by chimpanzees, orangutans, gorillas and, of course, by hominins. One species of gibbon (*Bunopithecus hoolock*) has also shown the ability to learn tool-use in captivity, extending this capacity across the apes (Cunningham *et al.* 2006). Orangutans rarely use or need tools in the wild, but in captivity have shown the capacity, when taught by humans, to make a stone flake and use it to cut through a cord to access food stored in a box (Wright 1972). Chimpanzees are the most intensively studied of the apes, with observations of stone tool-use commented on by Darwin (1871), who drew attention to their premeditated behaviours associated with nut cracking. They are also the most prolific tool-users and tool-makers among the great apes. Long-term field studies began in 1960 in Tanzania (Goodall 1964) and have since spread to other areas of eastern and western Africa where chimpanzee populations have survived human encroachment (see McGrew 2004a for overview). The common chimpanzee (*Pan troglodytes*) and, to a lesser extent, the bonobo (*Pan paniscus*) (Hohmann and Fruth 2003) habitually use a broad range of natural objects as tools, make tools, and have regionally and locally distinct toolkits (Whiten *et al.* 1999). The range of tools used and made exceeds those reported for capuchins and includes different contexts of use, such as social displays, defence against predators, and maintenance of personal hygiene. Chimpanzees also do something not seen among capuchin groups; they use two or more tools in a sequence (a toolset) to accomplish a task (McGrew 2004b). Toolsets have been used to penetrate beehives and termite mounds to extract food, and both activities involve considerable forethought and an understanding of cause and effect. Such sequential thinking is also seen in the earliest Mode 1 assemblages from eastern Africa (Wynn and McGrew 1989; Delanges and Roche 2005), which suggests that this cognitive capacity for goal-oriented, tool-based behaviours existed among the last common ancestors of apes and hominins.

The range of chimpanzee technical abilities also reveals another common ancestral trait – socially learned patterns of behaviour, or culture. The regionally diverse repertoires of tool-using and tool-making behaviours reflect the capacity to innovate and to transmit changes through social learning that together constitute evidence for distinctive chimpanzee cultures or traditions (Whiten *et al.* 1999). Across tropical Africa, broad differences exist between the behaviours of eastern and western chimpanzee populations, as well as intraspecific variations that reflect local cultures (Fig. 3.1). In West Africa, for example, the chimpanzees of the Taï Forest (Ivory Coast) and Bossou (Guinea) use wood and stone hammers to crack nuts (Boesch and Boesch 2000) (Fig. 3.2), but other groups do not, despite living in the same environment and being of the same

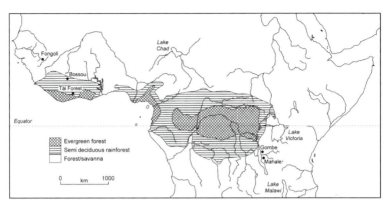

**Figure 3.1.** Chimpanzee traditions of tool-use vary across central Africa, including variation within the same subspecies living in similar environments, such as the West African sites of Bossou and the Taï Forest, which are inhabited by the subspecies *verus*. Nuts are available at both western sites, but the Taï chimps have a wider repertoire of learned nut-cracking activities (wood and stone hammers used with either wood or stone anvils or hammering directly onto the ground) than the Bossou group. Nut-cracking does not occur among eastern chimpanzee groups, but near neighbours on the shores of Lake Tanganyika (Tanzania) of the subspecies *schweinfurthii* do vary in their tool-use patterns. The Gombe chimps pound food on wood and stone, unlike the Mahale group who have fewer learned behaviours related to food gathering and processing. These variations among communities provide an analogue for examining the early archaeological record for subtle differences in tool-making that reflect socially transmitted behaviours rather than ecological limitations. (After Whiten *et al.* 1999.)

subspecies (*Pan troglodytes verus*). The Taï chimpanzees have also been observed to learn the craft of nut-cracking through imitation and occasionally by maternal guidance (Boesch 1993; but see Tomasello 1999 for an alternative interpretation). This is compelling evidence that the tradition of nut-cracking is socially rather than genetically transmitted between generations. The Taï tradition of nut-cracking has some antiquity too, with large stone hammers bearing traces of nuts (starch residues) excavated from deposits dated to 4300 bp (Mercader *et al.* 2007). The range of nuts exploited prehistorically closely resembles the range preferred today by local chimpanzees, which includes species not eaten by farmers in the area.[2] Learned behaviours in hunting technology and techniques have also been

Figure 3.2. Chimpanzees at Bossou (Guinea) using stone hammers and anvils to crack oil palm nuts. A juvenile watches his mother at work. (Photograph by Susana Carvalho [KUPRI].)

reported among chimpanzees living in the seasonally dry savanna of southeastern Senegal (Fig. 3.1). The chimpanzees of Fongoli fashion wood spears to immobilise small prosimian prey (bushbabies, *Galago senegalensis*) asleep in holes in trees (Preutz and Bertolani 2007). The making of these stabbing tools involves four or more sequential steps from selecting the raw material (branches), trimming the ends, sharpening the tip (using teeth), and applying the tools. The holes are then widened and the injured or dead prey removed and eaten. The Fongoli chimpanzees are the first to be observed using tools to procure meat and they are also unusual in that this form of hunting is largely the activity of females and immature individuals. Male chimpanzees more generally tend to hunt larger monkeys, often in coordinated hunts that may result in food sharing (Stanford 1998). At Fongoli, the small size of the bushbaby leaves little to share and the lack of a coordinated hunt removes this particular social context in which sharing can take place among non-kin members. Systematic observation of the Fongoli community only began in 2005, but already this savanna-based group living in a semi-arid environment looks set to provide insights into behavioural responses of early hominins living in similarly dry seasonal habitats. The Fongoli tradition of tool-making linked to hunting and associated with adults as well as immature individuals, both female and male, broadens our conceptual repertoire of group and individual dynamics under ecological conditions that became increasingly widespread during the Plio-Pleistocene.

## SOCIAL CONTEXTS OF LEARNING

Tomasello (1999:512) draws a clear distinction between human and chimpanzee cultures that has implications for reconstructions of the co-evolution of tool-making and cognition. He places childhood learning at the heart of a distinctively human ability to retain and transmit innovations over many generations. This ability is based on the human child's facility for cultural learning based on imitation, emulation and teaching by others, all of which allow the individual to absorb the technological and social heritage into which he or she is born. Through social learning, the human child and adult share a collective cultural inheritance that becomes a repository of knowledge and a basis for innovation. This inheritance is the foundation for a potential 'ratchet effect' in cultural evolution by which cumulative knowledge is retained but also transformed over time. Chimpanzees are less capable of learning new behaviours because they lack an understanding of the intention or goals of other tool-users, and instead focus on the physical act or environmental context of a behaviour, only rarely engaging in imitative learning and teaching. This vision of the distinction between chimpanzee and human social learning is controversial (cf. McGrew 2004a), and may have limited utility for distinguishing between early hominin as opposed to *Homo sapiens* tool-use, but it reinforces the concept that the social context in which learning takes place is of prime evolutionary importance.

Additional variation in the process of the social transmission of technical expertise among chimpanzees may be related to sex, and be learned rather than inherited. Among chimpanzees at Gombe, western Tanzania, females tend to learn precision tool-making skills (e.g., probing termite nests) more quickly from observing their mothers than do males (Lansdorf *et al.* 2004), and females show more persistence in their application as adults. The learned skills of termite fishing enable adult females who may be carrying offspring or pregnant to collect a critical source of fat and protein, whereas males usually obtain protein through active hunting of smaller mammals without the use of tools. These sex-based differences in foraging activities may have existed in the last common ancestor, but there is considerable variation among other chimpanzee communities in feeding behaviours, making evolutionary generalisations based on the Gombe pattern difficult to sustain (Stanford 1996). The use of spears by females and young chimpanzees at Fongoli highlights the likely diversity of feeding niches that existed among early hominins, with females potentially engaged in hunting small prey as well as gathering.

Archaeological evidence for sex-based differences in hominin tool-use and learning capacities will always remain elusive and prone to circularity based on underlying assumptions. For example, bone pieces from Swartkrans Cave, South Africa (1.8–1.0 mya), show signs of damage that may result from extracting termites from their hard mounds (d'Errico and Backwell 2003) (Fig. 3.3). Based on observations of contemporary chimpanzee behaviour, these artefacts are arguably the work of female hominins, but this interpretation cannot be tested independently of the primate analogy.

In summary, behaviour patterns among living primates, in particular the great apes, provide the foundations for reconstructing the conditions in which tool-use arose and the underlying tool-using abilities of a hypothetical last common ancestor. Tool-assisted feeding probably developed among primates that lived in environments offering nutrient-rich foods that were not accessible using hands or teeth alone, such as termites, hard-shelled nuts, tubers, and large carcasses (van Schaik *et al.* 1999). Also needed was some minimum level of manual dexterity and the cognitive capacity to innovate (van Schaik *et al.* 1999). Increased neocortex size among primates, which equates with enhanced information processing and memory, correlates with rates of both innovation and social learning (Reader and Laland 2002). Innovations are most likely to have taken hold among the most sociable communities where cultural selection retained new skills, especially those that enhanced learning during childhood (van Schaik and Pradham 2003:660). Social and physical environments that gave offspring the time to learn from others without being in competition with adults or at risk from predators will have been more conducive to the transgenerational transmission of innovations. An extended childhood and adolescence based on communal provisioning of offspring no doubt provided a stable foundation for social learning and innovation (Chapter 4).

We can now imagine a common ancestor, living in dry tropical woodlands, that used organic and inorganic (stone) objects, some modified but most not, for collecting and processing foods rich in energy and protein. Stone was used to access roots during times of seasonal nutritional stress and to process hard items such as nuts (Marchant and McGrew 2005). This ancestor had a limited capacity to innovate, but developed socially learned traditions of tool-use through observation and emulation that were transmitted across generations with gradual change. The traditions included non-food-related tool-use patterns in threat displays and maintenance of personal hygiene. The repertoire of tool-use was shared by all individuals, though with differences in emphasis among individuals and between sexes. Tool-use complemented rather than dominated feeding strategies. Finally, this imagined ancestor had the cognitive capacity to anticipate future needs and could match or modify materials to meet these needs.

Almost all these hypothesised behaviours would leave no archaeological traces, with the exception of use-wear on stone hammers and anvils and the occasional accidental stone flake. This is just the kind of debris found today associated with chimpanzee nut-cracking sites in the Taï Forest (Mercader *et al.* 2002). The Taï assemblages raise issues about the authorship of some early archaeological assemblages (chimpanzee ancestors or hominins?) but, more importantly, lead us to consider under what conditions incidental flake production might become intentional and how to recognise this threshold (Panger *et al.* 2002). This is not a recent concern, as Lubbock (1865:473) speculated that any use of flint-like stone would inevitably lead to the accidental creation of sharp splinters or flakes employable as tools. The next step from accidental to purposeful production of flakes was a small one, but took a long time to happen in Lubbock's

**Figure 3.3.** A possible bone tool from Swartkrans, South Africa, used for digging into termite mounds or for digging for tubers. The polished (darkened) tip is the working end.

view. We now know that stone tool-making is at least 2.6 million years old, but how much older both tool-use and tool-making might be remains a matter of informed speculation. The evidence for capuchin technology suggests an underlying anthropoid capacity that long preceded the first stone tool-making. There is, however, another route to examining the possible existence of a pre-Oldowan technology, and that is through comparative anatomy of the hands of apes and hominins, as well as experimental observations of tool-use among apes and humans.

## EARLIEST HOMININS

Hominin evolution can be characterised by the following trends based on the fossil record and on comparisons with the our closest living relatives, the chimpanzees: a shift to habitual (obligate) bipedal locomotion, decreased tooth size, increase in brain size, decrease in skeletal robusticity and sexual dimorphism, an increase in life span, extended childhood growth and period of dependency on others, and an increased reliance on technology and culture (Hughes *et al.* 2004). Since the early 1990s, the fossil evidence for the evolution of bipedalism has extended the time span of the earliest hominins to the late Miocene, ∼6–5 mya, in close agreement with the estimated date of the last common ancestor of humans and chimpanzees based on genetic data. Three genera of hominins have been reported from the late Miocene, including *Sahelanthropus tchadensis* (Chad) (Brunet *et al.* 2002), *Orrorin tugenensis* (Kenya) (Pickford 2001), and *Ardipithecus kadabba* (Ethiopia) (Haile-Selassie 2001). There is considerable disagreement among researchers about the evidence for bipedalism and about evolutionary relationships among these taxa, apes, and later hominins (e.g., Senut 2006; White 2006). The evidence for bipedalism in *Orrorin* derives from the morphology of its femur, but the anatomical and phylogenetic interpretation of this lower limb is contested (Begun 2004). For *Sahelanthropus*, the reconstructed position of the foramen magnum provides indirect evidence of bipedalism (Zollikofer *et al.* 2005), though some doubt remains about the accuracy of the reconstruction of this distorted fossil cranium. A small sample of foot bones of *A. kadabba* forms the basis of the claims for bipedalism in this species. Disputes about locomotion aside, the discoveries are significant in that they come from forested environments in eastern Africa and more open and varied habitats in central Africa. The selection pressures for the origins of bipedalism existed in the more forested landscapes of the late Miocene (Thorpe *et al.* 2007) rather than in the later savannas of the Pleistocene, though these had a significant impact on the behavioural ecology of early *Homo* (Chapter 4).

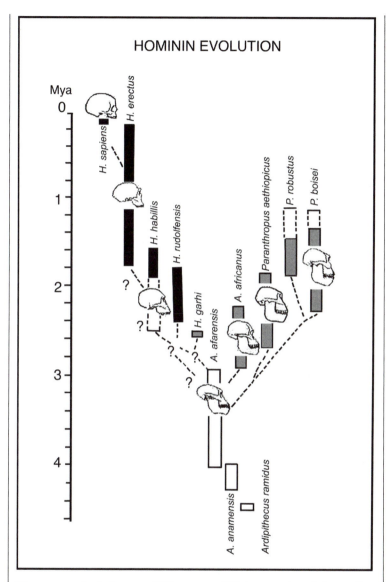

**Figure 3.4.** A phylogeny of Pliocene and Pleistocene hominins outlining possible evolutionary relationships among australopithecines, paranthropines, and early *Homo*. In this scheme, *A. afarensis* forms the root from which later hominins ultimately diverge. (After deMenocal 2004.)

The short-lived desiccation of the Mediterranean 5.9–5.3 mya as a result of tectonic movements would also have affected North Africa's biogeography and presumably its hominin populations.

The earliest Pliocene hominin currently known is *Ardipithecus ramidus* (4.4 mya) (Ethiopia) (originally called *Australopithecus aramis*) (Fig. 3.4), a likely descendant of *A. kadabba* and also associated with woodland habitats. The phylogenetic relationship is unclear between this taxon and the slightly later and much better known hominins attributed to the genus *Australopithecus*. The number of species assigned to *Australopithecus* varies depending on taxonomic approach, with some researchers splitting the fossil record into a number of genera and species based on differing morphological traits (cladistic analysis) (Tattersall 2000). Others recognise considerable regional and chronological variation within species, preferring to encompass this diversity within fewer genera until the biological significance of specific traits is better understood and the fossil record expands (T. White 2002). The fluidity of species boundaries among terrestrial primates (baboons) and the still-uncertain association of morphological variation in the fossil record with species-level variation (C. Jolly 2001) make current taxonomic debates a frustrating distraction from the more interesting questions about population adaptation, interaction, dispersal, and the development of those other traits that define humans generally. The australopithecines are recognised here as having brains similar in size to chimpanzees, expanded molars and pre-molars (megadonty), small canines, and a wide distribution across Africa (T. White 2002), and they are the likely root from which *Homo* evolved. *Australopithecus anamensis* (Kenya) is the earliest recognised representative (4.2–3.9 mya), and lived in a mosaic of woodland habitats and grassy floodplains. This species may be the ancestor of *A. afarensis* (3.6–2.9 mya) (Kimbel *et al.* 2006), which is well known from the fossil record as a habitual biped, though able to climb trees, highly variable in its morphology, and wide ranging across eastern Africa and possibly farther south. *A. africanus* (3–2 mya) is known solely from South African cave sites. *A. garhi* (2.5 mya) (Bouri, Ethiopia) is the earliest member of the genus possibly associated with stone tools, and has megadont back teeth in common with three other species that are often classified informally as robust australopithecines in recognition of their enlarged dentition and supporting cranial features. We treat them here as a separate genus, *Paranthropus*, to emphasise their differences from earlier australopithecines. *P. aethiopicus* (2.7 mya) is the earliest member of the genus, and *P. boisei* (2.3–1.3 mya) in eastern and south-central Africa is the latest known. In South Africa, the genus is represented by *P. robustus* (~2–1.3 mya). The paranthropines co-existed with early *Homo* and may have been tool-makers, though they became extinct between 1.4–1.1 mya, perhaps from the combined effects of competition with early *Homo* and climate change.

The definition of fossil *Homo* and the number of species in this genus continues to be debated, with arguments made in favour of expanding (Bermudez de Castro *et al.* 1997) or reducing membership (Wood and Collard 1999). The two earliest representatives, *H. habilis* and *H. rudolfensis* (~2.3–2.0 mya), have been argued to be morphologically and behaviourally closer to australopithecines than to *H. sapiens* (Wood and Collard 1999), and conversely both are considered as plausible long-legged ancestors of *H. erectus* (Haeusler and McHenry 2004). The recent discovery of an upper jaw attributed to *H. habilis* at Koobi Fora, Kenya (~1.4 mya), not only extends the time range of this species, but also throws some doubt on its position as the ancestor of *H. erectus* as both species seemed to have co-existed, at least in this part of East Africa (Spoor *et al.* 2007). The ancestor of *H. erectus* may have yet to be found. Uncertainty about the significance of character traits as taxonomic indicators also afflicts the status of *H. erectus* (~1.8–0.6 mya), which is viewed as either a single but regionally variable species that probably evolved in Africa then spread into Eurasia (Rightmire 2004) or an Asian species that developed distinctive robust features and that evolved from an African ancestor, *Homo ergaster*. We use *H. erectus* in preference to *H. ergaster* throughout this text and recognise the likelihood that regional subspecies co-existed (Antón 2003).

## FINGERING THE TOOL-MAKERS

Making stone tools is a deceptively simple act that involves a complex interplay between bone, muscle, and brain. A skilled knapper understands the flaking properties of stone, the relationships among angle, force, and placement of a blow, and the resulting length and thickness of a flake. These skills take time to learn, but also involve distinctive biomechanical features of human anatomy that are a likely consequence of the evolution of bipedalism. Apes use their hands for locomotion (e.g., climbing, brachiating, or walking as quadrupeds), as well as for manipulating objects. Humans, as terrestrial bipeds, have their arms and hands free from the constraints of locomotion and, compared with apes, have relatively short fingers and a long thumb (Napier 1960). The increased relative length of the thumb gives humans greater dexterity, and a unique pad-to-pad form of the precision grip (Fig. 3.5; Alba *et al.* 2003). Variations of this grip are typically involved in human tool-making (Marzke 1997), including the three-jaw chuck grip used to hold spherical objects, and precision cradle grips created between the fingers and palm that enable objects to be held and rotated with skill. Humans also have a wider range of power grips, including those involving support of the thumb as a buttress, compared with the great apes (Aiello and Dean 1990). In particular, humans have the unique ability to cup the palm of the hand that plays a central role in power grips. Cupping the hand has the added effect of increasing the area of skin in contact with an object, which means more sensory information can be relayed to the brain (Landsmeer 1993).

Experimental replication studies of early stone tools show that both power and precision grips are used in making and using stone tools (Marzke and Shackley 1986). The action of striking a hammerstone held in one hand against a core held in the other involves precision gripping of the hammerstone (e.g., a three-jaw chuck) and a firm power squeeze grip on the core. Electromyographic recordings of muscle activity in the hands during knapping show that the most actively engaged muscles are associated with the fifth finger in the hand supporting the core, and in the index finger/thumb regions in the hand controlling the hammerstone (Marzke *et al.* 1998).

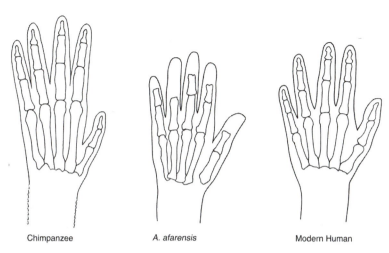

Chimpanzee              *A. afarensis*                Modern Human

**Figure 3.5.** Comparative skeletal structure of the hands of a chimpanzee, *Australopithecus afarensis*, and *Homo sapiens*. The elongated thumb of *A. afarensis* is similar to that of *H. sapiens* and would have enabled this australopithecine to form the precision grips commonly used by humans in tool manufacture and use. (The *A. afarensis* hand is a composite derived from several specimens, after Alba *et al.* 2003.)

Tool-use, such as cutting and scraping with a handheld flake, involves pad-to-pad precision grips between a strong thumb and the side of the index finger (Marzke and Shackley 1986). Among humans, the power squeeze grip comes into play when a stone is used for pounding or a club for striking.[3] A now classic study of the limitations of the ape hand for stone tool-making is the work of Toth *et al.* (1993) in showing a captive and enculturated bonobo, known as Kanzi, how to make stone flakes. Kanzi initially preferred to create flakes by throwing a stone core against a hard surface, but when forced to use two hands, showed a limited understanding of the interplay between the geometry of the core, and the angle and force of blow needed to remove large flakes with consistency. His hand-held knapping is characterised by repetitive and often unproductive banging together of two rocks (Fig. 3.6). The resulting flakes are small by comparison with those found in early Oldowan assemblages and Kanzi's limited precision grip means his application of force is also limited when holding a flake for cutting. After three years' of experimenting,

Kanzi had developed his own techniques of knapping and improved his understanding of the mechanics of flaking, including core shape and weight (Schick *et al.* 1999). He produced larger flakes as a result, but the fruits of his labours still do not mirror the controlled knapping seen in even the earliest Oldowan assemblages. Kanzi's more limited dexterity as a quadruped may account for his limitations as a knapper, but may also stem from not having been brought up among stone tool-makers whom he could observe and emulate.

Given the distinctive form of the human hand with its relatively long opposable thumb and ability to form a deeply cupped palm, it should be possible to assess the toolmaking abilities of early hominins based on fossil hands. Dated to 2.6–2.5 mya, the oldest stone tools currently known come from sites along the northern Awash River and its tributaries at Gona in the Afar region of Ethiopia (Fig. 3.7; Semaw *et al.* 2003). Stone flakes and cores have been found associated with faunal remains, some of which have cut-marks from processing animal carcasses, but as yet no hominins have been found with the Gona tools. Along the middle Awash River, just 96 km farther south, the contemporary site of Bouri has yielded indirect evidence of stone tool use in the form of cut-marked and splintered bones (de Heinzelin *et al.* 1999). Scattered fossils of *Australopithecus garhi* occur in the same stratigraphic horizon, but not in direct association with the modified animal bone. The other hominin in eastern Africa at this time is *Paranthropus aethiopicus*, known from the Omo-Turkana basin of southern Ethiopia-northern Kenya (A. Walker *et al.* 1986; Suwa *et al.* 1996) and also reported 700 km south at Laetoli, Tanzania (Harrison 2002). In southern Africa, the Oldowan appears later, at 2.0 mya (Kuman 1998), postdating *Australopithecus africanus* (3.3–2.5 mya), but coeval with two possible contenders as tool-makers, *Paranthropus robustus* and early *Homo* sp. Metacarpals attributed to *Paranthropus robustus* and capable of forming a precision grip have been recovered from Swartkrans Cave, Member 1, South Africa (Susman 1991; Susman *et al.* 2001) along with Oldowan artefacts. Member 1 also contains remains of *Homo* sp., which means either, or both, taxa could be responsible for the tools. They may also have been using bone tools, such as those identified at Swartkrans and Drimolen, which show microwear traces interpreted as evidence for digging into termite mounds or extracting underground sources of

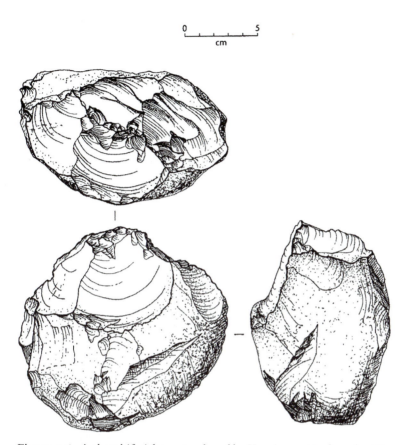

**Figure 3.6.** A chert bifacial core produced by Kanzi, a captive bonobo (*Pan paniscus*) using the technique of throwing one stone against another rather than by hand-held percussion with a stone hammer. His preference for throwing probably reflects the biomechanical features of bonobo anatomy, which limit the force and accuracy of hand-held blows. The core resembles a Mode 1 (Oldowan) bifacial side chopper in the classification system developed by Mary Leakey (Reprinted from Schick *et al.* 1999. 'Continuing investigations into the stone tool-making and tool-using capabilities of a bonobo (*Pan paniscus*)'. (*Journal of Human Evolution*, 26:821–832, with permission from Elsevier.)

plant foods such as roots, tubers, and corms (Backwell and d'Errico 2001). The bone tool evidence underlines how little we know of the use of organic materials by early hominins because of taphonomic biases in favour of durable stone.

In eastern Africa, the earliest dates associated with the genus *Homo*, at 2.4–2.3 mya (Schrenk *et al.* 1993; Kimbel *et al.* 1996; Deino and Hill 2002; Prat *et al.* 2005) postdate the appearance of the Oldowan by at least 100,000 years. Assuming this age for the emergence of early *Homo* remains unchanged by future research, then stone tool-making was already established by the time our genus appeared and was contemporaneous with *Australopithecus* and *Paranthropus* in eastern Africa. The fossil record does not currently provide enough evidence to assess the morphology of the hands of either *A. garhi* or *P. aethiopicus*, but there is sufficient material from an earlier lineage, *A. afarensis* (3.7–2.9 mya) to gauge this species' ability to make tools (Alba *et al.* 2003). At Sterkfontein Cave, South Africa, the ongoing extraction of the remarkably well-preserved australopithecine skeleton known as Little Foot (STW 573) from the Member 2 breccia promises an exceptionally complete hominin hand, but in the interim the *A. afarensis* sample provides the most informative database on manual dexterity.

A composite hand created from several fossils of *A. afarensis* found at Hadar, Ethiopia (site AL333/333w; ~3.2 mya), reveals the human pattern of an elongated thumb in relation to fingers that could perform pad-to-pad precision grasping. A separate three-dimensional modelling of a trapezium bone from *A. afarensis* (which articulates the thumb and wrist) also supports the interpretation that this species could form distinctively human grips, including pad-to-side and the three jaw chuck (Tocheri *et al.* 2003). The significance of these findings lies in the age of *A. afarensis*, which pre-dates the Oldowan by 1 million years. The emergence of a more terrestrial biped, such as *A. afarensis*, may have seen the relaxation of selection pressures associated with forelimb-based locomotion and increased selection operating on the manipulative skills of the hands (Alba *et al.* 2003:250). *Homo habilis* (2.3–1.6 mya), which probably evolved from the later australopithecines (Falk *et al.* 2000), also inherited an opposable thumb and precision grip (Napier 1962; Marzke and Marzke 2000).

As a potential tool-user and maker, *A. afarensis* may also have had the social and cognitive skills we have attributed to a common ancestor of hominins and apes. If chimpanzees have socially

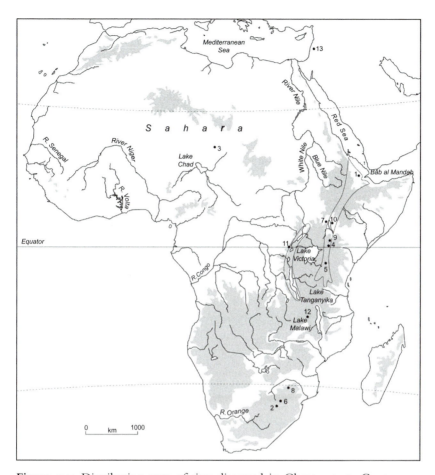

**Figure 3.7.** Distribution map of sites discussed in Chapter 3: 1. Gona, Bouri; 2. Swartkrans and Sterkfontein; 3. locality of *Sahelanthropus tchadensis* fossil (Djurab desert); 4. locality of *Orrorin tugenensis* (Tugen Hills); 5. Laetoli; 6. Drimolen; 7. Lokalalei localities; 8. Makapansgat; 9. Kapthurin Formation; 10. Koobi Fora (Lake Turkana); 11. Semliki Valley; 12. Luangwa Valley; 13. Yiron.

transmitted technological traditions and the ability to plan their tool-use, then these behaviours should also have existed among at least some australopithecines. Indirect evidence for the cognitive foundations for these traits can be inferred from a comparative analysis of cranial endocasts as indicators of relative brain size and neural organisation. Analyses of later australopithecine (*Australopithecus africanus*), *Paranthropus*, and early *Homo* endocasts show that the australopithecines underwent an expansion of the temporal and frontal lobes between ∼3.0 and 2.5 mya (Falk *et al.* 2000). The frontal lobe is associated with abstract thought, language, planning, and the execution of motor skills, and the australopithecine pattern of development resembles that of early *Homo*, whereas the morphology of the *Paranthropus* brain most closely resembles that of the great apes. The relative brain size of the australopithecines, including *A. afarensis*, is as large as or larger than, that of chimpanzees and gorillas (Kappelman 1996). These indirect indicators of cognitive ability, combined with the anatomical evidence for human-like grips, make the australopithecines prime candidates as early tool-makers and innovators of stone tool technology. *Paranthropus*, however, cannot be excluded as a possible stone tool-maker based on brain organisation and size alone. Brain size in this genus increased over time along with that of early *Homo* (Elton *et al.* 2001), and *Paranthropus* is found on Oldowan sites in both eastern and southern Africa. More generally, brain size as an indicator of technical ability is also challenged by the association of the small-brained *Homo floresiensis* (380 cm$^3$) with Mode 3 and 4 tools on the island of Flores (Indonesia), dated as recently as 13 kya (Falk *et al.* 2005).

Once the Oldowan industry makes its appearance, early *Homo* in the form of *Homo habilis* is found with stone tools in both eastern and southern Africa, supporting arguments for a behavioural and phylogenetic linkage between later australopithecines and early *Homo*. This lineal evolutionary sequence of tool-making from australopithecines to *Homo* is complicated by the association of *Paranthropus* with the Oldowan industry. Tool-making patterns need not be species-specific, and in the case of the early Oldowan, from 2.6 to 2.0 mya, there is the likelihood that multiple species of tool-makers co-existed, perhaps developing differing cultural traditions of tool use comparable to those seen today among chimpanzees and bonobos. This potential complexity in the archaeological record raises significant methodological issues of how to recognise traditions within the Oldowan including those that may not be typical of the flake and core content of this industry. All these issues also apply to the later

African archaeological record, but they first arise with the origins of the Oldowan.

## WHY STONE TOOLS AT 2.6 MYA?

The fundamental question of why stone tool-making developed when it did remains to be answered. If the capacity to use and make tools had evolved with the last common ape/hominin ancestor during the Miocene–Pliocene transition (8–5 mya) or perhaps much earlier with the common ancestors of Old and New World monkeys (35–30 mya), why did stone tool technology develop relatively late in the broad sweep of hominin evolution? There is the possibility that an earlier manifestation of stone tool-use exists, but has not been recognised by archaeologists because it does not closely resemble the Oldowan as currently understood. Much of Kanzi's efforts at knapping produced broken flakes and other fragments that would be difficult to distinguish from naturally fractured stone (Schick *et al.* 1999). An example of what a pre-Oldowan assemblage might look like is provided by the chimpanzees of the Taï Forest, Ivory Coast, who are currently creating archaeological deposits by systematically cracking hard nuts using stone hammers and anvils (Mercader *et al.* 2002). The deposits are characterised by an abundance of small fragments of shattered stone (<20 mm), a few flakes, no cores, and battered hammers and anvils. The rarity of flakes and lack of cores distinguishes these nut-processing areas from Oldowan sites. Such non-Oldowan sites would also be difficult to recognise in the context of naturally occurring accumulations of rock fragments and battered stones found in river and lakeshore deposits associated with early hominin sites. Actualistic studies are needed to develop criteria for distinguishing between deliberate and unintentional (natural) patterns of surface damage on stone (e.g., Mora and de la Torre 2005). The Taï Forest excavations are a salutary reminder of the possible diversity of archaeological sites that may have existed before, during, and after the Oldowan, but remain methodologically invisible. Likewise, the diversity of current chimpanzee and bonobo cultures (Whiten *et al.* 1999) remind us that regional variation can be expected across the spatial and temporal range of the Oldowan complex.

Adding to the argument for pre-Oldowan development of stone tool technology is the evidence for a well developed understanding of the mechanics of knapping seen in the very early assemblage at Lokalalei 2C, West Turkana, Kenya. The site is dated to 2.34 mya and contains clear evidence of hominin knapping of lava cobbles, with the excavators able to refit flakes to cores to reconstruct sequences of flake production. This evidence shows the use of carefully planned strategies of flake removal or *débitage* to produce systematically sharp flakes (Delanges and Roche 2005). The knappers combined well-controlled motor skills with an understanding of the physical and mechanical properties of the raw materials used, including an awareness of the importance of core angles in flake removal (see fig. 4.2). This evidence of sequential decision-making (*chaîne opératoire*) shows that these were not novice knappers with rudimentary abilities, but experienced makers and users of flakes.

The skills shown at Lokalalei 2C are more developed than those seen at the slightly older site of Lokalalei 1 and other contemporary Plio-Pleistocene sites in eastern Africa (e.g., Omo, Hadar, and Kanjera). They also challenge existing perceptions of the Oldowan as a long period of technological stasis characterised by a gradual accretionary development of technical abilities (Kibunjia 1994; Semaw 2000). *Homo habilis* and *Paranthropus aethiopicus* lived in the West Turkana area, and both species could have been tool-makers at Lokalalei (sites 2C or 1), each with pre-existing experience of stone tool-use as yet undiscovered or unrecognised. Current research in the Busidima Formation of the Gona area of Ethiopia hints at the possibility that the first Mode 1 tools were made as soon as the ancient Awash deposited coarse cobbles suitable for flaking, just after 3.0 mya (Quade *et al.* 2004:1543). The Gona knappers, like those at Lokalalei 2C, also carefully selected their cobbles for quality and demonstrated controlled flake removal, including bifacial flaking, showing both an awareness of the physical properties of differing raw materials and an understanding of the mechanics of flake production (Semaw 2000). This suite of knowledge based on experience speaks of an even older tradition of knapping that just remains to be discovered.

Whether Mode 1 technology emerged ~2.9 or 2.6 mya, the diversity of species and technological variability seen in the Plio-Pleistocene make any single theory of stone tool-making's origins much more difficult to conceptualise, evaluate, and support. For the time being, the archaeological evidence points to stone tool technology having developed first in eastern Africa by 2.6 mya, then spreading to southern and northern Africa and into Eurasia by 1.8 mya among hominins adapted to savanna habitats (mixed woodland and grasslands) (discussed subsequently). If the period 2.6–2.5 mya marks a genuine threshold of technological innovation, then we must consider what factors stimulated a shift towards greater use of stone technologies – in particular, cutting and pounding tools – to the extent they become archaeologically visible as distinctive Mode 1 accumulations. Our hypothetical last common ancestor used tools as an adjunct to its food procurement strategies, but was not dependent on technology for accessing essential foods. This may also have been the situation among the early australopithecines such as *A. afarensis*. With the appearance of the Oldowan, the relationships among technology, diet, physiology, and social traditions may have changed for some species, including early *Homo*, in ways that created new dependencies and adaptive opportunities.

## DIET AND PALAEOECOLOGY

Stone tools are assumed to have played a significant role in the feeding and social strategies of early hominins and explanations for the emergence of the Oldowan generally stress the adaptive value of flakes and hammerstones as tools for accessing meat and marrow (Stanford and Bunn 2001). The systematic incorporation of animal protein into the diet of early hominins has long been regarded as the catalyst for the evolution of distinctive hominin traits, including large brain size, increased intelligence (Washburn and DeVore 1961; Washburn and Lancaster 1968; Aiello and Wheeler 1995), increased body size, and delayed maturation with an extended childhood supported by food provisioning (Kaplan *et al.* 2000). Meat-eating has also been credited with the development of human forms of social organisation, including food sharing, nuclear families, base camps, and a sexual-based division of labour (Rose and Marshall 1996). How meat and marrow were acquired, whether through hunting of large game or scavenging, has remained a topic of intensive research and debate since the 1960s. Putting this issue aside for the moment, the addition of animal protein to the hominin diet is generally accepted as a basic development in human evolution that took place during the Plio-Pleistocene. Multiple lines of direct and indirect evidence exist for meat-eating in the form of hominin dental morphology, dietary isotopes, stone tool cutmarks on bone, life history data, and ethnographic and ethological analogues.

Given the association of *Australopithecus*, *Paranthropus*, and *Homo* with early Mode 1 assemblages, these genera warrant close examination in terms of their respective feeding strategies set against the backdrop of increasing climatic variability and aridity in the Plio-Pleistocene outlined subsequently. If the dietary range of these hominins can be broadly reconstructed, then the possible contribution of stone tools can be assessed, along with the likelihood that one or all species might have benefited from this technology. J. Robinson (1954) proposed a dietary hypothesis that remains an influential starting point for discussing the palaeoecology of early hominins. He and others observed that clear morphological differences exist between the dentition of *Paranthropus* and that of *Australopithecus* and early *Homo*. Dental morphology and craniofacial features linked to mastication were recognised as important indicators of hominin ecology. According to the dietary hypothesis, the large molars, pre-molars, and thick enamel associated with *Paranthropus* distinguish it as a genus of specialised feeders with teeth evolved to crush and grind hard plant foods. In contrast, the more human-like pattern of reduced molars and thin enamel seen in the australopithecines and early *Homo* reflects a more generalised, if not omnivorous diet. The specialised versus generalised distinction is supported by comparative studies of dental functional morphology (Luke and Lucas 1983; Ungar 1998, 2004), craniofacial morphology (Lucas 2004; Sakka 1984), analogies with baboon (*Theropithecus*) feeding patterns (C. Jolly 1970; C. Jolly and Plog 1987), and dental microwear analyses (Grine 1981, 1984, 1986; Grine and Kay 1988; Teaford 1994). Grine's research challenged the dietary hypothesis in part, however, by suggesting that *Australopithecus africanus* was a fruit and leaf eater, rather than a generalist omnivore. Dental morphology remains a significant source of inferences for reconstructing diet (see subsequent discussion), but whether alone, or combined with primate analogues, cannot provide direct evidence of feeding behaviours. Tooth shape may be controlled by phylogenetic history and not be an accurate reflection of actual feeding behaviours, especially among generalists that can consume a variety of plant and animal foods (Lee-Thorp 2000). Although dental microwear is not directly affected by evolutionary ancestry, the technique records only the relatively recent food intake of an animal, and soft foods such as meat leave ambiguous traces, such as fine scratches and small pits on occlusal surfaces, that may vary among individuals and sites (Organ *et al.* 2005). An additional source of dietary information that has emerged in recent years – stable isotope analysis – overcomes many of these problems (inset box) and is generating a sustained challenge to the original dietary hypothesis.

ISOTOPES AND DIET

Stable carbon isotopes and strontium/calcium (Sr/Ca) ratios are preserved in bone and tooth enamel and together provide direct evidence of long-term feeding strategies. The carbon isotope content of bone and Sr/Ca ratios can be affected by postdepositional leaching (Sillen 1992; Sillen *et al.* 1995; Sponheimer and Lee-Thorp 1999b), but the crystalline mineral structure of tooth enamel provides a more resilient environment for the preservation of isotopic signatures from foods eaten when the enamel was forming (Sponheimer *et al.* 2005). The use of late-developing permanent teeth for both stable carbon and Sr/Ca analyses captures the more typical dietary repertoire of the juvenile and perhaps young adult, depending on the age of tooth formation. Isotopes derived from bone represent a longer lifetime dietary average, but must take account of the effects of physical and chemical alteration after death (diagenesis).[4]

Carbon isotope analyses are based on the distinctive photosynthetic pathways of plants (Fig. 3.8). In summer rainfall zones and African savannas generally, most trees, shrubs, and herbs utilise the three-carbon form of photosynthesis ($C_3$ plants), whereas most tropical grasses and some sedges take the four-carbon pathway

($C_4$ plants) (Vogel 1978; Peters and Vogel 2005; Sponheimer *et al.* 2005). Each pathway can be recognised biochemically by its distinctive ratio of the stable carbon isotopes $^{12}C/^{13}C$ that gives a measurable value of $\partial^{13}C$. $C_3$ plants discriminate against the uptake of $^{13}C$ and $C_4$ plants do not, with the result that $\partial^{13}C$ values are lower in the $C_3$ plants and significantly higher in $C_4$ plants. Browsers such as giraffes feeding on $C_3$ trees and shrubs incorporate the lower $\partial^{13}C$ values typical of this carbon pathway into their tissues, including bones and teeth. Grazers, like zebras, likewise consume and incorporate the higher $\partial^{13}C$ values associated with the $C_4$ pathway. Carnivores incorporate into their tissues the ratios present in the animals they eat and omnivores can have the carbon signatures of plants and fruits consumed directly or indirectly through animals and insects eaten. Some variation in $\partial^{13}C$ values is caused by climatic and atmospheric conditions, with humidity, solar radiation, and carbon dioxide levels all affecting photosynthesis and the discrimination of $^{13}C$ uptake (van der Merwe *et al.* 2003). As a result, values in arid environments differ from those in tropical rain forests. These and other sources of variability need to be established for specific places and times as an essential framework for interpreting the isotopic values obtained from hominin specimens.

Dietary information derived from strontium/calcium ratios works on the principle that mammals discriminate against strontium in favour of calcium during metabolism. There is a trophic effect across the foodweb, with plants having the highest Sr/Ca ratios and carnivores, the lowest (Fig. 3.8 Sillen 1992). Sources of variation in Sr/Ca signals unrelated to diet need to be considered, including local variations in strontium content of soil, which control the amount of the element available for uptake by plants. As a result, different kinds of grazers, browsers, carnivores, and omnivores must be sampled at the same location in order to interpret their Sr/Ca ratios. Once local variations in soil geochemistry are mapped and their impact on isotope ratios is understood, they can be used to reconstruct the ranging behaviours of individual hominins across landscapes. This avenue of research has the

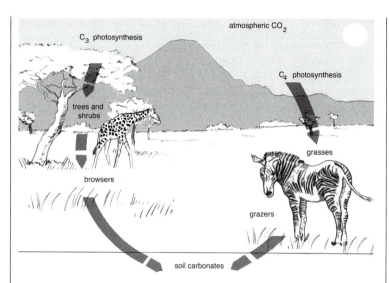

**Figure 3.8.** The stable carbon foodweb begins with the production of atmospheric $CO_2$ and uptake of carbon through the differing photosynthetic pathways of grasses ($C_4$) and trees and shrubs ($C_3$). Grazers and browsers as direct consumers of plant foods will have differing isotopic values in their tissues reflecting dietary patterns. Stable carbon isotopes also enter soils through the vegetation cover and provide an important source of data for reconstructing shifts in habitats.

potential to reveal nuances in feeding strategies between sympatric species. Differences in female/male physiology may also affect discrimination of strontium (J. F. Thackeray 1995), but this is not the case among contemporary chimpanzees (Schoeninger *et al.* 1999) and by extension is unlikely to alter significantly the results obtained for early hominins.

Isotopic approaches to dietary analysis have, to date, been largely applied to early hominins from the South African sites of Swartkrans, Sterkfontein, and Makapansgat. This regional bias reflects the pioneering work of South African biochemists in developing these techniques, and no doubt these analyses will be extended to the eastern African hominin record. For the time being, the dietary hypothesis is being tested in the region where it was first framed. Initial stable carbon isotope analyses of both *Paranthropus robustus* and *Homo* sp.

from Swartkrans (~1.7–1.5 mya) gave surprising results, with both taxa deriving 25% of their diets from $C_4$ plants, including grasses, sedges, or the animals and insects that ate them (Lee-Thorp *et al.* 1994, 2000). *Paranthropus* at this site appears to have been a generalist, rather than the specialised herbivore originally predicted by Robinson's dietary hypothesis. The recovery of bone tools from Swartkrans and the suggestion that they were used for breaking into termite mounds (d'Errico and Backwell 2003) strengthen the idea that termites were a source of $C_4$-based food for both hominins. The similarity in $C_4$ values for the two taxa does not mean they had identical diets given that carbon isotope analyses cannot yet discriminate between potential food sources. It can be said with certainty, however, that they did not consume plants from closed forest environments (van der Merwe *et al.* 2003).

At Makapansgat, four *Australopithecus africanus* specimens had varying amounts of $C_4$ foods in their diets, ranging from none to 50% (Sponheimer and Lee-Thorp 1999a). A larger sample of *A. africanus* individuals (n = 10) was analysed from Member 4 at Sterkfontein (2.5–2.0 mya) and compared with the $\partial^{13}C$ values of associated browsers and grazers at either end of the $C_3$ and $C_4$ spectrum, plus two non-human primate species, including the grazing baboon *Theropithecus oswaldi* (van der Merwe *et al.* 2003). The results for *A. africanus* show this species to have been a generalist feeder with average values indicating 60% of the diet derived from $C_3$ plants and the remaining 40% from $C_4$ sources (van der Merwe *et al.* 2003:592). The Makapansgat and Sterkfontein data combined reveal *A. africanus* to have been a very opportunistic feeder, with great variability in $C_4$ consumption among individuals. It may have consumed several potential sources of $C_4$, including grasses, sedges, insects, and grazing mammals, all pointing to *A. africanus* having lived in savanna habitats 3–2 mya.

As the number of fossil hominins analysed using carbon isotopes continues to grow, earlier dietary interpretations are being tested and revised. Nineteen *A. africanus* individuals and eighteen *Paranthropus robustus* have now been sampled, all from South Africa (Sponheimer *et al.* 2005). The combined results confirm that these two genera were distinct in their feeding strategies compared with browsing ($C_3$) and grazing ($C_4$) fauna, and that contrary to the dietary hypothesis, both consumed unexpectedly high quantities of $C_4$-based foods (*Australopithecus* = 40%, *Paranthropus* = 35%). A small sample of three teeth of *Homo erectus* from Member 1 at Swartkrans also indicates a significant contribution of $C_4$-based foods (25%) in the diet of this species (Lee-Thorp *et al.* 2000). *H. erectus* made Mode 1 and 2 tools, and accessed meat and marrow (see Chapter 4), but the isotopic data alone cannot discriminate between sources of $C_4$ foods; in the southern African context, termites may have contributed to this $C_4$ input (Sponheimer *et al.* 2005). Plant foods in the form of grass seeds, forbs, edible tubers, and roots of sedges are other possible $C_4$ sources, but, except for grasses, tend to be associated with wetland environments (Peters and Vogel 2005). Palaeoenvironmental data from the Sterkfontein Valley reflect a varying landscape of open woodland to savanna with only localised wetlands 3.0–1.1 mya. Most $C_4$ plants would have made a minor contribution to the diet under these conditions. Available animal sources would have included reptiles, birds, and rodents, as well as medium and large grazers (Peters and Vogel 2005). Scavenging or hunting large grazers without effective weapons would have exposed hominins to direct competition with dangerous predators, making this a risky source of food. A flexible pattern of omnivory may thus have existed among *Australopithecus*, *Homo*, and *Paranthropus*, with animal inputs involving a small fraction of scavenged or hunted meat and marrow. The assessment of individual dietary histories is also just beginning to reveal additional complexities introduced by seasonal and yearly changes in resource availability linked to climate variability. Analysis of the teeth of four *Paranthropus* individuals from Swartkrans shows evidence of seasonal differences in resource exploitation from predominantly $C_3$ to $C_4$ foods that probably reflect movement from wooded to more open savanna habitats on a seasonal basis (Sponheimer *et al.* 2006). The evident dietary flexibility of *Paranthropus* is not paralleled by contemporary chimpanzees, even those living in seasonally dry environments, nor by earlier *Australopithecus afarensis* at Hadar (Ethiopia, 3.6–3.2 mya), whose diet remained largely unchanged over time despite changes in habitat structure (Grine *et al.* 2006). The shift to greater dietary flexibility

seen with *Paranthropus*, the later australopithecines, and among early
*Homo* coincides with the onset of global glacial cycles after 2.7 mya
and the resulting selection pressures of increased aridity and environmental instability.

At present, stable carbon isotope analyses cannot discriminate
between sources of $C_4$ input consumed by these three taxa, but,
this significant limitation aside, they do challenge the foundations
of the dietary hypothesis. The enlarged molars and premolars of
*Paranthropus* and related craniofacial morphology were the basis of
J. Robinson's (1954) considering it a 'robust' group of feeding specialists that focused on hard fibrous plant foods in savanna habitats.
The stable carbon isotope evidence suggests these hominins were,
in fact, well-adapted omnivores whose unique dental, skeletal, and
muscular features enabled them to process a diverse range of foods
(Peters and Vogel 2005:231). Young paranthropines could have had a
weaning advantage over the young of *Australopithecus* and early *Homo*
by being able to consume difficult-to-access foods (i.e., hard seeds
and bone) at a critical time in their development. As a consequence,
they would have been less reliant on feeding support from adults,
with implications for the structure of *Paranthropus* social groups and
the life histories of individuals. The inherited ability to process tough
foods would have lessened the need for the pounding, cracking, or
grinding tools that form part of Oldowan assemblages. All three
genera, based on the carbon isotope data, were probably omnivores
able to consume plant and animal resources in a range of habitats.
They may have coexisted in the same landscape at low population
levels, each consuming similarly broad spectra of foods. The use of
stone tools for processing carcasses as well as vegetable foods could
have been part of their respective feeding strategies (discussed subsequently), though it seems *Paranthropus* would have had least need
for heavy processing equipment such as stone hammers and anvils.

## THE STRONTIUM/CALCIUM EVIDENCE

Dietary evidence from Sr/Ca analyses provides additional and independent information on the place of hominins in the foodweb. Initial
studies of Sr/Ca ratios in bone of *Paranthropus* and *Homo* sp. from

UNDERGROUND STORAGE ORGANS (USOs)

This collective name for roots, tubers, rhizomes, bulbs, and corms refers to their subterranean habitat and function as a reserve of nutrients and water for plants under seasonally harsh conditions of drought or cold. Once conditions improve, the stored nutrients enable rapid growth to occur. Tuberous roots are simply fleshy root tissue and tubers are thickened underground fleshy stems. Rhizomes are underground stems that grow horizontally. A bulb is composed of fleshy modified leaves or leaf bases enclosing each other, and these are the primary storage tissues, whereas a corm is a thickened stem base, and the stem serves as the storage tissue. For humans and other animals (e.g., baboons, capuchins, warthogs), USOs provide a source of carbohydrates, proteins, minerals, and vitamins, but humans lack the digestive physiology needed to process some USOs in their natural state. The edible fraction of wild tubers varies within and between species, and is lower than in cultivated varieties (Schoeninger *et al.* 2001). Cooking by baking or boiling breaks down indigestible cellulose, increases the availability of nutrients, changes the flavour, and kills harmful bacteria. The availability of these vegetable foods during the extended dry seasons of tropical woodlands and grasslands and their ability to be left in the ground until needed would have made them valuable fallback foods for early hominins (Kays and Paul 2004). Some basic digging tools, such as a sharpened stick or suitably shaped stone, are needed to access USOs and pounding technology (stone, wood, or bone hammers and anvils) helps reduce large tubers into edible portions, especially for the young or elderly.

Swartkrans showed unexpectedly higher levels of carnivory (low strontium) among *Paranthropus* compared with *Homo* (Sillen 1992). The higher strontium levels in *Homo* were also interpreted as evidence of hominins eating plant foods in the form of strontium-rich **underground storage organs** or USOs (Sillen *et al.* 1995). These results can be integrated with the stable carbon isotope-based model of widespread omnivory among hominins and the added advantage of evidence for dietary and niche differences among genera. Subsequent studies, however, have used Sr/Ca in tooth enamel, and the results differ significantly from those derived from bone. The integrity of the ecological signal preserved in enamel from fossil faunal assemblages has been demonstrated for the Sterkfontein Valley, and used to interpret dietary signals from hominin tooth enamel (excluding the small *Homo* sample from Swartkrans) (Sponheimer *et al.* 2005). Both *Paranthropus* and *Australopithecus* had relatively high levels of strontium, similar to those of contemporary browsers, rather than omnivores. This does not mean these taxa did not eat animal foods, but that the evidence is not seen in Sr/Ca ratios in the modern faunal sample. Some differences in diet among taxa have emerged from the enamel data, with *Australopithecus* (n = 7) having a higher strontium level than *Paranthropus* (n = 13), a finding that parallels the differences initially reported between *Homo* and *Paranthropus*.

These data are interpreted as tentative evidence that increased strontium values of *Australopithecus*, and possibly for *Paranthropus*, came from consuming USOs, as suggested by earlier bone analyses of *Homo* from Swartkrans. Additional, but still preliminary, analyses of the barium/calcium content (Ba/Ca) of the *Australopithecus* specimens reveal a low barium content, which is unlike that of contemporary grazers or termite-eating insectivores that have high Ba/Ca ratios and high strontium values. The nearest comparable mix of high strontium levels with low Ba/Ca is found among mammals, such as omnivorous warthogs that regularly eat underground plant resources. The bone tools from Swartkrans and Drimolen could, based on these isotopic data, have been used by *Paranthropus* and *Homo* to dig for roots and tubers rather than termites alone.[5] *Homo*, with its relatively reduced dentition and musculature, could have benefited from the use of stone tools to process tubers into edible pieces, as capuchins do today.

Despite the differing results between the two Sr/Ca analyses and the Sr/Ca and stable carbon isotope studies, some tentative conclusions can be drawn. The two techniques should be used in tandem, and ideally applied to the same specimens to ensure direct comparability and develop further the strontium-based evidence for dietary differences among taxa. For the time being, the number of specimens examined by Sr/Ca is smaller (n = 20) than that analysed for stable carbon isotopes (n = 37), and the number of specimens of *Homo* (n = 3) is too small to support meaningful generalisations. The option of omnivory for *Australopithecus* and *Paranthropus* remains a strong possibility, despite the negative results from recent Sr/Ca studies. Meat, grass seeds, and insects may have accounted for only a small fraction of the diet and their relative proportions remain invisible using both sources of dietary data. The combined high values for $C_4$ and strontium, however, could be accommodated by the exploitation of underground plant resources. Dietary flexibility seems the most likely adaptation for all taxa, especially in the context of the varying habitats that existed in the Sterkfontein Valley, and further Sr/Ca analyses may highlight the extent of niche overlap and differentiation. They also reveal that early hominins were unlike modern chimpanzees and gorillas in their foraging strategies and had developed behaviours that differed from those of the last common ancestor, including the making and use of stone and bone tools.

The preferred food of chimpanzees and bonobos is ripe fruit, with leaves and piths used as secondary or fallback foods when fruits are seasonally scarce (Laden and Wrangham 2005). The thin enamel and high shearing capacity of their molars are adaptations to processing fruits, but also leaves and piths (Taylor 2002). Even where $C_4$ foods are available, such as in dry woodlands with grassland components, chimpanzees largely ignore these resources in preference for $C_3$ foods (Sponheimer *et al.* 2006).[6] Both the functional morphology of chimpanzee dentition and consistent $C_3$ isotope values (Schoeninger *et al.* 1999) reflect a relatively specialised diet compared with that of australopithecines and paranthropines. The high proportion (35%–40%) of $C_4$ foods in the diets of these hominins indicates strategies based on either regular foraging for these foods or concentrated consumption during periods of seasonal abundance (Sponheimer *et al.* 2006:132). With either strategy, and it is not yet possible to discriminate between them, these early hominins were able to colonise increasingly open landscapes with more prolonged dry seasons.

Dental morphology and use-wear have not featured much in this overview of hominin ecology given their limitations as already outlined, but there are significant patterns between taxa that complement the isotopic and biochemical evidence for dietary flexibility. *A. afarensis*, with its large molars, thickened enamel, low shearing capacity, and heavy supporting mandible, was able to consume hard, brittle fallback foods, including nuts, seeds, roots, and rhizomes (Ungar 2004). This range of potential secondary foods would have allowed it to exploit a wider range of seasonal habitats than contemporary chimpanzees. The addition of tools such as digging sticks or hammerstones would have further increased its dietary flexibility, enabling it to extract roots more efficiently and process hard foods with less damage to tooth surfaces. The dentition of *Paranthropus*, like that of *Australopithecus*, was adapted not to leaf eating, but for processing hard, brittle fallback foods. Enlarged molars and premolars, combined with the supporting mandible and musculature for chewing, enabled *Paranthropus* to consume USOs on a regular basis (Laden and Wrangham 2005). A comprehensive overview of the direct and indirect evidence for resource use by this species interprets the balance of data as indicating a eurybiomic or ecological generalist pattern, with perhaps seasonal specialisation of fallback foods during times of stress (Wood and Strait 2004:149). The ability to use tools to extract rhizomes and other buried foods, including termites, would have contributed to *Paranthropus*' dietary flexibility, and enlarged chewing teeth and thick enamel would have made pounding tools unnecessary. The limited isotopic evidence currently available for early *Homo* combined with a larger sample of dental microwear analyses on molars, including early *Homo* from eastern and southern Africa (Ungar *et al.* 2006), supports generalist feeding strategies for this taxon. The microwear analyses also highlight subtle differences in diet among groups of early *Homo*, though all shared a similar mix of neither very hard nor very tough foods. In southern Africa, *Homo erectus* and *Homo* sp. indet. from Swartkrans Member 1 (1.7 mya) consumed foods that were more difficult to fracture than did *Homo habilis* and *Homo* sp. indet. from Sterkfontein Member 5C (2 mya). This dietary difference may reflect the use of harder fallback foods by the Swartkrans hominins, perhaps related to increasingly drier conditions globally and locally after 1.8 mya.

## CLIMATE, DIET, AND STONE TOOL-MAKING

Isotopic and dental analyses have, together, undermined the original dietary hypothesis of the 1950s with the distinction between specialist and generalist feeders now blurred, and differing patterns of omnivory evident across the major taxa over the period 3.3–1.7 mya. Plant foods – in particular, the USOs of savanna plants – have emerged as likely fallback foods for *Australopithecus, Paranthropus*, and early *Homo* in the context of seasonally dry environments. The isotopic evidence also highlights the likely input of animal and insect protein in the dietary mix, and observations of the hunting of small mammals by chimpanzees enhance the likelihood that this was a shared ancestral behaviour. A case can be made that more than one species could have benefited from the use of Mode 1 tools to access and process plant and animal foods. Given the obvious advantages of stone for cutting, scraping, and pounding (and for making other tools), we ask the question again – why did it take so long for hominins to develop this technology? The anatomical and cognitive capacity to make stone tools probably existed with *A. afarensis*, but this species became extinct by 2.9 mya (T. White 2002), before the earliest currently known tools from Gona, Ethiopia.

The answer may lie in two lines of evidence. The first is the association of butchered carcasses of medium and large grazers with early Mode 1 tools from the middle Awash valley site of Bouri (de Heinzelin *et al.* 1999) dated to 2.5 mya. Two localities at Bouri provide evidence of access to meat and marrow. The first site shows the processing of a medium-sized antelope, including the removal of its tongue, and broken fragments of the bones of a large bovid that bear stone tool cut-marks, chopping marks, and percussion fractures from stone hammers. At the second locality, leg bones of an extinct three-toed horse (*Hipparion*), bear the distinctive tool marks of dismemberment and defleshing. Meat and presumably marrow (from splintered bones) were being extracted at Bouri, and perhaps by the hominin found in the same stratigraphic unit as these tools and food remains, *Australopithecus garhi*. The molars and premolars of this species were robust, suggesting an ability to access tough plant foods, but if this descendant of *A. afarensis* (Asfaw *et al.* 1999) used stone tools to extract animal protein, it was living the life of an omnivore with a penchant for meat and marrow.

The second line of evidence comes from a combination of regional and local sources of environmental data that, when combined, show pronounced fluctuations in climate 3.4–1.8 mya. Looking more closely at the pattern of climate data reveals correlations among increased aridity, shifts in vegetation patterns, greater habitat variability, and the emergence of stone tool manufacture. A correlation is not necessarily causal, but climate change, by altering the distribution of plants, animals, and availability of surface water, can create adaptive stresses as well as new opportunities, depending on a species' ability to respond. Stenobiomic species that are resource and habitat specialists (Turner 1999:78) will have relatively narrow tolerances, with fewer behavioural and physiological options with which to respond to either short or longer term shifts in biogeography. With its distinctive dental and physiological adaptations to extracting nutrients from highly fibrous plant foods (Popovich *et al.* 1997), the western lowland gorilla (*Gorilla gorilla gorilla*) represents a stenobiomic species, in this case one dependent on tropical forest $C_3$ resources. Eurybiomic species, as resource and habitat generalists, can cope better with environmental change through their behavioural and morphological plasticity. The australopithecines and paranthropines were dietary and landscape generalists, and we can infer from primate analogies and the fossil record that tool-using was part of their respective behavioural repertoires. These taxa were thus pre-adapted to the pronounced changes in climate and biogeography that preceded and coincided with the emergence of stone tool manufacture.

The regional record of climate change for the early Pliocene to early Pleistocene, 5.0–1.7 mya, comes from ocean cores off northwest Africa and in the Arabian Sea. The cores contain pollen and dust records that reflect large-scale shifts in vegetation and wind speeds linked to changes in global climate driven by long-term variation in the earth's orbit. The cores have been calibrated with the orbital record of cyclical variation and with oxygen isotope stages to give remarkably precise age ranges for shifts in climate. As outlined in Chapter 2, there is a general correlation of glacial stages with more arid conditions and interglacials with more humid conditions. The periodicity and amplitude of the shifts between climate states (extremes of cool/dry and warm/humid) govern the distribution, stability, and variability in the distribution of the plant, animal, and water resources that were essential for early hominins. The northwest African coastal pollen record shows a long, warm, moist period before 3.5 mya with increased aridity between 3.5–3.2 mya that heralds a trend towards drier conditions across the Sahara and Sahel (Dupont and Leroy 1999:158). This trend towards aridity in North Africa culminated ~2.6 mya in association with the growth of ice sheets in the northern hemisphere, marking the start of global glacial cycles (deMenocal 2004). In North Africa, the onset of glaciation was associated with strengthened trade winds, reduced sea-surface temperatures, and the desertification of the Sahara. The fluctuating dust record in marine sediments from the Arabian Sea provides corroborating evidence of increased winds linked to the onset of global glaciation 2.6–2.5 mya (deMenocal 1995).

Turning to northeast Africa and closer to the Rift Valley basins, a marine core (Deep Sea Drilling Project, site 231) from the Gulf of Aden shows significant shifts towards more open grassland vegetation ($C_4$ pathway) and drier conditions after 3.4 mya. The evidence comes in the form of waxes on plant leaf surfaces abraded by monsoonal winds coming from the southwest up the Rift Valley and across northern Ethiopia and Somalia, depositing the waxes in marine sediments (Feakins *et al.* 2005). With a chronology based on geochemical correlation of tephra (ash) layers with dated volcanic eruptions in the Rift Valley, the core spans more than 9 million years. This long sequence shows an exclusively woodland vegetation ($C_3$) cover between 9.4 and 3.8 mya, with grassland appearing 3.8 mya and then expanding as the dominant vegetation type 3.4–3.2 mya. That expansion corresponds with evidence for increased aridity at this time in the northwest African marine record. Site 231 shows a progressive expansion of grassland 2.4–1.7 mya, a record similar to that seen in the terrestrial evidence described subsequently from the Eastern (Gregory) Rift Valley and Turkana Basin.

The terrestrial record of climate change is less straightforward to interpret, with complications introduced by discontinuous depositional sequences, taphonomic biases, and the inevitable variability introduced by geographical differences among sites. The most detailed records of biogeographical change from 4.0–2.0 mya come unsurprisingly from the same localities that preserve fossil hominins – the eastern African rift basins and South Africa's cave sites. The Turkana Basin, which includes the southern Omo Valley's Shungura Formation and the fossil-bearing deposits on either side of Lake Turkana (the Nachukui and Koobi Fora Formations; Fig. 3.9), provides one of the continent's most detailed and well-dated terrestrial records of biogeographical change (Behrensmeyer *et al.* 1997). Diverse lines of evidence have been used to assess the impacts of global climate change on this regional ecosystem, with data drawn from faunal assemblages (changes in taxa abundance and distribution), stable carbon isotope analyses of old land surfaces (palaeosols), palaeobotanical remains, and small mammal assemblages. The first two datasets provide very different degrees of habitat and temporal resolution and are the basis for large-scale palaeoenvironmental reconstruction. Faunal data are relatively coarse-grained by comparison with palaeosols, as they involve estimates of average habitat variability over periods often spanning more than 100,000 years and covering at best tens of square kilometres (Wynn 2004:107). These limitations aside, the Shungura Formation faunal record offers the best temporal and spatial resolution currently available for the period in question (Bobe *et al.* 2002). The changing abundance of three key ecologically sensitive taxa indicates significant shifts in vegetation cover that can be linked to global and regional shifts in climate. Forest-loving taxa (e.g. **suids**) dominate assemblages 4.0–3.2 mya and taxa adapted to more open vegetation become more abundant after 2.5 mya. The rise of this bovid-dominated fauna marks a shift towards increasing seasonal aridity and corresponding loss of forest habitats (Bobe *et al.* 2002:488). The transition from relatively closed forested environments to more open woodland and grasslands was

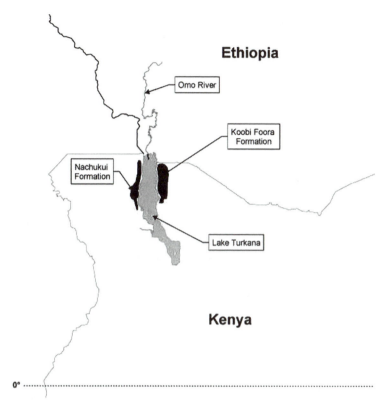

**Figure 3.9.** Lake Turkana Basin, Kenya showing location of key sedimentary formations on the west side of the lake (Nachuki) and the east side (Koobi Fora). The lower Omo River, Ethiopia, also cuts through the Shungura Formation. (After McDougall and Brown 2006.)

marked by an increase in large-bodied terrestrial primates like *Theropithecus*, able to range widely to exploit more dispersed resources and defend themselves against the risk of predators in more open landscapes. These gradual trends underlie two episodic shifts in the fauna of the Omo ecosystem that took place ~2.8 and 2.5 mya and are linked to global climate. The onset of orbitally driven glacial cycles 2.5 mya corresponds with increased variability in the Omo fauna and the appearance of stone tools in the sequence.

Stable carbon isotope studies of palaeosols farther south in the Turkana Basin provide a higher resolution record of vegetation shifts that can be correlated with climate forcing as inferred from the marine core records. Three episodes of aridity (3.58, 2.52, and 1.81 mya) punctuate a gradual trend towards drier conditions in the basin, as reflected in increased $C_4$ vegetation (grass) cover. The trend and peaks of aridity correspond in time with those derived from the offshore Saharan record and, in particular, the peaks at 2.52 and 1.81 mya appear to be linked to global glacial cycles. The isotopic and faunal data from the Turkana Basin agree that increased aridity at 2.5 mya resulted in greater habitat variability. Away from the perennial woodlands that flanked the river courses draining into the basin, the floodplain landscapes would have become more arid, open, and prone to seasonal fluctuations in rainfall. It is just this sort of mosaic of woodland and grassland habitats along and behind the river channels that was used by the first stone tool-makers in the Gona region as favoured places for knapping (Quade *et al.* 2004:1543) and perhaps for gathering in social groups. Cobbles exposed on the active channels of the Awash River were selected and transported to the less exposed wooded river banks and the tall grasslands of the floodplain.

The rich database from Turkana underlines the importance of multiple lines of evidence on which to base palaeoecological reconstructions. Global climate change 2.8–2.5 mya has been correlated with large-scale pulses of speciation among African fauna, including hominins (Vrba 1988), but regionally specific and high-resolution databases are necessary if the causal links are to be made among climatic instability, habitat variability, and hominin responses (Potts 1996). The South African cave-derived data lack the temporal resolution of East Africa's rift sequences. However, faunal and isotopic data from Makapansgat (Hopley *et al.* 2006) and the Sterkfontein Valley (Avery 2001) show a trend of increasingly arid conditions and a gradual shift from woodland savanna ($C_3$-$C_4$ mix) to more mosaic habitats from the mid- to late-Pliocene, characterised by woodlands of varying density and more open grasslands. The onset of global glaciation at 2.5 mya is less easy to detect, but was probably a cause of the shift to more open and seasonal habitats reflected in the dietary signals from the Sterkfontein Valley hominins. Further evidence for regional variability in the timing of the onset of aridity is emerging from central Africa. Pliocene faunas (5–3 mya) from the Djurab

Desert of Chad indicate that aridity began earlier here than in eastern Africa, and with a more homogeneous environment than in the Rift Valley basins (Boisserie *et al.* 2003).

The apparent correspondence in timing between the onset of global glaciation, increased aridity, and habitat variability and the appearance of stone tools could be coincidental, but there are other developments in hominin morphological evolution that, taken together, highlight the mid-Pliocene as a time of significant transition. The interval 2.9–2.5 mya saw the evolution of the paranthropines as a lineage of megadont hominins and the large-toothed, but less dentally robust, *A. garhi*. The evolution of large molars and premolars has already been remarked on in terms of dietary adaptations to processing hard, brittle, fallback foods. Megadontia, with its associated enlarged chewing muscles and areas of attachment (**sagittal cresting**), has been considered a defining feature of the paranthropines, but may also have evolved independently among several taxa, calling into question the legitimacy of the genus *Paranthropus* (T. White 2002:415, but see Wood 2002). Regardless of the ultimate resolution of this phylogenetic issue, an evolutionary trend emerges after 2.6 mya, with the extinction of 'gracile' australopithecines (*A. afarensis, A. africanus*) and the evolution of even more megadont forms (*P. aethiopicus, P. robustus, P. boisei*) linked to the spread of more seasonal, arid habitats in which USOs were potential fallback foods (Laden and Wrangham 2005). For the paranthropines at least, it seems that tool-use was unnecessary for processing USOs – their robust dental apparatus did the job – but digging sticks to access roots and hammerstones to split open marrow-rich bones, or flakes to remove scraps of meat from carcasses, might still have played a role in their feeding strategies.

Shortly after the appearance of stone tools, the fossil record reveals another trend, that of reduced or gracile masticatory apparatus and increased relative brain size. This trend starts with the earliest representatives of the genus *Homo* (2.4–2.3 mya), *Homo rudolfensis* and *Homo habilis*. Considerable uncertainty accompanies the morphological separation of these two taxa (Blumenschine *et al.* 2003) and even their attribution to the genus *Homo* rather than *Australopithecus* (Wood and Collard 1999), but we retain the view that whether one or two species, they mark an adaptive shift towards the *Homo* lineage. Genetic evidence points to a mutation about 2.4 mya that inactivated the gene coding for large chewing muscles, and this may have had the knock-on effect of releasing the physical constraints on brain size created by the force of massive muscle attachments on the skull and its sutures (Stedman *et al.* 2004:418). Stone pounding tools for processing USOs could have acted as surrogate molars and pre-molars, enabling those hominins with this mutation to coexist with the paranthropines as savanna omnivores. The release of constraints on **encephalisation** may be expressed in the increased brain size of early *Homo* notable after 2.0 mya (Wood and Collard 1999), but had its roots in the complex interplay among environment, physiology, and behaviour. The evolutionary roots may also lie with the gracile australopithecines who, as potential ancestors of *Homo* spp., lacked sagittal crests to support large chewing muscles and had relatively reduced molars compared with the paranthropines. Whether a genetic release took place or a more subtle combination of factors selected for increased relative brain size, the fossil evidence points to a late Pliocene threshold.

In the context of increased climatic instability and habitat variability in the mid- to late-Pliocene, eurybiomic or generalist species could be expected to adapt to the pronounced peaks in aridity, and, from 2.5 mya, to the cyclical waxing and waning of global glacial cycles. The first peak in aridity ~3.5 mya neatly corresponds with the time span of *A. afarensis*, which, on anatomical grounds, had the ability to use and make tools and probably the dietary plasticity inferred for later australopithecines. We presume that its descendants, such as *A. garhi*, responded to increasingly heterogeneous and dry environments ~2.5 mya with the innovation of stone tool manufacture, perhaps derived from a nut-cracking tradition. The Taï chimpanzees provide a useful analogue here as sharp flakes are accidentally struck from anvils and hammers during nut cracking (Mercader *et al.* 2002). If nut cracking localities were communal places where animal foods, such as scavenged limbs, were transported and consumed, then we have a context for the discovery of the advantages of a sharp flake. Mode 1 technologies, with their range of possible functions as cutting, scraping, and pounding tools, could have enhanced the reliability and predictability of food supplies, especially in savanna environments with long dry seasons. At the late Pliocene site of Kanjera South, western Kenya, for example, hominins lived in a relatively open, grass-dominated landscape (Bishop *et al.* 2006) (Fig. 3.10). Preliminary analyses from extensive excavations hint at highly mobile hominins who transported local and non-local lithics to places where small to medium-sized bovids were butchered, and, less frequently, horse and pig (Fig. 3.11). The extensive use and re-use of the stone tools at Kanjera emphasises the critical importance of technology in the lives of these landscape generalists. The limited use-wear data available for Oldowan flakes come from Koobi Fora (Keeley 1980; Keeley and Toth 1981) and Aïn Hanech, Algeria (Sahnouni and deHeinzelin 1998), and show that a variety of activities was undertaken, including processing of plant materials, as well as cutting of meat. The making of wooden tools is not yet known directly from Oldowan sites, but the use of organic tools should be expected given the primate heritage of tool-use. The amplification of stone tool-use and the innovation of flaking could have taken 100,000 or more years to have developed, but the coarse resolution of the archaeological record makes it appear as if it were a sudden innovation. The systematic fracture of silica-based rocks to produce cutting and scraping edges gave the Bouri hominins access to flesh, and stone hammers gave them access to marrow. We have already identified dietary flexibility as a feature of early hominin taxa, and the addition of meat and marrow could be particularly advantageous under conditions of seasonal scarcity of easily accessible plant foods. The use of stone for digging and processing fibrous, but energy and moisture bearing, USOs (Stahl 1984) would have had obvious adaptive value for savanna hominins, as it does today for capuchin monkeys in the dry woodlands of Brazil.

Tool-making was certainly not the only behavioural response to environmental pressures available to early hominins, but it is the one that leaves a mark on the landscapes of Africa and beyond. The distribution of Mode 1 sites in eastern, south-central, southern, and northern Africa between 2.6–1.8 mya shows tool-making hominins living in regions with increasingly open and seasonal habitats that emerged following the onset of global glacial cycles. The recognition

**Figure 3.10.** View of excavations of late Pliocence deposits at Kanjera South, western Kenya. (Courtesy and copyright the Homa Peninsula Project.)

of Oldowan sites in West Africa remains controversial, with early reports (Davies 1964:86) of rolled Mode 1 cores unsubstantiated (Casey 2003:35). The presence of *Australopithecus bahrelghazali* in Chad between 3.5–3 mya (Brunet *et al.* 1995) and later Mode 2 technologies in the dry woodlands of west Africa raises the likelihood that Mode 1 making hominins lived in the savannas and dry woodlands that extended west of Lake Chad towards the Atlantic coast, and in time these sites will be found. In the interim, it appears that Mode 1 hominins avoided tropical rain forests, as there is no evidence from West Africa or the Congo Basin of hominins before the Middle Pleistocene at the earliest. Mode 1 sites occur on the western margins of the Western Rift along the Semliki River (Democratic Republic of Congo) and are indirectly dated to between 2.35 and 2.0 mya by faunal correlation with East African assemblages (Harris *et al.* 1987:714). Across south-central Africa undated sites occur in northern Malawi (Juwayeyi and Betzler 1995), the Luangwa Valley, Zambia (Elton *et al.*, 2003), and south of the Zambezi in Angola (J. D. Clark 1966). In southern Africa the earliest evidence for Mode

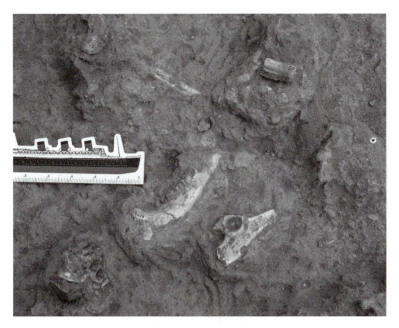

**Figure 3.11.** A lower mandible and postcranial remains of a medium-sized bovid in association with stone artefacts at Kanjera South, Kenya. (Courtesy and copyright the Homa Peninsula Project.)

1 technology comes from Member 5 of Sterkfontein cave, South Africa, which is estimated to be as early as 2.0 mya based on faunal correlations (Kuman 1999). A distance of 4000 km and a time span of 600,000 years separate Gona from Sterkfontein, suggesting a gradual expansion of eurybiomic stone tool-making hominins through savanna and woodland habitats. Early hominins adapted to the seasonality of savannas both anatomically (*Paranthropus* dentition) and behaviourally through tool-assisted access to meat, marrow, insects, and underground plant foods. Other behavioural developments such as food-sharing, pair-bonding, extended parenting, and the use of central gathering places in the landscape may also have enhanced individual and group survival, and these are discussed more fully in Chapter 4.

This typically African biome also extended eastwards across Asia as far as northern China (40°N) by ~3 mya, raising the possibility that australopithecines and paranthropines had extended their range

**Figure 3.12.** Hadza women collecting tubers using digging sticks. Similar digging tools of wood or bone may have been used by some early hominins to access underground storage organs as seasonal fallback foods. (Courtesy and copyright of Alyssa N. Crittenden.)

far beyond current known limits and entered Asia long before the appearance of *H. erectus sensu stricto* 1.8 mya (Dennell and Roebroeks 2005). The broad expanse of this transcontinental 'savannahstan' could have supported grassland-adapted taxa, and it is not surprising that the earliest Mode 1 technologies found outside Africa are in seasonal savanna habitats, such as Dmanisi, Georgia (1.7 mya and found with early *Homo* fossils, Gabunia *et al.* 2000), Erq el-Ahmar, Israel (~1.8 mya, Ron and Levi 2001), possibly and controversially at Riwat, Pakistan (~2 mya, Dennell *et al.* 1988), and in China's Nihewan Basin (1.66 mya, Zhu *et al.* 2004). Though *Homo* is assumed to have been the first tool-maker to spread from Africa, the possibility remains that even earlier hominins, as resource and landscape generalists, were part of this savanna biome. Flint artefacts found at Yiron, Israel, in the Levantine extension of the Rift Valley, may be 2.4 mya and, if so, they reflect a very early movement of Mode 1 makers out of Africa (Ronen 2006). Further research at Yiron is needed, however, to demonstrate a clear association of the tools with the dated volcanic deposits.

OVERVIEW

This chapter asked why stone tool-making appeared relatively late in hominin evolution. The answer lies in a combination of evolutionary processes, with global climate change being the most recent stimulus acting on a common hominin heritage of bipedalism, omnivory, and tool-use. The shift to global aridity starting roughly 3.5 mya with the build-up of northern hemisphere ice, and culminating with the start of orbitally driven glacial cycles at 2.5 mya, created both intermittent and sustained ecological pressures. Peaks of aridity interrupted a gradual drying trend followed by the onset of the rhythmic waxing and waning of glacial cycles. Climatic variability and increased seasonality altered the distribution of plant, animal, and water resources, creating strong selective forces that favoured ecological generalists over specialists. The early hominins – australopithecines and paranthropines – developed a range of morphological and behavioural responses to increasingly harsh and unpredictable conditions, with some species becoming extinct as well. Differing contexts of social learning combined with varying traditions of innovation and variations in neocortex size could have given some species greater behavioural plasticity than others. Stone tool technologies contributed to the ecological flexibility of at least one taxon by facilitating its ability to extract and process fallback foods in the context of seasonally dry habitats (Fig. 3.12).

The interaction of social intelligence, innovation, and brain size with the environment establishes an evolutionary framework for modelling the emergence of the human dependency on technology 2.6 mya. This is the framework on which the subsequent development of the human lineage was built, enabling it to cope in this new and climatically unstable world and, in the case of *Homo*, to thrive as the premier landscape generalists.

CHAPTER 4

# EARLY PLEISTOCENE TECHNOLOGIES
# AND SOCIETIES

The emergence and spread of stone tool technologies in the late Pliocene altered substantially the complex interplay between hominin behavioural and biological evolution. With the addition of cutting and pounding tools to their behavioural repertoire, some early hominins enhanced their dietary security and, ultimately, their reproductive success at a time of global climate change. In this chapter, we consider how a growing technological dependency manifested itself in the emergence of local traditions of tool-making, and explore the implications for the development of social mechanisms for the transmission of learned behaviours across generations. The time frame is restricted to the period 2.6–1.0 mya, during which changes in technology occurred that were built on Mode 1 foundations, including the development of bifacial cutting edges (Mode 2), the use of organic tools, and, possibly, the controlled use of fire. The overview ends with the onset of further disruptions to global climate cycles.

Our focus is not solely technological; we assess other aspects of the physiological and behavioural evolution of *Homo* that enabled this taxon to adapt to increased environmental variability and instability in the early Pleistocene. An arid peak 1.8–1.7 mya caused a further expansion of grasslands and coincides with the emergence of a new species – *Homo erectus* – characterised by an essentially modern postcranial skeleton with an elongated frame that enabled it to range long distances in increasingly open, arid environments. The high metabolic costs of feeding a large body combined with those of rearing large-brained offspring had a direct impact on the social lives of *erectus* individuals and groups. Fundamental elements of the human pattern of an extended life history from childhood to menopause may have arisen, alongside co-operative provisioning and parenting involving males and females.

## MODE 1 – CHANGE, STASIS, AND THE TRANSMISSION OF TRADITIONS – 2.6–1.7 MYA

The study of contemporary non-human primates underlines the importance of the social context of tool-making for the transmission of knowledge and habitual behaviours across generations, and for the process of innovation (van Schaik and Pradham 2003). Chimpanzees and, to a lesser extent, bonobos, have socially accepted ways of using and making tools (Whiten *et al.* 1999). By extension, so, too, did Mode 1 tool-makers, especially given their comparable, if not larger, relative brain sizes. We can assume that early hominins inherited from the last common ancestor the capacity to create traditions of behaviours grounded in the social acquisition of skills during development, and that the ability to innovate and transmit innovations was advantageous in environments – social as well as physical – undergoing pronounced changes. Before considering the archaeological evidence for tool-making traditions, a cautionary reminder is needed about the limitations of the archaeological record. Outside East Africa's rift basins, most open sites in the tropics suffer from poor dating resolution combined with unfavourable conditions for the preservation of discrete artefact assemblages, let alone organic remains. South Africa's cave sites, though generally having limited dating controls and affected by time-averaging of assemblages, nonetheless offer excellent conditions for fossil preservation. Also affecting assemblage composition regardless of location is the individual variability in tool-making proficiency based on age, experience, and learning opportunities that undoubtedly existed within and between hominin groups. Technological expertise need not have been evenly distributed even in the same landscape, with group composition affecting opportunities for transmission of knowledge across and between generations. The combined effect of taphonomic and social averaging is a highly variable archaeological record that probably under-represents the levels of technical expertise existing at any one time. In this context, the few well-dated and relatively undisturbed sites available from eastern Africa give a valuable impression of the evolving social, cognitive, and biological abilities of early stone tool-makers. We look here at the evidence from Gona in Ethiopia's Afar region, the Turkana Basin, and farther south along the western Rift Valley (Fig. 4.1). The combined data show local variations in stone tool-making patterns from the outset, analogous to chimpanzee cultures. Some variability reflects local differences in raw material availability, but real differences exist in knapping methods, raw material selection, and transport that reflect social learning.

The earliest known archaeological assemblages (2.6–2.5 mya) come from the Gona locality, Ethiopia, and provide clear evidence for raw material selectivity. Gona tool-makers had access to river gravels containing cobbles of a variety of volcanic rocks suitable for knapping, and deliberately selected the finer-grained trachyte, rhyolite, and latite in preference to the coarser basalt (Stout *et al.* 2005:367–8). This developed understanding of the physical properties of raw materials suggests an existing pool of socially transmitted knowledge, and raises the likelihood that even earlier sites will be found. The testing of cobbles to assess their flaking properties also seems to have taken place at Lokalalei 2C, West Turkana (2.34 mya), where hominins selectively collected and used river cobbles from a nearby channel deposit. Cobbles of coarse-grained trachyte were minimally flaked, whereas those of finer-grained phonolite were knapped extensively using clear strategies of sequential removals that show understanding of the geometry of the cores (Delagnes and Roche 2005:444–5). The dichotomy in raw material selection also extends to the use of trachyte cobbles as hammerstones and phonolite flakes for further retouching into cutting tools (Fig. 4.2). At the nearby and slightly older site of Lokalalei 1, the tool-makers also preferred phonolite cobbles for making sharp flakes, but used less planned and more opportunistic knapping techniques. A high

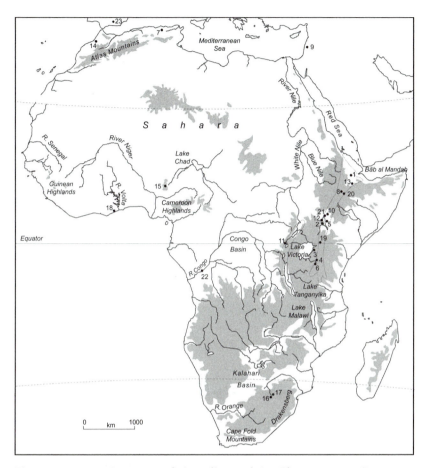

**Figure 4.1.** Location map of sites discussed in Chapter 4: 1. Gona; 2. Lokalalei localities; 3. Kanjera; 4. Peninj (Lake Natron Basin); 5. Koobi Fora; 6. Olduvai Gorge; 7. Aïn Hanech, El-Kherba; 8. Melka Kunturé; 9. Gesher Benot Yáaqov; 10. Lower Omo Valley; 11. Senga 5A; 12. Kokiselei; 13. Middle Awash Valley; 14. Thomas Quarry; 15. Jos Plateau; 16. Swartkrans, Sterkfontein; 17. Kromdraai; 18. Asokrochona; 19. Chesowanja; 20. Gadeb; 21. Nariokotome; 22. Gombe Point; 23. Baza Basin (Orce).

proportion of the core faces bear step fractures from misplaced hammer blows (Kibunjia 1994) or unrecognised subtle flaws in the raw material (Ludwig and Harris 1998). Taken together, Lokalalei 1 and 2C may be capturing the relatively rapid development of stone tool-making skills between ~2.5–2.3 mya, or simply reflecting differences in raw material quality, or differences in activities among the sites. The possibility also exists that the sites reflect expected variations in technical expertise and perhaps social learning between differing groups.

A molar attributed to *Homo* has been found in the same stratigraphic context as Lokalalei 1, suggesting that the tools at both sites could have been made by this taxon, but *Paranthropus aethiopicus* lived in the area as well and may have been a tool-maker, too (Delagnes and Roche 2005:437). The identity of the tool-makers aside, the Lokalalei and Gona sites have convincingly challenged the perception that Mode 1 technologies before 2.0 mya exhibited little variability, planning, or understanding of raw material properties (Kibunjia 1994). They have also undermined the more sweeping generalisation that the Oldowan Industry as a whole (2.6–1.5 mya) marked a long interval of technological stasis (Semaw 2000:1211).

Further support for local variability in tool-making traditions before 2.0 mya comes from the large archaeological assemblages recovered at Kanjera South, western Kenya (~2.2 mya), near the shores of modern Lake Victoria which, at that time, was a small lake or playa. Here, hominins used a range of locally available raw materials for flake-making, but also selected and transported non-local materials, including chert, quartz, and fine-grained quartzite (Plummer *et al.* 2001; Plummer 2004:131). Quartzite was probably valued for its tough cutting edges, with cores more thoroughly knapped than those of locally available rocks. Knappers also employed a variety of strategies for removing flakes not seen in earlier Mode 1 assemblages. These included centripetal flaking (radial, discoidal cores), multiplatform removals (polyhedral cores), and flakes re-used as cores (see inset) (Roche 2000; Plummer *et al.* 2001). The working life of cores was extended (core rejuvenation flakes) and small flakes retouched, often along a single edge creating a distinctive tool (Plummer 2004:131). The evident awareness of raw material properties, their transport, and the ability to control flake removals suggests considerable expertise among Kanjera knappers as well as a degree of planning that exceeds that seen among apes, even Kanzi, the bonobo discussed in Chapter 3. That expertise was put to use in

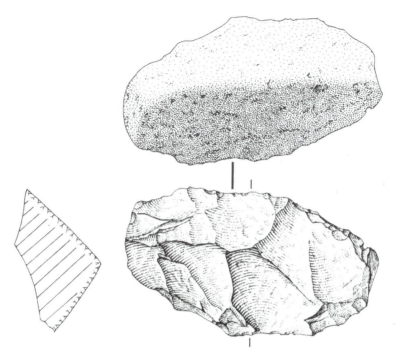

**Figure 4.2.** A phonolite core (10.1 cm long) from Lokalalei 2C (Kenya, 2.34 mya) showing the consistent removal of flakes around the periphery of one surface of a cobble. The cobble was first split lengthwise to provide a platform and a series of eight removals have been reconstructed by refitting flakes to the core. The knapper turned the core to use all the available natural platforms and clearly understood the need to maintain an acute platform angle. (Reprinted from Delagnes, A., and H. Roche, 2005, 'Late Pliocene hominid knapping skills: the case of Lokalalei 2C, West Turkana, Kenya', *Journal of Human Evolution*, 48:435–472, with permission from Elsevier.)

a relatively open semi-arid grassland landscape, in which the most abundant source of high-quality food came in the form of the carcasses of antelopes and horses (Bishop *et al.* 2006). Pigs also feature in the assemblage, indicating an element of woodland habitat available to hominins. The presence of carnivore damage on the archaeological fauna suggests multiple agents of accumulation, but hominins appear to be responsible for at least some of the collection and processing. The faunal assemblage has a notably high proportion of immature individuals of small to medium-sized animals (Bishop *et al.* 2006:37). These may be the prey of carnivores, but the defenceless young may also have been targeted by hominins working individually or in groups. The presence of some relatively complete carcasses at Kanjera South in association with flakes and cores provides persuasive evidence that this area was a butchery site where carcasses were processed. How the meat was obtained, whether by hunting or active scavenging, and how it was distributed is uncertain, but what is clear is that stone tools were an integral part of the adaptive strategy for hominins in this open landscape.

COMPLEXITY AMONG CORE TYPES

Archaeologists have traditionally classified core types by morphological and technological attributes, noting the direction and type of flake removals. The process of knapping to remove usable pieces is called *débitage*, not to be confused with the actual debris or waste from knapping. The deliberate shaping by retouch of stone is called *façonnage* and Mode 2 bifaces were generally shaped by retouch. Mode 1 knappers at Kanjera South applied a range of knapping techniques not commonly seen in earlier assemblages, including the direction of blows inward and around the periphery and either side of a block material. The resulting core forms, typically circular in plane view and disc-shaped or conical to biconical in section, collectively represent a strategy of centripetal flaking. The resulting flakes tend to be triangular to quadrilateral in form and thin with extensive cutting edges. Discoidal cores result from alternating flake removals from both sides, creating a bifacial form that may have been the precursor to Mode 2 tools such as handaxes which also have an artificial edge or plane created by alternate removals. More elaborate planning and management of the geometry of centripetal cores occurs ∼1.6 mya at Peninj (Tanzania), where late Mode 1 or early Mode 2 knappers deliberately planned their cores so that one surface was shaped in preparation for removing flakes of a predetermined size from the opposite or principal flaking surface (de la Torre *et al.* 2003)

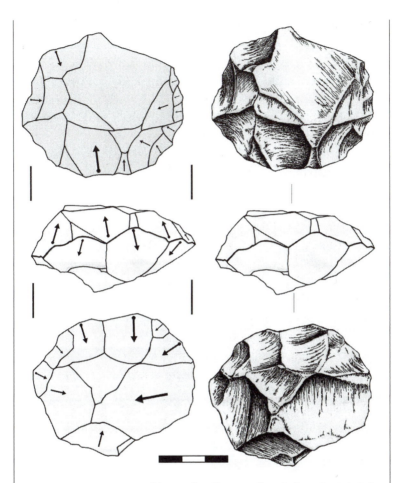

**Figure 4.3.** A 'centripetal hierarchical' core of basalt from Peninj, Lake Natron (Tanzania) showing the sequential, planned reduction of both surfaces (site ST51). (Courtesy and copyright of Ignacio de la Torre.)

(Fig. 4.3). Such sequential planning and understanding of core geometry long predates the development of prepared core technology (Levallois method, ~0.7 mya) and indicates that the ability to conceive and impose abstract forms on stone existed among Mode 1 and 2 makers of the early Pleistocene. Centripetal flaking remained a feature of African stone-working throughout the Pleistocene, occurring among Mode 2–5 assemblages.

Our understanding of the technical competence of early Mode 1 makers is increasing, not just with the discovery of new sites, but also with developments in methods of lithic analysis. The apparent simplicity of some flake assemblages may mask subtle adaptations to local conditions, as in the case of material from Koobi Fora (East Turkana Basin, Kenya, Fig. 4.4) (Braun and Harris 2003). A ratio of extent of flake cutting edge to mass (size) was calculated on assemblages from the KBS Member (~1.87 mya) and the Okote Member (~1.6 mya) as a measure of control over flake production. The resulting 'flake utility' measure shows that later Okote Member hominins, probably *Homo erectus*, produced more cutting edge per block of raw material than did earlier KBS hominins. The greater economy of stone use seen in the later member is tentatively linked to differing ecological pressures in a landscape with unevenly distributed food resources (Braun and Harris 2003:137). In this context, the extended cutting edge probably enabled hominins to range further by increasing the likelihood of encountering and processing foods without needing to replenish or resharpen raw material supplies so frequently. Variation in flake utility also occurs between sites within each Member, emphasising the flexibility of technological responses to local conditions. New analytical techniques, such as the utility index, will, when applied to Mode 1 assemblages from well-dated and relatively undisturbed contexts, almost certainly reveal more local, ecologically sensitive decision-making as distinct from chronological patterns that reflect longer-term evolutionary processes.

Outside eastern Africa, evidence of raw material selectivity is reported from the earliest Mode 1 sites in northern Africa found at the Aïn Hanech locality, northeastern Algeria. In the absence of directly datable deposits, the archaeological sequence at the site of Aïn Hanech itself and at nearby El-Kherba are estimated to date to 1.8 mya based on palaeomagnetic data, faunal correlations with East African sites and comparisons with Mode 1 assemblages from Olduvai Gorge's Bed I (Sahnouni *et al.* 2002, 2004). In Aïn Hanech's oldest layers (Levels B and C), the relatively undisturbed deposits contain fragmentary animal remains associated with stone tools. Large cobbles of siliceous limestone were knapped to produce flakes, with flakes removed on either side of a platform edge making for

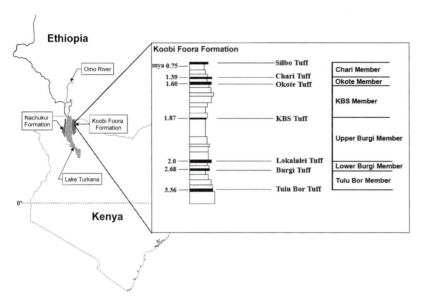

**Figure 4.4.** The Omo–Lake Turkana basin of northern Kenya and southern Ethiopia contains deeply stratified Pliocene to Pleistocene deposits (lacustrine, fluvial, and deltaic in origin) that extend more than 500 km north-south and up to 100 km across the East African Rift Valley (McDougall and Brown 2006). A regional stratigraphy and chronology have been developed by correlating the chemical signatures of widely dispersed volcanic tephra that have been radiometrically dated ($^{40}Ar/^{39}Ar$). The Koobi Fora Formation on the eastern shores of Lake Turkana has provided the earliest evidence for *Homo erectus* in Africa (KNM-E2598), and deposits on the western side of the Lake (Nachukui Formation) were the source of the most complete *H. erectus* skeleton found to date (WT-1500, Nariokotome boy).

a chopper-like core (Fig. 4.5) or towards the centre of the core and around its periphery (centripetal flaking). The understanding of core geometry resembles that seen at the older site of Kanjera, and shows a similar level of expertise gained from regular knapping of stone, and perhaps from observing others. Smaller cores of flint provided flakes that were preferentially selected over limestone flakes for further retouching into sharper-edged scrapers and notched or **denticulated** pieces (Fig. 4.6b).

**Figure 4.5.** A quartzite 'end chopper' or flake core from the Luangwa Valley, Zambia.

CHANGING METHODS OF ANALYSIS

Experimental replication studies of Mode 1 flakes show them to be effective butchery tools that can slice through thick hides and cut meat (Toth 1985). The limited use-wear data available on flakes made on fine-grained siliceous rock (at Koobi Fora) extend the range of Mode 1 activities to include woodworking, cutting soft plants, as well as animal butchery (Keeley and Toth 1981). The greater durability of lava and quartzite cutting edges makes these materials well suited to percussive tasks such as chopping wood or breaking bones. Cores could also have been used to chop wood, or break bone, particularly those with acute edge angles (Toth 1985:109). Mary Leakey's (1971) classification

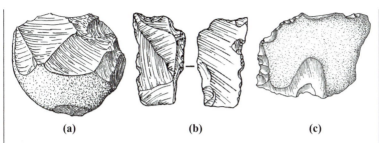

**(a)** **(b)** **(c)**

**Figure 4.6.** Mode 1 (Oldowan) artefacts from Aïn Hanech (Algeria), Level B, including a unifacial core or chopper of limestone (a), a retouched flint flake (denticulate?) (b), and a retouched limestone flake (scraper) (c). (Reprinted from Sahnouni *et al.* 2002, 'Further research at the Oldowan site of Ain Hanech, North-eastern Algeria', *Journal of Human Evolution*, 43:925–37, with permission from Elsevier.)

of cores at Olduvai emphasised their intentional design as distinct tool forms or templates in the minds of the makers. The Olduvai "core tools" included various forms of "choppers" with flakes as secondary or incidental byproducts from their manufacture (Fig. 4.6). More recently, researchers have not assumed the existence of tool templates and have created classifications that emphasise processes of flake production with flakes recognised as valued end-products in their own right. Isaac's (1984) scheme distinguishes between Flaked Pieces (cores), Detached Pieces (flakes and other knapping debris), and Pounded Pieces (hammerstone and grindstones). Toth's (1985) classification ranks the decreasing extent of cortex on a flake surface and butt on a scale of I–VI as an indicator of degree of core reduction. Raw material properties, including size, shape, and coarseness of grain are also recognised as variables affecting the choice of techniques and products of knapping. Leakey's classification scheme is still used to compare assemblages, and the chopper may still have utility as a distinctive tool, but more analysts now incorporate the dynamics of technical skills, such as decision-making processes (*chaînes operatoires*), as at Lokalalei 2C, or flake utility indices, as at Koobi Fora, for studying the cognitive and ecological foundations of Mode 1 technologies.

Other evidence for regional and temporal variation among Mode I technologies comes from Olduvai Gorge, Tanzania (see inset box) (Fig. 4.7). The earliest occupants at Olduvai were active around the palaeolake margins, now exposed as Bed I sediments (1.87–1.75 mya). They used locally available igneous rocks (basalt, phonolite) to make flakes, but preferred the more brittle quartzite for intensive flaking and the coarser lava for heavy-duty cutting tools (M. Leakey 1971). Following tectonic shifts combined with a hotter, drier interval (Hay 1976; Kimura 2002:297), the Bed I period lake shrank after 1.67 mya to expose a bed of fine-grained siliceous chert used by hominins to make tools until it was reburied 1.53 mya as lake levels rose. Comparing flake scar counts on chert cores derived from this Bed II outcrop with numbers of chert flakes recovered from selected Bed II sites shows an overabundance of flakes, indicating either the transport of chert cores away from the "factory" source (site MNK) or the bringing of flakes to the site. Neither of these behaviours is seen in Bed I, where lava and quartzite were knapped close to their sources. The deliberate selection and transport of chert seems to reflect new behaviours at Olduvai, but a re-analysis of the methodology of core scar analysis based on experimental replication data questions this interpretation. The initial results were heavily influenced by core size. Experimental knapping shows that large cores are more likely to preserve extended sequences of flake removals than the surfaces of smaller cores that are more readily reduced, erasing a higher proportion of previous scars (Braun *et al.* 2005:528). The increased erasure rate with continued knapping means small cores are also associated with a higher number of flakes relative to the surviving flake scars. Thus, the high ratio of chert flakes to cores in mid–Bed II does not necessarily indicate preferential knapping of this raw material or its transport. These qualifications aside, there was undoubtedly an awareness of the superior flaking properties of chert and the deliberate targeting of this material during its brief interval of availability.

## PERCUSSION TECHNOLOGIES IN MODE I ASSEMBLAGES

The gradual shift in analytical emphasis away from morphological classifications of core tools towards reconstructing knapping

DIAGRAMMATIC SECTION OF OLDUVAI GORGE

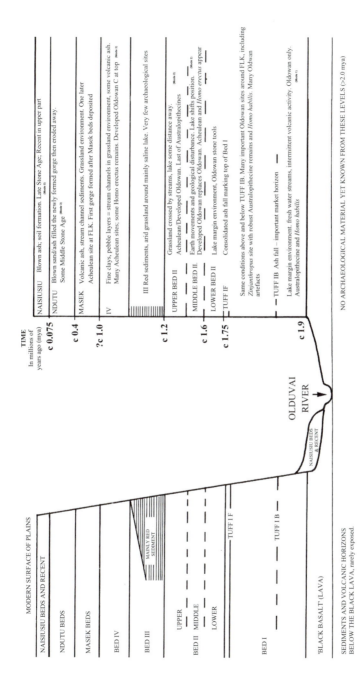

| | TIME In millions of years ago (mya) | |
|---|---|---|
| NAISIUSIU | | Blown ash; soil formation. Late Stone Age; Recent in upper part [Mode 5] |
| NDUTU | c 0.075 | Blown sand/ash filled the newly formed gorge then eroded away. Some Middle Stone Age [Mode 3] |
| MASEK | c 0.4 | Volcanic ash, stream channel sediments. Grassland environment. One later Acheulean site at FLK. First gorge formed after Masek beds deposited |
| IV | ?c 1.0 | Fine clays, pebble layers = stream channels in grassland environment, some volcanic ash. Many Acheulean sites; some Homo erectus remains. Developed Oldowan C at top [Mode 2] |
| | | III Red sediments, arid grassland around mainly saline lake. Very few archaeological sites |
| UPPER BED II | c 1.2 | Grassland crossed by streams, lake some distance away. Acheulean/Developed Oldowan. Last of Australopithecines [Mode 2] |
| MIDDLE BED II | | Earth movements and geological disturbance. Lake shifts position. Developed Oldowan replaces Oldowan. Acheulean and Homo erectus appear [Mode 2] |
| LOWER BED II | c 1.6 | Lake margin environment, Oldowan stone tools |
| TUFF IF | c 1.75 | Consolidated ash fall marking top of Bed I |
| | | Same conditions above and below TUFF IB. Many important Oldowan sites around FLK, including Zinjanthropus site with robust Australopithecine remains and Homo habilis. Many Oldowan artefacts |
| | | TUFF IB Ash fall – important market horizon |
| | c 1.9 | Lake margin environment. fresh water streams, intermittent volcanic activity. Oldowan only. Australopithecine and Homo habilis [Mode 1] |

NO ARCHAEOLOGICAL MATERIAL YET KNOWN FROM THESE LEVELS (>2.0 mya)

MODERN SURFACE OF PLAINS

NAISIUSIU BEDS AND RECENT

NDUTU BEDS

MASEK BEDS

BED IV

BED III

MAINLY RED SEDIMENT

UPPER
BED II  MIDDLE
LOWER

TUFF I F

TUFF I B

BED I

'BLACK BASALT' (LAVA)

SEDIMENTS AND VOLCANIC HORIZONS
BELOW THE BLACK LAVA, rarely exposed.

OLDUVAI RIVER

NAISIUSIU BEDS & RECENT

**Figure 4.7.** A diagrammatic section through Olduvai Gorge, Tanzania, showing the sequence of major depositional units (Beds and dated tuffs) with associated technologies, hominins, and general ecological conditions. (Used with the permission of Derek Roe and the Western Academic & Specialist Press and originally published in *The Year of the Ghost: An Olduvai Diary*, 2002, Bristol, Western Academic & Specialist Press.)

sequences and their cognitive implications (see inset) has also high-lighted variability in percussion-related tools and tasks among Mode 1 assemblages. These include the use of anvils and hammerstones in knapping, and of battered, rounded stones classified by shape as sub-spheroids and spheroids. The formation of spherical stone objects has been replicated experimentally (Schick and Toth1994; Sahnouni *et al.* 1997) and argued to be the unintended byproducts of continu-ous use of hammerstones. By contrast, other replication studies and analyses of archaeological assemblages favour a deliberate fashioning of spheroids as pounding tools (Willoughby 1987; Texier and Roche 1995; de la Torre and Mora 2005). If true, spheroids provide further evidence for the capacity to plan and broaden the range of activi-ties associated with Mode 1 tool-makers. Percussion tools in general seem more prevalent in Mode 1 assemblages than previously recog-nised (de Beaune 2004), especially at Olduvai and Melka Kunturé, Ethiopia (Chavaillon and Piperno 2004; Mora and de la Torre 2005). At the former, concentrations of anvils, battered objects including cores, basalt hammerstones, and quartzite spheroids certainly attest to multiple activities having taken place (de la Torre and Mora 2005:219). Mode 1 involved more than just making flakes.

As discussed in Chapter 3, percussion technology in the form of wood or stone hammers and anvils is used by capuchin mon-keys to pulverise roots and insects, and by some chimpanzees to crack hard nutritious nuts. Accessing foods by pounding may have a deep primate ancestry that precedes the earliest stone flake tech-nology (Marchant and McGrew 2005) and, in the context of drier and more seasonal later Pliocene habitats, may have given access to essential fallback foods such as nuts, tubers, and bone marrow. No direct evidence has yet been found for nut-cracking among African Mode 1 assemblages, but at the waterlogged Mode 2 site of Gesher Benot Yáaqov, Israel (0.76 mya), well-preserved nut remains were found with pitted anvils. Pitted anvils occur in Mode 1 contexts at Melka Kunturé Gombore 1 (1.7–1.4 mya), but only later, in Beds III and IV, of the Olduvai sequence (de la Torre and Mora 2005:216). The earlier Bed I and II Olduvai anvils are typically made of tabu-lar quartzite slabs with battered surfaces, and could have been used for multiple purposes, including knapping, nut-cracking or possibly bone breaking for accessing marrow. Residue analysis of the surfaces may resolve the issue of use, especially when combined with further experimental work that defines criteria for distinguishing between organic and inorganic sources of surface damage (de la Torre and Mora 2005). Unambiguous evidence of percussion tools used for food extraction occurs in the form of hammerstone impact marks on animal bone mid-shafts at the mid-Bed I FLK 22 (FLK Zinj) site, which dates to about 1.8 mya (Blumenschine 1995; Domínguez-Rodrigo and Barba 2006). Even earlier evidence for the use of stone hammers to break bone occurs in one of the earliest Mode 1 assemblages at Bouri, Ethiopia (2.5 mya). Here, the tibia of a large bovid bears distinctive impact scars on its surface along with conchoidal fracture scars, presumably from efforts to extract marrow (de Heinzelin *et al.* 1999:627).

The growing recognition of percussion technology as a significant part of the behavioural repertoire of tool-making hominins does not mean that these tools necessarily occur in all Mode 1 assemblages. Raw material availability and size can affect the frequency of percussion tools in an assemblage, as in the case of the lower Omo Valley where the local stone was largely limited to small angular quartz pebbles (Merrick and Merrick 1976). Some of the earliest Omo artefact assemblages (Shungura Member E, ~2.4 mya) are difficult to distinguish from naturally occurring fractured pebbles (de la Torre 2004), but slightly later assemblages (Member F, sites 57 and 123, 2.34–2.32 mya) show deliberate and careful exploitation of angled surfaces. The mixture of hand-held knapping and occasional use of an anvil to split small pebbles (**bipolar flaking**) show a degree of planning, concentration, and dexterity that exceeds chimpanzee nut-cracking abilities (de la Torre 2004:455). Bipolar flaking as an expedient method of accessing sharp flakes from rounded pebbles is also seen at the late Pliocene site (~2.3–2.0 mya) of Senga 5A, Democratic Republic of Congo (Harris *et al.* 1987; Ludwig and Harris 1998:90). The resulting assemblage of quartz fragments looks unsophisticated compared with the well-struck flakes from Gona or Lokalalei 2C, but at each of these sites hominins demonstrated an understanding of the physical properties of available materials and developed appropriate strategies to create flakes.

## VARIABILITY AND CHANGE: ~1.7–1.5 MYA

The accomplished flaking skills seen in even the earliest stone tool assemblages challenge our preconceptions about the pace and direction of behavioural evolution. The surprising tool-making abilities and awareness of raw material properties at Gona, Lokalalei 2C, and Kanjera South are likely to become less exceptional as the late Pliocene archaeological record improves and analyses continue to probe the cognitive abilities of these early hominins. For the time being, the early technological expertise and extent of local variability in selection of raw materials and knapping methods argue against a lineal sequence of increasing sophistication with time. The pre- and post-2.0 mya Mode 1 tool-makers seem to differ more in their increasing reliance on stone tools than in their abilities to make flakes and pounding tools. Tool dependency intensified after 1.7 mya, with the development of new standardised tool forms, greater selectivity of raw materials and increased site visibility. This brief interlude at 1.7–1.5 mya marks a technological shift, with Mode 1 assemblages amplified by the development of large bifacially flaked tools (Mode 2) made on flakes and cores.[1] These additions to the technological repertoire coincided with a marked increase in African climate variability and aridity 1.8–1.6 mya (deMenocal 2004) that led to a major expansion of grassland habitats in eastern and southern Africa (Bobe and Behrensmeyer 2004; Hopley *et al.* 2007). This step change in climate was also the likely stimulus for the evolution of *Homo erectus* as a large-bodied landscape generalist that developed a range of interlinked behavioural and biological attributes that distinguish it as the first recognisable human ancestor (Wood and Collard 1999).

---

### MODE 2 LARGE CUTTING TOOLS

The knapping strategies used by Mode 1 knappers were intended to produce sharp flakes, which were most often used without further modification. Makers of Mode 2 handaxes made large, typically teardrop shaped tools with a tip, perimeter, and rounded base by flake removals on either side of the long axis, creating a tool with bilateral symmetry, and a lenticular section (Fig. 4.8).

**Figure 4.8** Mode 2 tools: (a) handaxe; (b) cleaver; (c) pick.

The plane of intersection between the two convex surfaces forms an extended cutting edge. Experimental replication studies show handaxes to be multipurpose tools that can be used to butcher carcasses, chop wood, or dig (Schick and Toth 1993). They can also serve as cores for making sharp flakes, increasing their usefulness in environments where food resources are widely separated and tools need to be carried long distances (see Chapter 5). Cleavers differ in having a transverse cutting edge opposite the base rather than a pointed tip, with the cutting edge formed either by the intersection of the ventral face of the flake with retouch on the dorsal surface or by a deliberate blow perpendicular to the long axis (tranchet blow) on one or both faces. Picks are generally thicker and heavier than handaxes or cleavers, with triangular sections, and robust tips that may have been useful for digging or wood-working, but their uses, and those of cleavers, have yet to be tested experimentally. African handaxes and cleavers were typically made of large flakes, but cobbles, slabs, or cores were also used. Considerable variation exists within each artefact type and the significance of this variation is discussed in Chapter 5 along with general development in biface technology over time.

## THE DEVELOPED OLDOWAN AND ACHEULEAN – ONE AND THE SAME?

The starting point for examining behavioural variability during this interval is Olduvai Gorge. Observing that new tool types occurred through the Bed II sequence and in overlying Beds, Mary Leakey (1971) defined three typological and chronological variants, Developed Oldowan A, B, and C, that acknowledged links with the earlier Bed I (Mode 1) assemblages (M. Leakey and Roe 1994). Her typology remains the foundation for assessing local, regional, and continent-wide changes in stone tool-making during the early Pleistocene, and for considering which hominins were responsible for these changes.

The Developed Oldowan A (1.65–1.53 mya) appears in lower Bed II, just above Tuff IIA, and contains more spheroids and small flake

tools, many on chert, than the Oldowan, but otherwise essentially
the same range of tools as seen in Bed I assemblages. Developed
Oldowan B occurs in mid to upper Bed II (1.53–1.2 mya) and is
marked by the addition of a small percentage of bifacially flaked
tools (Mode 2), the peripheral shaping of anvils, and higher percentages of light-duty tools than in Developed Oldowan A. Developed
Oldowan C in Beds III and IV (1.2 mya to ~1.0 mya) is notable for
the prevalence of percussion-related tools, including pitted anvils,
small battered quartzite flakes (*outils écaillés*), and cylindrical pieces
with damaged ends called 'punches' (P. R. Jones 1994:288), as well
as the highly variable bifaces seen in Developed Oldowan B. In
Leakey's original scheme, the Oldowan and Developed Oldowan
were both the products of one species, *Homo habilis*, despite the presence of *Paranthropus boisei* in Beds I and II. Also occurring in mid-
Bed II are assemblages containing high frequencies of Mode 2 bifaces
(40–60% of retouched tools). Leakey attributed this new technology to a separate species, *Homo erectus*. The makers of Developed
Oldowan and Acheulean tools apparently coexisted in Beds II to IV,
each species with distinct cultural traditions, occupying separate ecological niches. Acheulean or Mode 2 biface makers created, with regularity, large flakes as blanks for their handaxes and cleavers, but makers of the shorter, thicker, and broader Developed Oldowan bifaces
lacked this ability and used cobbles or quartzite slabs as blanks. The
tendency for Acheulean sites to be located farther away from the
lake margins than Developed Oldowan sites (Hay 1976) emphasises
the differing adaptations of the two hominin groups, with *H. erectus*
more wide-ranging in its landscape use.

Mary Leakey's chronological phases of the Developed Oldowan
and two-species model have long been challenged, and the concept of species-specific technologies remains contentious (Foley and
Lahr 2003). In the case of Mode 2, the earliest unambiguous fossil
evidence for *Homo erectus* precedes the development of bifacial technology by more than 100,000 years and comes from Koobi Fora, East
Turkana (Kenya). A nearly complete cranium (KNM-ER 3733) (Fig.
4.9) is estimated to be 1.78 mya (Feibel *et al.* 1989), though it may
be as young as 1.63 mya based on a reassessment of the stratigraphic
relationship of deposits overlying and contemporaneous with the
KBS tuff (Gathogo and Brown 2006:478). Further fieldwork should

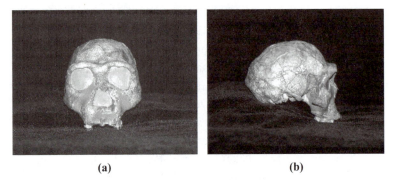

**(a)**                                                    **(b)**

**Figure 4.9.** *Homo erectus* cranium from Koobi Fora (Lake Turkana, Kenya)
(KNM-ER 3733) showing frontal and side views. (Courtesy and copyright
of Philip Rightmire.)

clarify the age of KNM-ER 3733 and other specimens linked to the
proposed stratigraphic revision (i.e., KNM-ER 1813), but regardless
of the outcome, the earliest widely accepted cranial evidence for
*erectus* is a partial occipital (KNM-ER 2598) estimated to be just
less than 1.9 mya (Feibel *et al.* 1989). This estimate remains uncon-
tested for the time being, and is slightly younger than the postcranial remains of two large-bodied hominins (KNM-ER 3228 and
1481) that may be as old as 2.0–1.9 mya. These specimens potentially extend the age range of *H. erectus*, but given the difficulty
of attributing postcranial remains to particular species, they could
also be assigned to *H. habilis* (Antón 2003:128). Regardless of the
taxonomic placement of these specimens, it is clear from the fossil
record that evolution of large-bodied and potentially wide-ranging
hominins precedes the innovation of Mode 2 technologies. Early
Mode 2 bifacial tools first appear in the archaeological record in
eastern Africa ~1.7–1.6 mya at the Kokiselei site complex, West
Turkana (Kenya) (Roche *et al.* 2003), and possibly about the same
time at the ST site complex (Peninj) in the Lake Natron Basin,
northern Tanzania (Domínguez-Rodrigo *et al.* 2005). Identifying
*H. erectus* as the primary maker of Mode 2 technology is reinforced
by the continued production of large cutting tools after the extinction of the paranthropines in eastern and southern Africa around
1.4 mya. Moreover, an *H. erectus* mandible found directly associated

with bifaces at Konso-Gardula in Ethiopia's Middle Awash Valley, Ethiopia, has a minimum age of 1.4 mya (Asfaw *et al.* 1992; Shigehiro *et al.* 2000). At Olduvai, the earliest *H. erectus* fossil (OH9) is even earlier, and comes from the Mode 2 site of EHFR in Bed II, which is dated to 1.53 mya (Kimura 2002).

Leakey's two-species model has now been bypassed by current approaches to lithic analysis that emphasise the dynamics of production, raw material constraints, and analyses of full assemblage variability rather than classifications based primarily on core (chopper) forms. Morphological differences between Developed Oldowan B and early Acheulean bifaces have also been reinterpreted as reflecting differing functions (Gowlett 1986, 1988), raw material selection (Stiles 1991), and stages of use and discard (P. R. Jones 1979, 1994). Experimental replication of Developed Oldowan C and Acheulean bifaces from Beds III–IV using local raw materials from the Olduvai area showed underlying similarities in shape among both groups and in the raw materials used. The apparent morphological differences between the smaller, thicker bifaces of the Developed Oldowan with their more obtuse edge angles and the thinner Acheulean tools were simply a matter of extent of use and resharpening (P. R. Jones 1994: 296). Only three or four resharpening episodes could transform a typical Acheulean biface into a typical Developed Oldowan form. The distribution of raw materials in the Olduvai landscape may also explain the apparent longevity and spatial separation of the two industries. Where large lava boulders were readily accessible to produce flake blanks, knappers had no incentive to extend the working lives of tools and they were discarded after use. Away from boulder outcrops, the working lives of tools were extended by resharpening and smaller cobbles were used opportunistically as well, with both strategies creating the typical Developed Oldowan form (P. R. Jones 1994).

Similar associations of raw material availability and intensity of use are suggested for the distribution of quartzite and phonolite bifaces. Where these raw materials were abundant, there was little necessity to resharpen tools, but where scarce they were used intensively. This association between raw material abundance and degree of re-use holds for Bed II, but not in Bed IV, where Developed Oldowan and

Acheulean sites are located within a few hundred metres of each other, and even contain similar ranges of percussion-related artefacts (pitted anvils, bipolar cores, and 'punches'). The coexistence of these Mode 2 variants cannot be attributed to separate hominin taxa because only one species is found in Bed IV, *H. erectus*. Developed Oldowan sites may simply represent specific areas where bifaces were used and maintained, alongside other activities represented by the range of small flake tools and percussion implements. An additional variable needs to be considered as well and that is the effect of differing levels of knapping skill on biface form, in particular on thickness. Inexperienced knappers often struggle to thin a biface through controlled flake removal on either side of the long axis. More controlled experiments are needed to eliminate the possibility that the small, thick Developed Oldowan bifaces simply reflect less developed skill levels.

Resolution of this issue lies in integrating further technological analyses of the artefacts themselves, combined with modelling of hominin landscape use to interpret patterns of site location, size, and content (Blumenschine and Peters 1998). Recent re-analysis of the Bed II assemblages attributed to the Developed Oldowan B has led to a substantial reduction in the number of pieces that can be classified as bifaces, and recognition that a similar range of artefacts occurs in both industries (de la Torre and Mora 2005). The primary technological distinction remaining between the Oldowan and the Acheulean is the preference for large flakes (>10 cm) as blanks for making large cutting tools (handaxes and cleavers) in the Acheulean. In this simplified vision of the Oldowan/Acheulean divide, the Developed Oldowan A is merged with the Oldowan and Developed Oldowan B, with its bifaces, is considered to be Acheulean (Mode 2). The essence of the Oldowan is the making and often immediate use of small flakes, with Mode 2 involving greater planning that includes the imposition of specific shapes on a blank, whether a flake, slab, or cobble. The conceptual understanding of the mechanics needed to produce the characteristic symmetry of a handaxe is the same whether it is made on a flake or cobble.

To this redefinition could be added the biface-maker's aim to create elongated tools with extensive working edges. The bifaces and large flakes of Mode 2 reflect a level of intentionality or forethought not seen previously. Mode 1 makers largely made and used tools at the time of need, though planned ahead in terms of moving raw materials from source to place of use (Potts 1988). Mode 2 bifaces (and large flakes) are deliberate tools that represent a range of potential or future tasks linked to the tool itself (Wynn 1993). They also involve an ability to coordinate shape recognition in the form of symmetry with the spatial cognition and dexterity needed to transform a volume of material into a predetermined shape (Wynn 2002, but see McPherron 2000). Precursors for these cognitive developments existed in the ability of hominins at Kanjera and Lokalalei 2C to consistently extract multiple flakes from single continuous edges. The knapping of bifaces builds on this capacity to envisage the consequences of future flake removals on the resulting shape of the tool.

REGIONAL PATTERNS

Terminological issues aside, looking broadly at the African record, a trend emerges from 1.7 mya towards greater technical complexity in the management of cores and the shaping of flakes. In eastern Africa, contemporary with developments in Bed II at Olduvai, a new technique for producing small flakes of a consistent size appears at Koobi Fora (Kenya) at sites along the Karari Escarpment (Okote Member). A large flake struck from a boulder, typically of basalt, was used as the platform for the systematic removal of flakes in the 20–40 mm size range from its perimeter (Isaac *et al.* 1997:279) (Fig. 4.10). The consistency in flake size and method of production clearly show these were the intended end product of a planned reduction process. What these small flakes were used for is unknown, but they effectively extended the amount of cutting edge available from a given volume of raw material. This efficient use of raw material could enhance an already mobile lifestyle (see later discussion), especially for a wide-ranging hominin foraging in stone-poor areas (Ludwig and Harris 1998:98). The flake cores, also known as Karari scrapers, share a technical feature with the Acheulean bifaces at Olduvai – they are both based on large flakes. If the ability to make large flakes consistently is a feature of the Acheulean, then Karari cores are arguably part

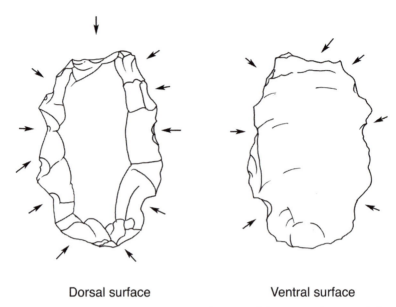

Dorsal surface                    Ventral surface

**Figure 4.10.** A Karari core/scraper showing flake removals around the perimeter of a large flake, with the ventral surface of the flake used as the platform. (After Isaac *et al.* 1997: Appendix 6EE.)

of this tradition rather than a regional expression of the Developed Oldowan A as once thought (Ludwig and Harris 1998:99).

## SOUTHERN AFRICA

In southern Africa, the period 1.7–1.5 mya sees comparable developments in techniques of tool-making that mark this as a period of widespread change. For the region as a whole, Sterkfontein provides the largest sample of Oldowan (Member 5 East, ~2.0–1.7 mya) and early Acheulean (Member 5 West, ~1.7–1.4 mya) artefacts (Kuman 1998; Kuman *et al.* 2005). Oldowan tool-makers used a variety of knapping strategies to produce flakes from the local quartz and quartzite, including bipolar flaking of small quartz pieces and radial flaking to remove a series of flakes around core perimeters. The awareness of raw material properties and understanding of core geometry resemble that seen in earlier eastern African Mode 1 sites. The Sterkfontein quartz flakes also provide microscopic traces of their use, with mammalian blood cells and tissue along with plant residues apparently bound to the silica surfaces (Loy 1998). These findings have been interpreted as evidence of hunting, based on the supposed freshness of the blood ruling out scavenging of old carcasses, and of the extraction of starchy tubers from the landscape. The claim for the preservation of blood in particular seems remarkable given how quickly blood degrades in the presence of air, water, sunlight, and microbes (Tuross *et al.* 1996). Further investigation of the geochemistry of the deposits will help resolve the process of preservation and further analysis of the Sterkfontein assemblage using more sensitive biomolecular detectors now available should address lingering doubts about the legitimacy of these claims.

In the early Acheulean breccia from Member 5 West, there is a shift towards greater use of quartzite, especially for making larger flakes as blanks for bifaces. Also embedded in the breccia was a single quartzite cleaver, with the distinctive transverse distal cutting edge of this tool type. For the excavators, this chance find transformed their assessment of the deposit from being Developed Oldowan A (without bifaces) to early Acheulean, especially when combined with the few bifaces found previously in Member 5 East (Kuman 1998:177). This experience is a salutary reminder that caution should be exercised when assigning small assemblages to particular industries; they may not be representative of the full technological repertoire of a place or time.

Nearby, at Swartkrans, the Member 1 and 2 deposits lack distinctive Mode 2 bifaces, but five large flakes (>10 cm) are associated with Member 2 ($\sim$1.5 mya), and a single large flake subspheroid with the younger Member 3 ($\sim$1.0 mya) (Kuman *et al.* 2005:73). A large flake also occurs in the small collection of artefacts and manuports from decalcified breccias in Kromdraai A (Kuman 1998) and one core and a few flakes in the somewhat older deposit, Kromdraai B ($\sim$1.9 mya) (J. F. Thackeray and Braga 2005). The rarity of artefacts in both deposits may reflect the use of the sites by large, dangerous carnivores, including the false sabre-toothed cat *Dinofelis* (Kromdraai A), or simply the scarcity of hominins in this part of the landscape for more prosaic reasons than a fear of big felines.

The presence of flake-based bifaces at Sterkfontein and large flakes at both Swartkrans and Kromdraai collectively indicates the presence of a post-Oldowan Mode 2 technology comparable to that recognised at Olduvai and Koobi Fora. The Developed Oldowan as an industry no longer seems to have counterparts in southern Africa, especially if we apply a simplified definition based on the making of bifacial forms on large flake blanks. The production of large flakes is not strictly a part of the current conception of Mode 2 technology, but a large flake, like a handaxe, offers an extended cutting edge without the need for extensive thinning or shaping and is easily transported (P. R. Jones 1979). The production of a large flake also shares the same level of understanding of raw material properties and application of force that is needed to produce flake blanks for making a handaxe or cleaver.

## NORTH AFRICA (AND SOUTHERN IBERIA)

The earliest Mode 2 technology in North Africa is still not well dated, with Mode 2 artefacts at Aïn Hanech (Algeria) overlying and postdating Mode 1 assemblages estimated to be 1.8 mya (Sahnouni 2005:108). The earliest indirectly dated assemblages come from the Atlantic coast of Morocco. Since the 1950s, this area has been investigated for its succession of ancient shorelines, now stranded by gradual vertical uplift, which provide evidence of a sequence of alternating high and low sea levels (Biberson 1964). These stratified deposits, exposed by quarrying, especially around Casablanca (e.g., Sidi Abderrahman quarry) contain stone artefacts and fauna in cemented dunes formed during periods of low sea level. Flaked cobbles discovered in the lower Casablanca sequence were once thought to be proof of an Oldowan presence, perhaps extending to the Pliocene, but these artefacts have since been reassessed as geofacts or as redeposited from younger sediments (Hublin 2001:103). More recently, the Casablanca sequence has been tied into the deep sea core record of alternating glacials and interglacials (Texier *et al.* 1994; Lefevre *et al.* 1999), along with efforts at long distance faunal correlation and radiometric dating. At Thomas Quarry 1 (Layer L), the fauna that is associated with handaxes, cleavers, large flakes, and picks (mostly on quartzite but with some flint) has been correlated with eastern African faunas dated 1.5–1.0 mya (Raynal *et al.* 2001; Geraads *et al.* 2004). Three OSL dates from Layer L5 range from

1683 ± 473 kya to 989 ± 208 kya (Raynal *et al.* 2002:68), but their large error ranges undermine our confidence in them. For the time being, the North African record documents the presence of Mode 1 tool-makers in the region, probably at the same time they were made at Olduvai (Bed I) and at Koobi Fora (KBS formation) – about 1.8 mya, but the development of Mode 2 cannot be dated with certainty to much before 1.0 mya.

The likely presence of Mode 1-making hominins in North Africa during the early Pleistocene raises the intriguing possibility of hominin dispersals into Europe via the Strait of Gibraltar and across southern Iberia (Gilbert *et al.* 2003). Mode 1 flakes and cores (limestone and flint) have been found in early Pleistocene deposits in the Orce region of southeastern Spain (Tixier *et al.* 1995; Martínez-Navarro *et al.* 1997) that also include some fauna originating in Africa (Martínez-Navarro and Palmqvist 1995). The case for a North African source of the hominins and fauna seems plausible, but further refinements in dating the Orce sequence and new palaeontological data have weakened the likelihood of a direct African connection. The extensive Pleistocene deposits are part of a larger geological feature, the Baza Basin, formed by tectonic activity that began in the late Miocene (Scott *et al.* 2007), and in the absence of volcanic deposits the age of the sequence is based on detailed magnetostratigraphic correlations. Recent refinements in the dating sequence place the Mode 1 tools at a minimum of ~1.3 mya, the associated large mammal fauna is of similar age, and assemblage composition resembles that of Dmanisi, Georgia (Scott *et al.* 2007:421). An earlier and compositionally different fauna dated to ~1.5 mya lacks any evidence of a hominin presence. The most parsimonious reading of this data is that Mode 1 making hominins entered Iberia from eastern Europe rather than crossing the Strait of Gibraltar.

## WESTERN AND CENTRAL AFRICA

Occurrences of Mode 2 assemblages in the large expanse of the continent represented by West and Central Africa are typically in contexts that offer little opportunity for biostratigraphic or radiometric dating, though developments in extending the age range of

OSL dating may alter this bleak picture. The discovery of a probable specimen of *H. erectus* in Chad (Coppens 1966) and the more recent find of *A. bahrelghazali* in this region of Central Africa (Brunet *et al.* 1995) highlight the early hominin occupation of regions west of the Rift Valley. The distribution of Mode 2 artefacts confirms this hominin presence, with bifaces reported as surface finds in the central and western Sahara (J. D. Clark 1980; Petit-Maire 1991; Tillet 1985), in the Sahel region of Niger (Haour and Winton 2003), in deeply buried alluvial contexts on Nigeria's Jos Plateau (Fagg 1956), in shallower deposits in Senegal (Camara and Duboscq 1990), and on the highlands of the Central African Republic (Bayle des Hermens 1975). In Ghana, Mode 2 Acheulean or Sangoan (see Chapter 5) overlain by Mode 3 artefacts have been reported from the coastal site of Asokrochona, but this sequence remains undated (Andah 1979). Mode 2 sites are rare in lowland West or Central Africa (Casey 2003; Mercader 2003), and their near absence may be an artefact of limited research, or reflect a genuine hominin avoidance of closed canopy rainforests. Profound changes have taken place in the region's biogeography during the past 18,000 years, with the rainforest belt reduced to discontinuous fragments in West and Central Africa as a result of aridity during the Last Glacial Maximum (18 kya) (Anhuf *et al.* 2006) and Lake Chad's expansion at times of higher rainfall (11–9 kya) also affecting the region's climate (Leblanc *et al.* 2006). Such recent fluctuations in climate and biogeography would have had parallels in the early to mid-Pleistocene, creating more seasonal forests and savannas associated with *H. erectus* in eastern and southern Africa. Mode 2 assemblages occur around the highlands of the southern and western margins of the Congo Basin (J. D. Clark 1966; van Noten 1983). The extensive sand deposits underlying the south-central Congo Basin attest to drier conditions in the past and expansions of the Mega-Kalahari (Thomas and Goudie 1984), but, unfortunately, artefacts move vertically through these sands, creating false assemblages and erroneous associations of Mode 2 and later assemblages with radiocarbon dates, such as at Gombe Point (Democratic Republic of Congo) (Cahen and Moeyersons 1977). For the time being, we assume that the age of early Mode 2 technologies in this vast region is comparable to that seen to its south, north, and east ($\sim$1.7–1.0 mya) and hope that future research will establish a chronology and behavioural ecology of hominins in West and Central Africa.

The broad distribution of Mode 2 assemblages across Africa, with the notable exception of the lowland tropics, suggests a spread from what appears to be an eastern African centre of development. Innovations can move with the gradual expansion of the range of associated hominins, most likely *Homo erectus* in this case, or through borrowing of ideas between adjacent groups. The spatial overlap of *H. erectus* with later paranthropines in eastern and southern Africa raises the possibility of inter-specific exchanges of technologies and knowledge through observation, but this option is untestable, as is the possibility of independent invention of bifacial technology by isolated Mode 1-using groups across Africa. As the chronological resolution of early Mode 2 assemblages improves for other regions, challenges may arise to the orthodoxy of an eastern African origin of *H. erectus* and Mode 2. In the interim, both seem to have developed at a time of climatic instability, with the innovation of bifaces and large-flake technology as part of a pattern of increasing manipulation of raw materials, including organic materials.

## NONLITHIC TECHNOLOGIES: BONE, WOOD, AND FIRE

The last common ancestor of chimpanzees and hominins probably used organic objects as tools (Chapter 3), but archaeological evidence for nonlithic tools appears only in the early Pleistocene of Africa. South Africa's cave sites currently provide the most extensive record of early bone use, and this is associated with more than one hominin species. At Sterkfontein and Swartkrans, *H. erectus* is the likely maker of Mode 2 stone tools, in contrast to the range of hominins contemporaneous with the Mode 1 (Oldowan) infills at Sterkfontein (*Paranthropus robustus*), Swartkrans (early *Homo* and *Paranthropus*), and Kromdraai B (*P. robustus*, early *Homo*) (J. F. Thackeray and Braga 2005:234). No hominin has been found in the Kromdraai A deposits. *H. erectus* may also have made the bone tools found at Swartkrans Members 1–3, ~1.8–1.0 mya (Brain and Shipman 1993; Backwell and d'Errico 2001); Sterkfontein Member 5 West, ~1.7–1.4 mya; and Drimolen, 2–1.5 mya (Backwell and d'Errico 2005). However, *Paranthropus* is also a candidate, and the only hominin associated with bone tools in Member 3 at Sterkfontein; the dietary evidence discussed in Chapter 3 indicates that it, along with *Homo*, consumed $C_4$-based foods such as termites. Use-wear analysis of the combined South African assemblages shows consistent selection of weathered long bone shaft fragments and horn cores from medium- to large-sized bovids, with some tips shaped by intentional grinding (see Fig. 3.3). Experimental evidence suggests these tools were used for digging into fine-grained sediments, such as termite mounds, and this remained their primary use for more than 600,000 years. Less likely is the use of bone for extracting tubers, as experimental replication produces different wear patterns for this activity in the soils of the Sterkfontein Valley (Backwell and d'Errico 2001). Wooden digging sticks may have been used for extracting underground storage organs, and though no such tools are as yet known from this period there is indirect evidence for early woodworking from the eastern African record (discussed subsequently).

The only bone tools reported from eastern Africa come from Olduvai Gorge, Beds I and II (M. Leakey 1971). They have subsequently been identified as flaked while fresh, with the bones of elephants and giraffes selected for a variety of purposes, including hide-working, digging, butchery, and as anvils (Shipman 1989). More recent use-wear and replication studies have reduced the number of likely tools because of uncertainties caused by postdepositional abrasion of bone surfaces (Backwell and d'Errico 2005). This smaller sample shows no evidence of hide-working or digging, and the anvils have been reinterpreted as hammers used with stone wedges for splitting other materials such as wood, bone, or hard fruits. One large bifacially worked flake from mid-Bed II resembles a hand-axe (Fig. 4.11), with *H. erectus*, its likely maker, transferring the concept and practice of bifacial knapping to bone. This particular artefact reminds us of the range of organic materials that were probably used as tools, but that simply do not survive. Replication studies show that bifaces are effective multipurpose cutting and chopping tools, including for wood-working (Schick and Toth 1993). Residue analysis of artefacts from Peninj, Tanzania ($\sim$1.6 mya), have found **phytoliths** that indicate that bifaces were used to cut hardwoods (*Acacia*) and flake softer wood (Domínguez-Rodrigo *et al.* 2001b).

**Figure 4.11.** A bifacially flaked bone, probably an elephant limb bone, from upper Bed II, Olduvai Gorge, Tanzania (site FC). The bone is approximately 17 cm long. (Courtesy and copyright of Francesco d'Errico and Lucinda Backwell.)

For the time being, Olduvai is the only eastern African site for which data exist on bone tool use. If the sample is representative for the region and period, then it is reasonable to suggest a different tradition of bone use compared with the South African pattern of weathered bone used for digging. These regional traditions, if they may be called that, arguably reflect differing local environments and needs, with termite mounds a feature of the Sterkfontein Valley landscape, whereas at Olduvai, the bones of large savanna mammals provided an additional raw material for making tools for butchery and percussion-related activities. The underlying significance of the two traditions is their common chronology: Bone tool-making seems to appear no earlier than 1.8 mya, and can be encompassed within a broadened range of technological behaviours that emerged shortly after, and probably in association with, the spread of *H. erectus*. *Paranthropus* cannot be excluded as an innovator of stone, bone, and wood technologies, but its extinction after 1.4 mya and the subsequent continuation of Mode 1 and 2 technologies makes this a less likely option.

FIRE AS A TOOL

The behavioural flexibility of *H. erectus* may have included the use
of natural sources of fire for warmth, protection, cooking, light,
pest control, tool-making, and perhaps hunting. Large areas of
Africa's savanna today maintain a balance of tree and grass cover only
through disturbance caused by natural and human use of fire and
extensive browsing (Sankaran *et al.* 2005). These 'unstable' savannas
extend across the Sahel and from southern Kenya across the broad
Zambezian *miombo* woodland zone into southern Africa. The antiquity of fire- and browse-maintained savanna is uncertain, but evidence of fire in the African record pre-dates the Quaternary (Scott
2000). Naturally occurring fires are generated by lightning strikes
that accompany the onset of seasonal monsoons, and in the late dry
season, the landscape offers fuel in the form of grass and wood to
support bush fires. A bush fire has an active moving front marked
by fleeing animals and insects (and their prey), and the aftermath
is an open landscape of smouldering fallen trees and perhaps the
charred remains of small animals unable to escape the flames. The
tool-assisted scavenger could also dig for burrowing animals that may
have suffocated in their holes. As well as ready-made meals, a pass-
ing bush fire provides a smouldering source of embers in the form
of logs and tree trunks that can last weeks. A hominin equipped
simply with combustion-resistant leaves, a burning brand, or a bark
tray could carry away coals for use elsewhere, and once a fire is
lit, embers can be maintained for weeks so long as fuel is supplied
(J. D. Clark and Harris 1985). Bush fires also promote grass regen-
eration, with new shoots appearing that in turn attract grazers and
their prey. Indirect evidence for the use of fire to manage landscapes
appears relatively late in the African record (see Klasies River, Chapter 6), but early hominins would certainly have recognised the effects
of fire on a landscape, and possibly on potential foods, both plant
and animal. Transforming that recognition into deliberate control or
making of fire requires some understanding of the physical processes
linked with burning as well as planning to maintain fires. Without the knowledge to kindle a fire, some kind of social network
would be necessary to ensure the supply of fuel, and perhaps even a

division of labour under conditions of environmental stress (Gowlett 2005:9). The nutritional and physical advantages of controlled fire would more than offset these costs.

The deliberate cooking of USOs could have given *H. erectus* access to a reliable energy source by neutralising toxins and improving nutrient yield (Stahl 1984; Wrangham *et al.* 1999). Cooked and dried meat resists bacterial decay longer than raw meat, and thorough cooking can kill parasites such as tapeworms. Other subsistence-related uses of fire include making tools such as wooden spears and digging sticks with fire-hardened tips, and controlling the movement of game for ambush hunting. As well as its obvious value in providing warmth and protection from predators, fire has significant social value as a focus of group interaction. Firelight effectively extends the daylight hours for making and maintaining tools, preparing food, and social bonding.

Archaeological evidence for the controlled use of fire 1.6–1.0 mya remains equivocal, with uncertainty existing about the anthropogenic origin of traces of burning and the role of taphonomic processes in creating fortuitous associations between artefacts and naturally burnt areas (James 1989). In eastern Africa, the evidence takes the form of oxidised patches of sediment in association with stone artefacts and sometimes bone. Two of the most thoroughly studied examples come from Koobi Fora and Chesowanja, both in Kenya. At Koobi Fora, areas of apparent burning have been discovered at sites within the Okote tuff, dated to 1.6 mya, which also preserves fossils of *H. erectus*. Among the most intensively investigated localities is FxJj 20 Main, which contains Karari core-scrapers and other stone artefacts along with fauna and discrete concentrations of fully oxidised sediment near the sequence's base. The oblong to circular form of the oxidised deposits and their basin-shaped profiles most closely resemble hearths rather than the more irregular shape of burnt stumps, which have little impact on surrounding sediment (Bellomo 1994:176). Palaeomagnetic analyses also show the patches to have been reheated several times, and at temperatures of 400°C and to a depth not normally associated with bush fires (Bellomo and Kean 1997). The areas of burning seem to have been revisited, perhaps as part of the site's seasonal use, as if it was a favoured place for camping, or at least tool-making. A spatial analysis of artefacts found within 5 cm depth of the uppermost patch of burning showed patterns consistent with tool-making and tool-use taking place nearby (Bellomo 1994). It is tempting to envisage a *H. erectus* group gathered around the glow and safety of firelight to share the company of others and process food, though we lack evidence for cooking meat (burnt bone) or roasting tubers.

Nearby at FxJj 20 East, phytoliths recovered from several burnt areas show that hominins used a variety of woods to make fires, including easily ignited palm wood (Peters and Rowlett 1999). The botanical knowledge for kindling fire seems to have existed by 1.6 mya, though it cannot be said with certainty that *H. erectus* made fire as opposed to sustained fires from curated embers gathered from natural sources. A similar association of oxidised sediment with artefacts occurs at Chesowanja, near Lake Baringo. Here, at site GnJj 1/6E, late or Developed Oldowan artefacts with some possible Mode 2 elements (picks) occur with fauna, including cranial remains of *Australopithecus/Paranthropus boisei*, in the same deposits as baked clay clasts dated to ~1.5 mya (Gowlett *et al.* 1981). The larger (5–7 cm) clay pieces occur in a concentration measuring approximately 1 × 1.5 m, with palaeomagnetic analyses showing exposure to temperatures of ~600°C, consistent with a campfire rather than the lower temperatures of a bush fire, though stumps can sometimes reach hearth-like temperatures (Gowlett 1999). The burnt clay cluster has been affected by water runoff and the possibility remains that the association of artefacts with baked sediment is fortuitous, though the stone and bone scatters show minimal disturbance (J. D. Clark and Harris 1985).

Chesowanja and Koobi Fora provide tantalising hints for the controlled use of fire, and brief mention should be made of fire-cracked rocks in a Mode 2 site at Gadeb (1.5–0.7 mya) in the Ethiopian highlands and of burnt tree stumps in the Middle Awash Valley associated with Mode 1 (Bodo A-4) and Mode 2 (HAR-A3) sites (J. D. Clark and Harris 1985). The Gadeb material is of interest as it comes from a highland context where warmth would be advantageous, but palaeomagnetic analysis of this material remains inconclusive. In the Middle Awash, the areas of burning are natural, but the associated artefacts may represent hominins gathering around these focal points, or they may simply be fortuitous associations.

In South Africa, taphonomic issues have also dogged the acceptance of early evidence of deliberate burning. In Member 3 at Swartkrans, 270 bone fragments from an assemblage of 108,098 specimens have been identified as affected by heat, with 47% of the burnt bone subjected to temperatures approaching or above 600°C (Brain and Sillen 1988). The observed changes to the bone structure and chemistry are tentatively supported by preliminary and as yet unpublished electron spin resonance (ESR) analyses that identify free radicals created by burning at high temperatures (Skinner pers. comm.). The burnt bone occurs throughout much of the six metres of the Member 3 deposit, which makes it a little less likely that it is intrusive (cf. Curnoe *et al.* 2001). That said, all the deposits are derived from external sources (washed in) and the potential for mixing cannot be excluded in any Member. The lack of obvious concentrations also undermines arguments in favour of spontaneous combustion in a cave deposit. The Member 3 burning appears to be the result of repeated use of fire by hominins, perhaps for cooking meat based on the more frequent association of cutmarks on the burnt than the unburnt bone. Members 1 and 2 contain fossils of *Paranthropus robustus* and early *Homo*, but only *Paranthropus* has been found in Member 3 with bone and stone tools. The small stone artefact assemblage includes a large flake (>10 cm) that suggests an Acheulean attribution (Kuman *et al.* 2005), and, on balance, the stone artefacts are probably the work of *Homo*, though *Paranthropus* cannot be excluded. Members 1–3 are thought to be broadly contemporaneous, based on their faunal content and correlations with 1.6 mya East African fauna from dated contexts (de Ruiter 2003). This accords with ESR estimates of ~1.6 mya for Member 1, but evidence of mixing of younger with older fauna in Members 2 and 3 (Curnoe *et al.* 2001) makes these deposits unreliably dated for the time being. The presence of *Paranthropus* in Member 3 does, however, suggest an age of at least 1.0 mya for the use of fire at Swartkrans.

Relatively close in age to the proposed minimum age of Member 3 is the Israeli Mode 2 site of Gesher Benot Ya'aqov. Dated to approximately 780 kya, it contains the most compelling evidence for the early use of fire in the form of multiple clusters of burnt flint and wood (Goren-Inbar *et al.* 2004; Alperson-Afil *et al.* 2007). On balance, the African database and that of its Near Eastern neighbour point to the use of fire possibly starting as early as 1.6 mya, but with more certainty in the mid-Pleistocene. The very earliest dates should not be too surprising, given the cognitive abilities of *H. erectus* (and perhaps *Paranthropus*) to shape organic and inorganic materials into tools and use them for a range of tasks. These hominins had an intimate awareness of the properties of living and inanimate resources and the effects of seasonal changes to savanna and woodland landscapes. Naturally occurring fire, even if infrequent, would be yet another resource to be harnessed and one that had the added effect of creating a focal point for interaction, observation, and learning. For most archaeologists, though, the bulk of the evidence points to a mid-Pleistocene development of the capacity to systematically make fire, with much of the evidence coming from high-latitude Eurasian sites younger than MIS 12 (430 kya) (Rolland 2004; Gowlett 2005). There is a gap in the African record between possible early traces of fire at 1.6–1.0 mya and the more widespread evidence found later in the mid-Pleistocene (Chapter 6). Given the obvious physical and social advantages of controlled fire use, the apparent slow uptake of this technology confounds expectations. The paucity of sites may reflect a combination of low population densities and poor preservation of hearths, especially in open sites as opposed to caves, or genuine cognitive limitations of early hominins before about 400 kya in Africa, Europe, and Asia. The latter interpretation seems less likely now given the recent support from thermoluminesence analysis of burnt flint pieces at Gesher Benot Ya'aqov that the hominins at this lakeside site were, indeed, making fire and structuring their social lives around hearths (Alperson-Afil *et al.* 2007).

A WEED IN THE GARDEN OF EDEN

The technological changes seen at 1.7–1.5 mya, perhaps including the controlled use of fire, reflect an increased reliance on tools as part of the behavioural repertoire of at least one hominin species.

These developments follow shifts in global climate, the evolution of *H. erectus*, and its dispersal across much of Africa and Asia, substantially before the development of the Mode 2 technology and use of fire once considered critical for this to happen. The near contemporaneity of *H. erectus* sites with Mode 1 tools in Africa and Eurasia at 1.8 mya (see Chapter 3) raises the possibility that this species originated outside Africa (Dennell and Roebrooks 2005). The hominin fossils from the Georgian site of Dmanisi, in particular, show African and East Asian craniodental traits at ~1.7 mya (Rightmire *et al.* 2006), but also have postcranial features suggestive of links with *Homo habilis* and early *H. erectus*, including the limb morphology to travel long distances (Lordkipanidze *et al.* 2007). For the time being, an African origin seems more likely, given the emergence of the anatomical capacity for long-distance travel with early *Homo*, either *H. habilis* or *H. rudolfensis* (Haeusler and McHenry 2004). Both taxa were long-legged and remain prime candidates for the ancestral population from which *H. erectus* evolved. The early age for *H. erectus* at Koobi Fora of ~1.9 mya (KNMR-2598) also provides a chronological anchor for considering subsequent movements of this species. The apparent rapidity of *H. erectus'* dispersal into Eurasia ~1.8 mya seems much less remarkable on closer examination. Assuming population expanded at a modest rate of just 1 km per year, starting from Lake Victoria, *H. erectus* would have reached Java within 15,000 years, or by 1.785 mya, a date well within one standard deviation of even the most precise dating techniques available for the period. The shorter amble to Dmanisi would be almost undistinguishable from an African origin.

The widespread occurrence of *H. erectus* and its ability to thrive in disrupted habitats make it analogous to a successful weed that develops a new adaptive niche in response to changing selection pressures (Cachel and Harris 1998). For early *Homo*, the selection pressures were caused by climate change ~1.8 mya, with increased aridity, especially in Africa, creating landscapes with more unevenly and widely dispersed food resources. The niche was filled by a large-bodied, relatively larger brained, tool-assisted forager with a high-quality diet based on a substantial meat input, a large home range, and a life history characterised by a slow maturation rate (Aiello and Wells 2002; Antón 2003). This combination of biological and behavioural attributes makes *H. erectus* more like modern humans in its lifestyle compared to earlier and contemporary hominins. Before looking briefly at each of these features in turn, we consider the record of climate change.

The marine and terrestrial indicators of climate and biogeographical change reviewed in Chapter 3 collectively highlight a pronounced trend from the late Pliocene through the early Pleistocene (2.5–1.7 mya) towards increased aridity and associated expansion of $C_4$ grasslands in eastern, southern, and northwestern Africa (deMenocal 2004). At a regional scale, the stable isotope and palaeosol data from the Turkana Basin point to a rapid shift towards greater aridity at 1.81 mya that continues to 1.58 mya (Wynn 2004) with consequently increased ecological diversity. Farther south along the Eastern Rift, pollen and phytolith records from the Lake Natron Basin's Humbu Formation record dry open grassland environment ~1.5 mya (Domínguez-Rodrigo *et al.* 2001a). At Olduvai, during mid-Bed II times, the palaeolake shrank in response to increased aridity (Decampo *et al.* 2002) combined with uplift (Hay 1976) to expose chert beds and increase the extent of open plain around the lake. Localised uplift in parts of the Eastern and Ethiopian Rift starting about 1.8 mya (Ebinger 2005) further contributed to the increasing diversity of habitats at this time. The general pattern of increased aridity and expansion of $C_4$ grasslands is mirrored in the shifting composition of large-mammal communities (Bobe and Behrensmeyer 2004). Before 1.8 mya, grazers account for 15%–25% of most fossil assemblages, with browsers and arboreal species making up the bulk of the large-mammal biomass (Vrba 1995). Thereafter, the balance shifted in favour of grazers, which account for up to 45% of fossil species. The shift is also reflected in the extinction of several taxa of large, predatory sabre-toothed cats (machairodonts) and hyenas that made a living by ambush-style hunting in more wooded habitats (Turner 1999:85). By 1.5 mya, the only feline families remaining were those found today.

In South Africa, the period between 1.8–1.7 mya sees a significant decrease in monsoonal rainfall and a shift to a more open landscape than existed in the late Pliocene, with its mosaic of habitats. The evidence for expanded savanna grasslands comes from the climate proxies of fauna and stable isotopes (carbon and oxygen). At Sterkfontein, the faunal assemblage shows significant increases in grazers and this, combined with carbon isotope data, indicate a more $C_4$-grass-dominated landscape than previously (Luyt *et al.* 2003). Supporting isotopic evidence for a similarly marked shift in vegetation at this time comes from a flowstone at Buffalo Cave, to the north of Sterkfontein (Hopley *et al.* 2007).

---

WHAT IS A SAVANNA?

Savanna ecosystems comprise two main plant communities – trees and grasses. Competing for soil nutrients and water, they coexist by having separate niches, with differing root systems, growth periods, and communities of herbivores (browsers and grazers). The proportion of tree to grass cover varies with rainfall and soil moisture, with wet savannas found in areas with rainfall above 1000 mm or on poorly draining soils, and dry savannas where rainfall is below 1000 mm or soils are easily drained. Savannas range in type from largely woodland with a sparse grass ground cover to open grassland with few trees. The balance of tree and grass cover is maintained across large parts of Africa through disturbance caused by fire and extensive browsing (Sankaran *et al.* 2005). Trees in these fire-based savannas typically have thick bark that protects them from short-lived grassfires. Pronounced seasonal variation in rainfall typifies savannas, with the result that grazing quality declines with long dry seasons and animals disperse or migrate to more nutritious pastures. Much plant growth takes place beneath the surface with USOs (roots, bulbs, and corms), an adaptation to storing water during long dry seasons. Drought and heat-adapted $C_4$ grasslands emerge in Africa with the onset of global glacial cycles after 2.7 mya, and more open grasslands appear from 1.8 mya (Bobe and Behrensmeyer 2004). *Homo erectus*, as a tool-equipped savanna dweller, would have been able to access meat protein by scavenging and hunting, and by collecting a range of seasonally available plant foods.

In this ecological setting of more open landscapes with patchy distributions of resources, including surface water, a large-bodied, longer-legged, energetically efficient biped would have been able to range widely during daylight hours and exploit more dispersed resources (Aiello and Wells 2002; Antón *et al.* 2002). The small African sample of postcranial fossils that can be unambiguously assigned to *H. erectus* comes from the Turkana Basin, and includes the relatively complete skeleton of a boy from Nariokotome (KNM-WT 15000) dated to 1.5 mya (A. Walker and Leakey 1993). His bones and those of others show that this was, indeed, the physique that characterised early *H. erectus*, which probably had home ranges exceeding those of all earlier and contemporary hominins, and approximating those of modern tropical foragers (Antón *et al.* 2002: Table 4). A linear physique also enabled *H. erectus* to minimise exposure to sunlight during daytime foraging, reducing the risk of over-heating and the need for water (Wheeler 1993). The combined effect of these developments in anatomy and physiology increased *H. erectus*' tolerance of aridity, and enabled it to expand, like a weed, into a variety of new habitats. If, as seems to have been the case, it was also able to increase the quality of its diet by regularly procuring meat and tubers (see inset), then it would have been able to expand its home range yet farther, and especially into grassland habitats with abundant grazers, not to mention predators. A large body size would also have been advantageous in this context, both in communal defence against predators and in competing with them for food (Brantingham 1998: Stiner 2002). The seemingly rapid dispersal of *erectus* into the 'savannahstan' of Eurasia about 1.8 mya thus seems less remarkable, given its biological adaptations and use of Mode 1 tools for cutting and pounding.

LANDSCAPE USE

The high-quality archaeological records from East Africa's rift basins provide evidence for the increasingly wide-ranging use of landscapes by early Pleistocene hominins, principally *H. erectus*. By integrating reconstructions of the palaeogeography and

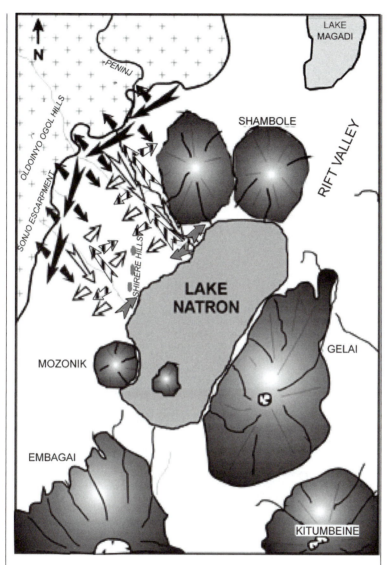

**Figure 4.12.** A hypothetical model of hominin land-use (*H. erectus*) in the Lake Natron Basin (Tanzania) ∼1.5 mya. Large arrows mark primary occupation areas along the slopes of the Sonjo Escarpment during the wet season when tree cover and surface water would be abundant. Smaller arrows mark secondary routes of movement onto the plains for accessing animal resources. (Image reproduced with the permission of the Western Academic & Specialist Press.)

palaeoecology of each basin with the distribution of raw material sources and then archaeological sites, it is possible to model changing patterns of landscape use over time. Spanning the period 2.3–1.6 mya, the Turkana Basin shows a gradual expansion of tool-making and using activities away from immediate sources of water and stone. At 2.3 mya, hominin tool transport remained within 1 km of the river systems, and still at 1.9–1.8 mya, hominins were tied to water and sources of stone for knapping (Rogers *et al.* 1994). By 1.6 mya, hominins were using a greater variety of habitats, including more open landscapes farther away from stone sources and water (Kibunjia 1994). Fluctuations in the basin's hydrology between river- and lake-dominated environments may account for these behavioural shifts, but similar patterns are seen at Olduvai Gorge and in the Lake Natron Basin. At Olduvai, a lake environment persisted between 1.9–1.4 mya with an interruption between 1.67–1.53 mya. In Bed II times (∼1.6 mya), hominin ranging patterns, as reflected in raw material transport, exceeded distances of 10 km, incorporating a variety of habitats with biface-rich sites located farther from the lake margins than the biface-poor Developed Oldowan sites (Hay 1976: Blumenschine *et al.* 2003). In the Lake Natron Basin, early Pleistocene (∼1.5 mya) *H. erectus* lived in more open, resource-poor environments than at Olduvai and the distribution of archaeological sites seems to reflect a seasonal strategy of moving between highland and lowland zones to maximise resource availability (Downey and Domínguez-Rodrigo 2002) (Fig. 4.12). As at Olduvai, sites with bifaces are located farther from the lake margins than those dominated by Mode 1 flakes that are also generally associated with butchered carcasses. In each basin, *H. erectus* shows attributes of a landscape generalist able to extract resources from open and closed habitats as well as integrating technology into its planning.

As well as a larger body to feed, *H. erectus* also had a relatively large brain to support. With its estimated cranial volume of 909 cm$^3$, the 1.5-million-year-old Nariokotome juvenile had a brain twice the predicted size for a non-human primate of similar body size and two-thirds the size of the modern human brain (1354 cm³) (Falk 2004). The metabolic and reproductive costs of a large brain are high, especially for females during pregnancy and lactation, as it consumes nine times more energy for its weight than other human tissues, and stores no significant energy reserves of its own (Aiello and Wheeler 1995:200). It is estimated that a *H. erectus* individual weighing 59 kg with a brain size of 800 cm³ would have devoted 17% of its resting energy to supporting its brain. The smaller bodied (36–39 kg) and smaller brained (450 cm³) australopithecines would have expended only 11% of their resting energy on their brain (Leonard and Robertson 1992). The added energy requirements of the larger *H. erectus* brain and body could have been met by increasing the energy and protein content of the diet, as well as by making an evolutionary trade off with other expensive tissues, such as the digestive system. The human gut is small in relation to our body size, and this loss of digestive facility was offset by increased consumption of high-quality and easily digestible foods, namely animal fat and protein (Aiello and Wheeler 1995). The narrow pelvis of the Nariokotome skeleton arguably reflects this reduction in gut size early in the evolution of *H. erectus*.

For the *erectus* female, pregnancy and, more especially, lactation added significantly to daily energy needs, with an estimated increase in expenditure of 47%–87% compared with smaller bodied australopithecines and paranthropines (Aiello and Key 2002; Steudel-Numbers 2006). These high costs could have been met by changes to feeding and reproductive strategies, but with significant implications for the social lives of *H. erectus* groups. Females could have found the additional calories needed by eating more and higher quality foods, such as meat and USOs. Accessing meat would have put the mother and child at risk from predators, but digging for tubers is far less dangerous and they are available year round today in parts of eastern Africa (O'Connell *et al.* 1999:474). Tubers, though, generally need to be cooked to be edible and maximise nutrient content (Stahl 1984), which, in turn, requires the control of fire. For *H. erectus*, the development of cooking may have solved this problem after 1.6 mya, but there is no direct evidence for the roasting of plant foods in the form of charred remains or phytoliths. If we accept the evidence for hearths at Koobi Fora and Chesowanja, then how did large-bodied and large-brained *Homo* meet its dietary needs before 1.6 mya? The archaeological and isotopic evidence points towards the consumption of animal-based foods – meat and marrow (see inset). The earliest Mode 1 assemblages with bone (Bouri, ~2.5 mya) show evidence of the butchery of carcasses with stone flakes and the extraction of marrow using stone hammers. By 1.8 mya, if not long before, hominins were sufficiently skilled at accessing meat from carcasses before other carnivores to make meat an important part of the diet (Domínguez-Rodrigo 2002; Domínguez-Rodrigo and Barba 2006). The predatory skills of *H. erectus* may have been another critical factor in enabling this species to disperse into the temperate environments of Eurasia with their seasonal shortages of fallback plant foods (Stiner 2002).

---

### HUNTING, SCAVENGING, AND CENTRAL PLACES

Until the early 1980s, archaeologists generally assumed that associations of stone tools with the remains of large mammals indicated evidence of a direct behavioural association with sites reflecting butchery areas or living floors in the case of dense concentrations of material, as at FLK 22 (FLK *Zinjanthropus*) and the stone outlines of a purported hut circle at site DK (see Binford 1981), both in Olduvai Bed I (M. Leakey 1971). Using contemporary ethnographic analogues, living floors were interpreted as hunter-gatherer campsites where social groups shared food derived from a gender-based division of labour, with males hunting and scavenging and females gathering. Such home bases were thought to have provided the social contexts for the evolution of other human traits, including language and monogamy (Isaac 1978). Subsequent testing of the home base model has combined comparative analyses of other sites like Koobi Fora (Isaac 1981), with taphonomic reassessments and experimental studies of assemblage formation at Olduvai, including the impact of human versus carnivore consumption of carcasses (Binford

1981,1988; Bunn 1981, 1986; Bunn and Kroll 1986). Observations of contemporary scavenging and plant gathering opportunities in savanna environments provided evidence on which to base alternative interpretations to the home base concept (Vincent 1984; Sept 1986, 2001; Blumenschine 1987, 1988). Associations of bone and stone have been explained as the result of hominins carrying stone to carnivore kill sites where only marrow and scraps remained (Binford 1981); by hominins carrying carcasses to caches of stone placed along strategic points in foraging ranges (Potts 1988, 1991); by repeated use of favoured places where food was abundant and protection offered by trees allowed hominins to eat, sleep, and socialise, creating dense concentrations of debris over time (Schick 1987; Sept 1992); and as places to which meat was transported and defended communally against competitors and that provided other resources to support a group (Rose and Marshall 1996). Except for Binford's, all these models share the active movement of meat away from places of danger to sites where stone and other resources were available. At issue is the quantity of meat available, the frequency of its consumption, and the methods of its procurement. Early access to a carcass either through active scavenging or hunting provides large packets of food that can be shared and encourages communal co-operation in transport and defence. A carnivore-scavenged carcass yields far less meat, with marrow as the main attraction for hominins (Blumenschine 1991). The low frequency of success in big game hunting by contemporary savanna hunters (e.g., the Hadzabe) underpins the argument that *H. erectus* males acquired meat by active scavenging primarily as a mate-attracting display rather than a contribution to group subsistence (O'Connell *et al.* 2002). In this challenge to the centrality of meat in the diet of early *Homo*, plant foods (roots, tubers) gathered by females and shared between grandmothers and daughters were the mainstay of hominin social life. Most palaeoanthropologists continue to regard the consumption of meat and marrow as essential components of the high-quality diet that underpinned the evolution of large-bodied and big-brained *Homo*. Still at issue is the role of food sharing in the life history of *H. erectus* (discussed subsequently) with its implications for a sexual division of labour, extended parenting through provisioning of young, and the coevolution of greater group size with increased social and technological intelligence (Kaplan *et al.* 2000). Methodological issues also remain unresolved for determining the timing of access to carcasses and the quantity of meat and marrow available (Blumenschine 1998; Domínguez-Rodrigo 1997, 2002). Given the fundamental importance of a high-quality diet to the evolution of *Homo*, this debate is likely to continue for some time, but more than two decades of experimental and field research are leading to a robust methodology for assessing faunal assemblages created by hominins as opposed to carnivores (Egeland *et al.* 2004; Domínguez-Rodrigo and Barba 2006).

An alternative approach to meeting the energy and nutrient demands of the reproductive cycle is to reduce the length of lactation, as has happened among humans compared with chimpanzees (Aiello and Key 2002:557). This, in turn, reduces the interval between births, enabling a female to have more children for lower energetic costs per child. For this strategy to work, though, infants have to be weaned at an early age and this poses significant problems of its own. The weanling obviously needs to be fed, and if it cannot dig and roast tubers or find meat on its own, or fend off predators, then it needs looking after. Very young children also have small deciduous dentition and immature digestive tracts that make it difficult for them to eat and digest adult foods (Kennedy 2003:564). As well as food and security, the *H. erectus* weanling, with its humanlike pattern of sustained and early brain growth, needed nutritious foods to support brain development (Kennedy 2005). *H. erectus* mothers could have met these needs with the added costs in calories of finding food for themselves and their offspring, plus the effort of carrying and protecting the weanling. Alternatively, they could have elicited the sharing of energetic costs with other group members as alloparents, including older siblings, grandmothers, and unrelated males (Hawkes *et al.* 1998; O'Connell *et al.* 1999, 2002; Aiello and Key 2002). An expanded support role for grandmothers may be the adaptive advantage that accounts for the uniquely human experience of a long postmenopausal life – something not experienced by chimpanzees. The evolution of such co-operative behaviours and extended life expectancy will be difficult to detect archaeologically or in the fossil record, but humans are distinctive in their habitual provisioning of children by both males and females (Kaplan *et al.* 2000). The extent of male and female involvement in provisioning and parenting varies considerably among hunter-gatherers today depending on existing social structures and ecological constraints on resources (Panter-Brick 2002), and would presumably have done so with early *Homo*.

The rearing of big-bodied and big-brained *H. erectus* offspring is inextricably linked with a series of related changes in its life history, including a distinctively human-like pattern of early weaning (childhood), high fertility, late maturation (adolescence), and greater longevity after menopause compared with other primates (Bogin and Smith 1996; Hawkes *et al.* 1998:1338). To this can be added the emergence of stable social structures where a nursing infant finds support from kith and kin (Kennedy 2003:566).[2] An extended childhood in such a protective environment would have provided added time to experience and learn about the social and material world. A costly brain and extended life history evolved under selection from the increased cognitive demands posed by large social groups, and, as discussed in Chapter 5, a strong positive correlation exists between social group size and brain size (Dunbar 2003). Ecological pressures also played a role in driving changes in cognition and life history. A large home range coupled with skill-intensive foraging correlates positively with increased longevity and group size (Walker *et al.* 2006). In the context of global climate change ∼1.8 mya, the corresponding innovation of Mode 2 technology by *H. erectus* not only enhanced its adaptive flexibility, but also acted as a further catalyst for the evolution of an extended childhood. The making of thin, well-shaped bifaces requires a mastery of motor and spatial skills that involves considerable time and practice to learn (see Chapter 5) (Winton 2005), and the making of wood and bone tools would have involved some degree of extended learning. Hunting as a meat-acquisition strategy would further select for enhanced cognitive and motor skills with an extended adolescence for learning. Finding and pursuing game takes time to observe, learn, and integrate the behaviours of prey with the cues and signs they leave in differing landscapes and at different times of the year. Among contemporary well-armed hunter-gatherers, indeed, the skills needed to capture even small game can take up to twenty years to master after adolescence (Gurven *et al.* 2006).[3] The active scavenging proposed for early *H. erectus* would also have involved some period of learning to manage the dangers involved. Collecting and processing vegetable foods, especially roots and tubers as fallback resources, would have embodied distinctive sets of knowledge and skills. Tubers can be difficult to locate in dry season landscapes, require tools (and adult strength) to extract them from the ground, and experience in making fire, though some varieties can be eaten raw (O'Connell *et al.* 2002).

The life history profile inferred for *H. erectus* derives largely from estimates of human-like energy demands on the reproductive cycle of females. Its brain size at birth falls within the lower end of the modern range (Hublin and Coqueugniot 2006), but the rate of maturation of the brain after birth is critical in determining whether a mother with infant would have needed the support of alloparents. Human brains are larger than those of early and later *H. erectus*, and this difference may reflect divergent growth rates after birth or a more sustained period of growth among humans (Leigh 2006). Reconstructing the maturation rate of *H. erectus* relies in part on the methodology of measuring brain size and estimates of the age of death of the very small number of juvenile specimens available, such as the Nariokotome child. Estimated rates of brain growth for this individual show a more human-like pattern of development before and after birth compared with that of chimpanzees (DeSilva and Lesnik 2006). The ancestry of the human pattern of delayed brain development may have its roots in the australopithecines based on the emerging evidence from a remarkably well-preserved skeleton of a juvenile *A. afarensis* (DIK-1–1) found in the Hadar Formation (3.3 mya), Ethiopia. This individual features a slower rate of brain growth than seen among extant apes (Alemseged *et al.* 2006:300), perhaps setting foundations in the mid-Pliocene for the later emergence of extended childhood, alloparenting, and increased brain size. These developments evolved in concert with increased technological complexity that underpinned the more efficient exploitation of high-quality plant and animal foods. Global climate change created the selective pressures favouring the evolution of these integrated changes in biology and behaviour, and continued to play a formative role in hominin evolution in the mid-Pleistocene.

## OVERVIEW

Hominin dependence on tool-making appears 2.6 mya with an already well-developed understanding of the mechanics of flaking, suggestive of an even earlier period of development that awaits discovery. The innovation of the sharp flake, possibly as an unintentional byproduct of nut-cracking, transformed the lives of some late Pliocene hominins by enabling them to access larger quantities of meat, whether as scavenged carcasses or hunted game. The importance of meat in hominin evolution has been much debated, but the archaeological evidence of cutmarked and smashed bones at sites like Bouri, Kanjera South, and FLK-Zinj shows without doubt that hominins sought animal protein and fat and did so with the aid of stone tools. At issue is the centrality of animal protein in the diet and social lives of these early tool-makers. Large packets of meat, such as limbs, provide a highly nutritious resource that can be shared and in the act of sharing lie the bonds of obligation and trust that underpin hominin sociality. A meat-centred vision of Mode 1 technology, however, risks undervaluing the input of plant foods in hominin diets and the role of gathering in the structuring of communal life. As stable isotope analyses now show, early hominins were generalist feeders. The likely repertoire of organic tools made by early hominins is under-represented by the vagaries of preservation, and underappreciated in the context of the spread of increasingly open and more seasonal landscapes from the late Pliocene onwards. Mode 1 and 2 tool-makers developed new technologies, including fire, in response to changing ecological conditions as well as maintaining that essential tool, the humble flake. Tool-assisted foraging and increased body size enabled early *Homo*, in particular *H. erectus*, to range widely and with this species we see the evolution of the interrelated social, anatomical, and physiological changes linked with the human pattern of an extended life history.

CHAPTER 5

# MID-PLEISTOCENE FORAGERS

The evolution of *Homo erectus* as a large-bodied, large-brained, tool-dependent hominin with extended social networks and life history took place in concert with large-scale shifts in Africa's climate. The increased variability and aridity experienced between 1.8–1.6 mya altered the continent's biogeography, creating the ecological conditions for genetic selection, behavioural innovation, and speciation. This chapter reviews the impact of a subsequent and more prolonged shift in the earth's climate that began about 1 mya and ended ~400 kya with the establishment of the current rhythm of extended glacial cycles lasting 100,000 years. The mid-Pleistocene transition led to greater climatic variability and instability, with direct effects on the distribution and predictability of the resources on which hominins depended. The poor fossil and archaeological record for this period limits our current perception of evolutionary trends, whether linked ultimately to fluctuations in climate or with their own internal dynamics (Foley 1994).

We review in some detail the climatic record for this 600,000-year interval to establish the broad patterns of biogeographical change with which to search the archaeological record for correspondences of change. Correlations are noted between mid-Pleistocene climate change and indirect evidence for the emergence of language, with increased group size and brain size seemingly linked. A speciation event at 0.6 mya marked the appearance of large-brained

*Homo heidelbergensis*, a descendant of *H. erectus* and a possible ancestor of modern humans in Africa and Neanderthals in Eurasia. Technological changes in the Mode 2 tradition of biface-making occurred at the onset of the mid-Pleistocene and again ~0.7 mya, perhaps associated with the evolution of *H. heidelbergensis*. The early Pleistocene strategy of using tools to extend home ranges is amplified with evidence for greater planning and transport of raw materials. As with earlier *H. erectus*, the ability to hunt large game, control fire, and form coalitions based on food sharing and a division of labour all remain speculative developments when applied to mid-Pleistocene hominins. The African archaeological record on its own provides a narrow window through which to view this period, revealing only glimpses of behaviours that underpin the lives of modern humans.

## VARIABILITY SELECTION AND CLIMATE CHANGE IN THE MID-PLEISTOCENE

Darwin's concept of evolution as descent with modification emphasises the biological and behavioural inheritance that any organism has when faced with changes to its environment. For *H. erectus*, this inheritance included a large body and brain with their high metabolic demands, a dependence on technology, and cooperative social groups involved in the raising of young. The intensification of global glacial cycles at the outset of the mid-Pleistocene accentuated the selective pressures already acting on this highly mobile landscape generalist. The concept of variability selection (Potts 1998, 2001) recognises the importance of differing temporal and spatial scales of change in environments as selective forces for genetic and behavioural change. Selective pressures are greatest at times of environmental instability driven by fluctuations in global climate between glacial and interglacial states. Across its African range, *Homo*, like other species, faced environmental changes ranging from annual variations in rainfall to long-term fluctuations in temperature and rainfall over tens of thousands of years linked to shifts in the amplitude and duration of glacial cycles. Most species adapt to very frequent changes to their surroundings through individual learning (Richerson and Boyd 2005:230), and among humans the exchange of information between individual members of a group enables us to formulate rapid responses based on accumulated experience and innovation. Social learning transmitted across generations provides an effective system for monitoring and responding to variations in habitat over the lifetime of group members. Communications systems play a central role in social learning, and the relative increase in brain size seen early in the evolution of *H. erectus* provided a foundation for the selection of more complex systems under conditions of heightened environmental variability that characterised the mid-Pleistocene (Potts 2001). Such an increase in the neurological capacity to process information would be advantageous for expanding social networks as well as enhancing the ability to respond rapidly to change. Both individual and social learning derive ultimately from mutations to the genetic inheritance of innate behaviours (Aoki *et al.* 2005). The gradual selection pressures that typify slowly changing environments favour innate behaviours as the most parsimonious response to change, and it is unlikely that under such conditions *Homo*'s large and costly brain would have evolved (Potts 2001:231). A complex web of interaction exists, then, among the physical processes that structure resource distributions, the behavioural responses of hominins, and genetic changes that underlie new behavioural and developmental responses (Fig. 5.1).

The available oceanic and terrestrial sources of data for reconstructing climate change in the mid-Pleistocene of Africa record large-scale changes linked to global glacial cycles (Fig. 5.2). Short-lived millennial-scale fluctuations in temperature and rainfall are now well known for the last glacial cycle (127–11 kya; MIS 5–2) (Blunier and Brook 2001), and may have been part of glacial cycles as far back as 430 kya (MIS 12) and perhaps even earlier based on evidence from the Antarctic Dome C ice cores (Jouzel *et al.* 2007). However, the resolution of the climate proxy data remains too coarse to bring these events into focus. They were undoubtedly stressful periods of rapid change for *Homo*, and placed a premium on socially mediated responses, including language and innovation. Future research may pinpoint the archaeological signatures of behavioural responses to millennial and even shorter events, but until then the analytical scale remains the broad sweep of glacial cycles.

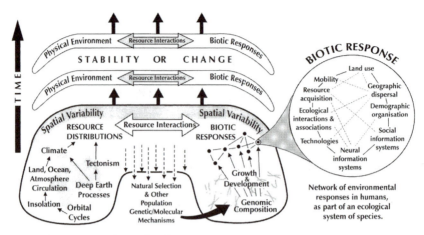

**Figure 5.1.** The web of interaction between changes in resource distribution caused by climate and local geological process with the network of potential hominin behavioural responses (right side). The biotic response is conditioned by existing variability in gene pools, but also acts as a selective force on gene frequencies and their expression in human growth, development, and cognitive capacities. Variability selection integrates physical and social environments as driving forces of evolutionary change. (Used with permission of the Western Academic & Specialist Press.)

With the onset of global glacial cycles 2.8 mya, the periodicity in the rhythm of glacial and interglacials was approximately 41,000 years, in tune with cyclical shifts in the tilt of the earth's axis (obliquity) that affected the latitudinal distribution of heat (deMenocal 2004). The 41,000-year-long glacial cycles were unevenly balanced between cold and warm, with long periods of gradual cooling followed by rapid warming and short interglacials lasting ~5000 years (Ashkenazy and Tziperman 2004). This pulse of climate change beat throughout the evolution of early *Homo* and *Paranthropus*, but its periodicity changed dramatically starting about 1 mya. The 'mid-Pleistocene revolution' (EPICA 2004:625) saw a shift to a dominant glacial cycle of 100,000 years and an increase in global ice volumes. Dust records in the Gulf of Aden (deMenocal and Bloemendal 1995) chart an early start to the revolution, and other proxies reflect its development 720–430 kya (Liu *et al.* 1999; Shackelton 1995; EPICA 2004). The lengthening of glacial cycles was also accompanied by an increase in the amplitude of the oscillations from

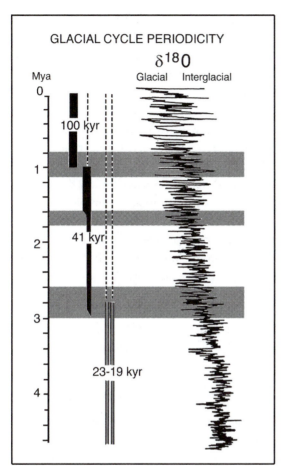

**Figure 5.2.** Global glacial cycles between 1.8 and 0.13 mya showing significant shifts in the duration and amplitude of glacial cycles between 1–0.6 mya and again at ∼0.4 mya. (After deMenocal 2004.)

warm/wet and cold/dry conditions (Fig. 5.2). The peaks of cold and dry were more pronounced than before and the interglacials became warmer and wetter. The asymmetry seen in the earlier 41,000-year cycle, with longer cold periods, was also maintained. In a typical 100,000-year cycle, a gradual build-up of polar ice takes place over 90,000 years, reaching a peak followed by rapid warming and a brief 10–11,000-year-long interglacial. The availability of energy, protein, and surface water for hominins would have changed dramatically at glacial/interglacial boundaries. Prolonged dry glacials with their reduced productivity and increased resource variability would also have amplified the selection pressures faced by early Pleistocene hominins. The extinction of the paranthropines about 1 mya may have been hastened by the mid-Pleistocene climate shift combined with competition for resources from *H. erectus*. The latter's existing capacity to range widely, along with its more humanlike life history, relatively larger brain, and tool dependence gave it the adaptive flexibility to survive these changes.

The duration of interglacials has also varied around the 10,000-years average (Forsström 2001), with the notable example of MIS 11, which lasted 16,000 years according to some estimates (Forsström 2001:1583), or as much as 28,000 years based on more recent evidence from the Dome C ice core, Antarctica (EPICA 2004). The intensity and duration of glaciations has varied as well, but more important from an evolutionary perspective is the further intensification in the amplitude of oscillations between warm/wet and cold/dry cycles that started 430 kya (EPICA 2004). Interglacials became warmer but slightly shorter than before; glacial phases, colder and slightly longer. Assuming that environmental productivity is higher during interglacials and lower during glacials, then this change in the duration of cycles and enhanced contrast between extremes of temperature created more marked variability in resource distributions. The rapid warming that marks the end of glacial phases would have been even more pronounced, placing a selective premium on culturally based responses. Again, the current limitations of the archaeological record mask such periods of short-lived, but pronounced ecological stress.

This model is made complex by fluctuating wetter-drier cycles over 100,000 years and differing regional controls on climate. In the subtropics, the dominant monsoonal climate is driven by the 23,000-year-long cycles of precessional variation in the earth's spin, and has been since the Pliocene (deMenocal 2004:11). The evidence comes from dark organic sediments (sapropels) deposited in the eastern Mediterranean that originated as increased monsoonal runoff, particularly from the Nile and its Ethiopian source (Rossignol-Strick 1983). After 2.8 mya, the orbital eccentricity and precessional cycles coexist in the monsoonal zones, with increased aridity (and winds)

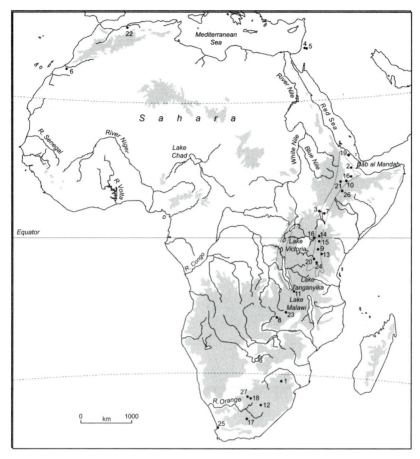

**Figure 5.3.** Location of sites discussed in Chapter 5: 1. Tswaing Crater (Pretoria Salt Pan); 2. Dikika; 3. Nariokotome; 4. Qafzeh; 5. Berekhat Ram; 6. Tan Tan; 7. Koobi Fora; 8. Mumbwa Caves; 9. Olorgesailie; 10. Middle Awash Valley; 11. Kalambo Falls; 12. Florisbad; 13. Isenya; 14. Kilombe; 15. Kariandusi; 16. Kombewa; 17. Seacow Valley; 18. Wonderwerk Cave; 19. Buia; 20. Olduvai Gorge; 21. Melka Kunturé; 22. Tighenif (Ternifine); 23. Kabwe (Broken Hill); 24. Ndutu; 25. Elandsfontein; 26. Gadeb; 27. Kathu Pan.

typical of glacial stages (deMenocal 2004). In South Africa, sediments from the Tswaing Crater (Pretoria Saltpan) (Fig. 5.3) also show an underlying monsoonal cycle within the longer 100,000-year glacial cycle of the mid- to late Pleistocene (Partridge *et al.* 1997). In Central Africa, the Intertropical Convergence Zone brings rain twice annually, but the availability of atmospheric moisture is governed by sea surface temperature differences between the tropics and subtropics in the South Atlantic Ocean (Schefuß *et al.* 2005). Millennial, and even shorter centennial to decadal changes in ocean circulation have had major impacts on rainfall in Central and West Africa (Garcin *et al.* 2006; Weldeab *et al.* 2007). They undoubtedly affected the availability and distribution of food sources for hominins, but for the time being these short-lived events remain archaeologically invisible. The 100,000-year rhythm of mid-Pleistocene glacial cycles appears in Central Africa's vegetation by 650 kya, preceded by substantial fluctuations in the amplitude and duration of cycles during a transitional phase between 920–650 kya (Schefuß *et al.* 2004). The evidence comes from a marine core off Angola (Ocean Drilling Program site 177) that preserves a biomolecular record (windborne leaf wax residues) of a mid-Pleistocene increase in arid-adapted $C_4$ plants linked to the colder sea surface of glacial stages.

The fossil record of African bovids also shows two phases of change, with increases in arid-adapted species taking place after 1.2 mya and again after 700 kya (deMenocal 2004:14,18). The modern range of bovids and other large mammals in eastern Africa was in place by ~450 kya, following the last mid-Pleistocene extinction phase (Potts and Deino 1995). Coinciding with the spread of $C_4$ savanna grasslands, especially in eastern Africa, these shifts in mammalian lineages were ultimately driven by orbital-scale changes in the periodicity and intensity of glacial cycles. As well as highlighting these intervals of marked change, the combined terrestrial and marine evidence reveals a distinctive mid-Pleistocene trend towards increasingly dry, variable, more open environments. Hominins had to adapt to these trends and the periodic transitions between them.

---

## THE HOMININ FOSSIL RECORD – WITH TABLE 5.1

In stark contrast to earlier periods, the fossil record for the period 1.0–0.4 mya is poor, with few specimens from well-dated contexts. Only eleven sites have produced fossils, mostly cranial specimens, with the majority from East Africa. No specimen has been

TABLE 5.1. *Early mid-Pleistocene hominin sites (∼1.0–0.4 mya)*

| Site | Specimen | Age (mya) | Reference |
|---|---|---|---|
| Olduvai (Bed IV) | OH 12 – cranium | 0.78–1.25 | Antón 2003 |
| Olduvai (Masek Bed) | OH 23 – mandible | <0.78 | Antón 2003 |
| Olduvai (Beds III & IV) | OH 28 & 34 – postcrania | <0.78 | Day & Molleson 1976 |
| Buia (Eritrea) | Cranium | 1–0.78 | Abbate *et al.* 1998 |
| Daka (Ethiopia) | Cranium | 1.0 | Gilbert *et al.* 2003 |
| Melka Kunture (Ethiopia) | Gombore II, cranium | 0.8–0.7 | White 2000 |
| Olorgesailie (Kenya) | Cranium | 0.97–0.9 | Potts *et al.* 2004 |
| Tighenif (Algeria) | Three partial mandibles | 0.7 | Hublin 2001 |
| Bodo (Ethiopia) | Cranium | 0.6 | Conroy *et al.* 2000 |
| Gawis (Ethiopia) Specimens with estimated ages | Cranium | 0.5–0.3? | unpublished |
| Kabwe (Zambia) | Cranium & postcrania | 0. 5–0.2? | Pycraft 1928 |
| Elandsfontein (South Africa) also known as Saldanha or Hopefield | Cranium & mandible fragment | 0.7–0.4? | Klein 1994a |
| Ndutu (Tanzania) | Cranium | 0.4–0.25? | Rightmire 1983 |

reported from West and Central Africa and the southern African fossils are indirectly dated, typically by long-distance faunal correlations with the East African record, as in the case of the Mode 2 site of Elandsfontein (Saldanha) (Klein and Cruz-Uribe 1991). The considerable morphological variability represented by this small group raises fundamental taxonomic issues about the validity of *Homo ergaster* as a distinctive African species separate from Asian

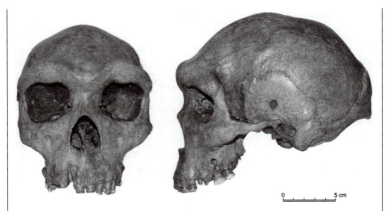

**Figure 5.4.** The cranium of the Kabwe (Broken Hill) (Zambia) specimen of *Homo heidelbergensis*. (Used with permission of Philip Rightmire and the Western Academic & Specialist Press.)

*H. erectus* (see Chapter 3) (Asfaw *et al.* 2002; Gilbert *et al.* 2003; Manzi *et al.* 2003; Potts *et al.* 2004) and the recognition of speciation in mid-Pleistocene *Homo* (Manzi 2004). The limited African sample does show a significant increase in absolute and relative brain size over time, with Bodo and other later specimens within the size range of recent humans (Rightmire 2004:115). The increase may have taken place gradually (Conroy *et al.* 2000), but the combined African and European records support a rapid change about 600 kya, marking a speciation event and the evolution of *H. heidelbergensis* (Fig. 5.4) as the ancestral population of both *Homo sapiens* in Africa and *Homo neanderthalensis* in Europe (Rightmire 2004; but see Bermúdez de Castro *et al.* 1997). This speciation event coincided with fundamental shifts in global climate in the mid-Pleistocene. The Buia cranium (Eritrea) and perhaps the Daka specimen (Ethiopia) can arguably be excluded from *H. erectus* based on their morphological variability. Moreover, the Buia specimen shares affinities with later mid-Pleistocene crania assigned to *H. heidelbergensis*, indicating an earlier splitting of lineages among ancestral *H. erectus* populations about 1 mya (Antón 2003:141).

## VARIABILITY SELECTION, GROUP SIZE, AND LANGUAGE

All parts of Africa were affected by the mid-Pleistocene shift in glacial periodicity, with the exception of some equatorial rainforests that remained relatively undisturbed (Marret *et al.* 1999) but apparently uninhabited by hominins. Across Africa, *H. erectus* groups faced long-term changes to local habitats driven by orbital cycles, and shorter-term but dramatic variations with rapid deglaciation at the poles. With a notable exception discussed subsequently, we lack the detailed local environmental data from well-dated sequences with which to reconstruct habitat shifts and model hominin responses to differing scales of variability. We can, however, anticipate potential responses for a landscape generalist like *H. erectus* based on ethnographic observations of contemporary hunter-gatherers and non-human primates living in savanna habitats. Among tropical hunter-gatherers, such as the Hadzabe and Ju/'hoansi, seasonal changes in resource availability are countered by range expansion, altering food preferences, reconfiguring group size by splitting into smaller foraging units (fission), and engaging in long-distance exchange. For longer-term changes to resource availability, foragers may respond by migration, technological innovation, intensified use of selected resources, birth control, intensified exchange, and formalised appeals for supernatural intervention (Kelly 1996). Some of these responses require not just co-operative social behaviours, but also those based on language.

Language has obvious benefits as a mechanism for gathering and transmitting essential information about resources and for long-term planning. It is also the glue that binds human social groups together to form lasting, co-operative entities, including the uniquely human form of monogamy based on mutual dependence and reciprocity. If extended parenting was a feature of early *H. erectus* societies, then some form of communication existed that enabled females to engage others to share the burden of provisioning young. Non-human primates create and sustain social bonds through mutual grooming, something that poses practical limits on the amount of daytime

available for other essential activities, including feeding and reproduction (Dunbar 1998). The 'social brain hypothesis' argues that
the demands of forming intense social bonds between members of a
group has placed a selective premium on the evolution of the cognitive capacities that support sociality (Dunbar 2004). These include
the ability to imagine the thoughts of others (theory of mind) and
use this mental modelling to anticipate and manipulate their desires,
intentions, and beliefs. No other primates, with the possible exception of the great apes, have the capacity to attribute intentions to
others or imagine the possibility of other states of reality, such as a
past or a future. Based on brain size alone, some minimum level of
intentionality (see inset) existed with early *H. erectus* that exceeded
that of apes, and was probably actively selected for by the demands
of extending parental investment beyond the mother.

Language frees its users from the physical limitations of one-to-
one grooming, enabling the formation of much larger social groups,
but also provides a medium for harnessing collective experience and
applying it to solve practical problems. The environmental pressures
operating following the mid-Pleistocene revolution and the bumpy
transition to the 100,000-year cycle would presumably have placed a
selective premium on effective communication and its genetic foundations (Potts 2001:16–17). Neurobiological research demonstrates
the brain's ability to quickly form new and strengthened neural connections within and between hemispheres in response to repeated
inputs from external stimuli, especially early in a child's life (Schenker
*et al.* 2005:563). This neural plasticity underlies rapid learning and
involves few genetic changes (T. Deacon 1997:202). Environmental
stimuli, such as changed configurations of resources in the landscape,
combined with the cognitive demands of maintaining social bonds
and learning increasingly complex technologies, constitute a package of selective forces for increased brain size and specific neural
systems, including those linked to communication. The discovery
of language-related genes that affect the learning and production of
speech, such as the *FOXP2* gene, provides insights into how natural
selection could reconfigure ancestral communications systems in the
brain to form language (Fisher and Marcus 2005). This neural flexibility and its genetic underpinnings form the biological foundation

LEVELS OF INTENTIONALITY

Intentionality refers to a conscious state of awareness of one's own state of mind and the beliefs, desires, and intentions one holds. The degree of awareness can be ordered into increasingly complex states of causal awareness or levels of intentionality that depend on the size of the neocortex for holding and processing information (Dunbar 2000):

0 =  no awareness
1 =  aware of the contents of your mind
2 =  awareness of beliefs about the intentions or beliefs of others (theory of mind)
3 =  belief about the intentions of another and their beliefs about you
4 =  intention that another believes what you want them to believe about your beliefs
5 =  intention that another believes that others have similar beliefs or intentions and can act on those beliefs

Second-order intentionality is essential for forming and managing social relationships and for planning (Barrett *et al.* 2003), and possibly exists among chimpanzees (Dunbar 2004). The ability to imagine alternative states of existence, including the past and future, underpins sequential behaviours such as the making of bifaces with three-dimensional symmetry (discussed subsequently). Theory of mind or Level 2 intentionality is also the foundation of the process of teaching or directed learning with teacher and pupil each needing to anticipate the intentions of the other for the relationship to work. Based on its estimated neocortex size alone, *H. heidelbergensis* would have been capable of fourth-order intentionality, which is well within the modern human range, and the foundation for complex beliefs in the supernatural and the creation of symbols (Dunbar 2003).

for individual and social learning that involved language. The challenge for palaeoanthropologists is to find evidence in the fossil and archaeological records for the evolution of language and to model the environmental and social selective pressures for its emergence.

Indirect evidence for *H. erectus'* communication systems comes from the strong correlation demonstrated among primates among social group size, the complexity of social relationships, and brain size, specifically neocortex ratio (Dunbar 2003). Neocortex ratios (Fig. 5.5) estimated from fossil cranial volumes show that group size among australopithecines fell within the range of living chimpanzees (50–55), but rose with *H. erectus* to 60–80 individuals, just beyond the size that can be comfortably maintained by grooming alone (Aiello and Dunbar 1993). An exponential increase to 150 individuals took place about 500 kya with *H. heidelbergensis*. Language would have been necessary to maintain bonds in a group of this size. Early *H. erectus* may have filled the gap in communication between grooming and language with vocal chorusing or singing, which has the effect of bonding individuals through a shared pleasurable experience reinforced physiologically by the release of endorphins in the brain (Dunbar 2004). Laughter, too, enhances bonding, but it is unclear how it might have been used as a form of communication. Tentative evidence for a correlation between the mid-Pleistocene climate shift and the emergence of systematic vocal communication comes from an apparent increase in the mean size of *H. erectus* groups to 93 individuals (with the removal of an anomalous early specimen from Olduvai) after 700 kya (Dunbar, pers. comm.). Bonding by vocalising (singing) may have become essential by this time according to the social brain hypothesis, with language emerging somewhat later in the mid-Pleistocene, as group size approached the 150 level.

The fossil record provides additional indirect evidence for the evolution of speech and language. Speech involves the articulation of breath with the shape of the throat and mouth (tongue, jaw, and lips) to produce distinctive sounds. The soft anatomy of the larynx or voice box containing the vocal chords does not fossilise, but indirect evidence for its shape and location in the throat comes from the morphology of the hyoid bone, which supports the upper larynx and is attached to the mandible. Apes have a shortened larynx relative to humans,[1] set high in the throat, which limits the range of sounds produced. This seems to have been the ancestral early

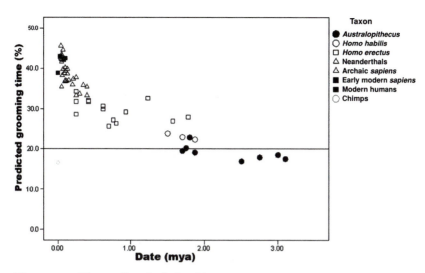

**Figure 5.5.** The predicted relationship among neocortex size, group size, and estimated grooming time for hominin taxa, showing a significant increase in grooming time in the mid-Pleistocene with *H. heidelbergensis* (archaic *sapiens*). (Courtesy and copyright of Robin Dunbar.)

hominin condition[2] based on the rare discovery of a fossilised hyoid beneath the palate of a juvenile *Australopithecus afarensis* (DIK-1-1) dated to 3.3 mya (Alemseged *et al.* 2006). The only other example of a hyoid in the hominin record comes from a Neanderthal specimen from Kebara, Israel, dated to 60 kya. It is fully modern in form, suggesting that this species had a large resonating chamber created by a lower larynx and the ability to produce a wide range of sounds (Arensburg *et al.* 1989). The long interval between the two specimens limits the usefulness of this particular indicator of speech, but fortunately other lines of cranial and postcranial evidence help fill the gap.

The nerve that controls the tongue enters the skull through the hypoglossal canal, and the size of this in fossil hominins provides a measure for increased use of the tongue involved in speech production. Among australopithecines from Sterkfontein, the canal is no larger than that seen in chimpanzees and bonobos, indicating a limited ability to produce controlled sounds (Kay *et al.* 1998). The modern canal size had evolved by >300 kya as seen in specimens of *H. heidelbergensis*, the last common ancestor of *H. sapiens* and Neanderthals (Kay *et al.* 1998). Just how much earlier enlargement took place is unclear, as no *H. erectus* specimens were included in the study. Analysis of the thoracic vertebrae on the most complete *H. erectus* postcranial specimen known, the Nariokotome boy (WT-15000, 1.5 mya), reveals a relatively small canal, and thus a probable inability to produce finely articulated speech (MacLarnon and Hewitt 1999). Early *H. erectus* vocalisation would have been characterised by short utterances, rather than the long and nuanced phrases modern humans can manage with a single breath. As the only postcranial specimen available for its taxon, WT-15000 provides a *terminus post quem* for the evolution of fine breath control. Specimens of *H. sapiens* from Qafzeh, Israel, with modern dimensions, provide a *terminus ante quem* at 100 kya.

Endocranial casts (natural and virtually reconstructed) have long been examined for morphological evidence for the presence of areas of the brain associated with speech and language, in particular, the imprints of the interconnected cellular masses that protrude on the left hemisphere as Broca's and Wernicke's areas (Fig. 5.6). Endocasts of *Homo habilis* show both areas present, and the argument has been made that this taxon possessed the neurological capacity for some form of language (Tobias 1991:840; Falk 1983). The traditionally defined language areas are now seen as part of a much more distributed network of areas of the brain involved with language, including cortical and subcortical structures (Fisher and Marcus 2005). Assessing the linguistic abilities of hominins from endocasts is far from straightforward. A homologue of Wernicke's area is also found in chimpanzees (Gannon *et al.* 1998) and macaques share humans' left hemisphere dominance for the processing of vocalisations that carry social meaning (Gil-da-Costa *et al.* 2006). Brain lateralisation seems to have deep evolutionary roots among primates, with the left hemisphere linked with vocal and gestural communication; the right hemisphere with visual and spatial tasks (Falk 1993). The left hemisphere is also closely linked in modern humans with the predominance of right-handed tool use (Steele and Uomini 2005), and tentative links have been made between archaeological evidence for

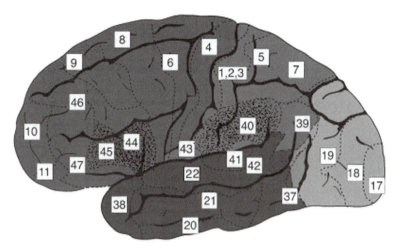

**Figure 5.6.** Location of areas of the brain traditionally linked to speech production (Broca's) and language comprehension (Wernicke's) on the left cerebral hemisphere. The numbers refer to Brodmann's map of cortical areas, with Broca's associated with areas 45 and 44 and Wernicke's with areas 40 and 22. Experimental knapping of Mode 1 cores shows areas 1–4 (primary motor cortex and somatosensory cortex) activated when imagining tool-use, Broca's area when naming tool-use, and Wernicke's when hearing the sounds of tool-use. Both general areas may also contain mirror neurons, which fire when an individual undertakes a particular action or simply observes another doing the same thing. Mirror neurons may, as a result, be involved in a gestural origin of speech, though this remains to be demonstrated (Glenberg 2006).

right-handedness and lateralisation as a pre-adaptation for language. Analysis of sequences of flake removals from Mode 1 cores and Karari scrapers at Koobi Fora (1.9–1.4 mya) shows a preference for right-handed knapping early in the Pleistocene (Toth 1985; Ludwig and Harris 1998). The potential links between lateralisation and tool-making have been investigated experimentally using Positron Emission Tomography to map those areas of the brain activated during knapping of Mode 1 cores. Preliminary analyses of a small number of subjects reveal connections across hemispheres and in comparable regions involved in visual, spatial, and motor skills (Stout *et al.* 2000; Stout 2005a). The left hemisphere was generally more active than the right, perhaps a reflection of the subjects' right-handedness and the tasks involved, but some activation of Broca's area was recorded in response to visualisation of knapping rather than actual knapping (Stout 2002:1218; Stout and Chaminade 2006). Other recent neuroimaging studies also show the engagement of both hemispheres during tool-use and perception of tools (seeing and hearing), but with the left hemisphere dominant among right-handers, including areas linked with language (Lewis 2006). Tool-making may have placed selective pressures on those structures of the brain linked to perceptual motor tasks, and contributed to the overall coordinated enlargement of the brain in human evolution. These studies support the hypothesis that tool-use and language share similar regions linked to the processing of information, and Mode 1 knapping may have selectively engaged regions later involved in language.

More extensive neuroimaging studies could involve other technological modes and left-handers to assess the integration of conceptual areas (the frontal and temporal cortices) with those involved with execution, including noncortical areas. Of particular interest would be an analysis of the brain regions engaged when creating the complex three-dimensional symmetry seen in some mid-Pleistocene bifaces. These tools reflect an essentially modern understanding of perspective and the ability to plan and impose such forms on raw materials (Wynn 1989). Unfortunately, current neuroimaging techniques only allow restricted movement by participants, with the result that robust modelling of a range of knapping activities remains a distant prospect.

Language undoubtedly simplifies the transmission of information about tool-making and use, but sustained observation and practice – a silent apprenticeship aided with gestures – could possibly have led to technical expertise. Proponents of a gestural origin of language give australopithecines the capacity to make some basic signals and attribute to *H. erectus* the ability to use complex gestures as symbols to convey abstract meanings (Calvin 1993; Corballis 2002). Following from these gestural roots, spoken language would have evolved much later, with *H. sapiens*. A supposed consequence and archaeological signature of the emergence of language is the freeing of the hands to make complex tools, like those of the European Upper

Palaeolithic (Corballis 2002). In Africa, though, the range of tool types associated with later Mode 2 (Acheulean) makers does not differ significantly from those with Mode 3- and Mode 4-making *H. sapiens* of the later Pleistocene. The three-dimensional complexity of later bifaces also would not be possible without full integration of the hands. If a transition from gestures to language took place, it left no clear archaeological signature in the African archaeological record.

The combined anatomical evidence of the hypoglossal canal and vertebral column give an approximate age range for the emergence of the modern capacity for controlled speech, and suggest language evolved after 1.5 mya and before 300 kya. This range can be narrowed further to 500 kya by including the correlation among neocortex ratios, group size, and language. The resulting interval overlaps in large part with significant shifts in mid-Pleistocene climates and the evolution of *H. erectus*. The endocast evidence is less well constrained in time and more difficult to interpret, given the long ancestry of lateralisation linked to communication. Endocasts of australopithecines (but not paranthropines) show increased brain size and reorganisation were underway 3.0–2.5 mya (Falk *et al.* 2000). Expansion took place in australopithecine frontal lobes, in an area associated with abstract thinking, memory, and planning in apes and humans (Brodmann's area 10), and also in an area of the temporal lobe that interconnects parts of the cortex associated with sound and vision, including facial recognition and naming among humans (area 38) (Fig. 5.6) (Falk *et al.* 2000:712). The neural architecture for engaging in complex social relations, and responding creatively to environmental adversity was, thus, already evolving in the australopithecine ancestors of *Homo*. Tool-making may have had a role in the later expansion of regions of the brain associated with visual, spatial, and motor skills. The endocast evidence highlights the underlying foundations for the emergence of language that existed in early *Homo*, but pinpointing the timing and outlining the process of its evolution require the integration of all lines of anatomical and genetic evidence. For now, they suggest a later, mid-Pleistocene origin for symbol-based communication.[3]

LANGUAGE, FIRE, AND FOOD

The linkages among group size, neocortex size, and forms of communication give added importance to the purported evidence for the controlled use of fire 1.6–0.78 mya. If communication by grooming places a practical limit on group size, then the light generated by hearths effectively extended the daytime hours for grooming, allowing larger group sizes to be sustained. Among primates, the maximum time spent grooming is 20% of daylight hours, but with campfires, the time for socialising can be stretched beyond the natural limits of daylight. For early *H. erectus*, an estimated group size of 60–80 individuals would require at least 25% of the day spent grooming for bonds to be maintained (Dunbar 2004). That additional demand on time could have been met by firelight socialising, reducing the need for alternative forms of communication, such as vocalising.

Campfires, like those at Koobi Fora (FxJj20), could also have stimulated the development of language by acting as foci for light, heat, protection, and interaction. Human societies differ from those of apes in repeatedly using favoured places as camps for sleeping and socialising, including the sharing of resources (reciprocity). Even if individuals do not forage as a group, they come together as a group, often at a central place, to consume at least some of their collected food (Winterhalder 2001:26). Adding controlled fire to such a gathering place would have increased its social and economic value, especially for females with dependent young reliant on food provisioning by others (alloparents). The more open landscapes of the early and mid-Pleistocene probably offered fewer opportunities for finding protection in trees and rocks, and *H. erectus* was anatomically unable to nest or sleep in trees, unlike earlier australopithecines (Ward 2002:203). Campsites provided an agreed upon location where dispersed foraging and scavenging groups could meet, with implications for the evolution of the human pattern of a gender-based division of labour based on a mutual exchange of resources (Lovejoy 1981; Panter-Brick 2002). The transition to sleeping on the ground may have incidentally extended the dream-related stages of sleep that are linked to enhanced memory, creativity, and visual–spatial awareness (Coolidge and Wynn 2006) These neurochemical changes associated with sleep and, by inference, with campsites would have contributed to *H. erectus*'s ability to range widely and respond innovatively to changes in its physical and social environment.

Language may have evolved from the demands of increasingly complex social lives, but it also enables its users to communicate more effectively about the mundane necessity of eating. Singing and grooming may cement bonds, but convey little practical information about the location of food and other resources. Food calls are well known among apes, but have a limited repertoire for expressing information about kinds of foods, their distance, quantity, size, and risks from competitors. The ability to label an object with a mutually understood sound, perhaps combined with a gesture, is a step towards symbols that represent the concept of the object without the necessity for direct physical association. Existing context-dependent vocalisations may have been the foundation from which labels or words emerged (Bickerton 2005). The limited vocal capabilities of early *H. erectus* as inferred from the Nariokotome juvenile may have sufficed to produce a limited range of words as labels, in addition to calls and gestures. The unfortunate rarity of mid-Pleistocene hominin fossils before 500 kya makes the development of fully symbolic and syntactic language difficult to track, but the emerging evidence of increased environmental instability after 1 mya provides a strong selective context for the evolution of enhanced communication. The ability to make informed choices about resources would have been advantageous given *H. erectus*'s need to provision metabolically demanding young in habitats with scattered, unpredictable foods, regardless of whether nutrients were scavenged, hunted, or extracted from the ground by helpful grandmothers (e.g., O'Connell *et al.* 1999). However obtained, the pooling and exchange of food at central places effectively minimises the impact of daily variations among individuals' contributions (Winterhalder 1990). The underlying motivations for food sharing among contemporary hunter-gatherers are complex and beyond mere risk minimisation (Winterhalder 2001:28), but with *H. erectus* the very basic need to provision young would have helped drive the development of social and economic relations. Some form of content-bearing vocal and gestural communication would have been part of the web of social life, and increasingly important against a background of environmental instability early in the mid-Pleistocene

## TECHNOLOGY AS AN ECOLOGICAL BUFFER

The network of environmental responses by humans clearly includes more than the development of social bonding, language, and strategies for sharing resources; technology offers a flexible, rapid means of responding to change at a range of scales from the immediate daily needs of the individual to long-term trends experienced over generations. We have already seen a close correlation between the emergence of Mode 1 flake and percussion technologies with the onset of global glacial cycles at 2.6 mya, and arguably the emergence of local adaptations or traditions of tool-making at the same time. Technological change accelerated in concert with climate change about 1.7 mya, with increasingly dry conditions in the early Pleistocene. If this pattern of hominin use of technology as a buffering mechanism has predictive value, then we should expect to see change again at key stress points in the mid-Pleistocene, notably ~1 mya, ~0.6 mya, and, after the MIS 12/11 transition, 430 kya. We can also expect a continuation and elaboration of the underlying pattern of local and socially transmitted technological traditions or cultures, with the added impact of language as a vehicle for learning and innovation. Before looking at the regional evidence for change, one particular Rift Valley basin – Olorgesailie, Kenya – warrants close examination. Its unusually high-quality database allows close examination of hominin responses to climate change over much of the mid-Pleistocene.

Decades of research since 1942 have produced a finely tuned chronological sequence spanning the period 1.2–0.49 mya in which several intervals of hominin activity have been excavated and their landscapes reconstructed (Potts *et al.* 1999; Sikes *et al.* 1999; Behrensmeyer *et al.* 2002). The basin covers approximately 300 km², with sedimentary and archaeological sequences most clearly exposed near the base of Mt. Olorgesailie. Three geological units are recognised, of which the oldest and most extensively investigated is the Olorgesaile Formation (L. Leakey 1952; Isaac 1977; Potts *et al.* 1999). The overlying Olkesiteti and Oltepesi Formations contain Mode 3 assemblages

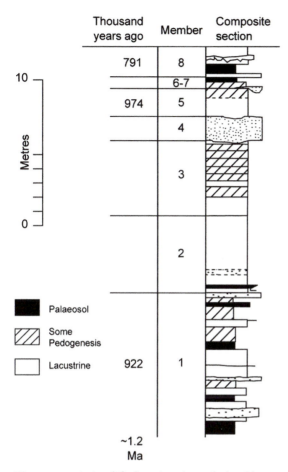

**Figure 5.7.** A simplified section through the Olorgesailie deposits showing the sequence from Members 1–8, and the alternation of lake phases with palaeosol formation. (After Potts 2001: Fig. 2.1.)

and are discussed in Chapter 6. The Olorgesailie Formation is sub-divided into 11 members, with Member 1 containing the old-est archaeological sites (~990 kya) (Fig. 5.7) and Member 11 the youngest (~662–625 kya). All the artefacts are attributed to the Acheulean or Mode 2, though bifaces are largely absent in Member 11 (Tryon and Potts 2006). The intervals separating the accumulated palaeolandscapes in each member are relatively short, generally on the order of hundred to a thousand years, and these intervals can be traced across the basin (Potts *et al.* 1999).

The basin itself offered few raw materials of sufficient size to knap, and all the stone found in the various sites had to be transported from the foothills of Mt. Olorgesailie and adjacent volcanic ridges, or from even more distant sources, up to 45 km away (Isaac 1977). With a fixed source of stone in the landscape, it is possible to assess changing strategies of raw material use against a background of ecological change, and this has been done for Members 1, 6/7, and 11 (Potts *et al.* 1999; Tryon and Potts 2006).

Members 1 (~990 kya) and 6/7 (~900 kya) are separated by just 90,000 years, but preserve very different ecological and behavioural signals. The Member 1 interval was warm and dry, with an environment of wooded grassland near a lake; open grassland existed elsewhere in the basin (Sikes *et al.* 1999). Evidence of hominin activity in the form of stone tools, often with animal bones, is distributed across the palaeolandscape in dense concentrations and diffuse scatters. One remarkable concentration (Site 15) preserves clear evidence for the butchery of an extinct elephant (*Elephas recki*) with sharp flakes around and in the carcass, along with two bifaces, plus cut marks found on one rib (Potts *et al.* 1999:768). Some of the lava flakes had been struck from large bifaces and discoidal cores, and then used in butchery, showing a degree of planning that included the transport of stone to the site from highland sources and more local outcrops. Well-preserved animal footprints and rootlets (Fig. 5.8) indicate that the elephant died in an old, damp river channel and that its carcass was the main reason hominins congregated at this low-lying place. The general association of artefact clusters with large mammal bones suggests hominins were attracted to the same areas of the landscape as the grazers, but also that *H. erectus* scavenged, and perhaps hunted as well.

The relatively homogeneity of the Member 1 habitat and the broadly continuous spread of artefacts contrasts markedly with conditions in Members 6/7. The Member 6 landscape was characterised by broad, shallow streams that deposited sands across the basin and by more extensive lake deposits than previously. The vegetation would have been more wooded and bushy than in Member 1. Later Member 7 saw the regression of the lake and the formation of a stable landscape (Potts *et al.* 1999:773). Artefacts in Members 6/7 occur in dense concentrations along stream channels and lake-margin

**Figure 5.8.** Footprints of a hippopotamus preserved in Member 1 sediments of the Olorgesailie Formation (∼990 ka).

floodplains, but are rarely found on the stable landscape of Member 7. A spectacular concentration of bifaces with the bones of the large-bodied extinct baboon *Theropithecus oswaldi* (Site DE/89) highlights the interpretive dilemma posed by the fluvial context of these sites (Fig. 5.9). The association of handaxes, cleavers, and spheroids with the fragmentary remains of at least 43 *Theropithecus* individuals could result from taphonomic mixing of unrelated assemblages (Binford and Todd 1982), a behaviourally meaningful deposit created by hominin butchery (Shipman *et al.* 1981) (see inset), or shared use of a specific area of the stream channel (Potts *et al.* 1999:777). The latter interpretation rests on more recent geomorphological evidence that shows Member 6/7 streams lacked the energy to move bifaces or bone any significant distance. The bone and stone concentrations are essentially intact, with minor reworking by water action. Their

**Figure 5.9.** Olorgesailie Formation, lower Member 7, Site DE/89, with its concentration of bifaces and at least 43 individuals of *Theropithecus oswaldi*.

distribution, then, reflects a hominin strategy of landscape use that involved the transport of raw materials from the volcanic highlands to the lowlands where foraging and scavenging/hunting took place. The concentrations of stone and bone were places for processing carcasses, though the evidence for this is equivocal in Member 6/7. These concentrations are also located near raised lava exposures that lay at the junction of the highlands and the lake basin. The geographical dichotomy between sources of stone versus food and water raises the intriguing possibility that hominins lived primarily in the highlands, and on returning after foraging in the lowlands left bifaces at the transitional zone where stone became abundant. The only hominin fossil known from Olorgesailie – a partial cranium of a small adult *H. erectus* – comes from the transitional zone, despite the obvious conditions favourable for the preservation of bone in the basin (Potts *et al.* 2004). As expected of a landscape generalist, it seems that hominins lived and died in the highlands, and were not tied to immediate sources of food and water.

## HUNTING IN THE MID-PLEISTOCENE

Evidence for the butchery of large mammals, including elephant, hippopotamus, and rhinoceros, from diverse localities, including Olorgesailie, Ethiopia's Middle Awash Valley (J. D. Clark and Schick 2000), Morocco's Oulad Hamida 1 quarry (Raynal *et al.* 1993), and outside Africa at Gesher Benot Ya'aqov, Israel (Goren-Inbar *et al.* 2004), raises the issue of the competence of *H. erectus* as a big game hunter. The ability to hunt large game systematically has significant ramifications for the structure of hominin communities, as the organisation of hunts – as opposed to individual hunting forays – probably placed further demands on the presumed sexual division of labour that emerged with the rising metabolic demands of reproduction. Based on contemporary ethnographic data, big game hunting is typically the work of males and involves a body of learned behaviours developed over time and transmitted across generations (Frison 2004). The incidence of failure is typically high (O'Connell *et al* 2002), and without the weaponry (bows and arrows, stone-tipped spears) used by modern hunters, the success rate was presumably lower for lightly armed mid-Pleistocene hominins.[4] Capturing game through exhaustive pursuit is arguably a strategy employed by *H. erectus* using its physiological and anatomical adaptations for long-distance running (Hilton and Meldrum 2004; Liebenberg 2006). This method of hunting, like trapping or the use of organic tools, would leave little archaeological evidence. Equally indistinguishable in terms of the distribution and frequency of butchery marks and body part representation is the early acquisition of large carcasses by hunting or active scavenging (Plummer 2004). Either involves some degree of co-operation between individuals. The large quantities of meat and marrow offered by early access to big carcasses would have fed several individuals, contributing to a group's ability to provision dependent offspring (Rose and Marshall 1996), as well as to other social bonds linked with food sharing (see text).

Member 11 (~662–625 kya) habitats were similar to those of
Members 6/7, with sites clustered in concentrations in the lowland landscape and relatively undisturbed by postdepositional processes (Tryon and Potts 2006). Bifaces are rare in Member 11, with
flakes the primary form of tool, made from local highland lavas.
These Mode 1 assemblages underline the continuing importance of
flakes as tools in the mid-Pleistocene at Olorgesailie from Member
1 onwards, and remind us that flakes remain a primary tool form
in Mode 2 assemblages generally. Closer analysis of the technological differences between Member 1 and Member 11 assemblages
shows a deliberate conservation of raw materials in Member 1, starting from the transport from the highlands to the final reshaping of
bifaces (Noll and Petraglia 2003). Member 1 bifaces were resharp-
ened more often than those in Members 6/7 and 11, and flakes in
Member 1 were thinner and less heavy for their size than in later
assemblages. Maximising the usefulness of bifaces and minimising
the weight of flakes in Member 1 reflect efforts to conserve raw
materials in the context of a more open grassland landscape with
less predictable and more scattered foods (Noll and Petraglia 2003;
Tryon and Potts 2006). Cores and bifaces would have had to be carried across the landscape to dispersed resources, with bifaces used as
cores as well. *H. erectus* shows the ability at Olorgesailie to anticipate
future needs (Hallos 2005:127) by developing a strategy of adjusting
raw material use to mobility needs in response to the distribution
of food resources. Considerable forethought was involved, given the
geographical and temporal separation between highland sources of
stone and lowland food resources.

The habitats in Members 6/7 and 11, with their more abundant
and clustered resources, would have enabled *erectus* groups to target
particular areas of the landscape and worry less about minimising
their use of stone. Hominins transported more unmodified material
into the lowlands, knapping it on site rather than removing the
cortex first in the highlands to reduce the weight and maximise the
amount of useful stone. Bifaces as portable multipurpose tools and
cores did not feature in the technological repertoire of Member 11
hominins, perhaps because they simply were not needed given the
abundance of foods and the quality of the raw materials available.

Varying resource distribution and linked transport costs may also explain similar sequences of interstratified Mode 1 and Mode 2 assemblages in eastern Africa, notably in the Middle Awash region, Ethiopia. The Awash floodplain lacked stone sources suitable for making large flakes and bifaces and these artefacts were transported from highland or upstream sources where carcasses of large animals, especially hippopotamus, were butchered. Smaller river cobbles were also used as expedient sources of flakes, with the result that both Modes occur together, but were perhaps used for different purposes (Schick and Clark 2003:26). The suggestion that the coexistence of Modes reflects a gender division of labour with males making bifaces because they had the greater strength and skill needed to produce blanks, with females restricted to knapping smaller flakes for butchery (J. D. Clark 2001b:3), seems counterintuitive: *H. erectus* males and females were similar in body size, and presumably strength (Antón 2003), and modern female student knappers can wield hefty boulders.

Mode 1 flake technology offered a highly flexible means of responding quickly to local variability in resource distribution (see Chapter 4 discussion of Koobi Fora), and this quality ensured the continued use of flakes until historic times in Africa and elsewhere. The co-occurrence of Modes 1 and 2 should not be surprising if we abandon lineal schemes of technological development that emphasise progression over continuity coupled with change. A similar phenomenon has long been observed in Britain, where flake assemblages (Clactonian Industry) are associated with mid-Pleistocene Mode 2 (Acheulean) occurrences (McNabb and Ashton 1995; Wenban-Smith *et al.* 2006). Close analytical parallels can be drawn between the evident technological flexibility seen in the Olorgesailie Formation or the Middle Awash and socio-ecological models offered in the British context (Mithen 1994; McNabb and Ashton 1995).

## TECHNOLOGICAL PATTERNS, SOCIAL LEARNING, AND CHANGE IN MID-PLEISTOCENE AFRICA

From its outset, tool-making enabled hominins to enhance their anatomical and physiological inheritance to extract food resources more effectively, saving energy and improving the reliability and quality of diets. The latter were particularly important developments in the evolution of large-bodied and brained early *Homo*, with its high reproductive costs. Mid-Pleistocene climate changes introduced significant resource-related stresses that favoured individual and social learning. Technological flexibility based on a repertoire of socially learned actions can be expected as a general response by *erectus* groups to the great variation in local habitats and raw material availability that existed across the continent. Innovation and its transmission across generations is, in part, a matter of demographics, with social groups smaller than 75 individuals offering fewer opportunities for novel solutions to problems to arise, to be observed, imitated, learned, and passed on within and across generations (Shennan 2001). Estimates of early *H. erectus* group size (60–80) based on correlations with neocortex ratios (Aiello and Dunbar 1993) fall within the range large enough to support innovation and its transmission, and if group size did increase to about 93 around 700 kya, this probably expanded the opportunities for technological, as well as social, change. If these estimates are correct, then we can expect to see an increase in the pace and range of technological change in the mid-Pleistocene, and this seems to be the case. The evolution of enhanced communication of content through language would also have contributed to a ratchet effect of increasingly rapid and varied responses transmitted by social learning. The combined anatomical evidence for language suggests a minimum date of ∼500 kya for its emergence, and provides a timeline for assessing behaviours that involved complex planning based on learning and perhaps symbolic communication.

Mode 2 has been characterised as technologically static over the course of more than a million years of biface-making (J. D. Clark 1969). Lumping assemblages together as a single entity inevitably reduces the amount of variability visible among sites, regions, and periods, contributing to a sense of uniformity and stasis. A subtle, often-unstated assumption also underlies some perceptions of Mode 2 assemblages as cognitively limited – namely, their association with pre-*Homo sapiens* (Gamble 1997). The strict linkage of cognitive with anatomical modernity has been challenged by evolutionary psychologists (Dunbar 2000) and some archaeologists (Wynn 1989, 2004). The focus of most lithic analyses remains the large cutting tools emblematic of the 'Acheulean World' – in particular, the handaxe. This has long attracted attention because of its broad distribution across a large area of the Old World and the relative homogeneity of its symmetrical form, regardless of raw materials used. Regularities in biface morphology and extent of retouch have been given various cognitive and social interpretations as markers of mental templates and cultural traditions based on social learning (Roe 1968; Gowlett 1996; Wynn 1995; Mithen 1994; Petraglia *et al.* 2005), sexual signals (Kohn and Mithen 1999), and expressions of individuality rather than group templates (Gamble 1999; White and Plunkett 2004). Often posed as alternative rather than complementary interpretations, functional analyses highlight the constraints of raw material size and shape on morphological variability (P. R. Jones 1979, 1994) and the convergence through repeated use on an unintended form (Davidson and Noble 1993; McPherron 2000). More synthetic approaches recognise the interplay of social, individual, and technological variables in reaching divergent views about the role of traditions and templates in shaping variability within and between sites (Crompton and Gowlett 1993; Gowlett and Crompton 1994; T. White 1998; Gamble and Marshall 2001; McNabb *et al.* 2004).

The handaxe has rightly been a focus of analysis given its distinctive shape, size, and ubiquity across Africa – with the exception of the interior of the Congo Basin – but this has been at the expense of obscuring other technological developments. At the continental level, the predominant form of biface manufacture is on flake blanks (*débitage*) and occurs from the very start of Mode 2 technology. Less common are bifaces made on thick nodules or cores (*façonnage*). A line drawn from West Africa east to India separates territories to the south typified by the use of flake blanks and to the north by nodules. This 'Roe Line' (Gamble and Marshall 2001:25) also divides the biface universe by shape with more ovate forms associated with *débitage*, more pointed forms with *façonnage*. These generalisations provide an analytical foundation for recognising shapes that fall outside the expectations for either method of knapping, and considering again the role of individual and social learning.

Ethnographic observations from highland Indonesia also highlight
the importance of directed social learning through apprenticeships
in achieving the technical competence to produce long, thin bifaces
(adzes in this case) that take years of effort (Stout 2002, 2005b). The
highly structured social environment supportive of learning in this
study may be an inappropriate analogue for early Mode 2 biface
production, but the development of finely crafted handaxes later
in the mid-Pleistocene demanded a level of skill challenging even
for experienced modern knappers (S. Edwards 2001; Winton 2005)
(Fig. 5.10). As a generalisation, early Mode 2 bifaces were shaped
using hard stone hammers that left large deep flake scars and sinuous
working edges. Later Mode 2 knappers introduced soft hammers of
bone, wood, or other stone that spread the force of the blow across
the face of the tool, giving a thinner profile and reducing volume.
Careful preparation of the tool edge before flaking also gave control over the regularity and sharpness of the working edge. Such
refinements in knapping techniques may have appeared ~700 kya
in eastern Africa, based on the replication of bifaces made at Isenya,
Kenya (Roche *et al.* 1988; Texier 1996). These studies revealed the
considerable understanding of the properties of woods underlying
the selection of effective soft hammers, a knowledge that rivalled
that used to produce bifaces themselves. Such botanical knowledge,
once learned through trial and error, could easily have been transferred to others through observation or teaching. Percussion marks
on some pieces of wood preserved at the Israeli site of Gesher Benot
Ya'aqov provide further evidence of the use of soft hammers to make
bifaces after 780 kya (Sharon and Goren-Inbar 1999). Whether this
technique developed first in eastern Africa or in the Levant is less
important than its correlation with the mid-Pleistocene transition
to the dominant 100,000-year glacial cycle. Thinner, less volumi-
nous bifaces produced by this method would have conserved raw
materials and have been lighter to carry, advantageous in more open
landscapes offering less predictable, more dispersed food resources
and placing a premium on mobility. Member 1 at Olorgesailie is a
case in point.

   Before the innovation of the soft hammer, biface makers already
possessed sufficient understanding of the mechanical properties of

**Figure 5.10.** Late Mode 2 handaxe from Kathu Pan (South Africa) made on banded ironstone using soft hammer flaking.

their raw materials to manipulate the relationship between geometry and volume to create different tools of specific size, shape, and weight, presumably for different purposes (Gowlett 1999). Multivariate statistical analyses of bifaces from the Kenyan sites of Kilombe (>780 kya) and Kariandusi (1.0–0.7 mya) reveal a common understanding among knappers of the relationship between handaxe length and weight. As length increases, the volume of material increases rapidly (as a cube of the dimensions), and the weight would soon be unwieldy if the dimensions were not managed by retouching (Crompton and Gowlett 1993; Gowlett and Crompton 1994). The usual response was to reduce the width so that long bifaces tend to be narrower for their size than shorter ones, but there are deliberate exceptions. At Kilombe, size-related variation, or allometry, in bifaces occurs across the site, but there are clusters of similarly shaped artefacts, including locality Z, where bifaces were made to be long, thick, and heavy, perhaps for use with two hands, and another cluster of six small, thin bifaces in locality AC/AH (Gowlett 2005). These internal differences in biface form may reflect activity areas with artefacts made to specific 'rule sets' that may be related to style, individual variability, or simply to the degree of reuse, with shorter, more pointed forms the result of resharpening the tip and upper edges over time (McPherron 2000). Even if the latter is the case, it suggests differing and repeated patterns of biface use across Kilombe that stand out against the normal range of variation. These variants need also to be considered in the context of a site that appears to have been a much-used, 'favoured place' in the landscape (Gowlett 1999), and, as such, we can see the local repertoire of tool-making behaviours.

At Kariandusi, specific rule sets about biface form seem linked to the two very different raw materials used – basalt and obsidian. Obsidian bifaces are significantly smaller, often with little retouch, and the basalt bifaces are larger and deliberately thicker at the butt and thinned at the tip (Gowlett and Crompton 1994:37). These metrical analyses highlight the extent of internal variation within these sites, probably linked to both use and traditions of social learning. That such local variability exists at the outset of the mid-Pleistocene seems almost unremarkable given the behavioural flexibility of *H. erectus* seen elsewhere at Olorgesailie and the long record of technological response to immediate needs apparent from the outset of stone toolworking.

Archaeologists remain divided about the extent to which biface variability reflects intentional designs or the convergence of forms at various stages of the process of use. This ongoing debate aside, patterns of change are evident in the mid-Pleistocene that are ultimately behavioural in origin. The development of soft-hammer flaking is one such innovation that spread widely as a concept and technique, or perhaps was developed independently in eastern Africa as well as in the Jordan Valley. Innovations in flake blank production also took place in the form of the Kombewa and prepared core techniques (see inset). Prepared core technology associated with later Mode 3 makers in the Levant is linked to land-use patterns, with the **Levallois technique** found in resource-poor environments as part of an adaptive strategy of high residential mobility (Wallace and Shea 2006). Mid-Pleistocene hominins may have pioneered this strategy, innovating prepared core technology and techniques of reducing tool weight linked to needs for mobility in semi-arid landscapes.

The southern African record provides a case study in which mid-Pleistocene technological change was linked to the colonisation of drier, cooler landscapes. Before 1 mya, Mode 2 hominins appear to have been restricted to the wetter northern and eastern borders of the region, but afterwards spread into the significantly drier interior and western margins, as well as southwards into the Fynbos Biome (H. J. Deacon 1975; Shackley 1980; Klein *et al.* 1999). Chronological controls are limited compared with eastern Africa, with biostratigraphic dating of time-sensitive taxa like elephants, pigs, and horses setting general boundaries for the regional expansion of Mode 2 populations at 1.0–0.4 mya (Klein 2000a). A few radiometrically dated sites confirm a mid-Pleistocene hominin presence and, at Wonderwerk Cave on the southern edge of the Kalahari, the Mode 2 use of this site may extend to ~0.78 mya (Beaumont and Vogel 2006), though the magnetostratigraphy of what appears to be the Brunhes-Matuyama boundary needs confirmation with further samples. The sparse Mode 2 assemblage from Wonderwerk includes a bifacial cleaver and a small prepared core, making this potentially the earliest evidence for Levallois technology in the region. Two chert bifaces also show use-wear traces that have been interpreted as evidence of plant working, in particular shaving wood and cutting sedges, possibly for bedding material (Binneman and Beaumont 1992). Charred and calcified grass stems have been found in the Mode 2 deposits, sometimes covering large areas, and these may be bedding or perhaps animal nesting material. A full comparative analysis of the vegetal remains is needed to assess the origin and uses of these unusual organic remains, along with a more extensive experimental replication programme to test the preliminary use-wear hypotheses.

## MID-PLEISTOCENE TECHNOLOGICAL VARIABILITY

The Kombewa technique of blank production was first described from sites in western Kenya (Owen 1938). It involves splitting a block of stone or boulder and removing a flake from the half with a positive bulb of percussion. The resulting flake has two bulbs of percussion, one on each face, creating a lenticular profile like that of a handaxe, with sharp cutting edges ready to be used or modified by retouch. Kombewa flakes were made in the Middle Awash Valley, Ethiopia, starting about 1.1 mya (Schick and Clark 2003), and occur in the Jordan Valley at Gesher Benot Ya'aqov (<780 kya) along with soft hammer flaking. The prepared core technique was first recognised in the South African interior and named the Victoria West technique after its place of discovery (Fig. 5.11; Goodwin and van Riet Lowe 1929). The preparation by flaking of the upper and lower face of a core to produce one or more flakes of desired shape, size, and thickness typifies both it and the Levallois technique normally associated with Mode 3 technologies. The conceptual differences between the large prepared cores associated with Mode 2 assemblages and smaller Levallois cores are more a matter of degree than kind, and the more general term of prepared core technology is preferred here. The flake blanks used for bifaces are usually struck from the side of an elongated core rather than perpendicular to the main axis as seen in the later Levallois concept, suggesting an origin in biface technology (Kuman 2001). The Victoria West technique (with its three variants) is widespread across the dry interior of South Africa (McNabb 2001), and, though undated with poor environmental data, looks to be a mid-Pleistocene development. The technique was also used to produce preformed cleavers in South Africa (Sharon and Beaumont 2006) and a remarkably similar method was developed independently in the northwestern Sahara, known as the Tachengit technique (J. D. Clark 1992). Prepared core technology also occurs in mid-Pleistocene contexts in eastern, central, and western Africa. Outside Africa, bifaces made on flakes from prepared cores are also found at Gesher Benot Ya'aqov (Goren-Inbar *et al.* 2004).

**Figure 5.11.** A Victoria West core from Canteen Kopje, South Africa, showing the large central flake scar from which a prepared biface blank was struck. Arrows indicate preparatory flake removals preceding the final blank removal.

The association of the Victoria West technique (see inset) with the semi-arid plateau of the Karoo could reflect a distinctive regional response to dispersed food and water sources. Mobility strategies as inferred from site distributions were based on surface water availability (springs, pans, rivers) and stone outcrops for making tools. The association of many sites with standing water may reflect a simple lack of containers for carrying liquid (H. J. Deacon 1975), such as the ostrich eggshell canteens with grass bungs used by later hunter-gatherers in the region. The most detailed record of Mode 2 mobility strategies comes from the Seacow Valley, where surface site distributions recorded across 5000 km² of Karoo plains and hills show that proximity to water was not always of primary importance, and may even have been a risky strategy (Sampson 2001; 2006). More than 400 sites and 600 quarries were found, and though they are undated, their distribution shows consistent clustering near better-quality outcrops of finer-grained hornfels rather than next to water sources, with effectively empty tracts separating the clusters (Fig. 5.12). Isolated finds of bifaces on the plains and in more mountainous areas show that these multipurpose tools were carried some kilometres from the main living and quarrying areas. Avoidance of predators may account in part for the decision not to live near springs that in historic times attracted game and lions in abundance.[5] Hominins in this dry landscape also weighed in the balance the need for large blocks of good-quality raw material for making bifaces with the essential requirement for water and security. The compromise solution was to locate living areas within 1–2 km of both water and good-quality stone (Sampson 2006:87). The large number of sites and pattern of clustering reflect a long-lived phenomenon, produced by repeated use of these favoured places. In the absence of dates for these sites, it is assumed that the Seacow Valley was used during interglacials, when semi-arid conditions like those of today prevailed, rather than during more inhospitable arid periods.

Evidence for the existence of social boundaries or territories among mid-Pleistocene groups is elusive, with modern foragers providing limited analogues given the differences in technology and constraints on landscape use caused by long interaction with nonforaging communities. We can assume that, like most modern hunter-gatherers in semi-arid tropics (Veth 2005), mid-Pleistocene groups in southern and eastern Africa probably had large home ranges that they varied depending on resource distribution, seasonality, and the proximity of other groups. The intensive surveys carried out in the Seacow Valley and at Olorgesailie show clear spatial patterning in the use of landscapes and, in the case of Olorgesailie, that patterning can be linked to managing resource distributions over many generations. Lacking direct data on territory size, the movement of stone raw materials across landscape can give minimal estimates of distances ranged. Geochemical fingerprinting of obsidian sources in parts of eastern Africa (Kenya, Ethiopia) shows this material moved over moderate distances of up to 50 km (Merrick and Brown 1984; Merrick *et al.* 1994; Negash *et al.* 2006). For modern hunter-gatherers in the tropics, this distance would be well within the average territorial range (Marlowe 2005). In rare cases, the distances travelled were large, with four obsidian handaxes at Gadeb, Ethiopia, derived from sources 150 km away (J. D. Clark 2001b). The distances may not, on the whole, be as large as those associated with some later Mode 3 users of obsidian, but they represent a significant increase in planning compared with earlier Mode 1 and 2 tool-makers, who rarely travelled more than a few kilometres to collect raw materials

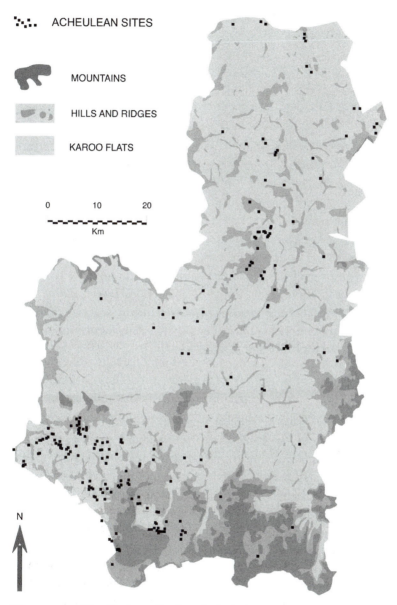

**Figure 5.12.** Distribution of archaeological sites in the Seacow Valley in the Karoo region of the South African interior. Clusters occur around outcrops of good-quality hornfels used for making artefacts, with isolated bifaces found on the plains in the highlands away from the main activity areas. The strength of association with springs is less than that seen with Mode 2 sites elsewhere in the region. (Courtesy and copyright of Garth Sampson.)

(Plummer 2004). Perhaps the preference among later biface makers for fine-grained raw materials stimulated the collection of materials from distant sources and, in doing so, expanded their range. The isolated handaxes found in the Seacow plains and highlands, away from surface water, highlights the utility of bifaces as enabling tools that allowed foragers to range widely and returns our attention to the woeful lack of evidence for water containers.

The considerable attention given to the analysis of biface variability has overshadowed the range of other tools in the behavioural repertoire, including the Mode 1 inheritance of pounding technologies (spheroids, anvils) and 'heavy-duty' core tools (choppers, picks), plus smaller retouched pieces, such as scrapers, that are part of the archaeological record from the outset. These nonbifacial tools warrant closer examination as they will undoubtedly provide further evidence of the development of local and regional traditions (Kleindienst 1961). The range of small tools found among later Mode 2 assemblages also presages tool forms found with early Mode 3 assemblages, emphasising a further element of continuity in the African record (Klein 2000a).

OVERVIEW

The central issue of this chapter has been the impact of climate change on the behavioural and biological evolution of mid-Pleistocene hominins in Africa. Perhaps such a broad question is premature, given the contrast between the frustratingly small database of well-dated archaeological sites and scarce fossils (Table 5.1) and the increasingly detailed marine and terrestrial records showing instability in mid-Pleistocene climates. With few exceptions, such as Olorgesailie, the African archaeological record lacks the fine-grained chronological, spatial, and ecological data needed to assess hominin responses to resource variability. At the intercontinental scale, a large-scale behavioural pattern exists in the form of the Roe Line, against which regional and local developments can be assessed in terms of socially or individually generated responses to environmental stimuli. Within Africa, broad correspondences do exist in the timing of biological, technological, and environmental changes suggestive of possible causal relationships. Variability selection provides a useful working model that explicitly recognises the complex interplay of genetic, phenotypic, and behavioural change in response to environmental instability at the local to global scale.

The onset of the mid-Pleistocene ~1.0 mya marks the onset of a transition in the periodicity of glacial cycles that took place over the next 600,000 years. The establishment of the 100,000-year glacial cycle in this interval and the greater amplitude of change between glacials and interglacials together created new adaptive stresses for hominins, especially those living in the drier parts of Africa. The meagre fossil and archaeological record hints at increased adaptive flexibility among *H. erectus* populations and their descendants during this interval. The extinction of the paranthropines ~1.1 mya may be coincidental with climate change, but the fossil record shows regional diversity in *H. erectus* morphology ~1 mya, including the emergence of forms such as those from Buia and Daka that may represent the emergence of a separate lineage at a time of environmental change. The interval between 1.0–0.6 mya is poorly represented in the fossil record, but by 600 kya, a larger-brained species, *H. heidelbergensis*, had evolved from *H. erectus*, probably in eastern Africa, as represented at Bodo.[6] The gradual encephalisation seen over the time span of *H. erectus* and the more rapid brain expansion associated with later mid-Pleistocene *Homo* imply increased metabolic costs with all they entail for provisioning of offspring and the emergence of extended human-like life history patterns. The advantages of greater cognitive capacity outweighed the costs and, in the context of mid-Pleistocene environmental change, those advantages included enhanced social learning as a means of responding rapidly and collectively to immediate challenges. The development of content-rich language, possibly with *H. heidelbergensis*, would have contributed greatly to the maintenance of increasingly complex social networks and the transmission of practical information about the physical world.

Technological innovation seems slow by comparison with these proposed social and cognitive developments, but significant changes took place in the integration of tools in strategies of landscape use, as well as in methods of tool-making that imply greater planning and the need for learning than seen previously. Mid-Pleistocene hominins economised on raw material use in landscapes with dispersed food resources, with bifaces carried as multipurpose implements. The spatial separation of place of manufacture from place of use also reflects a developed sense of planning that is less commonly seen in the Plio-Pleistocene. The near-contemporaneous innovations of prepared core technology and soft hammer thinning of bifaces are markers of mobility strategies in the face of ecological uncertainty. The soft hammer technique involves considerable expertise learned over time that evokes modern parallels of apprenticeships or, at the very least, less formalised teaching combined with long periods of observation and practice. The use of language would, of course, have expedited the learning process, and directed learning through teaching necessarily requires a theory of mind for such a social relationship to be meaningful and effective (Tomasello 1999). Proponents of the social brain hypothesis place the development of language and human-like levels of intentionality with *H. heidelbergensis* at a time (~600 kya) that saw not just ongoing climate change, but also refinements in biface-making and core preparation techniques and the expansion of hominins into increasingly arid environments in southern Africa. The controlled use of fire, the ability to hunt large game, a gender-based division of labour, and the use of base camps all remain controversial components of the behavioural repertoire of early and mid-Pleistocene *H. erectus*, but each of these activities would have undoubtedly contributed to the evolving human-like social support network needed to raise large-bodied and big-brained offspring. Perhaps the modern brain size of *H. heidelbergensis* marks the convergence of these related behavioural and biological changes, all against a background of pronounced environmental change.

CHAPTER 6

# TRANSITIONS AND ORIGINS

The gradual establishment of the 100,000-year pattern of glacial cycles in the mid-Pleistocene created a long interval of instability in Africa's climate that posed new selective pressures for hominin societies. Integrated technological, social, neurological, and genetic changes effectively broadened the range of habitats in which *Homo erectus* and its descendants lived, with many of these developments taking place in response to the variability of mid-Pleistocene climates. The archaeological record in particular shows the application of technological solutions by *H. erectus* and, later, by *Homo heidelbergensis* to challenges of mobility linked to shifting resource distributions. These patterns of integrated behavioural and biological change provide a framework for assessing the impact of climate change on hominin evolution to the end of the mid-Pleistocene and through the start of the late Pleistocene (~430–70 kya, MIS 12-MIS 5a). This relatively short period encompasses significant changes in technology and other behaviours, as well as the evolution of the anatomically modern human form. The innovation of composite tool technologies (Mode 3) took place ~300 kya, and before the evolution of *Homo sapiens* ~200 kya, though for some a correspondence may exist between the appearance of Mode 3 and the evolution of *Homo helmei*, a putative ancestor of *H. sapiens*. Regardless of the species involved, Mode 3 makers developed the first

distinctive regional artefact styles in the form of bifacial points, and
the earliest archaeological indicators of symbolic expression. Genetic
data also provide insights into changes in human population densities
and distributions within and outside Africa. The combined genetic
and fossil evidence supports an African origin with later dispersal of
anatomically modern humans into Eurasia, but the extent of interaction between dispersing and indigenous populations remains controversial. Throughout the period examined in this chapter, the African
archaeological record provides its own story of internal development
based on local innovation ultimately deriving from the Mode 2/3
transition.

NEW EXTREMES IN CLIMATE AND ENVIRONMENTAL
CONSEQUENCES

Before ~450 kya, the Earth's climate was characterised by 100,000-
year-long glacial cycles displaying smaller amplitudes between
extremes of cold and warm than have occurred since. These earlier mid-Pleistocene cycles were also characterised by cooler interglacials, but ones that lasted proportionately longer than in the
last four cycles (EPICA 2004; Jouzel *et al.* 2007). After 450 kya,
not only were the extremes of cold and warm greater, but the
warm intervals became increasingly shorter.[1] The notable exception to the rule was MIS 11 (430–402 kya), which, at 28,000
years long, was the warmest interglacial other than our own current interval. This prolonged period of warmth followed one
of the coldest troughs of MIS 12 (~430 kya), with the transition between the two states taking place relatively rapidly with
a steep rise in temperature. The impact on Africa's climate must
have been profound; the change from dry to moist conditions
affecting the continent's biogeography and thus the distribution
of hominin groups. Our understanding of these dramatic shifts
remains poor, with little direct evidence with which to model the
likely responses of hominins to heightened variable selection. The
quality of the terrestrial record of climate change will undoubtedly improve as results emerge from the current core-drilling

programme in Lake Malawi. This 706 m deep Rift Valley lake preserves a record of continuously deposited sediments that possibly spans the past 1.5 million years, offering a high-resolution millennial to centennial record of changes in rainfall and temperature. The Lake Malawi core data currently cover the past 145,000 years from the Holocene to late MIS 6 (Cohen *et al.* 2007; Scholz *et al.* 2007), with the promise of future drilling providing a terrestrial record of climate change to complement that of the deep sea and ice cores.

In the interim, we can be certain that the MIS 12/11 transition brought dramatic changes to the biogeography of tropical Africa. The Dome C ice core from Antarctica, which currently provides the most complete mid-Pleistocene climate record, shows that the deglaciation from MIS 12 to 11 took place over 5000 years and would have been imperceptible to the generations of humans who gradually responded to the consequences. If the end of the last glacial cycle (14.5–11 kya) was comparable, then some short-lived centennial fluctuations of warm to cold probably took place, but these are not visible in the ice core record. The gradual cooling that accompanied the end of the MIS 11 interglacial would also have been imperceptible to those living through the changes leading to an interval of maximum cold at 340 kya (Fig. 6.1). An echo of these changes in the amplitude and shortened duration of warm intervals may be reflected by the extinction of highly specialised grassland grazers in southern Kenya. Between 992 and 350 kya, several taxa of large-bodied grazers became extinct, including the massive baboon, *Theropithecus oswaldi*, found in abundance at site DE 89 (Member 1) at Olorgesailie; the widespread elephant species, *Elephas recki*, that was replaced by the smaller living form *Loxodonta africana*; the large hippopotamus *Hippopotamus gorgops*, with its aquatic adaptation of eyes on short stalks; the large zebra *Equus oldowayensis*; and large pigs (*Metridiochoerus* spp.) that were replaced by the living warthog (*Phacochoerus africanus*), noted for its adaptability to a range of habitats, including dry savannas (Potts and Deino 1995). These extinctions of specialised grazers and their replacement by smaller, extant species characterised by greater dietary flexibility reflect the variability of mid-Pleistocene habitats linked to the establishment of the 100,000-year cycle.

The combined terrestrial and marine records for the latter part of the Quaternary in southern, central, and western Africa confirm a pattern seen in earlier cycles of increasing aridity during cold glacial phases and wetter conditions during interglacials (Elenga *et al.* 1994; Dong *et al.* 1996; Gasse 2000; Gingele *et al.* 1998; Jolly *et al.* 1997; Marret *et al.* 1999; Mercader *et al.* 2000a; O'Connor and Thomas 1999; Partridge *et al.* 1997; Tyson 1999; Weldeab *et al.* 2007). Northern hemisphere ice core and deep-sea data also show the imprint of short-lived warm and cold oscillations over the periodicities of the last glacial cycle (see inset). The instability in climate seen during the past 100,000 years, with millennial scale alterations, looks to have been typical of later mid-Pleistocene glacial cycles. More than 50 short-lived peaks of cold (~2000 years duration) have been recorded in North Atlantic sediments spanning the past 500,000 years (McManus *et al.* 1999). Linked to massive iceberg discharges called Heinrich events, these cold peaks would have created spikes of aridity across northern Africa, as they did during MIS 5 (discussed subsequently). The North Atlantic and Antarctic cores emphasise the instability of climates during full glacials and at times of transition between glacials and interglacials, with interglacials being more stable. For African hominins, these periods of increased instability would have placed additional selective pressures on integrated biological and behavioural responses to increased resource variability. At the continental scale, populations distributed across Africa during warm, wet interglacials, including the Sahara at times of higher rainfall, would have become geographically isolated during times of increased aridity. Glacial phase expansion of the Sahara and Kalahari deserts would effectively have pushed populations outwards towards the better watered margins, such as the Mediterranean coast, the shores of southern Africa, and the deep lakes along the western Rift Valley highlands. Such repeated glacial cycle disruptions of landscapes were doubtless a force for isolating populations geographically and genetically, regularly disrupting gene flow between contiguous populations.

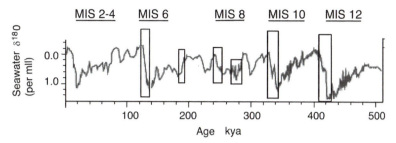

**Figure 6.1.** Marine isotope stages (MIS) from 500 kya to the present as reflected in changing seawater $\delta^{18}O$ values in the North Atlantic linked to ice sheet size (Ocean Drilling Program Site 980). Intervals of marked climatic instability during the mid-Pleistocene are highlighted (rectangles); in particular, the relatively rapid shifts between glacial and interglacial stages (after McManus *et al.* 1999: Fig. 3). In terms of variability selection, these periods of instability would have placed a premium on hominin behavioural flexibility.

A basic geographical point needs reiterating in this context: Africa's biomes are distributed longitudinally between 36°N and 35°S, in contrast to the latitudinal distribution of Eurasia's biomes (Foley and Lahr 1997). At a continental scale, expansions and contractions of Africa's environments would have drawn in or pushed out human populations from north to south, or *vice versa*, as well as eastwards into Eurasia during times of expansion or retreat from glacial aridity. Genetic evidence indicates at least one significant population reduction or bottleneck event between 300 to 100 kya during which human numbers were effectively reduced by 50% to 90%, to a few thousand individuals, with a consequent reduction in genetic diversity (Jorde *et al.* 2000; Ingman *et al.* 2000; Takahata *et al.* 2001; Voight *et al.* 2005; but see Hawks *et al.* 2000). The disruption of contact between regional populations combined with occasional severe downturns, causing local extinctions, would have contributed to the development of regional differences in morphology, gene pools, and behaviours (Stringer 2002). The periodicity and extremes of mid-Pleistocene glacial cycles underlay a process of accretional or mosaic emergence of human variation within Africa.

## GENE-BASED PHYLOGENIES AND DEMOGRAPHIC HISTORIES

The reconstruction of evolutionary relationships and population movements using genetic data has transformed the study of relatively recent African prehistory, complementing the fossil and archaeological evidence for an African origin of *H. sapiens* and adding an unexpected twist of one or more dispersals out of Africa into Eurasia. In the late 1980s, 'Mitochondrial Eve' made headlines as the putative female ancestor of all living humans (Cann *et al.* 1987). She evolved in Africa ~200 kya and her descendants dispersed across the Old World, replacing other hominin groups without interbreeding (admixture). That model has since been challenged and defended on methodological grounds (summarised by Relethford 2001), and it remains a watershed in the application of genetic analysis to issues of human evolution. Genetically based models of the interaction between African and Eurasian populations continue to be contested, with complete replacement still argued, as in the case of East Asia (Ke *et al.* 2001), but with more subtle gradualist models now proposed involving an African origin and spread of *H. sapiens* but with considerable admixture en route (Eswaran *et al.* 2005). Such divergent interpretations arise from the differing sources of data and methodologies used to analyse genetic diversity.

Most human genetic variation occurs between individuals within populations (~85%) with relatively little variation existing between populations. Widely used markers of genetic history and demographic change include gene variants or polymorphisms (e.g., blood group variants, Cavalli-Sforza *et al.* 1994), autosomal DNA (any DNA not from a sex chromosome, X or Y), nonrecombining mitochondrial DNA (mtDNA) inherited maternally, and the nonrecombining portion of the Y-chromosome (labelled NRY) inherited paternally. The X-chromosomes can recombine when there are two Xs, in a female, but the X and Y in a male can only recombine or pair in a small region (pseudoautosomal region), with the rest of Y being NRY. Nuclear DNA includes autosomal DNA and the X- and Y-chromosomes. Development in methods of extracting and sequencing DNA samples now enable the direct study of variations at the level of the single base pair changes and simplified comparisons of haplotypes (sets of genetic mutations inherited together) to map past population movements and derive genealogies based on estimated time of last shared ancestry (coalescence). Interpretations of variation between sequences have been based on the 'standard neutral model' that assumes past populations have been constant in size, mating was random (panmictic), all mutations were neutral, and all occur in different bases in the DNA (Przeworkski *et al.* 2000). With DNA that is subject to recombination, evidence of selection can be inferred from deviations from the predictions of the model, and sampling strategies refined (e.g., Voight *et al.* 2005). A comparison of the full chimpanzee and human genomes shows that strong positive selection took place among some haplotypes, with evidence of a 'selective sweep' of rare mutations that left its signature in the form of higher-than-predicted frequencies of the linked haplotype. The evidence of such sweeps can last up to 250,000 years before recombination reshuffles the haplotype and, in the case of humans, there is tentative evidence that the *FOXP2* gene, which is linked with the development of language, was part of a recent selective sweep (The Chimpanzee Sequencing and Analysis Consortium 2005). The apparent presence of this gene and its modern variants in ancient Neanderthal DNA suggests, however, that the sweep took place more than 400,000 years ago with the last common ancestor of moderns and Neanderthals, perhaps *H. heidelbergensis* (Krause *et al.* 2007). With human mtDNA, there is evidence, too, of considerable deviation from a strictly neutral model of no selection (Mishmar *et al.* 2003; Howell *et al.* 2004), and a potential effect of climate-related selection has been suggested for humans, but not yet substantiated (Ballard and Rand 2005:629).

Reconstructing genealogies or phylogenies from mtDNA involves inferring points of divergence and estimating rates of change along branches, and these can vary depending on the models and algorithms used to build the phylogenetic trees and the methods used to calibrate molecular clocks. The latter concept assumes a constant rate of mutation over time so that time since divergence can be estimated between species based on accumulated differences between matched sequences of DNA. Fossils or radiometrically dated archaeological events are used to calibrate DNA clocks. In the case of mtDNA, it is recognised that differing regions within the genome mutate at very different rates, in particular the D-loop or control region. For all DNA, the mutation that occurs least often is a change from one base to another. When this happens, the single base that now varies among individuals is described as a single nucleotide polymorphism (or SNP). These are typically used to study ancient lineage divergences. The human–chimpanzee divergence is now estimated to have taken place 7.13–4.17 mya with a 95% confidence interval, based on nuclear SNPs and in the absence of well-dated fossils for calibration (Kumar *et al.* 2005).

SNPs among mtDNA mutate so quickly in parts of the control region that the risk exists of reversals masking previous changes, underestimating divergence times and violating the assumptions necessary for a molecular clock to work (Howell *et al.* 2004). Comparisons of complete sequences of mtDNA can alleviate this problem, and the prospect now exists of whole-genome sequencing of Neanderthal autosomal DNA given recent discoveries of well-preserved ancient DNA combined with new sequencing techniques (Noonan *et al.* 2006). No ancient DNA has been recovered from African hominins, and the prospect is unlikely given the high rate of organic decay in the tropics.

Short tandem repeats (STRs) are brief strings of repeating base pair sequences (also known as microsatellites) that have a higher probability of mutating than SNPs and are typically used in forensic research to identify individuals within a population. A combination of slow-changing base pair changes with frequently mutating microsatellites has been used effectively with Y chromosomes to reconstruct population histories, as well as to improve the accuracy of divergence estimates (Ramakrishnan and Mountain 2004). The internationally agreed nomenclature of Y chromosome haplogroups (clusters of closely related haplotypes) labels them alphabetically from A-R (Y Chromosome Consortium 2002). African populations fall almost exclusively within haplogroups A and B, with all other lineages worldwide belonging to C-R (Underhill 2003). Group B includes the click-speaking Ju/'hoansi of the Kalahari and Hadzabe of Tanzania, suggesting a deep ancestral connection perhaps dating to the Last Interglacial, or independent invention of click-based consonants (Knight *et al.* 2003). The accumulated variation in A and B lineages and their position near the base of the Y-chromosome phylogenetic tree are used to argue for an African origin of all modern Y-chromosome lineages, following a period of diversification of lineages within Africa then dispersal into Eurasia. The Y-chromosome version of world prehistory sees no contribution of earlier non-African lineages in the modern Y range. The estimated date of the last common Y ancestor is just ~60 kya, which could mean that no African modern human was living outside the continent before then (Macaulay *et al.* 2005), or that it arose earlier but spread through the populations of Africa and Eurasia at this later date by selective advantage. The mitochondrial evidence supports a similar sequence of evolutionary development, with internal variation emerging within distinctive African haplogroups (labelled L1, L2, and L3) and L3 giving rise to the two basal non-African groups, M and N, from which all other variation is derived (Mishmar *et al.* 2003). L3 is estimated to have diverged from L2 about 85 kya in Africa, with divergence of M and N taking place ~60 kya, comparable in time to the purported spread of African Y chromosomes into Eurasia (Macaulay *et al.* 2005).[2]

Taken together, the NRY and mtDNA records tend to support a recent African origin (RAO) for modern humans and, by implication, all human diversity within the past 200,000 years, as was first proposed with Mitochondrial Eve. Significant challenges remain in refining chronologies of population genealogies and movements, but perhaps more important is the need to integrate these results with those derived from the nuclear genome. Nuclear DNA-based analyses of the RAO model provide conflicting results that are difficult to reconcile by the non-specialist. On the one hand, clear evidence of a RAO followed by dispersal with replacement has been claimed from a study of the geographical loss of genetic diversity (autosomal microsatellites) with increasing distance from East Africa (Prugnolle *et al.* 2005). In this model, a number of small bottlenecks occurred along routes of dispersal with little admixture. In contrast, a simulation study of the diffusion of nuclear DNA and mtDNA from an African origin shows a mismatch in estimated rates of mutation, expansion, and assimilation, as might be expected from the two different gene systems (Eswaran 2002; Eswaran *et al.* 2005). The more slowly mutating and more diverse nuclear DNA SNPs indicate a less clear pattern of expansion from Africa, with considerable incorporation of local non-African polymorphisms into the genome along a gradually expanding wave front that allowed time for assimilation between modern and archaic populations. Recent analyses of polymorphisms (microsatellites and extended haplotypes) on the X chromosome also support interbreeding between African moderns and non-African populations, including *H. erectus* in Asia (Garrigan *et al.* 2005; Hammer *et al.* 2005; Shimada and Hey 2005). The evident variations and contradictions between DNA analyses in part reflect varying sampling procedures, statistical analyses, and the use of different kinds of DNA data, each with its own limitations. The genetic signals of human expansion are, however, likely to be more complex than originally envisaged in the RAO model, with varying degrees of admixture to be expected given the fluidity of species boundaries in living primates (C. Jolly 2001), despite the NRY evidence to the contrary. Here, as discussed also later for more recent periods, the study of genetic variation has opened our eyes to the great diversity within Africa (Tishkoff and Williams 2002) and to processes of population expansion that would be largely invisible from the fossil and archaeological records alone.

## A VARIABLE FOSSIL RECORD

The hominin fossil record for the period between 430 kya (MIS 11) and 105 kya (MIS 5c), like that for the earlier range of the mid-Pleistocene, is represented by relatively few well-dated specimens, mostly from eastern Africa (Fig. 6.2; Table 6.1). Hominin fossils have yet to be found in West and Central Africa, except for cranial and postcranial material from cave deposits in south-central Africa. Farther south, caves and waterholes provided suitable environments for fossilisation in southern Africa. The largest fossil sample comes from the later end of the time range (~125–100 kya, MIS 5e-c) and from Levantine caves that, though not within Africa, nonetheless provide an important comparative sample. As with earlier hominin material, the strictly eastern African database derives from the Rift Valley basins of Ethiopia, Kenya, and Tanzania. Argon-argon dated volcanic deposits here provide the best framework on the continent for examining the sequence and process of evolutionary change during the middle to later Pleistocene. Currently, Ethiopia offers the most complete sequence documenting the likely evolution of *H. sapiens* from *H. heidelbergensis* as a single, but morphologically variable lineage. The term archaic *Homo sapiens* is commonly applied to mid-Pleistocene fossils from Africa and Europe that exhibit a mosaic of characteristics of *H. erectus* and *H. sapiens*, but that are clearly neither *H. erectus* nor fully anatomically modern (Antón 2003:141). *H. heidelbergensis* as used here subsumes the archaic group and includes the last common ancestor of *H. sapiens* and *H. neanderthalensis* (see Chapter 5). Considerable debate and uncertainty still surround the definition of what constitutes anatomical modernity (Howell 1978) and how to recognise the first appearance of *H. sapiens* in an evolving lineage (Stringer 2002; Trinkaus 2005). For some, the problem is solved by encompassing all Pleistocene hominins starting with *H. erectus* in a single evolving species, *H. sapiens*, characterised by regional morphological differences (Curnoe and Thorne 2003). Populations with mosaic or transitional characteristics are evidence from this perspective of a gradually evolving lineage with no speciation events (Lee and Wolpoff 2003). As outlined in Chapter 5, the apparent rapid increase in brain size in the mid-Pleistocene marks the speciation of *H. heidelbergensis* by 600 kya (Rightmire 2004), and

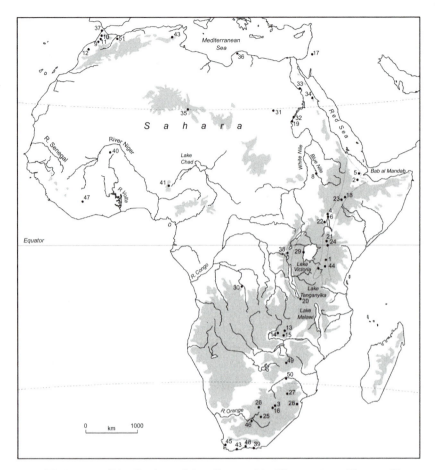

**Figure 6.2.** Distribution of sites discussed in Chapter 6: 1. Olorgesailie; 2. Middle Awash Valley (Bodo, Herto, Aduma); 3. Sterkfontein; 4. Omo (Omo I & II); 5. Gawis; 6. Ileret; 7. Lake Eyasi; 8. Singa; 9. Sidi Abderrahamane, Dar-es-Soltan; 10. Salé; 11. Kebitat; 12. Djebel Irhoud; 13. Kabwe; 14. Mumbwa Caves; 15. Twin Rivers; 16. Florisbad; 17. Qafzeh, Skhul; 18. Melka Kunturé; 19. Sai Island; 20. Kalambo Falls; 21. Kapthurin; 22. Eliye Springs; 23. Gademotta; 24. Cartwright's Farm; 25. Rooidam; 26. Wonderwerk; 27. Cave of Hearths; 28. Border Cave; 29. Sango Bay; 30. Lupemba; 31. Bir Tarfawi; 32. Arkin; 33. Taramsa; 34. Sodmein Cave; 35. Uan Tabu; 36. Haua Fteah; 37. Mugharet el'Aiya; 38. Katanda; 39. Klasies River; 40. Ounjougou; 41. Jos; 42. Blombos; 43. Bir-el-Ater; 44. Mumba; 45. Duinefontein; 46. Seacow Valley; 47. Bété I; 48. Mossel Bay; 49. Matopo Hills; 50. Kudu Koppie; 51. Taforalt.

TABLE 6.1. *Hominin fossil cranial specimens for the period 430–100 kya (MIS 12/11–5c)*

| Site | Species | Age (kya) | Reference |
|---|---|---|---|
| Gawis (Ethiopia) | *H. heidelbergensis?* | 400? | Unpublished |
| Salé (Morocco) | *H. heidelbergensis* | 455–400 | Hublin 2001 |
| Kebitat (Morocco) | *H. heidelbergensis?* | >250? | Hublin 2001 |
| Melka Kunturé (Ethiopia) | *H. heidelbergensis?* | 300–250? | Chavaillon *et al.* 1987 |
| Kabwe (Zambia) | *H. heidelbergensis** | 300? | Rightmire 2001 |
| Eliye Spring (Kenya) | *H. sapiens?*** | 300–200? | Brauer *et al.* 2003 |
| Florisbad (South Africa) | *H. sapiens?* | 260 | Grün *et al.* 1996 |
| Omo I& II (Ethiopia) | *H. sapiens* | 195 | Day 1969; McDougall *et al.* 2005 |
| Herto (Ethiopia) | *H. sapiens* | 160 | White *et al.* 2003 |
| Djebel Irhoud (Morocco) | *H. sapiens?* | 190–130 | Grün and Stringer 1991 |
| Ngaloba (LH18, Tanzania) | *H. sapiens?* | 200? | Magiori and Day 1983 |
| Ileret (Kenya) | *H. sapiens?* | >150 | Brauer *et al.* 1997 |
| Singa (Sudan) | *H. sapiens?**** | >130 | McDermott *et al.* 1996 |
| Lake Eyasi (Tanzania) | *H. sapiens?* | >130 | Mehlman 1987 |
| Klasies River (South Africa) | *H. sapiens* | 115 | Rightmire and Deacon 2001 |
| Skhul (Israel) | *H. sapiens* | 135–100 | Grün *et al.* 2005 |
| Qafzeh (Israel) | *H. sapiens* | 100–90 | Trinkaus 2005 |

A question mark following species attribution denotes uncertain taxonomic status. Those with a mosaic of archaic-*sapiens* traits are usually attributed to 'archaic *Homo sapiens*'. A question mark following the date indicates an estimated age, either on morphological grounds or by associated fauna.

* This poor individual suffered from extensive dental caries, perhaps induced by lead poisoning (Barstiokas and Day 1993). When first described, the Broken Hill (Kabwe) specimen was attributed to a new species, *H. rhodesiensis* (Pycraft 1928), but it is now generally considered a representative of *H. heidelbergensis* (Rightmire 2001).

** The unusually thickened bone of the Eliye cranial vault suggests the individual suffered from chronic anaemia as a juvenile (Braüer *et al.* 2003:203).

*** Computed tomography has revealed that the Singa cranium was also pathologically deformed with the right temporal bone lacking the inner ear bony labyrinth, probably as a result of a blood disease like anaemia (Spoor *et al.* 1998). The pathology would have led to permanent hearing loss in the one ear, and affected the individual's balance, suggesting it would have needed a greater-than-normal degree of communal support to survive to adulthood.

earlier variability in the specimens from Buia and Daka may indicate the emergence of non-*erectus* populations in eastern Africa at
the outset of the mid-Pleistocene (Antón 2003).

If *H. heidelbergensis* was the direct ancestor of *H. sapiens* in Africa,
we can expect considerable regional variability to exist in this lineage, with attendant problems of drawing an absolute distinction
between the two taxa. An intermediate species has been proposed,
'*Homo helmei*' (Foley and Lahr 1997; Lahr and Foley 2001), that
evolved about 300 kya in Africa, was responsible for the innovation
of Mode 3 technology, and then dispersed into Eurasia, where it
gave rise to Neanderthals as well as introducing the new technology
to a continent of biface-makers. The anatomical and genetic origins
of Neanderthals, however, have deeper roots in Europe than 300 kya
(Arsuaga *et al.* 1997; Stringer and Hublin 1999) and Mode 3 technology in Europe also pre-dates the putative arrival of *H. helmei* (M.
White and Ashton 2003). As discussed in Chapter 5, the use of prepared core technologies traditionally associated with Mode 3 has its
origins well before 300 kya, and may even precede or be coeval with
the Victoria West technique in South Africa (Sharon and Beaumont
2006). The 'Mode 3 Hypothesis' lacks support both from the fossil
record (see also Stringer 2002:567) and the archaeological evidence.
If we remove *H. helmei* as a likely direct ancestor of *H. sapiens*, then
the problem remains of how to define the morphological attributes
that distinguish *H. heidelbergensis* from early *H. sapiens*, since the transition between the two species may be subtle. The issue is further
confounded by morphological definitions of anatomical modernity
based on living or recent humans who, themselves, have changed in
the past 10,000 or so years (Lahr 1996), and may not be representative of earlier, more diverse populations of *H. sapiens*. This caveat
aside, most palaeoanthropologists recognise constellations of cranial
features that are distinctively *H. sapiens* (uniquely derived features
or autapomorphies), including a high, rounded globular vault with
a reduced face compared with *H. heidelbergensis* and Neanderthals
(Lieberman *et al.* 2002) and a bony chin, though this feature is not
present in all early specimens attributed to *H. sapiens* (Schwartz and
Tattersall 2000). Postcranial differences are less distinctive in comparing African specimens, but a pattern does emerge of a reduction
in robusticity or muscularity over time, particularly in the upper

body (Pearson 2000b). This may be linked to the development of hafted tools (Mode 3) that required less strength to use than hand-held Mode 2 tools. If the evolution of the constellation of *H. sapiens* attributes took place gradually, as seems to have been the case in Africa (Stringer 2002), then the range of shared characteristics of this clade will vary between early and more recent members.

## THE ETHIOPIAN LINEAGE

The oldest (600 kya) African specimen of *H. heidelbergensis* comes from Bodo in the Middle Awash Valley region of the Ethiopian Rift. The Bouri Formation from which the Bodo cranium was recovered is 80 m thick and divided into three members: Hata, Daka, and Herto (de Heinzelin *et al.* 2000). The Herto Member is later mid-Pleistocene in age and contains Mode 2 and 3 sites with significant evidence for the longevity of biface-making after the innovation of composite tool technology (discussed subsequently). Fossilised crania of two adults and one juvenile were recovered from the Herto Member and attributed to *Homo sapiens idaltu*, a sub-species that recognises the slight differences that distinguish the specimens from anatomically modern humans (T. White *et al.* 2003). The fossils were found in sandstone and gravel deposits in the Upper Herto Formation, which has been $^{40}Ar/^{39}Ar$ radiometrically dated to 160–154 kya (J. D. Clark *et al.* 2003). This was the coldest and driest interval of MIS 6, and these conditions may have contributed to a significant population decline, as inferred from autosomal DNA sequences (Voight *et al.* 2005). As well as providing much-needed anatomical data from a poorly represented period, the Herto specimens also contribute to the behavioural record of the mid-Pleistocene. The three crania show signs of intentional modification that can be interpreted as a mixture of mortuary and economic behaviours. Cutmarks occur on each cranium, with the varying patterns of placement, extent, and directions of cuts indicative of intentional defleshing using sharp stone flakes. The child's cranium also shows postmortem polish on its parietals. Cutmarks have been found within an eye orbit of the Bodo skull (T. White 1986) and on the lower mandible of a Plio-Pleistocene early *Homo* specimen from Sterkfontein Member 5, South Africa (Stw-53, ~1.7 mya) (Pickering *et al.* 2000). The defleshing of crania in general could reflect social conventions for commemorating the death of an individual or simply the removal of edible flesh. In the case of the Herto group, the polishing on the child's skull suggests some form of cultural activity such as curation by the family or group, and is the first such indication of mortuary practices in the African record.[3]

The earliest specimen of *H. sapiens* currently known also comes from Ethiopia. Two crania were found in 1967 in exposures of the Kibish Formation along the Omo River in southern Ethiopia (part of the Turkana Basin). Omo I is attributed to *H. sapiens*, Omo II, a surface find, is thought to be older, given its more archaic features (Day 1969). Attempts to date the site initially proved unsatisfactory, with Omo I correlated with deposits unreliably dated by uranium (U)-series measurements on shells to 130 $\pm$ 5 kya (Butzer *et al.* 1969). A well-dated stratigraphic sequence anchored by $^{40}$Ar/$^{39}$Ar-dated tuffs has since been developed, and the original find spots are confidently bracketed between tuffs dated to 104 $\pm$ 7 and 196 $\pm$ 2 kya (McDougall *et al.* 2005). Omo I came from deposits located just above the older tuff and the specimen is now thought to be ~195 kya (MIS 7), making it the oldest *H. sapiens* fossil known. Omo II has also been carefully linked with the 195 kya date, but as a surface find, some doubt remains about its stratigraphic association. If the age attribution of both specimens is correct, and if Omo II is also a specimen of *H. sapiens*, then we are seeing a highly variable morphology among early *H. sapiens* during this mid-Pleistocene interglacial. Three cranial fragments attributed to 'archaic' *H. sapiens* or *H. heidelbergensis* recovered from the riverside location of Melka Kunturé in the Upper Awash Valley add to this diversity. From the site of Garba III (level B, ~300–250 kya), they are associated with Mode 2 tools and overlain by Mode 3-containing deposits (Chavaillon *et al.* 1987).

Further finds from the period ~200 kya, and earlier, are needed to assess the extent of regional variability in our species, and ongoing research in the Afar region and the Middle Awash looks certain to contribute to the eastern African database. The recent discovery of a cranium at Gawis (Gona, Afar) associated with Mode 2 artefacts should address the *H. heidelbergensis/H. sapiens* transition as it appears to be morphologically intermediate between the two (Gona Palaeoanthropological Project 2006).

## SPECIMENS FROM FARTHER AFIELD

Elsewhere in eastern Africa, the mosaic of features indicative of an evolving lineage is seen in fossils from MIS 8–6 (304–130 kya) from Eliye Spring and Ileret (Guomde) in Kenya's Turkana Basin (Bräuer and Leakey 1986; Bräuer *et al.* 1997, 2003; Trinkaus 1993) and the Tanzanian sites of Lake Eyasi (Mehlman 1987) and Ngaloba (Magori and Day 1983). To the north, a single specimen from Singa, Sudan, represents northeastern Africa (McDermott *et al.* 1996). An evolutionary sequence from *H. heidelbergensis* to early *H. sapiens* is also found in mid-Pleistocene fossils from North Africa. Pre-dating MIS 6–7, crania from the Moroccan quarry sites of Sidi Abderrahmane and Salé show a mosaic of features shared by *H. erectus* and *H. sapiens* that suggest a single, evolving, but variable lineage, whereas the highly fragmented cranium from Kebitat near Rabat is of uncertain stratigraphic provenance and date, between ~400 and 250–350 kya (Hublin 2001). Within the time frame of Omo I and Herto, cranial and postcranial fossils from the cave of Djebel Irhoud are attributed to early *H. sapiens* (Hublin 2001). Attempts to date the overlying deposits by electron-spin resonance (ESR) produced wide-ranging results (>190–90 kya) (Grün and Stringer 1991), but recent resampling of the site should help constrain their age further.

In south-central Africa, the undated Kabwe (Broken Hill) cranium attributed to *H. heidelbergensis* (also called *Homo rhodesiensis*, its original attribution) and associated postcrania probably predate MIS 7 based on associated fauna (Rightmire 2001). The archaeological material from this now-destroyed cave falls within early Mode 3 (~300 kya), but no direct association can be made between the fossils and the tools (Barham *et al.* 2002). Postcranial material has been recovered from two other Zambian cave sites dating to the mid-Pleistocene and containing Mode 3 assemblages; Twin Rivers (a humeral fragment, ~177 kya, Pearson 2000b) and Mumbwa Caves (radius fragments, ~240–177 kya, Pearson *et al.* 2000). The most complete specimen from MIS 8–6 in southern Africa is a cranium from the spring mound site of Florisbad, South Africa. Found in deposits luminescence-dated to 260 kya (Grün *et al.* 1996), it is the type specimen of *H. helmei* (Foley and Lahr 1997) because of its mosaic of archaic and modern features. Along with Singa and Djebel

Irhoud, it falls within the *H. sapiens* clade, but is not anatomically modern in the sense of recent human variability (Stringer 2002). Variability in morphology is also seen in the later (~115 kya) fragmentary cranial and postcranial specimens from the Klasies River caves, South Africa. These specimens are generally attributed to *H. sapiens* (Rightmire and Deacon 1991, 2001), but robust or 'archaic' features remain and there is evidence of considerable sexual dimorphism in the postcrania (Churchill *et al.* 1996). The fragmentary Klasies material is also of considerable behavioural interest given that some of the cranial fragments show signs of burning and butchery (cutmarks, percussion impacts) suggestive of cannibalism. Some retention of archaic features, cranial and postcranially, is also seen in the large combined sample of 24 adult and juvenile skeletons from the two Israeli sites of Qafzeh and Skhul (135–100 kya, MIS 5), which are otherwise anatomically modern humans (Grün *et al.* 2005; Trinkaus 2005).

The combined African and Levantine database emphasises the gradual, piecemeal evolution of *H. sapiens* through the later part of the mid-Pleistocene and into the early late Pleistocene. In contrast to the evolution of *H. heidelbergensis*, there is no visible speciation event in the period 300–100 kya, though there is some genetic evidence for a population reduction or bottleneck ~160 kya. Periodic collapses or disruptions of population distributions caused by glacial cycles could have contributed to some of the morphological variability seen in eastern and other parts of Africa, but linkages need to be demonstrated between minor shifts in morphology and the remodelling of landscapes by climate change. The impact of technological change on the lifestyles of early *H. sapiens* also needs further consideration, as this interval encompasses a significant shift from hand-held to hafted tools.

## THE MODE 2 TO MODE 3 TRANSITION: THE EMERGENCE OF HAFTING AND REGIONAL TRADITIONS

The fossil evidence for the mosaic evolution of a recognisably modern morphology has its parallel in the archaeological record of changes in stone tool-making. *H. sapiens* at Herto and Melka

Kunturé is associated with Mode 2 bifaces and the Herto individuals plus *H. sapiens* from Omo, Mumbwa Caves, Twin Rivers, and Florisbad were also associated with Mode 3 sites. Significantly, at Herto and elsewhere the two technologies overlap in time. No direct linkage exists then between a hominin species and technological mode. The development of hafted tool technology marks the transition from Mode 2 to 3, but Mode 3 is also typically associated with the production of small flakes from prepared or Levallois cores, a method that, perhaps along with soft-hammer thinning of bifaces, perhaps had its origins with *H. heidelbergensis* in the early mid-Pleistocene. The tendency to equate behavioural with anatomical modernity still prevails among archaeologists (e.g., Henshilwood and Marean 2003), though the African fossil and behavioural records show a continuum of change with relatively few points of punctuated evolution. If brain size (neocortex ratios) correlates with a range of behaviours, including group size, co-operative social structures, extended learning, levels of intentionality and planning, capacity for language, and religion, then many of the traits we assume to be typically modern should be present in the mid-Pleistocene after 600 kya. The innovation of composite tool technology may signal the implementation of planning, social learning, and a high level of imagination and intentionality needed to conceive tools made from multiple components.

The construction of hafted tools, with a stone working bit set in a handle or shaft made of some organic material, such as bone, wood, ivory, or horn, involves an understanding of the properties of a range of raw materials and how they work together. Wood-working and bone-working both have some antiquity in the earlier Pleistocene (see Chapter 4) and the development of soft-hammer flaking (Chapter 5) shows an added awareness of the elastic properties of organic materials that could be relevant for the making of hafts. Composite technologies integrate these two spheres of knowledge to a degree not seen previously. The selection and shaping of hafts must be tailored to the task at hand, with drilling, scraping, cutting, adzing, or piercing involving different motor skills, actions, and stresses. The haft and the working edge, whether stone or other material, must be designed for each other. An often-neglected component of the hafting process is the adhesive or other materials used to bind a working edge to a handle to create a working whole. Plant- and animal-based glues have differing properties, and later Mode 3 makers in southern Africa had developed specific recipes for use with *Acacia* resin (Wadley 2005b). Experience and planning are required in the production of adhesives, as well as the selection of materials to haft, with implications for the transmission of social learning between generations. The additional thought and time involved in creating multi-component tools raises the obvious question of what practical and social advantages are offered by this technology over tried and tested hand-held tools. Extended handles or shafts give the user greater leverage when cutting, scraping, drilling, or thrusting and act as an extension of the limbs. Less force is needed to achieve the same effect, a saving in energy expenditure. More power applied to a working edge also saves on the amount of stone or other hard raw material needed to do the job, and once the working edge becomes blunt, it can be replaced and the haft reused. The saving on stone may be relevant in areas where raw materials are scarce or occur in small sizes, such as pebbles, and in such contexts extends the range of landscapes exploited by hominins.

Still at a practical level, hafting puts greater distance between the user and the contact material, reducing the risks associated with pro- cessing foods and hunting large game. Raw meat can be a source of infection and having a knife blade on a handle minimises dam- age to the user and direct contact with blood (J. D. Clark 1989b). A stone-tipped spear has greater penetrative power than a sharp- ened stick alone, thus reducing the risk of contact with an injured animal (or other human), as well as providing a nonabsorbent sur- face on which to place poisons. Composite technology also offers a means of responding quickly and effectively to shifting resource availability, especially in highly seasonal environments and where food is on the move (Torrence 2001). Specialised tools can be made to process abundant but short-lived resources, such as fish, and to target large, wide-ranging, and potentially dangerous game (Hayden and Gargett 1988). An alternative strategy is to create highly portable, multi-purpose hafted tools that can perform a range of tasks. Such tools are particularly valuable for reducing the risk of being ill-equipped in rapidly changing or unfamiliar environments as might be experienced by hunter-gatherers colonising new land-scapes (Hiscock 1994), or living in habitats with widely dispersed resources. Less obvious, but of potential social importance, is the platform offered by hafted tools as a medium for communicating individual and group identity through the design and decoration of hafts and shaping of inserts (Wiessner 1985). Unfortunately, no hafts survive from the African mid-Pleistocene, so this potential aspect of their use remains speculative. Despite this, a new range of stone and bone artefacts designed for hafting did emerge from the outset of Mode 3, and with these we recognise the first distinctive regional traditions in the African record (J. D. Clark 1988a).

Use-wear evidence for early hafting comes from the locality of Sai Island (site 8-B-11), along the southern Sudanese Nile, where early Mode 3 assemblages attributed to the Sangoan and Lupemban indus-tries (discussed subsequently) are dated to the late mid-Pleistocene. The majority of optically stimulated luminescence (OSL) and ESR dates provide a minimum age of >150 kya for these deposits (Van Peer, pers. comm.). Use-wear analyses of the edges and surfaces of Sangoan core-axes (thick, bifacially flaked tools with a retouched working end, Fig. 6.3) show edge damage in the form of scarring from hafting and use, an interpretation supported by experimen-tal replication studies (Rots and Van Peer 2006). The tools seemed to have been used for digging, perhaps to extract other stone for knapping, tubers, or even red and yellow iron oxides (haematite and limonite), which occur in abundance with some evidence of processing (Van Peer *et al.* 2004). There is evidence, too, of core-axes made on non-local raw materials having been brought to the site as complete tools, suggesting a strategy of production and use involving other sites in the area, with Sai Island a focal point for activities requiring heavy-duty tools.

Somewhat older (~265 kya) but indirect evidence for hafting comes from the deliberate **backing** of **blades** seen in the Lupemban industry (see inset) sites of Twin Rivers and Kalambo Falls, Zambia (Fig. 6.4) (Barham 2002a). These blunted pieces, because of their small size, are presumed to have been inserts in hafts rather than hand-held tools. Systematic blade-making appears in the African record in the Lupemban industry and in even earlier deposits at

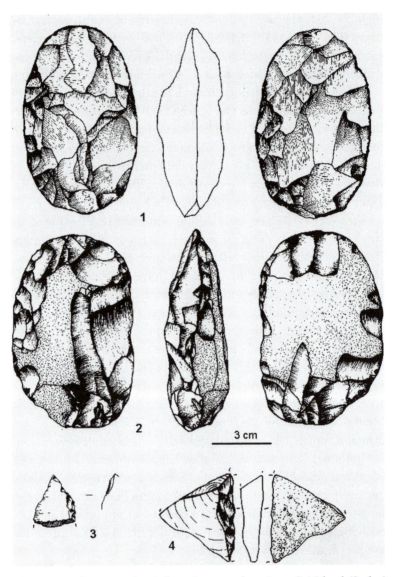

**Figure 6.3.** Core axes (1, 2) from Sangoan deposits at Sai Island (Sudan) and tranchets (3, 4). These artefacts currently provide some of the earliest evidence for hafting in the African record. (Used with permission of Philip Van Peer and the Western Academic & Specialist Press.)

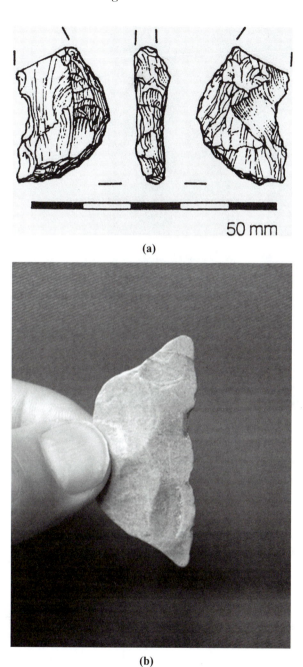

**(a)**

**(b)**

**Figure 6.4.** Lupemban backed tools from the Zambian sites of (a) Twin Rivers and (b) Kalambo Falls. Blade production (c) is also a feature of the Lupemban at these sites.

**(c)**

**Figure 6.4.** *Continued*

Kenya's Kapthurin Formation associated with small bifacial points, also presumed to be hafted (see inset).

The innovation of blade technology has long been used as an indicator of behavioural modernity given its association with early Upper Palaeolithic industries in western Europe made by *H. sapiens*. More recent evidence of blade-making by some Neanderthal populations (Bar Yosef and Kuhn 1999) and the early dates from the Kapthurin Formation, which predate the oldest known *H. sapiens*, provide a salutary reminder that technology makes for a poor phylogenetic marker. Blade-making is also the standard indicator of Mode 4 (see Chapter 1), and arguably Modes 2, 3, and 4 coexist below the K4 Tuff. A primary reliance on blades for making tools rather than flakes, however, does distinguish Mode 4 from 3,

## THE KAPTHURIN FORMATION AND THE MODE 2/3 TRANSITION

The Kapthurin Formation sediments that outcrop west of Lake Baringo in the Rift Valley of central Kenya provide a well-dated sequence of archaeological deposits that incorporate Mode 2 and Mode 3 sites. A series of $^{40}$Ar/$^{39}$Ar-dated tuffs provide the chronological framework, with tuffs K3 and K4 bracketing the Acheulean to Middle Stone Age (Mode 3) transition, 509–235 kya (Fig. 6.5). Bedded Tuff Member K4 is particularly important because it formed gradually from intermittent eruptions over a period of 50,000 years with archaeological sites on intervening land surfaces (palaeosols) buried by subsequent eruptions in a finely bedded sequence (Tryon and McBrearty 2006). The sites contained within K4 are dated between 284 kya at its base and 235 kya at its top, and the refitting of flakes to cores shows that they have undergone relatively little disturbance. Deposits within and below the base of the tuff include interstratified Mode 2 and Mode 3 sites, with the latter providing some of the earliest evidence in Africa for blade-making and small bifacial, presumably hafted retouched **points** indicative of the Middle Stone Age (Fig. 6.6). Of particular importance is the co-occurrence of sites below K4 with Levallois cores used to make large Mode 2 flakes for handaxes and cleavers with Mode 3 technologies. Few localities in Africa offer such chronological and spatial resolution covering this period of technological change. At 250–200 kya, the biface tradition is abandoned in the Kapthurin sequence in favour of diverse techniques of flake production using differing Levallois strategies typical of later eastern African Mode 3 assemblages (Tryon 2006). The smaller Levallois flakes (~5–10 cm) and cores found after 250 kya reflect a continuation and elaboration of the existing Mode 2 tradition of core preparation rather than an abrupt change.

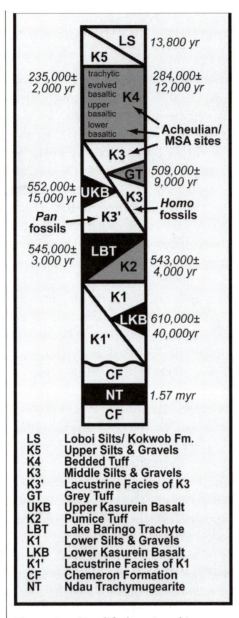

LS    Loboi Silts/ Kokwob Fm.
K5    Upper Silts & Gravels
K4    Bedded Tuff
K3    Middle Silts & Gravels
K3'   Lacustrine Facies of K3
GT    Grey Tuff
UKB   Upper Kasurein Basalt
K2    Pumice Tuff
LBT   Lake Baringo Trachyte
K1    Lower Silts & Gravels
LKB   Lower Kasurein Basalt
K1'   Lacustrine Facies of K1
CF    Chemeron Formation
NT    Ndau Trachymugearite

**Figure 6.5.** Simplified stratigraphic sequence of the Kapthurin Formation, Kenya, showing location of the K4 bedded tuffs (285–235 kya) within and below, which occur interstratified at Mode 2 and Mode 3 assemblages. (Courtesy and copyright of Christian Tryon.)

**Figure 6.6.** Artefacts from Bedded K4 Tuff showing the diversity of Mode 2 and 3 types represented: (a) unifacial handaxe on Levallois flake; (b, c) Levallois cores; (d) blades; (e) cores; (f) point rough out; (g) informal point; (h) point; (i) small handaxe; (j) pick. (Used with the permission of Western Academic & Specialist Press.)

but the early presence of this technology in Mode 3 again underlines the continuity of technological development in the African record. The presence of bifaces at Herto ~160 kya also points to a gradual replacement of Mode 2 tool types over the previous

100,000 years in parts of eastern Africa, and perhaps at a very local level. At Gademotta, near Lake Ziway in Ethiopia, the latest Mode 2 assemblages occur below Mode 3 deposits of potassium-argon dated to ~235 kya (Wendorf and Schild 1974; Wendorf *et al.* 1994), and their proximity to Herto reinforces the sense of local variability in traditions of tool-making. Perhaps differences in geography and raw material availability account for this striking discordance in the longevity of bifaces between highland Ethiopia and the Afar depression.

In Kenya, the site of Cartwright's Farm on the Kinangop Plateau is notable for controversial potassium argon dates of 440 kya that, at the time of its reporting, seemed far too old for a Mode 3 assemblage (Evernden and Curtis 1965). The subsequent discovery and dating of Mode 3 sites to ~285 kya has made this site less of a radical outlier, though it would still be the oldest Mode 3 occurrence by more than 150,000 years. There is still uncertainty about the association of its distinctive obsidian points with the dated tuff, and more recent excavations are addressing this stratigraphic issue (Waweru 2002). Current research at Olorgesailie in the Olkesiteti Formation, which postdates the Olorgesailie Formation, is targeting early Mode 3 sites beneath and between radiometrically dated tuffs that range from >340 to <166 kya ($^{40}$Ar/$^{39}$Ar), with the sediments preserving bone and ostrich eggshells (Brooks and Behrensmeyer 2007). In deposits sandwiched between tuffs dated to 220 kya (locality G) assemblages with Sangoan-like picks, core-axes, elongated bifacial points, and Levallois cores occur interstratified with Mode 3 assemblages lacking picks. The alternation of Sangoan and non-Sangoan assemblages resembles the local variability seen in the Kapthurin Formation, and suggests a functional explanation for the presence/absence of picks rather than evoking the need for separate hominin species in the landscape. Preliminary results from recent excavations of older deposits beneath a tuff dated to 340 kya (locality B) hint at an early non-Mode 2 technology with small flakes, some with faceted butts (Levallois), the transport of obsidian, and the presence of ochre. The absence of points or other obvious hafted tools, except possibly for the small flakes, means this is not clearly Mode 3 either. The Olkesiteti Formation sites look set to provide much-needed comparative data for assessing the Mode 2/3 transition from an area not far from the Kapthurin Formation, as well as pushing the age of the transition further back.

## EARLY MODE 3 INDUSTRIES IN SOUTHERN AND SOUTH-CENTRAL AFRICA

If local geographical and cultural factors did affect the rate of technological change, then the timing of the transition across the continent is likely to be very variable. Too few well-dated sites are available currently to establish regional patterns with any certainty. South of the Limpopo, the 'Fauresmith Industry' typically contains handaxes of varying size, but they tend to be small, and are generally associated with large points, Levallois cores, long blades, and flakes. This blend of Modes 2 and 3 has long made it a likely transitional industry (Goodwin and van Riet Lowe 1929), but until recently the Fauresmith has remained ill-defined and poorly dated. Reliable dates from excavated contexts have been lacking, with the pan site of Rooidam yielding a longstanding minimum age of ∼180 kya based on U-series dates (Szabo and Butzer 1979). Recent excavations at other pans in the Northern Cape Province, including Rooidam II and Bundu Farm, are addressing issues of typological definition, age, and ecological contexts. ESR dates on fauna from the stratified deposits at Bundu Farm place the Fauresmith in the time range ∼330–150 kya (Kiberd 2005). Wonderwerk Cave, also in the Northern Cape, provides the only stratified cave sequence containing Fauresmith artefacts, with two cultural units recognised. The latest, Major Unit 3, is dated by U-series to ∼286–276 kya (Beaumont and Vogel 2006:220), and contains large bifaces as well as blades, prepared cores, and Levallois unifacial points (Fig. 6.7). The underlying Major Unit 4 is less securely dated, with U-series results indicating an age of >350 kya. The artefacts in this 'Middle Fauresmith' include large blades, prepared cores, Levallois unifacial points, and smaller bifaces than those found in Unit 3.

Full publication of these regionally important cave and open-site assemblages will undoubtedly transform our understanding of the later mid-Pleistocene in southern Africa, especially given claims from Wonderwerk for grass bedding, pigment use, mobiliary art (engraved slabs), and the collection of exotic pebbles by its mid-Pleistocene inhabitants (Beaumont and Vogel 2006:222). For the time being, the least we can say is that the Mode 2/3 transition took place ~280–240 kya in southern Africa with the final disappearance of handaxes from the behavioural repertoire. (U-series dates of ~160 kya from the late Mode 2 dune deposits of Duinefontein 2, near Cape Town, provide a minimum age for the underlying landsurfaces with their well-preserved fauna [Klein *et al.* 1999; Cruz-Uribe *et al.* 2003].) The Wonderwerk sequence also highlights the continuity in the archaeological record that is often obscured by the labels Early and Middle Stone Age. Blades and unifacial points preceded the appearance of Mode 3 assemblages at Wonderwerk, and similarly at the Cave of Hearths (discussed subsequently) blades occur among late Mode 2 assemblages (Mason 1988). Hafting as a defining feature of Mode 3 assemblages may have originated among late Mode 2 communities, and use-wear analyses of Fauresmith tools could usefully address this possibility (Sharon and Beaumont 2006). The post-Fauresmith record is poorly known, with few well-dated assemblages available, perhaps reflecting the impact of glacial phase aridity during MIS 8–6 (~260–130 kya) on human population distributions, especially in the dry interior. In the spring deposits at Florisbad, non-diagnostic flakes and cores occur in the basal deposits (along with the cranium attributed to '*Homo helmei*') dated by thermoluminescence (TL) to ~260 kya (Grün *et al.* 1996; Kuman *et al.* 1999).

At the Cave of Hearths, a technological sequence attributed to the Mode 3 'Pietersburg Complex' (Sampson 1974) occurs in Beds 4–9 (Beds 1–3 contain late Mode 2 artefacts, including some blades), with the artefacts in the earliest Mode 3 level (Bed 4) characterised by minimal retouch on large quartzite and andesite blades and flake-blades, struck from boulder cores, as well as on Levallois flakes (Mason 1988). Average blade length decreases gradually in the overlying deposits (Beds 5–9) and this trend is accompanied by an increased frequency of more extensively retouched bifacial points. The points are made on finer-grained raw materials, such as chert, and some bear impact scars from use as hafted tips of projectiles, presumably spears (Sinclair, pers. comm.) The lithic raw materials used by the occupants of the site come from a range of near and distant sources in the Makapansgat Valley and reflect routines of

**Figure 6.7.** A unifacially retouched point of brown jasper from the 'Late Fauresmith' (MU3, ~270 kya) at Wonderwerk Cave, South Africa (Beaumont and Vogel 2006). The point is made on a large flake and reflects the shift to large flake and blade production seen in early Mode 3 assemblages in the region.

procurement and processing that took place beyond the cave. Recent re-investigation of the deposits indicate an age range for the early part of the Mode 3 sequence of ~250–115 kya, characterised by intermittent occupation, which is as yet difficult to attribute to specific isotope stages (Sinclair, pers. comm.). Brief mention should be made of fragmentary hominin remains found during earlier excavations, including a partial mandible in Bed 3 and a radius of uncertain stratigraphic origin (Tobias 1971). The radius shares morphological features with the common ancestor of Neanderthals and *H. sapiens*, taken here to be *H. heidelbergensis* (Pearson and Grine 1997), reinforces the association of late Mode 2 or early Mode 3 technologies with a highly variable, and evolving pre-*H. sapiens* morphology.

The long, and increasingly well-dated Mode 3 sequence from Border Cave[4] at the southern end of the Lebombo Mountains provides a comparable early assemblage of large, minimally retouched flakes and blades. The earlier part of the sequence (units 6BS to 4WA) corresponds with the occupation of the site during two successive interglacials (MIS 7 and 5e, discussed later), during which rainfall levels were higher than today, supporting a southerly extension of miombo woodland from what is now Zimbabwe (Grün and Beaumont 2001:480). The ESR age of the lowest, at ~227 kya, overlaps with the estimated age of the earlier Mode 3 at Cave of Hearths.

In southern Zimbabwe, early Mode 3 assemblages containing Sangoan-like picks and core-axes are known from the basal deposits at Bambata and Pomongwe Caves in the Matopos region and attributed to the 'Charama industry', also known as 'Proto-Stillbay' (Cooke 1969). These undated assemblages resemble Sangoan open sites in the Matopo Hills, as well as Sangoan material found along the Limpopo River Valley of South Africa, where excavations at the open site of Kudu Koppie have produced core-axes and prepared cores overlain by Mode 3 assemblages characterised by small flakes and retouched points (Kuman *et al.* 2004). This sequence from Sangoan to what might be considered a more conventional conception of the Middle Stone Age with points has parallels not just with the Matopos, but also with sequences in Zambia. The current absence of good chronological controls for this southern extension of the early Mode 3 Sangoan undermines suggestions of widespread cultural linkages in south-central Africa rather than local social traditions founded on similar underlying technologies.

At Kalambo Falls, northern Zambia, a stratified sequence of late Mode 2 and early Mode 3 assemblages (see inset) offers a potential minimum age for the transition in south-central Africa, but gaps in the depositional sequence make it impossible to characterise the change as gradual or rapid (Sheppard and Kleindienst 1996:172). Efforts to date the Kalambo sequence using luminescence are underway. U-series dates from Twin Rivers indicate that Mode 3 assemblages were being made by 265 kya, if not before (Barham 2000). Much farther north, in Egypt's Western Desert, repeated but separate occupations of lake and spring sites by late Mode 2 and Mode 3 communities provide a coarse measure of the time frame for the transition in this region. A suite of different dating techniques applied to the sediments and fauna produced a wide range of results of varying consistency between 540 and 160 kya for a late Mode 2 presence (Wendorf *et al.* 1993). The earliest Mode 3 assemblages date to the Last Interglacial (MIS 5e, ~130–116 kya) with gaps in time reflecting in terrupted occupation caused by aridity during MIS 6 (186–130 kya) rather than by late emergence of composite technology.

This brief overview highlights the rarity of sites that actually document the Mode 2/3 transition. Most Mode 3 sites are, in fact, later Pleistocene in age (<130 kya) (McBrearty and Brooks 2000). Given the limited archaeological visibility of mid-Pleistocene sites combined with poor chronological controls, much of our speculation on the causes of the Mode 2/3 transition will remain speculative for some time to come. The limited data do not show any obvious correlations between dramatic changes in climate and the earliest Mode 3 assemblages, but there is a convergence in dates ~280–240 kya for the adoption of Mode 3 in eastern and southern Africa. This interval overlaps with the coldest part of MIS 8. The correspondence may be coincidental, an artefact of the limited range of dates available, or perhaps a genuine reflection of human responses to ecological and demographic pressures engendered by this glacial stage. Well-dated sites are needed from western and northern Africa to test the apparent chronological association with MIS 8 on a continental scale. A refined chronology is also needed to develop models for the transmission of Mode 3, whether by population movement and interaction or by independent invention in more than one region.

Those rare sites that do show a temporal and spatial overlap of Modes raise important methodological and conceptual issues about the process of technological change. Archaeologists tend to classify lithic assemblages as belonging to one industry or another based on the presence of a diagnostic tool type such as handaxes, which, at Herto, account for less than 5% of the retouched assemblage from across the site (J. D. Clark *et al.* 2003:750). Most tools were made on flakes, and bifaces may have been made elsewhere and carried into the Herto area, or their small numbers reflect the end of a tradition of large cutting tools in an otherwise Mode 3 context.[5] At present, we know too little about the various uses of bifaces and hafted tools to be able to model the process of change. Which Mode 3 tools replaced the functions of a handaxe, a cleaver, and a pick, and how were points used? The light-duty tools such as scrapers, burins, and awls that continued to be made from one tradition to the next are also underrepresented in theorising about the transition. This period encompassed more than one species of *Homo*, raising the possibility that *H. sapiens* and late *H. heidelbergensis* coexisted, contributing to the technological variability seen in the archaeological record (McBrearty 2003). If technologies are not species-specific, and the handaxe spans several species, then the problem arises of how to recognise differing patterns of behaviour that may be culturally inherited. At Sai Island, Sudan, Van Peer *et al.* (2004) argue for a rapid shift from Mode 2 to 3 reflecting the arrival of a new population who brought not just new technologies, but differing economic strategies, including quarrying for stone, and symbolic behaviours. Such an argument displaces the search for the origins of Mode 3 technology southwards, but also raises the issue of how to differentiate between processes of *in situ* innovation and population replacement or coexistence (Rose 2004a).

## THE SANGOAN AND LUPEMBAN INDUSTRIES

In Central Africa and its border regions, the transition from Mode 2 to 3 has long been recognised in the Sangoan-Lupemban sequence (J. D. Clark 1957). The Sangoan, named after surface finds made near Sango Bay, Lake Victoria, Uganda (Wayland and Smith 1923), is characterised by few or no handaxes and cleavers, but by heavy-duty picks that show continuity with the Acheulean and the innovation of core-axes. Small flake tools are common, with Levallois cores and the first bifacial points also

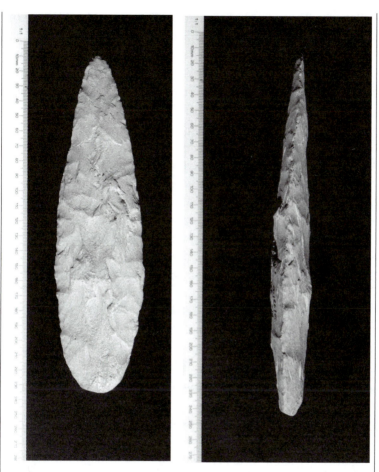

**Figure 6.8.** A Lupemban lanceolate made on quartzite from Kalambo Falls, Zambia, showing the distinctive elongated form of this bifacially flaked tool.

present. The Lupemban was named after the Lupemba river terraces in Kasai province, Democratic Republic of Congo, where mining uncovered deposits containing blades and elongated bifacially retouched points (Fig. 6.8; Breuil 1944). Neither type-site provided the secure contexts needed to establish the range of variability distinctive of each industry, and for some researchers the two industries were treated as a single entity in the absence of clear stratigraphic and typological distinctions (McBrearty 1988).

Kalambo Falls, Zambia, with its succession of late Acheulean (Mode 2), Sangoan, and Lupemban (both Mode 3) assemblages provides a key sequence (J. D. Clark 2001a). Core-axes and picks continued in the Lupemban at Kalambo, with backed blades and ochre use new features. At Sai Island, Sudan, the Sangoan is also older than the Lupemban, and its Sangoan occupants engaged in specialised activities, including core-axe production and ochre extraction (Van Peer *et al.* 2004). The age of the sequence at Kalambo Falls is currently being established by luminescence dating (Duller, pers. comm.), whereas at Sai Island, preliminary OSL age estimates place the Sangoan ~220–180 kya (Van Peer *et al.* 2003) with a minimum age of >150 kya. The collapsed Zambian cave site of Twin Rivers has provided U-series dates for deposits containing Lupemban artefacts of 265–170 kya (Barham 2000). Heavy-duty tools attributable to the Sangoan occur in the Kapthurin Formation ~285 kya interstratified with Mode 2 and 3 assemblages (Tryon and McBrearty 2002:228). Radiocarbon dates associated with Lupemban sites in the Congo Basin suggest it continued into the late Pleistocene (MIS 3), but should be treated with great caution given the vertical movement of charcoal in many Central African sites located on sand deposits (van Noten 1982; Cornelissen 2002).

Sangoan and Lupemban sites are found in currently forested areas of West and Central Africa (Lanfranchi 1996; Mercader and Martí 2003), and they may represent the first human occupation of the Congo Basin. The distribution of finds attributed to these early Mode 3 industries apparently extends far beyond the modern forest belt (J. D. Clark 1967), though most are from undated contexts and their attribution to either industry should also be treated with caution. In West Africa, the only dated Sangoan site is Bété I, Ivory Coast (lower layer 9) with a single TL date of 254 ± 51 kya from deposits underlying a sequence of Sangoan assemblages with picks and core-axes as well as bifaces (Liubin and Guédé 2000). The large error margin on the date makes it difficult to make firm comparisons with Sai Island or the Kapthurin Formation Sangoan, other than saying they all are late mid–Pleistocene occurrences with varying frequencies of picks and core-axes as well as flake tools. The relatively high frequency of bifaces at Bété I also distinguishes this assemblage from the Sangoan at Kalambo Falls, which has few Mode 2 elements. Regional variants may well exist that contain bifaces in meaningful numbers, but the possibility also exists that open sites like Bété I may have been subjected to taphonomic mixing with the vertical movement of artefacts creating false associations, as occurs in the Congo Basin (Cahen and Moeyersons 1977). The refitting of flakes to cores and the recovery of microdebitage as evidence for *in situ* knapping would help address any lingering concerns about the integrity of these and other surface sites.

The rarity of well excavated assemblages also contributes to continuing uncertainties about the efficacy of assigning material to one or another industry based on the presence of apparently diagnostic artefact types. The distinctive heavy-duty tools of the Sangoan and Lupemban have long been interpreted as wood-working tools (J. D. Clark 1963), but given the absence of supportive evidence from use-wear analyses and the presence of core-axes and picks outside modern forested zones, this hypothesis remains unsupported (McBrearty 1988; Van Peer *et al.* 2004). Sangoan core-axes at Sai Island were hafted, heavy-duty tools as shown by use-wear analyses, but were probably used for digging, not wood-working (Rots and Van Peer 2006). The combination of heavy-duty tools with blades, points, and lanceolates does, however, represent a new range of technologies that would have given its makers adaptive flexibility in a variety of environments. The earliest regional Mode 3 variants to emerge during and after the Mode 2/3 transition, the Sangoan and Lupemban, herald a trend towards greater geographical and chronological diversity built on composite technologies.

## BECOMING VISIBLE IN MIS 5

The observation that most Mode 3 African sites are younger than 130 kya (Tryon and McBrearty 2006:493) may seem odd given the mid-Pleistocene age of this technology, but the reality remains that we have few well-dated sites before the onset of MIS 5. A likely combination of generally low and periodically shifting population levels in glacial MIS 6 with highly variable conditions of preservation outside the Rift Valley has conspired to reduce the visibility of mid-Pleistocene sites. As a result, much of what is known about the behavioural abilities of Mode 3 makers comes from sites that post-date the evolution of *H. sapiens* by 70,000 years. The visibility of human populations increases markedly during the early part of MIS 5, especially in the Last Interglacial (~127–116 kya, MIS 5e), when temperature, rainfall, and vegetation patterns resembled those of today (see inset). New data from the Lake Malawi core suggest that just before the onset of the Last Interglacial, between 135 and 127 kya, semi-arid to arid conditions prevailed in the tropics creating a 'megadrought' (Cohen *et al.* 2007:16425). Such harsh conditions would have had profound implications for the distribution of human populations with large parts of the continent left sparsely inhabited or abandoned, and remaining wetter regions such as coastal margins seeing intensified occupation, and perhaps increased competition for limited resources. With the onset of MIS 5, these ecological and demographic pressures would have been relaxed and we see Mode 3 makers distributed across all parts of Africa, including the eastern Sahara where wetter conditions created permanent lakes and savanna habitats (Bir Tarfawi, Egypt) (Wendorf *et al.* 1993). An overview of some of the better-dated sites gives a glimpse of regional variation in technologies and behavioural developments that had their roots among earlier Mode 3 populations.

## REGIONAL OVERVIEWS

### North Africa

In northeast Africa, a new, distinctive regional Mode 3 variant emerged in MIS 5e with the Nubian Complex, characterised by use of Levallois reduction strategies, including a variant, the Nubian core, for producing pointed flakes alongside classic Levallois methods

## MARINE ISOTOPE STAGE 5

MIS 5 encompasses a sequence of alternating sub-stages of warmth and cold, each lasting about 10,000 years (Shackleton *et al.* 2003), and conventionally labelled with lower case letters e–a, though some researchers now prefer to number the sub-stages from 5–1 (Jouzel *et al.* 2007). MIS 5 as a whole was marked by an early interval of warmth (MIS 5e), followed by an irregular, but generally downward, trend in temperatures that culminated in the full glacial conditions of MIS 4 (Chapter 7). The sub-stage age boundaries vary depending on dating method, with estimates coming from sedimentation rates, deep-sea core correlations, or absolute uranium-thorium dates on raised coral reefs. The age ranges used here should be considered as guidelines. MIS 5e, also known as the Last Interglacial, began about 130–127 kya, reached a peak in temperature 125 kya, and ended at 116 kya. Global temperatures were as warm as, or even warmer than, today, with sea-level above current levels as ice sheets melted. Some uncertainty remains about the stability of climate during this interglacial, but current evidence indicates relatively little variability (Kukla 2000). In Africa, the tropical rainforest belt expanded and greater rainfall over North Africa enabled humans to live in areas of the Sahara that were subsequently abandoned. Temperatures dropped, ice sheets expanded, and sea-level fell with the onset of glacial substage 5d (~116–105 kya). Increased aridity resulted in an expansion of deserts in southern Africa (the Mega-Kalahari; Stokes *et al.* 1998) and northern Africa, and a marked decrease in water levels in Lake Malawi, Lake Tanganyika, and Lake Bosumtwi indicates a breakdown in the circulation of the African monsoon (Cohen *et al.* 2007; Scholz *et al.* 2007). MIS 5c (~105–94 kya) was warmer, but not an interglacial, with ice volumes greater and sea-level lower than today. Lake levels along the southern margin of the ITCZ rose indicating a partial return of the monsoon (Scholz *et al.* 2007). The lake cores aside, there is little terrestrial evidence available with which to reconstruct the distribution of Africa's biogeographical zones either for this period or for the colder, drier MIS 5b (∼94–84 kya). MIS 5a then followed as an interval of relative warmth (∼84–70 kya) with high tropical lake levels compared to MIS 5b and before the onset of full glacial conditions (MIS 4). Short-lived interstadials (Dansgaard–Oeschger events), characterised by rapid warming on a decadal scale followed by gradual cooling, have occurred periodically since MIS 5d (∼110 kya), as seen in Arctic ice cores, and there is evidence for contemporaneous, but less warm and rapid change in the Antarctic ice record (Alley 2000). Cold dry stadials (Heinrich events) associated with the North Atlantic phenomenon of ice rafting appear after 70 kya in deep-sea cores, and these events probably affected North Africa as pulses of aridity, though their impact in sub-Saharan Africa is less clear from the Antarctic ice core data (Jouzel *et al.* 2007).

(Van Peer 1998; Vermeersch *et al.* 2005a) (Fig. 6.9). Other distinctive tool types occur, including large, bifacial leaf-shaped (foliate) points, endscrapers, and truncated pieces. As defined by Van Peer (1989), this technocomplex encompasses various previously named industries, such as the Khormusan (Wendorf 1992), in recognition of the widespread occurrence of its technological and behavioural features that include specialised stone workshops and hunting camps. The Nubian Complex is widespread beyond the Lower Nile Valley, occurring during MIS 5 in the eastern Sahara. By contrast, the contemporaneous Lower Nile Valley Complex is constrained to the Nile Valley and has its own distinctive set of tools and behaviours. The coexistence of these two separate complexes has no parallel in the earlier African record, and it is argued that the Nubian Complex represents the arrival of new populations into the Lower Nile region late in the mid-Pleistocene, as seen at Sai Island. At issue is the linkage of constellations of technological strategies with separate cultural traditions, rather than seeing the variability as local expressions of a shared technological repertoire within a single cultural tradition.

The Sangoan tradition of quarrying at Sai Island ∼180 kya (Van Peer *et al.* 2004) continued into the Nubian Complex with evidence for the active extraction of chert by digging. This kind of specialised activity is more akin to a collector strategy (*sensu* Binford 1980) than

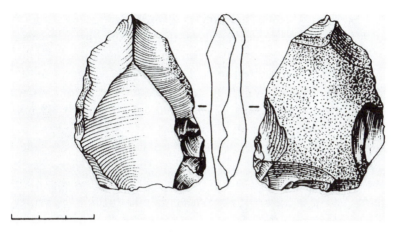

**Figure 6.9.** A Nubian Complex Levallois core showing the distinctive preparation of the distal end to form a strong central ridge, guiding the removal of a pointed flake (from Nazlet Khater 1, Egypt). (Courtesy and copyright of Philip van Peer.)

the image of foragers derived from recent hunter-gatherers in the Kalahari. Chert pits and areas of intensive Levallois reduction areas occur at various localities along the terraces of the Nile, such as Arkin 5 in Sudan (Chmielewski 1968) and Taramsa 1 and 8 in Egypt (Vermeersch 2002; Vermeersch *et al.* 2005b). The Nubian Complex also encompasses the lakeside sites of the eastern Sahara, including the site of BT-14, with its evidence for the butchery of gazelle and occasional large mammals (rhinoceros, giraffe, and buffalo), ochre use, and grinding stones that may have been used for processing plants, though no direct evidence exists to support this inference (Wendorf *et al.* 1993). Large, well-made foliate points, comparable in size to those of the Lupemban, occur in the Nubian Complex and may have been the weapons used by hunters. At Sodmein Cave, in Egypt's Red Sea Mountains, the early Nubian Complex level (∼115 kya) contains a large stone-lined firepit with the remains of large mammals (e.g., buffalo, elephant, and kudu), presumably hunted (Van Peer 2004). With the onset of colder, drier conditions from MIS 5d onwards, human occupation became sporadic, except in the eastern Sahara, where lakes and people remained until the onset of hyperarid conditions after 77 kya (Wendorf *et al.* 1993).

Elements of the Nubian Complex, in particular, the specific forms of Levallois-based points have been found in the Libyan Sahara at Uan Tabu shelter (~61 kya), and form the basis of the hypothesis that Mode 3 populations spread from the Nile Valley during the latter part of MIS 5 (Van Peer 1998, 2001b). A distinctive variant, the Aterian, characterised by the creation of a tang or extended base for hafting points and other tools (Fig. 6.10), emerged as a local adaptation to specific environmental conditions of the eastern and central Sahara. Van Peer's view of Aterian origins challenges the prevailing model of an origin in the Maghreb (Debénath 1994), with a subsequent spread across the Sahara from the Atlantic eastwards to Kharga Oasis, via the Mediterranean coast, and to the margins of the Sahel (see Wendorf and Schild 1992 for overview).[6] The limited number of well-dated sites, and the divergent results from different dating techniques (~90–60 kya by OSL, TL, and U-series; 60–35 kya by ESR; >40–24 kya by radiocarbon) (Cremaschi *et al.* 1998; Wrinn and Rink 2003; Bouzouggar *et al.* 2007) make resolution of this debate difficult as chronology determines the precedence of one area over another. The patterning in dates suggests a continuation of Aterian occupation in the Maghreb after the abandonment of the Sahara, probably in late MIS 5 to MIS 4.

The continuing emphasis on origins and the treatment of tanged tools as typological markers overshadow local cultural variations in the Aterian, including those Mode 3 ('Mousterian') sites with few or no tanged pieces. Moroccan sites provide evidence for the making of bone tools (El Harjraoui 1994) and structures within caves suggestive of long-term and varied use (Debénath 1992; Wengler 2001). In northern Niger, lithic quarries and workshops have been found (Holl 1989) and fine-grained raw materials were preferentially transported long distances (J. D. Clark 1993). Long-distance movement of materials is also evident on the Mediterranean margins with the transport of sea shells of the genus *Nassarius* from the coast to inland sites. At the cave of Taforalt, Morocco, thirteen perforated and ochre-stained shells have been recovered from recent excavations of Aterian deposits reliably dated by OSL, TL, and U-series to 82 kya (Bouzouggar *et al.* 2007). These shells were collected from the coast, which was at least 40 km distant at

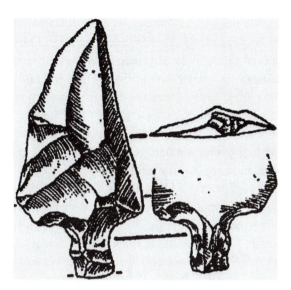

**Figure 6.10.** An Aterian stemmed Levallois point from Wadi el Hay Basin, Morocco. (Drawing from Luc Wengler in *Settlement Dynamics of the Middle Palaeolithic and Middle Stone Age*, 2; reproduced with the permission of Kerns Verlag.)

the time. A single *Nassarius* shells bead from Aterian deposits at Oued Djebanna, Algeria, was brought a distance of ~200 km. These examples of the movement of lithic raw materials and shells attest to the likely existence of exchange networks along which apparently utilitarian (stone) as well as symbolic items (shell) moved, gaining added social value in the process.

An Aterian component may also occur at the site of Haua Fteah (Great Cave), Libya, near the current Mediterranean coast. Possible tanged elements occur in a sequence of otherwise Mode 3 assemblages (Fig. 6.11) with retouched points, scrapers, burins, and prepared cores (the Mousterian layers, McBurney 1967). If an Aterian presence is genuine, then it extends the distribution of this technological tradition eastwards from the Maghreb along the coast, with implications for its spread, east, west, or from the Nile. In the absence of direct dates, however, the Haua assemblage cannot play a significant role in the Aterian origins debate for the time being. Underlying the possible Aterian and definite Mousterian levels is a small but technologically unusual assemblage recovered from the basal ∼5 m of the 1955 excavations (bedrock was not reached). This 'pre-Aurignacian' material contains long blades, some retouched and others with use damage, associated with burins, points, and rare bifaces (McBurney 1967:101). This assemblage probably dates to a post-MIS 5e period of intermittent use (after 115 kya) when the area was still sufficiently interglacial to support a range of sub-Saharan and Eurasian fauna. The Sahara may not have yet become a barrier to the movement of animals and people as it would by MIS 4, if not just before (Chapter 7). The occupants of Haua Fteah took advantage of the coastal and inland setting of the cave and gathered shellfish as well as hunted (probably) Barbary sheep, gazelle, and aurochs (wild cattle) (Klein and Scott 1986). The remains of some very large mammals are also present, with elephant and two species of rhinoceros represented, including the Eurasiatic form – Kirchberg's rhinoceros, *Dicerohinus kirchbergensis* (ibid:542). The role of humans in introducing these large animals is uncertain as there is evidence of hyaenas in the cave as well. The small size of the artefact sample makes it difficult to assess the true importance of blades in the technological tradition here, and for the time being, until further excavations are undertaken of the lower deposits, the site simply contributes to the technological diversity known across North Africa during MIS 5.

### Eastern Africa

In eastern Africa, human activity during sub-stages MIS 5d–a (∼100–80 kya) is well represented in the Aduma region of Ethiopia's Middle Awash Valley (Yellen *et al.* 2005). A distinct regional tradition of tool-making has been recognised as the 'Aduma Industry', characterised by the diminution of tool-size over time. Among the tool forms made preferentially on obsidian brought 30 km from the nearest source, are a range of point types, perforators, and small, specialised scrapers, the latter being generally uncommon in African Mode 3 assemblages. Flake and blade tools are made on blanks from Levallois cores, including 'micro-Levallois' cores, that may also occur in the Omo Kibish Formation of southern Ethiopia, indicating a larger regional tradition. At Aduma, the spatial distribution of

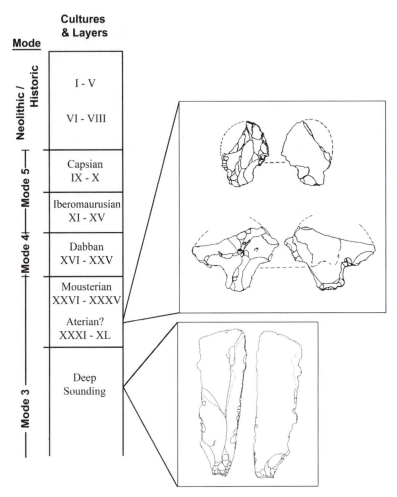

**Figure 6.11.** A schematic section of the Haua Fteah sequence showing a large blade from the 'pre-Aurignacian' from the deep sounding and possible 'Aterian' tanged pieces from the overlying 'Mousterian' layers. McBurney's sequence of archaeological cultures is grouped here within the Mode scheme (Artefact images after McBurney 1967.)

sites and ecological data indicate hunter-gatherers used a variety of habitats near and away from the river, but relied on the river for food, including hippopotamus, crocodiles, and probably large catfish. Fragmentary hominin remains from the locale confirm these Mode 3 makers were *H. sapiens*.

**Figure 6.12.** Excavation and reconstruction of a feature in Mumbwa Caves, Zambia (~130 kya), interpreted as a windbreak possibly designed to block the strong draught blowing through the cave, reducing the risk of fire and making the interior more comfortable. (Used with permission of the Western Academic & Specialist Press.)

## Central and Western Africa

The lack of well-dated sites in Central and West Africa for MIS 5 limits our view of regional variability across this vast area. On the southern margins of Central Africa, the site of Mumbwa Caves (Barham 2000) provides a glimpse of a range of behaviours during MIS 5e (~130–116 kya). The occupants built large hearths contained within stone surrounds and erected windbreaks (Fig. 6.12) to block the flow of wind through the site, perhaps to minimise the risk of fire and to make the cave more comfortable. The shelters may have been used as sleeping areas, with the interior of one seemingly swept clean of debris (Barham 1996). Locally collected ochres were brought to the cave and the range of Mode 3 tools included rare backed quartz blades, larger than those seen in the earlier Lupemban in the region. The site was abandoned during MIS 5d, at a time when drier conditions made the area less attractive to humans and animals reliant on seasonal standing water.

0    10    20    30    40    50 cm

**Figure 6.12.** *Continued*

The eastern border of the Congo Basin, formed by the western arm of the Rift Valley System, is characterised by a series of large, deep lakes. Draining Lake Rutanzige, the Semliki River has exposed Plio-Pleistocene to Holocene sediments containing archaeological deposits (Helgren 1997). Of interest in the context of MIS 5 are terrace deposits of the Katanda Formation that contain buried arte-fact horizons with dense concentrations of stone and bones, includ-ing large mammals such as hippopotamus and elephant, as well as catfish (Brooks *et al.* 1995). The sites are interpreted as likely base camps where small family groups made tools and processed animal carcasses, whether hunted or scavenged, and probably fish (Yellen 1996). Quartz flakes are abundant, largely made without preparation and rarely retouched, but well-shaped bone tools including barbed points occur in each of the three sites excavated (Katanda 2, 6, and 9; Yellen *et al.* 1995; Yellen 1998). The deposits were initially reported to be ~90 kya based on an averaging of results from a range of absolute dating techniques applied to the sediments and animal bone (Brooks *et al.* 1995). Subsequent luminescence analyses of sands from above the artefacts have reduced the average age range to 60–70 kya, but with older ages among these results (~117 kya, 95 kya) (Feathers and Migliorini 2001). The bone tools themselves have not been dated directly.

When initially published, the age of the deposits seemed untenable given the sophistication of the bone technology and the lack of evidence for similar bone-working abilities at other Mode 3 sites. Concerns about the stratigraphic integrity of the deposits and the possibility of intrusion of bone tools from much later periods have since been addressed (Yellen 1996, 1998). The more recent discovery of deliberately fashioned bone points and other tools from well-dated contexts at Blombos, South Africa (~77 kya, discussed subsequently), has also made the Katanda material seem less anomalous. Bone has been used as a raw material since the early Pleistocene (see Chapter 4), and the presence of shaped bone tools in probable mid-Pleistocene contexts at Kabwe suggests they may have been made by *H. heidelbergensis*, lending support to a continuum of bone-working in the African record (Barham *et al.* 2002).

Mode 3 sites occur across West Africa from Niger to Senegal, though usually as undated surface or secondary deposits (Allsworth-Jones 1987; Casey 2003). Mines on the Jos Plateau and in the Nok region of Nigeria provide evidence of Mode 3 technologies and some variation, perhaps chronological or functional, with sites like Mai Lumba (Allsworth-Jones 1987) and others in the area containing varying percentages of Levallois cores. The Jos sites underline the difficulty in the absence of dates of developing an understanding of patterns of landscape use, technological and ecological change, group interaction, and identity formation, as seen elsewhere, such as in the Nile Valley and along the Cape coast of South Africa (discussed later). The only absolute ages placing Mode 3 makers in MIS 5 come from the Sahel region of Mali. The locality of Ounjougou contains dozens of archaeological sites spread over an area of more than 10 km², in stratified deposits up to 16 m thick. OSL dating of sediments is the basis for building a chronology that so far extends to the end of MIS 5a and with the potential to span all of MIS 5, if not earlier periods, including Mode 2 sites (Robert *et al.* 2003). Preliminary results indicate the presence of Levallois and discoidal reduction techniques as well as the co-occurrence of Modes 1 and 3 where large cobbles are available for flaking. The site promises to reveal much about local variability in tool-making traditions and its location on the southern edge of the Sahara provides a window onto human responses in this ecologically unstable region. More generally, Ounjougou demonstrates the potential of luminescence dating to bring much-needed chronological resolution to the archaeological record of West and Central Africa and, with it, greater prominence in discussions of Mode 3 societies and their variability.

## Southern Africa

The most comprehensively dated MIS 5 record in southern Africa comes from south of the Limpopo River. A culture-stratigraphic framework has emerged from systematic investigation of long cave sequences, mostly from coastal sites, such as Klasies River, though with notable exceptions from the interior (e.g., Border Cave). Generally good organic preservation has provided the conditions for building chronologies based on multiple lines of evidence, as well as a range of behavioural information that would otherwise be invisible in the lithic record alone. The well-dated and published Klasies River lithic sequence forms the framework for regional comparisons of technological change through MIS 5 and later stages (Table 6.2; A. Thackeray 1992; H. J. Deacon and Wurz 2001; Wurz 2002). The 20 m sequence of deposits contains discrete occupation areas, mostly hearths and middens of shell and bone, separated by layers of sand. Fragmentary human remains occur in the basal deposits (MIS 5d, ~110 kya) and higher up, dating to MIS 5c, <100 kya, all attributed to a morphologically variable population of *H. sapiens*.

TABLE 6.2. *Existing nomenclature for Mode 3 sub-stages in South Africa showing the original sequence derived from Klasies River (Singer and Wymer 1982) and subsequent variations suggested by Volman (1984) and Wurz (2002)*

| Chronology (kya) | Singer & Wymer (1982) | Volman (1984) | Wurz (2002) |
|---|---|---|---|
| 65–22 | MSA III–IV | Post-Howiesons Poort | Post-Howiesons Poort |
| 70–65 | Howiesons Poort | Howiesons Poort | Howiesons Poort |
| 80–65 | – | – | Still Bay |
| 100–80 | MSA II | MSA 2b | Mossel Bay |
| 115–100 | MSA I | MSA 2a | Klasies River |
| ~260–115 | MSA 1 | ? | |

Evidence of cutmarks on some of the cranial and postcranial remains suggests cannibalism (H. J. Deacon and Deacon 1999), though alternative interpretations can be entertained given the apparent mortuary behaviours at Herto. Charred plant remains associated with the hearths, especially those from the later MIS 4 occupation, represent the gathering and roasting of **geophytes** (corms and bulbs) from the surrounding slopes. H. Deacon (1989:557) has argued that hunter-gatherers living in this fynbos habitat would have relied heavily on geophytes as a dietary staple, and used fire to burn the landscape as part of a strategy to promote the growth of this essential resource. If this was the case, and it is difficult to test, then it represents a form of landscape management with fire as an economic tool.

The large mammal faunal record from Klasies has been central to ongoing debates about the economic modernity of Mode 3 communities – were they competent hunters like their Mode 5 (Later Stone Age) descendants? The late Holocene occupants of Klasies hunted dangerous prey, including Cape buffalo and bushpig, but the MIS 5 occupants preyed on the young and old of these species and targeted less risky food sources such as eland. These differences in the frequencies and age profiles of game could reflect a limited ability to plan by Mode 3 hunters compared with their behaviourally modern counterparts (Klein 1989). Alternatively, the selection of prey was based on a careful assessment of their changing availability, defensive behaviours, and existing technologies and hunting strategies (H. J. Deacon 1989; Minichillo and Marean 2000). The later development of the bow and arrow with poisons would change the balance of risks, with dangerous prey seen as more accessible foods (Henshilwood and Marean 2003:632). Re-analysis of the assemblage has also provided evidence of active hunting of large game, including the giant buffalo (*Pelorovis antiquus*), with differing butchering strategies applied depending on carcass size (Milo 1998).[7] The evidence for access to large packets of meat combined with the presence of small hearths and associated middens with plant and shellfish remains provides compelling but circumstantial evidence that the early occupants engaged in food-sharing. The similarity of hearths throughout the Klasies sequence and their resemblance to those made by recent hunter-gatherers in the Kalahari extends the argument for continuity in food-sharing practices from the Last Interglacial to the present (H. J. Deacon 1992).

Further evidence for complex social and technological behaviours has emerged in recent years from excavations at the small site of Blombos Cave, also on South Africa's Indian Ocean coast (Fig. 6.13). The coastal zone was the source of dune sands that sealed and separated the Mode 3 deposits here from a later Mode 5 occupation. The culturally sterile sands have been well dated using OSL to ~68 kya, giving a minimum age for the underlying deposits (Jacobs *et al.* 2006). Burnt lithics have also been used to provide TL dates for each of the phases. The Mode 3 sequence is divided into three phases (M1, M2, M3), with further subdivisions. Phase M1 (~74 kya) contains a remarkable assemblage of artefacts, including 400 bifacial points typical of the local Still Bay Industry (Henshilwood *et al.* 2001b), at least two engraved pieces of ochre with abstract cross-hatched patterns along with abundant undecorated ochre (Henshilwood *et al.* 2002), ten bone tools plus an engraved bone fragment (d'Errico *et al.* 2001), and 39 beads made from the estuarine mollusc *Nassarius kraussianus* (d'Errico *et al.* 2005).[8] Phase M2 (85–77 kya) contains a more limited range of artefacts, with a few Still Bay points, some ochre, at least 20 deliberately shaped bone tools and two shell beads from upper M2. The earliest dated occupation in M3 took place ~100 kya (Jacobs *et al.* 2006) at a time of raised sea level (MIS 5c) that gave the occupants easy access to shellfish. As well as a dense shell midden and compact hearths, M3 contains thousands of pieces of ochre, much of it used. The human teeth from M3 are morphologically robust compared to those of modern humans, and they fit just within the modern range (Grine and Henshilwood 2002). The underlying sterile dune sand dated to 143 kya (MIS 6) provides a maximum age for the potential occupation of the cave. The faunal remains recovered from all three phases show a broad range of activities, including hunting of small and large game, fishing, collecting shellfish, and either hunting or scavenging of marine mammals (Henshilwood *et al.* 2001a).

The sequences at Klasies and that at Blombos Cave together show the range of behaviours existing along the southern Cape coast at roughly the same intervals of MIS 5. The two sites differ in lithic and bone technologies and the extent of symbolic activities represented (no *in situ* Still Bay points at Klasies and few bone tools), as might be expected of differing localities, times, and social traditions, but converge in having hunting and gathering economies based on the exploitation of diverse coastal and terrestrial resources. They also share a pattern of small hearths associated with food remains and, arguably, social systems based on food-sharing if we employ contemporary parallels. The careful excavation of comparable sequences with good organic preservation is needed to assess the extent to which Blombos and Klasies represent locally distinctive cultural traditions, and how communities responded to fluctuations in resources during MIS 5. A similar need for detailed local sequences applies to each of the regions highlighted earlier.

That need is being addressed on the southern Cape coast by an active programme of survey and excavation of caves and rock shelters along the coastal cliffs at Mossel Bay, located between Blombos and Klasies River. Excavations at one location in particular, Pinnacle Point (sites 13A and 13B), forms the basis of an emerging sequence of rare MIS 6 and MIS 5 occupations by Mode 3 makers. The sea cave site of 13B preserves two glacial phase MIS 6 occupation layers in sandy deposits that have been dated using OSL. The earliest occupation layer is dated to 164 ± 12 kya and contain the oldest evidence so far known for the use of shellfish, with a variety of species collected

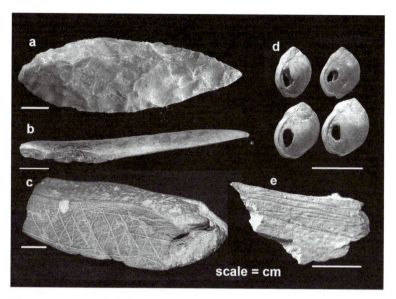

**Figure 6.13.** Artefacts from the c. 85–77 kya Still Bay levels (M1) at Blombos Cave: (a) silcreate bifacial foliate point; (b) shaped and polished bone point; (c) engraved ochre (SAM-AA 8938); (d) *Nassarius kraussianus* shell beads; (e) engraved mandibular bone fragment. (Courtesy and copyright of Chris Henshilwood and Francesco d'Errico.)

from the rocky coast nearby (Marean *et al.* 2007:906–7). The small lithic assemblage includes typical Mode 3 prepared core technology (flakes, points and blades), but also evidence for the making of bladelets long before this Mode 5 technology becomes established elsewhere in Africa (see Chapter 8). The use of red ochre is also associated with this earliest occupation, and perhaps we are seeing the expression of social identity through symbolic activities, such as body art, at a time of increased social and economic tension. The development of a shellfish based foraging system may have been a distinctive local response to lowered regional productivity during glacial MIS 6. The site is occupied again at the end of MIS 6 (132 ± 12 kya) and in MIS 5e (120 ± 7 kya), and fragmentary human remains have been recovered from this later occupation (Marean *et al.* 2004). The standards of survey and excavation are exemplary, employing state-of-the-art global positioning system (GPS) and geographical information system (GIS) data capture and analysis and multiple lines of independent dating techniques (U-series, ESR, OSL). As the results emerge from this project, they will contribute considerably to our understanding of social, technological, and ecological variability along the Cape coast spanning MIS 6 to MIS 5.

The interior of southern Africa was also inhabited by hunter-gatherers during the MIS 5 and the record from inland and mountainous regions is easily overlooked when compared with the detail available from coastal caves. Key early Mode 3-bearing sites like Wonderwerk Cave, the Cave of Hearths, Florisbad, and Border Cave also provide records for much of the span of MIS 5. Border Cave also offers well-preserved fossils of *H. sapiens*, though with limited stratigraphic controls given the history of uncontrolled digging at the site for guano in 1940s. Two specimens, BC1 (partial adult cranial vault) and BC2 (partial adult mandible) both lack contexts, but BC3, an infant skeleton, was recovered during controlled excavations in 1941 (Beaumont 1978). An adult mandible (BC5) was found during excavations in 1974, and other specimens are either relatively recent (BC4) or also lacking stratigraphic context (BC6–BC8) and not discussed further. Age range estimates for BC1 and BC2 have been made on assumed stratigraphic correlations with ESR-dated deposits, and these place the specimens between 91–71 kya (Millard 2006). BC3, with its more certain context, falls in a similar range, between 90–66 kya, and BC5 is more narrowly constrained to 72–61 kya. The direct dating of these specimens using ESR on tooth enamel and more recent developments in laser ablation extraction of U-series samples from bone (Pike and Pettitt 2003) promise to resolve lingering doubts about age and archaeological associations. The BC3 burial in particular deserves close attention as it appears to be the only deliberate burial known from the region during MIS 5–MIS 4. It may have come from a shallow grave, been covered with ochre (though this interpretation of the stained bone needs to be assessed geochemically), and buried with a grave good – a perforated *Conus* shell. The latter came from the Indian Ocean coast 80 km to the east (A. Thackeray 1992:415). Such a suite of symbolic behaviours remains unique in southern Africa.

## IMAGINATIVE THEORIES AND SYMBOLIC BEHAVIOURS

The Mode 3 African record is seen by some researchers as still pre-modern in the relative monotony of tool types over tens of thousands of years, providing limited evidence for hunting abilities and lack of symbolic expression, especially when compared with the apparent symbolic revolution in Europe that accompanied the arrival of anatomically modern humans ~40 kya (Conard and Bolus 2003). The sudden change in the European record recognised as the Middle (Mode 3) to Upper (Mode 4) Palaeolithic transition is typically attributed to a population replacement with *H. sapiens*, the bearer of sophisticated behaviours largely unknown to Neanderthals. Spirited, polarised debate continues to engulf the issue of Neanderthal behavioural abilities and their input, if any, to the development of Upper Palaeolithic societies (d'Errico 2003; Mellars 2005). No such population replacement occurred in Africa, but proponents of a relatively recent origin of behavioural modernity in Africa argue that a neural mutation took place about 50 kya, which gave African moderns something no other contemporary hominins had – fully syntactic language (Klein 2000). With this selective advantage, African populations were able to displace Eurasian hominins, the precursors of Upper Palaeolithic technologies being found in eastern Africa or in the Nile Valley (Ambrose 1998). The supposed neural-based shift to language is difficult to demonstrate both anatomically and genetically, though genetic candidates exist such as the *FOXP2* gene (Klein and Edgar 2002). Ancient DNA evidence now suggests that Neanderthals also shared the modern human variant of this gene (Krause *et al.* 2007) which, if substantiated through additional sequencing, undermines the argument for a recent African origin of syntactic language.

The archaeological evidence from Blombos, in particular, forms the foundation for an alternative view of an earlier MIS 5 origin of behavioural modernity. Henshilwood and Marean (2003) argue convincingly that many of the traits treated as general indicators of modernity are derived from the Upper Palaeolithic record and reflect the responses of hunter-gatherers to the specific ecological constraints of temperate to sub-arctic environments. Foraging theory predicts that hunter-gatherers in the tropics and sub-tropics of Africa would organise their material and social lives differently; a European-derived model of modernity is simply inappropriate for African contexts. In place of trait lists, they argue that modern behaviour is essentially about social relationships constructed through symbolic thought and actions. The material expressions of symbols used to organise behaviours can be seen archaeologically in forms of personal ornamentation, the creation of art, tool styles, and the socially defined use of space (Wadley 2001a). Based on this definition, the emergence of modern behaviour did not take place suddenly 50 kya, but gradually and earlier in the development of *H. sapiens*, perhaps during MIS 5e (e.g., Mumbwa Caves) and certainly by MIS 5a, given the evidence of beads and other symbolic behaviours from the southern and northern coasts of the continent (e.g., Blombos and Taforalt).

The association of anatomical with behavioural modernity has, however, been challenged from two perspectives, one based partly on the European record (McBrearty and Brooks 2000), the other from a purely African database showing behavioural continuity and the supposed evolution of symbolic thought in the mid-Pleistocene (H. J. Deacon and Wurz 2001). McBrearty and Brooks review the evidence from the African archaeological record for behaviours normally associated with behaviourally modern humans in Upper Palae-olithic Europe and among Mode 5 moderns in Africa. They see a gradual accumulation of the symbolic and other cognitive developments that characterise later populations, starting in the mid-Pleistocene ∼300 kya, with late *H. heidelbergensis* (or *H. helmei*). The appearance of pigment use, for example, with the Sangoan and Lupemban, heralds the ability to arbitrarily assign meaning to colours based on language. Well-made points first appeared at the same time, with backed tools, bone tools, long-distance transport of obsidian, personal ornamentation, and incised pigment occurring at different times, and in different places before 50 kya. No one trait signals the origin of modern cognitive abilities, as the African record since 300 kya shows a continuous and irregular accumulation of behaviours, each context specific. The Mode 2/3 transition nonetheless lies at the root of subsequent cognitive and behavioural flexibility.

H. J. Deacon and Wurz (2001:62) also argue for a continuum of change, but focus on the evolution of symbolic thought and communication as the key features of modern humans. They start with the premise that the large brain size of *H. heidelbergensis* provided the neural foundation for an early development of language and symbolic thought, probably between 400 and 200 kya. From this perspective, Neanderthals, as a closely related clade, should have had similar symbolic capacities. The challenge for this and any model that argues for the early development of language and symbolism lies in identifying traces of symbolic thought that may have existed before their expression in recognisable forms such as beads or engravings (Henshilwood and Marean 2003). The earliest symbolic behaviours may not be easily recognisable (as at Herto), having taken forms that are outside our realm of experience and for which no modern analogues exist (Davidson 2003:638). A long time lag can also be expected between the evolution of symbol use and its material expression (G. Clark 2002:60). In this context, the gap between the appearance of ochre use ~285 kya in the context of the Mode 2/3 transition – perhaps even earlier at Olorgesailie – and the engravings at Blombos (~74 kya) may reflect gradually changing demographic and social constraints rather than a later emergence of modern symbolic expression linked to *H. sapiens* (Barham 2007).

OVERVIEW

The archaeological record of the period 430–70 kya encompasses the gradual evolution of *Homo sapiens* as a descendant of *H. heidelbergensis* and significant technological and cognitive transitions, including the abandonment of bifaces, the widespread adoption of hafted tools, and the appearance of symbolic behaviours. No clear correlation exists among all these developments and climate change (Fig. 6.14), suggesting internal behavioural dynamics in the innovation of Mode 3 derived from Mode 2 foundations of prepared core technology. Once developed, composite technology offered new technological solutions to long-standing challenges of variable

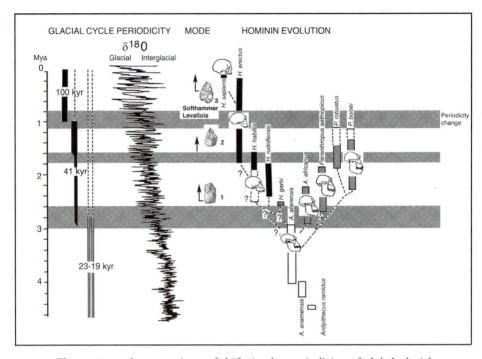

**Figure 6.14.** A comparison of shifts in the periodicity of global glacial cycles with speciation events and technological transitions in the archaeological record. The emergence of Mode 3 technology 280–240 kya takes place before the evolution of *H. sapiens* and probably during MIS 8, which was neither particularly cold nor especially prolonged in relation to previous and subsequent glacials. Cultural processes rather than climate-based stimuli seem to have driven the Mode 2/3 transition. The development of soft hammer flaking and Levallois core technology may coincide with climatic instability at 700–600 kya, but these are speculative correlations. The appearance of Modes 2 and 1 do coincide with step changes in global climate at ∼1.7 and 2.6 mya respectively, suggesting technological responses to increased aridity in Africa. (After deMenocal 2004.)

resource distribution caused by climatic instability. The colonisation of the tropical interior of the Congo Basin appears to have taken place by Mode 3 groups and the first recognisable regional traditions of artefact-making emerged based on the inherent flexibility of composite technology. The earliest of these industries, the Sangoan with its hafted core-axes and the Lupemban with its points and backed pieces, preceded the evolution of anatomically modern humans, and they challenge us to reconsider our assumptions about what constitutes behavioural modernity and how to recognise its appearance. The varied lines of genetic data reaffirm a mid-Pleistocene African origin of *H. sapiens* and its later dispersal into Eurasia, though disagreement remains about the timing and process of interaction with indigenous populations outside the continent. The archaeological record of MIS 5 also suggests population movement within Africa, linked ultimately to the underlying rhythm of glacial cycles.

# CHAPTER 7

# THE BIG DRY: THE ARCHAEOLOGY
# OF MARINE ISOTOPE STAGES 4–2

Some 73,500 years ago, the eruption of the Mt. Toba super-volcano (see inset) may have helped inaugurate 60,000 years of massive climatic change that incorporated both maxima of the Last Glaciation (Fig. 7.1). At higher latitudes, and especially in the northern hemisphere, the principal impact of those changes lay, as ever, in the realms of temperature and ice sheet expansion. In the tropics and subtropics, on the other hand, the main effect was one of lessened precipitation and greater aridity, even if lower temperatures helped reduce evaporation. It is for this reason that we title this chapter "The Big Dry," signalling that for the first Africans, the primary challenge lay not in coping with greater cold, but rather in surviving recurrent cycles of drought. The improved, and rapidly improving if still imperfect, accuracy of our chronometric tools makes investigating this question a more attainable goal for The Big Dry than for earlier glacial/interglacial cycles[1].

How African populations succeeded, or failed, to meet this challenge is among this chapter's themes. Developing topics raised in Chapter 6, we continue to explore the archaeological record for signs of behavioural modernity. Our chronological boundaries are deliberately structured to allow these data to feed into the broader issues raised by the widespread innovation and take-up of microlithic technologies and the transition, or transitions, between Mode 3 and Mode 5 industries. They thus question, rather than sustain, the traditional dichotomy between Middle Stone Age/Middle Palaeolithic

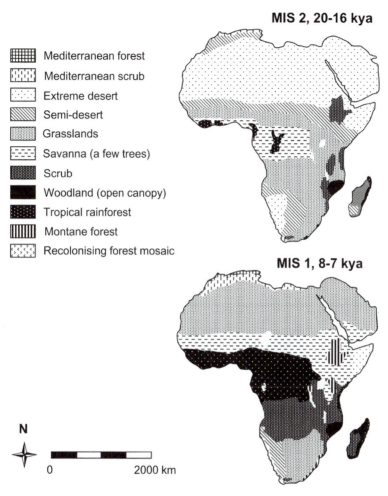

**MIS 2, 20-16 kya**

Mediterranean forest
Mediterranean scrub
Extreme desert
Semi-desert
Grasslands
Savanna (a few trees)
Scrub
Woodland (open canopy)
Tropical rainforest
Montane forest
Recolonising forest mosaic

**MIS 1, 8-7 kya**

N

0                    2000 km

Figure 7.1. The palaeoenvironmental situation in Africa during MIS 2 compared with that during the mid-Holocene. The situation described for MIS 2 is also likely to have prevailed during MIS 4.

and Later Stone Age/Upper Palaeolithic lifeways. Using genetic as well as archaeological sources, we examine the relevance of the African evidence to the expansion of anatomically modern humans into Eurasia, and the possibility of later population movements back *into* Africa. A further comparative element is also present: How far do the cultural patterns and strategies observable

THE BIGGEST BANG: THE MT. TOBA ERUPTION

Mt. Toba in the northwest of the Indonesian island of Sumatra
is an example of a super-volcano, one that erupts rarely but
on an unimaginably catastrophic scale. It erupted most recently
about 73.5 $\pm$ 2 kya according to potassium/argon dating, perhaps
c. 71 kya according to the position of its signature within the
Greenland icecore record. This was by far the largest volcanic
event of the Quaternary, ejecting a staggering 3000 km$^3$ of
material and depositing ash northwestward across the Indian
Ocean and India itself, where beds several metres thick occur
(see Rampino and Ambrose 2000 for more detail). There seems
little doubt (arguments by C. Oppenheimer 2002 and Gathorne-
Hardy and Harcourt-Smith 2003 notwithstanding) that an event
of this magnitude must have had a mass impact on the world's
climate. An impressive body of evidence indicates that the ash,
dust, and sulphur injected into the atmosphere produced a global
volcanic 'winter' some six years long, followed by a millennium of exceptionally cold temperatures before milder conditions
returned. Ecological impacts must have been severe, including
substantial lowering of plant (and thus animal) biomass, with obvious implications for hominins and other species. Although this
awaits confirmation from well-dated local palaeoenvironmental sequences, tropical Africa is unlikely to have been immune.
Indeed, cores from Lake Malawi show erosional disconformities
dated to 73 $\pm$ 3 kya that were produced by sudden drops in lake
level (Scholz *et al.* 2007) and likely result from the climatic changes
inspired by the Toba event. As described in the main text, a key
implication is that the eruption was also responsible for a substantial reduction in human numbers and genetic diversity (Ambrose
1998b, 2003).

across Africa resemble those elsewhere, northward in the much
better-studied parts of western Eurasia and eastward in other areas
of the tropics, such as southern Asia and newly settled Greater
Australia?

## THE IMPACTS OF ENVIRONMENTAL CHANGE

### *Palaeoenvironments of MIS 4–2*

Though not itself directly initiating the colder, drier conditions of MIS 4, the Toba eruption probably did have a serious impact on global climate for up to a millennium (Ambrose 1998b, 2003). Two millennia of milder, stadial conditions then intervened before MIS 4 itself began (Zielinski *et al.* 1996). The ensuing 10,000 years saw ecological effects similar to those of the better-documented Last Glacial Maximum (LGM), including sea levels that were depressed about 75 m relative to the present. Both the Sahara and the Kalahari expanded substantially, with other ecological zones compressed and grassland environments spreading at the expense of more closed vegetation types. Cooler temperatures (5–7°C below those of today), greater aridity (20%–40% less rainfall; Thomas 2000), and reduced atmospheric carbon dioxide levels also had an impact on the extent and composition of the equatorial forests (D. Jolly and Haxeltine 1997). Recent assessments suggest that although they probably fragmented, with more open forests developing in many areas, wholesale deforestation did not occur (Mercader 2003a). In fact, onshore and offshore pollen cores indicate that large areas of lowland forest remained intact in West and West-Central Africa (Jahns *et al.* 1998; Dupont *et al.* 2000). New species combinations are, however, likely as montane elements moved downslope and more seasonally adapted taxa shifted position.

Between 57 and 24 kya, conditions were generally more moderate than those just described, although frequent, rapid fluctuations on a decadal to centennial scale probably posed major adaptive challenges (Grootes 2001). Although temperatures were cooler than present, the extent to which things were more arid varied. Thus, in North Africa, conditions may not, on the whole, have been much drier than today, but in southern Africa, both wetter and drier extremes are noted. In northern Botswana, these included widespread arid events with extensive dune activity around 43–40 and 28–25 kya (Stokes *et al.* 1997). Conversely, permanent lakes existed for much of the intervening period, in an area where this is now impossible (Robbins *et al.* 2000). Conditions in South Africa's winter rainfall zone were wetter than, or as wet as, present (Cowling *et al.* 1999; Carr *et al.* 2006). Wetter conditions were not, however, found everywhere, and there is little, if any, evidence of increased precipitation within the Sahara (N. Brooks *et al.* 2003) or parts of the Namib Desert (Lancaster 2002). Conflicting evidence for moister (Lowe and Walker 1984) and drier (Runge 1996) conditions across eastern Central Africa and its highland margins also tell a story of regional variation, though Kiage and Liu's (2006) recent overview suggests a prevalence of warm conditions similar to today before 42 kya and cooler, drier conditions thereafter until around 30 kya when climate again turned moister.

From about 24 kya, temperatures again became significantly colder, with maximum depressions relative to today (averaging 6°C) registered around 18 kya, the LGM. Sea levels reached their lowest at the same time, their most dramatic African impact being the exposure of the continental shelf off South Africa's Agulhas Bank (Van Andel 1989). As peak aridity approached, desert dunes reactivated and the Sahara and the Kalahari again expanded, compressing climate and vegetation zones toward the Equator and the continent's northern and southern tips, the open tree savanna/open dry forest transition in West Africa, for example, shifting 3–4° south relative to its position today (Talbot 1983; T. O'Connor and Thomas 1999). Much of equatorial Africa saw renewed reductions in forests and the establishment of more open, mosaic forest/savanna environments (Runge 1996; D. Jolly *et al.* 1998). East and inland of the Gulf of Guinea (Dupont *et al.* 2000), major lowland forest refugia are likely in Cameroon/Gabon and the eastern Congo Basin (Maley 1996; Hamilton 2000). Lowering of vegetation belts is evident in these regions, East Africa (where prolonged episodes of dessication took hold and grasslands expanded significantly; Marean and Gifford-Gonzalez 1991; Kiage and Liu 2006), and the Maghreb (where cool, arid conditions and open steppe with little tree cover prevailed, except in sheltered locations west of the Atlas Mountains; Lubell 2000). Glaciers expanded on the highest mountains of both these mountains and those of East Africa. Further effects included the temporary disappearance – or at least extreme reduction – of Lake Victoria and other lakes (Johnson *et al.* 1996; Kiage and Liu 2006), the blocking of the White Nile's passage north by dunes (Williams and Adamson 1980), and the weakening of the monsoon's contribution to the Blue Nile, producing a lower, deeper, and much smaller river in Egypt and Nubia (Close and Wendorf 1990).[2] As another indication of changed rainfall levels, Partridge *et al.'s* (1997) isohyet reconstructions for southern Africa suggest reductions in annual precipitation compared with today of between 80% (southwestern Zambia) and 30% (KwaZulu-Natal). Following these extremes of aridity and cold at the LGM, moister, warmer conditions began to take hold in most regions about 14 kya, accelerating after 12.5 kya.

## *Demographic Effects of Palaeoenvironmental Change*

How did these changes affect the size and distribution of human populations? One dramatic consequence was the wholesale abandonment of some parts of the continent, most obviously the Sahara (Fig. 7.2). Contrary to earlier views that took at face value erroneous radiocarbon dates from ancient lake carbonates (e.g., Tillet 1985), mid-Upper Pleistocene aridity was so severe as to make continued human settlement impossible, although attenuated survival in the desert's central massifs cannot, pending further research, be wholly ruled out (A. Smith 1984). Dates now available for palaeolake sequences and Aterian assemblages from Egypt (Wendorf and Schild 1992) and Libya (Cremaschi *et al.* 1998) show that people had left the desert by 60 kya at the latest, and did not return for 50,000 years: The complete absence of Upper Palaeolithic-type occurrences anywhere in the Sahara confirms this. Whether the Maghreb was also abandoned is more moot (cf. Close 2002 with Wendorf and Schild 2005). As discussed in Chapter 6, the question hangs on the dates available for Aterian sites, mostly in Morocco, the relative merits of radiocarbon versus other dating techniques, and the dubious quality or stratigraphic inversions of many of the (bulk shell/sediment) samples on which those dates were run (Bouzouggar *et al.* 2002: Table 7). Our view is that whereas recent ESR dates from Mugharat el 'Aliya near Tangier suggest a persistence of Aterian occupation into MIS 3 (Wrinn and Rink 2003), perhaps reinforced by groups relocating out of an aridifying Sahara, there is otherwise little strong reason to date any Aterian assemblages as late as 40–20 kya (*pace* Debénath *et al.* 1986).[3] If so, then the Iberomaurusian Mode 5 industry of MIS 2, and its sketchily known Mode 4 predecessors, may represent a genuine *de novo* recolonisation of northernmost Africa (Close 2002).

Even the 'oasis' of the lower Nile offers little hard evidence of occupation for much of this time. Overviews of the industrial sequence there struggle to document sites dating to MIS 4/3 (Milliken 2003). Van Peer (1998), for example, notes just ephemeral Middle Palaeolithic occupations at Sodmein Cave in the Eastern Desert and evidence of chert quarrying at sites in Upper Egypt; of other possibilities, the Aterian is almost certainly of MIS 5 age (Wendorf *et al.* 1993), the Khormusan has infinite radiocarbon dates, and the Idfuan and Halfan are (*pace* Paulissen and Vermeersch 1987) probably younger than 20 kya (Wendorf and Schild 1989). Sampling bias may, of course, be at work, with sites lost to erosion or siltation, and in the Western Desert, the Khargan may be of post-Aterian date (Wiseman 1999). However, for the 40,000 years following the start of MIS 4, only these few, mostly OSL dates are certain: ~60 kya for chert quarrying at Nazlet Safaha; 55 kya for the Taramsa 1 burial; 65–45 kya for Late Mousterian occurrences in Wadi Kubbaniya; and 44–35 kya for the male burial from Nazlet Khater 4 and its associated chert mining activity (Vermeersch *et al.* 1984, 1998; Schild and Wendorf 1989; Stokes and Bailey 2002). Only after 25 kya is evidence of human activity widespread in southern Egypt and Lower Nubia (Milliken 2003).

These are but some of the settlement fluctuations that marked The Big Dry. At the continent's opposite end, Klein (1999) has argued, following H. J. Deacon and Thackeray (1984), that this period witnessed substantially lower population levels than either MIS 5 or the Holocene. Although some sequences do, indeed, show breaks at the start of MIS 4 (e.g., Blombos), other data fit such an analysis less comfortably. The Howiesons Poort industry, for example, is an extremely well-known phenomenon, from southern Namibia through the

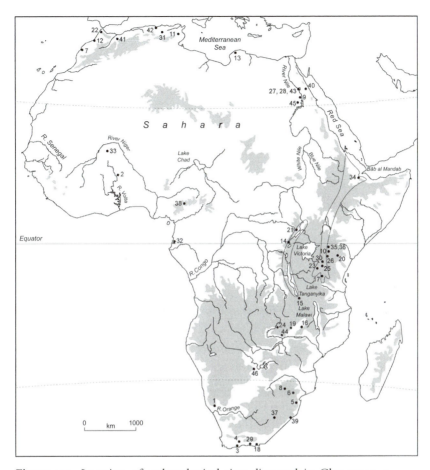

**Figure 7.2.** Location of archaeological sites discussed in Chapter 7: 1. Apollo 11 Cave; 2. Birimi; 3. Blombos; 4. Boomplaas; 5. Border Cave; 6. Bushman Rock Shelter; 7. Casablanca; 8. Cave of Hearths; 9. E71K13; 10. Enkapune ya Muto; 11. Gafsa; 12. Grotte Zouhra; 13. Haua Fteah; 14. Ishango; 15. Kalambo Falls; 16. Kalemba; 17. Kisese II; 18. Klasies River; 19. Leopard's Hill; 20. Lukenya Hill; 21. Matupi; 22. Mugharat el 'Aliya; 23. Mumba; 24. Mumbwa; 25. Naisiusiu; 26. Nasera; 27. Nazlet Khater 4; 28. Nazlet Safaha; 29. Nelson Bay Cave; 30. Ntumot; 31. Oued Djebanna; 32. Okala; 33. Ounjougou; 34. Porc-Epic; 35. Prolonged Drift; 36. Prospect Farm; 37. Rose Cottage Cave; 38. Shum Laka; 39. Sibudu; 40. Sodmein; 41. Taforalt; 42. Tamar Hat; 43. Taramsa 1; 44. Twin Rivers; 45. Wadi Kubbaniya; 46. White Paintings Shelter.

Fynbos Biome and into the Maloti-Drakensberg Mountains, with Zimbabwe's Matopo Hills a possible outlier (N. Walker 1995a). Yet its dates centre squarely in MIS 4 (Lombard 2005a). It might thus be expected that the apparent difficulty in attributing many more sites to MIS 3 reflects something other than a harsh environment, given the more humid conditions that repeatedly prevailed over this time: Problems in securing accurate dates beyond the radio-carbon barrier, especially for open-air sites of the kind common in South Africa's interior (Sampson 1985a), may be partly responsible. Overgeneralisation from a few relatively well-known, but perhaps quite specific, phenomena may also be at fault; sites 'up-country' from the Cape reveal repeated occupations across MIS 3 (e.g., Rose Cottage Cave, Wadley 2001a; Sibudu, Wadley and Jacobs 2004; Wadley 2005b, 2006), while back in the Fynbos, Die Kelders has a sequence of notch- and denticulate-dominated Mode 3 assemblages wholly unlike, but contemporary with, the Howiesons Poort (A. Thackeray 2000). As yet barely investigated, but potentially very productive coastal sites at Pinnacle Point, near Mossel Bay, were also occupied during MIS 4–3 (Marean *et al.* 2004). Global sea level changes pose another conundrum, given that the Cape is one of the few areas of Africa where substantial areas of continental shelf were exposed during MIS 4 and 2 (Van Andel 1989). The strikingly similar site distributions registered for the Howiesons Poort and the Robberg industry and its contemporaries around the LGM could reflect mostly coastal/coastal plain populations that made only occasional excursions inland; if so, then the remnant settlement pattern observable today is literally the tip of an iceberg (Mitchell 2002a).

*Seeking Stability: Can We Identify Refugia?*

If some areas were abandoned and settlement in others was spasmodic, which parts of the continent offered greatest ecological stability and maintained the largest, most persistent populations? Broadly speaking, those closest to the Equator fit this requirement best, because here, rainfall and temperature changes probably had least effect. Indeed, *if* equatorial rain forests are difficult for hunter-gatherers to occupy (R. Bailey *et al.* 1989, but see discussion in Chapter 8), then expansion of more open, mosaic environments may have had precisely the reverse effect on human settlement during MIS 4–2, not least because such environments probably favoured the growth of key plant foods. Cornelissen (2002), too, identifies the extent and distribution of ecotonal situations as a key variable in the attractiveness of the region to Upper Pleistocene people, emphasising that a simple forest/savanna dichotomy is unhelpful. A widespread, enduring human presence through Central Africa seems likely, but supportive dating evidence is sparse, emphasising a few rockshelters, almost all located toward the margins of the modern forest, such as Shum Laka, Cameroon (Cornelissen 2003), and Matupi, Democratic Republic of Congo (Van Noten 1977), plus a small, if growing, number of open air sites (Clist 1995; Mercader and Martí 2003). The situation is not helped by problems in relating some dates to archaeological occurrences, doubts over the stratigraphic integrity of others because of artefact displacement within unconsolidated deposits (Cahen and Moeyersons 1977), and uncertainty as to which, often very broadly defined, entity they should be ascribed (cf. Cornelissen 2002 and Clist 1999 on the site of Okala, Gabon). As we discuss later, similar cautions apply in West Africa's forest zone, although MIS 3 occupations are sporadically attested at Birimi, Ghana (Casey *et al.* 1997), and in central Mali (Robert *et al.* 2003).

East Africa, by contrast, presents a clearer picture, reflecting more intensive fieldwork and better conditions for chronometric dating and organic preservation. Though details still need working out, a sequence of Mode 3 and Mode 5 occurrences, as well as others transitional between the two technologies, is evident across The Big Dry in Kenya and northern Tanzania; it suggests that occupation there was, indeed, more continuous than in many other parts of Africa (Ambrose 1998a). Whether the same was true of Ethiopia, Eritrea, Somalia (Brandt 1986; Gresham and Brandt 1996), or southern Tanzania (Wynn and Chadderdon 1982; Willoughby and Sipe 2002), is difficult to say because of dating problems and less intensive research.

In concluding this section, we return to the Mt. Toba eruption and the argument that its impact on hominin populations was so severe that it precipitated the second of the genetic bottlenecks discussed in Chapter 6 (Ambrose 1998b; Rampino and Ambrose 2000). To be sure, its exact climatic impacts are debated and the bottleneck itself can also be explained through more conventional genetic processes (Lahr and Foley 1998). However, like Ambrose (2003), we are seized by the scale of the eruption and its close – though not immediate – conjunction with the start of MIS 4. Genetic data reported by Goldberg (1996) provide preliminary evidence that humans were not the only species affected by these two events,[4] and our own reading of the African record suggests that populations did, indeed, contract, or become extinct, at an early stage during The Big Dry, those inhabiting the Maghreb and the Sahara among them. Such events may have been more likely if their technologies or, more critically, social networks were less well developed than among recent hunter-gatherers.

MORE SIGNS OF 'MODERNITY'?

Like McBrearty and Brooks (2000), we have argued that there are good grounds for seeing in the MIS 5 archaeological record, and perhaps even before, evidence of behaviour similar to that of more recent hunter-gatherers. However, this evidence displays an accretionary pattern that probably reflects a gradual combining, and frequently situational expression, of those behaviours. Sudden breaching of a cognitive 'Rubicon' linked to the appearance of favourable mutations in genes coding for language skills seems to us a less satisfactory reading of the available data (*pace* Klein 2000b), a view supported by the still ill-defined dating of such mutations as the FOXP2 gene (Enard *et al.* 2002) and the latter's apparent presence in the Neanderthal genome (Krause *et al.* 2007). Stratigraphically indisputable evidence for art and jewellery from Blombos Cave, South Africa, at >70 kya is particularly important in refuting arguments for a 'human revolution' in cognitive abilities 50–40 kya (Henshilwood 2005).

*Jewellery and Exchange*

Indeed, the number and good context of the *Nassarius kraussianus* beads at Blombos (d'Errico *et al.* 2005) suggest that isolated examples of jewellery and decoration previously reported from African

Mode 3 contexts should be re-evaluated and considered more favourably. Possibly coeval, or even earlier in date, are Aterian examples like the (artificially?) perforated *N. gibbosulus* shell from Oued Djebanna, Algeria, mentioned in Chapter 5 (Morel 1974), and the (humanly produced?) bone pendant from Morocco's Grotte Zouhra (Debénath 1994). Much more certain are the recently published ~82,000-year-old *N. gibbosulus* shells, some of them ochre-stained and/or possibly worn, from Taforalt, also in Morocco (Bouzouggar *et al.* 2007). Farther south, one of several hundred beads from Layer V at Mumba, Tanzania (Mehlman 1989), is directly dated by amino-acid racemisation assay to 52 kya, though others certainly date to later in MIS 3 (Hare *et al.* 1993; Conard 2005:312); an MIS 3 age is also likely for ostrich eggshell beads from Boomplaas, Bushman Rock Shelter, Cave of Hearths, and, more convincingly, Border Cave in southern Africa, where several sites have also produced examples of incised ochre, bone, and ostrich eggshell (Cain 2006). Of these, Diepkloof in the Western Cape Province stands out: its upper Howiesons Poort levels, dated to 65–55 kya, have yielded almost 200 incised fragments of ostrich eggshell, some clearly from flasks, that document a variety of deliberate designs (Parkington *et al.* 2005; Rigaud *et al.* 2006).

From about 40 kya, and associated for the most part with micro-lithic industries, evidence of personal decoration becomes a little more plentiful. A date of 39,900 ± 1600 bp (Pta-4889 F2) for eggshells from a bead workshop in the Sakutiek industry levels at Enkapune ya Muto, Kenya (Ambrose 1998a), offers particularly good confirmation of their manufacture at this time depth and is readily paralleled in the Near East and Europe from about 40 kya (Vanhaeren 2005). As the Blombos evidence also indicates, jewellery, an inherently symbolic artefact, implies the existence of modern cognitive and language abilities (d'Errico *et al.* 2005). If (and it is a big 'if') it were appropriate to make the connection, then an analogy with recent Bushman practice would suggest that the manufacture of beads also marks the existence of reciprocal systems of gift-exchange comparable to the *hxaro* system Wiessner (1983) describes for the Ju/'hoansi. Though positive evidence for the movement of ostrich eggshell beads is difficult to obtain, other signs of long-distance connections do become more common during The Big Dry.

One such indicator is the recovery of marine shells at inland sites. However, except for two perforated *Conus* shells from early Howiesons Poort levels at Border Cave, 80 km from the Indian Ocean coast (Beaumont 1978; Grün *et al.* 2003), MIS 4 and 3 lack such evidence. More commonplace may have been the movement of stone, with Ambrose and Lorenz (1990) arguing that southern Africa's Howiesons Poort occurrences exemplify increased use of non-local raw materials as a result of wider-ranging movements and/or the intensification of intergroup alliances to cope with reduced resource abundance and predictability. It seems, however, that at many sites, including Klasies River, supposedly non-local rocks actually moved only a few kilometres, if that, well within the foraging distance of their occupants (Minichillo 2006), and that in some cases, moreover, no significant differences exist in raw material usage between Howiesons Poort and post-Howiesons Poort assemblages (Soriano *et al.* 2007). Alternative hypotheses are thus needed to explain the Howiesons Poort's preference for finer-grained raw materials, and we return to this point subsequently. In East Africa, on the other hand, there is some sound evidence for the movement of **toolstone**, facilitated by the readiness with which obsidian can be sourced (Fig. 7.3; Merrick and Brown 1984; Pleurdeau 2006). Increased access to more distant materials is evident, for example, at Prospect Farm in MIS 4/early MIS 3 (Merrick *et al.* 1994), but highest among late Mode 3 or transitional Middle Stone Age (MSA)/Late Stone Age (LSA) occurrences of MIS 3 age at Enkapune ya Muto, Ntumot, and Prolonged Drift (Ambrose 2001). Examples of obsidian travelling over distances in excess of 250 km are also known (Merrick and Brown 1984), with access probably gained through both intergroup exchange and increased embedded procurement as other activities were undertaken within expanded foraging ranges. Both practices may have been encouraged by the riskier, more unpredictable environments of The Big Dry (Ambrose 2002).

*Regional Industries and the Case of the Howiesons Poort*

As is widely appreciated, regional diversification is a pronounced feature of Africa's Mode 3 industries (J. D. Clark 1988a). Ecological

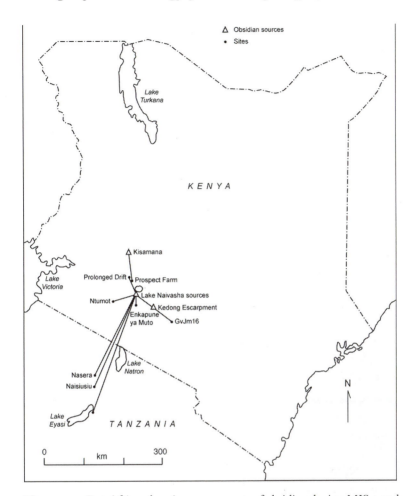

**Figure 7.3.** East Africa, showing movements of obsidian during MIS 4 and 3. (After Merrick and Brown 1984; Merrick *et al.* 1994; Ambrose 2001; S. Kusimba 2001.)

barriers to human movement, such as a hyper-arid Sahara, must have contributed to this development. More contested is the extent to which shorter-lived spatio-temporal patterning in artefact assemblages is discernible. Such patterning might allow the identification of the presence and practice of another of the forms of symbolic storage identified by Wadley (2001a), something generally perceived to be lacking, or at least much less well developed, in the contemporary

Neanderthal archaeological record of western Eurasia (Mellars 1996, 2005; cf. d'Errico 2003; Conard 2005). The Howiesons Poort, which we have already mentioned, has been in the thick of these discussions (Fig. 7.4). Long recognised as among Pleistocene Africa's most distinctive industries, it is characterised by enhanced use of fine-grained rocks, such as silcrete and **opaline**, and the production of backed pieces similar to, but typically larger than, those of terminal Pleistocene/Holocene Mode 5 industries. Now reasonably well dated to 70–55 kya, it belongs to MIS 4/early MIS 3 (G. Miller *et al.* 1999; Lombard 2005a; Tribolo *et al.* 2005; *pace* Parkington 1990a), with stratigraphic observations confirming that it is younger than the Still Bay industry discussed in Chapter 6 (Rigaud *et al.* 2006; Wadley 2006).

Non-Africanists have frequently identified (and been astounded by) purported resemblances between the Howiesons Poort and western Eurasia's Upper Palaeolithic (e.g., Binford 1984; Bar-Yosef 2002; Mellars 2005). Such comments emphasise the Howiesons Poort's backed artefacts and smaller blades, and a recent detailed study by Soriano *et al.* (2007) confirms that, at least at Rose Cottage Cave, its makers employed an Upper Palaeolithic-like direct marginal percussion technique using a stone hammer. However, it remains unclear whether this technique was now invented for the first time, and other studies show that the Howiesons Poort is clearly part of the overall sequence of southern African Mode 3 industries (A. Thackeray 1989; Harper 1997). Wurz (1999) also confirms that many of its backed artefacts are heavily standardised in size and morphology. This observation feeds into arguments that they, or rather the tools (spears?) incorporating them, were exchanged between individuals and groups, along the lines of Bushman *hxaro* gift-exchange. The tendency for such backed pieces to be preferentially made from fine-grained ('non-local') rocks is used to support this, the argument being that this would have enhanced the 'value' of the items concerned. These ideas appeal because they might explain why, following climatic amelioration in MIS 3, the same level of symbolic behaviour was deselected, provoking a return to more generalised Mode 3 traditions and the disappearance of the Howiesons Poort

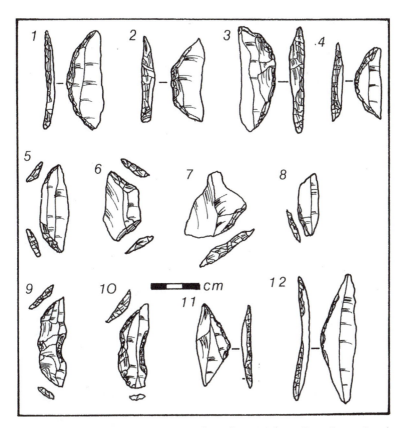

**Figure 7.4.** Howiesons Poort artefacts from Nelson Bay Cave, South Africa: 1–4. segments; 5–6. trapezoids; 7–8. truncated pieces; 9. trapezoid with notch; 10. strangulated and backed piece; 11–12. triangles. (Redrawn after Volman 1981; Figs. 27, 28, 30, 32; courtesy Tom Volman.)

(H. J. Deacon 1995; H. J. Deacon and Wurz 2005). However, they are grounded in little more than morphological similarities between Howiesons Poort backed artefacts and later Holocene **backed microliths,** the presumption, itself controversial (Binneman 1982), that the latter functioned as arrow inserts, and the fact that recent Bushmen have used arrows in gift-exchange and to define boundaries between linguistically different groups (Wiessner 1983). As already mentioned, the non-local origins of many of the rocks concerned can also be doubted (Minichillo 2006). Compelling evidence

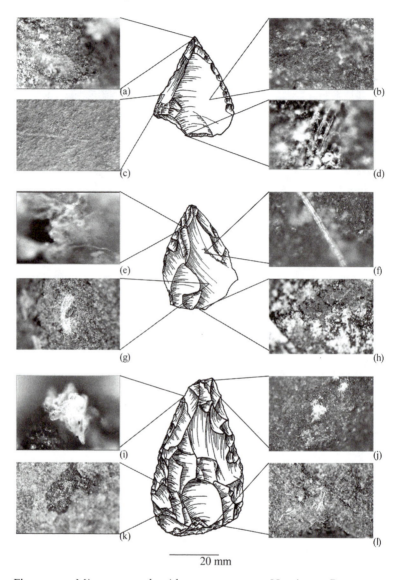

20 mm

**Figure 7.5.** Microwear and residue traces on post–Howiesons Poort stone points from Layer RSp, Sibudu Cave, South Africa. The residues illustrated are: (a) a thick blood residue deposit near the tip of the tool; (b) a diagonally deposited ochre smear on the medial portion; (c) a transverse striation associated with ochre and plant exudate (the grey stain) on the proximal surface (50×); (d) bark cells on the proximal edge (500×); (e) animal tissue on the distal surface (500×); (f) animal hair on the medial surface; (g) woody

for the uses of Howiesons Poort backed artefacts, or for why standardisation might reflect transmission of messages about social affiliation, also remains to be found.[5] Instead, arguments founded in understandings of how artefacts may have functioned within technological and subsistence strategies are needed (G. McCall 2006; see inset). Some design constraints may have been imposed by the very act of hafting (Gibson *et al.* 2004). Smaller, more blade-based, more standardised toolkits may also have been encouraged if, like provisioning sites with cores, they helped reduce the time needed to search out toolstone within less productive, less predictable stadial environments (Ambrose 2006). Climatic amelioration during MIS 3 may have deselected for such behaviour as resources became more abundant and predictable, with more expedient toolkits made on predominantly coarse-grained rocks once more sufficing for encounter-based, rather than more logistically organised, exploitation of a greater diversity of resources (Ambrose 2006).

## UNDERSTANDING STONE TOOL FUNCTION AT SIBUDU

What were stone tools used for? Despite well over a century of effort, answering this question is far from simple. However, recent work, exemplified here by studies of post-Howiesons Poort Mode 3 assemblages at Sibudu Cave (Fig. 7.5; Wadley

←————————————————————————————

**Figure 7.5.** (*continued*) residue trapped under a resin deposit on the proximal surface (100×); (h) a thick ochre deposit near the proximal edge associated with a diagonal striation and polish accompanied by a brown residue in the upper right corner that is resin and a whitish deposit that is macerated wood; (i) collagen with brown spots on the distal edge (500×); (j) a fatty deposit near the tip (100×); (k) a thick resinous deposit with wood imprint; (l) woody fibres and resin associated with polish near the proximal edge (100×). All the photographs were taken at a magnification of 200× unless otherwise stated. (This image was published in the *Journal of Human Evolution*, vol. 48, Lombard, M, 'Evidence of hunting and hafting during the Middle Stone Age at Sibudu Cave, KwaZulu-Natal, South Africa: a multianalytical approach', pp. 279–300, Copyright Elsevier, 2005).

and Whitelaw 2006), demonstrates how combining a variety of approaches offers the prospect of a solution. Analysis of organic residues trapped within the surface of more than 400 artefacts suggests that many had been used to process starchy and/or succulent plant foods, or other plant-derived materials, such as wood or medicines. Very few artefacts preserved collagen or blood residues consistent with butchery activities (B. Williamson 2005). Lombard's (2005b) study of a sample of points, on the other hand, combined organic residue analysis with investigations of macrofracture and use-wear patterns and experimental replication. She shows that most were used as hafted hunting tools and that plant twine, resin, and ochre were used as binding materials. The weapons themselves were probably handheld throwing or thrusting spears, and large game (including buffalo and bushpig) is a feature of the post-Howiesons Poort Sibudu fauna. The use of ochre in hafting stone artefacts has been further investigated by Wadley *et al.* (2004), who suggest that it may have been added as an emulsifier in mixing wax or resin and that it may also have encouraged mastic to harden as it dried. Such utilitarian uses do not, however, exclude the possibility that ochre was also selected for symbolic purposes, linked to its bright red colour, as discussed in Chapters 5 and 6.

Whether the Howiesons Poort's long duration is compatible with the rapid turnovers of artefact style noted for more recent human cultures has also been debated (Parkington 2006a). Wadley (2001b) suggests not, although multiple phases are present within the Howiesons Poort at Rose Cottage Cave (Wadley and Harper 1989; Soriano *et al.* 2007). Wurz (2002), on the other hand, offers an affirmative, if stretched, response. Because no absolute standard exists for inferring the presence/absence of 'style' from 'duration', a definite answer is elusive. The notorious conservatism of some lithic traditions reinforces this conclusion, as does the greater ease with which stylistic messages can be transmitted in more fluid, non-lithic media. The better dated East African sequence does, indeed, show a succession of often quite radically different industries across MIS 4–2, of the kind frequently cited as evidence for modern behaviour (Ambrose 1998a, 2002). Difficulties in paralleling this in southern Africa may be more apparent than real, a function of fewer well-defined, well-published sequences and of substantial variability in assemblage content. Observations from Rose Cottage Cave and Sibudu (Wadley 2001a, 2001b, 2005b, 2006) suggest quite volatile changes in assemblage character over time scales of only a few millennia later in MIS 3. The Still Bay phenomenon at Blombos (Henshilwood 2005) and evidence from pre-Howiesons Poort levels at Klasies River (A. Thackeray 1989) indicate that such volatility is even older. Still unclear, however, are the conditions under which it was encouraged and reinforced (Hiscock and O'Connor 2005), a question thrown into relief by the impression of enduring continuity conveyed by the 'Lupemban' and 'Lupembo-Tshitolian' traditions of Central Africa (J. D. Clark 1982b; Cornelissen 2002) and by the sharp contrasts in faunal associations between Howiesons Poort (ground game and small browsers) and post-Howiesons Poort (large grazing ungulates) levels reported from recent excavations in South Africa (Parkington *et al.* 2005; Wadley 2006).

### Other Signs of Modernity? Burials and Campsite Structure

Puzzling, too, is the extreme paucity of burials known from this period in Africa, in contrast to their practice by Neanderthals and early modern humans in western Eurasia (Klein 1999). Only Taramsa Hill, OSL-dated to $55.5 \pm 3.7$ kya, (Vermeersch *et al.* 1998), and the BC3 remains from Border Cave, which are of early Howiesons Poort age (Grün and Beaumont 2001), predate MIS 2; both are of children, with BC3 accompanied by one of the two *Conus* shells mentioned earlier. Evidence for Wadley's (2001a) final criterion, the formally structured use of domestic space, may also be at variance with that for the antiquity of style and symbolism. However, we wonder if rock-shelters, which almost invariably contain palimpsest deposits produced by repeated visits, are the best resource with which to tackle such issues. The paucity of comparative data from southern Africa or other parts of the continent, especially from open-air sites, offers a further stumbling block to generalising more widely from

Rose Cottage Cave alone. Even though clear contrasts are evident between that site's MSA and LSA components, only the latter exhibit discrete compartmentalisation of activities between different parts of the excavated area (Wadley 2001a).

## ONE TRANSITION OR MANY? BECOMING MICROLITHIC

If Blombos rewrites the framework within which other claims for art, jewellery, and signs of modern behaviour predating 50/40 kya should be interpreted, then collectively, such evidence also decouples the debate about the origins of such behaviour from large-scale changes in stone tool-making traditions. The transition(s) between Mode 3 and Mode 5 industries must be researched independently from other phenomena, and should not be expected to correlate with them (Mitchell 1994; A. Clark 1999). This conclusion, emphasised by the terminal MSA associations of Africa's oldest rock art at Apollo 11 Cave, Namibia (Wendt 1976), underlines the difficulties of retaining MSA and LSA as shorthand terms, and thus our preference for employing instead Grahame Clark's (1969) modal terminology. To tackle these questions, we first survey the main technological traditions in different parts of Africa during MIS 4–3, and then consider some of the explanations offered for the changes we observe.

### Africa South of the Zambezi

Backed artefacts are neither unique to the Howiesons Poort nor first found in that context (Chapter 5). In southern Africa, examples also occur in later Mode 3 assemblages. Once termed MSA 3 (Volman 1984), these are highly variable (Wadley 2005b). Thus, at Boomplaas, larger flake-blades characterise the uppermost part of the MSA sequence (Volman 1984), whereas at Border Cave, blades became shorter and squatter with time (Beaumont *et al.* 1978). Border Cave also offers the best example of a relatively early (±39 kya) microlithic industry (Grün and Beaumont 2001). Produced by bipolar reduction of opaline and quartz, it has large numbers of *pièces esquillées*, but almost no bladelets or formal tools. Similarly,

**Figure 7.6.** Sibudu, South Africa. (Courtesy and copyright Marlize Lombard.)

informal assemblages occur slightly later in MIS 3 at other sites in northern South Africa (Wadley 1987; Beaumont 1990a), but elsewhere, MSA retouched tools and patterns of flake reduction persisted, something that represents a real phenomenon, not problems of dating or definition (Mitchell 2002a). This was so, for example, beyond 32 kya at Boomplaas (H. J. Deacon 1995) and until

~25 kya in Namibia (Vogelsang 1996). Southeastern Africa shows this persistence particularly well, with extensive intra- and inter-site variation in assemblage composition. Emerging as the key regional reference point, Sibudu (Fig. 7.5) was occupied several times during MIS 3 by people who used Mode 3 methods to make diverse assemblages characterised by scrapers and bifacial and unifacial points, at least partly employed to hunt a wide range of large game, including zebra, buffalo, and bushpig (Wadley 2005b, 2006). Detailed technological studies of the kind undertaken by Villa *et al.* (2005) should help explain how such industries were replaced after 25 kya by informal, bipolar-reduced quartz assemblages or others described as transitional between MSA and LSA technologies (Mitchell 2002a). Events farther north, however, followed different paths. In Namibia, informal, macrolithic assemblages emerged (Wendt 1976), whereas in Zimbabwe's Matopo Hills, industries retaining a Mode 3 component seemingly survived until 13 kya, although the situation is confused by a substantial gap in occupation history and the complicating effects on the available radiocarbon dates of the downward migration of charcoal through rock-shelter stratigraphies (N. Walker 1995a; Larsson 1996). Botswana is different again. Recalling a pattern seen in East Africa, bladelet technologies are attested there from ~39–36 kya at White Paintings Shelter, accompanied by bone points and harpoons and extensive fish exploitation (Robbins *et al.* 2000; Brook *et al.* 2003).

*Zambia and Eastern Africa*

This exception noted, the generally late replacement of Mode 3 technologies south of the Zambezi is mirrored to its north. A key Zambian site is Kalemba, where a Mode 3 industry with unifacial points and scrapers in Horizon G is succeeded in Horizon H by one of slightly smaller dimensions and fewer formal tools; relevant dates of >37 kya (GX-2609) and 24600 ± 2000/1000 bp (GX-2610; D. Phillipson 1976) are on bone apatite, an often-unreliable medium. Slightly later is an apparently transitional industry, with smaller flakes, rare points and scrapers, and more backed flakes. The 'proto-LSA' described from Leopard's Hill, 450 km away but still within the *Brachystegia*-covered plateau, is remarkably similar, but has more bladelet cores and fewer radial cores; a charcoal radiocarbon determination places it ~22 kya (D. Phillipson 1976). Mumbwa may capture elements of the same succession, with an ephemeral late MSA occupation around 39 ± 7 kya, followed by a possibly transitional occurrence in Unit IV, in which centripetal flaking is reduced in favour of a broader mix of flake and blade forms (Barham 2000). Subsequent to the LGM, assemblages are unequivocally Mode 5 in character and variously termed Nachikufan I (D. Phillipson 1976) or, in the Lunsemfwa Basin, Group I (Musonda 1984). The one exception is the upper Zambezi Valley, where a Mode 3 industry may have persisted (was reinvented?) in the Holocene (L. Phillipson 1978).

Other Zambian sites help highlight possible connections between East and southern Africa. At Twin Rivers, a Mode 3 assemblage dating to terminal MIS 4/early MIS 3 combines bifacial points with large **segments** reminiscent of those of the Howiesons Poort (Barham 2000). Farther east at Kalambo Falls, the 'rubble component' of the Polungu industry, though not in primary stratigraphic context, also includes large segments, along with bladelet production and Levallois flakes, cores, and points (J. D. Clark 1974a). Backed artefacts, and specifically segments, also distinguish the Bed V assemblage from Mumba, in Tanzania's Eyasi Basin, where amino-acid racemisation and uranium assays suggest a possible, but potentially unreliable, age of 65–35 kya (Mehlman 1991; McBrearty and Brooks 2000). This Mumba industry is one of several described from East Africa in MIS 4/3 and is succeeded at Mumba itself by the Nasera industry, which has high frequencies of small, unstandardised points and fewer, smaller backed microliths. Uranium-series and radiocarbon dates suggest an age of 37–18 kya (Ambrose 2002), but this, too, may be an underestimate. The reason for thinking so concerns the overlying Lemuta industry at Nasera rock-shelter in the Serengeti, which has high frequencies of large backed tools, including examples of obsidian derived from sources more than 250 km away in the Central Rift Valley (Merrick and Brown 1984). The Lemuta industry is radiocarbon-dated to 22–18 kya at Nasera (Mehlman 1991) and to 17 kya at Naisiusiu, Olduvai Gorge (Leakey *et al.* 1972), but this is clearly an underestimate. The single crystal laser fusion

PROBLEMS WITH RADIOCARBON: SOME EAST
AFRICAN EXAMPLES

Radiocarbon dating, as is well known, has an effective upper
age limit of around 40 kya. However, this is far from being the
only problem with the technique when it is applied to MIS 3.
Ambrose's (1998a, 2002) work in Kenya elegantly demonstrates
some of the other pitfalls. One, which warrants more detailed investigation in African – and other – contexts, is the discrepancy
that arises when dates are run on materials that have been in storage for some time. For example, at Enkapune ya Muto, the basal
layer, RBL4, was dated within a few months of excavation to >26
kya and to 41.4 ± 0.7 kya (a clear underestimate given a date of
39.9 kya more than a metre above it). Yet, two samples submitted
four years after excavation produced a result of 29,280 ± 540 bp.
Almost certainly, they had absorbed modern contaminants during
storage, resulting in a false finite age (Haas *et al.* 1986). The moral
of the story is to minimise such errors by using complementary
dating techniques and alternative media, such as ostrich eggshell,
which has proved to be highly reliable and resistant to diagenesis.

A second problem highlighted by sites of probable MIS
3 age in the region is the unreliability of bone apatite as a
dating medium. It is now widely acknowledged that accurate
radiocarbon determinations on bone must employ the collagen
fraction of this material given that where apatite samples can
be checked against other dating techniques, they tend to be
significantly too young (e.g., Collett and Robertshaw 1983).
Whether what has been termed collagen is really so is also moot,
given that studies suggest it only rarely preserves in tropical Africa
beyond the early/mid Holocene (Ambrose 1990). The 'collagen'
used to date the Lemuta industry at Nasera and Naisiusiu is a
case in point, with other dating techniques suggesting a real age
perhaps three times that indicated by the radiocarbon dates (see
main text). Similar confusion exists over the exact antiquity and
interrelationships of sites at Lukenya Hill, and there is an urgent
need to deploy a more varied battery of dating techniques to try
and resolve such problems.

**Figure 7.7.** Enkapune ya Muto, Kenya. (Courtesy and copyright Stan Ambrose.)

$^{40}$Ar/$^{39}$Ar technique convincingly indicates that the industry's real age is >42 kya, and this is supported by similar ages from ostrich eggshell amino-acid racemisation and accelerator radiocarbon dating (Manega 1993), as well as a date of 60 kya produced by ESR (Skinner *et al.* 2003). Though additional work is required to evaluate and clarify the age, characteristics, and relationships of these industries, it seems increasingly clear that the production of microliths and backed artefacts reaches far back into MIS 3 in East Africa (see inset).

Ambrose's (1998a, 2002) excavations at Enkapune ya Muto (Fig. 7.7) offer the best-documented succession. The Nasampolai industry is the oldest LSA occurrence, given its large backed blades and geometric microliths and an absence of radial core preparation or faceted platform flakes. This combination differentiates it from the Mumba, Nasera, and Howiesons Poort industries, whereas the presence of low numbers of discoidal cores and facetted platform flakes in the overlying Sakutiek industry underlines the diverse, and frequently nonlinear, paths marking the transition between Mode 3 and Mode 5 technologies. Assemblages from various sites excavated at Lukenya Hill are also relevant. Dates are largely on bone apatite. In the absence of alternative estimates, it thus seems better to rely on typological similarities with other East African sites. If so, then the GVJm46 and 62 scraper-dominated microlithic occurrences (Lukenya Hill phase 1) may be broadly contemporary with the Sakutiek industry; those from GvJm16 and 22 (Lukenya Hill phase 2) comparable to the Lemuta industry at Naisiusiu and thus coeval, or even older, and those from GvJm19 (Lukenya Hill phase 3), of terminal Pleistocene age (S. Kusimba 2001).

## The Horn of Africa

Ethiopia and Somalia add few firm data to this picture. Late or transitional MSA assemblages have only poor chronological constraints (Kurashina 1978; Brandt 1986; Gresham and Brandt 1996), with those from Porc Epic, which include a backed microlith element, probably predating MIS 4 (Pleurdeau 2006). However, by the end of MIS 3, obsidian-based Mode 4 industries were already being made that included microliths and scrapers (Brandt 1986). Moving into Egypt and Nubia, the few Mode 3 industries of possible MIS 4/3 age belong to the so-called Nubian complex, except at Taramsa 1, where the classic Levallois system was adapted for systematic blade production (Van Peer 1998). A comparable technological transition is evident at Nazlet Khater 4. There, bifacial tools were combined with a fully developed blade production system made on chert quarried from vertical shafts and underground galleries using antelope horn picks and hammerstones (Vermeersch et al. 1990). Sadly, the paucity of immediately older or younger sites already noted means that the wider connections of these developments remain elusive. Only around 25 kya does the blade-based Shuwikhatian industry appear in Upper Egypt (Vermeersch 1992), followed from 21 kya by a plethora of microlithic assemblages (Milliken 2003). These dates match those available for the appearance of Mode 5 technologies in Cyrenaica and the Maghreb, both of which may have seen occupation hiatuses earlier in The Big Dry (Close 2002).

## West and Central Africa

In West and Central Africa, the continent's two remaining regions, acquiring a clear picture of assemblage variability is hampered by the lack of fieldwork, dating problems, and difficulties in typological characterisation that we have already noted. As these lacunae are filled, considerable interassemblage variability can be anticipated, judging from sites near Ounjougou, Mali, that may be vaguely related to Levallois-dominated industries of mostly uncertain age from Nigeria, Ghana, Burkina Faso, Senegal, and Guinea (Casey 2003; Robert *et al.* 2003). Mode 5 industries are unknown in this region for the period covered here. For Equatorial Africa, Cornelissen (2002) distinguishes two broad categories of assemblage between 40 and 10 kya. Those termed Lupemban emphasise bifacial core-tools, employ a wide variety of raw materials, and include some use of prepared core techniques (Fig. 7.8). However, although long-lasting typological continuities with Holocene Tshitolian assemblages in the same region are plausible, a firm chronology that would extend the Lupemban into later stages of The Big Dry is lacking: The few radiocarbon dates are infinite, nearly so, or of uncertain association (Lavachery 1990; Clist 1995). Dates for quartz, microlithic assemblages seem sounder (Cornelissen 2002:Table 1). Varying in reduction patterns among sites, they are informal, with backed microliths rare, and scrapers and denticulates the most common retouched artefacts. Grindstones and bone tools are also few, though sites at Ishango on the shores of Lake Edward form an important exception, discussed in greater detail subsequently. Comparisons between quartz assemblages there and in the Ituri rainforest show that the latter's settlement did not demand ecologically distinctive, or specialised, lithic technologies (Mercader and Brooks 2001).

## Transitions to Mode 5 Technologies

Where does this leave our understanding of the disappearance of Mode 3 technologies and the shift to microlithic ways of making stone tools? First, pathways were quite varied, even within quite small geographical regions. Second, microlithic (in the sense of producing small flakes or blades) is not necessarily synonymous with production of backed microliths, as the highly informal quartz microlithic assemblages of equatorial Africa and some southern African sites show, and as the unmodified bladelet emphasis of the same region's Robberg Industry confirms in a different way (Mitchell 2002a). Different explanations are needed to account for this variability – no single model is likely to work. To exemplify this further, consider Close's (2002) suggestion that the appearance of backed bladelet-rich microlithic assemblages across North Africa represents recolonisation after an occupational lacuna. Presumably, their origins lie in Mode 4 industries from Cyrenaica (the Dabban?), Egypt (the Shuwikhatian?), or the Levant, but no such connection is yet demonstrable, and the situation is further complicated by recently reported Mode 4 assemblages from northern Morocco (Barton *et al.* 2005) and northwestern Libya (Barich *et al.* 2006) that predate 23 kya. In contrast, the much older backed blade and microlithic technologies in East Africa have different origins and are older there than anywhere else, with roots in local Mode 3 technologies. This is shown not only at Enkapune ya Muto and by the Mumba, Nasera, and Lemuta industries already mentioned, but also by the recently discovered, deeply stratified sequence at Ntumot on the western margin of Kenya's southern Rift. Here, a transitional industry with backed microliths, small bifacial points, and a continued use of radial cores is probably older than 50 kya, with largely informal, microlithic (LSA) assemblages appearing about 30 kya (Ambrose 2002).

Residue, microwear, and experimental studies (Parsons and Badenhorst 2004; Lombard 2005b) confirm that neither microlithisation nor the production of backed microliths was directly related to the development of hafting or of composite tools; both innovations have much longer pedigrees (Chapter 6). Further work needs to be done to ascertain the uses to which Late Pleistocene microlithic artefacts, backed microliths, and other stone tools were actually put; studies in Egypt (Becker and Wendorf 1993) and southern Africa (Binneman 1982, 1997; Binneman and Mitchell 1997; B. Williamson 1997) document a multiplicity of uses. Hypotheses that explain the adoption of microlithic technology in terms of the

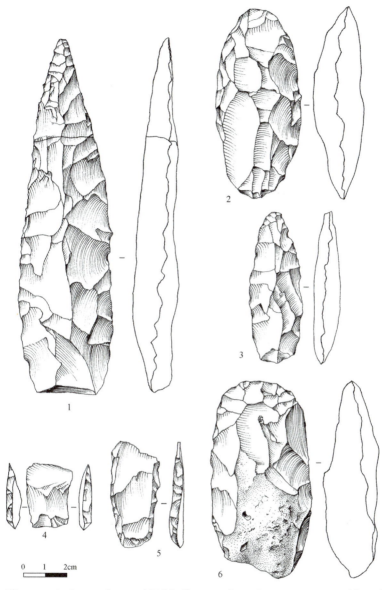

**Figure 7.8.** Lupemban and Tshitolian artefacts, Democratic Republic of Congo: 1. Lupemban elongated point; 2. Lupemban core-axe; 3. Lupemban arrowhead; 4–5. Tshitolian transverse arrowheads; 6. Tshitolian core-axe. All the artefacts are in silicified sandstone (*grès polymorphe*). The Lupemban artefacts come from Rivière Belgica near Kinshasa, the Tshitolian ones from the Bateke Plateau. (Courtesy Yvette Paquay and courtesy and copyright Els Cornelissen.)

advantages of lighter hunting equipment accompanying a shift to smaller, often more solitary, game in more closed habitats may hold in some quarters (Zambia? D. Phillipson 2005), but scarcely fit the more open environments that characterised so much of Africa during MIS 3/2, nor situations (such as the Robberg) where faunas vary, but often emphasise larger, more gregarious grazing species (Mitchell 2002a)[6]. For now, arguments that increasingly mobile settlement systems favoured the shift to microlithic technologies in order to conserve raw materials, lighten transport loads, and – perhaps most crucially – partly 'untether' people from fixed rock resources, seem among the most plausible suggestions (Bousman 1991, 2005; Ambrose 2002), not least because many of the critical East African assemblages do show intensified access to exotic raw materials at precisely the same time. Coping with the challenges posed by potentially drier, less productive, riskier environments during MIS 4/early MIS 3, could well provide the context for the development and spread of new technologies (and not just those hinted at by the stone tools that bulk so large in the archaeological record). The distinctive bladelet emphasis of the Robberg Industry can similarly be understood in terms of Bleed's (1986) concepts of maintainable and reliable design technologies (Mitchell 2002a). The shift to more complex, composite tools bearing microlithic inserts must have depended, however, upon an elaborate calculus involving artefact design principles, variation in, and knowledge of, resource patterns, and a range of social factors (Bar-Yosef and Kuhn 1999). One of African archaeology's continuing challenges is to identify and evaluate the elements of that calculus in order to explain the varied trajectories leading to the more general adoption of microlithic toolkits.

IN AND OUT OF AFRICA

If a core theme of Chapter 6 was the strengthening case for an early, African development of behavioural modernity, then a critical aspect of the time-period covered here has to be understanding the expansion into the rest of the world of populations equipped with those capacities. This is too large a topic for us to pursue in

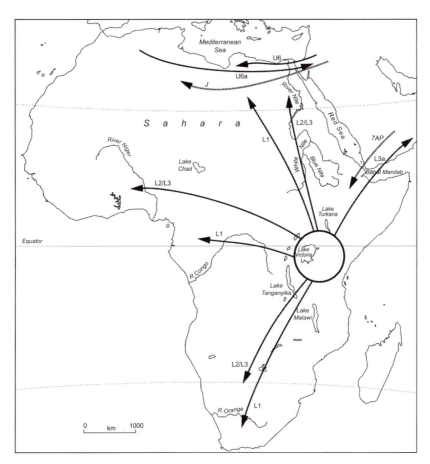

**Figure 7.9.** Africa, illustrating the genetic evidence for movements in and out of the continent during MIS 4 and 3 (after Watson *et al.* 1997; Maca-Meyer *et al.* 2003; Forster 2004; S. Oppenheimer 2004). Mitochondrial lineages are indicated in normal typeface; Y-chromosome lineages, in italics. For estimated dates and further information, please see the references and main text. Directions of movement indicated were not contemporary and are only schematically indicated here.

detail, but a couple of points deserve emphasis that relate to the timing and mode of modern human dispersals out of Africa and to the possibility of subsequent movements back into the continent (Fig. 7.9). Archaeology and genetics both contribute to this story.

*Exiting Africa: How and When?*

Of the routes by which people could have left Africa, the Straits of Gibraltar remained unused, despite claimed similarities between the Aterian and southwestern Europe's Upper Palaeolithic Solutrean Industry (Bouzouggar *et al.* 2002) most recently rebutted by Straus (2001) and Garcea (2002). This leaves Sinai and the Bab el-Mandab. The first route was almost certainly employed during MIS 5 when anatomically modern humans colonised the southern Levant. However, this colonisation failed, and Neanderthals lived in Israel early in MIS 3 (Klein 1999). Despite its attractions as the only land-based exit available, these facts suggest that Sinai was not used when modern humans again moved out of Africa into Eurasia. This process must have begun sufficiently early to permit them to enter Australia by 45–40 kya, the youngest possible age for the colonisation of Sahul (O'Connell and Allen 2004). Any older date for this settlement (see S. O'Connor 2007) only enhances the case for an exit via the Bab el-Mandab, followed by a spread around the Indian Ocean's northern perimeter (Forster and Matsumura 2005). Some capacity to build watercraft will have been necessary, however, as even at lower sea levels, the straits between Djibouti and Yemen did not close (Siddall *et al.* 2003).

DNA analyses indicate that all non-African populations have a single, African source, consistent with either a single major migration event out of Africa, or multiple migrations from one genetically homogenous source population (Underhill *et al.* 2000; Pearson 2004; Reed and Tishkoff 2006). The oldest subcluster of the L3a mitochondrial lineage, from which all Eurasian populations descend, is located in East Africa (Watson *et al.* 1997), and this is supported (though not definitely confirmed) by at least one recent analysis of nuclear DNA variation (Ray *et al.* 2005). The L3a lineage probably started expanding into Eurasia 65–50 kya (Mountain *et al.* 1995; Tishkoff *et al.* 1996; Forster *et al.* 2001), although Templeton (2002) proposes dates at the end of MIS 5, with limited interbreeding with resident Eurasian hominins, something also indicated by some DNA analyses and readings of the fossil record (Trinkaus 2005; Plagnol and Wall 2006). Other L2 and L3 mtDNA lineages expanded within Africa at and before this time, affecting all sampled populations except the Ju/'hoansi and the Aka (Watson *et al.* 1997; Forster 2004). It is tempting to link this expansion to a demographic rebound from the effects of the Toba eruption and the onset of The Big Dry, and/or to some new behavioural advantage, such as enhanced exchange systems or technologies (Ambrose 1998b, 2002; Mellars 2006). For now, however, the chronological parameters for both the genetic and the archaeological data remain unsettlingly broad, with mtDNA evidence unable to choose between an East African derivation for the Khoisan, or an expansion of modern humans from southern Africa into areas farther north (Salas *et al.* 2002). Note, too, that the derivation of North African mtDNA lines from others now characterising Europe and the Near East (Rando *et al.* 1998) means that North Africa was probably not the source of the modern humans who colonised western Eurasia, a conclusion reinforced by the pronounced genetic discontinuity between North African and Iberian populations (Bosch *et al.* 2001). All this is consistent with an East African origin for the L3a lineage and with mtDNA data from southern Arabia, the Andaman Islands, and Malaysia that collectively reinforce the case for a primary exit across the Bab el-Mandab, before or after the start of MIS 4 (Quintana-Murci *et al.* 1999; S. Oppenheimer 2004; Macaulay *et al.* 2005; Thangaraj *et al.* 2005).

The very sparseness of the lower Nile's archaeological record during MIS 4–3 reinforces the claims of the Bab el-Mandab as the primary exit route used by modern humans to enter Eurasia,[7] but supporting archaeological evidence is extremely scarce. Reports of Aterian-like tools from Yemen (McClure 1994) are alluring, but difficult to evaluate, and the Aterian itself has virtually no presence in the Nile Valley, and none to its east (Wendorf and Schild 2005). The recent discovery of an as yet undated bifacial foliate and scraper assemblage at Wadi Arah, southern Oman, is more compelling because its reduction technology strongly resembles that used at Station One, Sudan, and more broadly in Kenya and Ethiopia (Rose 2004b; Beyin 2006). However, much more basic fieldwork will be needed on both sides of the Bab el-Mandab to demonstrate whether what the genetic data currently indicate can be confirmed archaeologically. For the moment, some support for the alternative hypothesis of a second exit across the Sinai (Lahr and Foley 1998; Underhill *et al.* 2001) comes from similarities between the transitional Levallois/Upper Palaeolithic stone reduction technologies employed at Nazlet Khater 4 44–35 kya and those used at the Israeli site of Boker Tichtit (Marks 1983). Emireh stone points from the MPI level at Sodmein may also be relevant: They are typical of the latest Middle Palaeolithic in the Levant (Marks 1983), but unrecorded in the Nile Valley (Vermeersch *et al.* 1994).

### Re-Entering Africa?

Movements may also have been in more than one direction, given that the mtDNA signatures of North African populations provide intriguing evidence for a return to Africa from southwestern Asia around 45–40 kya (Olivieri *et al.* 2006). The arrival of these U6 and MI lineages, and of the more poorly dated J Y-chromosome line, may be reflected archaeologically at Haua Fteah in northeastern Libya (S. Oppenheimer 2004)[8]. An MIS 5 age for this site's Mousterian assemblages leaves a substantial gap before the appearance of the Mode 4 Dabban industry, probably around 40–34 kya (McBurney 1967; Klein and Scott 1986). Its general Upper Palaeolithic affiliations (which include burins and small backed blades), and more specific features like **chamfered blades**, indicate connections with broadly contemporary industries in the Levant (Bar-Yosef 1987). Such similarities could readily fit the genetic situation and perhaps indicate a broadly simultaneous colonisation by southwest Asian-derived populations of both North Africa (the Dabban) and Europe (the Aurignacian; Olivieri *et al.* 2006). An alternative correlation with the rapid, trans-North African appearance of backed bladelet industries early in MIS 2 (Close 2002) seems less likely because of its later date. The possibility of exploring such correlations underlines the importance of improving the chronological precision of both archaeological and genetic datasets.

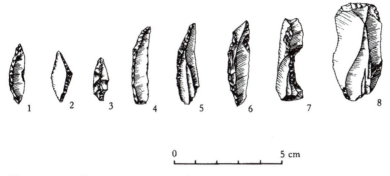

0                    5 cm

**Figure 7.10.** Iberomaurusian artefacts from the Maghreb: 1–6. backed bladelets; 7. notched bladelet; 8. scraper. (After P. Smith 1982: Fig. 5.9.)

## VARIATIONS ON A LAST GLACIAL MAXIMUM THEME

North Africa's backed bladelet industries offer some of the best evidence for how people made a living during MIS 2. In the Maghreb Iberomaurusian, assemblages[9] are dominated by small backed blades and backed points. A heavy-duty chopping/scraping component and a range of bone tools also occur (Fig. 7.10; Lubell *et al.* 1984). Though rarely extending into the mountains, Iberomaurusian sites occur across northernmost Morocco and Algeria (Lubell 2005). They are also known from northwestern Libya (Barich *et al.* 2006) and, under the name Eastern Oranian, at Haua Fteah (Close 2002).[10] Radiocarbon dates cluster after the LGM, and may imply a spread westward within Morocco around the end of Heinrich Event 1 (17.25–16.7 kya) when subtropical waters began re-entering the Mediterranean to produce significant vertical mixing of marine currents and enormously increased productivity in surface waters (Barton *et al.* 2005). Evidence of shellfish exploitation at some inland sites supports this hypothesis, or at least hints at seasonal movements to the coast, but many once littoral sites must have been lost to postglacial sealevel rises. Evidence is stronger for people procuring land-based resources, especially Barbary sheep (*Ammotragus lervia*) (Saxon *et al.* 1974), but also hartebeest, gazelle, and zebra; land snails were also intensively collected (Close and Wendorf 1990; Barton *et al.* 2005).

## North Africa and the Nile

The Iberomaurusian may be related historically to broadly contemporary backed bladelet industries along the lower Nile (Close 2002), though no close link is discernible between relevant skeletal samples (Irish 2000). Lower Nubia and Upper Egypt do, however, provide some of the best data anywhere in Africa for MIS 2, a tribute to exceptional preservation conditions and research intensity. At least five industries are recognised between 21 and 15 kya, with several more in later millennia, or following other schemes (e.g., Connor and Marks 1986). Four (the Fakhurian, Halfan, Kubbaniyan, and Silsilian) emphasise geometric microliths and backed microblades, often of **Ouchtata** type. A fifth, the Idfuan, is blade-based with few formal tools (Vermeersch 1992), and may be broadly contemporaneous with the Shuwikhatian, which is also of Mode 4 appearance (Schild and Wendorf 2002:453).

Reduced water flow and a relatively stronger flood regime meant that during MIS 2, the Nile's floodplain built up 25–30 m above today's level, but that outside the flood season, the river probably wandered through multiple braided channels (Close 1996). Sites were mostly located near the floodplain's edge, sometimes in commanding situations above these channels or in wadis several kilometres from the modern river. Exemplifying this situation, Wadi Kubbaniya provides some of our best evidence for subsistence, which focused around a broad spectrum of resources (Fig. 7.11; Wendorf *et al.* 1989). Fish and wetland plants were most important, with more limited use of migratory waterfowl and large mammals like hartebeest, gazelle, and aurochs, hunting of which is particularly well demonstrated at the possibly Fakhurian site of E71K12 near Isna (Gautier and van Neer 1989; Wetterstrom 1993; Wendorf *et al.* 1997). Fish faunas are overwhelmingly dominated by catfish (*Clarias*), probably taken en-masse during spawning runs at the start of the flood, as well as in residual autumn pools; preservation by drying or smoking for eating later in the year is likely. More than 25 plants have been recognised, though claims for early domesticated barley have proved false (Wendorf *et al.* 1984). *Cyperus rotundus* (nutgrass) is the most common foodplant. Rich in carbohydrate, young

All year round: *hunting aurochs, dorcas gazelle and hartebeest*

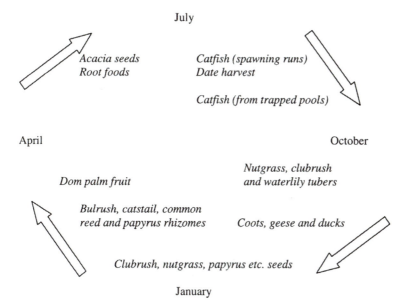

July

*Acacia seeds*
*Root foods*

*Catfish (spawning runs)*
*Date harvest*

*Catfish (from trapped pools)*

April                                                   October

*Dom palm fruit*

*Nutgrass, clubrush*
*and waterlily tubers*

*Bulrush, catstail, common*
*reed and papyrus rhizomes*

*Coots, geese and ducks*

*Clubrush, nutgrass, papyrus etc. seeds*

January

Figure 7.11. Reconstructed seasonal round from Wadi Kubbaniya, Egypt. (After Wetterstrom 1993.)

specimens could have been roasted, but more mature ones will have needed grinding and detoxifying; chemical analyses of grindstones confirm their use in processing such starchy vegetables, not seeds (C. Jones 1989). Nutgrass yields reach 3.3 kg/m$^2$ and exploitation probably stimulated further tuber production, mimicking the effects of farming. Other foodplants included *Scirpus* tubers (abundant and needing only minimal detoxification), and – it may be assumed – the archaeologically invisible rhizomes of reedmace (*Typha* spp.) and bulrushes (*Schoenoplectus* spp.). *Scirpus* and nutgrass, along with dom palm (*Hyphaene thebaica*) fruits, which have also been recovered, could all have been stored for several months. It therefore seems likely that these economies featured a strong delayed-returns element, at least from 19 kya, when grindstones first appear in the record.[11] Permanent settlement is unlikely, however, given the (seasonally?) contrasting subsistence profiles of some Halfan and

DEATH ON THE NILE: WADI KUBBANIYA
AND JEBEL SAHABA

As Agatha Christie would no doubt have appreciated, archaeology
shows that violent death has an antiquity along the Nile long predating the arrival of her Belgian detective hero, Hercule Poirot.
First evidence comes from a young man whose partially preserved
skeleton was excavated at Wadi Kubbaniya (Wendorf *et al.* 1986).
Dating ~21 kya, he had almost certainly been murdered, to judge
from the stone points found in his stomach cavity. Moreover, a
healed parry fracture on one arm and a stone chip embedded in his
partially healed right humerus suggest that he had been involved
in at least one previous violent confrontation. The dense pack-
ing of socially self-differentiating groups along the Nile discussed
in the main text presumably provoked such episodes, perhaps as
they competed for access to crucial resources. More telling evidence for this comes from the Pleistocene/Holocene transition,
the period reviewed in Chapter 8. Dating to perhaps 12.5 kya,
the Jebel Sahaba cemetery in Lower Nubia was the resting place
for 59 people, 24 of whom showed sure signs of having been
killed in the form of stone artefacts embedded in their bones or
bones with severe cutmarks. As many murders can be achieved
without penetrating bone, the real proportion of those killed may
have been much higher than 40. The backed microliths used by
the attackers belong to the Qadan industry, but it is not known
whether those killed would also have made the same kind of
artefacts. What is clear is that men, women, and children were all
attacked, suggesting the possibility that an entire group was targeted. The ecological havoc wreaked by what Close (1996) and
Butzer (1980) term the Wild Nile may well provide the context
for this event.

Kubbaniyan sites and the evidence for the acquisition of flint from
Wadi Kubbaniya by those responsible for the Kubbaniyan site of
E71K13 near Isna, some 150 km downstream (Close 1989). Groups
may nonetheless have been strongly territorial, to judge from the

**Figure 7.12.** Lukenya Hill, Kenya. (Courtesy and copyright, Chapurukha Kusimba and Sibel Barut Kusimba.)

evidence of interpersonal violence recorded at Wadi Kubbaniya (see inset).

*East Africa*

East Africa presents a different picture. At issue is the lack of ethnographic data for hunter-gatherers in such moist tropical grassland environments (Foley 1982). Marean (1997) explores three models predicting varying hunting and gathering strategies in the light of data from Lukenya Hill (Fig. 7.12). GvJm46, a large open-air site at a cliff base, was repeatedly used for mass-killing a now-extinct small alcelaphine (Marean 1992a). GvJm19 and 22, on the other hand, were probably residential bases from which several habitats were exploited. This pattern suggests that people combined tactical use of the landscape to procure mass kills during annual migrations with more generalised hunting/gathering at other seasons. Such a 'seasonal grassland model' may have been more practicable under stadial conditions, when lower temperatures and rainfall favoured more temperate grasslands, offering more seasonal resources and less dense and diverse foodplants. Pleistocene foragers, in other words, probably practised quite different lifeways from those of the Holocene (Marean 1997). Combining faunal and lithic data, S. Kusimba (2001) argues that her Lukenya Hill 1 phase combined tactical killing (GvJm46) with plant consumption (GvJm62) within a small foraging radius, whereas phase 2 witnessed greater mobility, enhanced access to non-local chert and obsidian, and hunting of a wider variety of game. Further fieldwork and better dating are needed to evaluate both this shift from processor to traveller strategy and Marean's (1997) quite different scheme, especially if both phase 1 and 2 sites are of MIS 3 age.

Turning now to other parts of the region, a heavy duty macrolithic assemblage is associated with evidence of hunting both small bovids and giraffe and zebra in basal levels at Kumbi Cave, Unguja (Zanzibar); a *terminus ante quem* of 21,695 ± 300 bp (Ua-24922) suggests that the island was still connected to the mainland at the time of this occupation, perhaps during MIS 3 or early MIS 2 (Sinclair *et al.* 2006). Browsers also played an important role in the diet of those occupying richer, grassland/woodland ecotones at Kisese II (S. Kusimba 2003:47), while Mumba demonstrates exploitation of fish and snails (Mehlman 1989). Westward, open-air sites at Ishango on the shores of Lake Edward are now convincingly dated to the LGM (25–20 kya; A. Brooks and Smith 1987; A. Brooks *et al.* 1990). They have produced fragmentary human remains and what may be some of the oldest evidence for human mathematical abilities (see inset). Faunal remains document exploitation of a wide range of terrestrial and lacustrine resources, including large nilotic fish species no longer found there (Peters 1989). Many were probably caught using uniserial or biserial bone harpoons, but K. Stewart (1989) notes successive changes in procurement focus from Nile perch (*Lates* sp.) and lungfish (*Protopterus* sp.) to taxa catchable during spawning runs to an eventual emphasis on others, like *Bagrus* sp. and catfish, probably taken by line, nets, and weirs. Whether such resources suggest anything like the more delayed-returns economies that may have been practised along the lower Nile remains a topic for future fieldwork.

## THE ISHANGO BONE

Found by de Heinzelin in 1950 during his original excavations at Ishango, Democratic Republic of Congo, this 10 cm long bone baton is engraved on three sides with several series of parallel, vertical marks (Fig. 7.13). It comes from the same stratigraphic

**Figure 7.13.** The Ishango Bone. (Courtesy Ivan Jadin and copyright Belgian Royal Institute of Natural Sciences.)

horizon that produced biserial bone harpoons and thus probably dates to 25–20 kya (A. Brooks and Smith 1987). Analysis of the marks suggests they are ordered in nonrandom fashion and show some understanding of multiplication and division, as well as of odd, even, and prime numbers. This makes the object one of the oldest examples of mathematics known. More speculatively, it may also represent a six-month lunar calendar (Marshack 1991), perhaps created by a woman tracking her menstrual cycle (Zaslavasky 1999). Now kept in the Musée des Sciences Naturelles, Brussels, the Ishango baton has become the symbol of a programme run by the government of Belgium's Brussels-Capital Region to attract high school pupils toward science and scientific careers (Ishango 2006).

## Southernmost Africa

Southern Africa, the fourth area we consider, differs again. Earlier suggestions of a specialised focus on hunting large, mobile, gregarious game have been replaced by an acceptance that plants, particularly geophytes with edible underground storage organs (USO), probably underpinned Late Pleistocene subsistence strategies (H. J. Deacon 1972, 1995; Opperman and Heydenrych 1990). People may have been as patch-bound as their Holocene successors (H. J. Deacon 1993), though undoubtedly integrating specific resources in different ways. Exploiting underground foodplants was facilitated by the innovation of **bored stone** digging stick weights of the kind known also from GvJm62 (S. Kusimba 2001) and Kalemba (D. Phillipson 1976), though some early examples seem too small to have been used in this way (e.g., Border Cave; Beaumont 1978). The diversity of faunal remains found in southern African sites during MIS 2 also refutes the idea of a single Late Pleistocene economy. Although the loss of sites on the continental shelf makes it difficult to evaluate the role of marine resources, contact with the sea is indicated by seashell ornaments found at sites up to 200 km from the then coast. Long-distance connections are also demonstrated by the technological uniformity of Robberg lithic assemblages from Swaziland to the Atlantic and by bone beads with virtually identical decoration found at sites many hundreds of kilometres apart (Mitchell 2002a). The exchanges to which these connections testify no doubt facilitated information flows and helped structure relations among groups and individuals (N. Walker 1990). However, while the Blombos and Taforalt finds reported in Chapter 6 suggest that such capacities may already have been tens of millennia old by this point, the rarity of surviving art and jewellery, with the notable exception of the Apollo 11 fragments (Lewis-Williams 1984), may indicate that the creation and manipulation of identities and relations with the natural and supernatural worlds took different forms from those recorded ethnographically.

## THE BIG DRY AND THE BIG COLD: AFRICAN PERSPECTIVES ON MIS 4–2

The global impact of the Last Glaciation invites comparisons between Africa and the rest of the world. Coping with often rapid and severe environmental changes and the challenges of regional abandonment and recolonisation are themes of worldwide relevance at the LGM (Gamble and Soffer 1990) and before. Comparing the African modern human record with that produced by other hominins on other continents also sits high on archaeology's agenda during The Big Dry.

First, we note recent arguments in favour of the parallel innovation among Neanderthals as well as modern humans of many of the features considered to mark behavioural modernity (d'Errico 2003). There can be little doubt that Neanderthals were highly accomplished hunters, used composite, hafted tools, and, on occasion, made blades. Nor that they sometimes exploited *r*-selected resources, buried their dead, used ochre, and produced artefact traditions with relatively tight spatio-temporal boundaries (Mellars 1996; Shea 1998; Stiner *et al.* 1999; Conard 2005). Recent comparisons of Mode 3 assemblages from Sibudu, South Africa, and western Europe reveal no fundamental differences between the two (Villa *et al.* 2005), a conclusion that some analyses extend to comparisons of Upper and Middle Palaeolithic tools (Hiscock 1996). However, when contrasting the limited African dataset before 40 kya with the far more detailed and prolific Neanderthal record, what strikes us is that only in the former is there unambiguous evidence of art or jewellery (Blombos, Border Cave, Taforalt, and other sites) or long-distance movement of raw materials (such as East African obsidian). The two records are not "indistinguishable" before 50/40 kya (*pace* Klein 2000b:509). Furthermore, Neanderthal "innovation" of many of the features adduced by d'Errico (2003) shows an uncanny temporal coincidence with the expansion of Upper Palaeolithic, anatomically modern populations across Europe, suggesting that they represent a bow-wave phenomenon moving ahead of that expansion through contact between moderns and Neanderthals and among Neanderthals themselves (Mellars 2005). Africa (and its short-lived extension of anatomically modern human settlement into Israel in MIS 5) thus retains chronological primacy in the appearance of archaeological evidence for art, personal decoration, ritualised burial, formal bone tools, and (if long-distance movements of stone and shell are correctly interpreted this way) gift-exchange (Mellars 2006). This fits both the genetic evidence for modern human dispersal from Africa and the fossil evidence that the first moderns to enter Europe had a recent, tropical ancestry (Holliday 1997). Given this primacy and the genetic hypothesis of a single emigration of modern humans from Africa (Forster 2004), it can be plausibly argued that the capacity for symbolising that lies at the core of modern human societies must already have been present when that dispersal took place. That it should have developed independently and to the same degree in another hominin lineage seems far less likely. That it may have crystallised first within a single core area, by analogy with the Near East's 'Neolithic Revolution' (Bar-Yosef 2002), is possible, but the chronometric resolution and wealth of archaeological data to assess this hypothesis properly are lacking. As he himself indicates, the same difficulties currently constrain attempts to define (one might go so far as to say, compellingly substantiate) Mellars's (2006:9383) recent argument that it was the cumulative effect of a suite of new behaviours (personal ornament, large-scale exchange, multiple-component composite weapons, a broader subsistence base in the form of marine fish and perhaps fire-managed geophytic plants) that supported the population increase and expansion indicated by genetic data *c.* 80–60 kya.

Our second point, then, draws on the evidence examined in this chapter and its predecessor to reaffirm the core model presented by McBrearty and Brooks (2000) of an early, African origin for modern behaviour. This process seems, as they point out, to have been gradual and accretionary, rather than sudden and transformative, something reinforced by the diverse (and nonlinear) pathways we have traced between Mode 3 and Mode 5 technologies. This no doubt partly reflects the still patchy nature of our evidence, the rarity of African sites that combine close, accurate dating, favourable conditions for organic preservation, and spatially extensive, high-standard excavations. We are confident that some of the contradictions between the timing of evidence for Wadley's (2001a) various symbolic storage media will ease as new data become available, and emphasise once more the revolutionary consequences for our understanding brought about by just a single site, Blombos. The dismissal of a 50/40 kya cerebral Rubicon to which Blombos and Taforalt both contribute also gains from a wider perspective that encompasses the whole of The Big Dry. This brings us to two further issues, one the nature and extent of hunter-gatherer interaction networks; the other, global patterning in the elaboration of material culture under stadial conditions.

Archaeologists typically seek order and directionality in the material they excavate and find it troubling when such patterning seems lacking. However, bearing in mind the likelihood of recurrent population contractions and extinctions during The Big Dry and the barriers to movement that climatic change must, at times, have thrown up[12], then it is not unlikely that real difficulties existed for the generation-to-generation and group-to-group transmission of new ideas and technologies. Yellen (1998), for example, has argued that more closed social networks operated during part of the MSA, and Ambrose (2006:368) proposes that the enhanced use of non-local toolstone in East Africa during MIS 4–3 signals 'a fundamental change in human behaviour and social and territorial organisation' that enhanced longer-distance information flows and reduced risk in unpredictable environments. Independently of how society was structured, fluctuations in regional demography probably also constrained the diffusion of innovations. Dissonance rather than directionality may therefore be a real component of the archaeology of The Big Dry, the pace at which innovations spread only picking up as long-distance contacts strengthened during MIS 3 (cf. Ambrose 2002). More generally, Wobst (1990) indicates how, on a global scale, low-latitude populations living around the LGM lacked the complexity of art, jewellery, ritual, or technology that characterised many Upper Palaeolithic Eurasian societies. The reason cannot, of course, be that they were cognitively unable to undertake the behaviours that these items imply, but rather that they chose to deploy them only rarely, if at all. In this respect, then, Africa's record for the LGM and, by extension, the rest of MIS 3 and 2 (Henshilwood and Marean 2003), resembles more those of India or Sahul than it does that of Europe. For the most part, people in all three low-latitude areas found it situationally inappropriate to over-invest in high-cost responses or narrowly focused hunting strategies, although those in Africa were the first to employ microlithic technologies. Instead, more stable adaptations could maintain themselves successfully (Gamble and Soffer 1990). Crucial to that success was the innovativeness of their (African) ancestors earlier in The Big Dry.

## SUMMARY

This chapter has reviewed the evidence for palaeoenvironmental change in Africa during MIS 4–2 and discussed some of its likely impacts on the size and distribution of human populations. Whereas areas such as East Africa appear to have maintained fairly continuous, perhaps relatively large, populations, other regions – among them the Maghreb and perhaps the lower Nile – show greater evidence for discontinuous occupation. The climatic effects of the Mt. Toba eruption and the glacial maximum of MIS 4 may be at work here. Following on from the unequivocal evidence for art and personal jewellery found at Blombos late in MIS 5, the archaeology of this period displays only limited signs of such external symbolic storage. In this respect, it more resembles the record of India, Sahul, and other low-latitude regions than the Upper Palaeolithic of Europe, suggesting that in Africa, people were able to survive without needing to invest as heavily in art or ritual as their counterparts closer to the northern ice sheets. The period reviewed is nonetheless of great interest for its evidence of technological innovation. One example of this is the Howiesons Poort industry of southern Africa, but this appears to have been a fairly short-lived and, as yet, incompletely understood, phenomenon dating to around 70–55 kya. Instead of leading directly into the Mode 5 technologies generally known as the Later Stone Age, the backed artefacts of the Howiesons Poort are followed south of the Zambezi by other Mode 3 industries and only later by a shift to microlithic assemblages. Different pathways to microlithic technologies can be traced in Zambia, East Africa, and North Africa, suggesting that no single explanation can account for them. The role of population movements in their spread remains one among many unknowns, but genetic analyses strongly suggest that it was during the earlier part of the period covered by this chapter that anatomically modern humans spread out beyond Africa. Of the two possible routes, DNA evidence currently supports a southward dispersal across the Bab el-Mandab and around the northern Indian Ocean, but archaeological data hint at a second, later movement from the lower Nile into the Levant. DNA studies and similarities between some Levantine industries and assemblages from Haua Fteah, Libya, also raise the possibility of subsequent movement back into Africa. Within the continent, diverse patterns of adaptation are evident on either side of the LGM, with the most informative data coming from the Maghreb, the lower Nile, East Africa, and South Africa. All told, the archaeological record for MIS 4–2 reaffirms the view expressed by McBrearty and Brooks (2000) and others that recognisably modern forms of behaviour have a greater time-depth in Africa than elsewhere, but lead us to question whether change followed unilinear pathways.

CHAPTER 8

# TRANSITIONS: FROM THE PLEISTOCENE INTO THE HOLOCENE

The Big Dry, the theme of Chapter 7, came to a temporary end around 10 kya. Comparative studies of cultural change across the Pleistocene/Holocene boundary identify several themes (Straus *et al.* 1996). Set against major shifts in climate and ecology, these include the (re)colonisation of previously uninhabited landmasses, the migration of human populations, the innovation of novel technologies, and the development of new subsistence strategies. Africa was not unaffected. This chapter collates and assesses the evidence for these themes on a continental scale and in a generally south-to-north direction. The archaeological record is, of course, more than a simple pattern of cultural response to environmental stimulus, and better-refined chronological controls and more plentiful archaeological observations render the Pleistocene/Holocene transition more suitable than earlier periods for developing alternative perspectives that take account of the social histories and cultural heritages of human groups. This chapter thus documents a diversity of transitions – cultural and environmental – between 15 and 8 kya, while it also illustrates the difficulty of generalising to Africa the standard narrative of agricultural origins generated from the Near East.

## ENVIRONMENTAL BACKGROUND

At the Last Glacial Maximum (LGM) Africa's climate was cooler and generally more arid than today. Consequences included the expansion of deserts and grasslands and the fragmentation, or at least substantial modification, of the tropical rainforests. The transition from this situation to that characterising the Holocene was far from straightforward. 'Complex' and 'oscillatory' better describe both the global and the African signatures of climate change. Recall, too, that changes in the tropics and the southern hemisphere were not necessarily synchronous with those in the better-studied higher latitudes of the northern hemisphere and that climatic variance in tropical Africa was, in any case, less than that found at higher latitudes. Climatic events in the Antarctic, for example, preceded those in the Arctic by up to a millennium and were considerably smaller in magnitude (Sowers and Bender 1995). Differences in climatic and ecological responses relative to the changes noted in higher latitudes may therefore be expected.

### A Broadly Ameliorating Climate: Africa Until the Younger Dryas

Signs of climatic amelioration are strongly evident from 15–14 kya, when, for example, some East African pollen records show expansion of montane forest (D. Taylor 1992) and there was a sudden switch to moister conditions in North Africa (deMenocal *et al.* 2000). Higher-altitude areas may have registered change first because of their greater receptivity to increased temperatures, even before precipitation also started rising (Zonneveld *et al.* 1997). By 12.5 kya, further rapid increases in temperature and precipitation are widely apparent. In Central and West Africa, rainforest taxa are more abundant in pollen profiles, suggesting expansion and reconstitution outward from glacial refugia (Hamilton and Taylor 1991; Marret *et al.* 2006), and forest expansion at higher altitudes is also widely evident in East Africa (Kiage and Liu 2006; Ryner *et al.* 2006) and offshore pollen records for Angola (Dupont and Behling 2006). Lake levels and river activity also rose, and the formation of stone-lines and hill

wash deposits that took place under earlier semiarid grassland conditions ceased (Kadomura and Huri 1990). Records for the Niger and
other West African rivers exhibit a burst of activity about 12.7 kya,
perhaps because a climate similar to today's was still accompanied by relatively unvegetated environments, lacking modern water
absorption and evapotranspirative capacities (Thomas and Thorp
1996). Around the same time, the summer monsoon, which supplies
much of northern and eastern Africa with rain, underwent substantial strengthening (Zonneveld *et al.* 1997). Higher rainfall recharged
the previously almost dry Lake Victoria, making it overflow northward into the Nile (Paulissen 1989). Compounded by substantially
higher rainfall in Ethiopia's highlands, a brief period of extraordinar-
ily high floods ensued around 12.5 kya, Butzer's (1980) Wild Nile.
This was soon followed by the river aggressively downcutting into
older sediments to become a single, deeply incised channel rather
than the more wandering, braided situation of the LGM (Close
1996). At the continent's opposite end, in contrast, changes in rainfall seasonality and intensity were less coherent. However, there is
good evidence of high lake levels in the Namib and Kalahari until 11
kya (J. Deacon and Lancaster 1988) and of increased precipitation
across the Fynbos Biome from 14 kya (H. J. Deacon *et al.* 1984).

By 11 kya, temperatures in Central Africa were similar to those of
today (Hamilton 1988). Elsewhere, conditions were probably much
more unstable: marine cores near Somalia suggest large, rapid variations in monsoon strength that must have provoked oscillating wet
and arid conditions across much of the continent (Zonneveld *et al.*
1997). Pollen cores from Aliwal North, South Africa, support the
case for repeated climatic oscillations. A particularly cold (but here
moister) interval 12.2–11.65 kya (Coetzee 1967) is also evident in the
oxygen isotope record from Bushman Rock Shelter, several hundred kilometres to the northeast (Abell and Plug 2000). A much
more severe oscillation took hold ∼10.8 kya with the onset of the
Younger Dryas stadial, a colder, drier interval of near-global impact.
Lake levels fell and forest regressed in both East and West Africa
(Talbot and Johannessen 1992; D. Williamson *et al.* 1993; Kiage and
Liu 2006; Ryner *et al.* 2006), and a distinctly drier episode is also
registered in the Sahel (Salzmann *et al.* 2002). Farther south, some

Kalahari dunes may have reactivated (Stokes *et al.* 1997), while multiple datasets register the drop in temperature across South Africa (J. F. Thackeray 1990; D. M. Avery 2000; Cohen *et al.* 1992; Abell and Plug 2000). The summer monsoon's very pronounced weakening at this time suggests that conditions approximated to those of the LGM over much (Zonneveld *et al.* 1997), but not all, of Africa; offshore pollen records from near Angola and Namibia do not seem to have been affected, for example (Dupont and Behling 2006).

## After the Younger Dryas

The Younger Dryas persisted for some 600 radiocarbon years. Its abrupt ending, as observed in the North Atlantic region, corresponds to the boundary between the Pleistocene and the Holocene. From 10.2 kya, temperature and rainfall both increased substantially. Moist conditions prevailed across Africa from 30°N to 9°S because greater insolation coincided with a stronger summer monsoon (Street-Perrott and Perrott 1994). In what is now the Sahara, the desert virtually disappeared 9.5–8.2 kya, replaced by a mixture of semiarid or even more humid vegetations (Guo *et al.* 2000). At Oyo, in hyperarid northern Sudan, for example, pollen samples show that a deciduous wooded grassland emerged, similar to that now found 500 km farther south (Ritchie 1994). At slightly lower latitude, Lake Chad grew 50-fold to cover over 300,000 km$^2$ (Pachur and Altmann 1997). Despite a briefly more arid phase around 8 kya (Guo *et al.* 2000), significantly wetter conditions persisted in the Sahara for several millennia and now dry rivers such as the Tilemsi and the Wadi Howar (the Yellow Nile) flowed with water, their former courses partly detectable using satellite imaging (Gaussen and Gaussen 1988; Keding 1996; Jousse 2006). Palaeolake stands provide good evidence of greater rainfall (Maley 1977; D. Jolly *et al.* 1998), as do the bones of savanna- or aquatic-adapted animals, many of which, like crocodiles, elephants and hippopotamus, are represented in the region's rock art (Mori 1998).

In equatorial regions, forests reached at least their present extent before 9 kya (Hamilton 1988), but strong coastal upwelling along the Gulf of Guinea may have curtailed their expansion around the

Bénin Gap to judge from the predominantly montane grassland species found in early Holocene deposits from Lake Bosumtwi, though not from offshore pollen records (Street-Perrott and Perrott 1994; cf. Dupont and Weinelt 1996; Dupont *et al.* 2000). Elsewhere, however, there is good evidence for an early Holocene expansion of tropical rainforest into what are today savanna regions in both Central and East Africa (Schwartz 1991; Maitima 1993; Lézine and Vernaud-Grazzini 1994). East Africa's pollen and lake records also register maximum moisture levels from virtually the start of the Holocene (Van Campo *et al.* 1982; Street-Perrott and Perrott 1994; Kiage and Liu 2006). Such evidence extends into both Ethiopia (Gasse *et al.* 1980) and Somalia, where tufa deposits were laid down at this time (Brandt and Brook 1984). Among changes in regional geography, Kenya's Lakes Nakuru and Elmenteita merged and Lake Turkana overflowed into the White Nile. The much higher lake-stands required for these changes facilitated the development of freshwater habitats vastly more productive than those characterising today's saline lakes (Gasse *et al.* 1980).

The continent's southern and northern extremes did not benefit from the ending of the Younger Dryas to the same degree. Because of stronger upwelling of the Canaries Current and an intensified North Atlantic anticyclone (Street-Perrott and Perrott 1994), relatively drier conditions persisted in the Maghreb until ∼8.5 kya, and even later in the northwestern Sahara. Drier early Holocene conditions also prevailed in southern Africa, in this case because of the prevalence of a weaker summer monsoon and adjacent oceanic anticyclones in the southern hemisphere (Partridge *et al.* 1990). Despite this, warmer temperatures facilitated the expansion of bushveld at the expense of grassland in much of the region's summer rainfall zone, though maximum temperatures were perhaps only reached after 8 kya (J. Smith *et al.* 2002). Out-of-phase, as usual, with the rest of southern Africa, moister conditions continued until this time in the southwestern Cape (Cartwright and Parkington 1997). Here, and in adjacent parts of the Fynbos Biome, a key effect of increased warmth and rainfall was the replacement of previously open grasslands and their associated grazer-dominated large mammal faunas by more closed shrub, browser-dominated communities (see inset).

## IT ALSO HAPPENED HERE: LARGE MAMMAL EXTINCTIONS IN AFRICA

In many parts of the world, the late Quaternary saw a wave of large mammal extinctions, a phenomenon that has provoked intense debate over the relative responsibilities for it of human hunting, anthropogenic landscape change, and climate (Martin and Klein 1984; Barnosky *et al.* 2004). The phenomenon is best known in the Americas, Eurasia, and Australia, but Africa, too, witnessed extinctions across the Pleistocene/Holocene transition (Fig. 8.1), partly countering arguments that its fauna was 'protected' by a much longer experience of human hunters. The record is most explicit in southern Africa's Fynbos Biome, where four ungulate taxa became extinct by 9.5 kya: the southern springbok (*Antidorcas australis*), the Cape horse (*Equus capensis*), the giant hartebeest (*Megalotragus priscus*), and the giant buffalo (*Pelorovis antiquus*). Their disappearance has sometimes been linked to the expansion of closed shrub communities at the expense of open grasslands. However, the fact that southern Africa's much larger summer-rainfall region and at least one other species (Bond's springbok, *A. bondi*) were also affected implies that other factors were involved. Evidence for targeted human hunting or improved hunting technologies is nonetheless lacking, and a more plausible scenario envisages the hyperspecialised grazing animals that disappeared having been linked in an ecological succession such that decline or extinction of just one precipitated a domino effect among the others (Klein 1984a). Perhaps something similar was true in the Maghreb, where the giant buffalo's loss was accompanied by that of a gazelle (*Gazella atlantica*), a camel (*Camelus thomasi*), and a giant deer (*Megaloceros algericus*). However, without greater chronological precision, preferably including direct dating of relevant faunal specimens, it is impossible to speculate usefully about the processes involved here, or in the Sahara and East Africa from which *Pelorovis* also disappeared.[1] Though all this may be limited relative to what happened on other continents, it should not be ignored. The well-established genetic bottleneck that affected eastern and southern African cheetah populations 12–10 kya, and

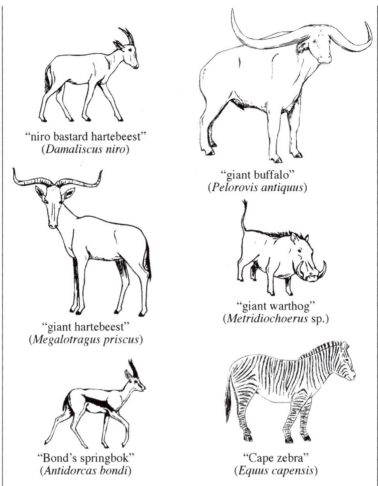

"niro bastard hartebeest"
(*Damaliscus niro*)

"giant buffalo"
(*Pelorovis antiquus*)

"giant hartebeest"
(*Megalotragus priscus*)

"giant warthog"
(*Metridiochoerus* sp.)

"Bond's springbok"
(*Antidorcas bondi*)

"Cape zebra"
(*Equus capensis*)

**Figure 8.1.** Some of the large mammals that became extinct in southern Africa at the Pleistocene/Holocene transition. (Courtesy and copyright Richard Klein.)

endangers their survival prospects today (Menotti-Raymond and O'Brien 1993), is a sign that other, still extant species came close to not surviving the Pleistocene/Holocene transition.

## *The Effects of Changing Sea Levels*

Finally, let us note that the continent's generally shallow continental shelf and smooth, unindented coastline meant that few parts of Africa experienced significant changes in coastline configuration across the Pleistocene/Holocene boundary. One exception is South Africa's southwest coast, where flooding of previously exposed areas of the Agulhas Shelf intensified the loss of grassland habitat just described. Other instances included the isolation of the islands of Bioko and Unguja,[2] the widening of the Bab el-Mandab, and the drowning of the Gulf of Gabès. However, even where effects were less dramatic, the loss of 10–20 km of coastal plain and the volatile effects of sea level change on coastal resources should not be ignored. Parkington's (1986, 1988) work at Elands Bay Cave, South Africa, provides a detailed study of the effects of sea level on coastlines, the availability of marine, littoral and estuarine resources, and the scheduling of human activities. The change from collecting limpets to gathering black mussels ∼10 kya was, for example, of more than local consequence given that it reflects the re-initiation of the cold water upwelling of the Benguela Current. At approximately the same time, a shift from black mussels (*Choromytilus meridionalis*) to thermophilous brown ones (*Perna perna*) along South Africa's Indian Ocean coast suggests strengthening of the warm-water Agulhas Current (Klein 1972). These current changes, which can be paralleled off Africa's other shores, underline once more the complexity of ecological change across the Pleistocene/Holocene transition.

## SOUTHERN AFRICA: SOCIAL AND ECOLOGICAL MODELS OF CULTURAL CHANGE

We start our survey in the south (Fig. 8.2). Southern Africa's relatively high density of archaeological research means that we have good data with which to work, but there are still regional and thematic lacunae. Many of the best observations, for example, come from coastal situations where changes in ecology and subsistence cannot be directly paralleled inland. Relative to areas farther north, southern Africa also displays a more complicated succession of industrial change, itself a longstanding research theme.

## The Stone Tool Industries

Chapter 7 showed the bladelet-emphasising Robberg Industry to be the best-defined stone tool industry in South Africa, Lesotho, and Swaziland during the millennia immediately following the LGM. More poorly defined assemblages occur farther north, of which those in Namibia are not microlithic. It was once thought that this situation persisted until all were replaced ~12 kya by a non-microlithic, but still informal, tradition frequently termed Oakhurst (Sampson 1974; Wadley 2000a). This remains generally true, but in southeastern southern Africa, Robberg assemblages continued to be made until 9.5 kya (Mitchell 2002a). Differences between Robberg and Oakhurst are striking: the latter has virtually no bladelet element, favours larger flakes, and generally prefers coarser rocks or those occurring in larger preforms. Large, D-shaped scrapers and naturally backed knives are among its few formal tools. Overall, the impression is one of considerable expediency, though formal tools do become more common after 9.5 kya, notably as end-retouched scrapers with adze-like lateral retouch, potentially used in a range of extractive and maintenance tasks (Bousman 1991). Several regional variants have been defined (Albany, Kuruman, Lockshoek, etc.), mostly reflecting differences in raw material usage. The Pomongwan of Zimbabwe's Matopo Hills is probably the best known of these beyond the Cape and includes rare backed tools, as well as bone matting needles (N. Walker 1995a). Farther northwest, bladelet technology persisted with little use of formal tools in Botswana's Kalahari (Robbins 1990; Robbins *et al.* 1996), but across the remainder of southern Africa, the Pomongwan's evident similarities with assemblages south of the Limpopo and others in central/southern Namibia (Wendt 1972) suggest that all these areas now formed part of the same broad interaction network. The complete absence of anything like the Oakhurst north of the Zambezi implies that this network did not reach into Zambia, where Mode 5 assemblages were made throughout the Pleistocene/Holocene transition.

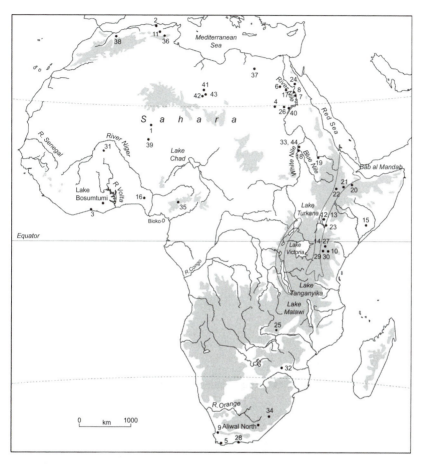

**Figure 8.2.** Location of archaeological sites mentioned in Chapter 8. 1. Adrar Bous 10; 2. Afalou; 3. Bingerville; 4. Bir Kiseiba; 5. Byneskranskop; 6. Dakhleh; 7. El-Hôsh; 8. El Kab; 9. Elands Bay Cave; 10. Enkapune ya Muto; 11. Faïd Souar 10; 12. FxJj12; 13. GaJj1; 14. Gamble's Cave; 15. Gogoshiis Qabe; 16. Iwo Eleru; 17. Kharga; 18. Khartoum; 19. Khasm el-Ghirba; 20. Laga Oda; 21. Lake Besaka; 22. Lake Ziway; 23. Lowasera; 24. Makhadma 2 and 4; 25. Mumbwa; 26. Nabta; 27. Nderit Drift; 28. Nelson Bay Cave; 29. Ntumot; 30. Ol Tepesi; 31. Ounjougou; 32. Pomongwe; 33. Sarabub; 34. Sehonghong; 35. Shum Laka; 36. Site 12; 37. Siwa; 38. Taforalt; 39. Tagalagal; 40. Tushka; 41. Uan Afuda; 42. Uan Muhuggiag; 43. Uan Tabu; 44. Umm Marrahi. Sites of special palaeoenvironmental significance are named.

The Oakhurst was followed by assemblages described as Holocene microlithic (J. Deacon 1984a) or Wilton (Sampson 1974; Wadley 2000b; Fig. 8.3). Increased use of finer-grained rocks, systematic production of backed microliths (segments, backed points, and bladelets) and small, standardised, often thumbnail-shaped, scrapers, and a greater variety of wood, bone, and shell items are characteristic. Size and raw material recall the Robberg, but the latter's bladelet emphasis is wholly lacking. Wilton assemblages show an interesting chronological pattern, being up to 4000 radiocarbon years older in Zimbabwe (Cooke 1979), Namibia (Wendt 1976), and possibly Angola (Beaumont and Vogel 1972) than in the Cape Fold Belt, where an east-to-west trend is also evident (H. J. Deacon 1976). Without obvious local antecedents in southern Africa, this chronology and the Wilton's emphasis on backed microliths and small scrapers suggest that Zambia's Nachikufan industry (discussed subsequently) might be a possible inspiration for it (J. Deacon 1984a).

## Changes in Food Resources

The availability of plants and animals must have altered considerably throughout the Pleistocene/Holocene transition, but at this time depth, only rare evidence of plant food consumption survives. At Bushman Rock Shelter, people shifted between collecting marula fruits and nuts and gathering *Hypoxis* corms depending on whether climate was warmer or cooler (Wadley 1987). Marula (*Sclerocarya birrea*) was also important in the Matopo Hills, where some levels at Pomongwe may have contained up to 400,000 fruits per cubic metre (N. Walker 1995a). In the Namib, not surprisingly, fruiting trees are absent, but people collected !nara melon seeds, a major staple of recent foragers (Sandelowsky 1977). Whether geophytes were collected in grassland and fynbos regions is uncertain, though it can probably be assumed that absence of evidence does not imply evidence of absence. Faunally, the period after 12 kya witnessed a shift toward a diet in which hunting, trapping, and snaring smaller antelope became more important, but much variability is apparent among sites and regions. Increased exploitation of more predictable

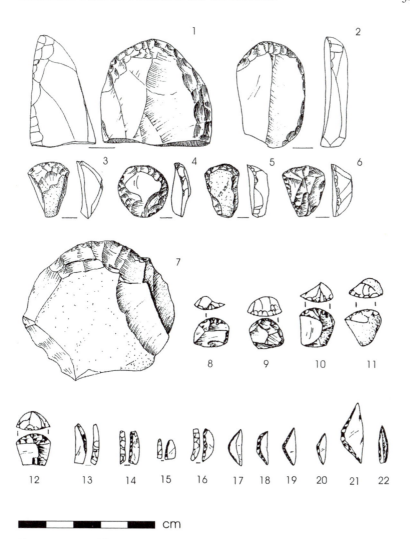

**Figure 8.3.** Oakhurst and Wilton artefacts from various sites in southern Africa. 1–7. Oakhurst scrapers; 8–12. Wilton scrapers; 13–22. Wilton backed microliths. (Redrawn after J. Deacon 1984a: Figs. 157 and 158 from Mitchell 2002: Figs 6.2 and 6.3; courtesy and copyright Janette Deacon.)

animals that occur in larger numbers, if smaller packages, was not restricted to antelope. Sites along the Cape coast register intensive shellfish, fish, rock lobster, and seabird exploitation from 11 kya, but this probably reflects coastline regression as much as genuinely new patterns of behaviour. Comparable intensification of terrestrial resources may be more novel: ostrich eggs and tortoises at Elands Bay Cave (Parkington 1990b) and Byneskranskop (Schweitzer and Wilson 1982); rock hyrax and rodents in the Matopo Hills (N. Walker 1995a).

*Explaining Change*

Archaeologists have tried to orchestrate these changes in environment, technology, and subsistence into a coherent score. Fieldwork in the southern Cape led H. J. Deacon (1976) to conceptualise changes in systemic terms, with Robberg, Albany (Oakhurst), and Wilton seen as homeostatic plateaux separated by brief episodes of more rapid organisational readjustment. Later, J. Deacon (1984b) recognised that the Robberg/Albany transition lagged some 2000 years behind the onset of climatic amelioration. Denying any direct functional link, she proposed that shifts in stone tool technology (such as scraper and flake size) indicate the 'social stress' experienced as people adapted to changing conditions. That most stone tools were probably never used directly to extract food (Isaac 1980) enhances her argument's attractiveness, but neither hypothesis fully takes on board the highly discontinuous nature of archaeological sequences, which augment differences between industries across time gaps (Sampson 1985b). Independently identifying stress also remains problematic.

A further issue concerns the scale of the phenomena being explained. Even if J. Deacon's (1984b) argument were valid in the Fynbos Biome, could it explain the disappearance of bladelet technologies where little faunal change is registered (e.g., Mpumalanga; Klein 1984b)? Furthermore, could the wholesale disappearance of bladelet production, after several thousand years, really proceed without technological or economic causes and/or consequences? Surely, in so far as artefacts *were* used for particular ends, those goals must have either changed, or been met in other ways by the makers of Oakhurst assemblages. Purely social factors, where left unspecified, are insufficient. More helpful is a model developed by

**Figure 8.4.** Elands Bay Cave, South Africa, looking outward to the Atlantic Ocean.

Ambrose and Lorenz (1990) that relates the organisation of technology, settlement-subsistence strategies, and exchange to ecology. They argue that increasingly plentiful resources led to a breakdown in earlier patterns of mobility and raw material exchange, promoting use of locally available rocks that then conditioned observed changes in flake and scraper size. The argument seems supported at some sites (e.g., Nelson Bay Cave), but fails to explain situations where, as in highland Lesotho, raw materials changed little, if at all (Mitchell 1995). However, by focusing on ecological variability, their model does offer a way of accommodating such issues of scale both spatially and temporally. The Robberg's persistence in southeastern southern Africa is one issue worth exploring afresh from this standpoint.

Different perspectives come from Parkington's (1986, 1988, 1992) work at Elands Bay Cave (Fig. 8.4). Eschewing cultural labels and emphasising the need to work with smaller, less lumped samples from tightly defined stratigraphic contexts, he views changes here as documenting the successive rescheduling of human activities in the face of environmental change. A key concept is that of place, defined as the opportunities that a location affords and thus the likelihood that people undertook particular activities there (Parkington 1980). Seen in this light, Elands Bay Cave shifted from being a short-term, expediently (male-only?) used hunting station ~13 kya to becoming a site exploited by larger groups on a much more regular, long-term basis: Increased artefact densities, including those associated ethnographically with women (grindstones, ostrich eggshell bead making), greatly enhanced use of gathered foods, and burials offer supporting evidence. Shifts in the site's position within the wider region as its catchment moved from riverine to estuarine to coastal must also have been critical (Poggenpoel 1987; Parkington 1988). Importantly, however, change was not unidirectional: after 9 kya, for example, visits became shorter once more (Parkington 1998). Successive, short-term adaptations to immediate problems that did not necessarily compromise long-term flexibility seem the rule. This emphasis on place warrants attention beyond South Africa's Atlantic coast, but it is worth stressing again the importance of researching differences in scale: place alone cannot suffice where the same technological or social processes can be identified across southern Africa, as with the 'explosion' in jewellery evident after 12 kya. Short-lived events, such as the overwhelming concentration of bone fish **gorges** at Elands Bay Cave in levels dating 9.6–8.6 kya (Parkington 1992), also need disentangling from more drawn out processes, such as the similar trajectories in ostrich eggshell bead size across the Pleistocene/Holocene transition shared between Elands Bay Cave and Sehonghong, 1200 km to the northeast.

Investigating demography and social relations must be an essential component of further work. Though site numbers are still few when compared with Europe, some patterning is evident, notably a rapid rise after 13 kya and a subsequent fall back, at least partly coinciding with the Younger Dryas, 12–10.5 kya. There is also good evidence for settlement of a wider range of environments as climate ameliorated. This is particularly so, for example, in South Africa's semiarid core (Sampson 1985a). As population densities rose, people presumably found it easier to locate marriage partners within more circumscribed areas, with consequences for gene flow rates within and between regional populations. Material culture may also have come to be used in different ways. Coherent patterning in toolstone use and access to ornaments of imported ostrich eggshell and marine/estuarine shell in southeastern southern Africa hints at the emergence of fairly self-contained zones of communication and exchange, though many forms of this may, of course, remain archaeologically invisible (Mitchell 1996). More generally, the much-increased evidence for bone points and ostrich eggshell beads after 12 kya may, for the first time, signal the presence of social relations founded on the reciprocal gift-exchange typical of many modern Bushman groups (Wadley 1987; J. Deacon 1990b). However, even leaving aside arguments about the universality of such *hxaro* practices and whether convincing evidence of actual movement of items exists in every case, Parkington (1998) disputes identifications of bone points as equivalent to ethnographically known arrowpoints before 9 kya; unequivocal evidence for the bow and arrow is even younger (H. J. Deacon 1976). If so, then, as Parkington points out, connections between hunting with bow and poisoned arrow and beliefs about sex, gender, and shamanism could not have existed in their ethnographically known form. This would imply major differences in social relations between Pleistocene and Holocene people; for example, in the organisation of hunting, where women perhaps played a more active role (Wadley 1998). Regrettably, burials and art are too scarce to inform this debate. However, it is worth considering if denser populations and greater evidence for exchange after 12 kya point to an enhanced use of social mechanisms for spreading risk. Moreover, as these became more entrenched, did they contribute to more expedient patterns of stone tool use, replacing the technological emphasis of reducing subsistence risks by combining reliable and maintainable design strategies characteristic of Robberg toolkits?

We have dwelt at length here on southern Africa, but this is only partly because of the quality of its data, for detailed observations also exist in the Maghreb, the Sahara, and along the Nile. Rather, it is because the issues that those data raise and the ways in which they have been explored identify many of the themes common to the

Pleistocene/Holocene transition elsewhere in Africa. We return to them at a more general level after reviewing developments elsewhere.

## THE PLEISTOCENE/HOLOCENE BOUNDARY IN CENTRAL AND EASTERN AFRICA

### Central and South-Central Africa

Greater technological continuity is evident farther north. In north-eastern Angola, associated with radiocarbon dates of 15–11 kya, and in much of the Congo Basin, it takes the form of the Tshitolian industry. This differs from the preceding Lupembo-Tshitolian in its artefacts' smaller size, changes in core-reduction, and a prolifera-tion of backed microliths, especially *petits tranchets* (D. Phillipson 1982). Poor preservation conditions mean that virtually nothing is known about subsistence, but in the Ituri region, accelerator mass spectrometer dating confirms exploitation of the oil-rich nuts of *Canarium schweinfurthii* ∼10 kya, a time when phytolith data iden-tify an abrupt increase in arboreal species compared with grasses (Mercader 2003b; Mercader *et al.* 2000a). Associated lithic assem-blages are not Tshitolian, but rather of the predominantly quartz, informal kind described more widely for Central Africa from MIS 3–2 (Cornelissen 2002). These data, and the persistence of the same lithic tradition into the late Holocene, suggest that humans stayed put, even as the forest became more closed (see inset). Claims that hunter-gatherers could only survive in this tropical rainfor-est environment by engaging in exchange with nearby (and at this period patently nonexisting!) farmers are therefore flawed (Bahuchet *et al.* 1991; Mercader 2003b *pace* Bailey and Headland 1991). Such claims are also refutable from Shum Laka, Cameroon. Here, too, an expedient, largely quartz microlithic industry with very few for-mally retouched tools continued into the early Holocene at a time (9–8 kya) when botanical remains indicate a mixed environment of forest and wooded savanna species and meat was principally obtained from giant forest hog (*Hylochoerus meinertzhageni*) and Cape buffalo (Lavachery 2001). The absence of dramatic cultural or ecological changes across the Pleistocene/Holocene transition may reflect the

**Figure 8.5.** Shum Laka, Cameroon: excavations in progress. (Courtesy and copyright Els Cornelissen.)

site's high elevation and favourable position, *vis-à-vis* orographic rainfall (Cornelissen 2003; Fig. 8.5).

In south-central Africa, where scarce pollen and faunal evidence suggests only limited environmental change (Klein 1984b; Street-Perrott and Perrott 1994), Zambia provides the largest number of observations. Nachikufan I Mode 5 assemblages with relatively high frequencies of scrapers and backed microliths (especially flakes) first appeared around the LGM in both the north and east of the country (D. Phillipson 1976). Farther west in the Lunsemfwa Basin, Musonda's (1984) Group I industry has a broadly similar age, but with backed bladelets the dominant formal tool type, as they are at Mumbwa 12–9 kya (Barham 2000). Although true geometric microliths are rare in all these assemblages, it seems likely that Zambia's subsequent, more localised stone tool industries evolved from this widely distributed tradition. The limited subsistence evidence indicates an emphasis on small to medium-sized, territorial antelope and suids that were often probably snared or trapped (S. Miller 1969a; D. Phillipson 1976; Gutin and Musonda 1985).

## THE GENES, SPEECH, AND ORIGINS OF AFRICA'S TROPICAL FORAGERS

The tropical forest foragers discussed here are often referred to as Pygmies because of their short stature, itself an adaptation to forest life (Cavalli-Sforza 1986). Apart from its potentially pejorative overtones, the term obscures the diversity present among such groups (Hewlett 1996) and we therefore avoid using it. Novel contributions to understanding the antiquity and origins of these peoples come from recent genetic research. Salas *et al.* (2002), for example, note that the L1a2 mtDNA lineage occurs in high proportions among the Mbuti of northeastern Democratic Republic of Congo and the Aka of the southern Central African Republic/northern Republic of Congo. This lineage may have spread through the equatorial rainforests during the early Holocene, perhaps linked to one or more episodes in the redistribution of human populations as the forests expanded once more after the LGM. More recently, Destro-Bisol *et al.* (2004) have used previously obtained genetic evidence and studies of the DNA of the Mbenzele of the Central African Republic to argue that the ancestors of groups living north and west of the Congo/Oubangui Rivers diverged from those of the eastern Congo Basin ≥18 kya. Although dating is necessarily imprecise, further support for the antiquity of rainforest foraging populations comes from linguistic studies of the Aka and the Baka, who live farther west in southern Cameroon, northern Congo, and northern Gabon. The two peoples share common vocabulary elements, especially in words dealing with gathering and hunting in the forest, despite otherwise speaking Niger-Congo languages of quite different affiliation. Such terms presumably represent traces of a now lost, but once shared, '*Baakaa*' language spoken before either acquired their present languages (Bahuchet 1989). This, in turn, supports the case for their ancestors having lived within the equatorial forests before the first agricultural settlement of the region (Bahuchet *et al.* 1991; cf. Blench 1999a:43 for an alternative view that has, however, won little support).

## East Africa

Moving north into East Africa, Enkapune ya Muto, a key sequence for the evolution of Mode 5 technologies, has a long occupational hiatus across the Pleistocene/Holocene boundary. Information must thus be pieced together from elsewhere. Dating to 14–13 kya in Kenya's Central Rift at Nderit Drift and Ol Tepesi, the obsidian-based Kiteko industry emphasises bladelets and bladelet cores and has virtually no backed microliths, although burins are common (Merrick 1975; Bower *et al.* 1977). A slightly older assemblage comes from Ntumot in the southern Rift Valley where, 60–90 km from the nearest obsidian sources, Middle Stone Age chert and obsidian arte-facts were recycled as cores for bladelet production (Ambrose 2002). At Nderit Drift and sites like Gamble's Cave near Lake Nakuru, a very different industry followed 12.0–10.5 kya. This is the Eburran, a Mode 4 industry making almost exclusive use of locally plenti-ful obsidian to produce large backed blades, crescents, scrapers, and other tools (L. Leakey 1931; Ambrose *et al.* 1980). The parallels between the Nakuru/Naivasha Basins and southern Africa warrant investigation, not only in the similarities between the Robberg and the Kiteko, but also in the fact that both industries were succeeded by others focused on producing much larger blanks (Ambrose 2002). Little is known about these early phases (1–2) of the Eburran, and an occupational hiatus between 10.5 and 8.5 kya means that we defer further discussion of it to Chapter 9. Farther west, south, and east – and no doubt reflecting the influence on technology of a quite different raw material base – relatively informal quartz microlithic assemblages were the rule in Uganda (Nelson and Posnansky 1970), central and northern Tanzania (Inskeep 1962; Mehlman 1977), and central Kenya (S. Kusimba 2001).[3]

## The Horn of Africa and Its Borderlands

In Ethiopia and Somalia, Mode 4 industries were already being made late in MIS 3. This largely obsidian 'Ethiopian Blade Tool Tradi-tion' included microliths, scrapers, and burins, as well as long, utilised blades (Brandt 1986). Following the LGM, it may be present at Laga Oda and can be paralleled by Mode 4 assemblages using fine-grained sandstone and mudstone from 10,000-year-old deposits at rockshelters outside the historic city of Aksum. Regrettably, none of these sites has yielded much useful subsistence evidence (D. Phillipson 1977a; Finneran 2000a, 2000b). This is not so of four ephemerally occupied sites reported by Marks (1987) near Khasm el-Ghirba on Sudan's Upper Atbara River. Here, a distinctive Mode 4 technology was made using chert pebbles, accompanied by bipolar flaking of quartz and agate, ~10.2 kya (Fig. 8.6). Characteristic, too, are large, lunate-shaped 'orange wedges', backed and truncated blades, and tiny scrapers. Although there is no direct sign of plant exploitation and grindstones are virtually absent, people hunted a range of large mammals typical of arid steppe, as well as making some use of hippopotamus, molluscs, and catfish[4]. Somewhat earlier than all these Mode 4 occurences, scraper-dominated microlithic assemblages come from terminal Pleistocene contexts at Ethiopia's Lake Ziway and Lake Besaka. In the latter area, they were followed ~11–7 kya by the aceramic phase of the Besaka industry, which is characterised by further reductions in tool size and significantly more backed microliths, especially segments (Brandt 1986). Sites there were now significantly thicker and more artefact-rich than before, perhaps reflecting opportunities under wetter early Holocene conditions for a more sedentary lifestyle partly geared to fish and other aquatic resources, although many land mammals were also hunted (Brandt 1986).

Southern Somalia provides a more detailed perspective. At Gogoshiis Qabe and other sites in the Buur Heybe inselberg, people used exotic cherts to produce highly distinctive pressure-flaked unifacial and bifacial points at the end of the Pleistocene. This microlithic Eibian industry was followed after 9.1 kya by another microlithic industry, the Baardale, which lacks the Eibian's distinctive points (Brandt 1986, 1988).[5] Small, sedentary antelope dominate its fauna, raw materials are almost wholly local in origin, and grindstones hint at more intensive plant consumption, features suggesting a more sedentary lifestyle than was previously possible. Further signalling this, the site yielded the remains of 14 individuals, 11 of them as almost complete burials, and all clearly associated with the Baardale industry's preceramic phase, which terminated ~8 kya

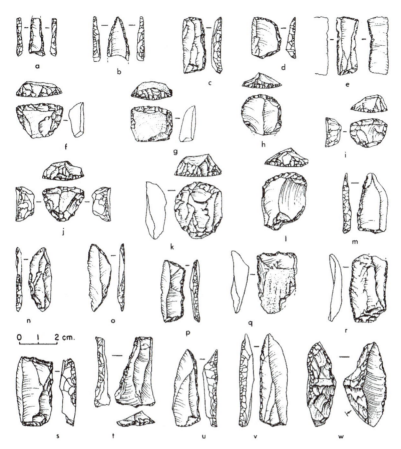

**Figure 8.6.** Artefacts from KG74, Khasm el-Ghirba, Sudan. a, b. double backed blades; c-e, p, s, t. backed trapezes; f-l. scrapers; m, u, v. backed points; n, o. lunates; q. denticulated flake; r. retouched flake; w. 'orange wedge'. (After Marks 1987: Fig. 3.)

(Brandt 1988). Four had been placed below cairns, another on a large granite slab accompanied by more than 30 lesser kudu (*Tragelaphus imberbis*) horns, most of them paired and still attached to their frontals. Coming from at least 16 adult males, this represents a substantial investment of time and effort, possibly linked to the individual's skill or status as a hunter. Other observable differences, however, relate to age or gender; there is no sign that other social dimensions received recognition. The significance of these burials is rather their demonstration that Gogoshiis Qabe was used as a formal disposal area for the dead, perhaps motivated by a desire to assert claims to land ownership by reference to ancestors (cf. Chapman 1981), but certainly consistent with the other evidence from the site for a more sedentary lifestyle under resource-richer early Holocene conditions.

Anthropological studies suggest that some of the closest affinities of the Gogoshiis Qabe individuals are with mid-Holocene burials from Lake Turkana in northern Kenya. Then and in the early Holocene, conditions there were much wetter than today and numerous sites are known. The oldest may be lithic scatters without bone points or pottery that occur in river drainages and near permanent water sources east of the lake (Barthelme 1985). By 9 kya, more substantial sites are associated with fossil beachlines 75–80 m higher than the current lakeshore.[6] Examples include Lowasera (D. Phillipson 1977b) to the west of the lake and GaJj11 and FxJj12 to its northeast (Barthelme 1977, 1985). Not surprisingly given their locations, fish bones are common finds. K. Stewart (1989) shows that only the Nile perch (*Lates* spp.) and the bigger cichlid species were consistently exploited, primarily by spearing and harpooning; *Clarias* may have been caught by hand or using the same techniques, but always on a minor scale. Barbed bone points, mostly uniserial, but sometimes biserial (exceptionally triserial), are plentiful (Fig. 8.7). As well as fishing, such points were probably used to hunt crocodiles, hippopotami, and terrestrial mammals. Differences in age, season of occupation, and lake alkalinity may be responsible for the intersite variability observed in the emphasis placed on these resources and fish (Barthelme 1985).

Most of the stone artefacts from these Lake Turkana sites were made on locally available lavas, crypto-crystalline silicas, and quartz, the finer rocks providing a backed microlith component of mostly segments and backed flakes, the lavas being used in larger, generally cruder artefacts that include rare scrapers and picks but mostly comprise flakes and cores. Obsidian is rare, obtained at Lowasera and GaJj1 from sources respectively 160 and 60 km distant (Merrick and Brown 1984). Such data provide some idea of the distances over which actual individuals moved, or at least interacted. However, they are dwarfed by the much greater area north of the

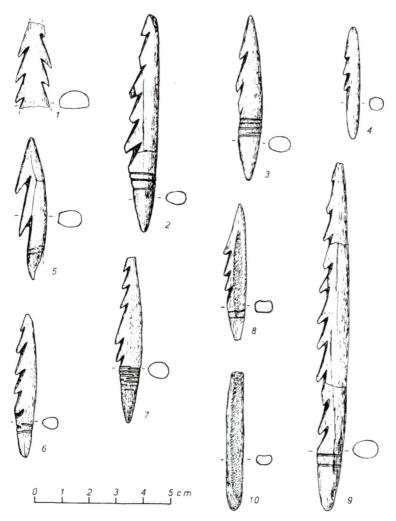

**Figure 8.7.** Barbed bone harpoon heads and an unbarbed bone point, Lowasera, Lake Turkana, Kenya. (After D. Phillipson 1977b; Fig. 16; courtesy and copyright David Phillipson and British Institute in Eastern Africa.)

Equator over which people exploited aquatic resources in the early Holocene, often using bone points and harpoons that appear similar to those found at Lake Turkana. Although this evidence can no longer be condensed under a single 'Aqualithic' rubric (MacDonald 1998 *pace* Sutton 1974), disentangling and understanding the social and economic processes behind this phenomenon remain concerns that unite the archaeologies of East Africa with those of the two regions to which we now turn, the Nile Valley and the Sahara.

## THE WILD NILE AND ITS AFTERMATH: TRANSITIONS IN EGYPT AND SUDAN

### *The Egyptian and Nubian Nile Valley*

At the LGM, even more than today, the lower Nile was an oasis of life within the deserts to either side. Succeeding the industries described in Chapter 7, new stone tool assemblages are recognised in southern Egypt and Lower Nubia 13.5–12.0 kya; as before, none is known upstream of the Second Cataract or downstream of Qena, perhaps because they lie buried by later silts (Close 1996). Interestingly, however, this period does provide evidence of contact between the Nile Valley and the Levant because North African-derived forms of backed microlith production occur in the Mushabian industry of Sinai *c.* 14–12 kya, which probably contributed to the subsequent emergence of the Natufian culture out of which grew some of the earliest Middle Eastern farming communities (Bar-Yosef 1987). The Afian and Qadan were both microlithic, though the latter emphasised flakes rather than bladelets, occasionally used the Levallois technique, and exhibits considerable (activity-related?) intersite variability (Vermeersch 1992). A third industry, the Isnan, employed a macrolithic flake technology. The fourth, the Sebilian, is more puzzling; a centripetal flaking technique sometimes termed Levallois, much more scattered distribution, and different economic focus (no fish or grindstones) may require its reattribution to the Middle Palaeolithic (Paulissen and Vermeersch 1987). However, Schild and Wendorf (2002) argue that its stratigraphic position points instead to a late Pleistocene age, with its technology and typology suggesting a derivation from the Tshitolian of equatorial Africa.

Except for the Sebilian, the economic basis was probably much the same as described in Chapter 7 – fish, game, and starchy wetland vegetables.[7] Excavations at Makhadma 4, an Afian site near Qena, document a primary concentration on *Tilapia*, complemented by

*Clarias*, a combination that suggests a specialist fishing operation late in the post-flood season (Vermeersch *et al.* 1989). Pits with large amounts of charcoal imply fish were preserved by smoking. Their small size suggests that thrust baskets, nets, and scoop baskets were used to catch them in shallow basins, and rock engravings at El-Hôsh near Idfu of possibly early/mid-Holocene age may record the use of such traps (Huyge *et al.* 2001). Other sites, like the repeatedly reused campsite at Makhadma 2 (Vermeersch *et al.* 2000), emphasised the capture of *Clarias*, perhaps in annual spawning runs (Close 1996).

Things changed with a vengeance with the onset of the Wild Nile around 12.5 kya. Its impact was disastrous (though see Schild and Wendorf 2002:455), greatly reducing the size of wetlands and the availability of the foodplants and fish that they hosted, though people may have tried to increase their resource base by controlled burning (Wendorf *et al.* 1970; J. D. Clark 1971). With the desert to either side completely dry, people had, literally, no way out, with increased conflict a likely result, as seen at the famous Jebel Sahaba cemetery discussed toward the end of Chapter 7. As people competed over dwindling resources, population shrank. From 11.5 to 10 kya, north of Khartoum, there is only a single Isnan site in Upper Egypt and a small cluster of artefact scatters near the Second Cataract (Close 1996; Vermeersch 2002). These Arkinian sites have very few grindstones and their faunas are dominated instead by aurochs and hartebeest, suggesting a radical reorientation of the economy (Schild *et al.* 1968) that may also have extended to trying to catch much larger deep-water fish (Wetterstrom 1993). As Close (1996:50) succinctly remarks, 'the Nilotic adaptations of the Late Palaeolithic were evidently no longer practised'. This hiatus was sustained far into the ninth millennium bp.[8] Thereafter, the centuries either side of 8 kya witnessed fishing and hunting (on a shortlived, seasonal basis?) near El-Kab and more intensively in the Fayum (the Qarunian industry, for which some evidence for foodplants also exists). Save, however, for poorly understood, pottery-equipped Tarifian assemblages in Upper Egypt that may date ~6.3 kya, there is no further evidence of occupation along the lower Nile until the advent of farming (Wetterstrom 1993).

*The Middle Nile*

The exceptions to this story of unmitigated disaster (Close 1996:54) lie upstream and in the Western Desert. Along the White Nile, the broader floodplain should have created attractive swamps and lakes (D. Edwards 2004), while along the Blue Nile more permanent riverine settlements were probably linked to hunting-oriented sites away from the river (Fernández 2003). Near their confluence at Khartoum, where there is no evidence of any immediately prior occupation, sites of the so-called Khartoum Mesolithic appear from ~9 kya, presumably taking advantage of the much more humid (±500 mm pa) early Holocene climate. They show extensive use of aquatic resources (especially fish), hunting of a wide range of medium and large mammals, and collection of a very different range of (typically savanna,) foodplants processed with numerous grindstones (Haaland 1993; Magid and Caneva 1998). The technology found at these sites was, however, very different from that of the late Pleistocene river-focused groups of the lower Nile, or the sites near Khasm el-Ghirba excavated by Marks (1987), in that it included barbed bone points alongside stone netsinkers, with blade production almost unknown and lunates the dominant retouched form. Faunal assemblages show that deepwater fish such as Nile perch, as well as shallow water species like *Clarias*, were now exploited (Elamin and Mohammed-Ali 2004). Pottery, too, is present, indicating new ways of acquiring and preparing food. Leaving their more detailed discussion until the next section, we merely note here the historical significance of the Khartoum Mesolithic in providing some of the first evidence for the association of bone points, ceramics, and aquatic resources that has variously been termed Aqualithic (Sutton 1974) or Neolithic of Sudanese Tradition (Camps 1967).

## THE DESERT BLOOMS: RECOLONISING THE SAHARA

Reoccupation of the Sahara had necessarily to await a return of rains sufficient to support the water, plants, and animals on which people could reliably depend. This process was clearly underway by 9.5 kya, although it may have begun earlier in places. As well as raising questions about how recolonisation was achieved and sustained,

Saharan archaeology for this period includes some of the world's oldest pottery and may relate to some of the region's prolific rock art. Detailed work in Libya's Tadrart Acacus region and Egypt's Western Desert, in particular, provides exceptionally rich datasets for exploring how people dealt with the opportunities and challenges of the Pleistocene/Holocene boundary, including intriguing evidence for the manipulation of wild animal resources.

## Resettling the Desert

Uranium/thorium-dated travertine deposits from the Acacus suggest that rainfall began increasing from its virtual absence at the LGM as early as 14 kya (Cremaschi and di Lernia 1999). If so, the Younger Dryas then brought greater aridity to both the Sahara and the Sahel (Gasse *et al.* 1990) before generally moister conditions returned after 10 kya. An important question is whether people resettled the Sahara before the end of the Pleistocene. Confirmation in the form of directly dated occurrences is still difficult to identify, but several sites with poorer chronological controls are known in Mali, Niger, Mauritania, and Algeria (MacDonald 1998). Typified by shouldered and/or tanged points made on blades (Ounan points), the blade-based Ounanian is the best described of these industries. Ceramics are lacking, except in the stratigraphically mixed situation of Adrar Bous 10 (Roset 1987), and are also absent from early Holocene backed bladelet-rich Mellalian assemblages in southern Algeria (Aumassip 1987). Tunisia's Horizon Collignon and the Iberomaurusian, both met with in Chapter 7, could provide a typological ancestry for these assemblages, matching physical anthropological evidence discussed subsequently (see inset: What bones can tell).

With these few possible exceptions, human resettlement of the Sahara was an entirely early Holocene affair, beginning ∼9.5 kya in Egypt's Western Desert where Mode 5 Epipalaeolithic assemblages are blade- and bladelet-based, with many backed artefacts (Gehlen *et al.* 2002; Milliken 2003). Nabta Playa and Bir Kiseiba are among the best-known localities, but the other major oases have also produced evidence of occupation. People had penetrated much closer to the heart of the Sahara even before this to judge from a stone windbreak constructed within the Uan Afuda shelter in the Acacus

~9.7 kya (di Lernia 1999). The western parts of the Sahara, how-ever, remained unoccupied, or at least were inhabited at archaeolog-ically invisible levels: Sites predating 7–6.5 kya are absent along the Atlantic coast and in northern Mali (Petit-Maire 1979; McIntosh and McIntosh 1986). Skeletal evidence indicates a North African source for the people concerned (Dutour 1989), but this was proba-bly only one of the directions from which resettlement came. With still little firm evidence for movement north from West Africa, an obvious additional source is the Nile Valley. Close (1996) notes sim-ilarities between artefacts at sites in the Western Desert and those from Arkinian occurrences near the Second Cataract, but the dearth of early Holocene settlement evidence in Egypt creates a difficulty here. If genuine, it could imply more of a movement north and west from the Sudanese Nile, following the northward movement of the monsoon (see inset).

---

AFRICA'S FIRST BOAT

Boats probably played an important part in early Holocene set-tlement of what is now the Sahara and Sahel, whether to travel along currently dead waterways, or to exploit the resources of lakes, swamps, and rivers. Jacquet (2000) notes an unmistakable representation of a boat being paddled in Chad's Ennedi massif, but even more spectacular evidence comes in the form of the wooden dugout canoe found at Dufuna, northeastern Nigeria (Fig. 8.8). Directly dated by radiocarbon to the mid-eighth mil-lennium bp, it is the oldest known boat in Africa and among the oldest anywhere in the world. It is almost intact, except for a few fragments at the top of its sides, over eight metres long, and has a pointed stern and prow. Made from the wood of *Khaya* sp. (mahogany), it was probably used for fishing on the tributaries of Lake Mega-Chad, the shoreline of which would have been only 50 km away. Though no other archaeological materials were directly associated with the boat, a rather later quartz assemblage with rocker-stamp–decorated pottery from the same locality con-firms the previously unsuspected early/mid-Holocene presence of people in the southwestern Chad Basin (Breunig *et al.* 1996).

**Figure 8.8.** The Dufuna boat, Nigeria. (Courtesy and copyright Peter Breunig.)

## The Tadrart Acacus

Two regions provide the most detailed evidence of these early Saharan/Sahelian communities. In the Tadrart Acacus, Early Acacus occupation from 9.8 kya took the form of multi-activity base camps within the Acacus range and of numerous small sites (hunting stations and raw material procurement sites) close to probable lakes in the surrounding lowlands (Barich 1987; Cremaschi and di Lernia 1999; di Lernia 1996, 1999; Garcea 2001, 2004). Stone tools consisted mostly of backed artefacts of various kinds made almost exclusively on bladelet blanks and included non-local raw materials (Cremaschi and di Lernia 1999). Hunting focused almost entirely on Barbary sheep (Corridi 1998), gathering on a narrow range of species that excluded cereals (Castelletti *et al.* 1999). After 8.9 kya, a different subsistence-settlement system is evident, probably reflecting drier conditions than before. Termed Late Acacus, sites are located mostly within the Acacus range itself. Stone artefacts are now largely made of local siliceous sandstone, with a reduced blade/bladelet component and shifts in backed microlith preference. This shift in raw material usage and the toolkit's more macrolithic character, along with more plentiful grindstones, more complex hearths and houses,

**Figure 8.9.** Round Head style paintings, Tadrart Acacus, Libya. (Courtesy and copyright Elena Garcea.)

and the introduction of pottery all suggest a more sedentary lifestyle (Cremaschi and di Lernia 1998).[9] Ceramics themselves are large, thick-walled, and often fibre-tempered, decorated using the rocker technique, mostly in packed zigzag motifs. Bone tools and basketry are also evident.[10] Barbary sheep are still dominant, but a much wider range of mammals (including small game such as hares and hyrax) was also taken (Cremaschi and di Lernia 1999; Garcea 2004). The diet was further broadened to include a wide range of grass seeds (Barich 1992), including *Pennisetum*, the ancestor of domesticated pearl millet (Wasylikowa 1993; Mercuri 2001). This pattern persisted until significantly more arid conditions precipitated a hiatus in regional occupation 8.0–7.4 kya that was ended by the introduction of a pastoralist lifestyle (Cremaschi and di Lernia 1999; Garcea 2004).

The Acacus is home to one of the Sahara's greatest concentrations of rock art. Others include the Tassili area of Algeria (Lhote 1959) and Jebel Uweinat at the meeting-place of Sudan, Libya, and Egypt (Zboray 2003). How much dates to the period reviewed here is hotly debated and attempts at direct dating have thus far been few in the extreme (Mori *et al.* 2006). Two styles are at issue: Round Head (Fig. 8.9) paintings from Tassili and the Acacus, which mostly show semi-naturalistic humans, often with globular heads, Barbary

**Figure 8.10.** Bubaline engravings, Messak Plateau, Libya. (Courtesy and copyright Elena Garcea.)

sheep, and roan antelope; and bubaline engravings and paintings that represent wild game (including the now-extinct giant buffalo *Pelorovis* (*Bubalus*) *antiquus*), cattle, and people in a highly realistic manner (Figs. 8.9, 8.10). Muzzolini (1993) argues that neither predates 6 kya

**Figure 8.11.** Masara Phase Type C stone hut circle, Dakhleh, Egypt. (Courtesy and copyright Mary McDonald and Dr P. Sheldrick).

and that all were therefore executed by people who kept domestic livestock. His identification of wild and domestic animals within the same styles is a major element of this synthesis. Mori (1998), on the other hand, places the bubaline style's onset as early as 12 kya. Yet other workers canvas an early Holocene date for both styles (e.g., Lutz and Lutz 1995), even when not differentiating between them (Le Quellec 1998); superpositioning of paintings of cattle on Round Head art at Uan Tabu supports a sequential relationship and, possibly, a hunter-gatherer origin (Garcea 2004). The matter cannot readily be resolved without direct dates and interpretation is also difficult without relevant ethnographic data. It is nevertheless interesting to note that women are more commonly represented in Round Head art and that they are depicted in roles different from men. Assuming that these paintings are (at least partly) later in age than the bubaline style, Barich (1998), among others (di Lernia 1996; Mori 1998), suggests that this indicates an enhanced status for women, consistent with an increased role for gathered foods in Late Acacus times.

### The Western Desert

Egypt's Western Desert is the second area to examine. Here, too, despite a probably earlier initial onset of higher rainfall, archaeologically visible populations are not evident much before 9.5 kya. Such populations were surely nomadic, and in some areas, toolstone choices document connections over as much as 400 km (Gehlen *et al.* 2002:93). More substantial campsites are known in the larger oases and playa basins. At Dakhleh, for example, people may have pursued a collector strategy (*sensu* Binford 1980). Type C Masara-phase sites in well-watered locations date to 8.9–8.3 kya and have stone hut circles, possible storage bins, and abundant grinding equipment, as well as a diverse toolkit, making substantial use of immediately local raw materials (Fig. 8.11). However, settlement is unlikely to have been permanent, with people probably dispersing into the surrounding desert in the wet season. Occupying different parts of the landscape and representing shorter-term occupations, some smaller sites emphasise burins made on local materials, others, microlith production from a formal blade core technology and a wider range of materials, some of them from up to 100 km away (McDonald 1991, 2003). Subsequently, microlithic technology was replaced by a macrolithic toolkit still within a context of partial sedentism (McDonald 2007). Sites at Kharga and Siwa show a similar close association with water resources and subsistence strategies making intensive use of hare, gazelle, and wild grains (Close 1980). Farther south at Nabta, direct evidence of plant exploitation includes *Zizyphus* fruits, legumes and grasses; sorghum, in particular, was intensively collected (Wasylikowa *et al.* 1997). The many grindstones found there and at other Saharan sites, even some of the most ephemeral, confirm the importance of wild grasses, just as in the subsistence economies of recent desert-dwelling nomads (Harlan 1982).

### Africa's First Pottery

Next to several regions of China and northeast Asia (Sadr and Sampson 2006:247), the Sahara is home to the oldest pottery in the world (Close 1995; Fig. 8.12), and provides evidence for the great antiquity within Africa of a porridge-rather than Middle Eastern-derived bread-based cuisine (Haaland 2006). The oldest examples from Tagalagal rockshelter in Aïr and Adrar Bous 10 exhibit a variety of vessel shapes and decoration and date ~9.5 kya. Examples are known from Bir Kiseiba in Egypt's Western Desert by 9.1 kya, and ~8.8 kya at Nabta Playa and in the Acacus (Garcea 2004). Those from sites in central Sudan like Sararub (Khabir 1987) and Umm Marrahi (Elamin and Mohammed-Ali 2004) are of comparable age, and include Arkell's (1949) 'Khartoum Mesolithic'. Considerable confusion has arisen as to the age and distribution of the decorative techniques employed on this pottery. So-called **dotted wavy line** decoration occurs on the oldest Saharan pottery, with **wavy line** motifs rare in the Sahara and of eighth/ninth millennium bp age (Mohammed-Ali and Khabir 2003). By contrast, wavy line is first along the Nile, where dotted wavy line only appears after 6.2 kya, perhaps introduced from the central Sahara (Caneva and Marks 1990). The Wadi Howar, which leads west from the Nile toward the Chad/Sudan border, may have been an important conduit for this introduction (Jesse 2000).

The sharing of similar decorative techniques across a broad expanse of northern Africa until – and beyond – 8 kya, contributed some decades ago to the lumping together of early Holocene settlement in the Sahara and the Sudanese Nile Valley under a single rubric. Focusing on the frequent association of these ceramics with barbed bone points, Sutton (1974) invented the term Aqualithic to describe this 'technocomplex', emphasising the potential causal links between fishing, mollusc exploitation, and cereal collection, and the invention of pottery, and the implications of all for more permanent settlement. Simultaneously, Camps (1974) wrote in similar terms about what he termed the Saharo-Sudanese Neolithic, employing the Francophone preference for defining Neolithic in terms of material culture (here ceramics) rather than subsistence. Subsequent work shows this to be an oversimplification (Hays 1975a, b; Haaland 1987). The ceramics themselves vary considerably, those using wavy line motifs in ways that still defy clear spatiotemporal definition. Furthermore, such variation does not co-occur with variability in lithic typologies or technologies. Lastly, numerous physicochemical analyses generally support local manufacture (Mohammed-Ali and Khabir 2003). The barbed bone points, too, vary typologically and in frequency through space and time. Nor does their patterning match that of the ceramics (Keding 1996; Yellen 1998). As MacDonald (1998:42) and Holl (2005) make plain, neither artefact category substantiates the notion of a single cultural complex, still less one that spread uniquely westward from a single Nilotic or East African source, as previously suggested by Haaland (1992) and Sutton (1977). Specific correlations with the Nilo-Saharan language family, as proposed by Sutton (1974) and Ehret (1993, 2002a), are thus difficult to substantiate, even apart from concerns about the dating methods and assumptions about language change that they may involve (Hassan 2002). Similar worries apply to the more radical grouping of Nilo-Saharan and Niger-Congo language families into a single macrophylum (Blench 1999b) and MacDonald's (1998) correlation of its southward spread with a resettlement of the Sahara from the Maghreb.

Such concerns with origins viewed in terms of population expansion or stimulus diffusion have deflected attention from alternatives,

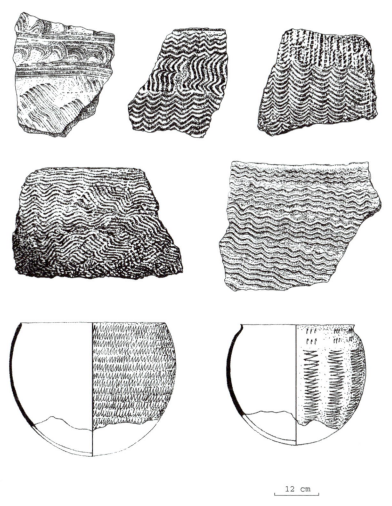

**Figure 8.12.** Early pottery from sites in the Sahara and Sudan. The top two rows show sherds from the Khartoum area, Sudan; the bottommost row, two pots from Amekni, Niger. (Redrawn after Camps 1982: Fig. 8.2 and D. Edwards 2004: Fig. 2.5.)

such as convergent cultural evolution (Holl 2005). They also detract from the significance of the ceramics themselves. In this respect, there may be much to salvage from Sutton's (1974) original model. Garcea (2004), for example, notes that in the Tadrart Acacus the appearance of pottery coincided with the dietary broadening and greater sedentism of the Late Acacus phase. Haaland (1992), too, argues for mutually reinforcing links among ceramics, increased use of wild grains, sedentism, and population growth, in her case along the Middle Nile. Pottery may have been used to cook shellfish, process fish to extract oil (J. D. Clark 1988b), store fats (Caneva 1988), prepare grain porridges, and make beer. Some vessels may also have had non–utilitarian uses, perhaps linked to prestige or the creation through exchange of mutual insurance systems against drought–induced resource failures (Garcea 2004); Livingstone Smith's (2001) analysis of Late Acacus sherds from Uan Tabu hints at this by documenting movement over distances of at least 70 km. The initial rarity of ceramics further suggests that their first function was not storage or cooking (Close 1995), though there is, as yet, insufficient evidence to substantiate Hayden's (1995) general model for the development of pottery as a prestige technology in a context of competitive feasting and display.

### Controlling the Wild: First Attempts at Domestication?

We have left until last tantalising evidence that early Saharan foragers also experimented with controlling and manipulating wild animals. The older, and more controversial, instance comes from the southern part of Egypt's Western Desert, where cattle bones at Nabta and Bir Kiseiba may date back to 9.2 kya (Gautier 2002). None, however, shows signs of morphological change consequent upon domestication. Arguments that they were domesticated are thus ecological ones, the water demands of cattle being such that they would not naturally occur in an environment otherwise populated only by nondrinking desert-adapted species like hare, gazelle, and oryx, where rainfall probably did not exceed 50 mm pa (Neumann 1989; Close 1996; Gautier 2002; Wendorf and Schild 2002). However, pastoralists could have forced their animals into drier areas, keeping them alive by providing them with water. Significantly, after 8.5 kya, there is considerable evidence for well-digging (Close 1984), whereas before this people perhaps used today's desert regions only in and after the summer rains, remaining close to the Nile for the rest of the year. The argument for domestication is countered by A. Smith

(2005a), who reasons that the relevant faunas are so impoverished that they cannot represent a real ecology. One might also ask, if water was so scarce, then what of fodder? And why is there no comparably early evidence for domestic cattle in the Nile Valley? DNA evidence nevertheless encourages the view that African cattle were independently domesticated in North Africa (Bradley *et al.* 1996; Hanotte *et al.* 2002), and at a date earlier than the oldest known instances in the Near East (Gautier 2002). Possible triggers may have been to access their fat (A. Smith 1986) or as living reservoirs of blood and milk, tappable on demand for protein, fat, and liquid (Close and Wendorf 1992). However, regular milk production would need selection, just like human tolerance for fresh milk, so this could not have been important at first; transport of water or housing are other possibilities (Wendorf and Schild 2002). The Nabta/Bir Kiseiba area may have occupied a crucial ecological position in all this: far enough south to receive some rain, but sufficiently north that this fell only in small, highly variable amounts. Domestication, if indeed it was taking place, could thus have enhanced the reliability and predictability of a moveable food resource (Marshall and Hildebrand 2002).

Human interest in managing another North African mammal is indicated by finds from Uan Afuda in the Tadrart Acacus. There, Late Acacus occupation of the inner part of the site produced a thick stratum of dung attributable to Barbary sheep (di Lernia 1999). Today, *Ammotragus* does not produce such deposits in rockshelters and analysis of the stratum's plant content indicates a non-natural range, probably collected in late winter/early spring (Mercuri 1999). Supporting the case for close human control, Mercuri also notes the high representation of *Echium* sp., a toxic species that does not normally form part of the animal's diet. She and A. Smith (2005a) both suggest that this was linked to some ritual aspect of confining *Ammotragus* at the site. This may be implied by its being the most commonly depicted animal in Round Head style paintings; one, from Tin Tezerift in the central Sahara, may depict a sheep being led on a rope (Cesarino 2000).[11] If, as may have been the case, the Late Acacus people spoke an early form of Nilo-Saharan, then the reconstructed term 'drive' (Ehret 1993:110) would also not be out of place. Summarising these data, di Lernia (2001) emphasises the connection with the other evidence already cited for the development of a less mobile settlement pattern in the Late Acacus phase, suggesting that people penned in *Ammotragus* individuals to facilitate continued access to them even as their local numbers declined. However, as Garcea (2006) has recently argued, this trend towards a more sedentary, delayed-returns waylife that employed pottery to store and cook food in new ways had limited potential for further intensification, or even survival, when conditions turned more arid: pastoralism, not cultivation, provided the basis for later central Saharan societies.

## BEYOND THE SAHARA: WEST AFRICA AND THE MAGHREB

### West Africa: The Forests and the Sahel

We turn now to the areas south and north of the modern Sahara. West Africa continues to remain largely enigmatic, with Iwo Eleru in southern Nigeria one of the more significant sites. From the basal horizon of a long sequence featuring a relatively informal microlithic industry comes a negroid skeleton dated ~11.2 kya, one of West Africa's oldest human burials (Shaw and Daniels 1984). Another terminal Pleistocene microlithic assemblage is known from Bingerville, in the Ivory Coast (Chenorkian 1983). Although chronological controls are few, similar occurrences are probable in Nigeria (Casey 2003) and Burkina Faso (Breunig and Wotzka 1991). It seems likely that a long-established microlith-making West African population played some part in resettling the Sahel and the southern Sahara during the Pleistocene/Holocene transition. However, defining connections requires much more sustained fieldwork to complement the scattered observations currently available (MacDonald 1997); the Phase 1 early Holocene occupation at Ounjougou in Mali's Dogon Country differs not only in raw material usage, but also in core-reduction and formal tool preferences from early Saharan assemblages (Huysecom *et al.* 2004). New research may pin down more precisely the age and associations of other macrolithic assemblages. In Mali's Vallée du Serpent, people used sandstone to make massive flakes and flake-blades direct from the native rock, as well as smaller flakes from prepared cores. Palaeohydrology and geomorphology suggest such occurrences may date 9–6 kya (MacDonald and Allsworth-Jones 1994), and it is relevant to note the presence of a sandstone macrolithic component in the Phase 2 toolkit used at Ounjougou in the ninth millennium bp (Huysecom *et al.* 2004). Wider parallels exist as far afield as Senegal (Camara and Duboscq 1987), Mauritania (Mauny 1955), and the Central African Republic (De Bayle des Hermans 1975). Their concentration in areas of open or wooded savanna or near rivers gainsays Shaw's (1985) opposition of microlithic/savanna to macrolithic/forest. The absence of microlithic artefacts (except at Ounjougou?) also suggests this is a very different phenomenon from the presence of prepared core techniques in mid-Holocene horizons at Shum Laka, still less of core tools in later Mode 5 industries in West Africa's forest zone (MacDonald and Allsworth-Jones 1994).

## Libya and the Maghreb

If the archaeology of the Sahara's southern margins remains relatively poorly understood, the Maghreb has long been the focus of sustained activity focused on the Pleistocene/Holocene transition (Lubell 2000, 2005). Here and at Haua Fteah in northeastern Libya, the Iberomaurusian industry introduced in Chapter 7 continued to be made into the terminal Pleistocene (McBurney 1967; Close and Wendorf 1990). Several unusual features are of interest, including evidence, rare at this time depth, for sculpture. This takes the form of anthropomorphic and zoomorphic ceramic figurines from Afalou, Algeria, baked from locally available clay to temperatures of 500°–800°C (Hachi 1996, Hachi *et al.* 2002). Dating 15–11 kya, they are complemented by an earlier fragmentary figurine from the nearby site of Tamar Hat (Saxon 1976). Distinctive, too, are the many burials known from these later Iberomaurusian contexts, including apparent cemeteries at Afalou (Hachi 1996) and Taforalt, Morocco (almost 200 individuals; Ferembach *et al.* 1962). Analysis of these remains (see inset) raises issues of territoriality, limited mobility, and group identity that economic data are still too few to explore further.

Knowing that people hunted Barbary sheep and other large mammals and that they collected molluscs, both terrestrial and marine, is
very different from being able to develop this checklist of ingredients
into a meaningful set of recipes or menus that could illuminate the
details of Iberomaurusian subsistence-settlement strategies.

> WHAT BONES CAN TELL: BIOLOGICAL
> PERSPECTIVES ON THE HUNTER-GATHERERS
> OF THE MAGHREB

The extremely large skeletal samples that come from sites such as
Taforalt (Fig. 8.13) and Afalou constitute an invaluable resource
for understanding the makers of Iberomaurusian artefacts, and
their number is unparalleled elsewhere in Africa for the early
Holocene. Frequently termed Mechta-Afalou or Mechtoid, these
were a skeletally robust people and definitely African in origin,
though attempts, such as those of Ferembach (1985), to establish
similarities with much older and rarer Aterian skeletal remains are
tenuous given the immense temporal separation between the two
(Close and Wendorf 1990). At the opposite end of the chronological spectrum, dental morphology does suggest connections
with later Africans, including those responsible for the Capsian
Industry (Irish 2000) and early mid-Holocene human remains
from the western half of the Sahara (Dutour 1989), something
that points to the Maghreb as one of the regions from which
people recolonised the desert (MacDonald 1998).

Turning to what can be learned about cultural practices and
disease, the individuals from Taforalt, the largest sample by far, display little evidence of trauma, though they do suggest a high incidence of infant mortality, with evidence for dental caries, arthritis,
and rheumatism among other degenerative conditions. Interestingly, Taforalt also provides one of the oldest known instances of
the practice of trepanation, the surgical removal of a portion of the
cranium; the patient evidently survived for some time, as there
are signs of bone regrowth in the affected area. Another form
of body modification was much more widespread and, indeed,
a distinctive feature of the Iberomaurusian skeletal sample as a

**Figure 8.13.** Taforalt, Morocco, under renewed excavation. The site preserves a long sequence of Iberomaurisian and, below these, Aterian deposits. (Courtesy and copyright Nick Barton and Ian Cartwright.)

whole. This was the practice of removing two or more of the upper incisors, usually around puberty and from both males and females, something that probably served as both a rite of passage and an ethnic marker (Close and Wendorf 1990), just as it does in parts of sub-Saharan Africa today (e.g., van Reenen 1987). Cranial and postcranial malformations are also apparent and may indicate pronounced endogamy at a much more localised level (Hadjouis 2002), perhaps supported by the degree of variability between different site samples noted by Irish (2000).

During or just after the Younger Dryas, new industrial traditions developed in the Maghreb, collectively known as Epipalaeolithic. Lubell *et al.* (1984) propose a broad grouping into western and eastern traditions, but their relationships are more complex than this and need reassessment (Rahmani 2002). The best known is the Capsian, initially found in a restricted area along the Algerian/Tunisian border south of Tebessa. This continued well into the early Holocene and shows substantial continuities in stone tool typology with the

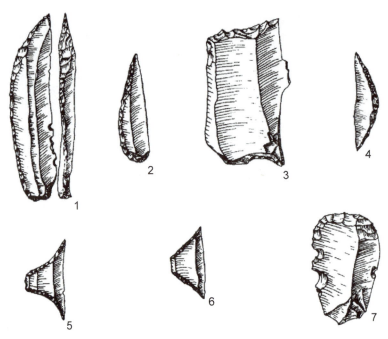

**Figure 8.14.** Capsian artefacts, Algeria: 1. backed blade; 2. backed bladelet; 3. burin; 4. segment; 5–6. trapezoidal backed microliths; 7. scraper. (After P. Smith 1982: Fig. 5.10.)

Iberomaurusian (Lubell *et al.* 1991). Comparison of human remains also attests to long-term biological continuity between the two (Irish 2000; *pace* Ferembach 1985). Rahmani (2004) recently clarified longstanding debates about the relationship between the Capsian's Typical and Upper variants, the change between which fell around $8 \pm 0.2$ kya (Sheppard 1987). Although both emphasised backed pieces, they used distinct *chaînes opératoires*, with blades larger and geometric microliths fewer in the former (Fig. 8.14).

Occupying a landscape of open wooded savanna with Mediterranean forest and scrub at higher altitudes, before 8 kya, the subsistence focus of Capsian groups was on large herbivores (cattle, zebra, hartebeest). However, a wide variety of other animals was also trapped or collected, including large landsnails like *Helix melanostoma*, the abundant remains of which form the *escargotières* (*ramadiyas*) or shell middens that are such a well-known feature of the Capsian archaeological record. Complementing this good faunal evidence, regrettably little is known about plant foods: garlic (*Allium* sp.) was recovered from the Logan Museum's excavations before World War II, and charcoal analyses demonstrate the availability of pine, pistachio, acorns, and other nuts (Lubell 2005). Sites are typically inland and distant from the sea, occupying both rockshelters and open-air locations. Human remains are relatively common, if fragmentary. Focusing on Site 12 in northeast Algeria, Haverkort and Lubell (1999) show that no difference is apparent in their treatment of either side of 8 kya, and that this could involve dismemberment, decapitation, and possible removal of internal organs soon after death. Ritual/utilitarian modification of human remains is also known from other Capsian sites (Camps-Febrer 1966), most spectacularly by a skull from Faïd Souar II possibly used as a mask (Vallois 1971). Haverkort and Lubell (1999) conclude that secondary burial, often including transport of remains over some distance, was probably commonplace and that this implies a strong sense of the 'right' place in which burial should occur. As at Gogoshiis Qabe, Somalia, concerns about landscape ownership and territoriality may be at work here, asserted through relationships with dead ancestors of the kind discussed by Chapman (1981) and Pardoe (1988).[12] Mediterranean northwest Africa thus stands out as an area in which both Iberomaurusian and Capsian populations may have structured their lives in ways quite different from any model of 'simple' immediate-returns hunter-gatherers. The historical and ecological underpinnings of this merit the increased attention that the region is now once again receiving (e.g., Barton *et al.* 2005).

OVERVIEW

Resettlement, colonisation, subsistence change, greater sedentism (at least in some areas), and technological innovation are all evident in the African record of the Pleistocene/Holocene transition. One further element that we have touched on several times is that of language (Fig. 8.15). Considerable attention has been given to mapping hypothetical linguistic entities onto the archaeological record and to using reconstructed proto-vocabularies to infer those aspects of past lifeways that may not be archaeologically recoverable (e.g., Ehret 2002b). However, although a loose correlation exists between the general distribution and glottochronologically inferred time-depth of Nilo-Saharan and Sutton's (1974) Aqualithic, the notion of a simple movement of people westward from the Nile into what are now the Sahara and the Sahel cannot be supported archaeologically (Holl 2005). Alternative classifications of Nilo-Saharan languages are also possible, each with its own potential archaeological correlations (MacDonald 1998).[13]

Another major language family, Afroasiatic, is also of interest, as its origin probably lies in the southeastern Sahara or toward the Horn, a view supported by Y-chromosome phylogeography (Ehret *et al.* 2004; Keita 2005). The connections between North African and southern Levantine backed microlith industries in the late Pleistocene, to which we referred earlier (Bar-Yosef 1987), could provide one possible, if early, context for its spread into Asia. However, as discussed in Chapter 9, other archaeological correlations can also be envisaged, including a later hunter-gatherer–led expansion broadly coinciding with the Pleistocene/Holocene boundary (Blench 1999b; Ehret 2002a), or an origin for the whole family within the Near East (D. McCall 1998), though this would then require a mechanism for its introduction to Africa. Farther south, and on a less grand scale, we wonder whether the apparently long-standing separation of Southern from Northern Khoisan languages (Westphal 1963) reflects the confinement of Robberg assemblages south of the Limpopo and the Orange and the presence of quite different industries to the north during MIS 2. Crawhall's (2006) provocative overview of Khoisan linguistics emphasises this separation and also reinforces the importance of undertaking genetic analyses that might establish whether such linguistic boundaries coincide with genetic ones.

If the potential archaeological correlations of Africa's language families constitute one potentially interconnecting theme for the issues discussed in this chapter, then sedentism – or at least reduced mobility – forms another. From the Maghreb through the Tadrart Acacus to southern Somalia and East Africa, the data we have reviewed suggest that, at varying times and in many different places,

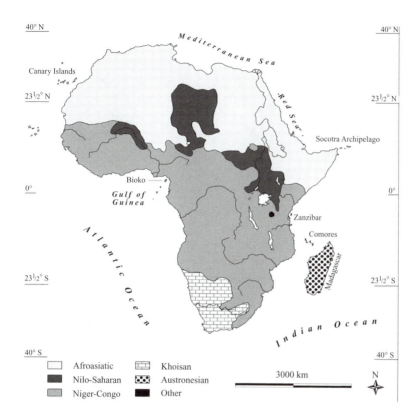

**Figure 8.15.** Africa, showing the current distribution of its major language families. Note that Austronesian was introduced to Madagascar around the time of Christ from Indonesia and that south of the Equator, the zone now covered by Bantu languages of the Niger-Congo family, in particular, also represents a relatively recent expansion, linked to the spread of food-production. Until this took place in the first millennium B.C./first millennium A.D., other language families were no doubt present there, and the Khoisan language family would have extended farther east and north to the Zambezi. The category 'other' includes Hadza and Sandawe.

some people were able to make a living in smaller territories and from increasingly local resources through the Pleistocene/Holocene transition. At least in some instances (the Iberomaurusian, the Capsian, Gogoshiis Qabe), increased group-definition and assertion of claims to the landscape through dead ancestors seem detectable. This was, of course, by no means a uniform process, as the evidence from the lower Nile examined in Chapter 7 makes plain, nor was it unique to this period. Indeed, intensive use of fish and shellfish reaches back tens of thousands of years in more than one part of the continent. Nevertheless, the African record for the Pleistocene/ Holocene boundary does allow this to be identified as a trajectory shared across many regions. As Sutton (1974) wrote when first formulating the concept of an Aqualithic, this provided an alternative pathway to increasing cultural complexity without requiring the domestication and cultivation of cereals as in the Near East. Manipulating the productivity of key animal resources (cattle, Barbary sheep) may have been a different matter, for it is probably to the Pleistocene/Holocene transition that the earliest evidence of one of the most transformational developments in African history, the domestication of livestock, belongs. The conjunction of this with the arrival of new domesticated resources from Western Asia (sheep, goats, and, ultimately, cereals and legumes), and the impacts that these resources had on African societies, forms part of the material covered in the next chapter.

## SUMMARY

Better chronological controls and a richer archaeological record allow the Pleistocene/Holocene transition to be studied in much greater detail than any previous glacial/interglacial switch. African climates ameliorated relatively rapidly from 15 kya but, as in many other parts of the world, this amelioration was punctuated by the Younger Dryas stadial. Once this ended, around 10.2 kya, temperature and rainfall increased substantially, equatorial forests expanded, and people recolonised previously inhospitable habitats. Limited, but locally important, losses of land to rising seas, the extinction of some large mammals, and the catastrophic impact of some climatic episodes, notably the Wild Nile floods, show, however, that the change to a warmer, wetter climate was not an entirely positive affair. Across the continent, it is southern Africa that offers some of the most detailed observations for this period, and several models have been developed to explain the changes observed in stone tool industries, population distribution, resource exploitation, and settlement pattern. A key question remains the degree to which terminal Pleistocene/early Holocene hunter-gatherers in the region practised social relations identical to those of ethnographically known Bushman foragers. Farther north, data are sparser in south-central Africa and the Congo Basin, but become richer in East Africa and the Horn. In several localities (e.g., southern Somalia, the Upper Atbara River, and around Khartoum) people developed more sedentary lifestyles, often geared to fish and other aquatic resources, but along the lower Nile, the success of such (by now millennia old) adaptations had a severe impact from the massive floods that occurred around 12.5 kya. Even then, the Sahara remained too dry to support human life, and though Ounanian assemblages hint that resettlement began before the end of the Pleistocene, it is only after the Younger Dryas closed that we find firm evidence for people in either of our two best-researched areas, the Tadrart Acacus and Egypt's Western Desert. In both, there are signs of a more sedentary lifestyle developing, and as part of this reduction in mobility, pottery was innovated and shared across a broad expanse of northern Africa, from the central Sahara to the Middle Nile. Rock art, in which the Tadrart Acacus is spectacularly rich, may have played a part in structuring relations between more sedentary populations, and in northwestern Africa, as in southern Somalia, people may have asserted claims to land resource ownership through the deliberate burial of their dead in well-defined cemeteries. The Maghreb, along with the Nile and sub-Saharan West Africa, is one area from which the desert may have been resettled, and correlations between archaeological evidence and the evidence of physical anthropology and historical linguistics now allow such suggestions to be explored over a wider dataset than hitherto. Foreshadowing a key theme of Chapter 9, there is also the intriguing possibility that some early Holocene foragers began to experiment with manipulating wild animals for food or other resources (such as transport): The confinement of Barbary sheep at Uan Afuda in the Tadrart Acacus and what may well be cattle bones at Nabta and Bir Kiseiba in Egypt's Western Desert hint at this, supported in the latter case by DNA evidence pointing to a separate domestication event for cattle within North Africa.

# CHAPTER 9

# HUNTING, GATHERING, INTENSIFYING: THE MID-HOLOCENE RECORD

Hunter-gatherers continued to occupy most of Africa throughout the Holocene, making it more similar in this respect to Australia and North America than to Eurasia. This generalisation, however crude, again highlights the importance of relating African hunter-gatherers to those on other continents. Our focus here falls on the mid-Holocene, from 8 kya to between 4 and 2 kya, an upper limit set by the regionally variable arrival or adoption of food-production. After sketching the history of livestock-keeping and cultivation in Africa, we review the continent region by region, emphasising areas south of the Sahara because food-production was adopted much earlier within the modern desert and to its north (Fig. 9.1). We examine evidence that African hunter-gatherers were engaging in processes of social and economic intensification at this time and ask how complex some of them may have been, how far they pursued experiments in domestication independently of connections with food-producers, and whether social and/or ecological factors constrained their ability to do this. Rock art is crucially important for understanding African hunter-gatherer societies during the period covered by this chapter and the next one. We therefore describe in some detail the diversity of African hunter-gatherer rock arts, showing how some can now be read in detail while discussing the challenges of integrating them with excavated data.

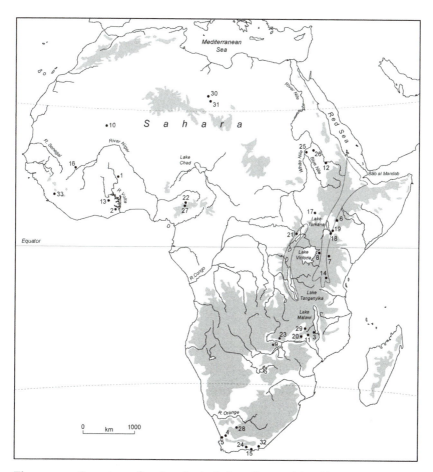

**Figure 9.1.** Location of archaeological sites discussed in Chapter 9: 1. Birimi; 2. Bosumpra; 3. Chencherere; 4. De Hangen; 5. Elands Bay Cave; 6. Ele Bor; 7. Enkapune ya Muto; 8. Gogo Falls; 9. Gwisho; 10. Hassi el-Abiod; 11. Kalemba; 12. Khasm el-Ghirba; 13. Kintampo; 14. Kisese II; 15. Klasies River; 16. Kourounkorokalé; 17. Lokabulo; 18. Lothagam; 19. Lowasera; 20. Makwe; 21. Matupi; 22. Mbi; 23. Mumbwa; 24. Nuwekloof; 25. Saggai; 26. Shaqadud; 27. Shum Laka; 28. Springbokoog; 29. Thandwe; 30. Ti-n-Torha; 31. Uan Muhuggiag; 32. Welgeluk; 33. Yengema.

## MID-HOLOCENE PALAEOENVIRONMENTS

The Holocene was far from being a period of environmental stasis, and we draw upon growing evidence for the importance of shortlived ecological changes at many points in our discussion. Hassan (2002) reviews such data as they relate to the spread of food-production, emphasising how recurrent drought episodes encouraged herders to move across the Sahara and into the Nile Valley. The picture is one of staggered pulses of expansion at varying scales and intensities, rather than a single wave. High-resolution palaeoenvironmental sequences using multiple datasets indicate that many of these abrupt changes were widely registered. Some, such as the sudden cooling, aridifying event ~7300 bp known as the 8.2 kya event, were clearly global in nature and must have had a powerful impact on African populations. With North Atlantic temperatures falling some 6°C, this major excursion in Greenland's oxygen isotope record (Alley *et al.* 1997) is paralleled by evidence for greater cold and/or aridity in many parts of Africa (Lario *et al.* 1997; Stager and Mayewski 1997; Cremaschi 2002; Thompson *et al.* 2002; Esterhuysen and Smith 2003; Stager *et al.* 2003).

After only one or two centuries, the 8.2 kya event was followed by generally warmer, wetter conditions, with higher lakestands and expanded woodland and forest habitats. Though climate became somewhat drier again after 6500 bp, pollen and charcoal records from the Sahel and the Sahara still document much more vegetated environments than those of today (Ritchie 1994). Further abrupt cooling/drying events ~4500 and ~4100 bp signalled more profound transformations. Southward retreat of the Inter-Tropical Convergence Zone provoked largescale, enduring aridification of the Sahara, lower lakestands, lower Nile floods (which may have contributed to the collapse of Egypt's Old Kingdom; Barker *et al.* 2004), and retreating forests in East and West Africa, including the abrupt reopening of the Bénin Gap savanna corridor (Bonnefille *et al.* 1990; Gasse and Van Campo 1994; Street-Perrot *et al.* 2000; Salzmann and Hoelzmann 2005; Kiage and Liu 2006). The hyperaridity then established across the Sahara has remained in place ever since.

Elsewhere, a key climatic episode was the Holocene altithermal, the postglacial temperature peak (± 2°C higher than today) attained between 7000 and 4500 bp. Its impact on rainfall patterns varied, with the Kalahari wetter, but the Karoo and much of Zimbabwe generally drier (Partridge *et al.* 1990). Thereafter, cooler, drier neoglacial episodes prevailed in southern Africa's summer rainfall zone around 4200 and 3500–2300 bp. Significantly, the winter rainfall region was out-of-synch with these trends, being drier from 7800 bp, but wetter again after 4500 bp (Jerardino 1996). In East Africa, Kenya's highlands were drier 5500–3300 bp (Ambrose and Sikes 1991), a period when Kilimanjaro's rapidly disappearing icecore record registers abrupt droughts ~4500 and ~3700 bp (Thompson *et al.* 2002); several pollen records document abrupt increases in drought-adapted taxa such as *Podocarpus* spp. at one or both of these events (Kiage and Liu 2006) and Lakes Elmenteita, Naivasha, and Nakuru may have temporarily dried up (Richardson 1972). Grasslands expanded during these drier phases, with more-or-less modern temperatures and precipitation, including today's bimodal Rift Valley rainfall pattern, only kicking in around 3000 bp (Marshall 1990). Progressive, if erratic, reductions in rainfall are also evident farther north. In highland Ethiopia, for example, lake levels that had recovered from the 8.2 kya event fell again 6200–5800 bp and more rapidly still after 4800 bp, declining gradually to modern stands from 3000 bp (Gillespie *et al.* 1983). Further testimony to the continent-wide significance of some of the dates we have been noting comes from West Africa, where the African Humid Period ended abruptly ~4500 bp (deMenocal *et al.* 2000), just as it did in the equatorial forests (Marret *et al.* 2006). Observations from Lake Bosumtwi suggesting a significantly later transition (Peck *et al.* 2004) better fit the dramatic decline in rainforest extent ~2500 bp that Maley and Chepstow-Lusty (2001) believe was climatically inspired (*pace* Sowunmi 1999, who emphasises clearance for cultivation).

## THE EARLY SPREAD OF FOOD-PRODUCTION IN AFRICA

Several recent syntheses summarise the spread of food-production for Africa as a whole (Marshall and Hildebrand 2002; Gifford-Gonzalez 2005; Mitchell 2005b; Neumann 2005; D. Phillipson 2005; cf. Clark and Brandt 1984). If, as previously discussed, cattle were domesticated in northeastern Africa independently of events in southwest Asia, then little beyond the most ephemeral campsites (Gabriel 1987) indicates they had spread far before 7500 bp. The sharp downturn to colder, more arid conditions that marked the 8.2 kya event may simultaneously have encouraged intensification of cattle herding, the introduction (by immigrants?) of domesticated sheep and goats from the Levant, and their combination with cattle into a more expansionist economy. Where, as in Libya's Tadrart Acacus, aridity may have created a widespread occupation hiatus, this spread probably took the form of colonising an empty niche once wetter conditions returned (A. Smith 2005a).

It must be remembered, however, that expanding pastoralists did not necessarily neglect or avoid hunting and gathering. In a pattern common across Africa, communities more-or-less heavily committed to food-production also used, and continue to use, wild resources. The pastoralist occupation at Nabta Playa itself ~8000 bp is a good example of this and shows cattle-keeping to have been part of a broad-spectrum economy involving fruits, tubers, and grasses, especially sorghum (Wasylikowa *et al.* 1997). Sites like Ti-n-Torha and Uan Muhuggiag reveal a similar story in the Acacus (Barich 1987; Cremaschi and di Lernia 1999). Much later, and at the continent's opposite end, early second millennium A.D. agropastoralists in southern Zimbabwe placed an impressively high emphasis on gathering wild grasses (Jonsson 1998). The inappropriateness of constructing farming in bipolar opposition to hunting and gathering is one that we shall revisit when considering the archaeological records of East Africa's 'Pastoral Neolithic' (Karega-Munene 2003) or South Africa's Western Cape (Sadr 2003). A second theme to reflect upon is the long-term persistence of hunting and gathering alongside and beyond areas inhabited by farmers and pastoralists. Differences in the reliability of these different subsistence modes may explain much of this persistence, along with the unevenness with which food-production itself spread (Gifford-Gonzalez 2000; Marshall and Hildebrand 2002) and the opportunities for hunter-gatherers to strike a variety of exchange-based connections with food-producers (Chapter 10).

The mobile land use patterns of early Saharan herders probably minimised competition with those who chose not to acquire livestock, or were unable to do so. Thus, hunter-gatherer camp-sites are known in Egypt's Western Desert until at least 6800 bp (McDonald 1998; Gehlen *et al.* 2002) and until 5500 bp in the west-central Sahara (Camps 1969). The trend toward aridification will, however, have increasingly swung the balance in favour of those able to control dependable food sources in the form of milk, blood (?), and meat that could, moreover, be readily moved to best exploit fluc-tuations in the availability of water and grazing. Critical here was an increasing emphasis on sheep and goats, which are better able than cattle to withstand, or recover from, drought. Faced with increas-ingly arid conditions, large areas of the Sahara underwent significant depopulation from the sixth millennium bp, a process that gathered pace as desertification intensified with the cold, dry events of ∼4500 and ∼4100 bp. These events not only left the Sahel relatively moist, but probably made it and parts of East Africa more inviting to pas-toralist settlement as grasslands expanded; the simultaneous south-ward shift of the 750–500 mm isohyet provoked a corresponding relocation of the tsetse fly (*Glossina* sp.) vector for sleeping sick-ness (trypanosomiasis), a major disease of livestock. Vernet's (1998a) radiocarbon database beautifully illustrates this process, which saw food-production's first significant expansion beyond today's Sahara, an expansion that ultimately supplanted hunting and gathering across virtually the whole African continent.

Fuelling that expansion was the synergy created by combining herding with cultivated crops. Climatic constraints curtailed the spread of the wheat/barley/legume complex introduced to Egypt around 5000 bp. Even with irrigation, its presence was limited to North Africa, some Saharan oases, the Middle Nile, and the Ethiopian/Eritrean highlands. Farther south, one is therefore look-ing at the domestication of wholly African foodplants, of which pearl millet (*Pennisetum glaucum*) and sorghum (*Sorghum bicolor*) are today the most important and widespread cereals. Current evidence sug-gests that pearl millet was first domesticated in southern Mauritania in the early fourth millennium bp (Neumann 2005).[1] A critical development may have been a shift in the balance of risk man-agement as pastoralists spread into previously unoccupied, more southerly zones and as climate deteriorated or recovered from the

4.5 and 4.1 kya events. Though domesticated pearl millet is attested over a wide zone of the Sahel before 1000 bp, the adoption of cultivation was still patchy and spasmodic, something well illustrated by recent fieldwork in the Chad Basin (Klee and Zach 1999). Here, too, there is evidence for the long-term persistence of foraging alongside the use of domesticates, and there seems little reason to suppose that elsewhere in West Africa hunting and gathering had given way to historically documented agricultural systems based on yam (*Dioscorea* spp.) and oil palm (*Elais guineensis*) or African rice (*Oryza globerrima*) much before the mid-first millennium B.C.[2] South of the Equator, dates for comparable transitions are almost invariably more recent. Until as recently as 2000 years ago, therefore, much of Africa remained the domain of hunters and gatherers. It is to their archaeological record that we now turn.

## HUNTER-GATHERERS OF NORTHERN AFRICA AND THE SAHEL

Africa's far north featured heavily in Chapter 8. Its omission from the thumbnail sketch just given is because, even though there is no evidence that hunter-gatherers persisted there into historic (i.e., first millennium B.C.) times, the dynamics by which the Near Eastern farming complex was installed along the North African littoral and its hinterland remain poorly understood. While **caprines** reached Algeria's Aurès Mountains as early as 6500 bp, the status of cattle there requires reassessment (Roubet 1979; Gautier 1987), and hard evidence for cultivation is scarce everywhere before 1000 B.C. (Aumassip 1987; Bensimon and Martineau 1987). The widespread presence of ground stone tools, pottery, and (to a lesser degree) livestock encourages a belief in its earlier diffusion, but only in Cyrenaica is it certain that mixed farming was firmly established by the mid-second millennium B.C., and this because of the scale of Bronze Age population implied by Egyptian texts (D. O'Connor 1993).[3] The processes by which hunting and gathering gave way to food-production remain very much under-researched, leaving us to discuss here only the later (Upper) phase of the Capsian tradition first introduced in Chapter 8.

## The Upper Capsian of Algeria and Tunisia

Several changes took place among Capsian hunter-gatherers at 8000 ± 200 bp, including the adoption of pressure-flaking to create more standardised tools and effect greater economies in raw material usage, intensified hunting of smaller herbivores (*Gazella* sp.) and lagomorphs, and a trend toward collecting smaller land snails. A causal link with the more arid conditions provoked by the 8.2 kya event is tempting (Lubell *et al.* 1984). Among other changes, the Upper Capsian's greater emphasis on core preparation may have reduced dependency on specific toolstone resources, opening up areas more distant from the high-quality, flint-rich Typical Capsian heartland around Gafsa and Tebessa. The increased skill that pressure-flaking demanded may also have introduced an element of craft specialisation, further enhancing opportunities for social differentiation (Rahmani 2004). Though all this – and the evidence previously discussed in Chapter 8 – might favour models for the take-up of food-production that emphasise the social advantages of new resources (cf. Hayden 1990), hunting and gathering survived until at least 6000 bp in much of the Maghreb, notwithstanding herding's expansion in the Sahara farther south (Aumassip 1987). Continuities in lithic technology between the Capsian and the coastal 'Neolithic of Mediterranean Tradition', as well as the 'Neolithic of Capsian Tradition' farther inland (Camps 1982), support a predominantly local transition to food-production in northwest Africa, rather than the introduction by demographic expansion from farther east indicated by Y-chromosome analyses of modern North African populations (Barker 2003; Hassan 2003; Arredi *et al.* 2004).

## Mauritania and Mali

Within the area covered today by the Sahara Desert, hunting and gathering survived longest in the far west. Mauritania's shoreline boasts numerous *Anadara senilis*-dominated shell middens accompanied by evidence of fishing, hunting, and consuming beached whales. The middens date to a time (6000–4000 bp) when rainfall was higher than today's combined with a marine transgression that

produced extensive lagoon and estuary environments. Vernet
(1998b) recognises three culturally distinct groups, and inland sites
are also known (Jousse *et al.* 2003). Recent work extends this to
include a series of older, aceramic 'Epipalaeolithic' sites sadly lacking in organics near the Banc d'Arguin (Fig. 9.2; Vernet *et al.*
2007). To the east, the then lake/swamp/steppe landscape of Mali's
Azawad Basin and areas to its north was apparently only first settled
after 7000 bp (Petit-Maire *et al.* 1983; R. McIntosh 1998), though
postdepositional disturbance and changes in settlement strategy may
have affected archaeological visibility there, just as in Niger (Haour
2003:209). What does seem clear is that none of these sites are sub-
sumable within any overarching Aqualithic phenomenon (McIntosh
and McIntosh 1986). In the Azawad, those on dune/lake interfaces
typically feature bone harpoons, fish, and hippopotamus. Sites with
few harpoons, but very rich in fish, lie deeper within the interdune
areas and playa interiors. Still others comprise middens of shellfish
and bone, whereas those with grindstones (and thus more intensively
committed to grain collection?) are most common in the far north.
Ceramic frequencies vary greatly among sites, and lithic assemblages
are also diverse, some emphasising backed bladelets and points; others, more generalised toolkits. Yet more variation is evident in the
burial practices of people whom physical anthropology suggests were
of Mechtoid-type, related to populations in the Maghreb (Dutour
1989). They included tumulus construction and, around Hassi el-
Abiod, the postmortem defleshing and truncation of bodies and
body parts, all practices that suggest concerns with ancestors, the
demarcation of access to territory and resources (Petit-Maire *et al.*
1983).

Seasonality may partly explain this variability, but was probably
linked to the increasing differentiation of communities pursuing sub-
tly different lifeways (R. McIntosh 1998:55–57). Work in Mali's
Méma Basin suggests that herding, or trade with pastoralists, was
added to the mix after 3800 bp, creating a social landscape of multiple
specialists, within which hunting, gathering, and fishing flourished
for some time (MacDonald 1998; R. McIntosh 1998:58–66). Aridification may have been a forcing factor contributing to the adoption
of livestock here and in Mauritania (Jousse 2006). Farther south, near
Bamako, a quartz microlithic industry (including geometric backed

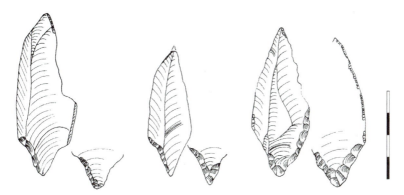

**Figure 9.2.** Stone points, Foum Arguin, Mauritania, from a hunter-gatherer context, probably dating 8-7 kya. (Courtesy and copyright Robert Vernet.)

microliths and unifacial and bifacial points) continued until perhaps 1 kya at Kourounkorokalé rockshelter. Comparable instances from Sierra Leone (Atherton 1972) to Nigeria (Switsur *et al.* 1994) may also reflect long-term hunter-gatherer persistence, perhaps in exchange relationships with agriculturalists (MacDonald 1997). Language isolates like Jalea in northeastern Nigeria could derive from such groups (MacDonald 1998). Recent work in Mali's Boucle du Baoulé region adds another dimension to this complexity by documenting a previously unknown naturalistic rock art tradition, the content of which (male figures holding bows; wild animals) implies a hunter-gatherer origin (Kleinitz 2001).

## FROM WEST AFRICA TO THE NILE

### *West Africa's Forest Zone and the Kintampo Complex*

Yengema, Sierra Leone, is among the few stratified mid-Holocene sites in West Africa's forest zone. It tracks the addition to a Mode 5 industry of first dolerite bifaces and then, from 4000 bp, of pottery and polished stone axes (Coon 1968). Such axes, frequently associated with Mode 5 assemblages from Senegal to Nigeria and beyond,[4] may have had multiple uses, among them clearing trees to manage oil palms and yams, two of today's regional staples (Posnansky 1984; MacDonald and Allsworth-Jones 1994). Direct information on subsistence strategies is nonetheless rare, though numerous shell middens occur in Senegal (Linares de Sapir 1971; Ravisé 1970) and Ivory Coast (Chenorkian 1983). One in Ghana suggests that pottery was present from 5900 bp (Nygaard and Talbot 1984) and ceramics also occur inland about this time in a Mode 5 context at Bosumpra Cave (A. Smith 1975). Much more extensive work has been undertaken at rockshelters in the Kintampo area (Stahl 1985; Watson 2005). Here, domesticated caprines and cattle have both been claimed for the Kintampo complex (3600–3200 bp), which shows a significant expansion in its scale of exchange networks and wealth of material culture over the preceding ceramic Mode 5 Punpun industry.[5] However, the cattle may well be buffalo and the caprines are few or stratigraphically ambiguous; evidence of yam cultivation is also highly indirect (Casey 2005). In short, there seems little reason, other than the pearl millet from Birimi in the environmentally distinct savannas of northern Ghana and a few domesticated cowpea (*Vigna unguiculata*) remains from Kintampo itself (D'Andrea *et al.* 2001, 2007), to treat the Kintampo complex as having had a significant food-production element. Instead, people may have engaged in a variety of management strategies to enhance resource access around regularly visited sites, now quite likely occupied on a more sedentary basis than before (Stahl 1993; Casey 2005). Enhancing continuities with the Punpun industry, which wholly lacks domesticates (Stahl 1985), this reading of the data also questions the likelihood of substantial population movements into Ghana by herder-farmers from the Sahel (an interpretation favoured by Watson 2005; cf. Casey 2005; Stahl 2005c).

*From Cameroon to Congo*

Farther east, Shum Laka remains a key sequence. The period 7000–6000 bp saw major changes in technology compared with the early Holocene: greater use of basalt and tuffs and the introduction of a macrolithic component, polished stone tools, and rare core tools. Four probably *in situ* potsherds are the oldest in the Gulf of Guinea region. Their impressed decoration leads Lavachery (2001) to posit a southward movement of people from the Sahel during a short, dry phase c. 7000 bp. Dating to about then, too, are four burials, broadly contemporary with another from Mbi Shelter (de Maret 1996); regrettably, their fragmentary nature precludes detailed study (Ribot *et al.* 2001). A further significant change in lithic technology (toward striking blades from carefully prepared cores and greater use of bifacial tools) took place around 5000–4000 bp when a different ceramic tradition becomes evident. Stone tools continued to be deposited at Shum Laka into the second millennium A.D., and hunting forest game and exploiting *Canarium* nuts are documented throughout. At some point, however, perhaps after 3000 bp in de Maret's (1994/95) 'Stone to Metal Age', yam cultivation took hold and foraging was substantially replaced by food-production.

In the equatorial rainforests, people continued making largely quartz microlithic assemblages after 8000 bp. The addition of pottery and ground stone tools around 3000 years ago (de Maret 1986; Clist 1995) is generally taken to denote the onset of food-production, but direct evidence of this is spectacularly scarce in pre metallurgical contexts, and still rare thereafter. Associations among such 'Neolithic' assemblages, a southward spread of yam and oil palm cultivation, and (speakers of?) Western Bantu languages are nonetheless widely advanced, as are linkages among microlithic assemblages, hunter-gatherers, and contemporary tropical forest foragers (Vansina 1990; Clist 1995). Given the problems of stratigraphic disturbance that plague many of the region's open-air sites and the logistical difficulties of fieldwork in the equatorial forests, outside Gabon, useful data remain confined to the northeastern Congo Basin.[6] There, at the forest/savanna ecotone, people still visited Matupi Cave, leaving behind quartz microlithic artefacts, a few bone tools, and some ostrich eggshell beads while accessing a range of bovids, suids, and smaller game (van Noten 1977). Farther into the Ituri, detailed observations that postdate the Pleistocene/Holocene boundary are only available for the second millennium A.D., but continued occupation is attested, in part based on consuming oil-rich nuts (Mercader 2003b).

## The Middle Nile

Happily, other regions have much fuller records, beginning with the Middle Nile, where sites of the Khartoum Mesolithic discussed in

Chapter 8 continued to flourish. The size of some, and the presence of burials, may indicate at least partial sedentism before domestic livestock were introduced in, or just before, the sixth millennium bp (Haaland 1996). It is tempting to link their arrival with that of dotted wavy line ceramic motifs from the central Sahara (Caneva and Marks 1990), the latter's ongoing aridification, and a limited degree of immigration. Such possibilities emphasise the significance of projects like that in the Wadi Howar, which sample areas connecting the Nile with others far to its west (Jesse 2000). Additional evidence of long-distance contacts comes from Saggai, near Khartoum, in the form of Red Sea marine shells and rhyolite from the Sixth Cataract, respectively 600 and 200 km away (Caneva 1983; Clark 1989b). Once introduced, herding did not spread quickly beyond the main rivers. Lithics and ceramics of the so-called Khartoum Neolithic at Shaqadud, for example, differ from those found along the Nile, and the site lacks domestic livestock (Caneva and Marks 1990). Hunting and gathering continued, too, in the Atbara/Gash area, mostly focused on smaller bovids, warthogs, molluscs, and – presumably – plants (Fattovich *et al.* 1984). This 'Saroba phase', in turn, followed earlier sites near Khasm el-Ghirba at which larger savanna ungulates complemented fish, shellfish, and smaller game; the associated lithic technologies and – at KG14 ~6200 bp – ceramics suggest at least two traditions are present, neither of them closely connected to the Khartoum Mesolithic. One tradition is flake-based, made heavy use of bipolar reduction, and has virtually no lunates; the other has many more geometric microliths and perforators with little bipolar flaking and chert (rather than agate) as its main raw material (Marks 1987).

## EASTERN AFRICA

### Southern Sudan and the Lake Turkana Basin

Geography suggests that southern Sudan and the Horn were instrumental in transmitting livestock to the southern two-thirds of Africa, but little is known about mid-Holocene foragers in either region. Along the Upper Nile, a preceramic quartz microlithic industry at

**Figure 9.3.** Lowasera, Kenya, showing the +80 m beach deposits overlying the old lava-strewn land surface. (Courtesy and copyright David Phillipson.)

Lokabulo Shelter was followed after 4800 bp by comb-impressed ceramics, but without evidence of domestic livestock (David *et al.* 1981). Comparable assemblages elsewhere in the region (and perhaps as far as central west Ethiopia; Fernández *et al.* 2007) hint that stone-using hunter-gatherers survived until a millennium ago (Robertshaw and Mawson 1981), despite evidence for livestock being in southern Sudan before 4000 bp (Kleppe 1984); difficulties in differentiating stone-using herders who also pursued wild resources from stone-using foragers may be involved here, something perhaps also relevant to the Shaqadud site mentioned earlier. Understanding how people in Ethiopia and Eritrea domesticated indigenous crops or acquired plants and animals of ultimately Near Eastern origin remains equally mired in uncertainty: Little evidence exists for either the processes involved or the speed at which they moved (Barnett 1999).

Moving south, people using Mode 5 assemblages and barbed bone points made intensive use of Lake Turkana's fish, mostly in the form of *Tilapia* and Nile perch (Fig. 9.3). Relevant campsites include Lowasera (reoccupied ~4500–3500 bp; D. Phillipson 1977b) and Lothagam (7–6000 bp; Robbins 1974); as with other East African foragers, the individuals buried at both these sites are best described as negroid (Rightmire 1984). Although coarse, poorly fired ceramics formed part of the toolkit at these Lake Turkana sites from before 7500 bp, livestock were absent until ~4500 bp, when they appeared in the Ileret area as part of an economy in which fishing and other wild resources remained important (Barthelme 1985). Only from ~3000 bp did this 'trickle' turn into a 'splash' associated with a much fuller, more widespread commitment to herding (Bower 1991). Recently published analyses of the genetics of lactose tolerance in East African populations support this broad time frame for the introduction of milk consumption (Tishkoff *et al.* 2007a). Even then, however, foraging adaptations persisted, especially in areas less well suited to herding, such as east of Lake Turkana where foraging may only have disappeared when camels made pastoralism more secure (see inset).

---

ELE BOR: SURVIVING ON THE EDGE

The rock outcrops of Ele Bor (Fig. 9.4) lie in what is now one of the most arid areas of northern Kenya and contain many different archaeological sites. Two rock-shelters excavated in 1976 document occupation by makers of a Mode 5 industry from the mid-Holocene into the second millennium A.D. (D. Phillipson 1984). Foetal and neonate remains confirm occupation by whole families, showing that the sites were residential camps for at least some of their history. It is thus of interest that Gifford-Gonzalez's (2003) analysis of the highly fragmented fauna indicates that the site's occupants ate a very wide range of foods, including carnivores, hares, birds, and reptiles, as well as antelope. Moreover, the extensive breakage of almost all first, second, and even some third phalanges suggests that they needed to extract all possible fats from their prey. The ceramics and grindstones introduced around 5200 bp facilitated this by allowing bones to be smashed up and boiled in pots to extract edible fat from them. These facts point up the precariousness of human survival in this arid part of East Africa, though the persistence of forager occupation at Ele Bor long after the onset of food-production in the wider region

**Figure 9.4.** Ele Bor, Kenya. (Courtesy and copyright David Phillipson.)

also attests to the success of the strategies followed by its inhabitants. The arrival of the camel may have undermined wild game stocks through competition for food and water, while simultaneously providing foragers with an alternative strategy in the form of becoming the clients of newly immigrating pastoralists.

## East Africa's Central Rift Valley and Great Lakes

Farther south in Kenya's Central Rift Valley, phase 5 of the Eburran industry is best known from Enkapune ya Muto, where the sequence spans what is otherwise a major data gap from 6000–3300 bp, when a drier climate elevated the forest/savanna ecotone. Ambrose (1984, 1986) argues convincingly that people shifted their settlement focus in line with this altitudinal variation, deploying subsistence strategies that resembled those of recent Okiek people: trapping and snaring forest/savanna game rather than hunting larger plains species, and using wild honey as a substitute for plant foods that are rare in the ecotone. Marean's (1992b) faunal analysis substantiates the faunal emphasis that the model demands. Earlier in the Holocene, however, at least some Eburran phase 3/4 groups may have heavily exploited aquatic resources (L. Leakey 1931), though how far these included fish is an open question (K. Stewart 1989). Eburran phase 5 assemblages differ from their immediate predecessors in the proportions and sizes of specific formal tool types, but the production of backed microliths, burins, and scrapers is common to both.

Enkapune ya Muto also registers the introduction to highland Kenya of first pottery (~4900 bp) and then caprines (~4000 bp). Though not precisely paralleling other East African traditions, the ceramics do resemble Nderit and Ileret pottery (Ambrose 1998a), perhaps indicating contacts to the north. Continuities in lithic typology suggest that the caprines were acquired on a small, sporadic scale by indigenous foragers, perhaps partly through the integration of immigrating herders who failed to make a success of pastoralism; rare Nderit ceramics at other sites with wild, or almost wholly wild, faunas in central Kenya/northern Tanzania may testify to this (Gifford-Gonzalez 1998).

The 'splash' made by pastoralism's expansion around 3000 bp remains undocumented south of the Serengeti grasslands.[7] Their northern Mara extension lacks Holocene hunter-gatherer sites, perhaps because a dearth of rockshelters offered few foci for repeated occupation, perhaps because a scarcity of edible plants and the seasonal migration of many game animals constrained population densities (Robertshaw 1990c). Holocene Mode 5 assemblages thought to be the work of foragers are better known from rockshelters in the Serengeti itself and the nearby Eyasi Basin (Mehlman 1977; Bower and Chadderdon 1986). Some of these sequences include another kind of pottery, Kansyore (Oltome) ware, which is widespread in East Africa and typically associated with relatively expedient, quartz-dominated microlithic toolkits that feature few formally retouched tools. Kansyore pottery has generally been attributed to hunter-gatherer-fishers, notably in the Lake Victoria Basin where it is most frequently found. Open-air shell middens there probably represent a phase of intensified aquatic resource exploitation (Robertshaw et al. 1983) perhaps dating 8250–4000 bp, though reliance on apatite and shell radiocarbon samples makes this uncertain. Multicomponent riverbank sites have different ichthyofaunas, lack harpoons, and were sited to exploit seasonal spawning runs of *Barbus* and other species (Lane 2004). The best known of these is Gogo Falls (Fig. 9.5;

**Figure 9.5.** Gogo Falls, Kenya: Trench I under excavation. (Courtesy and copyright Peter Robertshaw.)

Robertshaw 1991), from which claims of caprines in Kansyore contexts (Karega-Munene 2003) are now strengthened by observations at two nearby sites (Lane *et al.* 2007). Together with the high artefact densities characterising many Kansyore occupations, this suggests that at least some of those using Kansyore pottery engaged in a delayed-returns economy that included domesticated resources. We touch on this again subsequently.

## East African Rock Art

Surprisingly, no comparable evidence of lacustrine-focused adaptations has yet emerged around the other Rift Valley lakes, something that may, however, reflect lower levels of fieldwork in these areas. Little more, in truth, is known from central Tanzania, where the Kondoa area boasts a major concentration of hunter-gatherer rock art in the form of fine line paintings in red, mostly showing naturalistic animals (especially antelope), rare geometric motifs, and stylised human figures whose hairstyles, dress, and body decoration are elaborately depicted (Fig. 9.6). Red ochre was certainly used at the painted Kisese II site in the late Pleistocene (Inskeep 1962), but the age of the surviving paintings and the tradition to which they belong are unknown. Only limited further excavation has taken place (Masao 1979) and many interpretations of the art (M. Leakey 1983; Anati 1986) remain superficial. Greater insight comes from Ten Raa's (1971) demonstration that not far from Kondoa local Sandawe people still paint or use some painted sites in hunting rites and sacrifices. Lim (1992) confirms this, suggesting that one aspect of Sandawe rock art concerns how the act of painting in shelters reproduces the meaning of places within the landscape; another may involve the visual representation of images seen in altered states of consciousness experienced during *simbó* ritual dances (Lewis-Williams 1986; see inset). Though the Sandawe are now farmers, their own traditions recall that formerly they were hunter-gatherers and that other foragers also existed in their neighbourhood (Ten Raa 1969). They may thus provide the closest ethnographic analogue to the makers of the Kondoa painting, and ethnographically informed understandings may also be possible in the Eyasi Basin, where the

**Figure 9.6.** Rock paintings of stylised human figures, leopard, eland, and giraffe, Kolo, Tanzania.

still-foraging Hadzabe claim authorship of its rock art for their own ancestors (Mabulla 2003).

---

THE SANDAWE, THE HADZABE, AND THE KHOISAN

Lewis-Williams' (1986) interpretation of Kondoa region rock paintings draws on his earlier work with southern African Bushman rock art, discussed subsequently. It is, however, best judged independently of such parallels, despite longstanding attempts to connect southern Africa's Khoisan peoples with the Sandawe and Hadzabe of East Africa, both of whom, like the Khoisan, speak languages that make extensive use of various click sounds (e.g., Greenberg 1963). Recent studies show, however, that there is no convincing physical anthropological evidence for the former presence of Khoisan people in East Africa (Schepartz 1988; Morris 2003) and that, genetically, both the Hadzabe and Sandawe have East African affinities (Godber *et al.* 1976; Salas *et al.* 2002). Moreover, whereas click-using languages were perhaps once more widely distributed in Eastern Africa (Güldemann

2004), Hadzabe and Sandawe are genuine linguistic isolates that cannot be convincingly connected to any Khoisan languages (Güldemann and Vossen 2000). Any genetic links or other connections between them and southern African hunter-gatherers must thus be very ancient indeed (Knight *et al.* 2003). The most recent such study uses mtDNA and Y chromosome data to conclude that population divergence or genetic exchange between the Sandawe and southern Africa's Khoisan last took place >35 kya and that even Hadzabe and Sandawe have had no significant genetic exchange since ≥15–20 kya (Tishkoff *et al.* 2007b).

## SOUTH-CENTRAL AFRICA

### *Stone Tool Industries and Subsistence*

Rather more is known of mid-Holocene hunter-gatherers in Zambia, where several Mode 5 industries succeeded the Nachikufan discussed in Chapter 8. In the southeast, the Makwe industry includes ground stone axes and displays a dominance of backed microliths over scrapers. These observations, repeated across Zambia, contrast with contemporary industries in southern Africa, probably because people used different clothing media in the two regions: leather (prepared using scrapers) south of the Zambezi, bark cloth (removed using axes) to its north (H. J. Deacon and Deacon 1980). Backed microliths from Makwe itself offer further insights into how technology was organised: Mastic traces show that different types of geometrics were mounted in different ways (as chisels, arrow barbs, scrapers, or cutting tools), whereas backed points and scrapers probably went unhafted (Fig. 9.7; D. Phillipson 1976).

In northern and central Zambia, uncertainty prevails over how best to understand Holocene assemblage variability. Where S. Miller (1971) saw a clear succession of Nachikufan IIA (7000–5000 bp; emphasising backed flakes) and Nachikufan IIB (4000–2000 bp; relatively high frequencies of geometrics and concave scrapers), Sampson and Southard (1973) postulated differences between scraper-dominated processing locations and others marked by abundant

**Figure 9.7.** Possible hafting patterns of backed microliths from Makwe, Zambia. (After D. Phillipson 1976: Fig. 140; courtesy and copyright David Phillipson and British Institute in Eastern Africa.)

backed microliths used to make/repair hunting weapons. Analysing temporal changes in reduction sequences at Luano Hot Spring, Bisson (1990) reached a similar conclusion, but straightforward associations between backed microliths and hunting seem doubtful given the evidence just cited from Makwe. Even more diversity in the relative proportions of scraper and backed microlith types is evident in the post-3000 bp Nachikufan III phase (D. Phillipson 1976).

---

GWISHO: A FORAGER CAMP IN ZAMBIA

The Gwisho Hotsprings site on the southern edge of Zambia's Kafue Flats provides some of the most detailed evidence for the region's Holocene foragers because its largely waterlogged deposits preserved an unusual range of organic materials (Fagan and Van Noten 1971). These include grass-lined hollows that were probably used for sleeping and wooden post settings interpreted as the remains of windbreaks, though it is to be regretted that the excavation was unable to isolate the individual occupation phases that could have provided the basis for more detailed spatial studies. The many wooden and bone artefacts found demonstrate marked preferences in raw material selection (Fig. 9.8). For example, *Baikiaea plurijuga* and other hardwoods were chosen for bows, arrows, fire-drills, and some digging sticks, but softer woods for linkshafts and bone for points and awls. The *Swartzia* pods that were also recovered are a known source of arrow poison, while the Gwisho bow itself is the oldest surviving example of its kind known from south-central or southern Africa.

Connections between this Nachikufan series and mid-Holocene industries from the Lunsemfwa Basin (Musonda 1984) or Mumbwa (Barham 2000) are uncertain. Clearer is the emphasis on backed microliths in the open country of southern and western Zambia, which may reflect a greater role for bow-and-arrow hunting (D. Phillipson 1976). Gwisho is a key site for these Wilton assemblages, preserving an exceptional range of items and more than 30 burials (see inset). Farther west still, excavations in the Upper Zambezi Valley suggest manufacture of a Mode 3 industry, or one transitional between modes 3 and 5, until as recently as 3500 bp; its bifacial and core tools may find parallels in poorly known Tshitolian assemblages from the Congo Basin and Angola (L. Phillipson 1975, 1976).

Most of what is known about the subsistence ecology of Holocene foragers in Zambia comes from the work of D. Phillipson (1976), whose observation of a continuing trend toward greater use of smaller game animals like suids and small to medium territorial bovids is reinforced by Musonda (1984; Gutin and Musonda 1985). The fauna from Chencherere, south-central Malawi, provides a fuller picture, though one that only begins ∼2500 bp and extends well into the period of contact with farming communities. Significantly, Crader's (1984) analysis shows that even though smaller bovids dominate numerically, the much rarer zebras, suids, and large antelope, like wildebeest, provided most of the meat eaten, a caution that probably merits wider application were comparably detailed taphonomic studies only available elsewhere. Occupation at Chencherere emphasised the wet season and targeted animal migrations, but complementary evidence of movement to other sites at different times of the year, or of plant food exploitation, is lacking. Makwe does provide rare evidence for foodplants in the form of *Parinari parinari* nuts (D. Phillipson 1976) and the rarity of bored stones in Makwe toolkits suggests that underground plant foods were less important in eastern Zambia than elsewhere, though weighted digging sticks could, of course, have been used for other purposes (Ouzman 1997). Additional dietary information might be obtainable from isotopic analyses of human remains, but none has been attempted. Although Gwisho has the largest number of burials, Kalemba and Thandwe

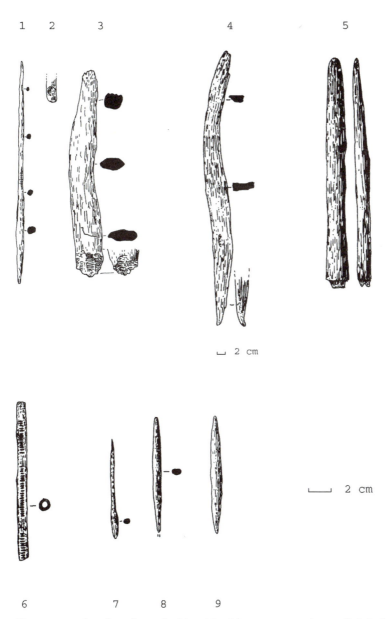

**Figure 9.8.** Artefacts from Gwisho, Zambia: 1. arrowpoint or linkshaft; 2. fire drill; 3–4. digging sticks; 5. end of bow(?); 6. carved bone tube; 7. arrowhead; 8. linkshaft; 9. arrowpoint or linkshaft. All artefacts are in wood unless otherwise stated. (Redrawn after D. Phillipson 1982: Fig. 6.12 and 2005: Fig. 51; Fagan and van Noten 1971; courtesy and copyright David Phillipson.)

in eastern Zambia also document mortuary rituals: burial of just partially broken skulls at the former, partial dismemberment, in one case associated with deposition of warthog skulls and tusks, at the latter (D. Phillipson 1976).

## Zambian Rock Art

Further insights into the beliefs of Zambian hunter-gatherers come from their rock art. B. Smith's (1997) recent overview distinguishes between Red Animal and Red Geometric Traditions, previously thought to form a temporal sequence (D. Phillipson 1976). The former is scattered across Zambia, but has its densest concentration around Kasama; recognisably different from paintings in the Kondoa and Lake Eyasi areas, it may also occur south of Lake Victoria in Tanzania (Mabulla 2005). Large red or yellowish-red paintings of animals, mostly antelope, that vary in their degree of stylisation, are characteristic, sometimes accompanied by people and often overlain by rows of dots. The art's animal associations may indicate that it was produced by men, while compositional details at some Kasama sites recall features relatable to shamans' experience of trance in southern Africa's Bushman rock art (B. Smith 1997). However, such parallels are few, and the human remains found at Kalemba and Thandwe (de Villiers 1976) show predominantly negroid, rather than Khoisan, traits, countering ideas of Khoisan presence in south-central Africa, except perhaps at Gwisho, in Zambia's far south (Fagan and Van Noten 1971).[8]

Much more widely distributed is the Geometric Tradition (B. Smith 1997, 2006a, 2006b; Fig. 9.9). Found from Uganda, Kenya, and the Lake Victoria Basin through the eastern Congo Basin and into Malawi, Angola, and Mozambique, Zambia is but one of the countries where it exists. Dominant motifs are simple geometric designs such as circles, some surrounded by dots or equipped with radiating lines, lines (some parallel), and dots, along with a few animal and human figures. Images occur as pecked or incised engravings and as paintings, usually finger-applied and in red; white paint survives at some well-protected sites, suggesting it, too, may have been widely used. Selection is evident in the choice of geometric figures and in how they are repeated and organised at particular sites. Recent

**Figure 9.9.** Red Geometric Tradition paintings, Zambia.

interpretations draw upon the ethnography of tropical forest foragers, especially the Mbuti. This is encouraged by oral traditions of Bantu-speaking Zambian farmers and nineteenth/twentieth-century traveller reports that seem to describe an aboriginal hunter-gatherer population in Zambia sometimes termed Twa[9] (B. Smith 1997). Closely resembling those of the Geometric Tradition, the designs Mbuti women use to scarify themselves and decorate bark cloth follow similar conventions about design construction and the use of space. That the rock art also shows what seem to be female genitalia and weather-related phenomena (sun, rain, rainbows, etc.) further supports its association with women because both sets of images have clear fertility connections, links reinforced by associations between many paintings or painted sites and modern rainmaking rituals (B. Smith 1997; Mabulla 2005). Demonstrable as these resemblances are, there is, as yet, little further evidence to connect the makers of Geometric rock art in south-central or eastern Africa with recent equatorial forest foragers: No connection is evident, for example, in the physical anthropological record, whereas the backed microlith and scraper-dominated artefact assemblages from Zambia and Malawi differ greatly from those of the Ituri, the only part of the Congo Basin with relevant excavated sequences (Mercader 2003b).[10] Finally, note that the contemporaneity of Red Animal (male-associated) and Geometric (female-associated) Traditions suggested by rare two-way superpositions and widespread spatial segregation of sites (B. Smith 1997) remains, for the moment, unsupported by absolute dating techniques.

## THE FAR SOUTH

### Stone Tools and Subsistence

Beyond the Zambezi, Mode 5 Wilton assemblages rich in small scrapers and backed microliths (especially segments) had wholly replaced their Oakhurst predecessors by 6000 bp. Varied local reasons involving changes in hafting design, tool standardisation, and innovation of new artefact types were probably important in this process (Bousman 2005), with risk-minimisation to cope with adverse climate changes a contributory factor in some cases (Mitchell 2000). Changes in the frequency and typology of backed microliths and scrapers distinguish successive phases within the Wilton, and a trend towards increased numbers of woodworking adzes after 4000 bp is widespread. Regional industries are also discernible (Wadley 2000b). Wilton-equipped foragers have left such a rich, intensively researched archaeological record (Mitchell 2002a:160–226) that we identify only a few key themes, emphasising how data have been explored as much as describing the record itself.

Across southern Africa, large ungulates were probably important socially for meat sharing and providing the wherewithal for groups to stay together in larger numbers, just as in ethnographically described recent Bushman societies. However, in the main, Holocene hunters focused on smaller, territorial game, developing a pattern already identified in Chapter 8.[11] Instead, plant foods underwrote the distribution and dynamics of Holocene foragers in southern Africa (H. J. Deacon 1993). Occupation was more sporadic, or at best at lower density, where highly variable rainfall rendered them less reliable, as in Bushmanland (Beaumont *et al.* 1995) or the Karoo (Sampson 1985a). Some savanna areas, in contrast, display more intensive occupation histories, geared to collecting nut/fruit-bearing trees like marula. Zimbabwe's Matopo Hills exemplify this (N. Walker 1995a), but in Limpopo and Mpumalanga known sites are few, perhaps because people used open-air camps more (cf. Korsman and Plug 1994), perhaps because earlier research biases are only now beginning to be corrected (Thorp 2004). The most dependable plant resource, however, was probably geophytes, the reproduction and productivity of which can be enhanced by burning. They were key resources on the highveld, but, combined with enhanced ecological diversity, more stable rainfall and abundant coastal resources such as shellfish, sustained even denser, more enduring populations in South Africa's Fynbos and Forest Biomes.

## Seasonality, Sedentism, and Storage

Earlier researchers emphasised seasonality and seasonal movements across the landscape when modelling how food resources were combined. Inspired by the palaeoeconomy school of Eric Higgs (1972), Carter (1970, 1978) followed this approach in the Maloti-Drakensberg Mountains, though his conclusions warrant further investigation and Cable's (1984) later suggestion of movement from within Lesotho to the Indian Coast seems farfetched (Opperman 1987). More detailed studies come from the Verlorenvlei area of South Africa's Atlantic coast (Parkington 1988), which it is now known was not abandoned after 7800 bp (Orton and Compton 2006), despite a long occupational hiatus in the key sequence from Elands Bay Cave. Contrasting seasonal indicators in the post-2000 bp deposits there and at De Hangen, 60 km inland, provided the initial basis for arguing that people spent summers inland and winters at the coast (Parkington 1977). Subsequent research restricted the model to the period 4300–2000 bp (Parkington *et al.* 1987), but even this is now questioned given the virtual lack of inland sites dating to the third millennium bp (Jerardino 1996).

Stable isotope analyses of human remains offer an independent line of evidence given that, in this region, coastal and terrestrial resources have quite distinct isotopic signatures. Results show that between 4000 and 2000 bp, individuals dying at the coast differed markedly in diet (and thus landscape use) from those dying inland (Sealy and van der Merwe 1988). Questions have been raised over the long-term stability of the region's isotope ecology (and thus the uniformitarian assumptions that the analyses require), the effects of dietary change over an individual's life, and whether the technique exaggerates marine protein over other foods, such as terrestrial plants (Parkington 1991, 2001). However, though results do, indeed, suggest that coastal people used terrestrial resources (Lee Thorp *et al.* 1989) as basic nutritional considerations dictate (Noli and Avery 1988), the isotopic data as a whole are inconsistent with regular seasonal movements between coast and interior (Sealy and van der Merwe 1992; Sealy *et al.* 2000). If this is so where resources do pattern markedly in space, then there seems even less likelihood of well-defined, regular seasonal rounds having been practised where ecological structure is less pronounced (Jacobson 1984; Humphreys 1987).

Across much of southern Africa, after 4500 bp (3500 bp around the Verlorenvlei and to its north; Jerardino 1996) people increasingly stressed resources that were predictable, productive, and low in risk (geophytes, shellfish, fish, tortoises, etc). This shift in the balance of subsistence strategies is explicable if they were choosing, or being compelled, to adopt less mobile lifestyles within more circumscribed regions as overall population sizes increased. Identifiable in KwaZulu-Natal and Zimbabwe, the trend is best documented in the Cape Fold Belt and its coastal forelands. North and south of Elands Bay Cave, for example, higher rainfall and cooler seas after 3000 bp greatly improved terrestrial and marine productivity, encouraging the growth of large, open-air 'megamiddens' that document exploitation of black mussels (*Choromytilus meridionalis*) on a massive scale. For Henshilwood *et al.* (1994), such sites reflect intensive drying of mussels for later consumption inland, perhaps by single-gender task groups, as male isotope signatures of this period show enhanced marine protein intake relative to women (Lee Thorp *et al.* 1989). However, the absence of contemporary sites inland on which we have already remarked, and the demonstrable presence of many other activities (Jerardino and Yates 1997), suggest that the megamiddens were residential camps, perhaps associated with nearby rockshelters (Jerardino 1998). Mussel-drying to prolong access to desired resources would be equally consistent with this interpretation, and is one of a suite of storage strategies for which there is evidence. In the Matopos, for instance, pits contain marula and (*mopane?*) caterpillars (N. Walker 1995a), whereas at many southern Cape sites pits were used to preserve the seeds of *Pappea capensis*, an edible fruit yielding a prized cosmetic oil (Binneman 2000; Fig. 9.10). Both areas, along with others where small package foods were increasingly pursued, also show the development of regionally circumscribed artefact styles and/or toolstone choices that may have signalled group identity (Mazel 1989; Binneman 1996; S. Hall 2000), just as was the case among nineteenth-century/Xam Bushman groups (J. Deacon 1986).

Isotope analysis of human remains confirms that in the Cape's Forest Biome at least, many Holocene individuals were relatively sedentary, living and dying within quite small areas, and maintaining distinctive diets, with implications for both body size and health (Sealy and Pfeiffer 2000; Sealy 2006). Other analyses also hint at regionally varied activity patterns and lifestyles (Stock and Pfeiffer 2001; Dewar and Pfeiffer 2004). Moreover, the exceptional concentration of burials in the Fynbos and Forest Biomes (Inskeep 1986) recalls an observation that we have already made – the likelihood that repeated placement of the dead at particular locations asserted claims to ownership of an increasingly crowded landscape. Welgeluk, a cemetery before it became a residential site after 4000 bp, is a particularly good example of this (S. Hall and Binneman 1987). That burials are fewer and generally less complex in this region after 3500 bp suggests still further changes in how social organisation and landscape affiliation were expressed. Perhaps rock art, which sometimes included depositing painted stones in pits or burials (Pearce 2005),[12] was another way of doing this?

### Social Approaches to Hunter-Gatherer Archaeology in Southern Africa

Recent analyses of burial practices are enriched by data drawn from Bushman ethnographies (Wadley 1997a; S. Hall 2000). Encouraged by developments in rock art research that we describe shortly, this forms part of a major reorientation of southern African hunter-gatherer archaeology towards addressing a broad gamut of questions about past social relations. Wadley (1987) led the way here, exploring how seasonal patterns of aggregation and dispersal may manifest themselves archaeologically and identifying possible correlates (ostrich eggshell beads, bone arrow points) for the systems of delayed, reciprocal gift-exchange known from the Ju/'hoansi and some other Bushman groups. Gender is another focus, with Mazel (1989), for example, in part, reading the post-4000 bp trend toward intensification of plant food and ground game exploitation in the Thukela Basin as a conscious struggle by women to enhance their status *vis-à-vis* men. As an example of how social variables should be considered when analysing technological choices, he also presents evidence that in some areas scrapers and backed microliths were preferentially made from exotic toolstone, adzes using local rocks, a pattern with potential gender connotations if the former were male-related (leatherworking, hunting); the latter, female-associated (shaping of digging sticks primarily for use in plant-gathering).

Such ideas have been widely taken up (e.g., S. Hall and Binneman 1987; Wadley 1989; Kinahan 1991; N. Walker 1995a; papers in

**Figure 9.10.** Storage pit at Nuwekloof Shelter, South Africa. (Courtesy and copyright Johan Binneman.)

Wadley 1997b), but important questions remain. Foremost among them, given the almost complete lack of ethnography about people living in rock-shelters or making stone tools, is the degree to which unambiguous correlations can be made between social processes and archaeological finds (Barham 1992). Ignorance of tool functions is another problem, one slowly being improved by microwear and residue studies (Binneman 1982; B. Williamson 1997). Uncertainties about how archaeological assemblages built up are also many: Jerardino (1995a) discusses the importance of finding ways of disentangling size, nature, and duration of occupation; Mitchell (2003), demonstrates that putative exchange items had actually moved, rather than merely assuming this from formal analogy with Ju/'hoan practice. Another consideration must be the degree of resolution attainable archaeologically. To situate social change in relations between people, rather than between people and environment, individuals must be identifiable. Burials and rock art offer most scope for this, but excavated evidence needs to be more highly resolved in space and time than is often the case: Large-scale excavations of short-lived occupation horizons offer one strategy, most promisingly perhaps at open-air locations that minimise re-occupation and disturbance relative to rock-shelters (Parkington 1992, 1998). Finally, archaeologists need to beware of using too narrow a range of Bushman ethnographies or of inadvertently creating a picture of undue stasis in hunter-gatherer lifeways: Greater attention should be directed to investigating the archaeology of ethnographically known groups like the /Xam or Ju/'hoansi (N. Walker 1995b), to reaching beyond them to other Bushman ethnographies, and to employing analogies and comparative theoretical frameworks drawn from beyond southern Africa (Parkington 1984; S. Hall 1990; Humphreys 2004/05). Sealy's (2006) recent demonstration of dietary difference and relative sedentism among people living in the Plettenberg Bay area of South Africa, to which we have already referred, provides a strong indication that patterns of social organisation among later Holocene foragers were more variable than anything recorded from the Kalahari or Karoo.

### Bushman Rock Art

We have already noted the importance of rock art research for informing recent hunter-gatherer archaeology in southern Africa as a whole. Like their contemporaries elsewhere, southern African foragers left an enormous heritage of rock paintings and engravings that emphasise naturalistic representations of people and animals (especially big game, such as eland, kudu, and gemsbok). Paintings are typically monochrome or bichrome, but polychrome examples also occur, some using shading to attain an exceptional quality. Paintings occur in most areas with suitable rock-shelter surfaces, the Maloti-Drakensberg and Cederberg Mountains (Fig. 9.11), the Matopo Hills, and Namibia's Dâures massif all being major centres. Engravings, on the other hand, dominate in the Karoo and western Free State: Fine-line forms are the oldest, but pecking and scraping were also employed after 2700 bp (Fig. 9.12). All together, many thousand sites are known.

Archaeological understanding of this art was transformed by Patricia Vinnicombe (1976) and David Lewis-Williams (2003), who

**Figure 9.11.** Rock paintings of antelope, Western Cape Province, South Africa.

**Figure 9.12.** Scraped rock engravings of eland and a human figure, Northern Cape Province, South Africa.

grasped that to comprehend its meanings it was essential to reject ear-lier interpretations grounded in a naïve empiricism or sympathetic magic, turning instead to Bushman ethnography (Lewis-Williams and Loubser 1986).[13] The result is an infinitely more detailed and nuanced picture than exists for other African hunter-gatherer rock arts, or for most others elsewhere in the world. A tripod of ethno-graphic data sustains current thought, drawn from the comments of the Maloti Bushman Qing (Orpen 1874), a much larger corpus of nineteenth-century material dictated by /Xam informants from the Northern Cape (Bleek and Lloyd 1911; Hollmann 2005a), and recent observations of Kalahari groups (e.g., Katz 1982; Keeney 2003). Showing surprising congruencies (Lewis-Williams and Biesele 1978; Lewis-Williams 1992), they are reinforced by ethnographic frag-ments from other sources (e.g., How 1962; P. Jolly 1986). Collec-tively, these data demonstrate how the art expresses the beliefs and religious practices of the people who made it — in particular, the experiences of shamans who, by tapping into supernatural potency within themselves, could enter altered states of consciousness, com-mune with God, cure the sick, control animals, make rain, and go on out-of-body travel. These experiences and actions were (and are) crucial to the social and economic reproduction of society (Lewis-Williams 2003). They can be widely recognised in the art, directly and through visual metaphors (notably the eland) explicable from Bushman ethnography (Lewis-Williams and Dowson 1999; Lewis-Williams and Pearce 2004).

A yet more profound understanding comes from learning that southern African Bushmen believe(d) that shamans can move among the three tiers (above, this world, below) of the cosmos (Lewis-Williams 1996). This helps explain, for example, depictions of ani-mals entering or exiting the rock face, which was probably thought of as a portal to the spirit world (Lewis-Williams and Dowson 1990). It also enriches understandings of past burial practices and the selection of some sites as cemeteries, others as living sites (Wadley 1997a; S. Hall 2000). Furthermore, this worldview can be success-fully applied to the full range of the art: nineteenth-century paintings previously seen as mere records of historic events (Campbell 1986); engravings (Dowson 1992); the paintings of the Maloti-Drakensberg Mountains (Lewis-Williams 1981), the Western Cape (Parkington

2003a), the central Limpopo Basin (Eastwood and Eastwood 2006), Namibia (Kinahan 1991), and still other regions; and even previously enigmatic images such as the 'formlings' known from Zimbabwe (Mguni 2006), or the thin red lines widely observed in the Maloti-Drakensberg (Lewis-Williams *et al.* 2000). But although shamanism is central, other levels of meaning may also exist (Lewis-Williams 1998). Solomon (1997a,b), for example, has argued that paintings, including the 'canonical' texts from sites in Lesotho interpreted by Qing (Orpen 1874), relate to beliefs about creation myths. However, no strong correspondence is discernible between the art's content and that of /Xam mythology (J. Deacon 1994) or that recounted by Qing, and any connections more likely reflect the common origin of both in a shamanistic cosmology (Lewis-Williams 1998; cf. Guenther 1994). Other perspectives suggest that the art references gender distinctions within forager societies, contains narrative elements, and expresses beliefs about hunting and the control of weather that are not directly linked to shamanism (Solomon 1992; Parkington 1989, 1996, 2003b). More recently, attention has been given to networking knowledge of animal behaviour with Bushman beliefs and to the importance of animals other than eland as key symbols (e.g., Challis 2005; Hollmann 2005b).

Redirecting southern African rock art research along ethnographically grounded lines has transformed both it and the wider discipline of hunter-gatherer archaeology, not least by introducing to rock arts elsewhere in the world a concern with understanding the representation of experiences gained in altered states of consciousness (Whitley 2000; Lewis-Williams 2002; Lewis-Williams and Pearce 2005). Much remains to be done, however, to draw parietal and excavated records into a closer working relationship, though it seems very plausible that rock art helped structure and reproduce social relations at times of social aggregation; Carter (1970) suggested this several decades ago, Wadley's (1987) aggregation/dispersal model implies it, and seasonality-related images in Drakensberg paintings offer support (Mazel 1983). One way to develop such arguments further is by building a reliable chronology for the art, given that excavated finds are temporally constrained and researchers otherwise run the risk of interpreting the art in a timeless 'ethnographic present' (see inset). More detailed, systematic studies of interregional variability are also required because differences certainly exist (Hampson *et al.* 2002); Zimbabwe, for instance, has little explicit trance or shaman-related imagery, emphasising instead different kinds of supernatural potency (Garlake 1995).

---

### DATING SOUTHERN AFRICAN ROCK ART

Dating rock art poses many challenges to archaeologists. In a few cases, painted or engraved stones, or exfoliated slabs and spalls of parietal art, may be preserved in stratified archaeological deposits, as at Steenbokfontein Cave (Jerardino and Swanepoel 1999) or the many painted stones found in pits or burials in the southern Cape (Pearce 2005). These are, however, special cases, and leave the vast bulk of rock paintings untouched. One strategy is to investigate the content of the art, given that images of cattle or sheep, for example, can only have been created after these animals were present in, or close to, the region concerned. This approach has been used, for example, in conjunction with distributional data to suggest a chronology for paintings in the Winterberg area of South Africa's Eastern Cape Province (Hall 1994), and for engravings in the Northern Cape (Beaumont and Vogel 1989). More recently, attempts have been made to develop Harris matrices that show the stratigraphic interrelationships of images at individual sites and to seek correlations among sites with a view to refining the stylistic sequences proposed by a previous generation of researchers. Work by Thembi Russell (2000) and Joané Swart (2004) in the Drakensberg Mountains exemplifies this well. Absolute dates have also now begun to be obtained for the same region, applying AMS-dating to paintings (where organic substances may have been used in their production) or to organic matter trapped above and/or below them (Mazel and Watchman 2003). Collectively, these approaches now suggest that painting on rock-shelter walls began by 6000 bp in the Matopo Hills, 3500 bp in the Western Cape, and 3000 bp in the Drakensberg. They also indicate that some open-air engravings are at least 7000 years old and show that potentially important temporal changes in imagery and belief can begin to be traced.

## INTENSIFICATION WITHIN LIMITS: A COMMON THEME?

### *Intensification: Definition and Critique*

Surveying the record left by mid-Holocene hunter-gatherers across Africa, we have more than once noted evidence for the emergence of economies characterised by elements of delayed, rather than immediate, forms of labour investment (Woodburn 1982). Intensive, often managed, exploitation of *r*-selected resources (seeds, nuts, fish, shellfish, etc.) that demand specialised procurement, processing, and storage 'gadget technologies' is typical of such systems (Hayden 1994). They are also frequently associated with such phenomena as range reduction, increased sedentism, the creation of cemeteries, enhanced intergroup competition and exchange, and greater regionalisation of material culture as a means of structuring social interactions and defining or contesting individual and group identities. Significantly less equal forms of social relations may also develop, with the institutionalisation of leadership roles. Privileged individuals may emerge by settling disputes previously resolved by moving away, facilitating/ controlling flows of information, regulating access to resources, or simply because sedentism permits accumulations of wealth and food that lend themselves to political manipulation and the lifting of previous constraints on self-aggrandising behaviour. Population increase and/or increased settlement of previously marginal environments are also common (Price and Brown 1985; Keeley 1988; Bowdler 1995), though disentangling cause and effect within the precise trajectories followed in an individual case is not easy (cf. Ames 2005).

Where discussed elsewhere, for example, in Australia, such phenomena are typically linked together under the rubric of intensification, with social and political factors, rather than ecological or demographic ones, given primacy in explanations inspired by structural Marxism (Lourandos 1983, 1997). A similar emphasis is discernible in some African work (Mazel 1989), but there is good reason to believe that spatial and temporal fluctuations in resource availability also influenced the scale and timing of such developments (Kelly 1995:321–28). Examples of social and economic intensification in mid-Holocene Africa might include South Africa's Fynbos and Forest Biomes, the Kansyore groups of the Lake Victoria area, Ghana's Kintampo complex, the Upper Capsian of the Maghreb, and the inhabitants of the Malian steppes and lakesides before final aridification of the Sahara. As more detailed regional pictures are developed, it will become easier to draw parallels and contrasts among such areas and those where intensification is less well marked or seems wholly absent. Exchange between groups practising different subsistence strategies is one factor to look out for, as in Mali (Petit-Maire *et al.* 1983; R. McIntosh 1998). Another common thread may lie in access to lacustrine, riverine, and coastal resources susceptible to long-term, sustained, bulk exploitation.

To assume too tight a set of linkages among dietary broadening, the specifics of resource ecology, and social change would, however, be wrong. Although increased emphasis on *r*-selected resources may be widely identifiable, it does not follow that the social consequences that this entailed were always identical. How resources were combined together within a total economic pattern, previous community history, and contemporary social organisation and ideology will all have played a part. Furthermore, caution must be exercised against the possibility that these changes reflect nothing more than the tendency of the archaeological record to favour the preservation of younger sites that are, by their very nature, more likely to contain organic remains. In other words, is it possible that supposed evidence for directional change reflects biases in archaeological preservation (Bird and Frankel 1991; Wadley 1989)? The much improved evidence for coastal resource exploitation across the Pleistocene/Holocene transition illustrates this well because we know from sites like Klasies River that shellfish and other marine foods were consumed at least as early as MIS 5, their scarcity for much of the later Pleistocene presumably being, at least in part, the result of the loss of sites to subsequent rises in sea level.

Linear models of social change that see intensification as a necessarily late phenomenon, a pre-adaptation for developing food-production, or as necessarily linked to sedentism, must also be avoided (Stahl 1999; Boyd 2006; Garcea 2006). In Europe, for instance, the disappearance of Upper Palaeolithic art and the richly decorated artefacts associated with it provides one well-attested example of change towards lower levels of social integration, even if part of the reason for such elaboration in the first place was the 'hysterical' deployment of material culture of all kinds to ensure human biological and social reproduction in the face of the Last Glacial Maximum (Wobst 1990). Transformation of central Canadian Arctic Thule groups into the Netsilik of the historical record provides another such instance, and in neither case, of course, did food-production follow (Rowley-Conwy 2001). Comparable African examples include the demographically and socially dense communities discussed in Chapters 7 and 8, whose aquatic resource base was demolished by changes in the Nile's flood regime at the Pleistocene/Holocene transition, and the transition from foraging to pastoralism in the Acacus region of Libya outlined in Chapter 8.

## The (Im)possibilities of Domestication South of the Sahara

The question of 'pre-adaptation' demands further clarification because there is good evidence that, in many parts of the world, farming spread through the demographic expansion of agricultural populations at least as much as by take-up or independent domestication on the part of local foragers (Rowley-Conwy 2004; Bellwood 2005). This issue is, of course, linked to the distribution of potentially domesticable plants and animals, and it is worth emphasising here the very narrow evolutionary pathways along which domestication has travelled (Rowley-Conwy 1986; Diamond 1997). Of 51 sub-Saharan bovid taxa, for example, none has ever been domesticated; cattle and donkeys, the two African ungulates for which domestication is likely, both lived north of the Sahel. No comparably detailed survey of potential African foodplants exists, but it is striking that Saharan and sub-Saharan Africa have few large-seeded grasses (Blumler 1992), that no significant foodplant is indigenous to Africa south of the Equator, and that African species were frequently superseded by higher-yielding Indonesian or American crops once these became available. Sorghum, African rice, finger millet (*Eleusine coracana*), and even yams have origins in the savanna belt immediately south of the Sahara, pearl millet within the desert (Harlan 1982,

1992). The situation thus seems to have been one in which, for most of Africa, opportunities for developing food-production were constrained, particular pressures may have been required to encourage cultivation rather than continued dependence on a broad range of wild species, and key domesticated resources were imported from beyond the Equator or even farther north.[14]

These conclusions feed into others, notably the likelihood that managing the risks of resource failure was a key concern in adopting food-production in Africa. Marshall and Hildebrand (2002) show how, in areas of low or variable rainfall, gathering a diversity of wild plants was more compatible with mobile herding than cultivation and how herding itself could extend the security of hunter-gatherers by providing a dependable, moveable source of fat and protein. They argue that this explains a key feature of the African situation, that pastoralist (more properly, herding/hunting/gathering) economies expanded first, with cereal cultivation developing substantially later (Neumann 2005). Climate and disease also placed real barriers on the spread of both herding and farming, especially given the transequatorial or extra-African origins of many plants and animals. Gifford-Gonzalez (2000) details this for domestic livestock, but even more impermeable were the frontiers set by rainfall patterns on the expansion of Near Eastern crops into the Sahara, or of sorghum and millet-based agriculture in southernmost Africa (Mitchell 2005b). Third, and finally, the potential for intensifying use of many of the *r*-selected resources we have mentioned in this chapter was probably limited: nut- and fruit-bearing trees (like *Canarium* or marula) have long maturation periods and high processing costs, geophytes show restricted productivity even if fire-managed, and many grasses, at least in southern Africa, have such low protein/carbohydrate contents that they were used only as famine foods or if ants had first harvested and stored the seeds (H. J. Deacon 1993). Unlike other Mediterranean environments, like California or the Levant, South Africa's Fynbos and Forest Biomes may thus have had ecological ceilings on the degree to which socio-economic intensification could 'take off'. Our discussion in Chapter 8 makes the same point for another intensively investigated region, Libya's Tadrart Acacus, where severe aridity ended the delayed-returns economic pattern of Late Acacus hunter-gatherers, Barbary sheep had only limited potential for domestication, and further intensification was achieved by shifting away from sedentism toward a more mobile, pastoralist economy (Garcea 2006). In other contexts, managing yams, oil palm, and *Canarium* in tropical forest areas may have enhanced access to desired resources without significantly altering the subsistence economy as a whole (Casey 2005). If confirmed by further research, the astonishingly early presence of banana phytoliths in Uganda before 4500 bp could provide an additional example of such plant-management integrated within the delayed-returns, but otherwise largely wild resource-focused, economy practised by makers of Kansyore pottery in the Lake Victoria region (Lejju *et al.* 2006).

Ecological determinism is scarcely the whole story, and social relations are also critical in explaining agricultural origins (Hayden 1990), a point recently reiterated by D. Edwards (2004) in an African context. We nonetheless suggest that, by the yardstick of temperate latitudes in Eurasia or North America (Fagan 1991; Mithen 2003), the African record shows, for the most part, relatively limited processes of transformation that did not – perhaps could not – transcend critical thresholds of social or economic intensification without the introduction of resources from outside. Except for the ceramics discussed in Chapter 8, greater dietary breadth – Flannery's (1969) broad-spectrum revolution – seems to have been but rarely linked with the emergence of hunter-gatherer societies characterised by permanent inequality or significant, transformative technological innovation. Unlike the rest of the Old World, societies geared to hunting and gathering therefore continued to flourish in Africa for much of the Holocene, often engaging in exchange relations with food-producers or benefiting from mobile, extensive pastoralist lifeways that offered them only minimal competition (Marshall and Hildebrand 2002). The two broad areas in which these limits to growth were exceeded were, we suspect, the eastern Sahara (with the domestication of cattle and the addition to them of sheep and goats) and one or more areas of the Sahel (when cereal cultivation was combined with livestock). It was these two processes that, working over several millennia, eventually resulted in most Africans ceasing to be hunter-gatherers and becoming farmers or pastoralists. How this happened in eastern, central, and southern Africa is the theme to which we now turn.

SUMMARY

The mid-Holocene is a period of great interest in African archaeology as it saw various systems of food-production take hold and expand in much of the continent. Climate seems to have been a significant force in promoting this expansion, most obviously seen in the spread of pastoralism across the Sahara and its later expansion into the Sahel and East Africa. Abrupt, drier events around 8.2, 4.5, and 4.1 kya were particularly significant, and help frame the chronological limits of this chapter. For hunter-gatherers, the expansion of herding (and later still of mixed farming economies that also included an element of cultivation) did not necessarily spell disaster. Numerous opportunities for exchange and survival presented themselves, as in Mali's Méma Basin, and it would, in any case, be wrong to draw too hard a distinction between farming and foraging. Regrettably, our database is still too poor to give colour to such generalisations in all parts of the continent, and the expansion of farming across Cyrenaica and the Maghreb is a good example of where research could usefully be directed. One general theme that emerges for this period in many regions is that of intensification, with data from areas as diverse as Algeria/Tunisia (the Upper Capsian), Ghana (the Kintampo Complex), and the shores of Lake Victoria (the Kansyore industry) pointing to greater commitments to sedentism and the exploitation of *r*-selected resources, sometimes incorporating some use of ceramics, cultigens, or domesticated livestock. Such resources seem, however, to have often been introduced from north of the Sahel, and we contend that neither sub-Saharan Africa's bovids nor its grasses offered much opportunity for successful domestication. Management of indigenous resources had its limits and only rarely – most notably perhaps with yams and oil palm in West Africa's tropical forests – were these ecological constraints transcended without diffusion from, or the immigration of, populations already engaged in food production. Exploring these processes is a key feature of the records of some of the areas reviewed here – for example, the tropical rain forests, the Middle Nile, and the northern part of East Africa. Farther south, domesticated resources were a much later introduction, first appearing only a little before 2 kya. The hunter-gatherer archaeologies of south-central and southern Africa are thus especially rich, complemented and strengthened by a wealth of rock paintings and engravings that speak to the social and ideological, rather than just the material, dimensions of their makers' existence. For southern Africa, Bushman ethnography provides the key to understanding this art, and also helps drive the investigation of more social questions that include gender, exchange, and the organisation of domestic space. Though less intensively studied in this way, the ethnographies of East African and tropical forest foragers hold out hope of developing comparable research strategies in their regions too.

# CHAPTER 10

# FORAGERS IN A WORLD OF FARMERS

The past 3000 years have seen the number of Africans pursuing a hunter-gatherer lifeway diminish to virtually zero. The contrast with the period covered thus far is stark. However, hunter-gatherers, and the descendants of people for whom hunting and gathering was still the primary means of making a living until recently, have not disappeared. They survive as recognisable communities in many African countries, while their cultural, linguistic, and genetic heritage is much more widely shared (Fig. 10.1). This chapter examines how this situation has come about, emphasising the diverse relations between hunter-gatherers and the pastoralist, agropastoralist, colonial, and postcolonial societies that first existed alongside, and now enclose, them.

Excavated archaeology, rock art, ethnography, linguistics, genetics, oral traditions, and written history track a myriad of relations: resistance, coexistence, adoption of food-production, displacement, and assimilation. After some preliminary remarks, we survey relationships between hunter-gatherers and their neighbours in four parts of the continent: East Africa; the equatorial forests; south-central Africa; and Africa south of the Zambezi. This completed, we address the so-called Kalahari debate, asking whether these relationships have so altered the hunter-gatherer societies known to anthropologists as to render invalid their use as baselines for understanding earlier foragers. Finally, we examine the current economic and political status of African foraging peoples. This, in turn, forms

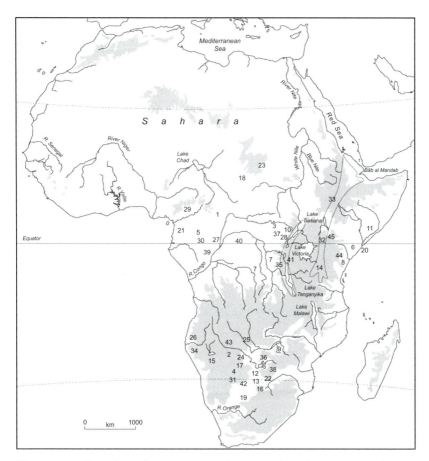

**Figure 10.1.** Location of contemporary forager and ex-forager groups in Africa. 1. Aka; 2. //Ani; 3. Asua; 4. ≠Au//eisi; 5. Baka; 6. Boni; 7. Cwa; 8. Dahalo; 9. Doma; 10. Efe; 11. Eyle; 12. G//ana; 13. G/wi; 14. Hadzabe; 15. Hai//om; 16. ≠Hoã; 17. Ju/'hoansi; 18. Kajakse; 19. ≠Khomani; 20. Kilii; 21. Kola; 22. Kua; 23. Kujarkse; 24. Kxoe; 25. Kwandu; 26. Kwisi; 27. Mbendjele Yaka; 28. Mbuti; 29. Medzan; 30. Mikaya; 31. Nharo; 32. Ogiek; 33. Ongota; 34. OvaTjimba; 35. Rhwa; 36. Shua; 37. Sua; 38. Tshwa; 39. Twa (Republic of Congo); 40. Twa (Democratic Republic of Congo); 41. Twa (Burundi and Rwanda); 42. !Xõ; 43. !Xu; 44. Waata; 45. Yaaku.

a bridge to Chapter 11, which considers archaeologists' responsibilities to those claiming descent from the groups they aim to study.

## FORAGERS AND FOOD-PRODUCERS

### Farming Frontiers

We preface our discussion with some general comments about the relations between foragers and food-producers. A key concept is that of frontiers, introduced to African history by Kopytoff (1987) and to African archaeology by Alexander (1984a, 1984b; see also, P. Jones 1984, Lane 2004). As outlined in Chapter 9 and the regional discussions that follow, Africa has seen multiple frontiers result from the staggered expansion and transformation of many different systems of food-production, each with its own specific characteristics. In general terms, however, three phases of expansion are distinguishable (after Zvelebil and Rowley-Conwy 1984): a pioneer phase, when food-producers explore, but do not permanently settle, areas ahead of their area of settlement; a substitution phase, when farmers or herders initiate permanent colonisation; and an end phase of consolidation, perhaps marked by agricultural intensification, the development of greater sociopolitical complexity, and the eventual disappearance of hunter-gatherer groups from the archaeological record.

The consequences for hunter-gatherers vary from one phase to another. Thus, during the pioneer phase, relations may have minimal impact and be confined to the more-or-less occasional exchange of domesticates or farmer/herder material culture for 'bush' or 'forest' products collected or made by foragers. As food-production takes hold during the substitution phase, hunter-gatherers may retreat, develop more structured, permanent relations of clientship with food-producers, be absorbed through intermarriage, commence losing access to land or resources, and gain greater access to new technologies and products. As expansion draws to an end, such processes gain strength, bringing loss of, or massive reduction in access to, crucial subsistence resources, deprivation of land, consolidation of client relations, and eventual disappearance of forager languages or recognisable forager communities.

Table 10.1 lists the likely archaeological correlates of these pro-cesses, which end when the 'moving' frontier of a territorially expanding food-producing society reaches the limits imposed by climate, geography, or successful resistance. Relations across such 'static' frontiers may variously include mutual avoidance, raiding, and exchange (Alexander 1984a). A final point worth noting is that, in general terms, foragers may find it easier to develop exchange rela-tions with farmers than with herders. Exchanges of the former kind are well documented globally (Spielmann and Eder 1994) because, examples such as the Ogiek and Maasai of East Africa notwith-standing, pastoralists often have less to offer (by way of foodstuffs, for example) than agriculturalists.

For those hunter-gatherers known from the ethnographic record, what needs to be understood is how they have been able to per-sist notwithstanding the expansion of food-producing economies around or alongside them (cf. papers in Kent 2002). Discussing this issue, Woodburn (1988) refers to the encapsulation of African hunter-gatherers, though noting that those involved may not per-ceive their situation as one of confinement. His emphasis lies rather on how farming or pastoralist neighbours asserted political domi-nance, stigmatising foragers as culturally inferior. Such views stem as much from ignorance (of language, mores, etc.) as from patterned contrasts with the values and lifestyles of food-producers. They are, nonetheless, real (and politically alive today), if frequently coupled with a degree of respect for foragers as possessors of supernatu-ral knowledge and aboriginal owners of the land. Examples as dis-parate as the Bushmen who once occupied Lesotho and the Aka and Baka of the northwest Congo Basin attest to this (Ellenberger 1953; Hewlett 1996). Crucially, encapsulation does not, of itself, imply subordination: so long as sufficient land and resources remain to sup-port a forager lifeway, stigmatisation and claims to dominance need not translate into political or economic dependency. In contrast, where foragers and food-producers were more equal in number and level of political organisation, as during the pioneer phase described earlier, then relations between them may have departed widely from those recorded ethnographically and in favour of hunter-gatherers (Woodburn 1988:49–50).

TABLE 10.1. *Characteristics of the expansion of food-producing economies after Alexander (1984a, 1984b) and Lane, (2004)*

| Farmers/herders | Hunter-gatherers |
|---|---|
| **A – Pioneer Phase (Moving Frontier)** | |
| Pioneers explore/exploit the 'wilderness', seeking land, pasture, metals, 'bush' products, and frequently using techniques/technologies similar to those of hunter-gatherers | Interact with pioneer farmers/herders, exchanging 'wild' products (bush meat, hides, ochre, honey, ivory, etc.) for domesticated plants/animals, farmer/herder material culture |
| *Archaeological signatures* | |
| Technologies may be similar to hunter-gatherer aborigines | Occasional traces of 'exotic' items of farmer/herder material culture and domesticated fauna or cultigens |
| Transient camps/settlements | |
| Occasional traces of domesticates and farmer/herder material culture | Some possible reduction in self-sufficiency |
| **B – Substitution Phase (Moving Frontier)** | |
| Farmers/herders begin substantive settlement and colonisation through infiltration, negotiation, or conquest. Manifestations include:<br><br>• acquisition of pasture, land, access to water and other local raw materials;<br>• creation of permanent settlements;<br>• intermarriage with hunter-gatherers;<br>• establishment of exchange or client relations;<br>• potential for more hostile interactions;<br>• adoption of loan words, material culture, and ritual practices from hunter-gatherers | Increasing interference from farmer/herder strategies, with possible consequences including:<br><br>• greater access to new technologies, products, and 'prestige goods';<br>• development of symbiotic or client relations with farmer/herder communities;<br>• absorption of some group members through intermarriage;<br>• adoption of loan words, material culture, and ritual practices from farmer/herders;<br>• habitat change/destruction through agricultural clearance/overgrazing and other impacts on the environment from food-production;<br>• retreat into more isolated areas |

| Farmers/herders | Hunter-gatherers |
|---|---|
| *Archaeological signatures* | |
| Modification of local habitats | Major changes in material culture inventories |
| Creation of more permanent settlements, monuments, rock art | Evidence for specialised hunting, craft production, collection of other 'bush products' |
| Changes in DNA of human populations | |
| Evidence for exchange in prestige goods or specialised products | Changes in diet, site occupation, seasonal round |
| Changes in social organisation of production | Changes in DNA of human populations |
| | Possible introduction of new disease pathologies |
| | Partial disappearance or spatial restriction of hunter-gatherer settlements |

## C – Consolidation Phase (Moving Frontier ends)

| | |
|---|---|
| Development of new farming technologies/intensification | Loss of, or massive reduction in access to, means of subsistence |
| Increased specialised exploitation of wild resources, especially animals | Consolidation of client-based/ symbiotic relations with farmers/ herders |
| Increased warfare | |
| Voluntary restriction of population increase | Endemic warfare with farmers/ herders |
| More competitive social relations, e.g., prestige goods systems | Encapsulation |
| | Disappearance of hunter-gatherer languages |
| *Archaeological signatures* | |
| Introduction of irrigation, field-terracing, and other systems of agricultural intensification | Disappearance of forager subsistence patterns and material culture inventories |
| Infilling of more marginal areas | Incorporation of surviving hunter-gatherers into farmer/ herder settlements |
| Partial migration to new land if available | |
| Growth in circulation of prestige goods/evidence for warfare | Absence of sites attributable to hunter-gatherers |
| Greater evidence of wealth/status differentiation | Evidence for site destruction, physical trauma suggestive of warfare |
| | Enhancement/maintenance of distinct material culture boundaries |

*Forager/Food-Producer Relations: Three Possibilities*

More recently, S. Kusimba (2003) identifies three broad possibilities about how forager/food-producer relationships may be structured.[1] The first is symbiosis, the development of ties that create and maintain a situation of mutual dependency between foragers and food-producers so tight that *neither* party can readily walk away. Strategies involved include coresidency, intermarriage, and, typically, intensive exchange. Tropical forest foragers provide one of the best contemporary examples of this situation, the intensity and longevity of their relationships with neighbouring farmers indicated by the fact that all now speak Bantu or Sudanic languages.[2] One example is that of the Efe of the Ituri forest, who, for part of the year, frequently visit and live near the villages of Lese farmers, trading meat and honey from the forest and helping to harvest crops in return for food, metal, and other goods, but returning deeper into the forest to hunt and gather during the dry season (R. Bailey 1991). Joiris's (1998) study of the Baka of Cameroon shows how political and military considerations can, in other circumstances, play much more crucial roles than concerns for protein and carbohydrate. In particular, farmers sought the spiritual and practical help of the Baka as both parties engaged in the precolonial ivory trade.

An alternative possibility is that of parallelism, the development of technologies and social forms that mimic those of nearby food-producers, allowing interaction while permitting foragers to retain a distinct identity. The Ogiek (previously Okiek) of East Africa, for example, survive where cattle-keeping and farming were historically unsustainable, generally in cold, high-altitude areas of Kenya's central highlands. Their subsistence depends on hunting small game and husbanding, and collecting and trading honey (as well as a wide range of other animal products) to Maa-speakers for whom honey is a ritual necessity. To facilitate such exchanges, Ogiek use Maa when trading, and take on Maasai clan names, age-set structures, initiation rituals, and patrilineal kinship systems, defining fictive kinship ties between themselves and their trade partners (Blackburn 1982, 1996). Privately owned beehives and the emphasis on property rights and storage that goes with them suggest that in at least one key respect the Ogiek practise a delayed-returns economy. They understand this as a direct analogy for Maasai cattle, something that helps to maintain 'a structural parallel to an institution of the dominant society while retaining a separate ethnic foraging identity' (S. Kusimba 2005:347).

The third option is the selection of a peripatetic lifestyle in which hunter-gatherers become flexible generalists, retaining connections with food-producers but otherwise managing their own economies, dealing freely with other societies and living in the interstices between them. S. Kusimba's (2003, 2005) own work concerning the Waata of eastern Kenya, who exemplify this strategy, is discussed subsequently. Symbiosis, parallelism, and peripateticism do not exhaust the processes of interaction taking place across the frontiers of which Alexander (1984a, 1984b) writes. All emphasise the retention of at least some degree of political autonomy, economic autarky, and a foraging-based lifestyle. In each individual case, the circumstances that allowed such a relationship to emerge or persist must also be established. Whether the foraging groups who survive today are themselves autochthonous, not 'devolved' farmers or pastoralists, has also to be problematised, not merely treated as axiomatic. We keep these points in mind as we approach the archaeological record.

## Late Holocene Palaeoenvironments

Before doing so, however, a few words on palaeoclimatic change for the period covered here. As with earlier phases of the Holocene, changes were, by Quaternary standards, of a relatively low order of magnitude, with increasing anthropogenic effects suspected in areas of pastoralist and agropastoralist settlement. Several episodes do, however, stand out, especially an abrupt regression of the equatorial rainforests and extension of savanna vegetation around 2800–2500 bp (Maley 2002; Marret *et al.* 2006). In East Africa, cooler conditions in the third millennium bp saw ice advance, heavier rainfall, and forest expansion on Mt. Kenya (Barker *et al.* 2001), though lacustrine records to the west and south pick up drier conditions only ~2200/2000 bp (Alin and Cohen 2003; Russell *et al.* 2003). In contrast, generally cooler, drier conditions prevailed in southern

Africa, where the late Holocene Neoglacial episode is well marked (Jerardino 1995b). The past 2000 years have, on the whole, been punctuated by a series of cooler, drier and warmer, wetter phases, though with some suggestion that these fluctuations were asynchronous between eastern and southern Africa (Tyson and Partridge 2000; Verschuren *et al.* 2000; D. Taylor *et al.* 2005; Kiage and Liu 2006). Such recurrent pulses of temperature and precipitation changes undoubtedly had an impact on human populations and their history. In particular, we can identify the Medieval Warm Epoch, from around A.D. 900–1300, and the ensuing Little Ice Age (from about A.D. 1300–1800) as periods characterised by important fluctuations in rainfall patterns that had demonstrable consequences for the growth and expansion of agropastoralist populations, and thus on the viability of an alternative, hunter-gatherer way of life (e.g., Huffman 1996; cf. Robertshaw 1999; Schoenbrun 1999).

## EAST AFRICA

East Africa is still home to several peoples for whom hunting and gathering remain, or were until recently, a mainstay. Oral traditions and archaeology hint that foragers were even more widely distributed on the landscape only a few centuries ago (Fig. 10.2). Rangi rock-shelter, Uganda, is but one example of a recent (<500 years old) Mode 5 assemblage (in this case, overwhelmingly quartz and with large numbers of scrapers and segments) found with an entirely wild fauna, perhaps partly derived from intercepting dry season movements by migrating ungulates (Robbins *et al.* 1977). Associated ceramics comprise Iron Age pottery and Akira ware, the latter a relatively late 'Pastoral Neolithic' type, but one generally found with wild, rather than domesticated, faunal assemblages. One explanation for this association may be that it represents a return to more mobile settlement strategies and greater use of foraged resources on the part of previously more specialised pastoralists (Bower 1991; cf. Gramly 1975). Alternatively, Akira ware's lightness, thinness, distinctive shape and decoration, and widespread distribution may imply manufacture by surviving forager groups for exchange (Robertshaw 1990c:198–200).

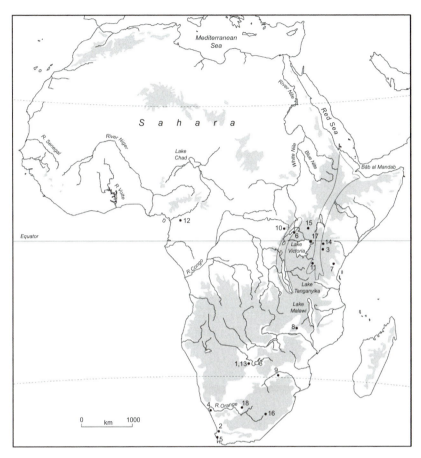

**Figure 10.2.** Location of archaeological sites discussed in Chapter 10. 1. Divuyu; 2. Dunefield Midden; 3. Enkapune ya Muto; 4. Jakkalsberg; 5. Kasteelberg; 6. Kibiro; 7. Kisio; 8. Makwe; 9. Mapungubwe; 10. Matengai Turu Northwest; 11. Mumba; 12. Nkang; 13. Nqoma; 14. Prolonged Drift; 15. Rangi; 16. Tandjesberg; 17. Usenge 3; 18. Wildebeest Kuil.

Lane's (2004) review of the expansion of food-production across East Africa emphasises the variability of initial hunter-gatherer responses during a prolonged pioneer phase of pastoralist expansion that ended ~3000 bp. One trajectory involved local foragers adopting ceramics, caprines, and ultimately cattle, as attested at Enkapune ya Muto (Marean 1992b). Another was the development and maintenance of exchange ties that provided occasional access to livestock and herder pottery and other goods through exchange, pacific or otherwise; the Prolonged Drift sequence may exemplify this (Gifford *et al.* 1980). The lack of evidence thus far for Pastoral Neolithic settlement south of the Serengeti, save for the few sherds reported by Chami and Kwekason (2003), implies that a static frontier developed here, with endemic livestock diseases perhaps inhibiting southward pastoralist expansion (Gifford-Gonzalez 2000). Limited research in central or southern Tanzania makes it impossible, however, to know what kinds of relations existed across such a frontier. By contrast, evidence does exist in two areas of Kenya where static frontiers are also suspected to have developed.

### The Ogiek And the Yaaku

The first of these areas is the Mau Escarpment, home to the modern Ogiek, where Eburran Phase 5 assemblages continued to be made until ∼2500 bp, the other on and near the Laikipia Plateau. In the latter locality, the absence of substantial pastoralist sites older than 700 bp suggests that Pastoral Neolithic pottery, domesticates, wild fauna, and Mode 5 lithic assemblages from open-air and rockshelter sites could be the residues of surviving hunter-gatherers, not expanding pastoralists. Farther west, and reaching almost to the Ugandan border, the **Sirikwa hole** phenomenon is attributed to mid-second millennium A.D. Kalenjin pastoralists (Sutton 1998). Lanet pottery found at such sites closely resembles modern Ogiek ceramics used to prepare and store honey (Blackburn 1973). The similarity may indicate that ethnographically described Ogiek-Maasai relations were preceded by similar relationships between the Ogiek and those responsible for the Sirikwa sites, or even that the Ogiek were specialist pottery producers in such exchanges. Presumably, they acquired Kalenjin as a mother tongue in this setting (Ehret 2002b:278).

Ethnohistoric data and excavations from the Mukogodo Hills indicate how rapidly such relationships can change. Here, as with the Ogiek, faunal assemblages emphasise small mammals (especially dikdik and hyrax), but also include cattle and caprines (Mutundu 1999). Such items, alongside glass beads, metal, and grain, were probably obtained from exchanging honey and other bush products with neighbouring Maasai. From the 1920s, the area's Yaaku-speaking inhabitants also acquired a Maa dialect and Maasai styles of dress, weaponry, and housing, as well as Maasai initiation and age-set practices. This cultural shift was facilitated by the marriage of Yaaku women to the Maasai, the acquisition of livestock as bridewealth, and the solidification of earlier exchange ties. The result was extensive cultural assimilation, provoked by the need of displaced pastoralists to acquire Yaaku wives in order to assert land claims within an area assigned by the British colonial authorities to cattle-less Yaaku and other 'Dorobo' (Cronk 2004; see inset). With an eye on the end of this chapter, Yaaku activists now seek to revive their original language, protect remnant forests, and reserve them for themselves (IPACC 2006).

## The Great Lakes

A farming economy based on a mix of cereals, legumes, and livestock was introduced to East Africa later than pastoralism itself. Linguistic data suggest that early Eastern Bantu-speakers moved along the northern edge of the equatorial forest to enter the Great Lakes region, acquiring sheep, cattle, and cultigens there, although relevant palaeobotanical and archaeological evidence for the presence of still earlier cultivators is totally lacking (Schoenbrun 1998). Pollen sequences suggestive of land clearance for cultivation are, however, apparent from ~500 B.C. They are associated with evidence for iron-smelting and Urewe ceramics typologically ancestral to those made by almost all subsequent early farming communities in eastern, south-central, and southern Africa (Lane 2004). Interaction between East African foragers and such early farmers is registered around Lake Victoria. Near Kavirondo, several sites (Fig. 10.3) document acquisition of rare domesticates and limited quantities of Urewe pottery, or attempts to make it, within otherwise forager contexts associated with Mode 5 lithic assemblages that are quartz-based and relatively expedient, though sometimes with a clear bladelet element (Gabel 1969; Lane *et al.* 2007). They are paralleled by others on Lake Victoria's western side and in Rwanda (Nelson and Posnansky 1970;

DOROBO: WHAT'S IN A NAME?

In East Africa, the term Dorobo has been widely applied to describe people who lived by hunting, gathering, fishing, and ivory trading. Derived from the Swahili Wandorobo, itself a corruption of the Maasai Il Toroboni, it refers to someone who is so poor that they have no cattle and must therefore eat game. Echoing the Kalahari debate in southern Africa, however, some researchers have proposed that many East African foragers are (or were) nothing of the sort. Van Zwanenberg (1976) and Chang (1982), for example, both argue that the Ogiek and others descend from pastoralists and farmers who lost land and livestock during the nineteenth and early twentieth centuries. Just as in southern Africa, European travel journals form a primary source of the evidence that they use, situated within the context of historically attested warfare, cattle epidemics, and the enforced crystallisation of tribal identities under colonial rule. There seems little doubt that the term Dorobo was sometimes applied by these writers and by colonial officials to people who were, in fact, impoverished pastoralists, nor that some of them later regained status as Maasai by acquiring and retaining livestock. However, as Blackburn (1982) underlines, the more than thirty known Ogiek groups share a distinctive suite of material culture, subsistence practices, and social relations, as well as a clear sense of self-identity, historical independence, and language affiliation that is recognised by other Kalenjin-speakers around them. Such features imply that the identity of most Ogiek transcends the specific political and economic events of the early colonial period (Distefano 1990). Indeed, linguistic evidence may suggest that one group, the Omotik, diverged from other Kalenjin-speakers at least 1500 years ago, which substantially reinforces the case for Ogiek autochthony (Blackburn 1982; cf. Blackburn 1996:193). Such data strengthen the likelihood that they descend from the hunter-gatherers who were present in central Kenya before largescale pastoralist settlement of the region (Ambrose 1986:12).

**Figure 10.3.** Usenge 3 shell midden, Kenya: close-up view of the excavated deposits. (Courtesy and copyright Paul Lane.)

Nenquin 1967), and they show considerable continuity from the stone tools found earlier in the same area, and sometimes on the same sites, with Kansyore pottery. However, little firm stratigraphic detail exists with which to work, and linguistic and genetic evidence suggests that the formation of societies speaking Bantu languages and practising a mixed farming economy resulted from a highly fluid situation (Lane 2004), one in which hunter-gatherers were more than mere bystanders.

### Other East African Foragers: Hadzabe, Sandawe, and Waata

Regrettably, there is little detailed archaeological evidence with which to consider what happened to hunter-gatherers as farming expanded farther south, nor to elucidate the history of groups such as the Hadzabe or the Sandawe. For the Hadzabe, potentially relevant archaeological material comes from Beds I, II, and upper/middle Bed III at Mumba Shelter. It includes ceramics (Early Iron Age Lelesu pottery, as well as Pastoral Neolithic Kansyore and Narosura wares), iron arrowheads, and stone pipes, but Mehlman (1979, 1989) offers few further details, though noting the existence nearby of several freshwater shell midden accumulations of presumed Hadzabe origin. Little new has been learned from excavation over the intervening decades (Seitsonen 2005), though the Hadzabe are well studied ethnoarchaeologically (e.g., O'Connell *et al.* 1988). Mabulla (2003), in particular, emphasises the potential that exists for developing observations capable of relating their current land-use strategies to those practised by past Eyasi Basin hunter-gatherers. The Sandawe past is even more obscure, with relatively little recent work undertaken in the rock art-rich Kondoa area to add to earlier observations that stone tool manufacture survived into the second millennium A.D. (Inskeep 1962; Masao 1979). Genetic data add a new twist to these discussions, given that, whereas Sandawe show little evidence for the lactase persistence phenotype that allows adults to digest raw milk, this is present at around 50% among the Hadzabe. Whether this does, indeed, imply that the latter descend from a pastoralist population, or whether it reflects selection for other reasons, perhaps to digest particular glycoside-rich foodplants, remains to be determined (Tishkoff *et al.* 2007a). Analysis of mtDNA and Y chromosome data suggests that both Hadzabe and Sandawe have experienced moderate levels of both male and female in-migration from agriculturalist/pastoralist neigbours during the last few thousand years (Tishkoff *et al.* 2007b).

Rather more is known about the recent past of foragers in eastern Kenya, principally from work in the Taita-Tsavo area (C. Kusimba and Kusimba 2005; S. Kusimba and Kusimba 2003). Here, Kisio rockshelter (Fig. 10.4) was occupied in the last thousand years by people who left an almost wholly expedient lithic assemblage made in the local quartz and a fauna that emphasises small package foods (bovids, hyrax, hare, birds, and snails). Glass beads, pottery, and metal artefacts attest to participation in regional trade networks, fitting ethnohistoric evidence that local Waata foragers procured ivory for trading caravans, which handed back grain, metal, and other goods in return. Rock crystal, rhinoceros horn, skins, and beeswax were among other products traded on to the Swahili towns of Kenya's coast, and the Waata also acquired fame as specialised manufacturers of arrow poison and became indispensable actors in the rites of passage of some of their pastoralist neighbours (S. Kusimba

**Figure** 10.4. Kisio Shelter, Taita-Tsavo region, Kenya. (Courtesy and copyright Chapurukha Kusimba and Sibel Barut Kusimba.)

2003:228). Using distinctive art forms to assert their own identity (Bollig 1987; Kassam 2000), this economic pliancy allowed them to persist in the interstices of the more stratified societies around them until colonial wildlife conservation policies and Britain's creation of 'tribal reserves' destroyed their mobility and place within the regional economy (Kassam and Bashuna 2004). Whether before then Waata pliancy extended to sporadic or seasonal engagement in herding or farming is uncertain (Thorbahn 1979), but trade probably provided an important means of reducing subsistence risks by mediating local scarcities in what was, and is, an area of low, unpredictable rainfall.

## CENTRAL AND SOUTH-CENTRAL AFRICA

### Foragers and Farmers in the Equatorial Forests

Tropical forest foragers constitute a classic instance of hunter-gatherer/farmer interaction, popularised in Colin Turnbull's (1961) account, *The Forest People*. At least a dozen distinct forager groups exist today within Africa's equatorial forests, varying in their social organisation and subsistence patterns,[3] but all characterised by exchange relations of some kind with farming neighbours (Köhler and Lewis 2002). Linguistic and archaeological evidence align to suggest that an economy based on oil palm, yams, and goats, complemented by hunting, gathering, and fishing, spread south through the western part of the equatorial rainforest from Cameroon after 3000 bp (Vansina 1994/95), perhaps encouraged by the onset of a drier climate (Schwartz 1992; Maley and Brennac 1998; Maley and Chepstow-Lusty 2001). Another crucial factor may have been the availability of an important new carbohydrate staple in the form of plantains and bananas (*Musa* sp), phytolith evidence for which comes from ceramics excavated at Nkang, Cameroon, dating to 2600–2200 bp (Mbida *et al.* 2000, 2004; cf. Vansina 2003). Initially stone-using, those practising this economy later smelted and worked iron, and by 2000 bp were present as far as the mouth of the Congo River, as well as inland along many of its tributaries (Eggert 1997). They are generally acknowledged to have spoken Bantu languages, a language family with origins along the Nigeria/Cameroon border. However, there is nothing in the archaeological record to exclude the possibility that Bantu languages and knowledge of domesticates proceeded through assimilation of, or take-up by, indigenous foragers, rather than by the demographic growth and territorial expansion of Bantu-speaking migrants alone (Vansina 1995; cf. Eggert 2005). As farming expanded, however, foragers could find themselves gradually displaced, unable to pursue hunting and gathering as their lands were encroached upon. Despite a degree of resistance, this was particularly so of Twa groups in Rwanda and Burundi, most of whom ultimately became specialist potters (Köhler and Lewis 2002).

### The Ituri

The most relevant archaeological dataset again comes from the Ituri forest, home today to Mbuti and Efe foragers. Observations are particularly rich for the second millennium A.D., for which all the rockshelters tested contain 'capping units' that provide a wide range of finds. Their microlithic quartz assemblages, made until some time after A.D. 1200, seem little different from those found in the same region earlier in the Holocene (Mercader and Brooks 2001). However, to earlier evidence of *Canarium* consumption, better preservation conditions now add oil palm and a wild forest fauna, including duiker, porcupine, primates, and large molluscs such as *Achatina*. Such features find parallels in recent forest forager adaptations. Though forager settlement in Africa's equatorial forests was evidently *not* dependent on the resources obtained from neighbouring agriculturalists (Mercader 2003b; *pace* R. Bailey *et al.* 1989), the fact that farmers have been present in central Africa for many centuries does suggest that forager adaptations have changed, challenging archaeologists to investigate how and why such changes came about. Access to iron tools may have been one crucial factor in the initiation of exchange relations, forager knowledge of forest resources previously unknown to expanding farmers a second (Bahuchet *et al.* 1991). Unanticipated consequences may have included increased forager populations, reduced mobility, and exposure to disease, all of which may have come to hinder largescale or complete returns to a purely foraging lifestyle (Wilkie and Curran 1993).

The capping units reported from the Ituri sites provide some relevant evidence for the shape and antiquity of such relationships in the form of pottery, iron artefacts, and metallurgical debris. The mostly rouletted ceramics resemble those from the Kibiro salt-producing site in Uganda (Connah 1996), and it was probably from this direction that agriculturalists first entered the Ituri. However, exchange, or scavenging from abandoned farmer villages, is unlikely to account for the observed abundance and decorative diversity of the pottery found, whereas two rockshelters produced objects interpreted as having been used in pottery manufacture. The ceramics may thus have been made by foragers, their close similarities in raw material choice and technology with ethnographically documented farmer pottery indicating the closeness of the relations between the two groups (Mercader *et al.* 2000b). Unless surviving evidence reflects a concern for ritual isolation of smelting on the part of farmers, ironworking was another technology transferred between them, with finds from rockshelters including iron slag, vitrified clay, ore, tuyère fragments, and rare finished artefacts, among them an arrow-point from Matengai Turu Northwest (Mercader *et al.* 2000c). The same site produced the only burial known from the Ituri. Examined largely *in situ* and very fragmentary, its size and lack of caries nonetheless hint at a forager affiliation and diet (Mercader *et al.* 2001).

Summarising this evidence, it seems that, relative to earlier periods, recent forager adaptations were characterised by longer-term settlement within rockshelters that were used for multiple purposes (ceramic and metal production, nut gathering, hunting, burial). Hunting techniques may have altered as iron-tipped arrows became available, while vegetable resources probably increased as forest clearance facilitated the growth of oil palm and perhaps other foodplants (Mercader 2003b). Transfers of technology, in particular, point to the development of close links with neighbouring farmers, something further evidenced by foragers' adoption of farmer languages, though great caution is required in generalising from the specifics of the Ituri situation to all African tropical forest foragers.

### South-Central Africa

Although few forager groups survive today between the equatorial forests and the Kalahari, they were more widespread in Zambia, Malawi, and adjacent areas of the Democratic Republic of Congo into the nineteenth and early twentieth centuries (see inset). In southwestern Zambia, ethnographic data record that Lozi and Subiya farmers exchanged pottery and metal for the meat, skins, and labour offered them by Hukwe Bushmen. Similar connections may be implied archaeologically by finds of agriculturalist pottery, metalwork, and grindstones at sites such as Makwe (Fig. 10.5), where rare cattle and goat bones also occur, albeit in a mostly wild fauna (D. Phillipson 1976). Farther north, in eastern Zambia, Chewa traditions record that such exchanges did not only involve the material: rain shrines and weather divination practices are both said to have been borrowed from foragers (Schoffeleers 1973). Elsewhere in south-central Africa, processes of interaction cannot yet be modelled in

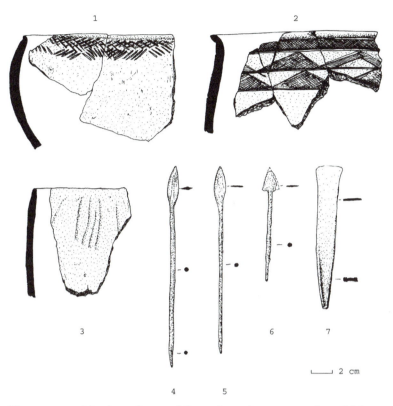

**Figure 10.5.** Metal artefacts and Later Iron Age pottery from Makwe, Zambia. 1–3. pottery; 4–6. iron arrowheads; 7. iron axe. (Redrawn after D. Phillipson 1976: Figs. 60 and 61; courtesy and copyright D. Phillipson and British Institute in Eastern Africa.)

detail, but one intriguing development is implied by observations from the Lunsemfwa Basin farther to the west. There, some four or five centuries elapsed between the first establishment of an agriculturalist presence and the appearance of farmer-made ceramics in Mode 5 assemblages within rockshelters, hinting that regular interaction between farmers and foragers perhaps took some considerable time to develop (Musonda 1987). Here, then, avoidance is suspected, instead of exchange or the more rapid displacement of hunter-gatherers seen where, as in southern and central Zambia, early farming settlement was relatively dense.

SEEKING THE TWA

Archaeological evidence shows that the Mode 5 industries of south-central Africa discussed in Chapter 9 continued to be made well into the second millennium A.D. (D. Phillipson 1976; Crader 1984; Barham 2000). Their makers are likely to have been among the ancestors of groups known variously in the region's oral histories as Akafula, Abatwa, or Batwa, the latter referring to communities living around Lake Bangweulu, Lukanga Swamp, and the Kafue Flats, who are, however, now culturally similar to their neighbours (J. D. Clark 1950). Described as skilled archers and ironsmiths, the Akafula/Abatwa/Batwa seem not to have practised agriculture and to have, at least sometimes, occupied caves or rockshelters. Moreover, they are recalled as having been relatively short in stature with physical characteristics reminiscent of those of tropical forest foragers in the Congo Basin or the Khoisan of southern Africa. The term Batwa itself (Abatwa is a variant) is the plural form of a word reconstructed as •-*tóa* in Proto-Bantu and now widespread in the Congo Basin and eastern, south-central, and southern Africa. Outside the equatorial forests themselves, where it is used with specific reference to so-called Pygmy peoples, its meaning is a general one: populations that are (were) non-Bantu-speaking hunter-gatherers thought to have been the aboriginal inhabitants of the country (Schadeberg 1999). As noted in Chapter 9, specific connections between the Twa of Zambia, mid/late Holocene rock art there, and the ethnography of today's equatorial forest foragers remain contentious.

*Southern Africa*

South of the Zambezi, as in East Africa, multiple frontiers played out between food-producers and foragers (Mitchell 2004). Overcoming or circumventing the barriers to pastoralist expansion created by endemic livestock diseases (Gifford-Gonzalez 2000), sheep and cattle reached northern Botswana and western South Africa (sheep only) by 2100 bp (Sealy and Yates 1994; Robbins *et al.* 2005). Their arrival was, from a regional standpoint, a little later than the appearance of a wide variety of ceramics (Sadr and Sampson 2006), but individual sequences show variability in the degree of association with livestock. By the time of European contact in the late 1400s, sheep- and cattle-keeping Khoe-speaking pastoralists dominated much of the western third of southern Africa. Mixed farming economies predicated on cereals, legumes, and livestock, on the other hand, were confined to its eastern half. Introduced in a complex series of movements from about 1800 bp, they reached a southernmost limit around 33.5°S when encountering the transition from summer- to year-round rainfall regimes (Nogwaza 1994). Subsequent expansion onto the highveld grasslands of South Africa's interior and western Lesotho began ~A.D. 1300, gathering pace after 1640. Limits to further expansion were set by low rainfall in the Karoo and much of the Kalahari and by cold temperature in the Maloti-Drakensberg Mountains. It was in these regions that foragers persisted longest, their ultimate dispossession from some areas the result of European settler expansion after 1652.

## Hunter-Gatherers, Herders, and Foragers-With-Sheep in Western Southern Africa

A crucial question in this region concerns the relations between sites with evidence of livestock-keeping and those without. Are these separate groups of people, or rich and poor components of a single society? And were sheep first introduced by ancestors of the historically known Khoekhoen, or acquired by hunter-gatherers through other means?

The first of these topics has provoked much debate and a recognition that the multiple criteria proposed for distinguishing forager and herder signatures in the material record of the Western Cape (A. Smith *et al.* 1991) are far from universally valid (Schrire 1992; Wilson 1996; Webley 1997; Sadr 2003; Sadr *et al.* 2003; cf. Parsons 2003).[4] Factors other than ethnicity warrant greater consideration, among them intersite functional variability and the practical arrangements of livestock management. So, too, does historical change in the kinds of herding economy practised; in the Western Cape, for example, cattle were apparently introduced significantly later than sheep (Klein and Cruz-Uribe 1989), as recent linguistic analyses also suggest (Crawhall 2004). Moreover, the numbers of both may also have substantially increased as trade with Europeans took hold (Sadr 1998).

Turning to the second question just posed, the case for sheep having been introduced to the Cape by an immigrant Khoe population is based on the latter's presence there at European contact and Khoe's origin within the Tshu-Khwe language group in northern-most Botswana ∼2000 years ago (Elphick 1985). Reinforcing this, A. Smith (1990) argues that egalitarian hunter-gatherers would have found it socially very difficult to establish viable, privately owned herds, whereas B. Smith and Ouzman (2004) use a distinctive geo-metric rock art tradition assigned to the Khoe to track their move-ment south.[5] Counterarguments abound: pottery with pierced lugs, thought to be made by Khoe-speakers, is nowhere reliably dated before 1200 bp; its arrival in the key Kasteelberg B sequence of the Western Cape broadly coincides with other changes in the arte-fact and faunal records, perhaps indicating a new population; and ceramics from first millennium A.D. contexts, including those with evidence of sheep-keeping, are typologically very diverse, some-thing inconsistent with a close common origin (Sadr 1998). Bam-bata ware, one of the kinds of pottery involved in this debate, has a particularly wide distribution (from northern Botswana through Zimbabwe as far as the Magaliesberg). Its presence in the Limpopo Valley, where numerous sheep paintings also occur, and some lin-guistic reconstructions suggesting one-time Khoe settlement, could support the spread of herding envisaged by B. Smith and Ouzman (2004). However, substantially more work needs to be done on clar-ifying its apparent associations with foragers, herders, and farmers, alike (cf. Huffman 2005).

If the appearance of sheep in Namibia and the Western Cape during the first millennium A.D. does not signal the arrival of Khoe migrants, what does it mean? One answer may lie in the Kala-hari, where some Bushman communities have acquired goats, but without (thus far) radically restructuring other aspects of their sub-sistence economy or social organisation; the goats are, as it were,

**Figure** 10.6. Kalahari Bushmen tending goats. (Courtesy and copyright Kazunobu Ikeya.)

tacked onto an existing *forager* structure of social and economic relations (Ikeya 1993; Kent 1993; Fig. 10.6). Such foragers-with-sheep may be visible in the archaeological record of the Cape (and other regions) in the first millennium A.D. (Sadr 2003). In further parallel with the trickle-and-splash model previously discussed in relation to East Africa (Bower 1991; Marean 1992b), rare instances such as Jakkalsberg where sheep are plentiful may document a later transformation into a fuller commitment to pastoralism (Sadr 1998; Sadr *et al.* 2003). However, the herder-with-sheep argument has still to address the problem of how to ensure the long-term viability of sheep-keeping. For this, at least 60 animals are required; too many, perhaps, for anything other than a pastoralist lifestyle (A. Smith 2005b).

The objection that hunter-gatherers cannot readily acquire livestock and become herders is more easily countered, not least by the fact that it clearly did happen on multiple occasions (Chapter 9 and below). Assuming that southern African hunter-gatherers were necessarily immediate-returns foragers like the Ju/'hoansi or G/wi of the Kalahari may also be flawed. Recalling the megamidden phenomenon and the constraints on individual mobility and group territory discussed in Chapter 9, we ask whether incorporating sheep was attractive as a means of minimising subsistence risks, acquiring additional sources of food, and accumulating wealth for people already moving to a more delayed-returns economic pattern. Did the settlement pattern and resource distribution changes noted by Jerardino (1996) in the westernmost Cape after 2400 bp form part of the context for this? And, in discussing the adoption of sheep and pottery in Namibia, is Kinahan (1991) correct to emphasise the potential of shamans as individuals capable of transcending constraints on egalitarianism by acquiring a prestigious new resource? The advantages of ceramic technology in offering new ways of cooking and storing food also merit consideration.

Still uncertain in all this is where the ceramics and livestock came from. Ehret (1998) argues on linguistic grounds for a still archaeologically invisible herder population in Zambia, whereas A. Smith (1992) identifies potential similarities (perhaps just functional coincidences?) between southern African ceramics and some East African Pastoral Neolithic wares. The alternative donor would have to be an early iron-working mixed farming society, but none is known in Zambia at a suitably early date (Mitchell and Whitelaw 2005:216). The puzzle remains, complicated by a recent analysis of radiocarbon dates for early pottery that floats the possibility of its independent invention within southern Africa (Sadr and Sampson 2006). Further work in the northern Botswana/western Zambia area is urgently needed, not least because aquatic resource exploitation by hunter-gatherers there could have encouraged the emergence of societies practising more delayed-returns economies who had an appetite for new technologies such as livestock and ceramics (cf. Robbins *et al.* 1998a). Even more desirable would be the extension of fieldwork to Angola, still a country of which the archaeology remains almost wholly unknown after more than four decades of civil war.

Turning back to the Cape, a key site is Dunefield Midden, a camp-site near the Atlantic coast occupied ~650 bp to collect shellfish, kill seals, hunt eland and other game, and roast whale meat (Parkington *et al.* 1992; Jerardino and Parkington 1993; see inset). Farther north, numerous sites are becoming known in Namaqualand: among them, SK400, a mass springbok killsite, recalls tactics employed by nineteenth-century /Xam Bushmen and challenges, by its very scale, notions that women were always excluded from the hunt (Dewar *et al.* 2006). Inland, in the Cederberg Mountains, an area unattractive to herders, site locations emphasise small rockshelters that typically exhibit a distinctive spatial arrangement of grass bedding around a central hearth; food debris stresses ground game, small bovids, and geophytes, a pattern recalling that of Dutch-recorded seventeenth-century Sonqua foragers, and lithic assemblages include high frequencies of adzes, thought to have been widely used to make and sharpen digging sticks (Parkington and Poggenpoel 1971; Parkington 1984). The rarity of sheep, and absence of cattle, in paintings at such sites and those closer to the coast suggest that a fine-line, forager tradition did not long survive the introduction of livestock (Yates *et al.* 1994). Important social changes between pre- and post-2000 bp forager societies are implied.

---

REFITTING THE PAST

Dunefield Midden is one of many open-air sites in a relict dune cordon near Elands Bay Cave, South Africa. It stands out from them, however, because of its comprehensive excavation and near-perfect preservation of organic materials, which together offer an unparalleled opportunity to investigate how people lived there 600–700 years ago. The site is sandwiched between a more recent aeolian sand and an underlying matrix, which forms the living floor on which the site's occupants left traces of their activities and preserves traces of an earlier, mid-Holocene occupation (Orton and Compton 2006). With this exception and some limited overprinting at its southern edge, Dunefield Midden comprises a single stratigraphic level. Excavated over an area of 860 m$^2$, it represents one or more relatively brief occupations that left features such as dumping areas, hearths, and roasting pits distributed among scatters of bone, stone, and shellfish (Fig. 10.7). Collectively, the finds recovered document the various activities

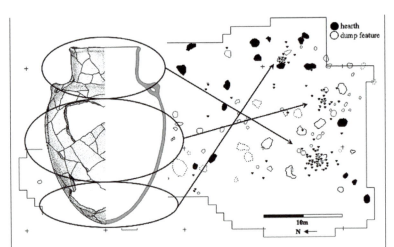

**Figure 10.7.** Spatial patterning at Dunefield Midden, South Africa. This example shows the use-life history of a large ceramic vessel: The neck and body sherds were the first to break off and lie at a distance in the dump; the still-useful base probably broke later, or was cached, near a hearth where it had been used. (Courtesy and copyright Brian Stewart.)

described in the main text. Moreover, detailed analysis of their distributions and the systematic refitting of a range of materials that includes tortoise shells, ostrich eggshells, ceramics, and the bones of sheep, steenbok, and eland offer unparalleled opportunities for investigating how people structured their use of space in acquiring, consuming, and discarding food and in making and using tools (Parkington *et al.* 1992; Orton 2002; Tonner 2002; Parkington 2006b; Parkington and Fisher 2006; B. Stewart 2007). One aspect of these studies is whether the kinds of pottery (B. Stewart 2005) and many sheep bones found point to herders, rather than foragers, having been the site's inhabitants.

Another area rich in hunter-gatherer archaeology for the past 2000 years is the Seacow Valley, where foragers developed their own suite of elaborately decorated grass-tempered wares and the area's upper reaches were later also settled by herders. A complex process of assimilation fed by recurrent droughts and the area's ecological fragility then saw herders and foragers increasingly integrate to the point at which the latter economy disappeared (Sampson 1988; Bollong and Sampson 1999). Still later deposits track the gradual appearance of European artefacts and loss of indigenous bone, stone, and ceramic technologies following European intrusion in the 1770s, sustained guerrilla warfare, the enslavement of many local foragers, and the eventual conversion of those who survived into a landless rural work-force (Saitowitz and Sampson 1992; Westbury and Sampson 1993; Sampson 1995).

## Hunter-Gatherers and Agropastoralists in Eastern Southern Africa

Examining the recent history of hunter-gatherers across southern Africa's eastern half, several themes stand out. First, is the uneven-ness with which they survived or were displaced. In Zimbabwe and Mozambique, for example, replacement of foragers by farmers pro-ceeded relatively rapidly (N. Walker and Thorp 1997). In contrast, foragers survived much later farther south and west, and especially so in areas beyond the ecological limits of farming, as in Lesotho's highlands and much of the Kalahari. In some areas, indeed, foragers acquired and retained livestock for themselves. Dating A.D. 1500–1830, the Type R sites of the western Free State are the best example of this, faunal and stable isotope analyses confirming the addition of livestock, but not cultivated cereals, to a diet otherwise made up of wild resources (Humphreys 1988; Lee Thorp *et al.* 1993). Cat-tle and sheep from late first millennium A.D. contexts in Lesotho's highlands raise the possibility of a yet older forager-with-livestock phenomenon (Mitchell and Whitelaw 2005:232–233), perhaps com-parable to that postulated for the Cape (Sadr 2003).

Several studies indicate the kinds of relations that existed between foragers and farmers. The widespread employment in southeastern southern Africa after 1700 bp of yet another distinctive ceramic technology (undecorated, thin-walled, often grit-tempered wares) was acquired early, ahead of, or during, the pioneer phase of farmer expansion (Mazel 1992, 1999). A little later, ostrich eggshell beads, bone arrow points, and stone tools found on farmer settlements in the Thukela Basin are probably the remnant 'hard' evidence for the transfer of many further 'invisible' plant, animal, and mineral products. In return, foragers acquired ceramics, iron, livestock, and cultivated foodstuffs, probably on an equitable basis, at least during the pioneer and availability phases of farming's expansion (Mazel 1989; Hobart 2003). As consolidation took hold, however, farming villages probably substituted for traditional aggregation foci, intermarriage patterns increasingly favoured farmers, and growing farmer and livestock numbers constrained forager movement and access to resources. Genetic evidence for intermarriage between farmers and foragers is strongest in southeastern southern Africa (Richards *et al.* 2004), and is supported by the numerous click sounds in today's Nguni languages that have Bushman or Khoe origins.[6] Cultural borrowings are also attested (Fig. 10.8), especially the reconfiguration of Bushman shamanistic beliefs into Nguni divination practices that Hammond-Tooke (1998) suggests was facilitated by the preferential marriage of hunter-gatherer women into farmer communities identified by DNA analyses (Salas *et al.* 2002). Though neither genetic nor linguistic evidence is tightly dated, and Nguni languages probably only entered the region ~ A.D. 1100 (Huffman 1989), within the frontier of farming expansion the totality of these processes led to the eventual assimilation of hunter-gatherer communities. As described by Wadley (1996), working farther north in the Magaliesberg, the process was one of progressive 'social strangulation' that undercut the social and biological reproduction of forager societies.

Loubser and Laurens' (1994) analysis of rock art and excavated evidence in the Caledon Valley reveals a similar pattern. Once farmers began settling there, perhaps ~ A.D. 1300 (Mitchell and Whitelaw 2005), richly decorated rock art sites such as Tandjesberg may have helped substitute for the 'real' coming together of a now more dispersed forager population (Wadley and McLaren 1998). Changes in ceramic preference further suggest that foragers refocused their exchange ties toward farmers (Thorp 2000). Beyond the limits of viable cereal cultivation, where autonomy could be maintained, hunter-gatherers selected sheep, cattle, and Sotho shields as potent symbols incorporated into their rock art (Loubser and Laurens 1994). Horses joined this repertoire in the mid-1800s, and

**Figure 10.8.** Rock painting of two human figures wearing bandoliers, part of a larger panel showing many more such figures, some with baboon tails, and many horses, Lesotho. (Redrawn after Vinnicombe 1976: Fig. 218.) The bandolier motif, which is is widely distributed among agricultural societies in tropical Africa, may have been borrowed by Maloti-Drakensberg Bushmen from Nguni-speaking agropastoralist neighbours (P. Jolly 2005).

nineteenth-century rock art in the Maloti-Drakensberg mountains compellingly records the many transformations in local forager societies as they sought to survive encroaching farmer and European settlement through strategies such as ivory-trading, cattle-raiding, clientship, warfare, and retreat. Paintings document the evolution from a previously more egalitarian background of pre-eminent individuals who used shamanistic skills to gain leadership roles, partly founded on success in raiding or in making rain for Nguni-speaking farmers (Campbell 1987; Blundell 2004). Though individuals survived and were absorbed, autonomous Bushman communities did not. A comparable history took shape in the Northern Cape homeland of the /Xam people, whose words, transcribed by Wilhelm Bleek and Lucy Lloyd, underwrite current understandings of Bushman rock art (J. Deacon 1996).[7]

This was not, however, the first time that southern African hunter-gatherers had to contend with expansionist state-level polities. Such societies first emerged in the late first/early second millennia A.D., partly on the basis of expanding trade with Swahili and other merchants visiting the region's Indian Ocean coast (Pikirayi 2001; Mitchell 2002a:300–341). In the Shashe-Limpopo Basin, which was crucial in these developments (Leslie and Maggs 2000), forager settlement first intensified in the early first millennium A.D., perhaps attracted by the possibilities of exchanging hides and meat with newly settling farmers. When Zhizo people re-established a much denser agricultural presence ~ A.D. 900, interaction patterns changed: foragers, now more constrained in using the landscape, engaged more heavily in supplying raw materials and (presumably) labour. However, as elite-controlled long-distance trade in skins, ivory, and gold intensified, foragers were increasingly relegated to the economic and political margins. Their role was taken over by commoners within the emerging K2/Mapungubwe polity, among whom they may have been subsumed. Former forager sites were appropriated by farmers, their art overpainted (Hall and Smith 2000). Surviving foragers developed into a marginalised class of dependent clients, taxed with providing labour, skins, and other products for their agropastoralist patrons (van der Ryst 2003).

## BEYOND THE KALAHARI DEBATE

### The Kalahari Debate in the Kalahari

This is, of course, part of the vision offered by the historical and archaeological research of so-called revisionist scholars such as Wilmsen (1989) and Denbow (1990), whose work calls into question ethnographic portrayals of surviving Kalahari foragers as autonomous communities. The implication is that the 'hunter-gatherers' observed by anthropologists were anything but pristine (Schrire 1980), a view echoed in East Africa (Chang 1982) and elsewhere (Headland and Reid 1989). Rather, many of their supposedly distinctive features (mobility, egalitarianism, etc.) may reflect a marginalised, oppressed status on the periphery of dominant,

more aggressive societies, as well as their impoverishment following the collapse of European-fostered commercial hunting in the
1890s (Wilmsen 1989; Wilmsen and Denbow 1990). Work by R.
Lee (1979) and others with the Ju/'hoansi has been a particular focus
of such critiques.

That many, perhaps all, Kalahari Bushman groups have had contacts of some kind with food-producers over the past 2000 years is
not in doubt (Solway and Lee 1990). For some, such as the Nharo
and ≠Au//eisi of Botswana's Ghanzi area, changes in trading and
hunting opportunities during the 1800s do appear to have promoted
important transformations in social organisation (Guenther 2002),
whereas in the Ju/'hoansi case, relevant historical evidence for this
is, in fact, lacking (R. Lee and Guenther 1993). What is not clear is
why contact should have led to forager subordination, as the revi-
sionists have sometimes been taken to suggest (R. Lee 2002:187).
Although today's Bushman societies include farm labourers, squat-
ters, and herdsmen, sometimes in century-old relationships, others
have remained much more autonomous (Guenther 1996; Vierick
and Hitchcock 1996; Barnard and Taylor 2002). Moreover, distinctive forager languages, kinship systems, cosmologies, technologies,
and social systems stressing sharing, reciprocity, and egalitarianism
also survived (Kent 1992). Ignoring such evidence, or overplaying
the significance accorded the few potsherds, metal items, and livestock bones recovered from otherwise Stone Age contexts, can only
contribute to denying Kalahari foragers a history of their own making (Sadr 1997; *pace* Wilmsen 1989; Denbow 1990).

A more nuanced view of forager-farmer relations within the Kalahari is thus developing – one that allows for considerable temporal
and spatial variation and avoids presuming that such relations developed along simple, linear trajectories (Reid 2005; Sadr 2005). In the
far northwest, for example, excavations support Ju/'hoansi traditions
of autonomy from, and limited exchange with, food-producers (A.
Smith and Lee 1997). By contrast, in southern Botswana, rockshelter
sequences identify an earlier phase of forager attraction toward agropastoralist villages, perhaps marked by trade in hides and ostrich eggshell beads. This gave way after Tswana arrival in the region to a pattern of gradual assimilation, the disappearance of stone-tool making,

and, eventually, the substitution of livestock and grain for hunted or gathered foods (Sadr 2005). The Tsodilo Hills in northwestern Botswana provide another example. Here, between A.D. 500 and 1100, a wetter climate supported an agricultural population with trading ties as far as the Atlantic and Indian Oceans. Stone tools from farmer settlements at Nqoma and Divuyu and farmer-made ceramics and metalwork in nearby rock-shelters may record mutual contact and exchange (Denbow 1990). If so, then one important item may have been the specularite intensively mined in the hills A.D. 800–1000; associated archaeological signatures are most parsimoniously understood as those of the foragers known to have occupied nearby rock-shelters at the same time (Robbins *et al.* 1998b). They and other hunter-gatherers *may* have contributed many of the items flowing through regional exchange networks (Denbow 1999), but this need not have placed them in a dependent or exploited position. As late nineteenth-century Hai//om control of northern Namibian copper and salt deposits shows (Gordon 1984), the ability of foragers to 'wheel and deal' to maintain themselves as pivotal, independent players in such exchange webs should not be underestimated.

### The Kalahari Debate Beyond the Kalahari

In other parts of Africa, too, research has increasingly focused on charting the degree to which present-day foragers may have long histories of participating in not just exchange relations with local food-producers, but also much larger, quasi-commercial trading systems. Such work is part of the growing, and welcome, recognition by archaeologists and others of Africa's dynamic, rather than passive, interaction with other landmasses (Mitchell 2005b). Waata involvement in supplying the nineteenth-century ivory trade in eastern Kenya is a case in point. Another, also involving ivory, comes from the western side of the Congo Basin, where, by the late seventeenth century, the Aka were procuring tusks for a trade oriented towards Europeans along the Atlantic coast. Their participation in such trade may have encouraged changes in hunting techniques and group organisation, as well as increasing their dependence on farmers, for example, for iron to use in weapons (Bahuchet and Guillaume

1982). Our comments that follow about Mbuti history, and those of Wilkie and Curran (1993) writing of the Efe, indicate that such changes and engagements characterise many African tropical forest foragers. Relations of dependency may, nonetheless, be restricted to the period of intensified trade that has marked equatorial Africa since the arrival of European merchants in the late fifteenth century. Before this, the second millennium A.D. probably witnessed foragers as well as farmers carving out new economic niches for themselves in expanding, indigenous systems of long-distance trade (Klieman 1999).[8]

Two points follow. On the one hand, and in contrast to much evo-lutionarily oriented work in the 1960s and 1970s, such interactions quite rightly emphasise the importance of understanding the specific historical context of the ethnographic record and of the impacts that contact with the wider world has had (Shott 1992). On the other, this does not negate the possibility of employing the ethnographic record in archaeological research where clearly demonstrable connections between past and present communities exist, or where empirically and theoretically robust patterns can be identified from compara-tive studies (Kelly 1995). Moreover, working back from the present archaeology can critically investigate the time–depth and associa-tions of ethnographically documented patterns of behaviour (Stahl 2001). To do this effectively may require more thorough attention to the archaeological records of areas still little known (for example, much of the Kalahari itself), but a great advantage of it would be to draw the work of archaeologists who study past hunter-gatherers yet closer to hunter-gatherer and ex-hunter-gatherer communities in the present.

## AFRICAN FORAGERS TODAY

Examining more than two decades of change in the lives of one Kalahari community, Marshall and Ritchie (1984) asked, "Where now are the Bushmen of Nyae Nyae?" The same question arises with respect to all those who retain strong links to hunter-gatherer ways of life, regardless of the degree to which they still practise them (Fig. 10.1). Literally dozens of self-identifying groups exist, strikingly diverse in their social organisation, beliefs, and subsistence practices (Kent 1996; R. Lee and Hitchcock 1998; Blench 1999a). Common to all, however, is their political and economic marginalisation within the states where they now live. Three regional super-groups can be defined: those of the equatorial rainforests, East Africa (principally Kenya, Tanzania and Rwanda), and southern Africa (especially Namibia and Botswana).

## Foragers of the Equatorial Forests

Tropical forest foragers have long related in complex ways to their horticulturalist neighbours. Today, some retain considerable self-sufficiency, deriving a significant part of their diet from forest sources, but most depend more on combining wage labour with cultivation and trade in forest products and crafts. An important development for groups such as the Baka has been a process of officially sponsored sedentarisation in permanent villages and agricultural projects that began in the colonial period and continued after Cameroonian independence (Hewlett 2000). For many Aka, in contrast, the primary vehicle for change has been different: overhunting and expanding commercial coffee production have decreased access to wild foods and increased use of cultivated plants, principally acquired through labouring on plantations where credit systems tie them into positions of indebtedness (Bahuchet *et al.* 1991). Although some Aka retain more autonomy, Bahuchet (1999) emphasises that lack of political organisation makes it difficult for them to oppose the pressures for sedentism brought to bear by government, religious missions, and international 'development' organisations.

The political turmoil prevailing in much of the Congo Basin since the early 1960s has not spared tropical forest foragers. The Mbuti, for example, have confronted military conscription, immigration by gold-seekers, deforestation, resource degradation, attempts to impose state control through taxation, and recruitment into wage labour as other challenges (Ichikawa 2000). More recently, they have been among the millions of victims of the region's civil wars, with many more Twa foragers and ex-foragers (mostly specialised potters) murdered during the 1996 Rwandan genocide (Waehle 1999). More

**Figure 10.9.** Baka foragers collecting honey, Cameroon. (Courtesy and copyright John Nelson.)

positively, some central African governments have made real efforts to respect the presence within their territories of forager groups. Burundi's 2005 constitution, for example, enshrines Twa participation in parliament, and Gabon and Cameroon have formally recognised the rights of indigenous forager communities (Fig. 10.9). More practically, some new ecotourism ventures actively involve foragers in conservation and revenue-generating efforts, providing employment, educational, and health care opportunities (R. Lee and Hitchcock 1998:22; IPACC 2006). Such efforts are supported by emerging pan-continental political alliances among forest peoples (Jackson 1999).

### East African Foragers

In East Africa, major concentrations of hunter-gatherers survive in and near the Rift Valley, Kenya's coast, and the Kenyan/Somali border. The various Ogiek communities are by far the largest, many now farming millet and maize. Land reforms undertaken by the Kenyan government in the 1970s crosscut traditional lineage land boundaries. Subdivision of these group-ranches into individually owned and marketable plots began in the 1980s. As a result, many Ogiek lost much of the land that they once owned and found it difficult to take collective action to arrest this process (Kratz 1999). Ongoing evictions from land claimed by the state as forest reserve continue a policy that began under colonial rule, the forests themselves becoming subject to unsustainable exploitation from incoming agricultural settlers and commercial loggers, actions against which Ogiek community organisations have started to protest (Ogiek 2006).

The Hadzabe find themselves in a similar position, though one tempered by the historic unsuitability of most of their homeland for herding or agriculture,[9] its rich wild plant and animal resources, and the opportunities thus created for engaging in exchange without experiencing assimilation. Post-independent Tanzania's promotion of a single, national culture has been at the expense of groups who are not sedentary farmers. Repeated attempts have accordingly been made to settle Hadzabe communities down, converting them into the peasants and workers required by the state's ideology (Kaare 1994).[10] As with similar ventures in the colonial period, such attempts failed as people returned to the bush, resisting policies that they felt might destroy their way of life (Ndagala 1988; Mabulla 2003). However, expansion into their home areas by farmers and herders, controls on hunting, and the growth of tourism (where not run in partnership with the Hadzabe) continue to threaten the long-term viability of a foraging way of life. Land loss is also of concern, with only part of historically inhabited Hadzabe territory registered to them (Kaare and Woodburn 1999; Marlowe 2002).

## The Bushmen of Southern Africa

In contrast to the areas just considered, southern Africa probably represents a more effective and co-ordinated regional network of forager organisations. This is for many reasons: the more contin-uous post-independence/post-apartheid democratic history of the three key states, Botswana, Namibia and South Africa; a more devel-oped role within them of indigenous (rather than Western-based) human rights organisations; a greater concentration of research by anthropologists, many of whom have become actively involved in human rights issues (R. Lee 2003); and a higher international profile that rides on the back of the portrayal of Bushmen in Western media as idyllic, prelapsarian people. The current reality is, of course, more prosaic, given that Bushmen find themselves faced with social and economic problems similar to other African foragers and only in a few instances retain, or have been able to reclaim, ownership of ancestral lands (R. Lee and Hitchcock 1998).

Consistent with this, the twentieth-century experience of south-ern Africa's Bushmen was dominated by dispossession and marginali-sation, producing a largely landless, impoverished underclass (Biesele and Royal-/O/oo 1999; Hitchcock 1999; RASSA 2001). In Namibia, eviction from land proclaimed as game reserves or white-owned farms (Gordon 1992) was exacerbated by the racial structures created under South African occupation, which culminated in estab-lishing a Bushmanland 'homeland'. The Tjum!kui administrative centre created there rapidly became a focus for a Ju/'hoansi popula-tion afflicted by crowding, hunger, violence, and alcohol abuse (Mar-shall and Ritchie 1984). Recruitment of men into the South African army to fight against Angolan, Cuban, and South West Africa Peo-ple's Organisation (SWAPO) forces in the 1970s and 1980s only worsened this situation. Angolan Bushmen were similarly employed and, at Namibia's independence, some 4000 of them fled to South Africa, fearing retribution from the new SWAPO government. Ending up at Schmidtsdrift in the Northern Cape Province (Sharp and Douglas 1996), they have only recently acquired permanent homes. One vehicle for community empowerment is the management of the nearby Wildebeest Kuil rock engraving site (Wildebeest Kuil 2006).

Establishing and maintaining land ownership remains a major challenge for Namibian Bushman communities. For the Ju/'hoansi, this began with an out-station, back-to-the-land movement away from Tjum!kui around 1980 that later gathered pace with the establishment of the Nyae Nyae Development Foundation of Namibia and what is now the Nyae Nyae Conservancy (Biesele and Hitchcock 2000). The two organisations have been instrumental in securing state recognition for traditional Ju/'hoansi land tenure practices, though this remains to be implemented. They have also succeeded in obtaining funds for the development of herding, cultivation, environmentally sustainable game management and ecotourism ventures, and community-based education programmes (Biesele and Hitchcock 2000; R. Lee 2003).

Botswana's experience has differed, notably in the creation (in 1974) of a development programme aimed directly at what were first termed Basarwa and then – to avoid focusing entirely on Bushmen – Remote Area Dwellers. Despite this, the socioeconomic status of most Botswanan Bushmen has declined, compounded by racial discrimination on the part of the Tswana majority, whose leaders paternalistically promote assimilation, development, and sedentism, while providing access to water (through boreholes), education, and health services (Hitchcock and Holm 1993). Many individuals and groups now herd, grow crops, or have entered the national economy as wageworkers or through selling craft goods. Others remain largely dependent on state handouts, and increased sedentism has often brought with it social problems akin to those experienced by the Ju/'hoansi of Tjum!kui (Tanaka and Sugawara 1999; R. Lee 2003). The ability to withstand state pressure is limited,[11] most revealingly in the Botswanan government's decision to remove G/wi and //Gana people from the Central Kalahari Game Reserve, ostensibly to provide better access to welfare facilities and promote game conservation (see Suzman 2002 for a summary of this complex issue). Disputed in the Botswanan courts to the at least partial advantage of the Bushmen, the case has attracted considerable, but not necessarily helpful, international attention (Zimbler 2007). As in Namibia, the HIV/AIDS epidemic and access to mother-tongue education are also major concerns, along with the development of viable wildlife conservancies and ecotourism ventures (R. Lee 2003).

In South Africa, yet a third trajectory can be mapped, starting from the fact that almost all hunter-gatherers there were killed, dispossessed, or assimilated in the nineteenth century. By the time apartheid ended in 1994, only a tiny community of N≠/u-speaking ≠Khomani appeared to survive, removed from their home in the Kalahari Gemsbok Park. Pursuing a policy of land restitution, post-apartheid South Africa restored control of this land to the ≠Khomani in 1997 and they now co-manage it, a far cry from their situation as 'exhibits' at the widely criticised Kagga Kamma theme park a decade earlier (H. White 1995; Robins 2001). Paralleling this development has been the reclamation of a Khoisan heritage by many of South Africa's 'Coloured' population,[12] and a yet wider respect for the country's hunter-gatherer past in the process of building a new nation. South Africa's coat of arms and motto (written in the /Xam language) are obvious examples of this (B. Smith *et al.* 2000), the massive investment in the new South African Museum of Rock Art and the emphasis placed on Bushman rock art in securing World Heritage Status for the uKhahambla-Drakensberg Park two more. In the latter case, the reclamation of cultural heritage has manifested itself in an unsuspected way, with the emergence of several hundred people who assert descent from, and knowledge of the customs of, nineteenth-century Maloti-Drakensberg hunter-gatherers (Derwent 2005).

These 'secret San' have been helped in reasserting their identity by various organisations linked to the much broader umbrella group known as the Working Group of Indigenous Minorities in Southern Africa (WIMSA) (WIMSA 2004, 2006). Founded in 1996, this brings together more than thirty member organisations from across southern Africa, aiming to win political recognition, secure access to resources and promote sustainable self-development (Barnard and Taylor 2002). Participating in the work of the United Nations Working Group on Indigenous Populations, it has had some success in areas such as developing education programmes. WIMSA also forms part of a much broader organisation, the Indigenous Peoples of Africa Co-ordinating Committee (IPACC), which includes many pastoralist groups and acts pan-continentally (IPACC 2006). Two particular developments are worth noting because WIMSA charges itself with protecting and upholding the cultural heritage and intellectual property rights of its member communities. First is its success in securing a share of profits from commercial development of P57, an appetite suppressant that uses Bushman knowledge of a Kalahari plant, *Hoodia* (WIMSA 2004). Second is its policy of allowing research on Bushman groups to proceed only with the permission of designated community leaders, something that embraces 'all aspects of the San heritage', including rock art and the remainder of the archaeological record (/Useb and Chennells 2004:99). Debate continues on who can justifiably advance such ownership claims, how they might be enforced, and what kind of limitations may thus be placed on research or publication. These questions are not unique to Africa, still less southern Africa. They serve as a reminder, however, that archaeology, though it draws on materials that survive from the past, is undertaken in the present and has real impacts on real people alive today. We take this theme with us into our final chapter.

## SUMMARY

Today, few, if any, Africans pursue a wholly hunting and gathering way of life. Its disappearance has been a feature of the last 2000–3000 years, but despite this, recognisable communities of forager descent survive in many parts of the continent. To understand how the present situation has come about, archaeologists have developed several models. The concept of the frontier has proved particularly popular, and the African record describes multiple frontiers resulting from the staggered expansion and transformation of several different systems of food-production. This chapter emphasises and describes those that developed in East Africa, the equatorial forests, and South and south-central Africa. The degree to which hunter-gatherer groups in any of these regions were encapsulated, i.e., territorially confined and economically and politically subordinate to farming or pastoralist neighbours, is a key question, but S. Kusimba's (2003) identification of symbiosis, parallelism, and peripateticism as three ways in which foragers structure their relations with nearby food-producers helps show that a simple model of dominance/subservience cannot adequately capture the complexity of what happened. Whether looking at groups such as the Ogiek and Hadzabe in East Africa, the Mbuti of the Congo Basin, or the many Bushman peoples of southern Africa, historical and archaeological sources emphasise the ability of foragers to maintain themselves as independent, often important, players in wide-ranging networks of interaction. Our reading of the evidence is thus at variance with that sometimes offered by revisionist scholars taking part in the (in)famous Kalahari debate and, instead, emphasises spatial and temporal variation in forager adaptation and the likelihood of nonlinear trajectories of change to the present. In some cases, for example the Ituri, in which a variety of contacts are now archaeologically documented, the initiation of exchange ties with farmers may eventually have hindered prospects for a return to a purely foraging lifestyle. In others, such as the more arid or high-latitude regions of southern Africa, independence was long retained in areas of little or no interest to food-producers. Foragers may also have chosen to adopt newly available domesticated resources for their own ends, and the Western Cape region of South Africa offers a particularly good example of this – by no means concluded – debate. Yet, where interactions undoubtedly did take place and hunter-gatherers came to be heavily involved in long-distance trading systems (as among the Waata of Kenya or the Aka of the western Congo Basin), real questions emerge as to how reliably recent ethnographies can serve as guides to long gone archaeologies. As to forager-descended groups today, they survive in close to twenty African countries. Surveying their position shows that although political and economic marginalisation are widespread, many retain a significant degree of autonomy from their neighbours as well as from the state. Moreover, they are also increasingly active politically, asserting claims to land and resources, access to development projects, tourism revenues, and intellectual property rights, and, not least through co-ordinating bodies that now operate on regional, pan-African, and intercontinental scales.

# CHAPTER II

# THE FUTURE OF THE FIRST AFRICANS' PAST

Who are, or were, the first Africans? The question may seem strange given all that has gone before, but it is pertinent to ask it now because it leads directly into several other important issues, such as the responsibilities of contemporary archaeologists to the present-day inhabitants of the African continent, what it means to be indigenous in an African context, and how academic researchers can best establish connections between the ethnographic and archaeological records. In this, our final chapter, we address these questions first, while briefly touching, too, on some of the infrastructural challenges facing archaeology in Africa. This done, we identify and summarise the key points that we feel emerge from our survey and look forward to new patterns of research in the future.

## THE PAST IN THE PRESENT

### Who Is Indigenous and What Does the Term Mean?

Our own usage of the phrase the first Africans has been, to a degree, deliberately ambiguous. One of the reasons for selecting it was to emphasise the importance of Africa in the human evolutionary story and of the archaeological evidence for this. In this sense, the phrase carries a clear chronological connotation. More specifically, it also draws attention to the fact that for all but a fraction of their existence, behaviourally modern humans have practised hunting and gathering

443

as a way of life. In that sense, hunter-gatherers, and not just earlier, now extinct hominin taxa, were indeed the first Africans. The
two should not, of course, be conflated, because our rejection of
progressivist evolutionary thinking (see Chapter 1 and discussion
later) most certainly extends to avoiding direct comparisons between
ethnographically *or* archaeologically observed hunter-gatherers and
those hominins for whom convincing evidence of modern linguistic, cognitive, and symbolising abilities is lacking. Rather, our choice
of terminology is designed to acknowledge and celebrate the fact
that hunter-gatherer societies once thrived across the entirety of the
African continent, just as they did everywhere else. This involves
more than merely echoing their importance as 'owners of the land',
a recognition frequently accorded hunter-gatherer communities by
African pastoralists or agriculturalists. It is to assert as well that peoples practising a hunting and gathering way of life have not been mere
bystanders in the creation of more recent African history, cut off from
the mainstream of events at the moment when food-production was
'invented' or introduced within a particular region of the continent.
Far from it: as we hope to have shown in Chapters 9 and 1, African
foragers have actively interacted with herders, farmers, state-level
polities, European settlers, and postcolonial societies for millennia,
and they continue to do so today. Opting for *The First Africans* as
the title for this book underscores all these points.

There is, nevertheless, danger in suggesting that some groups may
be more indigenous than others. This may be less obvious in countries demographically and politically dominated by populations of
European descent, more-or-less conscious that their ancestors dispossessed 'First Nations' of their lives and land and willing to make
some effort to overcome the marginalisation that resulted. However, it is certainly a valid point in an African context. Although the
Ogiek, Hadzabe, Baka, Mbuti, Ju/'hoansi and others have (at least
until recently) survived largely by hunting and gathering, this has
often been in the context of interaction with food-producing neighbours ensconced on the same landscapes as themselves for centuries,
if not millennia. Who, in such a situation, has the greater claim to
being indigenous, especially if that claim brings with it the assumption of special rights to land or other resources (Kuper 2003)? Is the

all-too-frequent combination of political and economic marginalisation, *de facto* discrimination by agriculturally based peoples in the
distribution of state resources, and some kind of special connection
to the environments in which they live sufficient to warrant the
'affirmative recognition' for which IPACC (2006) and other activist
organisations strive? The question is far from being an academic one,
because it, and related emphases on collective rather than individual rights (e.g., Boutros-Ghali 1994; /Useb and Chennells 2004),
have real consequences in how government policies work out; the
removal of the G/wi and G//ana Bushmen from the Central Kalahari
Game Reserve is a clear case in point (Suzman 2002; Zimbler
2007). However, the question *is* also an academic one, in that it concerns the relations among indigenous communities, African governments, and archaeologists. One of the most obvious areas in which
it does so is in the excavation and analysis of human remains.

*Excavation and Analysis of Human Remains, Repainting*
*of Rock Art*

This has become a controversial question in many parts of the world
where indigenous peoples hold – often with much justification –
that museums, anthropologists, and archaeologists have acquired,
displayed, and studied the remains of those whom they know, or
believe, to be their ancestors without due regard for their own
beliefs or feelings. Given South Africa's recent history and the fact
that the composition of its professional archaeological community
does not yet reflect the demographic makeup of the population as
a whole, it comes as little surprise that this issue resonates particularly strongly there (Meskell 2005). New legislation permits human
remains to be excavated only after concerted efforts to consult communities and individuals with an interest in the grave, as well as
agreement on what is to happen once excavation has taken place.
In some cases, as with two child burials excavated in the Pakhuis
Mountains north of Cape Town (Sealy *et al.* 2000), individuals
have been reinterred after study, but at least one institution, Iziko
Museums of Cape Town, has placed a moratorium on researching human remains. Such actions inevitably place serious question

marks over the future of physical anthropological and stable isotope studies that can, as we have seen, make immense contributions to understanding the past. Those question marks would be significantly enhanced were existing museum collections to be reburied, as some groups claiming Khoisan descent have urged (Jordan 1999). But what is the status of such groups? Who, ultimately, should make such decisions? Who, indeed, owns the past? There can be little doubt that archaeologists may often have done too little to explain their work to the wider community, or that the disturbance and scientific study of the dead is often a very emotive issue. However, the chain of reasoning by which present-day communities or organisations justify ownership of skeletons that may be centuries, even millennia, old does not necessarily always follow the pathways of scientific discourse. Compromise between archaeologically rooted understandings of the past and those with a nonscientific basis may thus not always be possible, something well exemplified by the Kennewick Man controversy in the United States (Watkins 2005). This may be especially so where interest in claiming ownership of archaeological resources has as much to do with seeking contemporary political empowerment as with genuine religious or emotional sensitivities.[1]

Human remains are not the only arena in which such debates have begun. Another, also southern African in its current focus, lies in the potential repainting or overpainting of Bushman rock art, given the claims to its ownership voiced by organisations such as the Working Group of Indigenous Minorities in Southern Africa (WIMSA; /Useb and Chennells 2004) or the emerging 'secret San' of the uKhahlamba-Drakensberg region of South Africa (Derwent 2005). Australia, where some rock paintings have been repainted and millennial-old human remains disposed of without any trace (Mowaljarlai *et al.* 1988; Mulvaney 1991), illustrates what can happen. It is, of course, possible, perhaps very likely, that in most of Africa and for most of the African past, the probability of something similar happening is very slight: the very different politics of African countries compared with the 'settler societies' of North America and Australasia, where such debates have arisen most sharply, suggests as much. Nonetheless, these concerns are now emerging as real issues in the practice of archaeology in southern Africa, and may do so more widely as foragers and forager-descended communities seek greater political empowerment. With regard to issues of cultural heritage, this may work most effectively where, as in the recent case of the Game Pass Shelter rock art site in South Africa, cultural and historical restitution and ownership have been made inclusive of the concerns and experiences of other stakeholders (Meskell 2005).

## Communicating Research Results to African Audiences

The challenge that this sets archaeologists is one of finding ways of making their research more relevant to those who may take greatest interest in its findings. Among the multiple audiences that need to be addressed, communicating with ordinary people and political leaders within Africa are of the highest importance (Kibunjia 1997; Thiaw 2003). This is not to underestimate the difficulties posed by language, culture, or the demands of research careers that measure success by prestigious grants and journal papers, not time spent communicating to local communities. However, such communication is essential, not only for protecting Africa's cultural heritage, but also for encouraging an informed, broadly based, local voice that demands such protection. Community-based museums and community-directed museum outreach projects, such as those developed in Botswana (Metz 1994; Phaladi 1998), suggest that such aspirations are not a mere pipedream, though they do, of course, require the commitment of resources. Within Africa itself, the difficulties posed by too few archaeologists and inadequate resources for excavation, curation, display, or access to books and journals are too well known to require citation, but neither should the constraints of researching the African past from within Western institutions be underestimated, hostage as they may be to changes in academic fashion and government-dictated financial constraints. The very fact that so much of the material we have covered in this book is relevant to the history – and ancestry – of everyone, from the earliest hominins to the origins and expansion of anatomically and behaviourally modern humans, helps insulate part of the archaeology of the first Africans from some of these difficulties. However, the very same interest in 'big splash' science may work to the detriment of research on more recent hunter-gatherers, where African evidence is, nevertheless, both superlatively rich and able to challenge models generated without taking it into account (Mitchell 2005a). Striking a balance will not be easy.

The other crucial audience with whom archaeologists must engage is, of course, African foragers themselves. Reid (2005) points out that Kalahari hunter-gatherer voices have been largely excluded from the Kalahari debate, a view echoed by Suzman (2004:203), who tellingly comments that despite a massive amount of research, 'we have learnt little of the past from a San perspective'. Much the same could be said of foragers or forager descendants in other parts of Africa, notwithstanding examples to the contrary, such as the work of Smith and Lee (1997) in Namibia, or the inclusion of indigenous groups (such as WIMSA) in the deliberations and conferences of the World Archaeological Congress (WAC 2006). To be effective, such engagement has to proceed on a basis of mutual respect. However, this does not itself resolve the tensions that may arise over questions such as rock art conservation or the excavation and analysis of human remains, still less those that may develop where archaeological findings are in direct contradiction to indigenous understandings of the past (Kuper 2003). There being no simple answers, the archaeological response has, perhaps, to be developed as much on a case-by-case basis as in terms of general principles, with Western institutions and expeditions doing as much as possible to assist in building capacity within African archaeology through the provision of training and other forms of effective collaboration. The interdisciplinary and international projects that have characterised hominin research in East Africa since the 1970s provide a historical model for the creation of training opportunities for African students. A second generation of African archaeologists and palaeontologists is now active, having benefited directly from long-running research programmes (e.g., at Koobi Fora) that offer close links between Western universities and museums and those in the host countries. National museums, such as those in Kenya and Ethiopia, play a central role in not just conserving and interpreting the past, but in instigating research. Endemic funding constraints in developing economies, however, will continue to limit the capacity of national institutions to undertake field research and engage in often-expensive post-excavation analyses. Collaborative partnerships with international researchers will thus remain a vital part of the development of archaeology across the continent, but this should not be construed as simply mutually convenient extensions of postcolonial legacies. Any notion that Stone Age archaeology was a servant of colonial interests has also dissolved with the engagement of African researchers in all periods of the continent's long past. Early hominin sites, in particular, are a source of national pride and tourist income, whether in the form of the famous fossil of "Lucy" (*Australopithecus afarensis*) conserved in the National Museum of Ethiopia, or the World Heritage Site of the Sterkfontein Valley and its environs, known collectively as the Cradle of Humankind. Hominin sites are rare, with few countries able to benefit from such associations, but every nation shares some part of the African continent's long and continuous human record, extending to at least the mid-Pleistocene.

## Conserving the Archaeological Heritage of the First Africans

Effective conservation of Africa's full archaeological heritage has to be a component of national and international collaborations. Although hominin-bearing fossil localities and stratified archaeological deposits are susceptible to damage through development in the form of road, dam, pipeline, or house construction, such attention is generally inadvertent, rather than deliberate. Regrettably, this is not so for Africa's thousands of rock art sites, many of which are exposed to growing threats from unregulated tourist activity that at best can stir up dust onto fragile paintings and at (a too frequent) worst involves spraying paintings with water or spitting on them, scribbling graffiti, or attempts at outright removal from the rockface. One area where such dangers are particularly evident is in the Sahara, which is increasingly accessible to tourism. Liverani *et al.* (2000) illustrate the level of the threat in southwestern Libya and the difficulties of creating a viable archaeological park in this World Heritage Site location, but their comments hold much more widely.

Systematic recording of threatened sites, provision of effective logistical support for tourism, effective regulation of tourist activity, and engagement with local inhabitants are all essential. In this respect, Mabulla (2000; Musiba and Mabulla 2004) makes a strong plea in an East African context for sustainable tourism to include not just the traditional African mainstay of game-viewing, but also visits to archaeological sites, with both involving the active participation of local communities.[2] This is emphatically *not* to present African societies, or their past, as standing outside time in some kind of Garden of Eden. However, the vitality of animal-based tourism and its frequent proximity to outstandingly significant archaeological localities (Olduvai, Laetoli, the Tsodilo Hills, and the Maloti-Drakensberg Mountains are but four examples) do suggest that archaeology *and* wildlife conservation could both gain from enhanced collaboration. The growing number of international projects developing under the auspices of the Peace Parks Foundation (2006) offer one avenue along which this might proceed, and emphasise the absolute necessity of tangible benefits flowing back from tourism into the lives of local communities. Without suggesting that they be turned into caricatures re-enacting a past that no longer exists and may not even be theirs (cf. White 1995), there are, as discussed in Chapter 10, undoubted opportunities for African foragers and forager-descended communities to benefit economically, socially, and politically from such ventures and others that stress different strands of ecotourism.

## THE PRESENT AND THE PAST

The danger of perpetuating the popular stereotype of timeless hunter-gatherers is nowhere more acute than where, in Reid's (2005:352) words, this may be 'used by governments to validate the systematic marginalization [of] and denial of basic rights to the people on whom the image was based'.[3] Employing neoevolutionary social models is one way in which such images can be conveyed and one of our own reasons for eschewing them here. But this is not to argue that archaeology ought to stand back from generalising, comparative studies, or that it should only emphasise the particularistic understanding of specific times, places, or peoples. The relationship between archaeological and ethnographic records lies at the heart of all these issues and some general discussion of it as it relates to the topics that we have broached in this book is thus warranted.

## Archaeology and Ethnography

One aspect of this relationship is, of course, the longstanding predilection of archaeologists to draw more-or-less direct analogies between ethnographically recorded societies and those of the remote past that they themselves seek to understand. As will by now be clear, for Africa, this is most strongly developed in the continent's south,[4] where the ethnography of Kalahari Bushmen and late-nineteenth-century Bushman societies in South Africa (notably the Bleek/Lloyd archives) has long been used to elucidate what Goodwin and van Riet Lowe (1929) termed the Later Stone Age. That relationship, strengthened immeasurably by the use of these ethnographic datasets to understand much of the region's rock art and the consequent sea-change in its archaeology away from largely ecological and toward much more sociological questions, has led some to write of the Later Stone Age as Khoisan history (H. J. Deacon and Deacon 1999:128). Material, genetic, biological, and anthropological connections are numerous, of that there can be no doubt, but does that mean that the prehistory of southern African hunter-gatherers should be written from a perspective that draws almost exclusively for its insights on the history and ethnography of Bushman societies in the Kalahari and the Karoo? The tension here is not a new one, and for more than twenty years, southern African archaeology has witnessed repeated statements calling for a wider set of analogies to be explored, both from within the Kalahari and beyond (Parkington 1984; Hall 1990; Humphreys 2004/05; Mitchell 2005a). Thus far, however, relatively little has been done to give effect to these statements, notwithstanding the growing recognition that many hunter-gatherer populations lived in radically different environments from those well known ethnographically and structured their lives in quite different ways: Parkington's (1998) arguments, explored in Chapter 8, that in the absence of bow-and-arrow technology many dimensions of hunter-gatherer social (i.e., not just ecological) relations must have differed from those known from the

Kalahari or the /Xam, and Sealy's (2006) demonstration of enormous variability in diet and landscape utilisation between neighbouring communities in the Holocene southern Cape are very much the exceptions here. More can be expected as investigation proceeds of Pleistocene hunter-gatherers for whom behavioural modernity seems certain, but the plausibility of projecting backward Bushman ethnography tens of millennia increasingly remote.

Another problem created by what Wobst (1978) termed the tyranny of the ethnographic record is that when archaeologists employ ethnographic material, they too rarely take into account that this is the product of its own historical process. In southern Africa, of course, this process centres on the potential consequences for hunter-gatherers of two millennia of contact with a range of food-producing societies, the nub of the Kalahari debate that, as discussed in Chapter 10, has resonances right across the continent, in the equatorial forests and East Africa, as well as (in the remote past covered in Chapters 8 and 9) the Sahara and the Sahel. We doubt that archaeological usages of ethnography can – or should – insulate themselves from these discussions and suggest the following as possible ways forward:

- Early hominin researchers have long used hunter-gatherer and primate analogues, and in addition to incorporating a wider range of known variability into existing models (e.g., the Grandmother Hypothesis) there is ample scope to expand multiple lines of behavioural evidence that integrate ethnographically derived *general* principles with experimental data and the material record itself. Landscape studies, such as those at Olorgesailie, Olduvai, Koobi Fora, and Peninj, have drawn successfully from a mix of foraging theory, actualistic studies, and artefact analyses (e.g., spatial distribution, use-wear, and flake-utility index approaches) to make testable predictions of hominin behaviours. Relatively new developments in methods of analysing the cognitive foundations of artefact variability, such as the *chaîne opératoire* applied to the Gona material or neural imaging, provide information independent of ethnographic parallels drawn specifically from hunter-gatherers;

- develop closely argued archaeologies of ethnographically known hunter-gatherer societies, borrowing here from the approach developed by Stahl (2001) in her work on late precolonial and early colonial communities at Banda, Ghana. The strategy here is to begin with the archaeology of the very recent past, working backwards from that to understand how the ethnographically described situation with its material manifestations has come about and thus establishing how things may once have been different from, not identical to, what has been recorded by anthropologists and other observers. For African foragers, the work of J. Deacon (1996) on nineteenth-century /Xam Bushman sites, Robbins *et al.* (1996, 2000) in the Tsodilo Hills, and Mercader *et al.* (2000a, 2000b, 2001) in the Ituri offers examples of this kind of approach;
- expand the sample of forager societies from which analogies are sought, with an eye on taking into account variability at both intra- and inter-societal levels. Papers in Kent (1996) make this point well, with Hewlett (1996) and Guenther (1996) emphasising it for tropical foragers and Bushman peoples in particular;
- reach beyond known African examples to consider whether the ethnographies of non-African hunter-gatherers offer relevant insights, not least, for example, in exploring instances of social and economic intensification. Comparisons with other low-latitude hunter-gatherers (in Australia, India, South America, and the Mediterranean) may prove more informative than those drawn with higher latitude, temperate, boreal, or Arctic groups;
- investigate further the potential of more explicit bodies of theory, such as behavioural ecology (Winterhalder 2001), and of systematically comparing variability within and between hunter-gatherer societies against known ecological gradients (Kelly 1995; Binford 2001). Although these suggestions may appear overly reductionist and environmentally deterministic, they can be defended on the grounds that foragers do employ their profound knowledge of the natural world for rational ends, such as finding food. Moreover, it would be a foolhardy archaeologist who suggested that variation in the natural world has no bearing on how people behave, even though economic

motives and ecological variables are clearly not the only ones influencing human actions. Ecology, in other words, is a necessary, though never wholly sufficient, prism through which to learn about hunter-gatherer societies, but – and it is an important but – it is a methodologically robust and powerful one. Bousman's (2005) study of lithic technologies at Blydefontein Shelter from a risk-minimisation perspective linked to tightly controlled palaeoenvironmental observations illustrates what can be done here. So too, of course, does Marean's (1997) modelling of tropical grassland forager settlement-subsistence patterns.

Pursuing these strategies will, we suspect, further challenge progressivist models of social change that lock hunter-gatherers into the earliest and lowest rungs of the evolutionary ladder and thus all too readily condemn African foragers, in particular, to the position of role models for the behaviour of earlier hominin taxa. The African record discussed in Chapters 7 through 10 already provides several instances in which more complex, potentially delayed-returns-based social formations were followed by more simple, immediate-returns-based societies, as well as others in which complex hunter-gatherers did not 'proceed' to adopt food-production: the Late Pleistocene populations of the lower Nile Valley, the Early Holocene communities of the Tadrart Acacus, and the Late (pre-2000 bp) Holocene inhabitants of South Africa's Forest and Fynbos Biomes are cases in point. The same record also reveals, for example in the case of the Kintampo Complex, the poverty of thinking about subsistence change in terms of straightforward bipolar oppositions between hunting and gathering and farming (Casey 2005). The archaeology of the first Africans, in other words, offers strong support for the view that sociocultural change has been far from unidirectional (S. McIntosh 1999; Rowley-Conwy 2001).

THE PAST IN THE FUTURE

Predicting the future of any discipline, still less one as fast moving as African archaeology, is fraught with risk, though we can be sure that here, too, change will not follow simple, linear pathways. What follows therefore should not just be taken with the proverbial pinch of salt, but also be recognised as a personal selection of topics that strike us as having particular potential for growth and exploration. One of these is undoubtedly the theoretical and methodological contributions that African-based research can make to the wider archaeological discipline. The development of so-called living floor excavations in the 1960s, taphonomy in the 1970s, and stable isotope analysis to investigate palaeodiet since the early 1980s are all examples of subdisciplines in which the contributions of African data and researchers have been fundamental. Another springs from the revolutionary consequences for rock art research of the shamanistic paradigm first developed in southern Africa (Lewis-Williams 2003) and applied more recently in situations as varied as western North America (Whitley 1992), Melanesia (Wallis 2002), Europe's Upper Palaeolithic parietal art (Lewis-Williams 2002), and the origins of farming in the Near East (Lewis-Williams and Pearce 2005). The richness of African ethnography and oral history, combined with the long time depth and multiple kinds of interactions between foragers and food-producers, identify this as another field from which models of more general relevance may spring.

## Methodologies for the Future

Thinking of the methodologies available to investigate the African past, obvious areas for growth include the application of molecular genetics and the development of more robust chronologies for Africa's rock art. The second of these topics, still very much a work in progress, is essential for articulating rock art with the remainder of the archaeological record. The combination of selective accelerator mass spectrometer dating with detailed stratigraphic, paint compositional, and stylistic studies is already paying dividends, and can be expected to produce many more (see box in Chapter 9, "Dating southern African rock art"). Molecular genetics is developing even faster, and we have referred to the insights that it is generating on numerous occasions. Such insights are bound to multiply, but for them to achieve their full potential, several issues will need detailed attention. Some of these have been usefully outlined by MacEachern (2000), who draws attention to the importance of acknowledging the complex ways in which the linguistic, genetic, and ethnic identities of present-day populations articulate; the certainty that those identities are dynamic, products of a complex history and subject to rapid change; and the need to have chronological controls on the conclusions drawn from genetic studies that are at least as tight as those operating in the relevant parts of the archaeological record.

Even more crucial – and challenging – than these concerns, however, is the importance of ensuring that molecular geneticists and archaeologists understand each other's *modus operandi* and have up-to-date knowledge of each other's activities. This is a tall order because of the immense amount of evidence available to each discipline and the different academic backgrounds of their practitioners, but it is essential to avoid matching second-hand knowledge of one set of reconstructions with more direct knowledge of another. Papers in Soodyall (2006), especially those by B. Smith (2006b) and Crawhall (2006), offer useful guidance here.

A third and, if anything, even more essential, area for development is upgrading the overall quality of archaeological excavation and recording on all kinds of sites to the highest international standards. The issues of cost and resourcing on which we have already touched are obviously germane here, but the routine use of global positioning systems and geographical information systems in field survey and site mapping, as well as the three-dimensional point-plotting of finds, have to be pursued if we are to try and extract the maximum amount of information from our data. Curtis Marean's ongoing work at Pinnacle Point, South Africa, is an exemplary methodology to emulate here (Marean *et al.* 2004, 2007).

*Filling the Gaps in Our Coverage*

More mundanely, there are obvious geographical and temporal lacunae in the archaeological coverage of the African continent. Two of these are the tropical forests of West Africa and the Congo Basin. The hypothesis that the scarcity of archaeological evidence within either region is an accurate reflection of reality brought about by disease, specifically malaria (Shaw 1984), seems highly unlikely: Recent research into the history and epidemiology of the malaria parasite suggests that *Plasmodium vivax* is only rarely fatal and that the more deadly *P. falciparum* only expanded once agricultural clearance of African forests took hold (Coluzzi 1994; Hume *et al.* 2003). Lack of fieldwork, problems with site visibility, use of perishable (i.e., non-lithic) technologies, and a reluctance to accept the validity of many possible Pleistocene sites because of overinterpretation in the past are all likely to be involved (Casey 2003). However, neither these issues, nor the difficulty of making sense of sites as badly compromised by stratigraphic disturbance as Gombe Point (Cahen and Moeyersons 1977) should be overstated; Mercader's (2003b) work in the Ituri forest shows that stratigraphically intact sequences can be recovered within the tropical rainforests, and Shum Laka (de Maret 1996; Lavachery 2001; Cornelissen 2003) demonstrates what is possible at their edge. The further development and wider application of luminescence dating looks set to provide the first absolute chronologies for West and Central Africa for sites beyond the range of radiocarbon dating, bringing this region into wider discussions of the development of behavioural variability in the Pleistocene. The relatively recent discoveries of Miocene and Pliocene hominins in Chad (Brunet *et al.* 1995, 2002) highlight the geographical biases in our understanding of evolutionary processes, with the Rift Valley basin sequences of East Africa inevitably driving models of origins and dispersals, as well as attracting considerable funding. More challenging than the methodological and logistical problems of working in West and Central Africa are the political difficulties that have, among their more minor consequences, for so long constrained archaeological research in countries such as the Democratic Republic of Congo, or, moving farther afield, Angola, Eritrea, and southern Sudan.

## Understanding Variability

As the spatial lacunae of the African past are increasingly filled in, we can also look forward to a much more nuanced appreciation of that past's variability than we have been able to attempt here. In discussing particular periods, we have, ourselves, chosen not to work within a spatial framework tied closely to either the ecological features of particular contemporary environments or the continent's physical geography. Instead, we have employed very broad geographical subdivisions, such as North Africa, the Sahara, or the equatorial forests. Our reasons are several: first, African environments have been nothing if not dynamic through the period we have covered; second, that dynamism has been both cyclical (as with the repeated contractions, expansions, and concomitant ecological changes of what is now the Sahara) and directional (as with the ongoing formation of the Rift Valley system). It follows that using the present ecology of Africa as a guide to that of the past is likely to be fraught with danger. Moreover, present-day ecological zones vary enormously in scale, from large biomes such as the Sahara to tiny ones, such as the Forest Biome of the southern Cape Fold Mountain Belt in South Africa. To structure our survey using analytical units of such widely different scales would be less than helpful. As detailed knowledge of Africa's palaeoenvironments is built up and more firmly anchored in time, we do, however, anticipate that it will become increasingly viable to examine the African archaeological record against analytical frameworks grounded in that knowledge; Gamble's (1986, 1999) work on Palaeolithic Europe provides an excellent example of what should be possible. In the context of early hominin evolution, we have argued that the concept of variability selection offers a uniquely integrated approach that explicitly links ecological change with morphological, genetic, and behavioural responses. Landscape-based studies with well-dated environmental and archaeological records are essential for archaeologists to reconstruct and assess hominin adaptive strategies in increasingly diverse environmental settings. The high-quality East African database currently provides the only real testing ground for this hypothesis.

Variability selection also encompasses processes of social learning and the transmission of innovation across generations. Archaeologists have, until recently, treated these behaviours as epiphenomena, or simply as processes not amenable to analysis. Observations of human and non-human primate societies are providing insights into the general social and demographic conditions that can promote or inhibit culturally based change (Shennan 2001; Stout 2002;

Van Schaik and Pradham 2003; Foley 2004), and these have direct relevance to the long perspective offered by the African record. That record also challenges progressivist assumptions about a lineal increase in complexity with time. The well-executed knapping strategies seen at Gona 2.6 mya and the symbolic excesses at Blombos Cave at 77 kya have surprised those accustomed to or expectant of certain behaviours at certain times, and not before. The hominins at both sites used their genetically inherited capacities in combination with culturally learned behaviours and individual experience to address specific ecological and social concerns. As argued in Chapter 3, the archaeological record presents us with a taphonomic and behavioural aggregate that obscures the true abilities that existed within a population at any one time. The occasional beacon, such as Blombos, shines through and seems the more startling against a dimly lit background. Genetic mutations are not required to explain such an occasional efflorescence. Instead, we should strive for careful, systematic accumulation of detailed, well-dated local sequences combined with behaviourally sensitive methodologies to reveal the range of abilities that existed at any one time, along with the external and internal conditions that stimulated their material expression. That challenge will take some time to meet. One likely and hoped for consequence will be the need to redefine the archaeological labels currently applied to large geographical areas and broad time spans, such as the Sangoan, Lupemban, and Aterian. For the time being, they mask rather than reveal behavioural variability and obscure local histories of human decision making.

As well as varying across space, African archaeology, like archaeology elsewhere, also varies in the intensity with which different periods have been investigated. The obvious attractions of researching the origins of the genus *Homo*, meat-eating, and stone tool manufacture, coupled with the ready availability in East Africa of relatively easily dated sediments of the right age, have encouraged a strong research emphasis on the archaeology of the Plio-Pleistocene boundary. In comparison, as seen in Chapters 5 and 6, the Middle Pleistocene has until recently (Barham 2000; McBrearty 2001) received little attention. The evidence now emerging that the latter part of this period (MIS 7 and 6) witnessed not just the appearance of anatomically modern humans, but also that of some key features of modern behaviour (such as the use of pigments), marks it as a priority for future study. MIS 4 and 3 form another such lacuna, albeit one that is a little better known. In this case, the Blombos finds, among others, indicate that we are dealing with hunter-gatherers who were probably no different cognitively from those of the ethnographic present. Despite this, we know remarkably little about how they structured their lives, or even how they coped with the challenges of fully stadial or rapidly changing environments (the extent to which Klasies River still dominates discussion of the archaeology of early modern humans in southern Africa underlines this point; important as it is, it is not a substitute for fieldwork elsewhere). That MIS 4–3 also saw Mode 4 or 5 technologies replace those of Mode 3 type and the expansion of modern humans out of Africa reinforces their identification as key targets for further research.

### New Frames of Reference

We conclude with two further points. The first is our conviction that in developing the study of the first Africans in a new century, the third in which archaeologists have pursued this goal, we should aim to do this using frames of reference that challenge earlier understandings. Our own use of J. G. D. Clark's (1969) modal terminology, rather than that inherited from Goodwin and van Riet Lowe (1929), is a small sign of that, as is our preference for a MIS-based chronology. A modal terminology also deliberately calls into question the longstanding tendency to bisect Africa at the Sahara and remove its far north from developments to the south, choosing instead to stress connections with Europe and the Levant. Such comparisons have tended to hinder, rather than facilitate, more holistic understandings of the African past itself. Nonetheless, at various stages of that past, it is undoubtedly appropriate to place Africa, or parts of Africa, within a much broader comparative setting. Examples of such studies have grown in recent years and now include volumes on the archaeologies of tropical rain forests (Mercader 2003a) and deserts (Veth *et al.* 2005), as well as older, more obviously time-linked studies (Gamble and Soffer 1990; Straus *et al.* 1996). For a much earlier period, Dennell and Roebroeks' (2005) emphasis on overcoming conventional geographical boundaries separating Africa from Asia by employing a biogeographically more valid 'Savannahstan' when thinking about Plio-Pleistocene hominins is another case in point. There is, no doubt, room for yet further work that might, for example, bring the hunter-gatherer records of all Mediterranean ecosystems, or those of the southern latitudes as a whole, into comparative focus.

Personally, we should welcome such developments because Africa's undoubted relevance to the history of all people has often been at the cost of relegating its own more recent history to the sidelines, a view encouraged by the intellectual legacy of European colonialism and the continent's often parlous economic and political condition since (Lane 2003). Comparative studies of this kind, so long as they do not begin from social evolutionary premises and so long as they use ecological variability as an analytical framework, not a deterministic explanation of first resort, can contribute much to the re-evaluation and re*valuation* of Africa's more recent, hunter-gatherer past. They may also have something to contribute to the continent's future, given that archaeological excavations typically generate varied and important palaeoenvironmental archives. With Africa, even more than other parts of the planet, set to experience significant and adverse climatic and environmental change in coming decades, more informed understandings of the long-term dynamics of the continent's ecosystems have never been more important. Archaeology is uniquely placed to contribute to the management and conservation of Africa's plant and animal communities and the sustainable economic development of its people (cf. Nyong 2005). As J. D. Clark (1974) famously argued three decades and more ago, African archaeology should indeed be paramount, rather than peripheral, within the discipline itself. That paramountcy is now as much about the future of Africa and of us all as it is about our common past.

# NOTES

## 1. Introducing the African Record

1. Surveys of several recent syntheses of world archaeology demonstrate this point. Thus, Fagan (2001) devoted only 5% of his Holocene coverage to Africa beyond Pharaonic Egypt; Wenke (1999), a mere two pages plus map. Price and Feinman's (2006) much used text similarly undersells the sub-Saharan African record. The fraction afforded African hunter-gatherers in all three instances is, of course, much smaller. Though still underplaying Africa relative to other continents (especially Europe and the Americas, where most purchasers presumably live), Scarre (2005) shows significant improvement on this score.

2. No term is ideal when referring to the aboriginal hunter-gatherer peoples of southern Africa and today different groups express different preferences (Lee and Hitchcock 1998). Rejecting any racist or sexist connotations that it may have held in the past, we, like Barnard (1992), see no reason to adopt 'San', a potentially derogatory Nama term, and still less, the Botswanan government's coinage of 'Basarwa', in place of the widely understood English word Bushmen. We also follow Barnard in spelling the names of individual Bushman groups, except for the Ju/'hoansi themselves, where we use the spelling employed by Lee (2003). Though still common in the literature, '!Kung' is the name of the language spoken by the Ju/'hoansi and others.

3. The reference to 'distance' is telling as it implicitly assumes the existence of a fixed reference point, whether the southern African focus of Goodwin and van Riet Lowe's (1929) original synthesis, or, as is perhaps more likely, Europe itself.

4. Note, however, that as part of his strategy to secure public support for his takeover of the Congo Basin, Belgium's King Leopold II had established the forerunner of today's Musée Royal de l'Afrique Centrale at Tervuren as early as 1897. Among the earliest European institutions dedicated to

African research, it remains today – in alliance with the Université Libre de Bruxelles – a major force in tropical African archaeology.

5. Which is not to say that archaeology has yet paid much attention to researching the particular pasts of specific Bushman peoples, more that limited research in East Africa, and still more so the equatorial rainforests, currently makes connections between their archaeological records and local hunter-gatherers even more tenuous. Whether this is the only, or even necessarily the most productive, strategy to follow in the southern African case is something we discuss further in Chapters 9 and 11.

6. Mitchell (1994) and A. Clark (1999), among others, have emphasised, for example, the degree to which radically different stone tool typologies automatically enhance differences between so-called Middle Stone Age and Later Stone Age lithic assemblages to the detriment of their comparison and a processual understanding of the lifeways of African hunter-gatherers during MIS 3 and 2. Harrold (1989) makes an analogous point with respect to the Middle/Upper Palaeolithic transition in Europe.

7. For the record, Barham took primary responsibility for writing Chapters 3–6, Mitchell for writing Chapters 7–10. All these chapters were, however, revised in the light of each other's comments, whereas the introductory and concluding parts of the book (Chapters 1, 2, and 11) represent much more of a joint effort.

## 2. Frameworks in Space and Time

1. A third major tributary, the so-called Yellow Nile, is represented by the Wadi Howar, a dried up valley system in the desert to the west of the modern river that reaches almost as far as Chad. It has been the subject of intensive research and was at times an east-west route of considerable importance (Jesse 2000).

2. Obsidian-hydration dating has a troubled history as a temperature-dependent technique (Ridings 1996; Anovitz et al. 1999, but see Hull 2001) and though it may have potential application to East African sites, we do not consider it sufficiently reliable to warrant further discussion. Amino-acid racemisation (AAR) is a means of dating the time since the death of an organism and has been applied to mollusc shells and ostrich eggshell. It is also temperature dependent and certainly not a routinely used method (Schwarcz and Rink 2001). In some caves with relatively stable climates, it has been used with relative success, especially when assessed against other independent dating techniques. At Border Cave, South Africa (Chapter 6), it has been used in association with ESR and TL (Miller et al. 1999).

## 3. First Tool-Users and -Makers

1. Tool use among insects is well-known, but beyond the scope of this volume.

2. The possibility remains that percussion tools were used by Mode 5 hunter-gatherers rather than chimpanzees, and this can be tested by further

comparative analysis of the technological characteristics of human and chimpanzee assemblages combined with residue analysis.

3. These experimental data raise the possibility that muscle marks on fossil bone could be examined as indicators of the tool-making abilities of early hominins, but no data exist yet on the correlation between muscle force generated during tool-making and the size of muscle markings (Marzke and Marzke 2000:132).

4. Bone collagen is an important source of carbon and nitrogen isotopes indicative of diet, but collagen does not survive long in the tropics and is unlikely to be found in hominins in Africa.

5. The smoothed, striated, and sometimes polished surface on these apparent bone tools may also have been produced by taphonomic processes such as porcupine gnawing followed by weathering under conditions specific to the dolomitic limestone cave infills (K. Kuman, pers. comm.). For the time being, until alternative interpretations of the purported bone tools are published, we accept the likelihood that they were deliberately used, and probably for digging.

6. The only chimpanzee fossil known, from the Kapthurin Formation in Kenya's eastern Rift Valley, extends this species' range by 600 km into an environment of woodlands and grasslands (McBrearty and Jablonski 2005). Dietary isotope analyses of the 500,000-year-old teeth would be of interest in the light of contemporary chimpanzee preferences for $C_4$ foods even in savanna environments.

## 4. Early Pleistocene Technologies and Societies

1. We use Mode 2 in preference to the Acheulean Industrial Complex as a label for assemblages containing both Mode 1 and Mode 2 technologies.

2. Perhaps a site like FxJj 20 East (Koobi Fora), with its possible hearths, was a place where just such a cooperative social group gathered; the development of prolonged childhood dependency would make such gathering places an important part of the behavioural ecology of *H. erectus* and later hominins.

3. Large game hunting has been emphasised in models of human evolution because of the excess meat available for sharing, the long-distance transport of meat, and the cooperative structure of big game hunting among modern hunter-gatherers. The cognitive demands of small game hunting versus large game are not yet known (Gurven *et al.* 2006), but among modern hunters, those who rely on small game tend to pursue a variety of different species, each with their own behaviours that need to be learned.

## 5. Mid-Pleistocene Foragers

1. The importance of the descended larynx in human speech has been questioned as it occurs in chimpanzees, and presumably evolved in the last common ancestor. The more significant anatomical change linked to speech is

the flattening of the face that reduced the horizontal length of the tongue. Initially, these changes were unrelated to the articulation of speech, but became part of a secondary evolution of language among hominins (Nishimura *et al.* 2006). The wider implication of this finding is that language evolved gradually and piecemeal rather than as a single, integrated step.

2. Analysis of rare fossil mid-ear bones suggests that both *A. africanus* and *H. habilis* had greater sensitivity to high-frequency sounds compared to modern humans (Moggi-Cecchi and Collard 2002). They may have used high-pitched vocalisation as a basic form of communication rather than lower pitched language.

3. Claims for symbolic behaviour in the mid-Pleistocene Mode 2 archaeological record are based on the apparent aesthetic sense exhibited by some particularly well-made bifaces (e.g., Le Tensorer 2006), and on the discovery of a naturally rounded piece of quartzite found in an undated biface-bearing deposit at Tan Tan, Morocco. The Tan Tan 'figurine' bears possible evidence of human modification to enhance the anthropomorphic shape of the stone and perhaps some traces of ochre (Bednarik 2003). Strong doubts remain about the intentionality of the modifications given the heavily weathered surfaces and the fluvial context of the find. Further publication is essential to demonstrate the association of the object with bifaces. Evidence for intentional modification of a naturally anthropomorphic pebble also exists at the Mode 2 site of Berekhat Ram, Israel (>230 kya) (Marshack 1997), and a wholly natural but human-like form has been reported among occupation debris at the Mode 3 site of Mumbwa Caves, Zambia (~120 kya; Barham 2000:137,140).

4. Evidence for the use of wood for possible hunting and gathering tools in Africa comes from the later mid-Pleistocene sites of Florisbad (South Africa, 260–125 kya; Bamford and Henderson 2003) and Kalambo Falls (Zambia, ~400 kya; J. D. Clark 2001a), where waterlogged conditions have preserved organic remains. The Florisbad specimen bears cutmarks from its shaping with stone tools, is lenticular in cross-section, with a pointed tip, and may have been a hunting stick. The Kalambo Falls assemblage, associated with late Mode 2 bifaces, has been abraded by river flow, but some evidence for deliberate modification occurs in the form of fire-hardened tips on possible digging tools and a club-like stick that could have been thrown to bring down small game.

5. Holocene and recent hunter-gatherers in the Seacow Valley located their camps near springs, creating a very different site distribution from that left by mid-Pleistocene foragers. The use of bonfires and the strategic placement of camps on ridges overlooking springs may have been effective means of countering the threat of predators.

6. Two species of *Homo* may have coexisted for a time in Africa, and the implications of this for the archaeological record are discussed in Chapter 6.

## 6. Transitions and Origins

1. Our current interglacial (MIS 1) most closely resembles MIS 11 in the nearly circular configuration of the Earth's orbit around the Sun, which may create an unusually extended warm interval by the standards of the past 400,000 years. Our own interglacial differs, though, in having rising carbon dioxide concentrations and their impact on its likely duration is not yet known.

2. L2 has, however, been shown to be an unreliable estimator of divergence times (Howell *et al.* 2004).

3. The apparent deposition of 28 individuals, including adults and children, in a cave shaft – Sima de los Huesos – at Atapuerca, Spain (~300 kya), along with a single soft hammer flaked handaxe, is the earliest evidence reported of possible mortuary behaviours (Carbonell and Mosquera 2006). The fossils are attributed to *H. heidelbergensis* or early *H. neanderthalensis* depending on taxonomic perspective (Arsuaga *et al.* 1997).

4. The Border Cave sequence has been dated using a variety of independent techniques, including radiocarbon, amino-acid racemisation (Miller *et al.* 1999), U-series, TL, and especially ESR on tooth enamel, which has been gradually refined to produce increasingly precise estimates of the age of the deposits and associated behaviours (Grün and Beaumont 2001; Millard 2006).

5. The Herto assemblage is a surface collection and potentially a palimpsest of Modes 2 and 3 with no behavioural significance to be drawn from their association, as contemporaneity cannot be assured. The apparently late survival of bifaces in an otherwise Mode 3 context remains to be demonstrated at Herto.

6. The human remains associated with the Aterian all come from North African cave sites such as Dar es Soltan and Mugharet el 'Aliya, Morocco, and the Haua Fteah, Libya. All are attributed to *H. sapiens*.

7. Binford (1984) interpreted the preponderance of non-meaty lower limbs and skulls of large game as evidence of passive scavenging by individuals of carnivore-ravaged carcasses. In this view, MIS 5 humans at Klasies could hunt small game, but not larger mammals, and brought lower limbs to the shelter of the cave for their personal consumption of marrow. No food-sharing took place. This interpretation was subsequently shown to be based on a miscalculation of lower limb frequencies (Outram 2000). Little evidence of carnivore damage exists in the assemblage and re-analysis has revealed clear evidence of butchery (cutmarks) and the ability to hunt large, dangerous game (a stone point was found embedded in the neck of a specimen of *Pelorovis*) (Milo 1998).

8. The earliest ornaments come from the Israeli site of Skhul, where two perforated shells of *Nassarius gibbosulus* were found in association with ten *H. sapiens* individuals, some intentionally buried and all dated to 135–100 kya (Vanhaeren *et al.* 2006). One bead of *Nassarius* has also been recognised

from the type site of the Aterian at Oued Djebbana, Bir-el-Ater, Algeria, though this open site remains effectively undated (Bouzouggar *et al.* 2007). Shells may also have been used as ochre containers at Qafzeh Cave, Israel (~90–100 kya), again associated with *H. sapiens*. The widespread distribution of *Nassarius* as the material of choice for early bead-making among coastal populations in North Africa, the Near East, and the Cape shows an independent convergence by MIS 5 hominins on shell beads as a form of personal ornamentation and, by implication, the existence of separate social traditions for the expression of identity.

### 7. The Big Dry: The Archaeology of Marine Isotope Stages 4–2

1. Of course, if the conclusions recently published by Scholz *et al.* (2007) and Cohen *et al.* (2007) are correct, then conditions between 135 and 90 kya in tropical Africa may have been repeatedly even more arid than those experienced during either of the maxima of the Last Glaciation (MIS 4 and MIS 2). Our use of the phrase 'Big Dry' is not meant to discount this new evidence, although the intensity and persistence of the aridity described warrant confirmation from other well-dated datasets.
2. The Nile nonetheless carried a relatively greater amount of sediment because lowered temperatures and vegetation belts in Ethiopia's highlands resulted in sparser vegetation, enhanced freeze–thaw effects at altitude, and led to a consequent increase in erosion (Close 1996).
3. Recently reported work from the Jebel Gharbi area of northwestern Libya supports this, though leaving open the possibility that there, too, (some) Aterian occurrences date to MIS 3 (Barich *et al.* 2006; Garcea and Giraudi 2006).
4. Goldberg's (1996) data show that eastern chimpanzees (*Pan troglodytes schweinfurthii*) underwent population expansion from a core montane refugium around 67 kya, only a few millennia after the Mt. Toba event.
5. Soriano *et al.* (2007) usefully point out that the almost total predominance of backed pieces among the formal tools in their 'classic' Howiesons Poort phase at Rose Cottage Cave may suggest that these artefacts were hafted into domestic/processing tools as well as hunting weapons. However, Lombard's (2007) residue analyses suggest that most of the Howiesons Poort segments from Sibudu were used as insets in hunting weapons that may have employed bone, as well as wooden, hafts and have been both hand- and projectile-delivered. None shows evidence of having been used to process plant materials. It may be that we should expect a degree of inter-site variability in how the same basic artefact type was employed.
6. We note, however, that this position may need to be revised if Mohapi's (2007) recent suggestion that 'terminal MSA' stone points from Layer Dc at Rose Cottage Cave (31–29 kya) functioned as arrowheads is supported by further experimental residue and morphological studies.
7. Field and Lahr (2006) argue that the Nile corridor offered a richer habitat than southern Arabia, noting, too, that sea level changes may have had an

adverse impact on the accessibility and productivity of key marine resources for people moving along the coastlines of Yemen and Oman. However this debate is ultimately resolved, movement into and through Egypt's Eastern Desert and thus into Sinai, as well as across southernmost Arabia, must have been constrained by aridity, and was perhaps thus largely restricted to warmer climatic phases, such as MIS 5 and 3 (Bar-Yosef 1995; Derricourt 2005).

8. The recent renewal of fieldwork at this critical North African site by Prof. Graeme Barker, University of Cambridge, promises greatly to refine our understanding of the region's prehistory.

9. We retain this term, though D. Phillipson (2005:135) prefers Oranian as being in keeping with the general pattern of naming industries after sites and avoiding the false imputation of an Iberian connection. For similar reasons, Barton *et al.* (2005) refer generically to Late Upper Palaeolithic assemblages.

10. The undated backed bladelet industry from the Horizon Collignon at Gafsa, Tunisia, may also be related (P. Smith 1982).

11. Or before. Hillman (1989) suggests that this merely marks a shift from using wooden pestles and mortars to employing stone processing equipment.

12. As our book goes to press, the recent papers by Scholz *et al.* (2007) and Cohen *et al.* (2007) on the ecological and demographic consequences of what they term 'megadroughts' in tropical Africa between 135 and 90 kya reinforce this point with reference to earlier – and more critical – periods of our species' evolutionary history. Such aridity must have constrained the availability of refugia for both human and non-human species and thus the distribution (and expansion) of early modern humans within and without of tropical Africa.

## 8. Transitions: From the Pleistocene into the Holocene

1. Peters *et al.* (1994) argued that the giant buffalo was conspecific with the surviving Cape buffalo (*Syncerus caffer*), but detailed examination of horn cores and dentition, overlapping distributions, and an absence of plausible intermediate forms refute this (Klein 1994b).

2. Whether a hunter-gatherer population survived on either island is unknown pending further fieldwork. On Bioko the aceramic basalt flake industry that precedes assemblages with pottery from a first and second millennia AD date could derive from a time when the island was still connected to the mainland, reflect the persistence of hunter-gatherers after sea levels rose, or even signal an earlier (pre-agricultural?) colonisation (Clist 1998). On Unguja, a substantial period of non-occupation intervened at Kumbi Cave ≤21 kya and it is not clear whether the overlying later Holocene assemblage is partly of forager origin, or should be wholly attributed to food-producers (Sinclair *et al.* 2006).

3. Note, however, the concerns expressed in Chapter 7 about the conflicting dates for Lukenya Hill, from which the assemblages in question come.

GvJm16 and GvJm22 are key here. S. Kusimba (2001) attributes them to her Lukenya Hill phase 2 group, which is typologically similar to early Mode 5 assemblages from Naisiusiu dating ≥40 kya (Ambrose 2002), but collagen-derived radiocarbon dates for GvJm22 suggest an age of only 16–13 kya.

4. Recent fieldwork north of the Ethiopian Blue Nile has identified apparently similar assemblages there too, although south of the river and toward the Sudanese border excavations hint at a surprisingly late (mid-Holocene?) persistence of Mode 3 technologies, as well as documenting the presence of first wavy line and then dotted wavy line ceramics of the kind discussed next (Fernández *et al.* 2007).

5. Much less well-defined Mode 5 assemblages, originally termed Somaliland Wilton (J. D. Clark 1954), are known in northern and central Somalia, Djibouti, and eastern Ethiopia. Featuring backed microliths, scrapers, rare burins, and even occasional potsherds, they are probably a mixture of assemblages of widely differing Upper Pleistocene to late Holocene ages (Brandt 1986).

6. An early Holocene age is supported in several cases by direct radiocarbon dates on archaeological materials, even though samples are shell and apatite. Owen *et al.* (1982) attribute all +75–80 m sites to before 7.5 kya, but Butzer (1980) argues for a second, shorter transgression to this elevation around 5.7 kya. Some, otherwise undated, sites may therefore be mid-Holocene in age.

7. Evidence for their continued consumption is, however, indirect, as no plant remains have been recovered from this time range. Cereal collection is possible, too, but unsupported by 'sickle gloss' on some Qadan and Isnan artefacts that results from sawing a hard, gritty material (Juel-Jensen *et al.* 1991; Becker and Wendorf 1993).

8. A fireplace at Nag El Busa in Middle Egypt dates to 9470 ± 50 bp (GrN-14909) and a single site in the Fayum predates 8.5 kya (Vermeersch 2002).

9. Strontium isotope analyses suggest that Late Acacus hunter-gatherers were more mobile than their pastoralist successors, but a lack of burials precludes comparisons with Early Acacus foragers that might strengthen the argument just made (Tafuri *et al.* 2006).

10. A Late Acacus adult male burial from Uan Muhuggiag shows dental wear consistent with using his teeth to process vegetable fibres, perhaps for making baskets, nets, or mats, rare direct evidence for male participation in such plant processing activities (Minozzi *et al.* 2003).

11. Ritual considerations may also be relevant to the domestication of cattle, given Late Pleistocene burials of wild cattle skulls at Tushka, Lower Nubia, which imply a significantly older symbolic significance for the species (Wendorf 1968). Might this mean that motives other than subsistence should be considered for its domestication in Africa, as already suggested in the Near East (Cauvin 2000; Lewis-Williams and Pearce 2005)?

12. Rock art, it should be mentioned, is not found in Capsian contexts, and stone sculptures and engraved stone plaques and ostrich eggshells do not seem to have specific associations with mortuary practices (Camps 1982).

13. Though not able to consult it while writing this or later sections of our study, we note the important contribution to African historical linguistics and the debates between its data and those of archaeology offered by Roger Blench's (2006) new book.

## 9. Hunting, Gathering, Intensifying: The Mid-Holocene Record

1. The situation is complicated by morphologically domesticated pearl millet and sorghum from sites in India and Pakistan dating to 2000–1500 B.C. Other African crops appear in the centuries immediately thereafter (Fuller 2003). Although the plant specimens themselves are not yet directly dated, there seems little doubt that their presence is genuine. We must therefore assume a prior history of cultivation in Africa. Proxy indicators for this may be the abundant grindstones, pottery, and morphologically wild sorghum found at sites along the Middle Nile if, as Haaland (1996) suggests, the harvesting methods used there precluded selection for physical traits diagnostic of domestication.

2. We find plausible Breunig and Neumann's (2002) arguments that this shift in emphasis was linked with other processes such as climate fluctuations, the take-up of iron metallurgy, and the development of social stratification.

3. Wheat and barley are reported from Initial Cardial contexts in northern Morocco, 8000–6500 bp (Ballouche and Marinval 2004). However, given the ease with which small items can move through archaeological stratigraphies, we note that this age has yet to be confirmed by accelerator mass spectrometer technology dating.

4. Note, however, D. Phillipson's (2005:198) highly appropriate caution about isolated finds of such ground stone artefacts, which were widely dispersed from quarry sites, and later also collected and valued for their supernatural properties, a practice that continues today (Connah 1964; Mitchell, pers. obs.).

5. Particularly distinctive artefacts include ground stone axes/adzes and rarer polished stone arm rings, as well as 'cigars', cylindrical objects made from fine-grained sedimentary rocks that are highly scored and worn. Stone arrowheads recall types known from the Sahel and Sahara, while the flaked stone assemblages are generally expediently made from local materials, often using a bipolar technique (Stahl 1994).

6. Mid-Holocene occupations with possible Tshitolian affinities reported from the Republic of Congo (de Maret *et al.* 1977) have yet to be followed up.

7. Apparently Pastoral Neolithic pottery reported from a few localities in southern Tanzania is not yet associated with evidence of herding (Chami and Kwekason 2003).

8. De Villiers' (1976) conclusion must, however, be treated with care because the comparative 'negroid' sample she used came from South Africa, where extensive intermarriage with Khoisan aborigines is known to have taken place (D. Phillipson 1976:206).

9. Schadeberg (1999) makes clear that no necessary connection exists between these Twa and other groups bearing this or cognate names elsewhere in Africa, including the Congo Basin. The term is a generic Bantu one applied to hunter-gatherers frequently regarded as aborigines and often non-Bantu-speaking.

10. One way of investigating the proposition further would, of course, be through the analysis of the DNA of modern populations, especially tropical rainforest foragers on the one hand and those from areas of south-central Africa where Batwa survived until very recently (B. Smith 2006b:89). The suggestion that the widespread distribution of Geometric Tradition rock art equates to an equally widespread pre-agricultural distribution of 'Pygmy' peoples certainly warrants such research.

11. The one area where large herd animals persist as the numerically dominant element of archaeological faunas is in the northeastern Eastern Cape (Opperman 1987), perhaps because vegetation there is exceptionally suitable for year-round grazing (H. J. Deacon 1993).

12. One wonders whether the cluster of more than 80 fine-line engravings at Springbokoog, Northern Cape Province, found associated with three small stone circles and dated 4400 bp, is another example of such practices (Morris 1988). Though contentious (B. Smith and Blundell 2004), there seems at least some scope for developing more landscape-oriented approaches to Bushman rock art (e.g., J. Deacon 1988; Solomon 1997; Taçon and Ouzman 2004).

13. Note, however, that some rock art researchers still emphasise documentation and style at the expense of ethnographically informed interpretation (e.g., Richter 2002; cf. Lewis-Williams 1990).

14. Keen (2006) has recently argued in a similar vein for Aboriginal Australia, at the same time noting that such ecological constraints do not prevent the development of inequalities (based there on controlling marriage and ritual knowledge) that were rarely, if at all, developed into inherited, institutionalised forms.

### 10. Foragers in a World of Farmers

1. Our use of the ethnographic present in this and the immediately succeeding paragraphs follows conventional anthropological usage. As our discussion later in this chapter hopefully makes clear, we are under no illusions that the relationships we are about to describe are preserved in some kind of unchanging timewarp. Far from it.

2. Note, however, that some equatorial forest hunter-gatherer communities may descend from farmers who abandoned horticulture to hunt and trade; the Lokaló and Kele are two possible examples (Vansina 1990).

3. Important variations exist among groups who hunt using bow and arrow (the Efe), nets (the Mbuti), or spears and traps (the Baka). Not only calorific returns, but also gender roles and degree of dependency on farmers may flow from these differences. Hewlett (1996) reviews the relevant literature,

emphasising the relevance of cultural history and socialisation, as well as the contemporary ecological and economic conditions that have traditionally dominated explanations of why such diverse hunting practices are found within broadly the same environment.

4. A. Smith *et al.*'s (1991) formulation of these signatures attributed sites marked by relatively high proportions of formal tools and silcrete, small ostrich eggshell beads, few grindstones, ceramics, sheep or seals, and large numbers of wild bovids to hunter-gatherers. Those showing the reverse pattern were attributed to herders.

5. As the comments attached indicate, this is a controversial proposition, developed further by Eastwood and Smith (2005). Matters that need clarification include the dating of the engravings themselves, their presence in areas where historical or archaeological evidence for herders is lacking, and the recovery of excavated evidence supportive of the links proposed with Red Geometric Tradition art in Zambia and beyond. Genetic analyses searching for markers characteristic of rainforest foragers among southern African Khoekhoen also need to be undertaken (B. Smith 2006b).

6. Gene flow was, however, clearly a two-way process (Chen *et al.* 2000). Within southern Africa, at least two physically negroid groups, the Dama of north-central Namibia and the 'River Bushmen' of northern Botswana, speak Khoe languages (Barnard 1992), suggesting assimilation of farmers by herders or foragers in areas that proved marginal to cultivation. That many ethnographically known Kalahari foragers, including the well-known G/wi, speak Khoe languages raises the further possibility that they descend from livestock-equipped groups who expanded into the desert relatively recently, only then to abandon herding (N. Walker 1995b).

7. Excavations here suggest few links to the expanding Cape Colony, but confirm informants' statements about material culture differences between /Xam dialect groups and hint at a gendered structuring of campsite spatial organisation (J. Deacon 1996). Much more such work could be done in this area.

8. Blench's (1999a) provocative argument that all contemporary and recent equatorial African forest foragers are specialised offshoots of colonising agricultural populations has not received wide support.

9. Tsetse fly control measures and land shortages in surrounding areas for rapidly growing agricultural and pastoralist populations have altered this situation since the 1950s (Ndagala 1988:69).

10. The implication that hunter-gatherers, and, indeed, pastoralists, lack an appropriate work ethic or suffer from 'backward attitudes' that require correction (cf. Nyerere 1971:5) carries eerie overtones of the racism implicit in nineteenth-century models of social evolution, as well as the stigmatisation of foragers typical of food-producing societies, African and non-African alike (Bahuchet and Guillaume 1982).

11. Though River Bushmen did, along with other ethnic groups, successfully oppose development projects in the Okavango Delta in the early 1990s (R. Lee and Hitchcock 1998:27).

12. This includes numerous descendant groups brought together in 2002 under the aegis of the National Khoi-San Consultative Conference of South Africa.

## 11. The Future of the First Africans' Past

1. The extended controversy over the rights and wrongs of excavating, and then studying, the several thousand historical period burials from the Prestwich Place cemetery in Cape Town, South Africa, offers an excellent example here. Opposition to excavation and archaeological analysis drew on community activists' resistance to the forced removal of 'Coloured' people from the city's District Six during the *apartheid* period, while also being linked to the distinctive post-apartheid racial politics of the Western Cape Province (Zimbler 2005).

2. The deliberate vandalism of the DK, JK, and MNK sites at Olduvai Gorge illustrates what can too readily happen when local communities are excluded from the management of, or economic benefits generated by, archaeological tourism (Karoma 1996:199–200).

3. Comments attributed to Botswana's president, Festus Mogae, with reference to his government's controversial removal of Bushmen from the Central Kalahari Game Reserve illustrate this well: 'How can you have a Stone Age creature continue to exist in the age of computers. If the Bushmen want to survive, they must change or, otherwise, like the dodo, they will perish' (Daley 1996). Change for whom and at what price, one might ask.

4. Why similar identifications between the ethnographic present and the archaeological record have not been pursued elsewhere is an interesting question. The relatively early start of intensive hunter-gatherer archaeological research in southern Africa and the emphasis originally placed by Lee and DeVore (Lee 1979:xvii) on the relevance of Kalahari Bushmen ethnography to evolutionary generalisations about the human past are two factors. Others presumably include the sheer number of anthropological studies of Kalahari hunter-gatherers and the relative ease of working in southern Africa compared with the equatorial forests.

# GLOSSARY

**Adze** In southern Africa, a stone tool with straight or concave working edges retouched by characteristic step-flaking that is partly
deliberate, partly the result of use; principally employed in wood-
working.

**Backing** The blunting of a stone tool's edge by abrupt vertical
retouch, for example, by creating a blunt edge opposite a sharper,
cutting edge, done in order to alter its shape or to facilitate hafting.

**Backed microliths** Formally designed microlithic tools, the shape
of which is defined by their backing.

**Bipolar flaking** A way of flaking stone in which a core (often small
and/or of quartz) is flaked using a hammer and anvil technique
such that flakes are detached from both ends simultaneously when
it is struck. Those that can be flaked no further are termed *pièces
esquillées* or *outils écaillés* or core-reduced pieces.

**Blade** Parallel-sided flake, at least twice as long as it is wide, with
one or more dorsal ridges and ≥25 mm long. Bladelets have the
same properties but a length of ≤25 mm.

**Bored stone** Spherical stone, the centre of which has been hol-
lowed out for use as a digging-stick weight.

**Caprines** Sheep and goat, the two being difficult to distinguish
osteologically in many archaeological samples.

**Chaîne opératoire** Sequence of actions in reducing toolstone from
its initial selection to the discard of exhausted tools.

**Chamfered blade** Blades from which a spall has been removed transversely to the long axis. Sometimes erroneously termed burins, they occur in the Dabban industry of Cyrenaica and the early Upper Palaeolithic of the southern Levant.

**Denticulated** Refers to retouched stone artefacts with one or more multiply notched edges.

**Dotted wavy line** A diagnostic ceramic motif found on early pottery in the Sahara and the Central Nile, produced either by a cord-wrapped stick rolled on the surface or by rocking. Found confined to the upper part of vessels, usually in conjunction with others.

**Encephalisation** Brain expansion relative to body size.

**Geophyte** Plant with **underground storage organs**, such as roots, tubers, or rhizomes. Many were important foods for hunter-gatherers in southern Africa.

**Glottochronology** Estimation of the age at which two languages diverged by comparing the degree to which their core vocabularies share cognate words. The assumption made that vocabulary change proceeds at a constant rate is widely held to be suspect.

**Gorges** Small, double-pointed slivers of ground and polished bone, believed to have been used for catching fish by tying them in the middle so that the they would lodge in the fish's mouth when the line was pulled.

**Ground game** Small, *r*-selected animal resources typically trapped or collected rather than hunted with projectile weapons. Examples include hare, springhare, hyrax, and tortoise.

**Holocene** The geological epoch spanning the last 10,000 years.

**Hominid** Traditionally describes human-like primates ancestral, or closely related to, modern humans, but in the light of recent genetic studies now extended to embrace bonobos, chimpanzees, and gorillas.

**Hominin** In the light of the previous point, this term is now the appropriate one to describe modern humans and their immediate bipedal fossil ancestors and relatives.

**Homotaxial** The occurrence of artefact types, cultures, or patterns of behaviour in the same relative position within two or more sequences, even if their absolute ages are not the same.

**Intermediate Periods** A term invented at the 1955 Pan-African Congress of Prehistory to draw together stone tool industries thought at that time to be transitional between either the Earlier and Middle Stone Ages or the Middle and Later Stone Ages. The **First Intermediate** included the Fauresmith and Sangoan, while the **Second Intermediate** included the Howiesons Poort. The terms were abandoned at the 1965 Burg-Waternstein conference.

**Last Glacial Maximum** The time of maximum ice sheet expansion and temperature depression during the Last Glaciation, coinciding broadly with MIS 2, but more narrowly with the period between ~21,000 and 18,000 radiocarbon years ago.

**Levallois method** A specialised method of obtaining flakes by preparing the surfaces of cores before the removal of one or more flakes (Inizan *et al.* 1992: 90). The Victoria West Technique of preparing large blocks of stone to produce large flakes for making Mode 2 bifaces (handaxes and cleavers) is considered here a variant of the Levallois method. Levallois cores and flakes first occur in the African record during the Middle Pleistocene, though a precise date for the method's development is lacking.

**Marine isotope stage (MIS)** Climatic stage defined by changes in the relative frequency of $^{18}O$ to $^{16}O$ in the global deep-sea core record and thus largely reflecting the growth and decline of ice sheets on a global scale.

**Miocene** Geological period from 23.8 to 5.3 mya.

**Opaline** Fine-grained rocks frequently employed to make stone tools. Also known as crypto-crystalline silicas, they include chalcedony, jasper, and agate. The term is specifically used in South Africa and Lesotho.

**Ouchtata retouch** Named after a group of Epipalaeolithic sites in northern Tunisia, this refers to light, usually semi-abrupt blunting along the edges of blades and bladelets.

*Petit tranchet* Short sections of straight-edged flakes, generally much broader than long, retouched almost completely and along two converging straight lines to meet at a rounded point.

**Phytolith** Silica body in plant cell walls identifiable to genus or species.

**Pleistocene** Geological period from ~1.7 mya to 10,000 years ago.

**Pliocene** Geological period from 5.3 to 1.7 mya.

**Plio–Pleistocene** The period spanning the boundary between the Pleistocene and the Pliocene.

**Point** A flake or blade retouched on two converging edges to a point, sometimes with additional unifacial or bifacial working. Classically considered a hallmark of Middle Stone Age assemblages and found in Mode 3 toolkits.

**Quaternary** The Pleistocene and Holocene periods together.

**Sagittal cresting** Bony ridge along the midline of the skull for attaching the temporalis (jaw) muscles.

**Scraper** Formally designed stone tool with a convexly retouched working edge, principally used to work hides.

**Segment** Formally designed stone tool with a straight, sharp edge opposite to a curved arc backed by abrupt retouch.

**Sirikwa holes** Archaeological phenomenon associated with early Kalenjin speakers found in Kenya's western highlands and dating to ~AD 1200–1800. Characteristic are groups of hollows with associated mounds, the remains of sunken, defensible cattle pens and attached houses.

**Suids** Members of the pig family, including warthogs (*Phacochoerus africanus*) and bushpig (*Potamochoerus porcus*).

**Toolstone** Raw materials used to make stone tools.

**Underground storage organ (USO)** Edible bulbs, rhizomes, tubers, and corms, typically accessed using a digging stick. **Geophyte** is a synonym for this category of plant foods.

**Ungulates** Hoofed mammals, including antelopes, zebras, and rhinoceri.

**Wavy line** A diagnostic ceramic motif found on early pottery in the Sahara and the Sudanese Nile Valley, produced by dragging a catfish spine or a comb horizontally in a wavy manner on the surface of the pot. Spacing, number, and angularity of lines can vary greatly, even on the same vessel.

# REFERENCES

Abbate, E., Albianelli, A., Asszaroli, A., Benvenuti, M., Tesfamania, B., Brun, P., Cipriani, N., Clarke, R. J., Ficcarelli, G., Macchiarelli, R., Napoleone, G., Papini, M., Rook., L., Sagri, M., Tecle, T. M., Torre, D. and Villa, I. 1998 A one million year old *Homo* cranium from the Danakil (Afar) depression of Eritrea, *Nature* 393: 458–460.

Abell, P. I. and Plug, I. 2000 The Pleistocene/Holocene transition in South Africa: evidence for the Younger Dryas event, *Global and Planetary Change* 26: 173–179.

Adams, W. M., Goudie, A. S. and Orme, A. R. 1996 *The physical geography of Africa*, Oxford: Oxford University Press.

Adams, W. Y. 1977 *Nubia: corridor to Africa*, Harmondsworth: Penguin.

Aiello, L. C. and Dean, C. 1990 *An introduction to human evolutionary anatomy*. London: Academic Press.

Aiello, L. C. and Dunbar, R. I. M. 1993 Neocortex size, group size and the evolution of language, *Current Anthropology* 34: 184–193.

Aiello, L. C. and Key, C. 2002 Energetic consequences of being a *Homo erectus* female, *American Journal of Human Biology* 14: 551–565.

Aiello, L. C. and Wells, J. C. K. 2002 Energetics and the evolution of the genus *Homo*, *Annual Review of Anthropology* 31: 323–338.

Aiello, L.C and Wheeler, P. 1995 The expensive tissue hypothesis: the brain and digestive system in human and primate evolution, *Current Anthropology* 36: 199–221.

Alba, D. M., Moyá-Solá, S. and Köhler, M., 2003 Morphological affinities of the *Australopithecus afarensis* hand on the basis of manual proportions and relative thumb length. *Journal of Human Evolution* 44: 225–254.

Alemseged, Z., Spoor, F., Kimbel, W. H., Bobe, R., Geraads, D., Reed, D. and Wynn J. G. 2006 A juvenile early hominin skeleton from Dikika, Ethiopia, *Nature* 443: 296–301.

Alexander, J. A. 1984a The end of the moving frontier in the Neolithic of north-eastern Africa, in L. Krzyzaniak and M. Kobusiewicz (eds.), *Origin and early development of food-producing cultures in north-eastern Africa*, Pozn án: Polish Academy of Sciences, pp. 57–63.

1984b Early frontiers in southern Africa, in M. Hall, G. Avery, D. M. Avery, M. L. Wilson and A. J. B. Humphreys (eds.), *Frontiers: southern African archaeology today*, Oxford: British Archaeological Reports, pp. 12–23.

Alin, S. R. and Cohen, A. S. 2003 Lake-level history of Lake Tanganyika, East Africa, for the past 2500 years based on ostracode-inferred water-depth reconstruction, *Palaeogeography, Palaeoclimatology, Palaeoecology* 199: 31–49.

Alley, R., 2000 *The two-mile time machine*, Princeton: Princeton University Press.

Alley, R. B., Mayewski, P. A., Sowers, T., Stuiver, M., Taylor K. C. and Clark, P. U. 1997 Holocene climatic instability – a prominent, widespread event 8200 yr ago, *Geology* 25: 483–486.

Allsworth-Jones, P. 1987 The earliest settlement in West Africa and the Sahara, *West African Journal of Archaeology* 17: 87–129.

Alperson-Afil, N., Richter, D., and Goren-Inbar, N. 2007 Phantom hearths and the use of fire at Gesher Benot Ya'aqov, Israel, *Paleoanthropology* 1–15.

Ambrose, S. H. 1984 The introduction of pastoral adaptations to the highlands of East Africa, in J. D. Clark and S. A. Brandt (eds.), *From hunters to farmers: the causes and consequences of food production in Africa*, Berkeley: University of California Press, pp. 212–239.

1986 Hunter-gatherer adaptations to non-marginal environments: an ecological and archaeological assessment of the Dorobo model, *Sprache und Geschichte in Afrika* 7(2): 11–42.

1990 Preparation and characterization of bone and tooth collagen for isotopic analysis, *Journal of Archaeological Science* 17: 431–451.

1998a Late Pleistocene human population bottlenecks, volcanic winter and the differentiation of modern humans, *Journal of Human Evolution* 34: 623–651.

1998b Chronology of the Later Stone Age and food production in East Africa, *Journal of Archaeological Science* 25: 377–392.

2001 Middle and Later Stone Age settlement patterns in the Central Rift Valley, Kenya: comparisons and contrasts, in N. J. Conard (ed.), *Settlement dynamics of the Middle Palaeolithic and Middle Stone Age*, Tübingen: Kerns Verlag, pp. 21–43.

2002 Small things remembered: origins of early microlithic industries in sub-Saharan Africa, *Archaeological Papers of the American Anthropological Association* 12: 9–30.

2003 Did the super-eruption of Toba cause a human population bottleneck? Reply to Gathorne-Hardy and Harcourt-Smith, *Journal of Human Evolution* 45: 231–237.

2006 Howiesons Poort lithic raw material procurement patterns and the evolution of modern human behavior: a response to Minichillo (2006), *Journal of Human Evolution* 50: 365–369.

Ambrose, S. H., Hivernel, F. and Nelson, C. M. 1980 The taxonomic status of the Kenya Capsian, in R. E. Leakey and B. A. Ogot (eds.), *Proceedings of the VIIIth Panafrican Congress of Prehistory and Quaternary Studies*, Nairobi: International Louis Leakey Memorial Institute for African Prehistory, pp. 248–252.

Ambrose, S. H. and Lorenz, K. G. 1990 Social and ecological models for the Middle Stone Age in southern Africa, in P. A. Mellars (ed.), *The emergence of modern humans*, Edinburgh: Edinburgh University Press, pp. 3–33.

Ambrose, S. H. and Sikes, N. 1991 Soil carbon isotope evidence for Holocene habitat change in the Kenya Rift Valley, *Science* 253: 1402–1405.

Ames, K. M. 2005 Tempo and scale in the evolution of social complexity in western North America: four case studies, in T. D. Pauketat and D. D. Loren (eds.), *North American archaeology*, Oxford: Blackwell Publishing, pp. 56–78.

Anati, E. 1986 The rock art of Tanzania and the East African sequence, *Bolletino del Centro Camuno di Studi Preistorici* 23: 15–68.

Andah, B. W. 1979 The early Palaeolithic in West Africa: the case of Asokro-chona coastal region of Accra, Ghana, *West African Journal of Archaeology* 17: 87–129.

Anhuf, D., Ledrou, M.-P., Behling, H., Da Cruz, Jr., F. W., Cordiero, R. C., Van der Hammen, T., Karmann, I., Marengo, J. A., De Oliveira, P. E., Pessenda, L., Siffedine, A., Albuquerque, A. L. and Da Silva Dias, P. L. 2006 Paleo-environmental change in Amazonian and African rainforest during the LGM, *Palaeogeography, Palaeoclimatology, Palaeoecology* 239: 510–527.

Anovitz, L. M., Elam, J. M., Riciputi, L. R. and Cole, D. R. 1999 The failure of obsidian hydration dating: sources, implications, and new directions, *Journal of Archaeological Science* 26: 735–752.

Antón, S. C. 2003 Natural history of *Homo erectus*, *Yearbook of Physical Anthropology* 46: 126–170.

Antón, S. C., Leonard, W. R. and Robertson, M. L. 2002 An ecomorphological model of the initial hominid dispersal from Africa, *Journal of Human Evolution* 43: 773–785.

Aoki, K., Yuichiro Wanako, J. and Feldman, M. W. 2005 The emergence of social learning in a temporally changing environment: a theoretical model, *Current Anthropology* 46: 334–340.

Arensburg, B., Tillier, A. M., Vandermeersch, B., Duday, H., Schepartz, L. and Rak, Y. 1989 A Middle Palaeolithic hyoid bone, *Nature* 338: 758–760.

Arkell, A. J. 1949 *Early Khartoum*, London: Oxford University Press.

Arredi, B., Poloni, E. S., Paracchini, S., Zerjal, T., Fathallah, D. M., Makrelouf, M., Pascali, V. L., Novelletto, A. and Tyler-Smith, C. 2004 A predominantly Neolithic origin for Y-chromosomal DNA variation in North Africa, *American Journal of Human Genetics* 75: 338–345.

Arsuaga, J. L., Martinez, I., Gracia, A. and Lorenzo, C. 1997 The Sima de los Huesos crania (Sierra de Atapuerca, Spain). A comparative study, *Journal of Human Evolution* 33: 219–281.

Asfaw, B., Beyene, Y., Suwa, G., Walter, R. C., White, T. D., WoldeGabriel, G. and Yemane, T. 1992. The earliest Acheulean from Konso-Gardula, *Nature* 360: 732–735.

Asfaw, B., Gilbert, W. H., Beyene, Y., Hart, W. K., Renne, P. R., Wolde-Gabriel, G., Vrba, E. A., and White, T. D. 2002 Remains of *Homo erectus* from Bouri, Middle Awash, Ethiopia. *Nature* 21: 317–320.

Asfaw, B., White, T., Lovejoy, O., Latimer, B., Simpson, S. and Suwa, G. 1999 *Australopithecus garhi*: a new species of early hominid from Ethiopia, *Science* 284: 629–635.

Ashkenazy, Y. and Tziperman, E. 2004 Are the 41 kyr glacial oscillations a linear response to Milankovitch forcing? *Quaternary Science Reviews* 23: 1879–1890.

Atherton, J. H. 1972 Excavations at Kamabai and Yagala rock shelters, Sierra Leone, *West African Journal of Archaeology* 2: 39–74.

Aumassip, G. 1987 Le Néolithique en Algérie: état de la question, *L'Anthropologie* 91: 585–622.

Avery, D. M. 2000 Micromammals, in T. C. Partridge and R. R. Maud (eds.), *The Cenozoic of Southern Africa*, Oxford: Oxford University Press, pp. 305–338.

Avery D. M. 2001 The Plio-Pleistocene vegetation and climate of Sterkfontein and Swartkrans, South Africa, based on micromammals *Journal of Human Evolution* 41: 113–132.

Backwell, L. and d'Errico, F. 2001 Evidence of termite foraging by Swartkrans early hominids, *Proceedings of the National Academy of Sciences* 98: 1358–1363.

2005 The origin of bone tool technology and the identification of early hominid cultural traditions, in F. d'Errico and L. Backwell (eds.), *From tools to symbols. From early hominids to modern humans*, Johannesburg: Witwatersrand University Press, pp. 238–275.

Bahuchet, S. 1989 Les pygmées Aka et Baka: contribution de l'ethnolinguistique à l'histoire des populations forestières d'Afrique centrale, Thèse de doctorat d'état, Université René Descartes, Paris.

1999 Aka Pygmies, in R. B. Lee and R. Daly (eds.), *The Cambridge encyclopaedia of hunters and gatherers*, Cambridge: Cambridge University Press, pp. 190–194.

Bahuchet, S. and Guillaume, H. 1982 Aka-farmer relations in the northwest Congo Basin, in E. Leacock and R. B. Lee (eds.), *Politics and history in band society*, Cambridge: Cambridge University Press, pp. 189–211.

Bahuchet, S., McKey, D. and de Garine, I. 1991 Wild yams revisited: is independence from agriculture possible for rain forest hunter-gatherers? *Human Ecology* 19: 213–243.

Bailey, G. N. 1983 Concepts of time in Quaternary prehistory, *Annual Review of Anthropology* 12: 165–192.

Bailey, R. 1991 *The behavioural ecology of Efe Pygmy men in the Ituri forest, Zaire*, Ann Arbor: Anthropological Papers of the Museum of Anthropology, University of Michigan.

Bailey, R., Head, G., Jenike, M., Owen, B., Rechtman, R. and Zechenter, E. 1989 Hunting and gathering in tropical rainforest: is it possible? *American Anthropologist* 91: 59–82.

Bailey, R. and Headland, T. N. 1991 The tropical rain forest: is it a productive environment for human foragers? *Human Ecology* 19: 261–285.

Ballard, J. W. O. and Rand, D. M. 2005 The population biology of mitochondrial DNA and its phylogenetic implications, *Annual Review of Ecology, Evolution and Systematics* 36: 621–642.

Ballouche, A. and Marinval, P. 2004 At the origins of agriculture in the Maghreb: palynological and carpological data on the early Neolithic of northern Morocco, in K. Sanogo and T. Togola (eds.), *Acts of the Eleventh Congress of the Pan-African Association of Prehistory and Related Fields*, Bamako: Institut des Sciences Humains, pp. 74–82.

Bamford, M. K. and Henderson, Z. L. 2003 A reassessment of the wooden fragment from Florisbad, South Africa, *Journal of Archaeological Science* 30: 637–650.

Bar-Yosef, O. 1987 Pleistocene connexions between Africa and Southwest Asia: an archaeological perspective, *African Archaeological Review* 5: 29–38.

2002 The Upper Palaeolithic revolution, *Annual Review of Anthropology* 31: 363–393.

Bar-Yosef, O. and Kuhn, S.L 1999 The big deal about blades: laminar technologies and human evolution, *American Anthropologist* 101: 322–338.

Barham, L. S. 1992 Let's walk before we run: an appraisal of historical materialist approaches to the Later Stone Age, *South African Archaeological Bulletin* 47: 44–51.

1996 Recent research on the Middle Stone Age at Mumbwa Caves, central Zambia, in G. Pwiti and R. Soper (eds.), *Aspects of African archaeology*, Harare: University of Zimbabwe Press, pp. 191–200.

2000 *The Middle Stone Age of Zambia, south central Africa*, Bristol: Western Academic and Specialist Press.

2002a Backed tools in Middle Pleistocene central Africa and their evolutionary significance, *Journal of Human Evolution* 43: 585–603.

2002b Systematic pigment use in the Middle Pleistocene of south central Africa, *Current Anthropology* 43: 181–190.

2007 Modern is as modern does? Technological trends and thresholds in the south-central African record, in P. Mellars, K. Boyle, O. Bar-Yosef & C. Stringer (eds.) *Rethinking the human revolution: new behavioural and biological perspectives on the origin and dispersal of modern humans*, Cambridge: McDonald Institute for Archaeological Research, pp. 165–176.

Barham, L. S., Pinto, A. C. and Stringer, C. 2002 Bone tools from Broken Hill (Kabwe) cave, Zambia, and their evolutionary significance, *Before Farming* [print version] 2(3): 88–103.

Barich, B. E. 1987 *Archaeology and environment in the Libyan Sahara. The excavations in the Tadrart Acacus, 1978–1983*, Oxford: British Archaeological Reports.

1992 The botanical collections from Ti-n-Torha/Two Caves and Uan Muhuggiag (Tadrart Acacus, Libya) – an archaeological commentary, *Origini* 16: 109–123.

1998 Social variability among Holocene Saharan groups: how to recognize gender, in S. Kent (ed.), *Gender in African archaeology*, Walnut Creek: AltaMira Press, pp. 105–114.

Barich, B. E., Garcea, E. A. A. and Giraudi, C. 2006 Between the Mediterranean and the Sahara: geoarchaeological reconnaissance in the Jebel Gharbi, Libya, *Antiquity* 80: 567–582.

Barker, G. W. W. 2003 Transitions to farming and pastoralism in North Africa, in P. Bellwood and A. C. Renfrew (eds.), *Examining the farming/language dispersal hypothesis*, Cambridge: McDonald Institute for Archaeological Research, pp. 151–162.

Barker, P. A., Street-Perrott, F. A., Leng, M. J., Greenwood, P. B., Swain, D. L., Perrott, R. A., Telford, R. J. and Ficken, K. J. 2001 A 14,000-year oxygen isotope record from diatom silica in two alpine lakes on Mt Kenya, *Science* 292: 2307–2310.

Barker, P. A., Talbot, M. R., Street-Perrot, F. A., Marret, F., Scourse, J. and Odada, E. O. 2004 Late Quaternary climatic variability in intertropical Africa, in R. W. Battarbee, F. Gasse and C. E. Stickley (eds.), *Past climate variability through Europe and Africa*, Dordrecht: Springer, pp. 117–138.

Barlow, G. W. 2002 *The cichlid fishes: Nature's grand experiment in evolution*, Cambridge: Perseus Publishing.

Barnard, A. 1992 *Hunters and herders of southern Africa: a comparative ethnography of the Khoisan peoples*, Cambridge: Cambridge University Press.

Barnard, A. and Taylor, M. 2002 The complexities of association and assimilation: an ethnographic overview, in S. Kent (ed.), *Ethnicity, hunter-gatherers and the "Other": association or assimilation in Africa*, Washington: Smithsonian Institution Press, pp. 230–246.

Barnett, T. 1999 *The emergence of food production in Ethiopia*, Oxford: British Archaeological Reports.

Barnosky, A., Koch, P., Feranec, R., Wing, S. and Shabel, A. 2004 Assessing the causes of Late Pleistocene extinctions on the continents, *Science* 306: 70–75.

Barrett, L., Henzi, P. and Dunbar, R. I. M. 2003 Primate cognition: from 'what now' to 'what if?' *Trends in Cognitive Sciences* 7: 494–497.

Barthelme, J. 1977 Holocene sites north-east of Lake Turkana: a preliminary report, *Azania* 12: 33–42.

1985 *Fisher-hunters and Neolithic pastoralists in East Turkana*, Oxford: British Archaeological Reports.

Barton, R. N. E., Bouzouggar, J., Collcutt, S. N., Gale, R., Higham, T. F. G., Humphrey, L., Parfitt, S., Rhodes, E., Stringer, C. B. and Malek, F. 2005 The Late Upper Palaeolithic occupation of the Moroccan northwest Maghreb during the Last Glacial Maximum, *African Archaeological Review* 22: 77–100.

Bartsiokas, A., and Day, M. H. 1993 Lead poisoning and dental caries in the Broken Hill hominid, *Journal of Human Evolution* 22: 243–249.

Bayle des Hermens, R. 1975 *Recherches prehistoriques en Republique Centrafricaine*, Paris: Lebethno.

Beaumont, P. B. 1978 Border Cave, MA thesis, University of Cape Town.

1990 Kathu, in P. B. Beaumont and D. Morris (eds.), *Guide to archaeological sites in the Northern Cape*, Kimberly: McGregor Museum, pp. 75–100.

Beaumont, P. B., de Villiers, H. and Vogel, J. C. 1978 Modern man in sub-Saharan Africa prior to 49000 years BP: a review and evaluation with particular reference to Border Cave, *South African Journal of Science* 74: 409–419.

Beaumont, P. B., Smith, A. B. and Vogel, J. C. 1995 Before the Einiqua: the archaeology of the Frontier Zone, in A. B. Smith (ed.), *Einiqualand: studies of the Orange River frontier*, Cape Town: University of Cape Town Press, pp. 236–264.

Beaumont, P. B. and Vogel, J. C. 1972 On a new radiocarbon chronology for Africa south of the equator. Part 2, *African Studies* 31: 155–181.

1989 Patterns in the age and context of rock art in the northern Cape, *South African Archaeological Bulletin* 44: 73–81.

2006 On a timescale for the past million years of human history in central South Africa, *South African Journal of Science* 102: 217–228.

Becker, M. and Wendorf, F. 1993 A microwear study of a late Pleistocene Qadan assemblage from southern Egypt, *Journal of Field Archaeology* 20: 389–398.

Bednarik, R. G. 2003 A figurine from the African Acheulian, *Current Anthropology* 44: 405–413.

Beerten, L., and Stesmans, A. 2005. Single quartz grain electron spin resonance (ESR) dating of a contemporary desert surface deposit, Eastern Desert, Egypt, *Quaternary Science Reviews* 24: 223–231.

2006 The use of Ti centers for estimating burial doses of single quartz grains: a case study from an aeolian deposit $\sim$2 Ma old, *Radiation Measurements* 41: 418–424.

Begun, D. R. 2004 The earliest hominins – is less more? *Science* 303: 1478–1480.

Behrensmeyer, A. K. 2006 Climate change and human evolution, *Science* 311: 476–478.

Behrensmeyer, A. K. and Hill, A. 1980 *Fossils in the making: vertebrate taphonomy and palaeoecology*, Chicago: University of Chicago Press.

Behrensmeyer, A. K., Potts, R., Deino, A. and Ditchfield, P. 2002 Olorgesailie, Kenya: A million years in the life of a rift basin, in R. W. Renaut and G. M. Ashley (eds.), *Sedimentation in continental rifts*, Tulsa: Society for Sedimentary Geology Special Publication No. 73, pp. 97–106.

Behrensmeyer, A. K., Todd, N. E., Potts, R. and McBrinn, G. E. 1997 Late Pliocene faunal turnover in the Turkana basin, Kenya and Ethiopia, *Science* 278: 1589–1594.

Bellomo, R. V. 1994 Methods of determining early hominid behavioral activities associated with the controlled use of fire at FxJj 20 Main, Koobi Fora, Kenya, *Journal of Human Evolution* 27: 173–195.

Bellomo, R. V. and Kean, W. F. 1997 Appendix 4A. Evidence of hominid-controlled fire at FxJj20 site complex, Karari Escarpment, in G. Ll. Isaac and B. Isaac (eds.), *Koobi Fora Research Project, Volume 5, Plio-Pleistocene archaeology*, Oxford: Oxford University Press, pp. 224–233.

Bellwood, P. 2005 *First farmers: the origins of agricultural societies*, Oxford: Blackwell Publishing.

Bensimon, Y. and Martineau, M. 1987 Le néolithique marocain en 1986, *L'Anthropologie* 91: 623–652.

Bermúdez de Castro, J.-M., Arsuaga, J.-L., Carbonell, E., Rosas, A., Martinez, I. and Mosquera, M. 1997 A hominid from the Lower Pleistocene of Atapuerca, Spain: possible ancestor to Neandertals and modern humans, *Science* 276: 1392–1395.

Beyin, A. 2006 The Bab al Mandab vs the Nile-Levant: an appraisal of the two dispersal routes for early modern humans out of Africa, *African Archaeological Review* 23: 5–30.

Biberson, P. 1964 La place des hommes du paléolithique marocain dans la chronologie du Pléistocène atlantique, *L'Anthropologie* 68: 475–526.

Bickerton, D. 2005 The origin of language in niche construction, www.derekbickerton.com/blog/archives/2005/3/28/486319/html. Accessed 26 September, 2006.

Biesbrouck, K., Elders, S. and Rossel, G. (eds.) 1999 *Central African hunter-gatherers in a multidisciplinary perspective: challenging elusiveness*, Leiden: University of Leiden Press.

Biesele, M. and Hitchcock, R. K. 2000 The Ju/'hoansi San under two states: impacts of the South West African Administration and the Government of the Republic of Namibia, in P. P. Schweitzer, M. Biesele and R. K. Hitchcock (eds.), *Hunters and gatherers in the modern world: conflict, resistance and self-determination*, Oxford: Berghahn, pp. 305–326.

Biesele, M. and Royal-/O/oo, K. 1999 Ju/'hoansi, in R. B. Lee and R. Daly (eds.), *The Cambridge encyclopaedia of hunters and gatherers*, Cambridge: Cambridge University Press, pp. 205–209.

Binford, L. R. 1980 Willow smoke and dogs' tails: hunter-gatherer settlement systems and archaeological site formation, *American Antiquity* 45: 4–20.

1981 *Bones: ancient men and modern myths*, New York: Academic Press.

1984 *Faunal remains from Klasies River Mouth*, New York: Academic Press.

1988 Fact and fiction about the *Zinjanthropus* floor: data, arguments and interpretation, *Current Anthropology* 29: 123–135.

2001 *Constructing frames of reference: an analytical method for archaeological theory building using hunter-gatherer and environmental data sets*, Berkeley: University of California Press.

Binford, L. R. and Todd, L. C. 1982 On arguments for the "butchering" of giant geladas, *Current Anthropology* 23: 108–111.

Binneman, J. N. F. 1982 Mikrogebruikstekens op steenwerktuie: eksperimentele waarnemings en 'n studie van werktuie afkomstig van Boomplaasgrot, MA thesis, University of Stellenbosch.

1996 Symbolic construction of communities during the Holocene Later Stone Age in the south-eastern Cape, DPhil thesis, University of the Witwatersrand.

1997 Usewear traces on Robberg bladelets from Rose Cottage Cave, *South African Journal of Science* 93: 479–481.

2000 Results from two test excavations in the Baviaanskloof Mountains, Eastern Cape Province, *Southern African Field Archaeology* 9: 83–96.

Binneman, J. and Beaumont, P. 1992 Use-wear analysis of two Acheulean handaxes from Wonderwerk Cave, Northern Cape, *Southern African Field Archaeology* 1: 92–97.

Binneman, J. N. F. and Mitchell, P. J. 1997 Microwear analysis of Robberg bladelets from Sehonghong Shelter, Lesotho, *Southern African Field Archaeology* 6: 42–49.

Bird, C. F. M. and Frankel, D. 1991 Problems in constructing a prehistoric regional sequence: Holocene south-east Australia, *World Archaeology* 23: 179–192.

Bishop, L. C., Plummer, T. W., Ferraro, J. V., Braun, D., Ditchfield, P. W., Hertel, F., Kingston, J. D., Hicks, J., and Potts, R. 2006 Recent research into Oldowan hominin activities at Kanjera South, Western Kenya, *African Archaeological Review* 23: 31–40.

Bishop, W. W. and Clark, J. D. (eds.) 1967 *Background to evolution in Africa*, Chicago: University of Chicago Press.

Bisson, M. S. 1990 Lithic reduction sequences as an aid to the analysis of Later Stone Age quartz assemblages from the Luano Hot Spring, Chingola, Zambia, *African Archaeological Review* 8: 103–138.

Blackburn, R. 1973 Okiek ceramics: evidence for Central Kenya prehistory, *Azania* 8: 55–70.

1982 In the land of milk and honey: Okiek adaptations to their forests and neighbours, in E. Leacock and R. B. Lee (eds.), *Politics and history in band societies*, Cambridge: Cambridge University Press, pp. 283–305.

1996 Fission, fusion and foragers in East Africa: micro- and macroprocesses of diversity and integration among Okiek groups, in S. Kent (ed.), *Cultural diversity among Twentieth Century foragers: an African perspective*, Cambridge: Cambridge University Press, pp. 188–212.

Bleed, P. 1986 The optimal design of hunting weapons: maintainability and reliability, *American Antiquity* 51: 737–747.

Bleek, W. H. I. and Lloyd, L. 1911 *Specimens of Bushman folklore*, London: Allen.

Blench, R. M. 1999a Are the African pygmies an ethnographic fiction? in K. Biesbrouck, S. Elders and G. Rossel (eds.), *Central African hunter-gatherers in a multidisciplinary perspective: challenging elusiveness*, Leiden: University of Leiden Press, pp. 41–60.

Blench, R. M. 1999b The languages of Africa: macrophyla proposals and implications for archaeological interpretation, in R. M. Blench and M. Spriggs (eds.), *Archaeology and language, Volume IV*, London: Routledge, pp. 29–47.

Blench, R. M. 2006 *Archaeology, language and the African past*, Walnut Creek: AltaMira Press.

Blockley, S. P. E., Blockley, S. M., Donahue, R. E., Lane, C. S., Lowe, J. J., and Pollard, A. M. 2006 The chronology of abrupt climate change and

Late Upper Palaeolithic human adaptation in Europe, *Journal of Quaternary Science* 21: 575–584.

Blumenschine, R. J. 1987 Characteristics of an early hominid scavenging niche, *Current Anthropology* 28: 383–407.

1988 An experimental model of the timing of hominid and carnivore influence on archaeological bone assemblages, *Journal of Archaeological Science* 15: 483–502.

1991 Hominid carnivory and foraging strategies, and the socio-economic function of early archaeological sites, *Philosophical Transactions of the Royal Society of London (Biology)* 334: 211–221.

1995 Percussion marks, tooth marks, and experimental determinations of the timing of hominid and carnivore access to long bones at FLK Zinjanthropus, Olduvai Gorge, Tanzania, *Journal of Human Evolution* 29: 21–51.

Blumenschine, R. J. and Peters, C. R. 1998 Archaeological predictions for hominid land use in the paleo-Olduvai basin, Tanzania, during lowermost Bed II times, *Journal of Human Evolution* 34: 565–607.

Blumenschine, R. J., Peters, C. R., Masao, F. T., Clarke, R. J., Deino, A. L., Hay, R. L., Swisher, C. C., Stanistreet, I. G., Ashley, G. M., McHenry, L. J., Sikes, N. E., van der Merwe, N. J., Tactikos, J. C., Cushing, A. E., Deocampo, D. M., Njau, J. K. and Ebert, J. I. 2003 Late Pliocene *Homo* and hominid land use from Western Olduvai Gorge, Tanzania, *Science* 299: 1217–1221.

Blumler, M. 1992 Seed weight and environment in Mediterranean-type grasslands in California and Israel, PhD thesis, University of California, Berkeley.

Blundell, G. 2004 *Nqabayo's Nomansland: San rock art and the somatic past*, Uppsala: Uppsala University Press.

Blunier, T. and Brook, E. J. 2001 Timing of millennial-scale climate change in Antarctica and Greenland during the last glacial period, *Science* 291: 109–112.

Bobe, R. and Behrensmeyer, A. K. 2004 The expansion of grassland ecosystems in Africa in relation to mammalian evolution and the origin of the genus *Homo*, *Palaeogeography, Palaeoclimatology, Palaeoecology* 207: 399–420.

Bobe, R., Behrensmeyer, A. K. and Chapman, R. E. 2002 Faunal change, environmental variability and late Pliocene hominin evolution, *Journal of Human Evolution* 42: 475–497.

Boesch, C. 1993 Aspects of transmission of tool-use in wild chimpanzees, in K. R. Gibson and T. Ingold (eds.), *Tools, language and cognition in human evolution*, Cambridge: Cambridge University Press, pp. 171–183.

Boesch, C. and Boesch, H. 2000 *The chimpanzees of the Tai Forest: behavioural ecology and evolution*, Oxford: Oxford University Press.

Bogin, B. and Smith, B. 1996 Evolution of the human life cycle, *American Journal of Human Biology* 8: 703–716.

Boissserie, J.-R., Brunte, M., Andossa, L. and Vignaud, P. 2003 Hippotamids from the Djurab Pliocene faunas, Chad, Central Africa, *Journal of African Earth Sciences* 36: 15–27.

Bollig, M. 1987 Ethnic relations and spatial mobility in Africa: a review of the peripatetic niche, in A. Rao (ed.), *The other nomads: peripatetic minorities in cross-cultural perspective*, Köln: Bohlau Verlag, pp. 179–228.

Bollong, C. A. and Sampson, C. G. 1999 Later Stone Age herder-hunter interactions reflected in ceramic distributions in the upper Seacow River valley, *South African Journal of Science* 95: 171–180.

Bonnefille, R., Roeland, J. C. and Guiot, J. 1990 Temperature and rainfall estimates for the past 40,000 years in equatorial Africa, *Nature* 346: 347–349.

Borland, C. H. 1986 The linguistic reconstruction of prehistoric pastoralist vocabulary, *South African Archaeological Society Goodwin Series* 5: 31–35.

Bosch, E., Calafell, F., Cornas, D., Oefner, P. J., Underhill, P. A. and Bertran-petit, J. 2001 High-resolution analysis of human Y-chromosome variation shows a sharp discontinuity and limited gene flow between Northwestern Africa and the Iberian Peninsula, *American Journal of Human Genetics* 68: 1019–1029.

Bousman, C. B. 1991 Holocene palaeoecology and Later Stone Age hunter-gatherer adaptations in the South African interior plateau, PhD thesis, Southern Methodist University.

2005 Coping with risk: Later Stone Age technological strategies at Blydefontein Rock Shelter, South Africa, *Journal of Anthropological Archaeology* 24: 193–226.

Boutros-Ghali, B. 1994 Foreword, in A. Ewen (ed.) *Voice of indigenous peoples*, Santa Fe: Native American Council of New York City.

Bouzouggar, A., Barton, N., Vanhaeren, M., d'Errico, F., Collcutt, S., Higham, T., Hodge, E., Parfitt, S., Rhodes, E., Schwenninger, J.-L., Stringer, C., Turner, E., Ward, S., Moutmir, A., and Stambouli, A. 2007 82,000-year-old shell beads from North Africa and implications for the origins of modern human behaviour, *Proceedings of the National Academy of Sciences* 104: 9964–9969.

Bouzouggar, A., Kozlowski, J. K. and Otte, M. 2002 Étude des ensembles lithiques atériens de la grotte d'El Aliya à Tanger (Maroc), *L'Anthropologie* 106: 207–248.

Bowdler, S. 1995 Offshore islands and maritime explorations in Australian prehistory, *Antiquity* 69: 945–958.

Bower, J. R. F. 1991 The Pastoral Neolithic of East Africa, *Journal of World Prehistory* 5: 49–82.

Bower, J. R. F. and Chadderdon, T. J. 1986 Further excavations of Pastoral Neolithic sites in Serengeti, *Azania* 21: 129–133.

Bower, J. R. F., Nelson, C. M., Waibel, A. F. and Wandibba, S. 1977 The University of Massachusetts, Later Stone Age/Pastoral 'Neolithic' comparative study in central Kenya: an overview, *Azania* 12: 119–146.

Boyd, B. 2006 On 'sedentism' in the Later Epipalaeolithic (Natufian) Levant, *World Archaeology* 38: 164–178.

Bradley, D. G., MacHugh, D. E., Cunningham, P. and Loftus, R. T. 1996 Mitochondrial diversity and the origins of African and European cattle,

*Proceedings of the National Academy of Science of the United States of America* 93: 5131–5135.

Brain, C. K. and Shipman, P. 1993 The Swartkrans bone tools, in C. K. Brain (ed.), *Swartkrans, a cave's chronicle of early man*, Pretoria: Transvaal Museum, pp. 195–215.

Brain, C. K. and Sillen, A. 1988 Evidence from the Swartkrans cave for the earliest use of fire, *Nature* 336: 464–466.

Brandt, S. A. 1986 The Upper Pleistocene and early Holocene prehistory of the Horn of Africa, *African Archaeological Review* 4: 41–82.

1988 Early Holocene mortuary practices and hunter-gatherer adaptations in southern Somalia, *World Archaeology* 20: 40–56.

1996 the ethnoarchaeology of flaked stone tool use in southern Ethiopia, in G. Pwiti and R. Soper (eds.), *Aspects of African archaeology*, Harare: University of Zimbabwe Press, pp. 733–738.

Brandt, S. A. and Brook, G. 1984 Archaeological and palaeoenvironmental research in northern Somalia, *Current Anthropology* 25: 119–121.

Brandt, S. A. and Fattovich, R. 1990 Late Quaternary archaeological research in the Horn of Africa, in P. T. Robertshaw (ed.), *A history of African archaeology*, London: James Currey, pp. 95–108.

Brantingham, P. J. 1998 Hominid-carnivore coevolution and invasion of the predatory guild, *Journal of Anthropological Archaeology* 17: 327–353.

Bräuer, G., Groden, C., Delling, G., Kupczik, K., Mbua, E. and Schultz, M. 2003 Pathological alterations in the Archaic *Homo sapiens* cranium from Eliye Springs, Kenya, *American Journal of Physical Anthropology* 120: 200–204.

Bräuer, G. and Leakey, R. E. 1986 The ES-11693 cranium from Eliye Springs, West Turkana, Kenya, *Journal of Human Evolution* 15: 289–312.

Bräuer, G., Yokoyama, Y., Falguères, C. and Mbua, E. 1997 Modern human origins backdated, *Nature* 386: 337–338.

Braun, D. R. and Harris, J. W. 2003 Technological developments in the Oldowan of Koobi Fora: Innovative techniques of artifact analysis, in J. M. Moreno, R. M. Torcal and I. de la Torres Sainz (eds.), *Oldowan: rather more than smashing stones*, Barcelona: University of Barcelona Press, pp. 117–144.

Braun, D. R., Tactikos, J. C., Ferraro, J. V. and Harris, J. W. K. 2005 Flake recovery rates and inferences of Oldowan hominin behaviour: a response to Kimura 1999, 2002, *Journal of Human Evolution* 48: 525–531.

Breuer, T., Ndoundou-Hockemba, M. and Fishlock, V. 2005 First observation of tool use in wild gorillas, *PLoS Biology* 3 (11): e380.

Breuil, H. 1944 La paléolithique au Congo Belge d'apres les recherches du Docteur Cabu, *Transactions of the Royal Society of South Africa* 30: 143–160.

Breunig, P. and Neumann, K. 2002 Continuity or discontinuity? The 1st millennium BC crisis in West African prehistory, in Jennerstrasse 8; (eds.) *Tides of the desert. Contributions to the archaeology and environmental history of Africa in honour of Rudolph Kuper*, Köln: Heinrich-Barth-Institut, Africa Praehistorica 14, 491–505.

Breunig, P., Neumann, K. and van Neer, W. 1996 New research on the Holocene settlement and environment of the Chad Basin in Nigeria, *African Archaeological Review* 13: 111–145.

Breunig, P. and Wotzka, H.-P. 1991 Archäologische Forschungen im Südosten Burkina Faso 1989/90 Vorbericht über die erste Grabungskampagne des Frankfurter Sonderforschungsbereiches 268 'Westafrikanisches Savanne,' *Beitrage zur Allgemeinen und Vergleichenden Archaeologie* 11: 145–199.

Brook, G. A., Robbins, L. H. and Campbell, A. C. 2003 Forty thousand years of environmental change in the Kalahari as evidenced by sediments in the Depression Rock Shelter, Tsodilo Hills, Botswana, *Nyame Akuma* 59: 2–10.

Brooks, A. S. and Behrensmeyer, A. K. After the Acheulean: stratigraphy, dating and archaeology of two new Formations in the Olorgesailie Basin, Southern Kenya Rift. Abstract: Paleoanthropology Society Meeting 2007, Philadelphia, USA, http://www.paleoanthro.org/meeting.htm. Accessed 1 June 2007.

Brooks, A. S., Hare, P. E., Kokis, J. E., Miller, G. H., Ernst, R. D. and Wendorf, F. 1990 Dating Pleistocene archaeological sites by protein diagenesis in ostrich eggshell, *Science* 248: 60–64.

Brooks, A. S., Helgren, D. M., Cramer, J. S., Franklin, A., Hornyat, M., Keating, J. M., Klein, R. G., Rink, W. J., Schwarcz, H., Smith, J. N. L., Stewart, K., Todd, N., Verniers, J. and Yellen, J. 1995 Dating and context of three Middle Stone Age sites with bone points in the Upper Semliki Valley, Zaire, *Science* 268: 548–553.

Brooks, A. S. and Smith, C. C. 1987 Ishango revisited: new age determinations and cultural interpretations, *African Archaeological Review* 5: 65–78.

Brooks, K., Scholz, C. A., King, J. W., Peck, J., Overpeck, J. T., Russell, J. M. and Amoako, P. Y. O. 2004 Late-Quaternary lowstands of Lake Bosumtwi, Ghana: evidence from high-resolution seismic-reflection and sediment-core data, *Palaeogeography, Palaeoclomiatology, Palaeoecology* 216: 235–249.

Brooks, N., Drake, N., McLaren, S. and White, K. 2003 Studies in geography, geomorphology, environment and climate, in D. Mattingly (ed.), *The archaeology of Fazzan, Volume 1, synthesis*, London: Society for Libyan Studies, pp. 37–74.

Brown, A. J. V. and Verhagen, B. T. 1985 Two *Antidorcas bondi* individuals from the Late Stone Age site of Kruger Cave 35/83, Olifantsnek, Rustenburg District, South Africa, *South African Journal of Science* 81: 102.

Brunet, M., Beauvilain, A., Coppens, Y., Heintz, E., Moutaye, A. H. E. and Pilbeam, D. 1995 The first australopithecine 2,500 kilometres west from the Rift Valley (Chad), *Nature* 378: 273–275.

Brunet, M., Guy, F., Pilbeam, D., Mackaye, H., Likius, A., Ahounta, D., Beauvilain, A., Blondel, C., Bocherons, H., Boisseries, J.-R., de Bonis, L., Coppens, Y., Dejax, J., Denys, C., Duringer, P., Eisenmann, V., Fanone, G., Fronty, P., Geraads, D., Lehman, T., Lihoreau, F., Louchar, A., Mahamat, A., Merceron, G., Mouchelin, G., Otero, O., Campomanes,

P., Ponce de Leon, M., Rage, J.-C. and Sapanet, M. 2002 A new hominid from the Upper Miocene of Chad, Central Africa, *Nature* 418: 145–151.

Bunn, H. T. 1981 Archaeological evidence for meat-eating by Plio-Pleistocene hominids at Koobi Fora, Kenya and Olduvai Gorge, *Nature* 291: 574–577.

  1986 Patterns of skeletal representation and hominid subsistence activities at Olduvai Gorge, Tanzania, and Koobi Fora, Kenya, *Journal of Human Evolution* 15: 673–690.

Bunn, H. T. and Kroll, E. M. 1986 Systematic butchery by Plio/Pleistocene hominids at Olduvai Gorge, Tanzania, *Current Anthropology* 27: 431–452.

Burkitt, M. C. 1928 *South Africa's past in stone and paint*, Cambridge: Cambridge University Press.

Burling, R. 2005 *The talking ape: how language evolved*, Oxford: Oxford University Press.

Butzer, K. W. 1980 Pleistocene history of the Nile Valley in Egypt and Lower Nubia, in M. A. J. Williams and H. Faure (eds.), *The Sahara and the Nile*, Rotterdam: A. A. Balkema, pp. 253–280.

Butzer, K. W., Brown, F. H. and Thurber, D. L. 1969 Horizontal sediments of the lower Omo Valley: the Kibish Formation, *Quaternaira* 11: 15–29.

Byrne, R. W. 1997 What's the use of anecdotes? Distinguishing psychological mechanisms in primate tactical deception, in R. W. Mitchell, N. S. Thompson and H. L. Miles (eds.), *Anthropomorphism, anecdotes, and animals*, New York: University of New York Press, pp. 134–150.

  2004 The manual skills and cognition that lie behind hominid tool use, in A. E. Russon and D. R. Begun (eds), *The evolution of thought: evolutionary origins of great ape intelligence*, Cambridge: Cambridge University Press, pp. 31–44.

Byrne, R. W. and Whiten, A. 1988 *Machiavellian intelligence: social expertise and the evolution of intellect in monkeys, apes and humans*, Oxford: Clarendon Press.

Cable, J. H. C. 1984 *Late Stone Age economy and technology in southern Natal*. Oxford: British Archaeological Reports.

Cachel, S. and Harris, J. W. K. 1998 The lifeways of *Homo erectus* inferred from archaeology and evolutionary ecology: a perspective from East Africa, in M. D. Petraglia and R. Korisettar (eds.), *Early human behaviour in the global context: the rise and diversity of the Lower Palaeolithic record*, London: Routledge, pp. 108–132.

Cahen, D. and Moeyersons, J. 1977 Subsurface movements of stone artefacts and their implications for the prehistory of Central Africa, *Nature* 266: 812–815.

Cain, C. R. 2006 Implications of the marked artifacts of the Middle Stone Age of Africa, *Current Anthropology* 47: 675–681.

Calvin, W. 1993 The unitary hypothesis: a common neural circuitry for novel manipulation, language, plan-ahead, and throwing? in K. R. Gibson and T Ingold (eds.), *Tools, language and cognition in human evolution*, Cambridge: Cambridge University Press, pp. 230–250.

Camara, A. and Duboscq, B. 1987 Contexte chronostratigraphique des outillages du paléolithique evolué dans l'est du Sénégal, *L'Anthropologie* 91: 511–520.

1990. La fouille d'un site Acheuléen à Djita (basse vallée de la Falémé, Sénégal, *L'Anthropologie* 94: 293–304.

Campbell, C. 1986 Images of war: a problem in San rock art research, *World Archaeology* 18: 255–268.

1987 Art in crisis: contact period rock art in the south-eastern mountains of southern Africa, MSc thesis, University of the Witwatersrand.

Camps, G. 1967 Le néolithique de tradition capsienne au Sahara, *Travaux de l'Institut des Recherches Sahariennes* 21: 85–96.

1969 *Amekni: Néolithique ancien du Hoggar*, Paris: Arts et Métiers Graphiques.

1974 *Les civilisations préhistoriques de l'Afrique Nord et du Sahara*, Paris: Doin.

1982 Beginnings of pastoralism and cultivation in north-west Africa and the Sahara: origins of the Berbers, in J. D. Clark (ed.), *Cambridge history of Africa Volume I: from the earliest times to c. 500 B.C.*, Cambridge: Cambridge University Press, pp. 548–623.

Camps-Febrer, H. 1966 *Matières et art mobilier dans la préhistoire nord-africaine et saharienne*, Paris: Arts et Métiers Graphiques.

Caneva, I. 1983 Pottery-using gatherers and hunters at Saggai (Sudan): preconditions for food-production, *Origini* 13: 7–278.

1988 El Geili. *The history of a Middle Nile environment, 7000 BC-AD 1500*, Oxford: British Archaeological Reports.

Caneva, I. and Marks, A. E. 1990 More on the Shaqadud pottery evidence for Saharo-Nilotic connections during the 6th-4th millennium B.C., *Archéologie du Moyen Nil* 4: 11–35.

Cann, R. L., Stoneking, M. and Wilson, A. C. 1987 Mitochondrial DNA and human evolution, *Nature* 325: 31–36.

Carbonell, E., and Mosquera, R. 2006 The emergence of symbolic behaviour: the sepulchral pit of Sima de los Huesos, Sierra de Atapuerca, Burgos, Spain. *Comptes Rendus Palevol* 5: 155–160.

Carr, A. S., Thomas, D. S. G., Bateman, M. D., Meadows, M. E. and Chase, B. 2006 Late Quaternary palaeoenvironments of the winter-rainfall zone of southern Africa: palynological and sedimentological evidence from the Agulhas Plain, *Palaeogeography, Palaeoclimatology, Palaeoecology* 239: 147–165.

Carter, P. L. 1970 Late Stone Age exploitation patterns in southern Natal, *South African Archaeological Bulletin* 25: 55–58.

1978 The prehistory of eastern Lesotho, PhD thesis, University of Cambridge.

Cartwright, C. and Parkington, J. E. 1997 The wood charcoal assemblages from Elands Bay Cave, southwestern Cape: principles, procedures and preliminary interpretation, *South African Archaeological Bulletin* 52: 59–72.

Casey, J. L. 2003 The archaeology of West Africa from the Pleistocene to the mid-Holocene, in J. Mercader (ed.), *Under the canopy: the archaeology of tropical rain forests*, London: Routledge, pp. 35–63.

2005 Holocene occupations of the forest and savanna, in A. B. Stahl (ed.), *African archaeology: a critical introduction*, Oxford: Blackwell Publishing, pp. 225–248.

Casey, J. L., Sawatsky, R., Godfey-Smith, A. C., Quickert, N., d'Andrea, A. C., Wollstonecraft, M. and Hawkins, A. 1997 Report on investigations at the Birimi Site in Northern Ghana, *Nyame Akuma* 48: 32–38.

Castelletti, L., Castiglioni, E., Cottini, M. and Rottoli, M. 1999 Archaeobotanical analysis of charcoal, wood and seeds, in S. di Lernia (ed.), *The Uan Afuda Cave. Hunter-gatherer societies of the Central Sahara*, Firenze: Edizioni all'Insegna del Giglio, pp. 131–148.

Cauvin, J. 2000 *The birth of the gods and the origins of agriculture*, Cambridge: Cambridge University Press.

Cavalli-Sforza, L. L. (ed.) 1986 *African Pygmies*, Orlando: Academic Press.

Cavalli-Sforza, L. L., Menozzi, P. and Piazza, A. 1994 *The history and geography of human genes*, Princeton: Princeton University Press.

Cesarino, F. 2000 Cani e mufloni protagonisti della più antica forma di controllo culturale delle risorse animali nel Sahara? *Sahara* 12: 107–120.

Challis, W. 2005 'The men with rhebok's heads: they tame elands and snakes': incorporating the rhebok antelope in the understanding of southern African rock art, *South African Archaeological Society Goodwin Series* 9: 11–20.

Chami, F. A. and Kwekason, A. 2003 Neolithic pottery traditions from the islands, the coast and the interior of East Africa, *African Archaeological Review* 20: 65–80.

Chang, 1982 Nomads without cattle: East African foragers in historical perspective, in E. Leacock and R. B. Lee (eds.), *Politics and history in band societies*, Cambridge: Cambridge University Press, pp. 269–282.

Chapman, R. 1981 The emergence of formal disposal areas and the 'problem' of megalithic tombs in prehistoric Europe, in R. W. Chapman, I. A. Kinnes and K. Randsborg (eds.), *The archaeology of death*, Cambridge: Cambridge University Press, pp. 71–81.

Charnov, E. L. 2001 Evolution of mammal life histories, *Evolutionary Ecology Research* 3: 521–535.

Chavaillon, J., Hours, F. and Coppens, Y. 1987 Découverte des restes humains fossiles associés à un outillage acheuléen final à Melka-Konturé (Ethiopie), *Comptes Rendus de l'Académie des Sciences, S. II, 10*, 304: 539–542.

Chavaillon, J. and Piperno, M. (eds.) 2004 *Studies on the Early Palaeolithic site of Mekla Kunture, Ethiopia*, Florence: Instituto Italiano di Preistoria e Protoistoria.

Chen, Y. S., Olckers, A., Schurr, T. G., Kogelnik, A. M., Huoponen, K. and Wallace, D. C. 2000 mtDNA variation in the South African!Kung and Khwe and their genetic relationships to other African populations, *American Journal of Human Genetics* 66: 1362–1383.

Chenorkian, R. 1983 Ivory Coast prehistory: recent developments, *African Archaeological Review* 1: 127–142.

Childe, V. G. 1934 *New light on the most ancient East: the oriental prelude to European prehistory*, London: Kegan Paul.

Chimielewski, W. 1968 Early and Middle Paleolithic sites near Arkin, Sudan, in F. Wendorf (ed.), *The Prehistory of Nubia*, Dallas: Fort Burgwin Research Center and Southern Methodist University Press, pp. 110–147.

The Chimpanzee Sequencing and Analysis Consortium. 2005 Initial sequence of the chimpanzee genome and comparison with the human genome, *Nature* 437: 69–87.

Churchill, S. E., Pearson, O. M., Grine, F. E., Trinkaus, E. and Holliday, T. W. 1996 Morphological affinities of the proximal ulna from Klasies River Mouth Main Site: archaic or modern? *Journal of Human Evolution* 31: 213–237.

Clark, A. M. B. 1999 Late Pleistocene technology at Rose Cottage Cave: a search for modern behaviour in a MSA context, *African Archaeological Review* 16: 93–120.

Clark, G. A. 2002 Neanderthal archaeology – implications for our origins, *American Anthropologist* 104: 50–67.

Clark, J. D. 1950 A note on the pre-Bantu inhabitants of Northern Rhodesia and Nyasaland, *South African Journal of Science* 47: 80–85.

1954 *The prehistoric cultures of the Horn of Africa*, Cambridge: Cambridge University Press.

(ed.) 1957 *Proceedings of the Third Panafrican Congress on Prehistory, Livingstone, 1955*, London: Chatto & Windus.

1959 *The prehistory of southern Africa*, Harmondsworth: Penguin.

1963 *Prehistoric cultures of northeast Angola and their significance in tropical Africa*, Lisbon: Museo do Dundo.

1966 *The distribution of prehistoric cultures in Angola*, Lisbon: Companhia de Diamantes de Angola.

1967 *Atlas of African Prehistory*. Chicago: University of Chicago Press.

1969 *Kalambo Falls prehistoric site Volume I: the geology, palaeoecology and detailed stratigraphy of the excavations*, Cambridge: Cambridge University Press.

1971 A re-examination of the evidence for agricultural origins in the Nile Valley, *Proceedings of the Prehistoric Society* 37: 34–79.

1974a *Kalambo Falls prehistoric site Volume II: the late prehistoric remains*, Cambridge: Cambridge University Press.

1974b Africa in prehistory: peripheral or paramount? *Man* 10: 175–198.

1980 Human populations and cultural adaptations in the Sahara and Nile during prehistoric times, in M. A. J. Williams and H. Faure (eds.), *The Sahara and the Nile – Quaternary environments and prehistoric occupation in northern Africa*, Rotterdam: A. A. Balkema, pp. 527–582.

(ed.). 1982a *Cambridge history of Africa Volume I: from the earliest times to c. 500 B.C.*, Cambridge: Cambridge University Press.

1982b Cultures of the Middle Palaeolithic/Middle Stone Age, in J. D. Clark (ed.), *Cambridge history of Africa Volume I: from the earliest times to c. 500 B.C.*, Cambridge: Cambridge University Press, pp. 248–341.

1988a The Middle Stone Age of East Africa and the beginnings of regional identity, *Journal of World Prehistory* 2: 235–303.

1988b A review of the archaeological evidence for the origins of food production in Ethiopia, in T. Beyene (ed.), *Proceedings of the 8th International Conference of Ethiopian Studies, Volume 1*, Addis Ababa: Institute of Ethiopian Studies, pp. 55–69.

1989a Shabona: an Early Khartoum settlement on the White Nile, in L. Krzyzaniak and M. Koubsiewicz (eds.), *Late prehistory of the Nile Basin and the Sahara*, Poznán: Poznán Museum, pp. 387–410.

1989b The origins and spread of modern humans: a broad perspective on the African evidence, in P. Mellars and C. Stringer (eds.), *The human revolution*, Edinburgh: Edinburgh University Press, pp. 565–588.

1990 A personal memoir, in P. T. Robertshaw (ed.), *A history of African archaeology*, London: James Currey, pp. 189–204.

1992 The Earlier Stone Age/Lower Palaeolithic in North Africa and the Sahara, in F. Klees and R. Kuper (eds.), *New light on the northeast African past*, Köln: Heinrich-Barth Institut, pp. 17–37.

1993 The Aterian of the Central Sahara, in L. Kryzaniak, M. Kobusiewicz and J. Alexander (eds.), *Environmental change and human culture in the Nile Basin and Northern Africa until the second millennium B.C.*, Poznán: Poznán Archaeological Museum, pp. 49–67.

2001a *Kalambo Falls prehistoric site, Volume III*, Cambridge: Cambridge University Press.

2001b Variability in primary and secondary technologies of the Later Acheulian in Africa, in S. Milliken and J. Cook (eds.), *A very remote period indeed: papers on the Palaeolithic presented to Derek Roe*, Oxford: Oxbow Books, pp. 1–18.

Clark, J. D. and Brandt, S. A. (eds.) 1984 *From hunters to farmers: the causes and consequences of food production in Africa*, Berkeley: University of California Press.

Clark, J. D., Beyenne, J., WoldeGabriel, G., Hart, W. K., Renne, P. R., Gilbert, H., Defleur, A., Suwa, G., Katoh, S., Ludwig, K. R., Boisserie, J-R., Asfawe, B. and White, T. D. 2003 Stratigraphic, chronological and behavioural contexts of Pleistocene *Homo sapiens* from Middle Awash, Ethiopia, *Nature* 423: 747–752.

Clark, J. D. and Harris, J. W. K. 1985 Fire and its roles in early hominid lifeways, *African Archaeological Review* 3: 3–27.

Clark, J. D. and Schick, K. D. 2000 Overview and conclusion on the Middle Awash Acheulean, in J. de Heinzelin, J. D. Clark, K. D. Schick and W. H. Gilbert (eds.), *The Acheulean and the Plio-Pleistocene deposits of the Middle Awash Valley, Ethiopia*, Tervuren: Royal Museum of Central Africa, pp. 193–202.

Clark, J. G. D. 1969 *World prehistory: a new outline*, Cambridge: Cambridge University Press.

Clist, B. 1995 *Gabon: 100,000 ans d'histoire*, Libreville: Centre Culturel Français St Exupery.

1998 Nouvelles données archéologiques sur l'histoire ancienne de la Guinée-Equatoriale, *L'Anthropologie* 102: 213–217.

1999 Traces de très anciennes occupations humaines de la forêt tropicale au Gabon, in K. Biesbrouck, S. Elders and G. Rossel (eds.), *Central African hunter-gatherers in a multidisciplinary perspective: challenging elusiveness*, Leiden: University of Leiden Press, pp. 75–87.

Close, A. E. 1980 Current research and recent radiocarbon dates from northeastern Africa, *Journal of African History* 21: 145–167.

1984 Report on Site E-80–1, in F. Wendorf, R. Schild and A. E. Close (eds.), *Cattle-keepers of the Eastern Sahara the Neolithic of Bir Kiseiba*, Dallas: Southern Methodist University Press, pp. 251–297.

1989 Identifying style in stone artefacts: a case study from the Nile Valley, *Archaeological Papers of the American Anthropological Association* 1: 3–26.

1995 Few and far between: early ceramics in North Africa, in W. K. Barnett and J. W. Hoopes (eds.), *The emergence of pottery technology and innovation in ancient societies*, Washington: Smithsonian Institution Press, pp. 23–37.

1996 *Plus ça change*: the Pleistocene-Holocene transition in Northeast Africa, in L. G. Straus, B. V. Eriksen, J. M. Erlandson and D. R. Yesner (eds.) *Humans at the end of the Ice Age: the archaeology of the Pleistocene-Holocene transition*, New York: Plenum Press pp. 43–60.

2002 Backed bladelets are a foreign country, *Archaeological Papers of the American Anthropological Association* 12: 31–44.

Close, A. E. and Wendorf, F. 1990 North Africa at 18,000 BP, in C. S. Gamble and O. Soffer (eds.), *The World at 18,000 BP, Volume II, low latitudes*, London: Unwin Hyman, pp. 41–57.

1992 The beginnings of food production in the eastern Sahara, in A. E. Gebauer and T. D. Price (eds.), *Transitions to agriculture in prehistory*, Madison: Prehistory Press, pp. 63–72.

Cloudsley-Thompson, L. (ed.) 1984 *The Sahara*, Oxford: Pergamon Press.

Coetzee J. A. 1967 Pollen analytical studies in East and southern Africa, *Palaeoecology of Africa* 3: 1–146.

Cohen, A. L., Parkington, J. E., Brundrit, G. B., and van der Merwe, N. J. 1992 A Holocene marine climate record in mollusc shells from the southwest African Coast, *Quaternary Research* 38: 379–385.

Cohen, A. S., Stone, J. R., Beuning, K. R. M., Park, L. E., Reinthal, P. N., Dettman, D., Scholz, C. A., Johnson, T. C., King, J. W., Talbot, M. R., Brown, E. T., and Ivory, S. J. 2007 Ecological consequences of early Late Pleistocene megadroughts in tropical Africa. *Proceedings of the National Academy of Sciences, USA* 104: 16422–16427.

Collett, D. and Robertshaw, P. T. 1983 Problems in the interpretation of radiocarbon dates: the Pastoral Neolithic of East Africa, *African Archaeological Review* 1: 57–74.

Coluzzi, M. 1994 Malaria and the Afrotropical ecosystems: impact of man-made environmental changes, *Parassitologia* 36: 223–227.

Conard, N. J. 2005 An overview of the patterns of behavioural change in Africa and Eurasia during the Middle and Late Pleistocene, in F. d'Errico and

L. Backwell (eds.), *From tools to symbols: from early hominins to modern humans*, Johannesburg: Witwatersrand University Press, pp. 293–332.

Conard, N. J. and Bolus, M. 2003 Radiocarbon dating the appearance of modern humans and timing of cultural innovations in Europe: new results and new challenges, *Journal of Human Evolution* 44: 331–371.

Connah, G. 1964 *Polished stone axes in Benin*, Lagos: Nigerian Federal Department of Antiquities.

1996 *Kibiro: the salt of Bunyoro, past and present*, Nairobi: British Institute in Eastern Africa.

2005 *Forgotten Africa: an introduction to its archaeology*, London: Routledge.

Connor, D. R. and Marks, A. E. 1986 The terminal Pleistocene on the Nile: the final Nilotic adjustment, in L. G. Straus (ed.), *The end of the Palaeolithic in the Old World*, Oxford: British Archaeological Reports, pp. 171–199.

Conroy, G. C., Weber, G. W., Seidler, H., Recheis, W., zur Nedden, D. and Mariam, J. H. 2000 Endocranial capacity of the Bodo cranium determined from three-dimensional computed tomography, *American Journal of Physical Anthropology* 113: 111–118.

Cooke, C. K. 1969 A re-examination of the 'Middle Stone Age' industries of Rhodesia. *Arnoldia Rhodesia* 4(7): 1–20.

1979 Excavations at Diana's Vow Rock Shelter, Maroni District, Zimbabwe Rhodesia, *Occasional Papers of the National Museum of Rhodesia A* 4: 115–148.

Coolidge, F., and Wynn, T. 2006 The effects of the tree-to-ground sleep transition in the evolution of cognition in early *Homo*. *Before Farming* (online version) 4, 11: 1–18.

Coon, C. S. 1968 *Yengema cave report*, Philadelphia: University of Pennsylvania Museum.

Coppens, Y. 1966 Le Tchadanthropus, *L'Anthropologie* 70: 5–16.

Corballis, M. C. 2002 *From hand to mouth: the origins of language*, Princeton: Princeton University Press.

Cornelissen, E. 2002 Human responses to changing environments in Central Africa between 40,000 and 12,000 BP, *Journal of World Prehistory* 16: 197–235.

2003 On microlithic quartz industries at the end of the Pleistocene in Central Africa: the evidence from Shum Laka (NW Cameroon), *African Archaeological Review* 20: 1–24.

Corridi, C. 1998 Faunal remains from Holocene archaeological sites of the Tadrart Acacus and surroundings (Libyan Sahara), in M. Cremaschi and S. di Lernia (eds.), *Wadi Teshuianat. Palaeoenvironment and prehistory in south-western Fezzan (Libyan Sahara)*, Firenze: All'Insegna del Giglio, pp. 89–94.

Cowling, R. M., Cartwright, C. R., Parkington, J. E. and Allsopp, J. C. 1999 Fossil wood charcoal assemblages from Elands Bay Cave, South Africa: implications for Late Quaternary vegetation and climates in the winter-rainfall fynbos biome, *Journal of Biogeography* 26: 367–378.

Crader, D. 1984 Faunal remains from Chencherere II rock shelter, Malawi, *South African Archaeological Bulletin* 39: 37–52.

Crawhall, N. 2004 !Ui-Taa language shift in Gordonia and Postmasburg districts, South Africa, PhD thesis, University of Cape Town.

2006 Languages, genetics and archaeology: problems and the possibilities in Africa, in H. Soodyall (ed.), *The prehistory of Africa: tracing the lineage of modern man*, Johannesburg: Jonathan Ball Publishers, pp. 109–124.

Cremaschi, M. 2002 Late Pleistocene and Holocene climatic changes in the Central Sahara: the case study of the southwestern Fezzan, Libya, in F. A. Hassan (ed.), *Droughts, food and culture: ecological change and food security in Africa's later prehistory*, New York: Kluwer Academic/Plenum Publishers, pp. 65–82.

Cremaschi, M. and di Lernia, S. (eds.) 1998 *Wadi Teshuinat: palaeoenvironment and prehistory in southwestern Fezzan (Libyan Sahara)*, Milan: Quaderni di Geodinamica Alpina e del Quaternario.

Cremaschi, M. and di Lernia, S. 1999 Holocene climatic changes and cultural dynamics in the Libyan Sahara, *African Archaeological Review* 16: 211–238.

Cremaschi, M., di Lernia, S. and Garcea, E. A. A. 1998 Some insights on the Aterian in the Libyan Sahara: chronology, environment and archaeology, *African Archaeological Review* 15: 261–286.

Crompton, R. H. and Gowlett, J. A. J. 1993 Allometry and multidimensional form in Acheulean bifaces from Kilombe, Kenya, *Journal of Human Evolution* 25: 175–199.

Cronk, L. 2004 *From Mukogodo to Maasai: ethnicity and cultural change in Kenya*, Boulder: Westview Press.

Cruz-Uribe, K., Klein, R. G., Avery, G., Avery, M., Halkett, D., Hart, T., Milo, R. G., Sampson, C. G., and Volman, T. P. 2003 Excavation of buried late Acheulean (mid-Quaternary) land surfaces at Duinefontein 2, Western Cape Province, South Africa. *Journal of Archaeological Science* 30:559–575.

Culotta, E. 2005 What genetic changes made us uniquely human? *Science* 309: 91.

Cunningham, C. L., Anderson, J. R. and Mootnick, A. R. 2006 Object manipulation to obtain a food reward in hoolock gibbons, *Bunopithecus hoolock*, *Animal Behaviour* 71: 621–629.

Curnoe, D., Grun, R., Taylor, L. and Thackeray, J. F. 2001 Direct ESR dating of a Pliocene hominin from Swartkrans, *Journal of Human Evolution* 40: 379–391.

Curnoe, D. and Thorne, A. G. 2003 Number of ancestral human species: a molecular perspective, *Homo* 53: 201–224.

Daley, S. 1996 Botswana is pressing Bushmen to leave reserve, *New York Times* July 14th 1996, section 1, page 3.

D'Andrea, A. C., Klee, M. and Casey, J. 2001 Archaeobotanical evidence for pearl millet (*Pennisetum glaucum*) in sub-Saharan West Africa, *Antiquity* 75: 341–348.

D'Andrea, A. C., Kahlheber, S., Logan, A. L. and Watson, D. J. 2007 Early domesticated cowpea from central Ghana, *Antiquity* 81:686–698.

Daniel, G. 1975 *150 years of archaeology*, London: Duckworth.

Dart, R. A. 1925 *Australopithecus africanus*: the man-ape of South Africa, *Nature* 115: 195–199.

Darwin, C. 1871 *The descent of man, and selection in relation to sex*, London: John Murray.

David, N., Harvey, P. and Goudie, C. J. 1981 Excavations in the southern Sudan, 1979, *Azania* 16: 7–54.

Davidson, I. 2003 Comment on C. Henshilwood and C. Marean, The origin of modern human behaviour, *Current Anthropology* 43: 637–638.

Davidson, I. and Noble, W. 1993 Tools and language in human evolution, in K. R. Gibson and T Ingold (eds.), *Tools, language and cognition in human evolution*, Cambridge: Cambridge University Press, pp. 363–388.

Davies, O. 1964 *The Quaternary in the coastlands of Guinea*, Glasgow: Jackson, Son and Company.

Davies, W. 1990 The study of rock art in Africa, in P. T. Robertshaw (ed.), *A history of African archaeology*, London: James Currey, pp. 271–295.

Day, M. H. 1969 Omo human skeletal remains, *Nature* 222: 1135–1138.

Day, M. H., and Molleson, T. I. 1976. The puzzle from JK2 – a femur and a tibial fragment (OH 34) from Olduvai Gorge, Tanzania, *Journal of Human Evolution* 5: 455–465.

de Barros, P. 1990 Changing paradigms, goals and methods in the archaeology of francophone West Africa, in P. T. Robertshaw (ed.), *A history of African archaeology*, London: James Currey, pp. 155–172.

De Bayle des Hermans, R. 1975 *Recherches préhistoriques en République Centrafricaine*, Nanterre: Labethno.

de Beaune, S. 2004 The invention of technology: prehistory and cognition, *Current Anthropology* 45: 139–162.

de Heinzelin, J., Clark, J. D., Schick, K. D. and Gilbert, W. H. (eds.) 2000 *The Acheulean and the Plio-Pleistocene deposits of the Middle Awash Valley, Ethiopia*, Tervuren: Musée Royal de l'Afrique Centrale, Belgium Annals of Science and Geology 104.

de Heinzelin, J., Clark, J. D., White, T. W., Hart, W., Renne, P., WoldeGabriel, G., Beyenne, Y. and Vrba, E. 1999 Environment and behavior of 2.5-million-year-old Bouri hominids, *Science* 284: 625–629.

de la Torre, I. 2004 Omo revisited. Evaluating the technological skills of Pliocene hominids, *Current Anthropology* 45: 439–465.

de la Torre, I. and Mora, R. 2005 *Technological strategies in the Lower Pleistocene at Olduvai Beds I & II*, Liège: ERAUL 112.

de la Torre, I., Mora, R., Domínguez-Rodrigo, M., de Luque, L., and Alcalá, L. 2003 The Oldowan industry of Peninj and its bearing on the reconstruction of the technological skills of Lower Pleistocene hominids. *Journal of Human Evolution*, 44: 203–224.

de Maret, P. 1986 The Ngovo Group: an industry with polished stone tools and pottery in Lower Zaire, *African Archaeological Review* 4: 103–133.

　　1990 Phases and facies in the archaeology of Central Africa, in P. T. Robertshaw (ed.), *A history of African archaeology*, London: James Currey, pp. 109–134.

1994/95 Pits, pots and the far-west streams, *Azania* 29/30: 318–323.

1996 Shum Laka (Cameroon): human burials and general perspectives, in G. Pwiti and R. Soper (eds), *Aspects of African archaeology*, Harare: University of Zimbabwe Press, pp. 275–280.

de Maret, P., Van Noten, F. and Cahen, D. 1977 Radiocarbon dates from West Central Africa: a synthesis, *Journal of African History* 18: 481–505.

de Mortillet, G. 1867 *Promenades préhistoriques à l'Exposition Universelle: Matériaux pour l'histoire positive et philosophique de l'homme, guide de collections de l'Exposition Universelle de Paris*, Paris: C. Reinwald.

de Moura, A. and Lee, P. C. 2004 Capuchin stone tool use in Caatinga dry forest, *Science* 306: 1909.

de Ruiter, D. J. 2003 Revised faunal lists for Members 1–3 of Swartkrans, South Africa, *Annals of the Transvaal Museum* 40: 29–41.

De Villiers, H. 1976 Thandwe: human skeletal remains and Kalemba: human skeletal remains, in D. Phillipson, *Prehistory of eastern Zambia*, Nairobi: British Institute in Eastern Africa, pp. 61–63 and 163–165.

Deacon, H. J. 1972 A review of the post-Pleistocene in South Africa, *South African Archaeological Society Goodwin Series* 1: 26–45.

1975 Demography, subsistence and culture during the Acheulean in southern Africa, in K. W. Butzer and G. L. Issac (eds.), *After the Australopithecines*, The Hague: Mouton, pp. 543–569.

1976 *Where hunters gathered: a study of Holocene Stone Age people in the eastern Cape*, Claremont: South African Archaeological Society.

1989 Late Pleistocene palaeoecology and archaeology in the southern Cape, South Africa, in P. Mellars and C. Stringer (eds.), *The human revolution: behavioural and biological perspectives on the origins of modern humans*, Edinburgh: Edinburgh University Press, pp. 547–564.

1992 Southern Africa and modern human origins, *Philosophical Transactions of the Royal Society, London B* 337: 177–183.

1993 Planting an idea: an archaeology of Stone Age gatherers in South Africa, *South African Archaeological Bulletin* 48: 86–93.

1995 Two late Pleistocene-Holocene archaeological depositories from the southern Cape, South Africa, *South African Archaeological Bulletin* 50: 121–131.

Deacon, H. J. and Deacon, J. 1980 The hafting, function and distribution of small convex scrapers with an example from Boomplaas Cave, *South African Archaeological Bulletin* 35: 31–37.

1999 *Human beginnings in South Africa*, Cape Town: David Philip.

Deacon, H. J., Deacon, J., Scholtz, A., Thackeray, J. F., Brink, J. S. and Vogel, J. C. 1984 Correlation of palaeoenvironmental data from the Late Pleistocene and Holocene deposits at Boomplaas Cave, southern Cape, in J. C. Vogel (ed.), *Late Cainozoic palaeoclimates of the Southern Hemisphere*, Rotterdam: A. A. Balkema, pp. 339–352.

Deacon, H. J. and Thackeray, J. F. 1984 Late Pleistocene environmental changes and implications for the archaeological record in southern Africa, in J. C. Vogel (ed.), *Late Cainozoic palaeoclimates of the Southern Hemisphere*, Rotterdam: A. A. Balkema, pp. 375–390.

Deacon, H. J. and Wurz, S. 2001 Middle Pleistocene populations of southern Africa and the emergence of modern behaviour, in L. Barham and K. Robson-Brown (eds.), *Human roots: Africa and Asia in the Middle Pleistocene*, Bristol: Western Academic & Specialist Press, pp. 55–63.

2005 A late Pleistocene archive of life at the coast, Klasies River, in A. B. Stahl (ed.), *African archaeology a critical introduction*, Oxford: Blackwell Publishing, pp. 130–149.

Deacon, J. 1984a Later Stone Age people and their descendants in southern Africa, in R. G. Klein (ed.), *Southern African prehistory and palaeoenvironments*, Rotterdam: A. A. Balkema, pp. 221–328.

1984b *The Later Stone Age of southernmost Africa*, Oxford: British Archaeological Reports.

1986 "My place is the Bitterputs": the home territory of Bleek and Lloyd's /Xam San informants, *African Studies* 45: 135–156.

1988 The power of a place in understanding southern San rock engravings, *World Archaeology* 20: 129–140.

1990a Weaving the fabric of Stone Age research in southern Africa, in P. T. Robertshaw (ed.), *A history of African archaeology*, London: James Currey, pp. 39–58.

1990b Changes in the archaeological record in South Africa at 18,000 BP, in C. S. Gamble and O. Soffer (eds.), pp. *The World at 18 000 BP, Volume II low latitudes*, London: Unwin Hyman, 170–188.

1994 Rock engravings and the folklore of Bleek and Lloyd's /Xam San informants, in T. A. Dowson and J. D. Lewis-Williams (eds.), *Contested images: diversity in southern African rock art research*, Johannesburg: Witwatersrand University Press, pp. 237–256.

1996 Archaeology of the Flat and Grass Bushmen, in J. Deacon and T. A. Dowson (eds.), *Voices from the past:/Xam Bushmen and the Bleek and Lloyd collection*, Johannesburg: Witwatersrand University Press, pp. 245–270.

Deacon, J. and Lancaster, I. N. 1988 *Late Quaternary palaeoenvironments of southern Africa*, Oxford: Clarendon Press.

Deacon, T. 1997 *The symbolic species: the co-evolution of language and the human brain*. London: Allen Lane, Penguin Press.

Débénath, A. 1992 Hommes et cultures matérielles de l'Atérien Marocain, *L'Anthropologie* 96: 711–720.

1994 L'Atérien du nord de l'Afrique et du Sahara, *Sahara* 6: 21–30.

Débénath, A., Raynal, J.-P., Roche, J., Tixier, J.-P. and Ferembach, D. 1986 Stratigraphie, habitat, typologie et devenir de l'Atérien marocain: données récentes, *L'Anthropologie* 90: 233–246.

Decampo, D. M., Blumenschine, R. J. and Ashley, G. M. 2002 Wetland diagenesis and traces of early hominids, Olduvai Gorge, Tanzania, *Quaternary Research* 57: 271–281.

Deino, A. L. and Hill, A. 2002 40Ar/39Ar dating of the Chemeron Formation strata encompassing the site of hominid KNM-BC 1, Tugen Hills, Kenya, *Journal of Human Evolution* 42: 141–151.

Delanges, A. and Roche, H. 2005 Late Pliocene hominid knapping skills: the case of Lokalalei 2C, West Turkana, Kenya, *Journal of Human Evolution* 48: 435–472.

deMenocal, P. B. 1995 Plio-Pleistocene African climate, *Science* 270: 53–59.

2004 African climate change and faunal evolution during the Pliocene-Pleistocene, *Earth and Planetary Science Letters* 220: 3–24.

deMenocal, P. B. and Bloemendal, J. 1995 Plio-Pleistocene climatic variability in subtropical Africa and the paleoenvironment of hominid evolution, in, E. S. Vrba, G. H. Denton, T. C. Partridge and L. H. Burckle (eds.), *Paleoclimate and evolution with emphasis on human origins*, New Haven: Yale University Press, pp. 262–288.

deMenocal, P. B., Ortiz, J., Guilderson, T., Adkins, J., Sarnthein, M., Baker, L. and Yarusinsky, M. 2000 Abrupt onset and termination of the African Humid Period: rapid climate responses to gradual insolation forcing, *Quaternary Science Reviews* 19: 347–361.

Denbow, J. R. 1990 Congo to Kalahari: data and hypotheses about the political economy of the western stream of the Early Iron Age, *African Archaeological Review* 8: 139–175.

1999 Material culture and the dialectics of identity in the Kalahari: AD 700–1700, in S. K. McIntosh (ed.), *Beyond chiefdoms: pathways to complexity in Africa*, Cambridge: Cambridge University Press, pp. 110–123.

Dennell, R., Rendell, H. M. and Hailwood, E. 1988 Early toolmaking in Asia: two-million year-old artifacts in Pakistan, *Antiquity* 62: 98–106.

Dennell R. and Roebroeks, W. 2005 An Asian perspective on early human dispersal from Africa, *Nature* 438: 1099–1104.

d'Errico, F. 2003 The invisible frontier: a multiple species model for the origin of behavioural modernity, *Evolutionary Anthropology* 12: 188–202.

d'Errico, F. and Backwell, L. R. 2003 Possible evidence of bone tool shaping by Swartkrans early hominids, *Journal of Archaeological Science* 30: 1559–1576.

d'Errico, F., Henshilwood, C. S. and Nilssen, P. 2001 An engraved bone fragment from ca. 75 kyr Middle Stone Age levels at Blombos Cave, South Africa: implications for the origin of symbolism and language, *Antiquity* 75: 309–318.

d'Errico, F., Henshilwood, C.S, Vanhaeren, M. and van Niekerk, K. 2005 *Nassarius kraussianus* shell beads from Blombos Cave: evidence for symbolic behaviour in the Middle Stone Age, *Journal of Human Evolution* 48: 3–24.

Derricourt, R. 2005 Getting "Out of Africa": sea crossings, land crossings and culture in the hominin migrations, *Journal of World Prehistory* 19: 119–132.

Derwent, S. 2005 The secret San, *Africa Geographic* 13(1): 59–63.

DeSilva, J. and Lesnik, J. 2006 Chimpanzee neonatal brain size: implications for brain growth in *Homo erectus*, *Journal of Human Evolution* 51: 207–212.

Destro-Bisol, G., Coia, V., Boschi, I., Verginell, F., Caglia, A., Pascali, V., Spedini, G. and Calafell, F. 2004 The analysis of variation of mtDNA hypervariable region 1 suggests that Eastern and Western Pygmies diverged before the Bantu expansion, *The American Naturalist* 163: 212–226.

Dewar, G., Halkett, D., Hart, T., Orton, J. and Sealy, J. C. 2006 Implications of a mass kill site of springbok (*Antidorcas marsupialis*) in South Africa: hunting practices, gender relations and sharing in the Later Stone Age, *Journal of Archaeological Science* 33: 1266–1275.

Dewar, G. and Pfeiffer, S. 2004 Postural behaviour of Later Stone Age people in South Africa, *South African Archaeological Bulletin* 59: 52–58.

di Lernia, S. 1996 Changing adaptive strategies: a long-term process in the Central Saharan massifs from Late Pleistocene to Early Holocene. The Tadrart Acacus perspective, in G. Aumassip, J. D. Clark and F. Mori (eds.), *The prehistory of Africa, Proceedings of the XIIIth Congress of the International Union of Prehistoric and Protohistoric Sciences, Colloquim XXX, Volume 15,* Forlì: ABACO, pp. 195–208.

  1999 (ed.) *The Uan Afuda Cave. Hunter-gatherer societies of the Central Sahara,* Firenze: Edizioni all'Insegna del Giglio.

  2001 Dismantling dung: delayed use of food resources among early Holocene foragers of the Libyan Sahara, *Journal of Anthropological Archaeology* 20: 408–441.

Diamond, J. 1997 *Guns, germs and steel,* London: Jonathan Cape.

Distefano, J. A. 1990 Hunters or hunted? Towards a history of the Okiek of Kenya, *History in Africa* 17: 41–57.

Dobson, M. 1998 Mammal distributions in the western Mediterranean: the role of human intervention, *Mammal Review* 28: 77–88.

Domínguez-Rodrigo, M. 1997 Meat-eating by early hominids at the FLK 22 Zinjanthropus site, Olduvai Gorge (Tanzania): an experimental approach using cut-mark data, *Journal of Human Evolution* 33: 669–690.

  2002 Hunting and scavenging by early humans: the state of the debate, *Journal of World Prehistory* 16: 1–53.

Domínguez-Rodrigo, M., Alcala, L., Luque, L. and Serrallonga, J. 2005 Quelques apercus sur les significations paléoécologique et comportemen-tale de sites oldowayens anciens et acheuléens du Peninj (Upper Humbu Foramtion, Ouest du Lac Natron, Tanzanie), in M. Sahnouni (ed.), *Le Paléolithique en Afrique: l'histoire la plus longue,* Paris: Artcom, pp. 129–156.

Domínguez-Rodrigo, M. and Barba, R. 2006 New estimates of tooth mark and percussion mark frequencies at the FLK Zinj site: the carnivore-hominid-carnivore hypothesis falsified, *Journal of Human Evolution* 50: 170–194.

Domínguez-Rodrigo, M., Lopez-Saez, J. A., Vincens, J. A., Alcala, L., Luque, L. and Serralonga, J. 2001a Fossil pollen from the Upper Humbu Formation of Peninj (Tanzania): hominid adaptation to dry open Plio-Pleistocene savanna environment, *Journal of Human Evolution* 40: 151–157.

Domínguez-Rodrigo, M., Serralonga, J., Juan-Treserras, J., Alcala, L. and Luque, L. 2001b Wood working activities by early humans: a plant residue analysis on Acheulian stone tools from Peninj, Tanzania, *Journal of Human Evolution* 40: 289–299.

Dong, B., Valdes, P. J. and Hall, N. M. J. 1996 The changes of monsoonal climates due to Earth's orbital perturbations and Ice Age boundary conditions, *Palaeoclimates* 1: 203–240.

Downey, C., and Domínguez-Rodrigo, M. 2002 Palaeoecological reconstruction and hominid land use of the Lake Natron basin during the early Pleistocene. *Before Farming* [print version] 1: 188–223.

Dowson, T. A. 1992 *Rock engravings of southern Africa*, Johannesburg: Witwatersrand University Press.

Drake, R. E., Curtis, G. H., Cerling, T. E., Cerling, B. W., and Hampel, J. KSB Tuff dating and geochronology of tuffaceous sediments in the Koobi Fora and Shungura Formations, East Africa. 1980 *Nature* 283: 368–372.

Dubow, S. 2004 Earth history, natural history and prehistory at the Cape, 1860–1875, *Comparative Studies in Society and History* 46: 107–133.

Duller, G. A. T., Bøtter-Jensen, L., and Murray, A. S. 2000 Optical dating of single sand-sized grains of quartz: sources of variability, *Radiation Measurements* 32: 453–457.

Dunbar, R. I. M. 1998 The social brain hypothesis. *Evolutionary Anthropology* 6: 178–189.

    2000 On the origin of the human mind, in P. Carruthers and A. Chamberlain (eds.), *Evolution and the human mind: modularity, language and meta-cognition*, Cambridge: Cambridge University Press, pp. 238–253.

    2003 The social brain: mind, language, and society in evolutionary perspective, *Annual Review of Anthropology* 32: 163–181.

    2004 *The human story*, London: Faber & Faber.

Dupont, L. and Behling, H. 2006 Land-sea linkages during deglaciation: high-resolution records from the eastern Atlantic off the coast of Namibia and Angola (ODP site 1078), *Quaternary International* 148: 19–28.

Dupont, L. M., Jahns, S., Marret, F. and Ning, S. 2000 Vegetation change in equatorial West Africa: time slices for the last 150ka, *Palaeogeography, Palaeoclimatology, Palaeoecology* 155: 95–122.

Dupont, L. M. and Leroy, S. A. G. 1999 Climatic changes in the Late Pliocene of NW Africa from a pollen record on an astronomically tuned timescale, in J. H. Wrenn, J.-P. Suc and S. A. G. Leroy (eds.), *The Pliocene: time of change*, Baton Rouge: American Association of Stratigraphic Palynologists Foundation, pp. 145–161.

Dupont, L. and Weinelt, M. 1996 Vegetation history of the savanna corridor between the Guinean and the Congolian rain forest during the last 150,000 years, *Vegetation History and Archaeobotany* 5: 273–292.

Dutour, O. 1989 *Hommes fossiles du Sahara peuplements holocènes du Mali septentrional*, Paris: Centre National de la Recherche Scientifique.

Eastwood, E. and Eastwood, C. 2006 *Capturing the spoor: an exploration of southern African rock art*, Cape Town: David Philip.

Eastwood, E. B. and Smith, B. W. 2005 Fingerprints of the Khoekhoen: geometric and handprinted rock art in the central Limpopo Basin, South Africa, *South African Archaeological Society Goodwin Series* 9: 63–76.

Ebinger, C. J. 2005 Continental break-up: The East African perspective, *Astronomy & Geophysics* 46: 2.16–2.21.

Edwards, D. N. 2004 *The Nubian past: an archaeology of the Sudan*, London: Routledge.

Edwards, S. W. 2001 A modern knapper's assessment of the technical skills of the Late Acheulean biface workers at Kalambo Falls, in J. D. Clark (ed.), *Kalambo Falls Prehistoric Site, Volume III*, Cambridge: Cambridge University Press, pp. 605–611.

Egeland, C. P., Pickering, T. R., Domínguez-Rodrigo, and Brain, C. K. 2004 Disentangling Early Stone Age palimpsests: determining the functional independence of hominid- and carnivore-derived portions of archaeofaunas. *Journal of Human Evolution* 47: 343–357.

Eggert, M. K. H. 1997 Equatorial African Iron Age, in J. Vogel (ed.), *Encyclopaedia of precolonial Africa*, Walnut Creek: AltaMira Press, pp. 429–435.

    2005 The Bantu problem and African archaeology, in A. B. Stahl (ed.), *African archaeology: a critical introduction*, Oxford: Blackwell Publishing, pp. 301–326.

Ehret, C. 1993 Nilo-Saharans and the Saharo-Sudanese Neolithic, in T. Shaw, P. Sinclair, B. Andah and A. Okpoko (eds.), *The archaeology of Africa: food, metals and towns*. London: Routledge, pp. 104–125.

    1998 *An African classical age: Eastern and southern Africa in world history, 1000 B.C. to A.D. 400*, Oxford: James Currey.

    2002a Language family expansions: broadening our understandings of cause from an African perspective, in P. Bellwood and A. C. Renfrew (eds.), *Examining the farming/language dispersal hypothesis*, Cambridge: McDonald Institute for Archaeological Research, pp. 163–176.

    2002b *The civilizations of Africa: a history to 1800*, Oxford: James Currey.

Ehret, C, Keita, S. O. Y. and Newman, P. 2004 The origins of Afroasiatic, *Science* 306: 167–168.

Elamin, Y. M. and Mohammed-Ali, A. S. 2004 Umm Marrahi an early Holocene ceramic site, north of Khartoum (Sudan), *Sahara* 15: 97–110.

Elango, N., Thomas, J. W., NISC Comparative Sequencing Program and Yi, S. V. 2006 Variable molecular clocks in hominoids, *Proceedings of the National Academy of Sciences* 103: 1370–1375.

Elenga, H., Schwartz, D. and Vincens, A. 1994 Pollen evidence of Late Quaternary vegetation and inferred climate changes in Congo, *Palaeogeography, Palaeoclimatology, Palaeoecology* 109: 345–356.

El Hajraoui, M. A. 1994 L'industrie osseuse atérienne de la grotte d'El Mnasra (Région de Témara, Maroc). *Préhistoire Anthropologie Méditerranéennes* 3: 91–94.

Ellenberger, V. 1953 *La fin tragique des Bushmen*, Paris: Amiot Dumont.

Elphick, R. 1985 *Khoikhoi and the founding of white South Africa*, Johannesburg: Ravan Press.

Elton, S., Bishop, L. C. and Wood, B. 2001 Comparative context of Plio-Pleistocene hominin brain evolution, *Journal of Human Evolution* 41: 1–27.

Elton, S., Barham, L., Andrews, P., and Sambrook Smith, G. H. 2003 Pliocene femur of *Theropithecus* from the Luangwa Vally, Zambia. *Journal of Human Evolution* 44: 133–139.

Ember, C. 1978 Myths about hunter-gatherers, *Ethnology* 4: 439–448.

Enard, W., Przeworski, M., Fisher, S. E., Lai, C. S. L., Wiebe, V., Kitano, T., Monaco, A. P. and Paabo, S. 2002 Molecular evolution of FOXP2, a gene involved in speech and language, *Nature* 418: 869–887.

EPICA community members. 2004 Eight glacial cycles from an Antarctic ice core, *Nature* 429: 623–628.

Esterhuysen, A. B. and Smith, J. M. 2003 A comparison of charcoal and stable carbon isotope results for the Caledon River valley, southern Africa, for the period 13,500–5000 yr BP, *South African Archaeological Bulletin* 58: 1–5.

Estes, R. D. 1992 *The behavior guide to African mammals*, Berkeley: University of California Press.

Eswaran, V. 2002 A diffusion wave out of Africa: the mechanism of the modern human revolution? *Current Anthropology* 44: 559–561.

Eswaran, V., Harpending, H. and Rogers, A. R. 2005 Genomics refutes an exclusively African origin of humans, *Journal of Human Evolution* 49: 1–18.

Evernden, J. F. and Curtis, G. H. 1965 Potassium argon dating of Late Cenozoic rocks in East Africa and Italy, *Current Anthropology* 6: 343–385.

Fagan, B. M. 1991 *Ancient North America: the archaeology of a continent*, London: Thames and Hudson.

——— 2001 *People of the Earth*, New York: HarperCollins.

Fagan, B. M. and Van Noten, F. L. 1971 *The hunter-gatherers of Gwisho*, Tervuren: Musée Royal de l'Afrique Centrale.

Fagg, B. 1956 An outline of the Stone Age of the Plateau minesfield, *Proceedings of the Third International West African Conference, Ibadan, Nigeria, 12–21 December 1949*, Lagos: Nigerian Museum, pp. 203–222.

Fairbanks, R. G., Mortlock, R., Chiu, T-C., Cao, L., Kaplan, A., Guilderson, T. P., Fairbanks, T. W., Bloom, A. L., Grootes, P. M., and Nadeau, M-J. 2005 Radiocarbon calibration curve spanning 0 to 50,000 years BP based on paired $^{230}$Th/$^{234}$U/$^{238}$U and $^{14}$C dates on pristine corals, *Quaternary Science Reviews* 24: 1781–1796.

Falk, D. 1983 Cerebral cortices of East African early hominids, *Science* 221: 1072–1074.

——— 1993 Sex differences in visuospatial skills: implications for hominid evolution, in K. R. Gibson and T Ingold (eds.), *Tools, language and cognition in human evolution*, Cambridge: Cambridge University Press, pp. 216–229.

——— 2004 Prelinguistic evolution in early hominins: Whence motherease? *Behavioral and Brain Sciences* 27: 491–503.

Falk, D., Hildebolt, C., Smith, K., Morwood, M. J., Sutikna, T., Brown, P., Jatmiko, Saptomo, E. W., Brunsden, B. and Prior, F. 2005 The brain of LB1, *Homo floresiensis, Science* 308: 242–245.

Falk, D., Redmond Jr., J. C., Guyer, J., Conroy, G., Recheis, W., Weber, G. W. and Seidler, H. 2000 Early hominid brain evolution: a new look at old endocasts, *Journal of Human Evolution* 38: 695–717.

Fattovich, R, Marks, A. E. and Mohammed-Ali, A. 1984 The archaeology of the eastern Sahel, Sudan: preliminary results, *African Archaeological Review* 2: 173–188.

Feakins, S. J., deMenocal, P. B. and Eglinton, T. I. 2005 Biomarker records of late Neogene changes in northeast African vegetation, *Geology* 33: 977–980.

Feathers, J. K., and Migliorini, E. 2001 Luminescence dating at Katanda – a reassessement. *Quaternary Science Reviews* 20: 961–966.

Feibel, C. S., Brown, F. H., and McDougall, I. 1989 Stratigraphic context of fossil hominids from the Omo Group desposits, northern Turkana Basin, Kenya and Ethiopia. *American Journal of Physical Anthropology* 78: 595–622.

Ferembach, D. 1985 On the origin of the Iberomaurusians. A new hypothesis, *Journal of Human Evolution* 14: 393–397.

Ferembach, D., Dastugue, J. and Poitrat-Targowla, M.-J. 1962 *La nécropole épipaléolithique de Taforalt (Maroc oriental): etude des squélettes humains*, Paris: Centre National de la Recherche Scientifique.

Fernández, V. (ed.) 2003 The Blue Nile project: Holocene archaeology in central Sudan, *Dossier de Complutum* 14: 199–425.

Fernández, V. M., de la Torre, I., Lueque, L., González-Ruibal, A. and López-Sáez, J. A. 2007 A Late Stone Age sequence from West Ethiopia: the sites of K'aaba and Bel K'urk'umu (Assosa, Benishangul-Gumuz Regional State), *Journal of African Archaeology* 5: 91–126.

Ferrer i Cancho, R., Riordan, O. and Bollobás, B. 2005 The consequence of Zipf's law for syntax and symbolic reference, *Proceedings of the Royal Society B: Biological Sciences* 272: 561–565.

Field, J. S. and Lahr, M. M. 2006 Assessment of the southern dispersal: GIS-based analyses of potential routes at Oxygen Isotope Stage 4, *Journal of World Prehistory* 19: 1–45.

Finneran, N. 2000a A new perspective on the LSA of the northern Ethiopian highlands: excavations at Anqqer Baahti, Aksum, Ethiopia, 1996, *Azania* 35: 21–52.

2000b Excavations at the LSA site of Baahti Nebait, Aksum, northern Ethiopia, 1997, *Azania* 35: 53–74.

Fisher, S. E. and Marcus, G. F. 2005 The eloquent ape: genes, brains and the evolution of language, *Nature Reviews: Genetics* 7: 9–20.

Fitzhugh, B. 2001 Risk and invention in human technological evolution, *Journal of Anthropological Archaeology* 20: 125–167.

Flannery, K. 1969 Origins and ecological effects of early domestication in Iran and the Near East, in P. J. Ucko and G. W. Dimbleby (eds.), *The domestication and exploitation of plants and animals*, London: Duckworth, pp. 73–100.

Flint, R. F. 1959 On the basis of Pleistocene correlation in East Africa, *Geological Magazine* 96: 265–284.

Foley, R. A. 1981 *Off-site archaeology and human adaptation in eastern Africa*, Oxford: British Archaeological Reports.

1982 A reconsideration of the role of predation on large mammals in tropical hunter-gatherer adaptation, *Man* 17: 222–242.

1994 Speciation, extinction and climatic change in hominid evolution, *Journal of Human Evolution* 26: 275–289.

1995 *Humans before humanity*, Oxford: Blackwells.

2002 Parallel tracks: human evolution and archaeology, in B. W. Cunliffe, W. Davies and A. C. Renfrew (eds.), *Archaeology: the widening debate*, Oxford: Oxford University Press, pp. 3–42. 2004.

2004. The evolutionary ecology of linguistic diversity in human populations, in Jones, M. (ed.): *Traces of Ancestry: studies in honour of Colin Renfrew*. Cambridge: McDonald Institute Monographs, 61–71.

Foley, R. and Lahr, M. 1997 Mode 3 technologies and the evolution of modern humans, *Cambridge Archaeological Journal* 7: 3–36.

2003 On stony ground: lithic technology, human evolution and the emergence of culture, *Evolutionary Anthropology* 12: 109–122.

Forsström, L. 2001 Duration of interglacials: a controversial question, *Quaternary Science Reviews* 20: 1577–1586.

Forster, P. 2004 Ice Ages and the mitochondrial DNA chronology of human dispersals: a review, *Philosophical Transactions of the Royal Society of London B* 359: 255–264.

Forster, P. and Matsumura, S. 2005 Did early humans go north or south? *Science* 308: 965–966.

Forster P., Torroni A., Renfrew A. C., and Röhl A 2001 Phylogenetic star contraction applied to Asian and Papuan mtDNA evolution, *Molecular Biology and Evolution* 18: 1864–1881.

Frison, G. C. 2004 *Survival by hunting: prehistoric human predators and animal prey*, Berkeley: University of California Press.

Fuller, D. Q. 2003 African crops in prehistoric South Asia: a critical review, *Africa Praehistorica* 15: 239–271.

Gabel, C. 1969 Six rockshelters on the Northern Kavirondo shore of Lake Victoria, *African Historical Studies* 11: 205–254.

Gabriel, B. 1987 Palaeoecological evidence from neolithic fireplaces in the Sahara, *African Archaeological Review* 5: 93–104.

Gabunia, L., Vekua, A., Lordkipanidze, D., Swisher III, C. C., Ferring, R., Justus, A., Nioradze, M., Tvalchrelidze, M., Antón, S. C., Bosinski, G., Jöris, O., de Lumley, M.-A., Majsuradze, G. and Mouskhelishvili, A. 2000 Earliest Pleistocene hominid cranial remains from Dmanisi, Republic of Georgia: taxonomy, geological setting, and age, *Science* 288: 1019–1025.

Gamble, C. S. 1986 *The Palaeolithic settlement of Europe*, Cambridge: Cambridge University Press.

1997 The skills of the Lower Palaeolithic world, *Proceedings of the Prehistoric Society* 63: 407–410.

1999 *The Palaeolithic societies of Europe*, Cambridge: Cambridge University Press.

Gamble, C., and Marshall, C. 2001 The shape of handaxes, the structure of the Acheulian world, in Milliken, S., and Cook, J., (eds.) *A very remote period indeed: papers on the Palaeolithic presented to Derek Roe*, Oxford: Oxbow Press, pp. 19–27.

Gamble, C. S. and O. Soffer (eds.) 1990 *The World at 18,000 BP, Volume II, low latitudes*, London: Unwin Hyman.

Gannon, P. J., Holloway, R. L., Broadfield, D. C., and Braun, A. R. 1998 Asymmetry of chimpanzee planum temporale: human like pattern of Wernicke's brain language area homology. *Science* 279: 220–222.

Garcea, E. A. A. (ed.) 2001 *Uan Tabu in the settlement history of the Libyan Sahara*, Firenze: All'Insegna del Giglio.

2002 Crossing deserts and avoiding seas: Aterian North African-European relations, *Journal of Anthropological Research* 60: 27–53.

2004 An alternative way towards food production: the perspective from the Libyan Sahara, *Journal of World Prehistory* 18: 107–154.

2005 Postcolonial criticism in One World archaeology: where is North Africa's place? *Archaeologies* 1: 110–117.

2006 Semi-permanent foragers in semi-arid environments of North Africa, *World Archaeology* 38: 197–219.

Garcea, E. A. A. and Giraudi, C. 2006 Late Quaternary human settlement patterning in the Jebel Gharbi, *Journal of Human Evolution* 51: 411–421.

Garcin, Y., Williamson, D., Taieb, M., Vincens, A., Mathé, P-E. and Majule, A. 2006 Centennial to milliennial changes in maar-lake deposition during the last 45,000 years in tropical Southern Africa (Lake Masoko, Tanzania), *Paleogeography, Palaeoclimatology, Palaeoecology* 239: 334–354.

Garlake, P. S. 1995 *The hunter's vision: the prehistoric art of Zimbabwe*, London: British Museum Press.

Garrigan, D., Mobasher, Z., Severson, T., Wilder, J. A. and Hammer, M. F. 2005 Evidence for archaic Asian ancestry on the human X chromosome, *Molecular Biology and Evolution* 22: 189–192.

Gasse, F. 2000 Hydrological changes in the African tropics since the Last Glacial Maximum, *Quaternary Science Reviews* 19: 189–211.

Gasse, F., Rognon, R. and Street, F. A. 1980 Quaternary history of the Afar and Ethiopian Rift lakes, in M. A. J. Williams and H. Faure (eds.), *The Sahara and the Nile*, Rotterdam: A. A. Balkema, pp. 361–400.

Gasse, F. and van Campo, E. 1994 Abrupt post-glacial climate events in West Asia and North Africa monsoon domains, *Earth and Planetary Science Letters* 126: 435–456.

Gasse, F., Tehet, R., Durand, A., Gibert, E. and Fontes, J.-C. 1990 The arid–humid transition in the Sahara and the Sahel during the last deglaciation, *Nature* 346: 141–146.

Gathogo, P. N., and Brown, F. H. 2006 Revised stratigraphy of Area 123, Koobi Fora, Kenya, and new age estimates of its fossil mammals, including hominins, *Journal of Human Evolution* 51: 471–479.

Gathorne-Hardy, F. J. and Harcourt-Smith, W. E. H. 2003 The super-eruption of Toba, did it cause a human bottleneck? *Journal of Human Evolution* 45: 227–230.

Gaussen, J. and Gaussen, M. 1988 *Le Tilemsi préhistorique et ses abords: Sahara et Sahel malien*, Paris: Centre National de la Recherche Scientifique.

Gautier, A. 1987 Prehistoric men and cattle in North Africa: a dearth of data and a surfeit of models, in A. E. Close (ed.), *Prehistory of North Africa*, Dallas: Southern Methodist University Press, pp. 163–187.

2002 The evidence for the earliest livestock in North Africa or adventures with large bovids, ovicaprids, dogs and pigs, in F. A. Hassan (ed.), *Droughts, food and culture: ecological change and food security in Africa's later prehistory*, New York: Kluwer Academic/Plenum Publishers, pp. 195–208.

Gautier, A. and van Neer, W. 1989 Animal remains from the late prehistoric sequence at Wadi Kubbaniya, in A. E. Close (ed.), *The prehistory of North Africa, Volume 2 palaeoeconomy, environment and stratigraphy*, Dallas: Southern Methodist University Press, pp. 119–158.

Gehlen, B., Kindermann, K., Linstädter, J. and Riemer, H. 2002 The Holocene occupation of the Eastern Sahara: regional chronologies and supra-regional developments in four areas in the absolute desert, in Jennerstrasse 8 (eds.), *Tides of the desert. Contributions to the archaeology and environmental history of Africa in honour of Rudolph Kuper*, Köln: Heinrich Barth Institute, pp. 85–116.

Geraads, D., Raynal, J-P. and Eisenmann, V. 2004 The earliest human occupation of North Africa: a reply to Sahnouni *et al.* (2002), *Journal of Human Evolution* 46: 751–761.

Gibert, J., Gibert, L., and Iglesias, A. 2003 The Gibraltar Strait: a Pleistocene door of Europe? *Journal of Human Evolution* 18: 147–160.

Gibson, N. E., Wadley, L. and Williamson, B. S. 2004 Microscopic residues as evidence of hafting on backed tools from the 60,000 to 68,000 year-old Howiesons Poort layers of Rose Cottage Cave, South Africa, *Southern African Humanities* 16: 1–11.

Gifford, D. P., Isaac, G. L. and Nelson, C. M. 1980 Evidence for predation and pastoralism at Prolonged Drift: a Pastoral Neolithic site in Kenya, *Azania* 15: 57–108.

Gifford-Gonzalez, D. 1998 Early pastoralists in East Africa: ecological and social dimensions, *Journal of Anthropological Archaeology* 17: 166–200.

2000 Animal disease challenges to the emergence of pastoralism in sub-Saharan Africa, *African Archaeological Review* 17: 95–139.

2003 The fauna from Ele Bor: evidence for the persistence of foragers into the later Holocene of arid north Kenya, *African Archaeological Review* 20: 81–119.

2005 Pastoralism and its consequences, in A. B. Stahl (ed.), *African archaeology: a critical introduction*, Oxford: Blackwell, pp. 187–224.

Gilbert, W. H., White, T. D. and Asfaw, B. 2003 *Homo erectus, Homo ergaster, Homo "cepranensis,"* and the Daka cranium, *Journal of Human Evolution* 45: 255–259.

Gil-da-Costa, R., Martin, A., Lopes, M., Muñoz, M., Fritz, J., and Braun, A. 2006 Species-specific calls activate homologs of Broca's and Wernicke's areas in the macaque. *Nature Neuroscience* 9: 1064–1070.

Gillespie, R., Street-Perrott, F. A. and Switsur, R. 1983 Post-glacial arid episodes in Ethiopia have implications for climate prediction, *Nature* 306: 680–682.

Gingele, F. X., Müller, P. M. and Schneider, R. R. 1998 Orbital forcing of freshwater input in the Zaire Fan area – clay mineral evidence from the last 200 kyr, *Palaeogeography, Palaeoclimatology, Palaeoecology* 138: 17–26.

Glenberg, A. M. 2006 Naturalizing cognition: The integration of cognitive science and biology. *Current Biology* 16: R802–804.

Godber, M., Kopec, A. C., Mourant, A. E., Teesdale, P., Tills, D., Weiner, J. S., El-Niel, H., Wood, C. H. and Barley, S. 1976 The blood groups, serum groups, red cell isoenzymes and haemoglobins of the Sandawe and Nyaturu of Tanzania, *Annals of Human Biology* 3: 463–473.

Goldberg, T. L. 1996 Genetics and biogeography of East African chimpanzees (*Pan troglodytes schweinfurthii*), PhD thesis, Harvard University.

Gona Palaeoanthropological Project 2006 Press release on a new hominid from Gona, Afar, Ethiopia, Indiana University, Bloomington, March 21, 2006.

Gooch, W. D. 1881 The Stone Age of South Africa, *Journal of the Anthropological Institute* 11: 124–182.

Goodall, J. 1964 Tool-using and aimed throwing in a community of free-living chimpanzees, *Nature* 201: 1264–1266.

Goodwin, A. J. H. and van Riet Lowe, C. 1929 The Stone Age cultures of South Africa, *Annals of the South African Museum* 27: 1–289.

Gordon, R. J. 1984 The !Kung in the Kalahari exchange: an ethnohistorical perspective, in C. Schrire (ed.), *Past and present in hunter-gatherer studies*, Orlando: Academic Press, pp. 195–224.

  1992 *The Bushman myth: the making of a Namibian underclass*, Boulder: Westview Press.

Goren Inbar, N., Alperson, N., Kislev, M. E., Simchoni, O., Melamed, Y., Ben-nun, A. and Werker, E. 2004 Evidence of hominin control of fire at Gesher Benot Ya'aqov, Israel, *Science* 304: 725–727.

Goren Inbar, N., Sharon, G., Melamed, Y. and Kisler, M. 2002 Nuts, nut cracking, and pitted stones at Gesher Benot Yáqov, Israel, *Proceedings of the National Academy of Sciences (USA)* 99(4): 2455–2460.

Gosden, C. 1994 *Social being and time,* Oxford: Blackwell Publishing.

  1999 *Anthropology and archaeology: a changing relationship*, London: Routledge.

Gowlett, J. A. J. 1986 Culture and conceptualisation: the Oldowan-Acheulian gradient, in G. N. Bailey and P. Callow (eds.), *Stone Age prehistory: studies in memory of Charles McBurney*, Cambridge: Cambridge University Press, pp. 243–260.

  1988. A case of Developed Oldowan in the Acheulean? *World Archaeology*, 20: 13–26.

  1990 Archaeological studies of human origins and early prehistory in Africa, in P. T. Robertshaw (ed.), *A history of African archaeology*, London: James Currey, pp. 13–38.

  1996 Mental abilities of early *Homo*: elements of constraint and choice in rule systems, in P. Mellars and K. Gibson (eds), *Modelling the early human mind*, Oxford: Oxbow Books, pp. 191–215.

1999 Lower and Middle Pleistocene archaeology of the Baringo Basin, in P. Andrews and P. Banham (eds.), *Late Cenozoic environments and hominid evolution: a tribute to Bill Bishop*, London: Geological Society, pp. 123–141.

2005 Seeking the Palaeolithic individual in East Africa and Europe during the Lower-Middle Pleistocene, in C. Gamble and M. Porr (eds.), *The hominid individual in context: archaeological investigations of Lower and Middle Palaeolithic landscapes, locales and artefacts*, Abingdon: Routledge, pp. 50–67.

2006 The early settlement of northern Europe: fire history in the context of the climate change and the social brain, *Comptes Rendu Palevol* 5: 299–310.

Gowlett, J. A. J. and Crompton, R. H. 1994 Kariandusi: Acheulean morphology and the question of allometry, *African Archaeological Review* 12: 3–42.

Gowlett, J. A. J., Harris, J. W. K., Walton, D. and Wood, B. A. 1981 Early archaeological sites, hominid remains and traces of fire from Chesowanja, Kenya, *Nature* 294: 125–129.

Gramly, R. M. 1975 Pastoralists and hunters: recent prehistory in southern Kenya and northern Tanzania, PhD thesis, Harvard University.

Greenberg, J. H. 1963 *The languages of Africa*, The Hague: Mouton.

Gregory, J. W. 1921 *The Rift Valleys and geology of East Africa*, London: Seeley, Service.

Gresham, T. H. and Brandt, S. A. 1996 Variability in the MSA of the Horn of Africa, in G. Pwiti, G. and R. Soper (eds.), *Aspects of African archaeology*, Harare: University of Zimbabwe Press, pp. 157–164.

Grine, F. E. 1981 Trophic differences between gracile and robust *Australopithecus*: a scanning electron microscope analysis of occlusal events, *South African Journal of Science* 77: 203–230.

1984 Deciduous molar microwear of South African australopithecines, in D. J. Chivers, B. A. Wood and A. Bilsborough (eds.), *Food acquisition and processing in primates*, New York: Plenum, pp. 525–534.

1986 Dental evidence for dietary differences in *Australopithecus* and *Paranthropus*: a quantitative analysis of permanent molar microwear, *Journal Human Evolution* 15: 783–822.

Grine, F. E. and Henshilwood, C. S. 2002 Additional human remains from Blombos Cave, South Africa: (1997–2000 excavations), *Journal of Human Evolution* 42: 293–302.

Grine, F. E. and Kay, R. F. 1988 Early hominid diets from quantitative image analysis of dental microwear, *Nature* 333: 765–768.

Grine, F. E., Ungar, P. S., Teaford, M. F., and El-Zaatari, S. 2006. Molar microwear in *Preanthropus afarensis*: evidence for dietary stasis through time and under diverse paleoecological conditions. *Journal of Human Evolution* 51: 297–319.

Grootes, P. M. 2001 Climate variability on centennial to millennial timescales in ice cores from Greenland and Antarctica, *Nova Acta Leopoldina* 84(331): 89–98.

Grün, R. and Beaumont, P. 2001 Border Cave revisited: a revised ESR chronology, *Journal of Human Evolution* 40: 467–482.

Grün, R., Beaumont, P., Tobias, P. V. and Eggins, S. 2003 On the age of Border Cave 5 human mandible, *Journal of Human Evolution* 45: 155–167.

Grün, R., Brink, J., Spooner, N., Taylor, L., Stringer, C., Franciscus, R. and Murray, A. 1996 Direct dating of Florisbad hominid, *Nature* 382: 500–501.

Grün, R. and Stringer, C. 1991 Electron spin resonance dating and the evolution of modern humans, *Archaeometry* 33: 153–199.

Grün, R., Stringer, C., McDermott, F., Nathan, R., Porat, N., Robertson, S., Taylor, L., Mortimer, G., Eggins, S. and McCulloch, M. 2005 U-series and ESR analyses of bones and teeth relating to the human burials from Skhul, *Journal of Human Evolution* 49: 316–334.

Guenther, M. G. 1994 The relationship of Bushman art to ritual and folklore, in T. A. Dowson and J. D. Lewis-Williams (eds.), *Contested images: diversity in southern African rock art research*, Johannesburg: Witwatersrand University Press, pp. 257–274.

1996 Diversity and flexibility: the case of the Bushmen of southern Africa, in S. Kent, (ed.) *Cultural diversity among twentieth-century foragers: an African perspective*, Cambridge: Cambridge University Press, pp. 65–86.

2002 Independence, resistance, accommodation, persistence: hunter-gatherers and agropastoralists in the Ghanzi veld, early 1800s to mid-1900s, in S. Kent (ed.), *Ethnicity, hunter-gatherers and the "Other": association or assimilation in Africa*, Washington: Smithsonian Institution Press, pp. 127–149.

Güldemann, T. 2004 Clicks, genetics and "proto-world" from a linguistics perspective. http://email.eva.mpg.de/~gueldema/pdf/ProtoClick.pdf. Site accessed 17 March 2006.

Güldemann, T. and Vossen, R. 2000 Khoisan, in B. Heine and D. Nurse (eds.), *African languages*, Cambridge: Cambridge University Press, pp. 99–122.

Guo Z., Petit-Maire N. and Kroepelin S. 2000 Holocene non-orbital climatic events in present-day arid areas of northern Africa and China, *Global and Planetary Change* 26: 97–103.

Gurven, M., Kaplan, H. and Gutierrez, M. 2006 How long does it take to become a proficient hunter? Implications for the evolution of extended development and long life span, *Journal of Human Evolution* 51: 454–470.

Gutin, J. A. and Musonda, F. B. 1985 Faunal remains from Mufulwe rock shelter, Zambia, and their implications, *South African Archaeological Bulletin* 40: 11–16.

Haaland, R. 1987 *Socio-economic differentiation in the Neolithic Sudan*, Oxford: British Archaeological Reports.

1992 Fish, pots and grain: Early and Mid-Holocene adaptations in the Central Sudan, *African Archaeological Review* 10: 43–64.

1993 Aqualithic sites of the Middle Nile, *Azania* 28: 47–86.

1996 A socio-economic perspective on the transition from gathering to cultivation and domestication: a case study of sorghum in the middle Nile region, in G. Pwiti and R. Soper (eds.), *Aspects of African archaeology*, Harare: University of Zimbabwe Press, pp. 391–400.

2006 Africa and the Near East: pot and porridge, bread and oven – two food systems maintained over 10,000 years ago, in H.-P. Wotzka (ed.), *Beitrage zur europaischen und africanischen Archaeologie für Manfred Eggert*, Tübingen: Francke Verlag, pp. 243–255.

Haas, H., Holliday, V. and Stuckenrath, R. 1986 Dating of Holocene stratigraphy with soluble and insoluble organic fractions at the Lubbock Lake archaeological site, Texas: an ideal case study, *Radiocarbon* 28: 473–485.

Hachi, S. 1996 L'Ibéromaurisian, découverte des fouilles d'Afalou (Bédjaîa, Algérie), *L'Anthropologie* 100: 55–76.

Hachi, S., Fröhlich, F., Gendron-Badou, A., de Lumley, H., Roubet, C. and Abdessadok, S. 2002 Figurines du Paléolithique supérieur en matière minérale plastique cuite d'Afalou Bou Rhummel (Babors, Algérie). Premières analyses par spectroscopie d'absorption Infrarouge, *L'Anthropologie* 106: 57–97.

Haddon, A. C. 1905 Presidential Address, Section H, *Reports of the British Association for the Advancement of Science (South Africa)* 1905: 511–527.

Hadjouis, D. 2002 Les hommes du Paléolithique supérieur d'Afalou Bou Rhummel (Bedjaia, Algérie). Interprétation nouvelle des cinétiques cranio-faciales et des effets de l'avulsion dentaire. Malformations crâniennes, troubles de la croissance, anomalies et maladies alvéolo-dentaires, *L'Anthropologie* 106: 337–375.

Haeusler, M. and McHenry, H. M. 2004 Body proportions of *Homo habilis* reviewed, *Journal of Human Evolution* 46: 433–465.

Haile-Selassie, Y. 2001 Late Miocene hominids from the Middle Awash, Ethiopia, *Nature* 412: 178–181.

Hall, S. L. 1990 Hunter-gatherer-fishers of the Fish River Basin: a contribution to the Holocene prehistory of the Eastern Cape, DPhil thesis, University of Stellenbosch.

1994 Images of interaction: rock art and sequence in the eastern Cape, in T. A. Dowson and J. D. Lewis-Williams (eds.), *Contested images: diversity in southern African rock art research*, Johannesburg: Witwatersrand University Press, pp. 61–82.

2000 Burial sequence in the Later Stone Age of the Eastern Cape Province, South Africa, *South African Archaeological Bulletin* 55: 137–146.

Hall, S. L. and Binneman, J. N. F. 1987 Later Stone Age burial variability in the Cape: a social interpretation, *South African Archaeological Bulletin* 42: 140–152.

Hall, S. L. and Smith, B. 2000 Empowering places: rock shelters and ritual control in farmer-forager interactions in the Northern Province, *South African Archaeological Society Goodwin Series* 8: 30–46.

Hallos, J. 2005 "15 Minutes of Fame": Exploring the temporal dimension of Middle Pleistocene lithic technology, *Journal of Human Evolution* 49: 155–179.

Hamilton, A. C. 1988 Guenon evolution and forest history, in A. Gautier-Hion (ed.), *A primate radiation evolutionary biology of the African guenon*, Cambridge: Cambridge University Press, pp. 13–34.

2000 History of forests and climate, in J. A. Sayer, C. Harcourt and N. Collins (eds.), *The conservation atlas of tropical forests: Africa*, New York: Simon and Shuster, pp. 17–25.

Hamilton, A. C. and Taylor, D. M. 1991 History of climate and forests in tropical Africa during the last 8 million years, *Climate Change* 19: 65–78.

Hammer, M. F., Garrigan, D., Wilder, J. A., Mobasher, Z., Severson, T., Kingan, K. B. and Kingan, S. B. 2005 Sequence data from the autosomes and X chromosome: evidence from ancient admixture in the history of *H. sapiens*? *American Journal of Physical Anthropology* S40: 111.

Hammond-Tooke, W. D. 1998 Selective borrowing? The possibility of San shamanistic influence on Southern Bantu divination and healing practices, *South African Archaeological Bulletin* 53: 9–15.

Hampson, J., Challis, W., Blundell, G. and De Rosner, C. 2002 The rock art of Bongani Mountain Lodge and its environs, Mpumalanga Province, South Africa: an introduction to problems of southern African rock-art regions, *South African Archaeological Bulletin* 57: 15–30.

Hanotte, O., Bradley, D. G., Ochieng, J. W., Verjee, Y., Hill, F. W. and Rege, J. F. O. 2002 African pastoralism: genetic imprints of origins and migrations, *Science* 296: 336–339.

Haour, A. C. 2003 One hundred years of archaeology in Niger, *Journal of World Prehistory* 17: 181–234.

Haour, A. C. and Winton, V. 2003 A Palaeolithic cleaver from the Sahel: freak or fact? http://www.antiquity.ac.uk/ProjGall/haour/haour.html. Accessed 28 September, 2006.

Hare, P. E., Goodfriend, G. A., Brooks, A. S., Kokis, J. E. and von Endt, D. W. 1993 Chemical clocks and thermometers: diagenetic reactions of amino acids in fossils, *Carnegie Institute of Washington Yearbook* 92: 80–85.

Harlan, J. R. 1982 The origins of indigenous African agriculture, in J. D. Clark (ed.), *Cambridge history of Africa, Volume I: from the earliest times to c. 500 B.C.*, Cambridge: Cambridge University Press, pp. 624–657.

Harlan, J. R. 1992 Indigenous African agriculture, in C. W. Cowan and P. J. Watson (eds.), *The origins of agriculture: an international perspective*, Washington: Smithsonian Institution Press, pp. 59–70.

Harpending, H. C., Sherry, S. T., Rogers, A. L. and Stoneking, M. 1993 The genetic structure of ancient human populations, *Current Anthropology* 34: 483–496.

Harper, P. T. N. 1997 The Middle Stone Age sequences at Rose Cottage Cave: a search for continuity and discontinuity, *South African Journal of Science* 93: 470–475.

Harris, J. W. K., Williamson, P. G., Vernieres, J., Tappen, M. J., Stewart, K., Helgren, D., de Heinzelin, J., Boaz, N. T. and Bellomo, R. V. 1987

Late Pliocene hominid occupation of the Senga 5A site, Zaire, *Journal of Human Evolution* 16: 701–728.

Harrison, T. 2002. The first record of fossil hominins from the Ndolanya Beds, Laetoli, Tanzania. *American Journal of Physical Anthropology* 119: 83.

Harrold, F. J. 1989 Mousterian, Châtelperronian and early Aurignacian in western Europe: continuity or discontinuity? in P. A. Mellars and C. B. Stringer (eds), *The human revolution: behavioural and biological perspectives on the origins of modern humans*, Edinburgh: Edinburgh University Press, pp. 677–713.

Hassan, F. A. (ed.) 2002 *Droughts, food and culture: ecological change and food security in Africa's later prehistory*, New York: Kluwer Academic/Plenum Publishers.
   2003 Archaeology and linguistic diversity in North Africa, in P. Bellwood and A. C. Renfrew (eds.), *Examining the farming/language dispersal hypothesis*, Cambridge: McDonald Institute for Archaeological Research, pp. 127–134.

Haverkort, C. M. and Lubell, D. 1999 Cutmarks on Capsian human remains: implications for Maghreb Holocene social organization and palaeoeconomy, *International Journal of Osteoarchaeology* 9: 147–169.

Hawkes, K., O'Connell, J. F. and Blurton Jones, N. G. 1991 Hunting income patterns among the Hadza: big game, common goods, foraging goals, and the evolution of the human diet, *Philosophical Transactions of the Royal Society (London)* 334B: 243–251.

Hawkes, K., O'Connell, J. F., Blurton Jones, N. G., Gurven, M., Hill, K., Hames, R., Kano, T., Nishida, T., White, F. J., Churchill, S. E. and Worthman, C. M. 1997 Hadza womens' time allocation, offspring provisioning, and the evolution of post-menopausal lifespans, *Current Anthropology* 38: 551–577.

Hawkes, K., O'Connell, J. F., Blurton Jones, N. G., Charnov, E.L and Alvarez, H. 1998 Grandmothering, menopause, and the evolution of human life histories, *Proceedings of the National Academy of Sciences (USA)* 95: 1336–1339.

Hawks, J., Hunley, K., Lee, S.-H. and Walpoff, M. 2000 Population bottlenecks and Pleistocene human evolution, *Molecular Biology and Evolution* 17: 2–22.

Hay, R. L. 1976 *Geology of the Olduvai Gorge*, Berkeley: University of California Press.

Hayden, B. 1981 Subsistence and ecological adaptation of modern hunter-gatherers, in R. S. O. Harding and G. Teleki (eds.), *Omnivorous primates: gathering and hunting in human evolution*, New York: Columbia University Press, pp. 344–421.
   1987. Alliances and ritual ecstasy: human responses to resource stress, *Journal for the Scientific Study of Religion* 26: 81–91.
   1990 Nimrods, piscators, pluckers and planters: the emergence of food production, *Journal of Anthropological Archaeology* 9: 31–69.
   1994 Competition, labour and complex hunter-gatherers, in E. S. Burch and L. J. Ellanna (eds.), *Key issues in hunter-gatherer research*, Oxford: Berg, pp. 223–239.

1995 The emergence of prestige technologies and pottery, in W. K. Barnett and J. W. Hoopes (eds.), *The emergence of pottery: technology and innovation*, Washington: Smithsonian Institution Press, pp. 257–266.

Hayden, B. and Gargett, R. 1988 Specialization in the Paleolithic, *Lithic Technology* 17: 12–18.

Hays, T. R. 1975a Neolithic settlement patterns in Saharan Africa, *South African Archaeological Bulletin* 30: 29–33.

1975b Neolithic settlement of the Sahara as it relates to the Nile Valley, in F. Wendorf and A. E. Marks (eds.) *Problems in prehistory: North Africa and the Levant*, Dallas: Southern Methodist University Press, pp. 193–204.

Headland, T. N., and Reid, L. A. 1989 Hunter-gatherers and their neighbours from prehistory to the present, *Current Anthropology* 30: 43–66.

Helgren, D. M. 1997 Locations and landscapes of Palaeolithic sites in the Semliki Rift, Zaire, *Geoarchaeology* 4: 337–361.

Henderson, Z. 1992 The context of some Middle Stone Age hearths at Klasies River Mouth Cave, *Southern African Field Archaeology* 1: 14–26.

Henshilwood, C. S. 2005 Stratigraphic integrity of the Middle Stone Age levels at Blombos Cave, in F. d'Errico and L. Backwell (eds.), *From tools to symbols: from early hominins to modern humans*, Johannesburg: Witwatersrand University Press, pp. 441–458.

Henshilwood, C. S., d'Errico, F., Marean, C. W., Milo, R. G. and Yates, R. 2001b An early bone tool industry from the Middle Stone Age at Blombos Cave, South Africa: implications for the origins of modern human behaviour, symbolism and language, *Journal of Human Evolution* 41: 631–678.

Henshilwood, C. S., d'Errico, F., Yates, R., Jacobs, Z., Tribolo, C., Duller, G. A. T., Mercier, N., Sealy, J. D., Valladas, H., Watts, I. and Wintle, A. G. 2002 Emergence of modern human behaviour: Middle Stone Age engravings from South Africa, *Science* 295: 1278–1280.

Henshilwood, C. S. and Marean, C. A. 2003 The origin of modern human behaviour: critique of the models and their test implications, *Current Anthropology* 44: 627–651.

Henshilwood, C. S., Nilssen, P. and Parkington, J. E. 1994 Mussel drying and food storage in the late Holocene, south-west Cape, South Africa, *Journal of Field Archaeology* 21: 103–109.

Henshilwood, C.S, Sealy, J. C., Yates, R., Cruz-Uribe, K., Goldberg, P., Grine, F. E., Klein, R. G., Poggenpoel, C. A., van Niekerk, K. and Watts, I. 2001a Blombos Cave, southern Cape, South Africa: preliminary report on the 1992–1999 excavation of the Middle Stone Age levels, *Journal of Archaeological Science* 28: 421–448.

Hewlett, B. S. 1996 Cultural diversity among African pygmies, in S. Kent (ed.), *Cultural diversity among Twentieth Century foragers: an African perspective*, Cambridge: Cambridge University Press, pp. 215–244.

2000 Central African governments' and international NGOs' perceptions of Baka Pygmy development, in P. P. Schweitzer, M. Biesele and R. K.

Hitchcock (eds.), *Hunters and gatherers in the modern world: conflict, resistance and self-determination*, Oxford: Berghahn, pp. 380–390.

Higgs, E. S. (ed.) 1972 *Papers in economic prehistory*, Cambridge: Cambridge University Press.

Hillman, G. C. 1989 Late Palaeolithic plant foods from Wadi Kubbaniya in Upper Egypt: dietary diversity, infant weaning and seasonality in a riverine environment, in D. R. Harris and G. C. Hillman (eds.), *Foraging and farming: the evolution of plant exploitation*, London: Unwin Hyman, pp. 297–239.

Hilton, C. E., and Meldrum, D. J. 2004 Striders, runners and transporters, in D. J. Meldrum and C. E. Hilton (eds.), *From biped to strider: the emergence of modern human walking, running and resource transport*. New York: Kluwer Academic, pp. 1–8.

Hiscock, P. 1994 Technological responses to risk in Holocene Australia, *Journal of World Prehistory* 8: 267–292.

1996 Transformations of Upper Palaeolithic implements in the Dabba industry from Haua Fteah (Libya), *Antiquity* 70: 657–664.

Hiscock, P. and O'Connor, S. 2005 Arid paradises or dangerous landscapes: a review of explanations for Palaeolithic assemblage change in arid Australia and Africa, in P. Veth, M. Smith and P. Hiscock (eds.), *Desert peoples archaeological perspectives*, Oxford: Blackwell Publishing, pp. 58–78.

Hitchcock, R. K. 1999 Tyua, in R. B. Lee and R. Daly (eds.), *The Cambridge encyclopaedia of hunters and gatherers*, Cambridge: Cambridge University Press, pp. 225–229.

Hitchcock, R. K. and Holm, J. D. 1993 Bureaucratic domination of hunter-gatherer societies: a case study of the San in Botswana, *Development and Change* 24: 305–338.

Hobart, J. H. 2003 Forager-farmer relations in southeastern southern Africa: a critical reassessment, DPhil thesis, University of Oxford.

Hohmann, G. and Fruth, B. 2003 Culture in bonobos? Between species and within species variation in behaviour, *Current Anthropology* 44: 563–571.

Holl, A. 1989 Social issues in Saharan prehistory, *Journal of Anthropological Archaeology* 8: 313–354.

2005 Holocene "aquatic" adaptations in tropical North Africa, in A. B. Stahl (ed.), *African archaeology: a critical introduction*, Oxford: Blackwell Publishing, pp. 174–186.

Holliday, T. W. 1997 Body proportions in Late Pleistocene Europe and modern human origins, *Journal of Human Evolution* 32: 423–447.

Hollmann, J. C. (ed.) 2005a *Customs and beliefs of the/Xam Bushmen*, Johannesburg: Witwatersrand University Press.

2005b 'Swift-people': therianthropes and bird symbolism in hunter-gatherer rock-paintings, Western and Eastern Cape Provinces, South Africa, *South African Archaeological Society Goodwin Series* 9: 21–33.

Hopley, P. J., Latham, A. G., Marshall, J. D. 2006 Palaeoenvironments and palaeodiets of mid-Pliocene micromammals from Makapansgat

Limeworks, South Africa: a stable isotope and dental microwear approach. *Palaeogeography, Palaeoclimatology, Palaeoecology* 233: 235–251.

Hopley, P. J., Weedon, G. P., Marshall, J. D., Herries, A. I. R., Latham, A. G., and Kuykendall, K. L. 2007 High- and low-latitude orbital forcing of early hominin habitats in South Africa. *Earth and Planetary Science Letters* 256: 419–432.

How, M. W. 1962 *The Mountain Bushmen of Basutoland*, Pretoria: Van Schaik.

Howell, F. C. 1978 Hominidae, in V. J. Maglio and H. B. S. Cooke (eds.), *Evolution of African mammals*, Cambridge: Harvard University Press, pp. 154–248.

Howell, F. C., Cole, G. H. and Kleindienst, M. R. 1962 Isimila: an Acheulean occupation site in the Iringa highlands, Southern Highlands Province, Tanganyika, in G. Mortelmans and J. Nenquin (eds.), *Actes du IVeme Congrès Panafricain de Préhistoire*, Tervuren: Musée Royal de l'Afrique Centrale, pp. 43–80.

Howell, N., Elson, J. L., Turnbull, D. M. and Herrnstadt, C. 2004 African haplogroup L mtDNA sequences show violations of clock-like evolution, *Molecular Biology and Evolution* 21: 1843–1854.

Hublin, J.-J. 2001 Northwest African Middle Pleistocene hominids and their bearing on the emergence of *Homo sapiens*, in, L. Barham and K. Robson-Brown (eds.), *Human roots: Africa and Asia in the Middle Pleistocene*, Bristol: Western Academic & Specialist Press, pp. 99–121.

Hublin, J.-J. and Coqueugniot, H. 2006 Absolute or proportional brain size: that is the question. A reply to Leigh's (2006) comments, *Journal of Human Evolution* 50: 109–113.

Huffman, T. N. 1989 Ceramics, settlements and late Iron Age migrations, *African Archaeological Review* 7: 155–182.

1996 Archaeological evidence for climatic change during the last 2000 years in southern Africa, *Quaternary International* 33: 55–60.

2005 The stylistic origin of Bambata and the spread of mixed farming in southern Africa, *Southern African Humanities* 17: 57–79.

Hughes, D. A., Cordaux, R., and Stoneking, M., 2004 Humans. *Current Biology* 14: R367–R369.

Hull, K. L. 2001 Reasserting the utility of obsidian hydration dating: a temperature-dependent empirical approach to practical temporal resolution with archaeological obsidians, *Journal of Archaeological Science* 28: 1025–1040.

Hume, J. C. C., Lyons, E. J. and Day, K. P. 2003 Malaria in antiquity: a genetic perspective, *World Archaeology* 35: 180–192.

Humphreys, A. J. B. 1987 Prehistoric seasonal mobility: what are we really achieving? *South African Archaeological Bulletin* 42: 34–38.

1988 A prehistoric frontier in the Northern Cape and western Orange Free State: archaeological evidence in interaction and ideological change, *Kronos* 3: 3–13.

1991 On the distribution and dating of bifacial barbed and tanged arrowheads in the interior of South Africa, *South African Archaeological Bulletin* 46: 41–43.

2004/05 "De-!Kunging" the Later Stone Age of the central interior of South Africa, *Southern African Field Archaeology* 11/12: 36–41.

Humphreys, A. J. B. and Thackeray, A. I. 1983 *Ghaap and Gariep: Later Stone Age studies in the Northern Cape*, Cape Town: South African Archaeological Society.

Hunt, G. R., and Gray, R. D. 2004 The crafting of hook tools by wild New Caledonian crows, *Proceedings of the Royal Society of London B* 271: S88–S90.

Huyge, D., Watchman, A., De Papper, M. and Marchi, E. 2001 Dating Egypt's oldest 'art': AMS $^{14}$C age determinations of rock varnishes covering petroglyphs at El-Hôsh (Upper Egypt), *Antiquity* 75: 68–72.

Huysecom, E., Ozainne, S., Raeli, F., Ballouche, A., Rasse, M. and Stokes, S. 2004 Ounjougou (Mali): a history of Holocene settlement at the southern edge of the Sahara, *Antiquity* 78: 579–593.

Ichikawa, M. 1999 Interactive process of man and nature in the Ituri forest of the Democratic Republic of Congo: an approach from historical ecology, in K. Biesbrouck, S. Elders and G. Rossel (eds.), *Central African hunter-gatherers in a multidisciplinary perspective: challenging elusiveness*, Leiden: University of Leiden Press, pp. 141–152.

2000 "Interest in the present" in the nationwide monetary economy: the case of Mbuti hunters in Zaire, in P. P. Schweitzer, M. Biesele and R. K. Hitchcock (eds.), *Hunters and gatherers in the modern world: conflict, resistance and self-determination*, Oxford: Berghahn, pp. 263–274.

Ikeya, K. 1993 Goat-raising among the San in the central Kalahari, *African Study Monographs* 14(1): 39–52.

Imbrie, J. and Imbrie J. Z. 1980 Modeling the climatic response to orbital variations, *Science* 207: 943–953.

Ingman, M., Kasessmann, H., Pääbo, S. and Gyllensten, U. 2000 Mitochondrial genome variation and the origin of modern humans, *Nature* 408: 708–713.

Inizan, M.-L., Roche, H., and Tixier, J. 1992. *Technology of knapped stone.* Meudon: CREP.

Inskeep, R. R. 1962 The age of the Kondoa rock paintings in light of recent excavations at Kisese II rock shelter, in G. Mortelmans and J. Nenquin (eds.), *Actes du IVᵉ Congrès Panafrican de Préhistoire et de l'Etude du Quaternaire*, Tervuren: Musée Royal de l'Afrique Centrale, pp. 249–256.

1967 The Late Stone Age, in W. W. Bishop and J. D. Clark (eds.), *Background to evolution in Africa*, Chicago: University of Chicago Press, pp. 557–582.

1986 A preliminary survey of burial practices in the Later Stone Age, from the Orange River to the Cape coast, in R. Singer and K. Lundy (eds.), *Variation, culture and evolution in African populations*, Johannesburg: Witwatersrand University Press, pp. 221–240.

1987 *Nelson Bay Cave, Cape Province, South Africa: the Holocene levels*, Oxford: British Archaeological Reports.

IPACC 2006 Indigenous Peoples of Africa Co-ordinating Committee, http://www.ipacc.org.za/eng/home.asp?sPage=regional.asp. Site accessed 10 July 2006.

Irish, J. 2000 The Iberomaurusian enigma: North African progenitor or dead end? *Journal of Human Evolution* 39: 393–410.

Isaac, G. Ll. 1975 Sorting out the muddle in the middle: an anthropologist's post-conference appraisal, in K. W. Butzer and G. Ll. Isaac (eds.), *After the australopithecines*, The Hague: Mouton, pp. 875–887.

1977 *Oloregesailie: Archaeological Studies of a Middle Pleistocene Lake Basin in Kenya*, Chicago: University of Chicago Press.

1978 The food-sharing behaviour of protohuman hominids, *Scientific American* 238: 90–108.

1980 Comment on time and place, *South African Archaeological Bulletin* 35: 96–98.

1981 Archaeological tests of alternative models of early hominid behaviour: excavations and experiments, *Philosophical Transactions of the Royal Society of London (Biology)* 292: 177–188.

1989 *The archaeology of human origins*, Cambridge: Cambridge University Press.

Isaac, G. Ll., Harris, J. W. K. and Kroll, E. M. 1997 The stone artefact assemblages: a comparative study, in G. Ll. Isaac and B. Isaac (eds.), *Koobi Fora Research Project, Volume 5, Plio-Pleistocene archaeology*, Oxford: Oxford University Press, pp: 262–362.

Ishango 2006 Autour d'Ishango, http://www.ishango.be/. Site accessed 28 September 28 2006.

Jackson, D. 1999 Some recent international initiatives in Equatorial Africa and their impacts on forest peoples, in K. Biesbrouck, S. Elders and G. Rossel (eds.), *Central African hunter-gatherers in a multidisciplinary perspective: challenging elusiveness*, Leiden: University of Leiden Press, pp. 279–290.

Jacobs, Z., Duller, G. A. T., Wintle, A. G. and Henshilwood, C. S. 2006 Extending the chronology of deposits at Blombos Cave, South Africa, back to 140 ka using optical dating of single and multiple grains of quartz, *Journal of Human Evolution* 51: 255–273.

Jacobson, L. 1984 Hunting versus gathering in an arid ecosystem: the evidence from the Namib Desert, in M. Hall, G. Avery, D. M. Avery, M. L. Wilson and A. J. B. Humphreys (eds.), *Frontiers: southern African archaeology today*, Oxford: British Archaeological Reports, pp. 75–79.

Jacquet, G. 2000 Piste oubliée en Haut-Ennedi (Tchad), *Sahara* 10: 141–149.

Jahns, S., Huls, M. and Sarnthein, M. 1998 Vegetation and climate history of west equatorial Africa based on a marine pollen record off Liberia (site GIK 16776) covering the last 400,000 years, *Review of Palaeobotany and Palynology* 102: 277–288.

James, S. R. 1989 Hominid use of fire in the Lower and Middle Pleistocene: a review of the evidence, *Current Anthropology* 30: 1–26.

Jennerstrasse 8 (T. Lenssen-Erz, Y. Tegtmeier, S. Kröpelin, H. Berke, B. Eichhorn, M. Herb, F. Jesse, B. Keding, K. Kindermann, J. Linstädter, S. Nussbaum, H. Riemer, W. Schuck and R. Vogelsang (eds.), 2002 *Tides of the desert. Contributions to the archaeology and environmental history of Africa in honour of Rudolph Kuper*, Köln: Heinrich Barth Institut.

Jerardino, A. 1995a The problem with density values in archaeological analysis: a case study from Tortoise Cave, Western Cape, South Africa, *South African Archaeological Bulletin* 50: 21–27.

1995b Late Holocene Neoglacial episodes in southern South America and southern Africa: a comparison, *The Holocene* 5: 361–368.

1996 Changing social landscapes of the western Cape coast of southern Africa over the last 4500 years, PhD thesis, University of Cape Town.

1998 Excavations at Pancho's Kitchen Midden, Western Cape coast, South Africa: further observations into the megamidden period, *South African Archaeological Bulletin* 53: 16–25.

Jerardino, A. and Parkington, J. E. 1993 New evidence for whales on archaeological sites in the south-western Cape, *South African Journal of Science* 89: 6–7.

Jerardino, A. and Swanepoel, N. 1999 Painted slabs from Steenbokfontein Cave: the oldest known parietal art in southern Africa, *Current Anthropology* 40: 542–548.

Jerardino, A. and Yates, R. 1996 Preliminary results from excavations at Steenbokfontein Cave: implications for past and future research, *South African Archaeological Bulletin* 51: 7–16.

Jesse, F. 2000 Early Khartoum ceramics in the Wadi Howar (northwest Sudan), in L. Krzyzaniak, K. Kroper and M. Kobusiewicz (eds.), *Recent research into the Stone Age of northeastern Africa*, Poznán: Poznán Museum, pp. 77–87.

Johnson, A. W. and Earle, T. 1987 *The evolution of human societies*, Stanford: Stanford University Press.

Johnson, T. C., Scholz, C. A., Talbot, M. R., Kelts, K., Ricketts, R. D., Ngobi, G., Beuning, K., Ssemmanda, I. and McGill, J. W. 1996 Late Pleistocene dessication of Lake Victoria and rapid evolution of cichlid fishes, *Science* 273: 1091–1093.

Joiris, D. V. 1998 La chasse, la chance, le chant: aspects du système rituel des Baka du Cameroun, PhD thesis, Université Libre de Bruxelles.

Jolly, C. J. 1970 The seed-eaters: a new model of hominid differentiation based on baboon analogy, *Man* 5: 1–26.

2001 A proper study of mankind: analogies from the papionin monkeys and their implications for human evolution, *Yearbook of Physical Anthropology* 44: 177–204.

Jolly, C. J. and Plog, F. 1987 *Physical anthropology and archaeology*, New York: Random House.

Jolly, D., Harrison, S., Damnati, B. and Bonnefille, B. 1998 Simulated climate and biomes of Africa during the late Quaternary comparison with pollen and lake status data, *Quaternary Science Reviews* 17: 629–658.

Jolly, D. and Haxeltine, A. 1997 Effect of low glacial atmospheric $CO_2$ on tropical African montane vegetation, *Science* 276: 786–787.

Jolly, D., Taylor, D., Marchant, R., Hamilton, A., Bonnefille, R., Buchet, G. and Riollet, G. 1997 Vegetation dynamics in central Africa since 18000 yr

BP: pollen records from the interlacustrine highlands of Burundi, Rwanda and western Uganda, *Journal of Biogeography* 24: 495–512.

Jolly, P. 1986 A first generation descendant of the Transkei San, *South African Archaeological Bulletin* 41: 6–9.

1996 Symbiotic interactions between Black farmers and south-eastern San: implications for southern African rock art studies, ethnographic analogy and hunter-gatherer cultural identity, *Cultural Anthropology* 37: 277–306.

2005 Sharing symbols: a correspondence in the ritual dress of black farmers and the southeastern San, *South African Archaeological Society Goodwin Series* 9: 86–100.

Jones, C. E. R. 1989 Archaeochemistry: fact or fancy? in F. Wendorf, R. Schild and A. E. Close (eds.), *Egypt during the Last Interglacial: the Middle Palaeolithic of Bir Tarfawi and Bir Sahara*, New York: Plenum Press, pp. 260–266.

Jones, P. 1984 Mobility and migration in traditional African farming and Iron Age models, in M. Hall, G. Avery, D. M. Avery, M. L. Wilson and A. J. B. Humphreys (eds.), *Frontiers: southern African archaeology today*, Oxford: British Archaeological Reports, pp. 289–296.

Jones, P. R. 1979 Effects of raw materials on biface manufacture, *Science* 204: 835–836.

1994 Results of experimental work in relation to the stone industries of Olduvai Gorge, in M. D. Leakey and D. A. Roe (eds), *Olduvai Gorge: excavations in Beds III, IV, and the Masek Beds 1968–1971*, Cambridge: Cambridge University Press, pp. 254–298.

Jonsson, J. 1998 *Early plant economy in Zimbabwe*, Uppsala: Uppsala University Press.

Jordan, B. 1999 Row erupts as Khoisan call for return of old bones, *Sunday Times* (South Africa) 17 January 1999.

Jorde, L., Watkins, W., Bamshad, M., Dixon, M., Ricker, C., Seilstad, M. and Baxter, M. 2000 The distribution of human genetic diversity: a comparison of mitochondrial, autosomal, and Y-chromosome data, *American Journal of Human Genetics* 66: 979–988.

Jousse, H. 2006 What is the impact of Holocene climatic changes on human societies? Analysis of West African Neolithic populations' dietary customs, *Quaternary International* 151: 63–73.

Jousse, H., Kaber, N. O. M. and Raimbault, M. 2003 Aperçu archéozoologique d'un site de chasseurs au Néolithique ancien à Berouâga (Mauritanie nord-occidentale), *Sahara* 14: 81–88.

Jouzel, J., Masson-Delmotte, V., Cattani, O., Dreyfus, G., Falourd, S., Hoffmann, G., Minster, B., Nouet, J., Barnola, J. M., Chappellaz, J., Fischer, H., Gallet, J. C., Johnsen, S., Leuenberger, M., Loulergue, L., Luethi, D., Oerter, H., Parenin, F., Raisbeck, G., Raynaud, D., Schilt, A., Schwander, J., Selmo, E., Souchez, R., Spahni, R., Stauffer, B., Steffensen, J. P., Stenni, B., Stocker, T. F., Tison, J. L., Werner, M., and Wolff, E. W. 2007 Orbital and millennial Antarctic climate variability over the past 800,000 years. *Science* 317: 793–796.

Juel-Jensen, H., Schild, R., Wendorf, F. and Close, A. E. 1991 Understanding the Late Palaeolithic tools with lustrous edges from the Lower Nile Valley, *Antiquity* 65: 122–128.

Juwayeyi, Y. M. and Betzler, C. 1995 Archaeology of the Malawi Rift: the search for Early Stone Age occurrences in the Chiwondo Beds, northern Malawi. *Journal of Human Evolution* 28: 115–116.

Kaare, B. T. M. 1994 The impact of modernization policies on the hunter-gatherer Hadzabe: the case of education and language policies of postindependence Tanzania, in E. S. Burch and L. J. Ellanna (eds.), *Key issues in hunter-gatherer research*, Oxford: Berg, pp. 315–332.

Kaare, B. T. M. and Woodburn, J. 1999 Hadza, in R. B. Lee and R. Daly (eds.), *The Cambridge encyclopaedia of hunters and gatherers*, Cambridge: Cambridge University Press, pp. 200–204.

Kadomura, H. and Nori, N. 1990 Environmental implications of slope deposits in humid tropical Africa: evidence from southern Cameroon and western Kenya, *Geographical Reports, Tokyo Metropolitan University* 25: 213–236.

Kaplan, H., Hill, K., Lancaster, J. and Hurtado, A. M. 2000 A theory of human life history evolution: diet, intelligence and longevity, *Evolutionary Anthropology* 9: 156–185.

Kaplan, J. 1990 The Umhlatuzana Rock Shelter sequence: 100,000 years of Stone Age history, *Natal Museum Journal of Humanities* 2: 1–94.

Kappelman, J. 1996 The evolution of body mass and relative brain size in fossil hominids, *Journal of Human Evolution* 30: 243–276.

Karega-Munene 2003 The East African Neolithic, in C. Kusimba and S. B. Kusimba (eds.), *East African archaeology: foragers, potters, smiths and traders*, Philadelphia: University of Pennsylvania Museum of Archaeology and Anthropology, pp. 17–32.

Karoma, N. J. 1996 The deterioration and destruction of archaeological and historical sites in Tanzania, in P. R. Schmidt and R. J. McIntosh (eds.), *Plundering Africa's past*, Bloomington: Indiana University Press, pp. 191–200.

Kassam, A. 2000 When will we be people as well? Social identity and the politics of cultural performance: the case of the Waata Oromo of East and Northeast Africa, *Social Identities* 6: 189–206.

Kassam, A. and Bashuna, A. B. 2004 Marginalisation of the Waata Oromo hunter–gatherers of Kenya: insider and outsider perspectives, *Africa* 74: 194–216.

Katz, R. F. 1982 *Boiling energy: community healing among the Kalahari !Kung*, Cambridge: Harvard University Press.

Kay, R. F., Cartmill, M. and Barlow, M. 1998 The hypoglossal canal and the origin of human vocal behaviour, *Proceedings of the National Academy of Sciences (USA)* 95: 5417–5419.

Kays, S. J. and Paul, R. E. 2004 *Postharvest biology*. Athens: Exon Press.

Ke, Y., Bing, S., Song, X., Lu, D., Chen, L., Li, H., Qi, C., Marzuki, S., Deka, Underhill, P., Xiao, C., Shriver, M., Lell, J., Wallace, D., X., Daru, L., Cheng, L., Hongyu, L., Chunjian, Qi, Sangkot, M., Ranjan, D., Wells,

R. S., Seielstad, M., Oefner, P., Zhu, D., Jin, J., Huang, W., Chakraboty, R., Chen, Z. and Jin, L. 2001 African origin of modern humans in East Asia: a tale of 12,000 Y chromosomes, *Science* 292: 1151–1153.

Keding, B. 1996 *Djabarona 84/3: Untersuchungen zur Besiedlungsgeschichte des Wadi Howar*, Köln: Heinrich Barth Institut.

Keeley, L. 1980 *Experimental determination of stone tool uses*, Chicago: University of Chicago Press.

1988 Hunter-gatherer economic complexity and "population pressure": a cross-cultural analysis, *Journal of Anthropological Archaeology* 7: 373–411.

Keeley, L. and Toth, N. 1981 Microwear polishes on early stone tools from Koobi Fora, Kenya, *Nature* 293: 464–465.

Keen, I. 2006 Constraints on the development of enduring inequalities in Late Holocene Australia, *Current Anthropology* 47: 7–38.

Keeney, B. (ed.). 2003 *Ropes to God: experiencing the Bushman spiritual universe*, Philadelphia: Ringing Rocks Press.

Keita, S. O. Y. 2005 Explanation of the pattern of P49a,f *Taq*I RFLP Y-chromosome variation in Egypt, *African Archaeological Review* 22: 61–76.

Kelly, R. L. 1995 *The foraging spectrum: diversity in hunter-gatherer lifeways*, Washington: Smithsonian Institution Press.

Kennedy, G. E. 2003 Palaeolithic grandmothers? Life history theory and early *Homo*, *Royal Anthropological Institute* (N.S.) 9: 549–572.

2005 From the ape's dilemma to the weanling's dilemma: early weaning and its evolutionary context, *Journal of Human Evolution* 48: 123–145.

Kent, S. 1992 The current forager controversy: real versus ideal views of hunter-gatherers, *Man* 27: 45–70.

1993 Sharing in an egalitarian Kalahari community, *Man* 28: 479–514.

(ed.) 1996 *Cultural diversity among Twentieth Century foragers: an African perspective*, Cambridge: Cambridge University Press.

(ed.) 1998. *Gender in African prehistory*, Walnut Creek: AltaMira Press.

(ed) 2002 *Ethnicity, hunter-gatherers, and the "other": association or assimilation in Africa*, Washington: Smithsonian Institution Press.

Kenward, B., Weir, A. A. S., Rutz, C., & Kacelnik, A. 2005 Tool manufacture by naive juvenile crows. *Nature* 433: 121.

Khabir, A. M. 1987 New radiocarbon dates for Sarurab 2 and the age of the Early Khartoum tradition, *Current Anthropology* 28: 377–380.

Kiage, L. M. and Liu, K. 2006 Late Quaternary palaeoenvironmental changes in East Africa: a review of multiproxy evidence from palynology, lake sediments, and associated records, *Progress in Physical Geography* 30: 633–658.

Kiberd, P. 2005 Investigation of archaeological deposits at Bundu Farm Pan, South Africa: implications for modern human origins, unpublished MSc dissertation, Southampton University.

Kibunjia, M. 1994 Pliocene archaeological occurrences in the Lake Turkana basin, *Journal of Human Evolution* 27: 159–171.

1997 The management of archaeological collections and resources in Africa, *African Archaeological Review* 14: 137–142.

Kibunjia, M., Roche, H., Brown, F. H. and Leakey, R. E. 1992 Pliocene and Pleistocene archaeological sites west of Lake Turkana, Kenya, *Journal of Human Evolution* 23: 431–438.

Kimbel, W. H., Lockwood, C. A., Ward, C. V., Leakey, M. G., Rak, Y. and Johanson, D. C. 2006 Was *Australopithecus anamensis* ancestral to *A. afarensis*? A case of anagenesis in the hominin fossil record, *Journal of Human Evolution* 51: 134–152.

Kimbel, W. H., Walter, R. C., Johanson, D. C., Reed, K. E., Aronson, J. L., Assefa, Z., Marean, C. W., Eck, G. G., Bobe, R., Hovers, E., Rak, Y., Vondra, C., Yemane, T., York, D., Chen, Y., Evensen, N. M. and Smith, P. E. 1996 Late Pliocene *Homo* and Oldowan tools from the Hadar Formation (Kada Hadar Member), Ethiopia, *Journal of Human Evolution* 31: 549–561.

Kimura, Y. 2002 Examining time trends in the Oldowan technology at Beds I and II, Olduvai Gorge, *Journal of Human Evolution* 43: 291–321.

Kinahan, J. 1991 *Pastoral nomads of the central Namib Desert: the people history forgot*, Windhoek: New Namibia Books.

Kingston, J., and Harrison, T. 2007 Isotopic dietary reconstructions of Pliocene herbivores at Laetoli: implications for hominin paleoecology, *Palaeogeography, Palaeoclimatology, Palaeoecology* 243: 272–306.

Klee, M. and Zach, B. 1999 The exploitation of wild and domesticated food plants at settlement mounds in north-east Nigeria (1800 cal B.C. to today), in M. van der Veen (ed.), *The exploitation of plant resources in ancient Africa*, New York: Kluwer Academic/Plenum Publishers, pp. 89–100.

Klein, R. G. 1972 The Late Quaternary mammalian fauna of Nelson Bay Cave (Cape Province, South Africa): its implications for megafaunal extinctions and environmental and cultural change, *Quaternary Research* 2: 135–142.

1984a Mammalian extinctions and Stone Age people in Africa, in P. S. Martin and R. G. Klein (eds.), *Quaternary extinctions: a prehistoric revolution*, Tucson: Arizona University Press, pp. 553–573.

1984b Later Stone Age faunal samples from Heuningneskrans Shelter, Transvaal, and Leopard's Hill Cave, Zambia, *South African Archaeological Bulletin* 39: 109–116.

1989 Biological and behavioural perspectives on modern human origins in southern Africa, in P. Mellars and C. Stringer (eds.), *The human revolution: behavioural and biological perspectives on the origins of modern humans*, Edinburgh: University of Edinburgh Press, pp. 529–546.

1994a Southern Africa before the Iron Age, in R. S. Corrucini and R. L. Ciochon (eds.), *Integrative paths to the past: paleoanthropological advances in honor of F. Clark Howell*, Englewood Cliffs: Prentice Hall, pp. 471–519.

1994b The long-horned African buffalo (*Pelorovis antiquus*) is an extinct species, *Journal of Archaeological Science* 21: 725–733.

1999 *The human career*, Chicago: University of Chicago Press.

2000a The Earlier Stone Age of southern Africa, *South African Archaeological Bulletin* 55: 107–122.

2000b Archaeology and the evolution of human behaviour, *Evolutionary Anthropology* 9: 17–36.

Klein, R. G., Avery, G., Cruz-Uribe, K., Halkett, D., Hart, T., Milo, R. G. and Volman, T. P. 1999 Duinefontein 2: an Acheulean site in the Western Cape Province of South Africa, *Journal of Human Evolution* 37: 153–190.

Klein, R. G. and Cruz-Uribe, K. 1989 Faunal evidence for prehistoric herder-forager activities at Kasteelberg, western Cape Province, South Africa, *South African Archaeological Bulletin* 44: 82–97.

1991 The bovids from Elandsfontein, South Africa, and their implications for the age, palaeoenvironment, and origins of the site. *African Archaeological Review* 9: 21–79.

1996 Exploitation of large bovids and seals at Middle and Later Stone Age sites in South Africa, *Journal of Human Evolution* 31: 315–334.

Klein, R. G. and Edgar, B. 2002 *The dawn of human culture*, New York: John Wiley.

Klein, R. G. and Scott, K. 1986 Re-analysis of faunal assemblages from the Haua Fteah and other Late Quaternary archaeological sites in Cyrenaica, Libya, *Journal of Archaeological Science* 13: 515–542.

Kleindeinst, M. R. 1961 Variability within the late Acheulean assemblage in eastern Africa, *South African Archaeological Bulletin* 16: 35–52.

Kleinitz, C. 2001 Rock art in sub-Saharan Mali, *Antiquity* 75: 799–800.

Kleppe, E. J. 1984 Village life in the upper White Nile region over a period of 3500 years. Unpublished paper presented at the Second Dymaczewo Conference on the Nile Basin and the Sahara, Poznán, Poland.

Klieman, K. 1999 Hunter-gatherer participation in rainforest trade-systems: a comparative history of forest vs ecotone societies in Gabon and Congo, c. 1000–1800 AD, in K. Biesbrouck, S. Elders and G. Rossel (eds.), *Central African hunter-gatherers in a multidisciplinary perspective: challenging elusiveness*, Leiden: University of Leiden Press, pp. 89–104.

Knight, A., Underhill, P. A., Mortensen, H. M., Zhivotovsky, L. A., Lin, A. A., Henn, B. M., Louis, D., Ruhlen, M. and Mountain, J. L. 2003 African Y-chromosome and mtDNA divergence provides insight into the history of click languages, *Current Biology* 13: 464–473.

Köhler, A. and Lewis, J. 2002 Putting hunter-gatherer and farmer relations in perspective: a commentary from Central Africa, in S. Kent (ed.), *Ethnicity, hunter-gatherers, and the "other": association or assimilation in Africa*, Washington: Smithsonian Institution Press, pp. 276–305.

Kohn, M. and Mithen, S. 1999 Handaxes: products of sexual selection? *Antiquity* 73: 518–526.

Kopytoff, I. (ed.) 1987 *The African frontier: the reproduction of traditional African societies*, Bloomington: Indiana University Press.

Korsman, S. and Plug, I. 1994 Two Later Stone Age sites on the farm Honingklip in the eastern Transvaal, *South African Archaeological Bulletin* 49: 24–32.

Kratz, C. 1999 Okiek, in R. B. Lee and R. Daly (eds.), *The Cambridge encyclopaedia of hunters and gatherers*, Cambridge: Cambridge University Press, pp. 220–224.

Krause, J., Lalueza-Fox, C., Orlando, l., Enard, W., Green, R. E., Burbano, H. A., Hublin, J.-J., Hänni, C., Fortea, J., de la Rasilla, M., Bertranpetit, J., Rosas, A. and Pääbo, S. 2007 The derived *FOXP2* variant of modern humans was shared by Neandertals, *Current Biology Online Version* http://www.current-biology.com/content/article/abstract?uid=PIIS0960982207020659 Accessed 18 October 2007.

Kukla, G. J. 2000 The Last Interglacial, *Science* 287: 987–988.

Kuman, K. 1998 The earliest South African industries, in M. Petraglia and R. Korisettar (eds), *Early human behaviour in global context: The rise of diversity of the Lower Palaeolithic record*, London: Routledge Press, pp. 151–186.

Kuman, K. 2001 An Acheulean factory site with prepared core technology near Taung, South Africa. *South African Archaeological Bulletin* 173–174: 8–22.

Kuman, K. and Clarke, R. J. 1986 Florisbad: new investigations at a Middle Stone Age hominid site in South Africa, *Geoarchaeology* 1: 103–125.

Kuman, K., Field, A. S. and McNabb, A. J. 2005 La Préhistoire ancienne de l'Afrique méridionale: contribution des sites à hominids d'Afrique du Sud, in M. Sahnouni (eds.), *Le Paléolithique en Afrique: l'histoire la plus longue*, Paris: Artcom, pp. 53–82.

Kuman, K., Inbar, M. and Clarke, R. J. 1999 Paleoenvironments and cultural sequence of the Florisbad Middle Stone Age hominid site, South Africa, *Journal of Archaeological Science* 26: 1409–1425.

Kuman, K., LeBaron, J. C., and Gibbon, R. J. 2004 Earlier Stone Age archaeology and the Vhembe-Dongola National Park (South Africa) and vicinity, *Quaternary International* 120: 23–32.

Kumar, S., Filipski, A., Swarna, V., Walker, A. and Hedges, S. B. 2005 Placing confidence limits on the molecular age of the human-chimpanzee divergence, *Proceedings of the National Academy of Sciences (USA)* 102: 18842–18847.

Kuper, A. 2003 The return of the native, *Current Anthropology* 44: 389–402.

Kurashina, H. 1978 An examination of prehistoric lithic technology in East/Central Ethiopia, PhD thesis, University of California, Berkeley.

Kusimba, C. M. and Kusimba, S. B. 2005 Mosaics and interactions: East Africa, 2000 b.p. to the present, in A. B. Stahl (ed.), *African archaeology: a critical introduction*, Oxford: Blackwell Publishing, pp. 392–419.

Kusimba, S. B. 2001 The Early Later Stone Age in East Africa: excavations and lithic assemblages from Lukenya Hill, *African Archaeological Review* 18: 77–123.

2003 *African foragers: environment, technology, interactions*, Walnut Creek: AltaMira Press.

2005 What is a hunter-gatherer? Variation in the archaeological record of eastern and southern Africa, *Journal of Archaeological Research* 13: 337–366.

Kusimba, S. B. and Kusimba, C. M. 2003 Comparing prehistoric and historic hunter-gatherer mobility in southern Kenya, in C. M. Kusimba and S. B. Kusimba (eds.), *East African archaeology: foragers, potters, smiths and traders*, Philadelphia: University of Pennsylvania Museum of Archaeology and Anthropology, pp. 1–16.

Laden, G. and Wrangham, R. 2005 The rise of the hominids as an adaptive shift in fallback foods: plant underground storage organs (USOs) and australopith origins, *Journal of Human Evolution* 49: 482–498.

Lahr, M. M. 1996 The Multiregional Model of modern human origins: a reassessment of its morphological basis, *Journal of Human Evolution* 26: 23–56.

Lahr, M. M. and Foley, R. A. 1998 Toward a theory of modern human origins: geography, demography and diversity in recent human evolution, *Yearbook of Physical Anthropology* 41: 137–176.

2001 Mode 3, *Homo helmei*, and the pattern of human evolution in the Middle Pleistocene, in L. Barham and K. Robson-Brown (eds.), *Human roots: Africa and Asia in the Middle Pleistocene*, Bristol: Western Academic & Specialist Press, pp. 23–39.

Lancaster, N. J. 2002 How dry was dry? Late Pleistocene palaeoclimates in the Namib Desert, *Quaternary Science Reviews* 21: 769–782

Landsmeer, J. M. F. 1993 Evolution and the hand, in H. Preuschoft and D. J. Chivers (eds.), *Hands of primates*, London: Springer, pp. 91–108.

Lane, P. J. 2003 African archaeology in Britian: a commentary on current trends and contexts, in P. J. Mitchell, A. Haour and J. H. Hobart (eds.), *Researching Africa's past: new contributions from British archaeologists*, Oxford: Oxford University School of Archaeology, pp. 145–152.

2004 The 'moving frontier' and the transition to food production in Kenya, *Azania* 39: 243–264.

Lane, P. J., Ashley, C., Seitsonen, O., Harvey, P., Mire, S. and Odede, F. 2007 The transition to farming in Eastern Africa: new evidence from Wadh Lang'o and Usenge, Kenya, *Antiquity* 81: 62–81.

Lanfranchi, R. 1996 Une industrie MSA de stone-line en forêt dense: le site de Mokeko (Congo), in G. Pwiti and R. Soper (eds.), *Aspects of African archaeology*, Harare: University of Zimbabwe Press, pp. 165–175.

Lansdorf, E. V., Pusey, A. E. and Eberly, L. 2004 Sex differences in learning in chimpanzees, *Nature* 428: 715–716.

Lario, J., Sanchez-Moral, S., Fernández, V. M., Jimeno, A. and Menendez, M. 1997 Palaeoenvironmental evolution of the Blue Nile (central Sudan) during the Early and Mid-Holocene (Mesolithic-Neolithic transition), *Quaternary Science Reviews* 16: 583–588.

Larsson, L. 1996 The Middle Stone Age of Zimbabwe: some aspects of former research and future aims, in G. Pwiti and R. Soper (eds.), *Aspects of African archaeology*, Harare: University of Zimbabwe Press, pp. 201–206.

Lavachery, P. 1990 L'Age de la Pierre Récent au Bas-Zaire: étude du matériel lithique des missions Bequaert 1950–1952 et de Maret 1973, Mémoire de licence, Université Libre de Bruxelles.

2001 The Holocene archaeological sequence of Shum Laka rock shelter (Grassfields, western Cameroon), *African Archaeological Review* 18: 213–247.

Le Gros Clark, W. E. 1952 Anatomical studies of fossil hominoidea from Africa, in L. S. B. Leakey (ed.), *Proceedings of the Pan-African Congress on Prehistory*, Nairobi, Oxford: Basil Blackwell, pp. 111–115.

Le Quellec, J.-L. 1998 *Art rupestre et préhistoire du Sahara. Le Messak libyen*, Paris: Payot et Rivages.

Le Tensorer, J.-M. 2006 Les cultures acheuléenes et la question de l'émergence de le pensée symbolique chez *Homo erectus* à partir des données relatives à la forme symétrique et harmonique des bifaces, *Comptes Rendus Palevol* 5: 127–135.

Leakey, L. S. B. 1931 *The Stone Age cultures of Kenya Colony*, Cambridge: Cambridge University Press.

1934 The Oldoway Culture sequence, *Proceedings of the First Congress of Prehistoric and Protohistoric Sciences, London, 1932*, London: Oxford University Press, pp. 73–74.

1952 The Olorgesailie Prehistoric Site, in L. S. B. Leakey (ed.), *Proceedings of the Pan-African Congress on Prehistory, 1947*, New York: Philosophical Library, pp. 209.

Leakey, M. D. 1967 Preliminary survey of the cultural material from Beds I and II, Olduvai Gorge, Tanzania, in W. W. Bishop and J. D. Clark (eds.), *Background to evolution in Africa*, Chicago: University of Chicago Press, pp. 417–446.

1971 *Olduvai Gorge: excavations in Beds I & II, 1960–1963, Volume 3*, Cambridge: Cambridge University Press.

1983 *Africa's vanishing art: the rock paintings of Tanzania*, London: Hamish Hamilton Ltd.

Leakey, M. D., Hay, R. L., Thurber, R., Protsch, R. and Berger, R. 1972 Stratigraphy, archaeology and age of the Ndutu and Naisiusiu Beds, Olduvai Gorge, Tanzania, *World Archaeology* 3: 328–341.

Leakey, M. D. and Roe, D. A. 1994 *Olduvai Gorge, Volume 5*, Cambridge: Cambridge University Press.

Leakey, R. E. and Walker, A. 1985 Further hominids from the Plio-Pleistocene of Koobi Fora, Kenya, *American Journal of Physical Anthropology* 67: 135–163.

Leblanc, M., Favreau, G., Maley, J., Nazoumou, Y., Leduc, C., Stagnitti, F., van Oevelen, P. J., Declaux, F. and Lemoalle, J. 2006 Reconstruction of Megalake Chad using Shuttle radar topographic mission data, *Palaeogeography, Palaeoclimatology, Palaeoecology* 239: 16–27.

Lee, R. B. 1979 *The !Kung San: men, women and work in a foraging society*, Cambridge: Cambridge University Press.

2002 Solitude or servitude? Ju/'hoansi images of the colonial encounter, in S. Kent (ed.), *Ethnicity, hunter-gatherers and the "Other": association or assimilation in Africa*, Washington: Smithsonian Institution Press, pp. 184–205.

2003 *The Dobe Ju/'hoansi*, Toronto: Nelson Thomson Learning.

Lee, R. B. and DeVore, I. (eds.) 1968 *Man the hunter*, Chicago: Aldine.

(eds.) 1976 *Kalahari hunter-gatherers: studies of the !Kung San and their neighbours*, Cambridge: Harvard University Press.

Lee, R. B. and Guenther, M. G. 1993 Problems in Kalahari historical ethnography and the tolerance of error, *History in Africa* 20: 185–235.

Lee, R. B. and Hitchcock, R. K. 1998 African hunter-gatherers: history and the politics of ethnicity, in G. Connah (ed.), *Transformations in Africa: essays on Africa's later past*, Leicester: Leicester University Press, pp. 14–45.

Lee, S. H. and Wolpoff, M. H. 2003 The pattern of evolution in Pleistocene human brain size, *Paleobiology* 29: 186–196.

Lee-Thorp, J. A. 2000 Preservation of biogenic carbon isotopic signals in Plio-Pleistocene bone and tooth enamel, in S. H. Ambrose and M. A. Katzenberg (eds.), *Biogeochemical approaches to paleodietary analysis*, New York: Kluwer Academic/Plenum Press, pp. 89–115.

Lee-Thorp, J. A., Sealy, J. C. and Morris, A. G. 1993 Isotopic evidence for diets of prehistoric farmers in South Africa, in J. B. Lambert and G. Grupe (eds.), *Prehistoric human bone: archaeology at the molecular level*, Berlin: Springer Verlag, pp. 99–120.

Lee-Thorp, J. A., Sealy, J. C. and van der Merwe, N. J. 1989 Stable carbon isotope ratio differences between bone collagen and bone apatite, and their relationship to diet, *Journal of Archaeological Science* 16: 585–599.

Lee-Thorp, J. A., Thackeray, J. F. and van der Merwe, N. J. 2000 The hunters and the hunted revisited, *Journal of Human Evolution* 39: 565–576.

Lee-Thorp, J. A., van der Merwe, N. J. and Brain, C. K. 1994 Diet of *Australopithecus robustus* and associated fauna from Swartkrans, *Journal of Human Evolution* 27: 361–372.

Lefèvre, D., Raynal, J.-P., Texier, J.-P., and Graoui, M. 1999. Où l'océan rencontre le continent, in J. P. Raynal, F. Z. Sbihi-Alaoui and A. El Hajraoui (eds.), *Maroc terre d'origines*, Le Puy-en-Velay: CDERAD, pp. 15–17.

Leibenberg, L. 2006 Persistence hunting by modern hunter-gatherers. *Current Anthropology* 47: 1017–1026.

Leigh, S. R. 2006 Brain ontogeny and life history in *Homo erectus*, *Journal of Human Evolution* 50: 104–108.

Lejju, B. J., Robertshaw, P. and Taylor, D. 2006 Africa's earliest bananas? *Journal of Archaeological Science* 33: 102–113.

Leonard, W. R. and Robertson, M. L. 1992 Nutritional requirements and human evolution: a bioenergetics model, *American Journal of Human Biology* 4: 179–195.

Leslie, M. and Maggs, T. M.O'C. (eds.) 2000 African naissance: the Limpopo Valley 1000 years ago, *South African Archaeological Society Goodwin Series* 8: 1–126.

Lewin, R. and Foley, R. 2004 *Principles of human evolution*, Oxford: Blackwells.

Lewis, J. W. 2006 Cortical networks related to human use of tools, *The Neuroscientist* 12: 211–231.

Lewis-Williams, J. D. 1981 *Believing and seeing: symbolic meanings in southern San rock paintings*, New York: Academic Press.

1982 The economic and social context of southern San rock art, *Current Anthropology* 23: 429–449.

1984 Ideological continuities in prehistoric southern Africa: the evidence of rock art, in C. Schrire (ed.), *Past and present in hunter-gatherer studies*, New York: Academic Press, pp. 225–252.

1986 Beyond style and portrait: a comparison of Tanzanian and southern African rock art, in R. Vossen and K. Keuthmann (eds.), *Contemporary studies on Khoisan 2*, Hamburg: Helmut Buske Verlag, pp. 95–139.

1990 Documentation, analysis and interpretation: dilemmas in rock art research, *South African Archaeological Bulletin* 45: 126–136.

1992 Ethnographic evidence relating to 'trance' and 'shamans' among Northern and Southern Bushmen, *South African Archaeological Bulletin* 47: 56–60.

1993 Southern African archaeology in the 1990s, *South African Archaeological Bulletin* 48: 45–50.

1996 'A visit to the Lion's house': the structure, metaphors and sociopolitical significance of a Nineteenth Century Bushman myth, in J. Deacon and T. A. Dowson (eds.), *Voices from the past: /Xam Bushmen and the Bleek and Lloyd collection*, Johannesburg: Witwatersrand University Press, pp. 122–141.

1998 *Quanto?*: the issue of many meanings in southern African San rock art research, *South African Archaeological Bulletin* 53: 86–97.

2002 *The mind in the cave: consciousness and the origins of art*, London: Thames and Hudson.

2003 *A cosmos in stone: interpreting religion and society through rock art*, Walnut Creek: AltaMira Press.

Lewis-Williams, J. D. and Biesele, M. 1978 Eland hunting rituals among northern and southern San groups: striking similarities, *Africa* 48: 117–134.

Lewis-Williams, J. D., Blundell, G., Challis, W. and Hampson, J. 2000 Threads of light: re-examining a motif in southern African San rock art, *South African Archaeological Bulletin* 55: 123–126.

Lewis-Williams, J. D. and Dowson, T. A. 1990 Through the veil: San rock paintings and the rock face, *South African Archaeological Bulletin* 45: 5–16.

1999 *Images of power: understanding Bushman rock art*, Johannesburg: Southern Books.

Lewis-Williams, J. D. and Loubser, J. N. H. 1986 Deceptive appearances: a critique of southern African rock art studies, *Advances in World Archaeology* 5: 253–289.

Lewis-Williams, J. D. and Pearce, D. G. 2004 *San spirituality: roots, expression and social consequences*, Walnut Creek: AltaMira Press.

2005 *Inside the Neolithic mind*, London: Thames and Hudson.

Lézine, A-M. and Vergaud-Grazzini, C. 1994 Evidence of forest extension in west Africa since 22,000 BP: a pollen record from the eastern tropical Atlantic, *Quaternary Science Reviews* 12: 203–210.

Lhote, H. 1959 *The search for the Tassili frescoes: the story of the prehistoric rock-paintings of the Sahara*, London: Hutchinson.

Lieberman, D. E., McBratney, B. M. and Krovitz, G. 2002 The evolution and development of cranial form in *Homo, Proceedings of the National Academy of Sciences (USA)* 99: 1134–1139.

Lim, I. 1992 A site-oriented approach to rock art: a study from Usandawe, PhD thesis, Brown University.

Linares de Sapir, O. 1971 Shell middens of Lower Casamance and problems of Diola protohistory, *West African Journal of Archaeology* 1: 23–54.

Liu, T., Ding, Z. and Rutter, N. 1999 Comparison of Milankovitch periods between continental loess and deep sea records over the last 2.5 Ma, *Quaternary Science Reviews* 18: 1205–1212.

Liubin, V. P. and Guédé, F. Y. 2000 *Paleolit Respubliki Kot d'Ivuar (Zapadnaya Afrika) (The Palaeolithic of the Republic of Côte d'Ivoire (West Africa))*. St. Petersburg: Russian Academy of Sciences, Institute of the History of Material Culture Proceedings, Volume 3.

Liverani, M., Cremaschi, M. and Di Lernia, S. 2000 The "archaeological park" of the Tadrart Acacus and Messak Setafet (south-western Fezzan, Libya), *Sahara* 12: 121–140.

Livingstone Smith, A. 2001 Pottery manufacturing processes: reconstruction and interpretation, in E. A. A. Garcea (ed.), *Uan Tabu in the settlement history of the Libyan Sahara*, Firenze: All'Insegna del Giglio, pp. 113–152.

Lombard, M. 2005a The Howiesons Poort of South Africa: what we know, what we think we know, what we need to know, *Southern African Humanities* 17: 33–55.

2005b Evidence of hunting and hafting during the Middle Stone Age at Sibudu Cave, KwaZulu-Natal, South Africa: a multianalytical approach, *Journal of Human Evolution* 48: 279–300.

2007 Finding resolution for the Howiesons Poort through the microscope: micro-residue analysis of segments from Sibudu Cave, South Africa, *Journal of Archaeological Science* 34: 1–16.

Lordkipanidze, D., Jashashvili, T., Vekua, A., Ponce de León, M. S., Zollikofer, C. P. E., Rightmire, G. P., Pontzer, H., Ferring, R., Oms, O., Tappen, M., Bukhsianidze, M., Agusti, J., Kahlke, R., Kiladze, G., Martinez-Navarro, B., Mouskhelishvili, A., Nioradze, M., and Rook, L. 2007 Postcranial evidence from early *Homo* from Dmanisi, Georgia. *Nature* 449: 305–310.

Loubser, J. N. H. and Laurens, G. 1994 Depictions of domestic ungulates and shields: hunter/gatherers and agro-pastoralists in the Caledon River Valley area, in T. A. Dowson and J. D. Lewis-Williams (eds.), *Contested images: diversity in southern African rock art research*, Johannesburg: Witwatersrand University Press, pp. 83–118.

Lourandos, H. 1983 Intensification. A late Pleistocene-Holocene archaeological sequence from southwestern Victoria, *Archaeology in Oceania* 18: 81–94.

1997 *Continent of hunter-gatherers: new perspectives in Australian prehistory*, Cambridge: Cambridge University Press.

Lovejoy, O. 1981 The origin of man, *Science* 211: 341–350.

Lowe, J. J. and Walker, M. J. C. 1984 *Reconstructing Quaternary environments.* London: Longman.

Loy, T. H. 1998 Organic residues on Oldowan tools from Sterkfontein Cave, South Africa, in M. A. Raath, H. Soodyall, K. L. K. D. Barkhan and P. V. Tobias (eds.), *Dual Congress of the International Association for the Study of Human Paleontology, and International Association of Human Biologists,* Johannesburg: University of the Witwatersrand Medical School, pp. 74–75.

Lubbock, J 1865 *Prehistoric times,* London: Williams and Norgate.

Lubell, D. 2000 Late Pleistocene-Early Holocene Maghreb, in P. N. Peregrine and M. Ember (eds.), *The Encyclopaedia of Prehistory, Volume 1 Africa,* New York: Plenum Press, pp. 129–149.

    2005 Continuité et changement dans l'Epipaléolithique du Maghreb, in M. Sahnouni (ed.), *Le Paléolithique en Afrique: l'histoire la plus longue,* Paris: Artcom, pp. 205–226.

Lubell, D., Sheppard, P. and Gilman, A. 1991 The Maghreb II, in R. W. Ehrich (ed.), *Chronologies in Old World archaeology,* Chicago: University of Chicago Press, pp. 257–267.

Lubell, D., Sheppard, P. and Jackes, M. 1984 Continuity in the Epipalaeolithic of northern Africa with emphasis on the Maghreb, *Advances in World Archaeology* 3: 143–191.

Lucas, P. W. 2004 *Dental functional morphology: how teeth work.* Cambridge: Cambridge University Press.

Ludwig, B. V. and Harris, J. W. K. 1998 Towards a technological reassessment of East African Plio-Pleistocene lithic assemblages, in M. Petraglia and R. Korissetar (eds.), *Early human behavior in the global context: the rise and diversity of the Lower Paleolithic Period,* New York: Routledge, pp. 84–107.

Luke, D. A. & Lucas, P. W. 1983 The significance of cusps. *Journal of Oral Rehabilitation* 10: 197–206.

Lutz, R. and Lutz, G. 1995 *The secret of the desert: the rock art of the Messak Sattafet and Messak Mellet, Libya,* Innsbruck: Golf Verlag.

Luyt, C. J., and Lee-Thorp, J. A. 2003 Carbon isotope ratios of Sterkfontein fossils indicate a marked shift to open environments c. 1.7 myr ago. *South African Journal of Science* 99: 271–273.

Mabulla, A. 2000 Strategy for cultural heritage management (CHM) in Africa: a case study, *African Archaeological Review* 17: 211–233.

    2003 Archaeological implications of Hadzabe forager land use in the Eyasi Basin, Tanzania, in C. M. Kusimba and S. B. Kusimba (eds.), *East African archaeology: foragers, potters, smiths and traders,* Philadelphia: University of Pennsylvania Museum of Archaeology and Anthropology, pp. 33–58.

    2005 The rock art of Mara region, Tanzania, *Azania* 40: 19–42.

Macaulay, V., Hill, C., Achilli, A., Rengo, C., Clarke, D., Meehan, W., Blackburn, J., Semino, O., Scozzari, R., Cruciani, F., Taha, A., Kassim Shaari, N., Maripa Raja, J., Ismail, P., Zainuddin, Z., Goodwin, W., Bulbeck, D., Bandelt, H.-J., Oppenheimer, S., Torroni, A. and Richards, M. 2005

Single, rapid coastal settlement of Asia revealed by analysis of complete mithochondrial genomes, *Science* 308: 1034–1036.

MacDonald, K. C. 1997 Kourounkorokalé revisited: the Pays Mande and the West African microlithic technocomplex, *African Archaeological Review* 14: 161–200.

1998 Archaeology, language, and the peopling of West Africa: a consideration of the evidence, in R. M. Blench and M. Spriggs (eds.), *Archaeology and language Volume II,* London: Routledge, pp. 33–66.

MacDonald, K. C. and Allsworth-Jones, P. 1994 A reconsideration of the West African macrolithic conundrum: new factory sites from the Malian Sahel, *African Archaeological Review* 12: 71–102.

MacEachern, S. 2000 Genes, tribes and African history, *Current Anthropology* 41: 357–384.

MacLarnon, A. M. and Hewitt, G. P. 1999 The evolution of human speech: the role of enhanced breathing control, *American Journal of Physical Anthropology* 109: 341–363.

Magid, A. A. and Caneva, I. 1998 Exploitation of food plants in the early Holocene central Sudan: a reconsideration, in S. di Lernia and G. Manzi (eds.), *Before food production in North Africa,* Forlí: ABACO, pp. 79–89.

Magori, C. C. and Day, M. H. 1983 Laetoli Hominid 18: an early *Homo sapiens* skull, *Journal of Human Evolution* 12: 747–753.

Maitima, J. W. 1991 Pollen records from the Lake Victoria region, *Quaternary Research* 35: 234–245.

Maley, J. 1977 Palaeoclimates of the central Sahara during the early Holocene, *Nature* 269: 573–577.

1996 The African rain forest – main characteristics of changes in vegetation and climate from the Upper Cretaceous to the Quaternary, *Proceedings of the Royal Society of Edinburgh* 104B: 31–73.

2002 A catastrophic destruction of African forests about 2500 years ago still exerts a major influence on present vegetation formations, *Institute of Development Studies Bulletin* 33: 13–30.

Maley, J. and Brenac, P. 1998 Vegetation dynamics, palaeoenvironments and climatic change in the forests of western Cameroon during the last 28000 years B.P., *Review of Palaeobotany and Palynology* 99: 157–187.

Maley, J. and Chepstow-Lusty, A. 2001 *Elaeis guineensis* Jacq. (oil palm) fluctuations in Central Africa during the late Holocene: climate or human driving forces for this pioneering species? *Vegetation History and Archaeobotany* 10: 117–120.

Manega, P. C. 1993 Geochronology, geochemistry and isotopic study of the Plio-Pleistocene hominid sites and the Ngorongoro volcanic highland in northern Tanzania, PhD thesis, University of Colorado, Boulder.

Manzi, G. 2004 Human evolution at the Matuyama-Brunhes boundary, *Evolutionary Anthropology* 13: 11–24.

Manzi, G., Bruner, E. and Passarello, P. 2003 The one-million-year-old *Homo* cranium form Bouri (Ethiopia): a reconsideration of its *H. erectus* affinities, *Journal of Human Evolution* 44: 731–736.

Marchant, L. F. and McGrew, W. C. 2005 Percussive technology: chimpanzee baobab smashing and the evolutionary modelling of hominin knapping, in V. Roux and B. Brill (eds.), *Stone knapping: the necessary condition for a uniquely hominin behaviour*, Cambridge: McDonald Institute Monographs, pp. 341–350.

Marean, C. W. 1990 Late Quaternary palaeoenvironments and faunal exploitation in East Africa, PhD thesis, University of California, Berkeley.

1992a Implications of Late Quaternary mammalian fauna from Lukenya Hill (south-central Kenya) for palaeoenvironmental change and faunal extinction, *Quaternary Research* 37: 239–255.

1992b Hunter to herder: large mammal remains from the hunter-gatherer occupation at Enkapune ya Muto rock-shelter, Central Rift, Kenya, *African Archaeological Review* 10: 65–128.

1997 Hunter-gatherer foraging strategies in tropical grasslands: model building and testing in the East African Middle and Later Stone Age, *Journal of Anthropological Archaeology* 16: 189–225.

Marean, C. W. and Gifford-Gonzalez, D. 1991 Late Quaternary extinct ungulates of East Africa and palaeoenvironmental implications, *Nature* 350: 418–420.

Marean, C. W., Nilssen, P. J., Brown, K., Jerardino, A. and Stynder, D. 2004 Paleoanthropological investigations of Middle Stone Age sites at Pinnacle Point, Mossel Bay (South Africa): archaeology and hominid remains from the 2000 field season, *PaleoAnthropology* 5(2): 14–83.

Marean, C.W, Bar-Matthews, M., Bernatchez, J., Fisher, E., Goldberg, P., Herries, A. I. R., Jacobs, Z., and Jerardi, A. 2007 Early human use of marine resources and pigment in South Africa during the Middle Pleistocene, *Nature* 449: 905–908.

Marks, A. E. 1983 The Middle to Upper Palaeolithic transition in the Levant, *Advances in World Archaeology* 2: 51–98.

1987 Terminal Pleistocene and Holocene hunters and gatherers in the eastern Sudan, *African Archaeological Review* 5: 79–92.

Marlowe, F. W. 2005 Hunter-gatherers and human evolution, *Evolutionary Anthropology* 14: 54–67.

Marlowe, P. 2002 Why the Hadza are still hunter-gatherers, in S. Kent (ed.), *Ethnicity, hunter-gatherers and the "Other": association or assimilation in Africa*, Washington: Smithsonian Institution Press, pp. 247–275.

Marret, F., Soucrse, J., Jansen, J. H. F. and Schneider, R. 1999 Climate and palaeoceanographic changes in west Central Africa during the last deglaciation: palynological investigation, *Comptes Rendus de l'Academie des Sciences Série II Fascicule A-Sciences de la Terre et des Planètes* 329: 721–726.

Marret, F., Maley, J. and Scourse, J. 2006 Climatic instability in west equatorial Africa during the Mid- and Late Holocene, *Quaternary International* 150: 71–81.

Marshack, A. 1991 *The roots of civilization*, Mount Kisco: Moyer Bell Ltd.

1997 The Berekhat Ram figurine: a late Acheulian carving from the Middle East, *Antiquity* 71: 327–337.

Marshall, F. B. 1990 Origins of specialized pastoral production in East Africa, *American Anthropologist* 92: 873–894.

Marshall, F. B. and Hildebrand, E. 2002 Cattle before crops: the beginnings of food production in Africa, *Journal of World Prehistory* 16: 99–143.

Marshall, J. and Ritchie, C. 1984 *Where are the Bushmen of Nyae Nyae? Changes in a Bushman society, 1958–1981*, Cape Town: University of Cape Town Centre for African Studies.

Martin, P.S and Klein, R. G. (eds.) 1984 *Quaternary extinctions: a prehistoric revolution*, Tucson: Arizona University Press.

Martínez-Navarro, B., and Palmqvist, P. 1995 Presence of the African machairodont *Megantereon whitei* (Broom, 1937) (Felidae, Carnivora, Mammalia) in the Lower Pleistocene site of Venta Micena (Orce, Granada, Spain), with some considerations on the origin, evolution and dispersal of the genus, *Journal of Archaeological Science* 22: 569–582.

Martínez-Navarro, B., Turq, A., Agustí Ballester, J., and Oms, O. 1997 Fuente Nueva-3 (Orce, Granada, Spain) and the first human occupation of Europe. *Journal of Human Evolution* 33: 611–620.

Marzke, M. W. 1997 Precision grips, hand morphology and tools, *American Journal of Physical Anthropology* 102: 91–110.

Marzke, M. W. and Marzke, R. F. 2000 Evolution of the human hand: approaches to acquiring, analysing and interpreting the anatomical evidence, *Journal of Anatomy* 197: 121–140.

Marzke, M. W. and Shackley, M. S. 1986 Hominid hand use in the Pliocene and Pleistocene: evidence from experimental archaeology and comparative morphology, *Journal of Human Evolution* 15: 439–460.

Marzke, M. W., Toth, N., Schick, K., Reece, S., Steinberg, B., Hunt, K., Linscheid, R. L. and An, K-N. 1998 EMG study of hand muscle recruitment during hard hammer percussion manufacture of Oldowan tools, *American Journal of Physical Anthropology* 1005: 315–332.

Masao, F. T. 1979 *The Later Stone Age and the rock paintings of central Tanzania*, Wiesbaden: Franz Steiner Verlag.

Mason, R. J. 1988 *Cave of Hearths, Makapansgat, Transvaal.* Johannesburg: Archaeological Resesarch Unit, University of Witwatersrand, Occasional Paper No. 21.

Mauny, R. 1955 Contribution à l'étude du Paléolithique au Mauritanie, *Proceedings of the Second Pan-African Congress of Prehistory*, pp. 461–479.

Mazel, A. D. 1983 Eland, rhebuck and cranes: identifying seasonality in the paintings of the Drakensberg, *South African Archaeological Society Goodwin Series* 4: 34–37.

1987 The archaeological past from the changing present: towards a critical assessment of South African Later Stone Age studies from the early 1960's to the early 1980's, in J. E. Parkington and M. Hall (eds.), *Papers in the prehistory of the Western Cape, South Africa*, Oxford: British Archaeological Reports, pp. 504–529.

1989 People making history: the last ten thousand years of hunter-gatherer communities in the Thukela Basin, *Natal Museum Journal of Humanities* 1: 1–168.

1992 Early pottery from the eastern part of southern Africa, *South African Archaeological Bulletin* 47: 3–7.

1999 iNkolimahashi Shelter: the excavation of Later Stone Age rock shelter deposits in the central Thukela Basin, KwaZulu-Natal, South Africa, *Natal Museum Journal of Humanities* 11: 1–21.

Mazel, A. D. and Watchman, A. L. 2003 Dating rock paintings in the uKhahlamba-Drakensberg and the Biggarsberg, KwaZulu-Natal, South Africa, *Southern African Humanities* 15: 59–73.

Mbida, C. M., Doutrelepont, H., Vrydaghs, L., Swennen, R. L., Swennen, R. J., Beeckman, H., de Langhe, E. and de Maret, P. 2004 Yes, there were bananas in Cameroon more than 2000 years ago, *InfoMusa* 13: 40–42.

Mbida, C. M., van Neer, W., Doutrelepont, H. and Vrydaghs, L. 2000 Evidence for banana cultivation and animal husbandry during the first millennium B.C. in the forest of southern Cameroon, *Journal of Archaeological Science* 27: 151–162.

McBrearty, S. 1988 The Sangoan-Lupemban and Middle Stone Age sequence at the Muguruk site, western Kenya, *World Archaeology* 19: 388–420.

2001 The Middle Pleistocene of east Africa, in L. S. Barham and K. Robson-Brown (eds.), *Human roots: Africa and Asia in the Middle Pleistocene*, Bristol: Western Academic and Specialist Press, pp. 81–98.

2003 Patterns of technological change at the origin of *Homo sapiens*, *Before Farming* [print version] 3(9): 22–26.

McBrearty, S. and Brooks, A. S. 2000 The revolution that wasn't: a new interpretation of the origin of modern human behaviour, *Journal of Human Evolution* 39: 453–563.

McBrearty, S. and Jablonski, N. G. 2005 First fossil chimpanzee, *Nature* 437: 105–108.

McBurney, C. B. M. 1967 *The Haua Fteah (Cyrenaica) and the Stone Age of the south-east Mediterranean*, Cambridge: Cambridge University Press.

McCall, D. F. 1998 The Afroasiatic language phylum: African in origins or Asian? *Current Anthropology* 39: 139–144.

McCall, G. S. 2006 Multivariate perspectives on change and continuity in the Middle Stone Age lithics from Klasies River Mouth, South Africa, *Journal of Human Evolution* 51: 429–439.

McClure, H. 1994 A new Arabian stone tool assemblage and notes on the Aterian industry of North Africa, *Arabian Archaeology and Epigraphy* 5: 1–16.

McDermott, F., Stringer, C., Grün, R., Williams, C. T., Din, V. and Hawkesworth, C. 1996 New Late-Pleistocene uranium-thorium and ESR dates for the Singa hominid (Sudan), *Journal of Human Evolution* 31: 507–516.

McDonald, M. M. A. 1991 Systematic reworking of lithics from earlier cultures in the early Holocene of Dakhleh Oasis, Egypt, *Journal of Field Archaeology* 18: 269–273.

1998 Early African pastoralism: view from Dakhleh Oasis (south central Egypt), *Journal of Anthropological Archaeology* 17: 124–142.

2003 The early Holocene Masara A and Masara C cultural sub-units of Dakhleh Oasis, within a wider cultural setting, in G. E. Brown and C. A. Hope (eds.), *The Oasis papers 3: Proceedings of the Third International Conference of the Dakhleh Oasis Project*, Oxford: Oxbow Books, pp. 43–69.

2007 Twilight of the microlith in the Late Epipalaeolithic of North East Africa? Locality 268 in Dakhleh Oasis, Egypt, *Journal of African Archaeology* 5: 79–90.

McDougall, I. and Brown, F. H. 2006 Precise $^{40}$Ar/$^{39}$Ar geochronology for the upper Koobi Fora Formation, Turkana Basin, northern Kenya, *Journal of the Geological Society London* 163: 205–220.

McDougall, I., Brown, F. H. and Fleagle, J. G. 2005 Stratigraphic placement and age of modern humans from Kibish, Ethiopia, *Nature* 433: 733–736.

McGrew, W. C. 2004a *The cultured chimpanzee: reflections on cultural primatology*, Cambridge: Cambridge University Press.

2004b Primatology: advanced ape technology, *Current Biology* 14: R1046–R1047.

McIntosh, R. J. 1998 *Peoples of the Middle Niger*, Oxford: Blackwell Publishing.

McIntosh, S. K. (ed.) 1999 *Beyond chiefdoms: pathways to complexity in Africa*, Cambridge: Cambridge University Press.

McIntosh, S. K. and McIntosh, R. J. 1986 Recent archaeological research and dates from West Africa, *Journal of African History* 27: 413–442.

McManus, J. F., Oppo, D. W. and Cullen, J. L. 1999 A 0.5–million-year record of millennial scale climate variability in the North Atlantic, *Science* 283: 971–975.

McNabb, J. 2001 The shape of things to come. A speculative essay on the role of the Victoria West phenomenon at Canteen Koppie, during the South African Earlier Stone Age, in S. Milliken and J. Cook (eds.), *A very remote period indeed: papers on the Palaeolithic presented to Derek Roe*, Oxford: Oxbow Books, pp. 37–46.

McNabb, J. and Ashton, N. M. 1995 Thoughtful flakers, *Cambridge Archaeological Journal* 5: 289–298.

McNabb, J., Binyon, F. and Hazelwood, L. 2004 The large cutting tools from the South African Acheulean and the question of social traditions, *Current Anthropology* 45: 653–677.

McPherron, S. P. 2000 Handaxes as a measure of the mental capabilities of early hominids, *Journal of Archaeological Science* 27: 655–663.

Meadows, J., Barclay, A., and Bayliss, A. 2007 A short passage of time: the dating of the Hazelton Long Cairn revisited, *Cambridge Archaeological Journal* 17: 45–64.

Mehlman, M. J. 1977 Excavations at Nasera Rock, Tanzania, *Azania* 12: 111–118.

1979 Mumba-Höhle revisited: the relevance of a forgotten excavation to some current issues in East African prehistory, *World Archaeology* 11: 80–94.

1987 Provenience, age and associations of archaic *Homo sapiens* crania from Lake Eyasi, Tanzania, *Journal of Archaeological Science* 14:133–162.

1989 Late Quaternary archaeological sequences in northern Tanzania, PhD thesis, University of Illinois, Urbana.

1991 Context for the emergence of modern man in eastern Africa: some new Tanzanian evidence, in J. D. Clark (ed.), *Cultural beginnings*, Bonn: Dr Rudolf Habelt GMBH, pp. 177–196.

Mellars, P. A. 1996 *The Neanderthal legacy: an archaeological perspective from western Europe*, Princeton: Princeton University Press.

2005 The impossible coincidence. A single-species model for the origins of modern human behaviour, *Evolutionary Anthropology* 14: 12–27.

2006 Why did modern human populations disperse from Africa ca. 60,000 years ago? A new model, *Proceedings of the National Academy of Sciences (USA)* 103: 9381–9386.

Menotti-Raymond, M. and O'Brien, S. J. 1993 Dating the genetic bottleneck of the African cheetah, *Proceedings of the National Academy of Sciences (USA)* 90: 3172–3176.

Mercader, J. 2003a Introduction, in J. Mercader (ed.), *Under the canopy: the archaeology of tropical rain forests*, London: Routledge, pp. 1–31.

2003b Foragers of the Congo: the early settlement of the Ituri Forest, in J. Mercader (ed.), *Under the canopy: the archaeology of tropical rain forests*, London: Routledge, pp. 93–115.

(ed.) 2003c *Under the canopy: the archaeology of tropical rain forests*, London: Routledge.

Mercader, J., Barton, H., Gillespie, J., Harris, J., Kuhn, S., Tyler, R., and Boesch, C. 2007 4,300-year-old chimpanzee sites and the origins of percussive stone technology, *Proceedings of the National Academy of Sciences (USA)* 104: 3043–3048.

Mercader, J. and Brooks, A. S. 2001 Across the forest and savannas: Later Stone Age assemblages from Ituri and Semliki, Democratic Republic of Congo, *Journal of Anthropological Research* 57: 197–217.

Mercader, J., Garcia-Heras, M. and Gonzalez-Alvarez, I. 2000b Ceramic tradition in the African forest: characterisation analysis of ancient and modern pottery from Ituri, D. R. Congo, *Journal of Archaeological Science* 27: 163–182.

Mercader, J., Garralada, M. D., Pearson, O. M. and Bailey, R. C. 2001 Eight hundred-year-old human remains from the Ituri tropical forest, Democratic Republic of Congo: the rock shelter site of Matangai Turu Northwest, *American Journal of Physical Anthropology* 115: 24–37.

Mercader, J. and Martí, R. 2003 The Middle Stone Age occupation of Atlantic Central Africa: new evidence from Equatorial Guinea and Cameroon, in J. Mercader (ed.), *Under the canopy: the archaeology of tropical rain forests*, London: Routledge, pp. 64–92.

Mercader, J., Panger, M. A. and Boesch, C. 2002 Excavation of a chimpanzee stone tool site in the African rainforest, *Science* 296: 1452–1455.

Mercader, J., Rovira, S. and Gómez-Ramos, P. 2000c Forager-farmer interaction and ancient iron metallurgy in the Ituri rainforest, Democratic Republic of Congo, *Azania* 25: 107–122.

Mercader, J., Runge, F., Vrydaghs, L., Doutrelepont, H., Corneille, E. and Juan, J. 2000a Phytoliths from archaeological sites in the tropical forest of Ituri, Democratic Republic of Congo, *Quaternary Research* 54: 102–112.

Mercuri, A. M. 1999 Palynological analysis of the Early Holocene sequence, in S. di Lernia (ed.), *The Uan Afuda Cave. Hunter-gatherer societies of the Central Sahara*, Firenze: Edizioni all'Insegna del Giglio, pp. 149–181.

2001 Preliminary analysis of fruits and seeds from the Early Holocene sequence, in E. A. A. Garcea (ed.), *Uan Tabu in the settlement history of the Libyan Sahara*, Firenze: All'Insegna del Giglio, pp. 189–210.

Merrick, H. V. 1975 Change in later Pleistocene lithic industries in eastern Africa, PhD thesis, University of California, Berkeley.

Merrick, H. V. and Brown, F. H. 1984 Obsidian sources and patterns of source utilization in Kenya and northern Tanzania: some initial findings, *African Archaeological Review* 2: 129–152.

Merrick, H. V., Brown, F. H. and Nash, W. P. 1994 Use and movement of obsidian in the Early and Middle Stone Ages of Kenya and northern Tanzania, in S. T. Childs (ed.), *Society, culture and technology in Africa*, Philadelphia: MASCA, pp. 29–44.

Merrick H. V. and Merrick, J. P. S. 1976 Archaeological occurrences of earlier Pleistocene age from the Shungura Formation, in Y. Coppens, F. C. Howell, G. Ll. Isaac and R. E. F. Leakey (eds.), *Earliest man and environments in the Lake Rudolf Basin*, Chicago: University of Chicago Press, pp. 574–584.

Meskell, l. 2005 Recognition, restitution and the potentials of postcolonial liberalism for South African heritage, *South African Archaeological Bulletin* 60: 72–78.

Metz, G. 1994 Working with comunities in Botswana, in B. Krafchik (ed.), *The South African Museum and its public: negotiating partnerships*, Cape Town: South African Museum, pp. 11–14.

Mguni, S. 2006 King's monuments: identifying 'formlings' in southern African San rock paintings, *Antiquity* 80: 583–598.

Millard, A. R 2006. Bayesian analysis of ESR dates, with application to Border Cave. *Quaternary Geochronology* 1: 159–166.

Miller, G. H., Beaumont, P. B., Deacon, H. J., Brooks, A. S., Hare, P. E. and Jull, A. J. T. 1999 Earliest modern humans in southern Africa dated by isoleucine epimerization in ostrich eggshell, *Quaternary Science Reviews* 18: 1537–1548.

Miller, S. E. F. 1969a The Nachikufan industries of the Later Stone Age in Zambia, Ph.D. thesis, University of California, Berkeley.

1969b Contacts between the Later Stone Age and the Early Iron Age in south central Africa, *Azania* 4: 81–90.

1971 The age of the Nachikufan industries in Zambia, *South African Archaeological Bulletin* 26: 143–146.

Milliken, S. 2003 *Catalogue of Palaeolithic artefacts from Egypt in the Pitt Rivers Museum*, Oxford: British Archaeological Reports.

Milo, R. G. 1998 Evidence for hominid predation at Klasies River Mouth, South Africa, and its implications for the behaviour of early modern humans, *Journal of Archaeological Science* 25: 99–133.

Minichillo, T. 2006 Raw material use and behavioral modernity: Howiesons Poort lithic foraging strategies, *Journal of Human Evolution* 50: 359–364.

Minichillo, T. and Marean, C. W. 2000 Behavioral ecological modelling and faunal resource use in the Middle and Later Stone Age of southern Africa, *Journal of Human Evolution* 38: A22.

Minozzi, S., Manzi, G., Ricci, F., di Lernia, S. and Borgognini Tarli, S. M. 2003 Nonalimentary tooth use in prehistory: an example from the early Holocene in the central Sahara (Uan Muhuggiag, Tadrart Acacus, Libya), *American Journal of Physical Anthropology* 120: 225–232.

Mishmar, D., Ruiz-Pesini, E., Golik, P., Macaulay, V., Clark, A. G., Hosseini, S., Brandon, M., Easley, K., Chen, E., Brown, M. D., Sukernik, R. I., Olckers, A. and Wallace, D. C. 2003 Natural selection shaped regional mtDNA variation in humans, *Proceedings of the National Academy of Sciences (USA)* 100: 171–176.

Mitchell, P. J. 1994 Understanding the MSA/LSA transition: the pre-20,000 BP assemblages from new excavations at Sehonghong Rock Shelter, Lesotho, *Southern African Field Archaeology* 3: 15–25.

1995 Revisiting the Robberg: new results and a revision of old ideas at Sehonghong Rock Shelter, Lesotho, *South African Archaeological Bulletin* 50: 28–38.

1996 Prehistoric exchange and interaction in southeastern southern Africa: marine shells and ostrich eggshell, *African Archaeological Review* 13: 35–76.

2000 The organization of Later Stone Age lithic technology in the Caledon Valley, southern Africa, *African Archaeological Review* 17: 141–176.

2001 Andrew Anderson and the nineteenth century development of archaeology in southern Africa, *Southern African Humanities* 13: 37–60.

2002a *The archaeology of southern Africa*, Cambridge: Cambridge University Press.

2002b Catalogue of the Southern African Stone Age collections of the British Museum, *British Museum Occasional Papers* 108: 1–232.

2003 Anyone for *hxaro*? Thoughts on the theory and practice of exchange in southern African Later Stone Age archaeology, in P. J. Mitchell, A. Haour and J. H. Hobart (eds.), *Researching Africa's past: new perspectives from British archaeologists*, Oxford: Oxford University School of Archaeology, pp. 35–43.

2004 Reflections on the spread of food production in southernmost Africa, *Before Farming* [print version] 3: 212–225.

2005a Why hunter-gatherer archaeology matters: a personal perspective on renaissance and renewal in southern African Later Stone Age research, *South African Archaeological Bulletin* 60: 64–71.

2005b *African connections: archaeological perspectives on Africa and the wider world*, Walnut Creek: AltaMira Press.

Mitchell, P. J. and Whitelaw, G. 2005 The archaeology of southernmost Africa *c*. 2000 BP to the early 1800s: a review of recent research, *Journal of African History* 46: 209–241.

Mithen, S. 1994 Technology and society during the Middle Pleistocene: hominid group size, social learning, and industrial variability, *Cambridge Archaeological Journal* 3: 3–36.

2003 *After the ice*, London: Weidenfeld and Nicholson.

Moggi-Cecchi, J. and Collard, M. 2002 A fossil stapes from Sterkfontein, South Africa, and the hearing capabilities of early hominids, *Journal of Human Evolution* 42: 259–265.

Mohammed-Ali, A. S. and Khabir, A. M. 2003 The wavy line and dotted wavy line pottery in the prehistory of the Central Nile and the Sahara-Sahel Belt, *African Archaeological Review* 20: 25–558.

Mohapi, L. 2007 Rose Cottage Cave MSA lithic points: does technological change imply change in hunting techniques, *South African Archaeological Bulletin* 62: 9–18.

Mora, R. and de la Torre, I. 2005 Percussion tools in Olduvai Beds I and II (Tanzania): implications for early human activities, *Journal of Anthropological Archaeology* 24: 179–192.

Morel, J. 1974 La station eponyme de l'Oued Djebbana à Bir-el-Ater (Est algérien), contribution à la connaissance de son industrie et de sa faune, *L'Anthropologie* 78: 53–80.

Mori, F. 1998 *The great civilizations of the ancient Sahara*, Turin: Einaudi.

Mori, F., Ponti, R., Messina, A., Flieger, M., Havlicek, V. and Sinibaldi, M. 2006 Chemical characterization and AMS radiocarbon dating of the binder of a prehistoric rock pictograph at Tadrart Acacus, southern west Libya, *Journal of Cultural Heritage* 7: 344–349.

Morris, A. G. 2003 The myth of the East African 'Bushmen,' *South African Archaeological Bulletin* 58: 85–90.

Morris, D. 1988 Engraved in place and time: a review of variability in the rock art of the northern Cape and Karoo, *South African Archaeological Bulletin* 43: 109–120.

Mountain, J. L., Herbert, J. M., Bhattacharyya, S., Underhill, P. A., Ottolenghi, C., Gadgil, M. and Cavalli-Sforza, L. L. 1995 Demographic history of India and mtDNA-sequence diversity, *American Journal of Human Genetics* 56: 979–992.

Mowaljarlai, D., Vinnicombe, P., Ward, G. K. and Chippindale, C. 1988 Repainting images on rock in Australia and the maintenance of aboriginal culture, *Antiquity* 62: 690–696.

Mulvaney, D. J. 1991 Past regained, future lost: the Kow Swamp Pleistocene burials, *Antiquity* 65: 12–21.

Musiba, C. and Mabulla, A. 2004 Politics, cattle and conservation: Ngorongoro Crater at a crossroads, in C. M. Kusimba and S. B. Kusimba (eds.), *East African archaeology: foragers, potters, smiths and traders*, Philadelphia: University of Pennsylvania Museum of Archaeology and Anthropology, pp. 133–148.

Musonda, F. B. 1984 Late Pleistocene and Holocene microlithic industries from the Lunsemfwa Basin, Zambia, *South African Archaeological Bulletin* 39: 24–36.

1987 The significance of pottery in Zambian Later Stone Age contexts, *African Archaeological Review* 5: 147–158.

Mutundu, K. 1999 *Ethnohistoric archaeology of the Mukogodo in north-central Kenya: hunter-gatherer subsistence and the transition to pastoralism in secondary settings*, Oxford: British Archaeological Reports.

Muzzolini, A. 1993 Chronologie raisonnée des diverses écoles d'art rupestre du Sahara central, in G. Calegari (ed.), *L'arte e ambiente del Sahara preistorico. I dati e interpretazioni*, Milan: Società Italiana di Scienze Naturali e Museo Civico di Storia Naturale di Milano, pp. 387–397.

Napier, J. R. 1960 Studies of the hands of living primates, *Proceedings of the Zoological Society of London* 134: 647–657.

1962 The evolution of the hand, *Scientific American* 207: 56–62.

Ndagala, D. K. 1988 Free or doomed? Images of the Hadzabe hunters and gatherers, in T. Ingold, D. Riches and J. Woodburn (eds.), *Hunters and gatherers: Volume 1, History, evolution and social change*, Oxford: Berg, pp. 65–72.

Negash, A., Shackeley, M. S. and Alene, M. 2006 Source provenance of obsidian artefacts from the Early Stone Age (ESA) site of Melka Konture, Ethiopia, *Journal of Archaeological Science* 33: 1647–1650.

Nelson, C. M. and Posnansky, M. 1970 The stone tools from the re-excavation of Nsongezi Rock Shelter, *Azania* 5:119–172.

Nenquin, J. 1967 *Contributions to the study of the prehistoric cultures of Rwanda and Burundi*, Tervuren: Musée Royal de l'Afrique Centrale.

Neumann, K. 1989 Zur Vegetationsgeschichte der Ostsahara in Holozän. Holzkohlen aus Prähistorischen Fundstellen, *Africa Praehistorica* 2: 13–181.

2005 The romance of farming: plant cultivation and domestication in Africa, in A. B. Stahl (ed.), *African archaeology: a critical introduction*, Oxford: Blackwell Publishing, pp. 249–275.

Nishimura, T., Mikami, A., Suzuki, J. and Matsuzawa, T. 2006 Descent of the hyoid in chimpanzees: evolution of face flattening and speech, *Journal of Human Evolution* 51: 244–254.

Nogwaza, T. 1994 Early Iron Age pottery from Canasta Place, East London District, *Southern African Field Archaeology* 3: 103–106.

Noli, D. and Avery, G. 1988 Protein poisoning and coastal subsistence, *Journal of Archaeological Science* 15: 395–401.

Noll, M. P. and Petraglia, M. D. 2003 Acheulean bifaces and early human behavioral patterns in East Africa and South India, in M. Sorressi and H. L. Dibble (eds.), *Multiple approaches to the study of bifacial technologies*, Philadelphia: University Museum Monograph 115, pp. 31–53.

Noonan, J. P., Coop, G., Kudaravalli, S., Smith, D., Krause, J., Alessi, J., Chen, F., Platt, D., Pääbo, S., Pritchard, J. K. and Rubin, E. M. 2006 Sequencing and analysis of Neanderthal genomic DNA, *Science* 314: 1113–1118.

Nyerere, J. 1967 *Socialism and development*, Dar es-Salaam: Government Printer.

Nygaard, S. and Talbot, M. 1984 Stone Age archaeology and environment on the southern Accra plains, Ghana, *Norwegian Archaeological Review* 17: 19–38.

Nyong, A. 2005 The economic, developmental and livelihood implications of climate induced depletion of ecosystems and biodiversity in Africa, http://www.wwf.org.uk/news/n_0000001454.as. Site accessed 14 July 2005.

Oakley, K. P. 1956 (3rd ed) *Man the tool-maker* London: British Museum.

O'Connell, J. F. and Allen, F. J. 2004 Dating the colonization of Sahul (Pleistocene Australia-New Guinea): a review of recent research, *Journal of Archaeological Science* 31: 835–853.

O'Connell, J. F., Hawkes, K. and Blurton-Jones, N. G. 1988 Hadza scavenging: implications for Plio-Pleistocene hominid subsistence, *Current Anthropology* 29: 356–363.

   1999 Grandmothering and the evolution of *Homo erectus*, *Journal of Human Evolution* 36: 461–485.

O'Connell, J. F., Hawkes, K., Lupo, K. D. and Blurton Jones, N. G. 2002 Male strategies and Plio-Pleistocene archaeology, *Journal of Human Evolution* 43: 831–872.

O'Connor, D. 1993 Urbanism in Bronze Age Egypt and northeast Africa, in T. Shaw, P. Sinclair, B. Andah and A. Okpoko (eds.), *The archaeology of Africa: food, metals and towns*, New York: Routledge, pp. 570–586.

O'Connor, P. W. and Thomas, D. S. G. 1999 The timing and environmental significance of Late Quaternary linear dune development in western Zambia, *Quaternary Research* 52: 44–55.

O'Connor, S. 2007 New evidence from East Timor contributes to our understanding of earliest modern human colonisation east of the Sunda Shelf, *Antiquity* 81: 523–535.

Ogiek 2006 http://www.ogiek.org/. Site accessed 10 July 2006.

Olivieri, A., Achilli, A., Pala, M., Battaglia, V., Fornarino, S., Al-Zahery, N., Scozzari, R., Cruciani, F., Behar, D. M., Dugoujon, J.-M., Coudray, C., Santachiara-Benerecetti, A. S., Semino, O., Bandelt, H.-J. and Torroni, A. 2006 The mtDNA legacy of the Levantine Early Upper Palaeolithic in Africa, *Science* 314: 1767–1770.

O'Malley, R. C. and Fedigan, L. 2005 Variability in food-processing behaviour among white-faced capuchins (*Cebus capucinus*) in Santa Rosa National Park, Costa Rica, *American Journal of Physical Anthropology* 128: 68–73.

Oppenheimer, C. 2002 Limited global change due to the largest known Quaternary eruption, Toba ≈ 74 kyr? *Quaternary Science Reviews* 21: 1593–1609.

Oppenheimer, S. 2004 *Out of Eden: the peopling of the world*, London: Constable and Robinson.

Opperman, H. 1987 *The Later Stone Age of the Drakensberg Range and its foothills*, Oxford: British Archaeological Reports.

Opperman, H. and Heydenrych, B. 1990 A 22,000 year old Middle Stone Age camp site with plant food remains from the north-eastern Cape, *South African Archaeological Bulletin* 45: 93–99.

Organ, J. M., Teaford, M. F. and Larsen, C. S. 2005 Dietary inferences from dental occlusal microwear at Mission San Luis de Apalachee, *American Journal of Physical Anthropology* 128: 801–811.

Orpen, J. M. 1874 A glimpse into the mythology of the Maluti Bushmen, *Cape Monthly Magazine* 9: 1–13.

Orton, J. 2002 Patterns in stone: the lithic assemblage from Dunefield Midden, Western Cape, South Africa, *South African Archaeological Bulletin* 57: 31–37.

Orton, J. and Compton, J. S. 2006 A reworked mid-Holocene lithic assemblage at Dunefield Midden 1, Elands Bay, South Africa, *South African Archaeological Bulletin* 61: 90–95.

Outram, A. K. 2000 Hunting meat and scavenging marrow? A seasonal explanation for the Middle Stone Age subsistence strategies at Klasies River Mouth, in A. Rowley-Conwy (ed.), *Animal bones: human societies*, Oxford: Oxbow Books, pp. 20–27.

Ouzman, S. 1995 The fish, the shaman and the peregrination: San rock art paintings of Mormyrid fish as religious and social metaphors, *Southern African Field Archaeology* 4: 3–17.

   1997 Between margin and centre: the archaeology of southern African bored stones, in L. Wadley (ed.), *Our gendered past: archaeological studies of gender in southern Africa*, Johannesburg: Witwatersrand University Press, pp. 71–106.

Ouzman, S. and Wadley, L. 1997 A history in paint and stone from Rose Cottage Cave, South Africa, *Antiquity* 71: 386–404.

Owen, R. B., Barthelme, J. W., Renault, B. W. and Vincens, A. 1982 Palaeolimnology and archaeology of Holocene deposits north-east of Lake Turkana, Kenya, *Nature* 298: 523–529.

Owen, W. E. 1938 The Kombewa Culture, Kenya Colony, *Man* 38: 203–205.

Pachur, H.-J. and Altmann, N. 1997 The Quaternary (Holocene, *ca.* 8,000 yrs BP), in H. Schandelmeier and P.-O. Reynolds (eds.), *Palaeogeographic-palaeotectonic atlas of north-eastern Africa, Arabia and adjacent areas*, Rotterdam: A.A Balkema, pp. 111–125.

Panger, M. A., Brooks, A. S., Richmond, B. G. and Wood, B. 2002 Older than the Oldowan? Rethinking the emergence of hominin tool use, *Evolutionary Anthropology* 11: 235–245.

Panter-Brick, C. 2002 Sexual division of labor: energetic and evolutionary scenarios, *American Journal of Human Biology* 4: 627–640.

Pardoe, C. 1988 The cemetery as symbol: the distribution of prehistoric Aboriginal burial grounds in southeastern Australia, *Archaeology in Oceania* 23: 1–16.

Parkington, J. E. 1977 Follow the San, PhD thesis, University of Cambridge.

   1980 Time and place: some observations on spatial and temporal patterning in the Later Stone Age sequence in southern Africa, *South African Archaeological Bulletin* 35: 75–83.

   1984 Soaqua and Bushmen: hunters and robbers, in C. Schrire (ed.), *Past and present in hunter-gatherer studies*, Orlando: Academic Press, pp. 151–174.

1986 Landscape and subsistence changes since the Last Glacial Maximum along the western Cape coast, in L. G. Straus (ed.), *The end of the Palaeolithic in the Old World*, Oxford: British Archaeological Reports, pp. 201–227.

1988 The Pleistocene/Holocene transition in the western Cape, South Africa: observations from Verlorenvlei, in J. Bower and D. Lubell (eds.), *Prehistoric cultures and environments in the late Quaternary of Africa*, Oxford: British Archaeological Reports, pp. 349–363.

1989 Interpreting paintings without a commentary, *Antiquity* 63: 13–26.

1990a A critique of the consensus view on the age of Howieson's Poort assemblages in South Africa, in P. A. Mellars (ed.), *The emergence of modern humans*, Edinburgh: Edinburgh University Press. pp. 34–55.

1990b A view from the south: southern Africa before, during and after the Last Glacial Maximum, in C. S. Gamble and O. Soffer (eds.), *The World at 18,000 BP, Volume II low latitudes*, London: Unwin Hyman, pp. 214–228.

1991 Approaches to dietary reconstruction in the Western Cape: are you what you have eaten? *Journal of Archaeological Science* 18: 331–342.

1992 Making sense of sequence at the Elands Bay Cave, western Cape, South Africa, in A. B. Smith and B. Mütti (eds.), *Guide to archaeological sites in the southwestern Cape*, Cape Town: Southern African Association of Archaeologists, pp. 6–12.

1993 The neglected alternative: historical narrative rather than cultural labelling, *South African Archaeological Bulletin* 48: 94–97.

1996 What is an eland? N!ao and the politics of age and sex in the paintings of the Western Cape, in P. Skotnes (ed.), *Miscast: negotiating the politics of the Bushmen*, Cape Town: University of Cape Town Press, pp. 281–290.

1998 Resolving the past: gender in the Stone Age archaeological record of the Western Cape, in S. Kent (ed.), *Gender in African prehistory*, Walnut Creek: Altamira Press, pp. 25–38.

2001 Mobility, seasonality and southern African hunter-gatherers, *South African Archaeological Bulletin* 56: 1–7.

2003a *Cederberg rock paintings*, Cape Town: Krakadouw Trust.

2003b Eland and therianthropes in southern African rock art: when is a person an animal? *African Archaeological Review* 20: 135–148.

2006a Africa's creative explosion, in G. Blundell (ed.), *Origins: the story of the emergence of humans and humanity in Africa*, Cape Town: DoubleStorey, pp. 66–117.

2006b *Shorelines, strandlopers and shell middens*, Cape Town: Cresta Communications.

Parkington, J. E. and Fisher, J. W. 2006 Small mammal bones on Later Stone Age sites from the Cape (South Africa): consumption and ritual events, *Archaeological Papers of the American Anthropological Association* 16: 71–79.

Parkington, J. E., Nilssen, P., Reeler, C. and Henshilwood, C. 1992 Making sense of space at Dunefield Midden campsite, western Cape, South Africa, *Southern African Field Archaeology* 1: 63–70.

Parkington, J. E. and Poggenpoel, C. A. 1971 Excavations at De Hangen 1968, *South African Archaeological Bulletin* 26: 3–36.

Parkington, J. E., Poggenpoel, C. A., Buchanan, W., Robey, T., Manhire, A. H. and Sealy, J. C. 1987 Holocene coastal settlement patterns in the western Cape, in G. N. Bailey and J. E. Parkington (eds.), *The archaeology of prehistoric coastlines*, Cambridge: Cambridge University Press, pp. 22–41.

Parkington, J. E., Poggenpoel, C. A., Rigaud, J.-P. and Texier, P.-J. 2005 From tool to symbol: the behavioural context of intentionally marked ostrich eggshell from Diepkloof, Western Cape, in F. d'Errico and L. Backwell (eds.), *From tools to symbols: from early hominins to modern humans*, Johannesburg: Witwatersrand University Press, pp. 475–492.

Parsons, I. 2003 Lithic expressions of Later Stone Age lifeways in the Northern Cape Province, South Africa, *South African Archaeological Bulletin* 58: 33–37.

Parsons, I. and Badenhorst, S. 2004 Analysis of lesions generated by replicated Middle Stone Age lithic points on selected skeletal elements, *South African Journal of Science* 100: 384–387.

Partridge, T. C. 2000 Hominid-bearing cave and tufa deposits, in T. C. Partridge and R. R. Maud (eds.), *The Cenozoic of Southern Africa*, New York: Oxford University Press, pp. 100–129.

Partridge, T. C., Avery, D. M., Botha, G. A., Brink, J. S., Deacon, J., Herbert, R. S., Maud, R. R., Scholtz, A., Scott, L., Talma, A. S. and Vogel, J. C. 1990 Late Pleistocene and Holocene climate change in southern Africa, *South African Journal of Science* 86: 302–306.

Partridge, T. C., deMenocal, P. B., Lorentz, S. A., Paiker, M. J. and Vogel, J. C. 1997 Orbital forcing of climate over South Africa: a 200,000 year rainfall record from the Pretoria Saltpan, *Quaternary Science Review* 16: 1125–1133.

Partridge, T. C., Granger, D. E., Caffee, M. W., and Clarke, R. J. 2003 Lower Pliocene hominid remains from Sterkfontein, *Science* 300: 607–612.

Paulissen E. 1989 The inundations of the Saharan Nile around 12,500 BP: unique catastrophic floods of an exotic river, *Abstracts of papers, Second International Conference on Geomorphology, Frankfurt/Main 1989, Geoko-plus*, p. 216.

Paulissen, E. and Vermeersch, P. M. 1987 Earth, man and climate in the Egyptian Nile Valley during the Pleistocene, in A. E. Close (ed.), *Prehistory of arid North Africa: essays in honour of Fred Wendorf*, Dallas: Southern Methodist University Press, pp. 29–67.

Peace Parks Foundation 2006 http://www.peaceparks.org. Site accessed 4 October 2006.

Pearce, D. G. 2005 Iconography and interpretation of the Tierkloof painted stone, *South African Archaeological Society Goodwin Series* 9: 45–53.

Pearson, O. M. 2000a Appendix 8: human remains from Twin Rivers, in L. Barham, *The Middle Stone Age of Zambia, south central Africa*, Bristol: Western Academic & Specialist Press, pp. 281–282.

2000b Postcranial remains and the origin of modern humans, *Evolutionary Anthropology* 9: 229–247.

2004 Has the combination of genetic and fossil evidence solved the riddle of modern human origins? *Evolutionary Anthropology* 13: 145–159.

Pearson, O. M., and Grine, F. 1997 Re-analysis of the hominid radii from Cave of Hearths and Klasies River Mouth, South Africa. *Journal of Human Evolution* 32: 577–592.

Pearson, O. M., Grine, F., Barham, L. and Stringer, C. 2000 Human remains from the Middle and Later Stone Age of Mumbwa Caves, in L. Barham, *The Middle Stone Age of Zambia, south central Africa*, Bristol: Western Academic & Specialist Press, pp. 149–164.

Peck, J. A., Green, R. R., Shanahan, T., King, J. W., Overpeck, J. T. and Scholz, C. A. 2004 A magnetic mineral record of Late Quaternary tropical climate variability from Lake Bosumtwi, Ghana, *Palaeogeography, Palaeoclimatology, Palaeoecology* 215: 37–57.

Peters, C. and Rowlett, R. M. 1999 *Koobi Fora*, Oxford: Oxford University Press.

Peters, C. R. and Vogel, J. C. 2005 Africa's wild $C_4$ plant foods and possible early hominid diets, *Journal of Human Evolution* 48: 219–236.

Peters, J. 1989 Late Pleistocene hunter-gatherers at Ishango (eastern Zaire): the faunal evidence, *Revue de Paléobiologie* 9: 73–112.

Peters, J., Gautier, A. and Brink, J. S. 1994 Late Quaternary extinction of ungulates in sub-Saharan Africa: a reductionist's approach, *Journal of Archaeological Science* 21: 17–28.

Petit-Maire, N. (ed.) 1979 *Le Sahara atlantique à l'Holocène, peuplement et écologie*, Algiers: CRAPE.

  1991 Recent Quaternary climatic change and man in the Sahara, *Journal of African Earth Sciences* 12: 125–132.

Petit-Maire, N., Celles, J. C., Commelin, D., Delibrias, G. and Raimbault, M. 1983 The Sahara in northern Mali: man and his environment between 10,000 and 3500 years bp (Preliminary results), *African Archaeological Review* 1: 105–126.

Petraglia, M. D., Shipton, C. and Paddayya, K. 2005 Life and mind in the Acheulean: a case study from India, in C. Gamble and M. Porr (eds.), *The individual hominid in context: archaeological investigations of Lower and Middle Pleistocene landscape, locales, and artefacts*, London: Routledge, pp. 197–219.

Phaladi, S. 1998 The organisation of archaeology, in P. J. Lane, D. A. M. Reid and A. K. Segobye (eds.), *Ditswa mmung: the archaeology of Botswana*, Gaborone: The Botswana Society, pp. 233–239.

Phillipson, D. W. 1976 *The later prehistory of Zambia*, Nairobi: British Institute in Eastern Africa.

  1977a The excavation of Gobedra rock-shelter, Axum: an early occurrence of cultivated finger millet in northern Ethiopia, *Azania* 12: 53–82.

  1977b Lowasera, *Azania* 12: 1–32.

  1982 The Later Stone Age in sub-Saharan Africa, in J. D. Clark (ed.), *Cambridge history of Africa Volume I: from the earliest times to c. 500 B.C.*, Cambridge: Cambridge University Press, pp. 410–477.

  1984 Aspects of early food production in northern Kenya, in L. Krzyzaniak (ed.), *Origins and early development of food-producing cultures in northeastern Africa*, Poznán: Polish Academy of Sciences, pp. 489–495.

  2005 *African archaeology*, Cambridge: Cambridge University Press.

Phillipson, L. 1975 Survey of the Stone Age archaeology of the Upper Zambezi Valley: I. The northern part of the valley, *Azania* 10: 1–48.

1976 Survey of the Stone Age archaeology of the Upper Zambezi Valley: II. Excavations at Kandanda, *Azania* 11: 49–82.

1978 *The later prehistory of the upper Zambezi Valley*, Nairobi: British Institute in Eastern Africa.

Pickering, T., White, T. D. and Toth, N. 2000 Cutmarks on a Plio-Pleistocene hominid from Sterkfontein, South Africa, *American Journal of Physical Anthropology* 111: 579–584.

Pickford, M. 2001 'Millennium Ancestor,' a 6-million-year-old bipedal hominid from Kenya, *South African Journal of Science* 97: 22.

Pike, A. W. G. and Pettitt, P. B. 2003 U-series dating and human evolution, *Reviews in Mineralogy and Geochemistry* 52: 607–629.

Pikirayi, I. 2001 *The Zimbabwe Culture: origins and decline of southern Zambezian states*, Walnut Creek: AltaMira Press.

Plagnol, V. and Wall, J. D. 2006 Possible ancestral structure in human populations, *PloS Genetics* 2: e105.

Pleurdeau, D. 2006 Human technical behaviour in the African Middle Stone Age: the lithic assemblage of Porc-Epic Cave (Dire Dawa, Ethiopia), *African Archaeological Review* 22: 177–197.

Plummer, T. 2004 Flaked stones and old bones: biological and cultural evolution at the dawn of technology, *Yearbook of Physical Anthropology* 47: 11–164.

Plummer, T., Ferraro, J., Ditchfield, P., Bishop, L. and Potts, R. 2001 Pliocene Oldowan excavations at Kanjera South, Kenya, *Antiquity* 75: 809–810.

Poggenpoel, C. A. 1987 The implications of fish bone assemblages from Eland's Bay Cave, Tortoise Cave and Diepkloof for changes in the Holocene history of the Verlorenvlei, in J. E. Parkington and M. Hall (eds.), *Papers in the prehistory of the western Cape, South Africa*, Oxford: British Archaeological Reports, pp. 212–236.

Popovich, D. G., Jenkins, D. J. A., Kendall, C. W. C., Dierenfeld, E. S., Carroll, R. W., Tariq, N. and Vidgen, E. 1997 The western lowland gorilla diet has implications for the health of humans and other hominoids, *Journal of Nutrition* 127: 2000–2005.

Posnansky, M. 1984 Early agricultural societies in Ghana, in J. D. Clark and S. A. Brandt (eds.), *From hunters to farmers: the causes and consequences of food production in Africa*, Berkeley: University of California Press, pp. 147–151.

Potts, R. 1988 *Early hominid activities at Olduvai*, New York: Aldine de Gruyter.

1991 Why the Oldowan? Plio-Pleistocene toolmaking and the transport of resources, *Journal of Anthropological Research* 47: 153–176.

1996 *Humanity's descent: the consequences of ecological instability*. New York: Avon.

1998 Variability selection in hominid evolution, *Evolutionary Anthropology* 7: 81–96.

2001 Mid-Pleistocene environmental change and human evolution, in L. S. Barham and K. Robson-Brown (eds.), *Human roots: Africa and Asia in the Middle Pleistocene*, Bristol: Western Academic & Specialist Press, pp. 5–21.

Potts, R., Behrensmeyer, A. K. and Ditchfield, P. 1999 Paleolandscape variation and Early Pleistocene hominid activities: Members 1 and 7, Olorgesailie Formation, Kenya, *Journal of Human Evolution* 37: 747–788.

Potts, R., Behrensmeyer, A. K., Deino, A., Ditchfield, P., and Clark, J. 2004 Small Mid-Pleistocene hominin Associated with East African Acheulean technology, *Science* 305: 75–78.

Potts, R. and Deino, A. R. 1995 Mid-Pleistocene change in large mammal faunas of the southern Kenya rift, *Quaternary Research* 43: 106–113.

Prat, S., Brugal, J-P., Tiercelin, J-J., Barrat, J-A., Bohn, M., Delagnes, A., Harmand, S., Kimeu, K., Kibunjia, M., Texier, P-J. and Roche, H. 2005 First occurrence of early *Homo* in the Nachukui Formation (West Turkana, Kenya) at 2.3–2.4 myr., *Journal of Human Evolution* 49: 230–240.

Preutz, J. D., and Bertolani, P. 2007. Savanna chimpanzees, *Pan troglodytes verus*, hunt with tools, *Current Biology* 17: 412–417.

Price, T. D. and Brown, J. A. (eds.) 1985 *Complex hunter-gatherers*, New York: Academic Press.

Price, T. D. and Feinman, G. 2006. *Images of the past*, London: McGraw-Hill.

Prugnolle, F., Manica, A. and Balloux, F. 2005 Geography predicts neutral genetic diversity of human populations, *Current Biology* 15: R159–R160.

Przeworski, M., Hudson, R. R. and Di Rienzo, A. 2000 Adjusting the focus on human variation, *Trends in Genetics* 16: 296–302.

Pycraft, W. P. 1928 Description of the human remains, in F. A. Bather (ed.), *Rhodesian Man and associated remains*, London: British Museum (Natural History), pp. 1–51.

Quade, J., Semaw, S., Stout, D., Renne, P., Rogers, M. and Simpson, S. 2004 Paleoenvironments of the earliest stone toolmakers, Gona, Ethiopia, *Geological Society of America Bulletin* 116: 1529–1544.

Quintana-Murci, L., Semino, O., Bandelt, H.-J., Passarino, G., McElreavey, K. and Santachiara-Benerecetti, A. S. 1999 Genetic evidence of an early exit of *Homo sapiens sapiens* from Africa through eastern Africa, *Nature Genetics* 23: 437–441.

Rahmani, N. 2002 *Le Capsien typique et le Capsien supérieur, évolution ou contemporanéité? Les données technologiques*, Oxford: British Archaeological Reports.

2004 Technological and cultural change among the last hunter-gatherers of the Maghreb: the Capsian (10,000–6000 B. P.), *Journal of World Prehistory* 18: 57–105.

Ramakrishnan, U. and Mountain, J. L. 2004 Precision and accuracy of divergence time estimates from STR and SNPSTR variation, *Molecular Biology and Evolution* 21: 1960–1971.

Rampino, M. R. and Ambrose, S. H. 2000 Volcanic winter in the Garden of Eden: the Toba supereruption and the late Pleistocene human population crash, *Geological Society of America Special Paper* 345: 71–82.

Rando, J. C., Pinto, F., González, A. M., Hernández, M., Larruga, J. M., Cabrera, V. M. and Bandelt, H.-J. 1998 Mitochondrial DNA analysis of northwest African populations reveals genetic exchanges with European, Near-Eastern and sub-Saharan populations, *Annals of Human Genetics* 62: 531–550.

RASSSA 2001 *Regional assessment of the status of the San in southern Africa, Volumes 1–5*, Windhoek: Legal Assistance Centre.

Ravisé, A. 1970 Une industrie néolithique en os de la région de St Louis, Sénégal, *Notes Africaines* 128: 97–102.

Ray, N., Currat, M., Berthier, P. and Excoffier, L. 2005. Recovering the geographic origin of early modern humans by realistic and spatially explicit simulations, *Genome Research* 15: 1161–1167.

Raynal, J-P., Geraads, D., Magoga, L., El Hajraoui, A., Texier, J-P., Lefevre, D. and Sbihi-Alaoui, F. Z. 1993 La Grotte des Rhinocéros (Carrière Oulad Hamida 1, anciennement Thomas III, Casablanca), nouveau site acheuléen du Maroc atlantique, *Comptes Rendus de l'Academie des Sciences* 316: 1477–1483.

Raynal, J.-P., Sbihi-Alaouti, F.-Z., Geraads, D., Magoga, L., and Mohib, A. 2001. The earliest occupation of North-Africa: the Moroccan perspective, *Quaternary International* 75: 65–75.

Raynal, J.-P., Sbihi-Alaoui, F.,-Z., Magoga, L., Mohib, A., and Zouak, M. 2002. Casablanca and the earliest occupation of North Atlantic Morocco, *Quaternaire* 13: 65–77.

Reader, J. 1988 *Missing links: the hunt for earliest man*, Harmondsworth: Penguin.

Reader, S. M. and Laland, K. N. 2002 Social intelligence, innovation and enhanced brain size in primates, *Proceedings of the National Academy of Sciences, U. S. A.* 99: 4436–4441.

Reck, H. 1914 Erste Vorläufige Mitteilung über den Fund eines fossilen Menschenskelets auz Zentral-afrika, *Sitzungsberichte der Gesselschaft Naturforschender Freunde* 3: 81–95.

Reed, F. A. and Tishkoff, S. A. 2006 African human diversity, origins and migrations, *Current Opinion in Genetics and Development* 16: 597–605.

Reid, D. A. M. 2005 Interaction, marginalization and the archaeology of the Kalahari, in A. B. Stahl (ed.), *African archaeology: a critical introduction*, Oxford: Blackwell Publishing, pp. 353–377.

Relethford, J. H. 2001 *Genetics and the search for modern human origins*, New York: Wiley-Liss.

Renne, P. R., Sharp, W. D., Deino, A. L., Orsi, G., and Civetta, L. 1997 $^{40}$Ar/$^{39}$Ar Dating into the historical realm: calibration against Pliny the Younger. *Science* 277: 1279–1280.

Reygasse, M. 1922 Etudes de paléthnologie maghrébine (deuxième serie), *Recueil des Notes et Mémoires de la Société Archéologique de Constantine* 53: 159–204.

Ribot, I, Orban, R. and de Maret, P. 2001 *The prehistoric burials of Shum Laka Rockshelter (northwest Cameroon)*, Tervuren: Musée Royal de l'Afrique Centrale.

Richards, M., Macaulay, V., Carracedo, A. and Salas, A. 2004 The archaeogenetics of the Bantu dispersals, in M. Jones (ed.), *Traces of ancestry: studies in honour of Colin Renfrew*, Oxford: Oxbow Press, pp. 75–88.

Richardson, J. L. 1972 Palaeolimnological records from Rift lakes in central Kenya, *Palaeoecology of Africa* 6: 131–136.

Richerson, P. J., Boyd, R. and Bettinger, R. L. 2001 Was agriculture impossible during the Pleistocene but mandatory during the Holocene? A climate change hypothesis, *American Antiquity* 66: 387–411.

Richerson, P. J., and Boyd, R. 2005 *Not by genes alone: how culture transformed human evolution*, Chicago: University of Chicago Press.

Richter, J. 2002 The giraffe people: Namibia's prehistoric artists, in Jennerstrasse 8, *Tides of the desert. Contributions to the archaeology and environmental history of Africa in honour of Rudolph Kuper*, Köln: Heinrich-Barth Institut, pp. 523–534.

Ridings, J. 1996 Where in the world does obsidian hydration dating work? *American Antiquity* 61: 136–148.

Rigaud, J.-P., Texier, J.-P., Parkington, J. E. & Poggenpoel, C. A. 2006 Le mobilier Stillbay et Howiesons Poort de l'abri Diepkloof. La chronologie du *Middle Stone Age* sud-africain et ses implications, *Comptes Rendus Palevol* 5: 839–849.

Rightmire, G. P. 1984 Human skeletal remains from eastern Africa, in J. D. Clark and S. Brandt (eds.), *From hunters to farmers: the causes and consequences of food production in Africa*, Berkeley: University of California Press, pp. 191–199.

2001 Comparison of Middle Pleistocene hominids from Africa and Asia, in L. Barham and K. Robson-Brown (eds.), *Human roots: Africa and Asia in the Middle Pleistocene*, Bristol: Western Academic & Specialist Press, pp. 123–147.

2004 Brain size and encephalization in early to mid-Pleistocene *Homo*, *American Journal of Physical Anthropology* 124: 109–123.

Rightmire, G. P. and Deacon, H. J. 1991 Comparative studies of Late Pleistocene human remains from Klasies River Mouth, South Africa, *Journal of Human Evolution* 20: 131–156.

2001 New human teeth from Middle Stone Age deposits at Klasies River, South Africa, *Journal of Human Evolution* 41: 535–544.

Rightmire, P., Lordkipanidze, D., Vekua, A. 2006 Anatomical descriptions, comparative studies and evolutionary significance of the hominin skulls from Dmanisi, Republic of Georgia. *Journal of Human Evolution* 50: 115–141.

Ritchie, J. C. 1994 Holocene pollen spectra from Oyo, northwestern Sahara: problems of interpretation in a hyperarid environment, *The Holocene* 4: 9–15.

Robbins, L. H. 1974 *The Lothagam site: a Later Stone Age fishing settlement in the Lake Rudolf Basin, Kenya*, East Lansing: Michigan State University Museum Anthropological Series.

1990 The Depression site: a Stone Age sequence in the northwest Kalahari Desert, Botswana, *National Geographic Research* 6: 329–338.

1999 Direct dating of worked ostrich eggshell in the Kalahari, *Nyame Akuma* 52: 11–16.

Robbins, L. H., Campbell, A. C., Murphy, M. L., Brook, G. A., Srivastava, P. and Badenhorst, S. 2005 The advent of herding in southern Africa:

early AMS dates on domestic livestock from the Kalahari Desert, *Current Anthropology* 46: 671–677.

Robbins, L. H., McFarlin, S. A., Brower, J. L. and Hoffman, A. E. 1977 Rangi: a Late Stone Age site in Karamoja District, Uganda, *Azania* 12: 209–233.

Robbins, L. H., Murphy, M. L., Brook, G. A., Ivester, A. H., Campbell, A. C., Klein, R. G., Milo, R. G., Stewart, K. M., Downey, W. S. and Stevens, N. J. 2000 Archaeology, palaeoenvironment and chronology of the Tsodilo Hills White Paintings Rock Shelter, northwest Kalahari Desert, Botswana, *Journal of Archaeological Science* 27: 1085–1113.

Robbins, L. H., Murphy, M. L., Campbell, A. C., Brook, G. A., Reid D. M., Haberyan, K. H. and Downey, W. S. 1998a Test excavation and reconnaissance palaeoenvironmental work at Toteng, Botswana, *South African Archaeological Bulletin* 53: 125–132.

Robbins, L. H., Murphy, M. L., Campbell, A. C. and Brook, G. A. 1998b Intensive mining of specular haematite in the Kalahari, *ca.* AD 800–1000, *Current Anthropology* 39: 144–150.

Robbins, L. H., Murphy, M. L., Stevens, N. J., Brook, G. A., Ivester, A. H., Haberyan, K. A., Klein, R. G., Milo, R., Stewart, K. M., Matthiesen, D. G. and Winkler, A. J. 1996 Paleoenvironment and archaeology of Drotsky's Cave western Kalahari Desert, Botswana, *Journal of Archaeological Science* 23: 7–22.

Robert, A., Soriano, S., Rasse, M., Stokes, S. and Huysecom, E. 2003 First chrono-cultural reference framework for the West African Palaeolithic: new data from Ounjougou, Dogon Country, Mali, *Journal of African Archaeology* 1: 151–170.

Roberts, A. F. 1984 "Fishers of men": religion and political economy among colonized Tabwa, *Africa* 54(2): 49–70.

Roberts, R. H., Jones, R. and Smith, M. A. 1994 Beyond the radiocarbon barrier in Australian prehistory: a critique of Allen's commentary, *Antiquity* 68: 611–616.

Robertshaw, P. T. (ed.) 1990a *A history of African archaeology*, London: James Currey.

1990b The development of archaeology in East Africa, in P. T. Robertshaw (ed.), *A history of African archaeology*, London: James Currey, pp. 78–94.

1990c *Early pastoralists in southwestern Kenya*, Nairobi: British Institute in Eastern Africa.

1991 Gogo Falls: a complex site east of Lake Victoria, *Azania* 26: 63–195.

1999 Seeking and keeping power in Bunyoro-Kitara, Uganda, in S. K. McIntosh (ed.), *Beyond chiefdoms: Pathways to complexity in Africa*, Cambridge: Cambridge University Press, pp. 124–135.

Robertshaw, P. T., Collett, D. P., Gifford, D. and Mbae, N. B. 1983 Shell middens on the shores of Lake Victoria, *Azania* 18: 1–44.

Robertshaw, P. T. and Mawson, A. 1981 Excavations in eastern Equatoria, southern Sudan, 1980, *Azania* 16: 55–96.

Robins, S. 2001 NGOs, 'Bushmen' and double vision: the Khomani San land claim and the cultural politics of 'community' and 'development' in the Kalahari, *Journal of Southern African Studies* 27: 833–853.

Robinson, J. T. 1954 The genera and species of the Australopithecinae, *American Journal of Physical Anthropology* 12: 181–200.

Roche, H. 2000 Variability of Pliocene lithic productions in East Africa, *Acta Archaeologia Sinica* 19: 98–103.

Roche H., Brugal J.-P., Delagnes A., Feibel C., Harmand S., Kibunjia M., Prat S. and Texier P.-J. 2003 Les sites archéologiques plio-pléistocènes de la Formation de Nachukui (Ouest Turkana, Kenya): bilan préliminaire 1996–2000, *Comptes Rendus Palévol* 2(8): 663–673.

Roche, H., Brugal, J.-P., Lefevre, D., Ploux, S. and Texier, P.-J. 1988 Isenya: état des recherches sur un nouveau site acheuléen d'Afrique orientale, *African Archaeological Review* 6: 27–55.

Roe, D. A. 1968 British Lower and Middle Palaeolithic handaxe groups, *Proceedings of the Prehistoric Society* 34: 1–82.

Rogers, M. J., Harris, J. W. K. and Feibel, C. S. 1994 Changing patterns of land use by Plio-Pleistocene hominids in the Lake Turkana Basin, *Journal of Human Evolution* 27: 139–158.

Rolland, N. 2004 Was the emergence of home bases and domestic fire a punctuated event? A review of the Middle Pleistocene record in Eurasia, *Asian Perspectives: the Journal of Archaeology for Asia and the Pacific* 43: 248–280.

Ron, H. and Levi, S. 2001 When did hominids first leave Africa? New high-resolution paleomagnetic evidence from the Erk-El-Ahmar formation, Israel, *Geology* 29: 887–890.

Ronen, A. 2006 The oldest human groups in the Levant, *Comptes Rendus Palevol* 5: 343–351.

Rope, D. A. (ed.) 1980 Early man: some precise moments in the remote past, *World Archaeology* 12: 107–229.

Rose, J. I. 2004a New evidence for the expansion of an Upper Pleistocene population out of East Africa, from the site of Station One, Northern Sudan, *Cambridge Archaeological Journal* 14: 205–216.

Rose, J. 2004b The question of Upper Pleistocene connections between East Africa and South Arabia, *Current Anthropology* 45: 551–555.

Rose, L. and Marshall, F. 1996 Meat eating, hominid sociality, and home bases revisited, *Current Anthropology* 37: 307–338.

Roset, J.-P. 1987 Palaeoclimatic and cultural condition of Neolithic development in the Early Holocene of northern Niger (Aïr and Ténéré), in A. E. Close (ed.), *Prehistory of arid North Africa*, Dallas: Southern Methodist University Press, pp. 211–234.

Rossignol-Strick, M. 1983 African monsoons, and immediate climate response to orbital insolation, *Nature* 304: 46–49.

Rots, V. and van Peer, P. 2006 Early evidence of complexity in lithic economy: core-axe production, hafting and use at Late Middle Pleistocene site 8-B-11, Sai Island (Sudan), *Journal of Archaeological Science* 33: 360–371.

Roubet, C. 1979 *Economie pastorale préagricole en Algérie occidentale: le néolithique de tradition capsienne*, Paris: Centre Nationale de La Recherche Scientifique.

Rowley-Conwy, P. 1986 Between cave painters and crop planters: aspects of the Temperate European Mesolithic, in M. Zvelebil (ed.), *Hunters in transition: Mesolithic societies of Temperate Eurasia and the transition to farming*, Cambridge: Cambridge University Press, pp. 17–32.

2001 Time, change and the archaeology of hunter-gatherers: how original is the "Original Affluent Society"? in C. Panter-Brick, R. H. Layton and P. Rowley-Conwy (eds.), *Hunter-gatherers an interdisciplinary perspective*, Cambridge: Cambridge University Press, pp. 39–72.

2004 How the West was lost: a reconsideration of agricultural origins in Britain, Ireland and southern Scandinavia, *Current Anthropology* 45: S83–113.

Runge, J. 1996 Palaeoenvironmental interpretation of geomorphological and pedological studies in the rain forest "core-areas" of eastern Zaire (Central Africa), *South African Geographical Journal* 78: 91–97.

Russell, J. M., Johnson, T. C., Kelts, K. R., Laerdal, T. and Talbot, M. R. 2003 An 11000-year lithostratigraphic and palaeohydrologic record from equatorial Africa: Lake Edward, Uganda-Congo, *Palaeoclimatology, Palaeogeography, Palaeoecology* 193: 25–49.

Russell, T. 2000 The application of the Harris Matrix to San rock art at Main Caves North, KwaZulu-Natal, *South African Archaeological Bulletin* 55 60–70.

Ryner, M. A., Bonnefille, R., Holmgren, K. and Muzuka, A. 2006 Vegetation changes in Empakaai Crater, northern Tanzania, at 14,800–9300 cal yr BP, *Review of Palaeobotany and Palynology* 140: 163–174.

Sadr, K. 1997 Kalahari archaeology and the Bushman debate, *Current Anthropology* 38: 104–112.

1998 The first herders at the Cape of Good Hope, *African Archaeological Review* 15: 101–122.

2003 The Neolithic of southern Africa, *Journal of African History* 44: 195–209.

2005 Hunter-gatherers and herders of the Kalahari during the late Holocene, in P. Veth, M. Smith and P. Hiscock (eds.), *Desert peoples archaeological perspectives*, Oxford: Blackwell Publishing, pp. 206–221.

Sadr, K. and Sampson, C. G. 2006 Through thick and thin: early pottery in southern Africa, *Journal of African Archaeology* 4: 235–252.

Sadr, K., Smith, A. B., Plug, I., Orton, J. and Mütti, B. 2003 Herders and foragers on Kasteelberg: interim report of excavations 1999–2002, *South African Archaeological Bulletin* 58: 27–32.

Sahlins, M. 1968 *Tribesmen*, Englewood Cliffs: Prentice Hall.

Sahnouni, M. 2004 On the earliest occupation in North Africa: a response to Geraads *et al.*, *Journal of Human Evolution* 46: 763–775.

Sahnouni, M. (ed.) 2005a *Le Paléolithique en Afrique: l'histoire la plus longue*, Paris: Artcom.

2005b Point des connaisssances du Paléolithique ancien d'Afrique du Nord et la question de la première occupation humaine au Maghreb, in M.

Sahnouni (ed.), *Le Paléolithique en Afrique: L'histoire la Plus Longue*, Paris: Artcom, pp. 99–128.

Sahnouni, M., Hadjouis, D., van der Made, J., Derradji, A.-El-K., Canals, A., Medig, M., Belahrech, H., Harichane, Z. and Rabhi, M. 2002 Further research at the Oldowan site of Ain Hanech, North-eastern Algeria, *Journal of Human Evolution* 43: 925–937.

Sahnouni, M., Schick, K., and Toth, N. 1997 An experimental investigation into the nature of faceted limestone "spheroids" in the Early Palaeolithic. *Journal of Archaeological Science* 24 (8): 701–713.

Sahnouni, M., and deHeinzelin, J. 1998 The site of Ain Hanech revisited: New investigations at this Lower Pleistocene site in northern Algeria, *Journal of Archaeological Science* 25: 1083–1101.

Saitowitz, S. J. and Sampson, C. G. 1992 Glass trade beads from rock shelters in the Upper Karoo, *South African Archaeological Bulletin* 47: 94–103.

Sakka, M. 1984 Cranial morphology and masticatory adaptations. In *Food acquisition and processing in primates* (D. J. Chivers, B. A. Wood and A. Billsborough, eds.), pp. 415–427. New York: Plenum Press.

Salas, A., Richards, M., De la Fe, T., Lareu, M.-V., Sobrino, B., Sánchez-Diz, P., Macaulay, V. and Carracedo, A. 2002 The making of the African mtDNA landscape, *American Journal of Human Genetics* 71: 1082–1111.

Salzmann, U., Hoelzmann, P. and Moerczinek, I. 2002 Late Quaternary climate and vegetation of the Sudanian zone of northeast Nigeria, *Quaternary Research* 58: 73–83.

Salzmann, U. and Hoelzmann, P. 2005 The Dahomey Gap: an abrupt climatically induced rain forest fragmentation in West Africa during the late Holocene, *The Holocene* 15: 190–199.

Sampson, C. G. 1974 *The Stone Age archaeology of southern Africa*, New York: Academic Press.

    1985a Atlas of Stone Age settlement in the Seacow Valley, *Memoirs of the National Museum (Bloemfontein)* 20: 1–116.

    1985b Review of Janette Deacon's The Later Stone Age of southernmost Africa, *South African Archaeological Bulletin* 40: 56–58.

    1988 *Stylistic boundaries among mobile hunter-foragers*, Washington: Smithsonian Institution Press.

    1995 Acquisition of European livestock by the Seacow River Bushmen between A. D. 1770–1890, *Southern African Field Archaeology* 4: 30–36.

    2001 An Acheulian settlement pattern in the Upper Karoo region of South Africa, in S. Milliken and J. Cook (eds.), *A very remote period indeed: papers on the Palaeolithic presented to Derek Roe*, Oxford: Oxbow Books, pp. 28–36.

    2006 Acheulean quarries at hornfels outcrops in the Upper Karoo region of South Africa, in N. Goren-Inbar and G. Sharon (eds.), *Axe age: Acheulian tool-making from quarry to discard*, London: Equinox, pp. 75–107.

Sampson, C. G. and Southard, M. D. 1973 Variability and change in the Nachikufan industry of Zambia, *South African Archaeological Bulletin* 28: 78–89.

Sandelowsky, B. H. 1977 Mirabib – an archaeological study in the Namib, *Madoqua* 10: 221–283.

Sankaran, M., Hanan, N. P., Scholes, R. J., Ratnam, J., Augustine, D. J., Cade, B. S., Gignoux, J., Higgins, S. I., Le Roux, X., Ludwig, F., Ardo, J., Banyikwa, F., Bronn, A., Bucini, G., Caylor, K. K., Coughenour, M. B., Diouf, A., Ekaya, W., Feral, C. J., February, E. C., Frost, P. G. H., Hiernaux, P., Hrabar, H., Metzger, K. L., Prins, H. H.T, Ringrose, S., Sea, W., Tews, J., Worden, J. and Zambatis, N. 2005 Determinants of woody cover in African savannas, *Nature* 438: 846–849.

Saxon, E. 1976 The evolution of domestication: a reappraisal of the Near Eastern and North African evidence, in E. S. Higgs (ed.), *Origine de l'élévage et de la domestication*, Prétirage Colloque XX, Ninth Congress of the International Union of Pre- and Protohistoric Sciences, pp. 180–226.

Saxon, E., Close, A. E., Cluzel, C., Morse, V. and Shackleton, N. J. 1974 Results of recent investigations at Tamar Hat, *Libyca* 22: 49–91.

Scarre, C. (ed.) 2005 *The human past: world prehistory and the development of human societies*, London: Thames and Hudson.

Schadeberg, T. 1999 Batwa: the Bantu name for the invisible people, in K. Biesbrouck, S. Elders and G. Rossel (eds.), *Central African hunter-gatherers in a multidisciplinary perspective: challenging elusiveness*, Leiden: University of Leiden Press, pp. 21–40.

Schefuß, E., Schouten, S., Jansen, J. H. F. and Sinninghe Damsté, J. S. 2004 African vegetation controlled by tropical sea surface temperatures in the mid-Pleistocene period, *Nature* 422: 418–421.

Schefuß, E., Schouten, S. and Schneider, R. R. 2005 Climatic controls on central Africa during the past 20,000 years, *Nature* 437: 1003–1006.

Schenker, N. M., Desgouttes, A-M. and Semendeferi, K. 2005 Neural connectivity and cortical substrates of cognition in hominoids, *Journal of Human Evolution* 49: 547–569.

Schepartz, L. A. 1988 Who were the later Pleistocene eastern Africans? *African Archaeological Review* 6: 57–72.

Schick, K. D. 1987 Modeling the formation of early stone age artifact assemblages, *Journal of Human Evolution* 16: 789–808.

Schick, K. and Clark, J. D. 2003 Biface technological development and variability in the Acheulean Industrial Complex in the Middle Awash region of the Afar Rift, Ethiopia, in M. Sorressi and H. L. Dibble (eds.), *Multiple approaches to the study of bifacial technologies*, Philadelphia: University Museum Monograph 115, pp. 1–30.

Schick, K. D. and Toth, N. 1993 *Making silent stones speak. Human evolution and the dawn of technology*, London: Weidenfeld & Nicholson.

1994 Early Stone Age technology in Africa: a review and case study into the nature and function of spheroids and subspheroids, in R. S. Corruchinin and R. L. Ciochon (eds.), *Integrative paths to the past: palaeoanthropological advances in honour of F. Clark Howell*, Englewood Cliffs: Prentice Hall, pp. 429–449.

Schick, K. D., Toth, N., Garufi, G., Savage-Rumbaugh, S., Rumbaugh, D. and Sevcik, R. 1999 Continuing investigations into the stone tool-making and tool-using capabilities of a bonobo (*Pan paniscus*), *Journal of Archaeological Science* 26: 821–832.

Schild, R., Chmielewska, M. and Wieckowska, H. 1968 The Arkinian and Shamarkian industries, in F. Wendorf (ed.), *The prehistory of Nubia*, Dallas: Southern Methodist University Press, pp. 651–767.

Schild, R. and Wendorf, F. 1989 The Late Pleistocene Nile in Wadi Kubbaniya, in F. Wendorf, R. Schild and A. E. Close (eds.), *Prehistory of Wadi Kubbaniya Volume Two*, Dallas: Southern Methodist University Press, pp. 15–100.

Schild, R. and Wendorf, F. E. 2002 Palaeolithic living sites in Upper and Middle Egypt: a review article, *Journal of Field Archaeology* 29: 447–461.

Schlanger, N. 2002 Making the past for South Africa's future: the prehistory of Field-Marshal Smuts (1920s-1940s), *Antiquity* 76: 200–209.

   2003 The Burkitt affair revisited: colonial implications and identity politics in early South African prehistoric research, *Archaeological Dialogues* 10: 5–26.

   2005 The history of a special relationship: prehistoric terminology and lithic technology between the French and South African research traditions, in F. d'Errico and L. Backwell (eds.), *From tools to symbols: from early hominids to modern humans*, Johannesburg: Witwatersrand University Press, pp. 9–37.

Schoenbrun, D. L. 1998 *A green place, a good place: a social history of the Great Lakes Region, earliest times to the fifteenth century*, London: Heinemann.

   1999 The (in)visible roots of Buynoro-Kitara and Buganda in the Lakes region: AD 800–1300, in S. K. McIntosh (ed.), *Beyond chiefdoms: pathways to complexity in Africa*, Cambridge: Cambridge University Press, pp. 136–150.

Schoeninger, M., Moore, J. and Sept, J. M. 1999 Subsistence strategies of two "savanna" chimpanzee populations: the stable isotope evidence, *American Journal of Primatology* 49: 297–314.

Schoeninger, M. J., Bunn, H. T., Murray, S. S., Marlett, J. A. 2001 Composition of tubers used by Hadza foragers of Tanzania. *Journal of Food Composition Analysis* 14: 15–25.

Schoffeleers, J. M. 1973 Towards the identification of a Proto-Chewa culture: a preliminary contribution, *Journal of Social Science* 2: 47–60.

Scholz, C. A., Johnson, T. C., King, J. W., Cohen, A. S., Lyons, R. P., Kalindekafe, L., Forman, S. L., McHargue, L. R. and Singer, B. S. 2005 Initial results of scientific drilling on Lake Malawi, East African rift: EOS, *Transactions of the American Geophysical Union* 86: 13C–03.

Scholz, C. A., Cohen, A. S., Johnson, T. C., King, J. W. and Moran, K. 2006 The 2005 Lake Malawi Scientific Drilling Project, *Scientific Drilling* 2: 17–19.

Scholz, C. A., Johnson, T. C., Cohen, A. S., King, J. W., Peck, J. A., Overpeck, J. T., Talbot, M. R., Brown, E. T., Kalindekafe, L., Amoako, P. Y. O.,

Lyons, R. P., Shanahan, T. M., Castañeda, I. S., Heil, C. W., Forman, S. L., McHargue, L. R., Beuning, K. R., Gomez, J., and Pierson, J. 2007 East African megadroughts between 135 and 75 thousand years ago and bearing on early-modern human origins. *Proceedings of the National Academy of Sciences (USA)* Early Edition www.pnas.org/cgi/doi/10.1073/pnas.0703874104 Accessed 7 October 2007.

Schrenk, F., Bromages, T. G., Betzler, C. G., Ring, U. and Juwayeyi, Y. 1993 Oldest *Homo* and Pliocene biogeography of the Malawi Rift, *Nature* 365: 833–836.

Schrire, C. 1980 An inquiry into the evolutionary status and apparent identity of San hunter-gatherers, *Human Ecology* 8: 9–29.

1992 The archaeological identity of hunters and herders at the Cape over the last 2000 years: a critique, *South African Archaeological Bulletin* 47: 62–64.

Schwarcz, H. P. 2001 Chronometric dating of the Middle Pleistocene, in L. Barham and K. Robson-Brown (eds.), *Human roots: Africa and Asia in the middle Pleistocene*, Bristol: Western Academic & Specialist Press, pp. 41–53.

Schwarcz, H. P., and Rink, W. J. 2001 Dating methods for sediments of caves and rockshelters with examples from the Mediterranean region, *Geoarchaeology* 16: 355–371.

Schwartz, D. 1991 Intéret de la mesure du delta-13C des sols en milieu naturel équatorial pour la connaissance des aspects pédologiques et écologiques des relations savane-foret, *Cahiers Orstom, Séries Pédologiques* 16: 327–341.

1992 Assèchement climatique vers 3000 BP et expansion Bantu en Afrique centrale atlantique: quelques réflexions, *Bulletin de la Société Géologique de France* 163: 353–361.

Schwartz, J. H. and Tattersall, I. 2000 The human chin revisited: what is it and who has it? *Journal of Human Evolution* 38: 367–409.

Schweitzer, F. R. and Wilson, M. L. 1982 Byneskranskop 1: a late Quaternary living site in the southern Cape Province, South Africa, *Annals of the South African Museum* 88: 1–203.

Scott, A. C. 2000 The Pre-Quaternary history of fire, *Palaeogeography, Palaeoclimatology, Palaeoecology* 164: 281–329.

Scott, G. R., Gibert, L. L., and Gibert, J. 2007. Magnetostratigraphy of the Orce region (Baza Basin), SE Spain: new chronologies for Early Pleistocene faunas and hominid occupation sites, *Quaternary Science Reviews* 26: 415–435.

Sealy, J. C. 2006 Diet, mobility and settlement pattern among Holocene hunter-gatherers in southernmost Africa, *Current Anthropology* 47: 569–595.

Sealy, J. C. and Pfeiffer, S. 2000 Diet, body size and landscape use among Holocene people in the southern Cape, South Africa, *Current Anthropology* 41: 642–655.

Sealy, J. C., Pfeiffer, S., Yates, R., Willmore, K., Manhire, A., Maggs, T. M.O'C. and Lanham, J. 2000 Hunter-gatherer child burials from the

Pakhuis Mountains, Western Cape: growth, diet and burial practices in the late Holocene, *South African Archaeological Bulletin* 55: 32–43.

Sealy, J. C. and van der Merwe, N. J. 1988 Social, spatial and chronological patterning in marine food use as determined by $\partial^{13}C$ measurements of Holocene human skeletal remains from the south-western Cape, South Africa, *World Archaeology* 20: 87–102.

1992 On "Approaches to dietary reconstruction in the Western Cape: are you what you have eaten?" – a reply to Parkington, *Journal of Archaeological Science* 19: 459–466.

Sealy, J. C. and Yates, R. 1994 The chronology of the introduction of pastoralism to the Cape, South Africa, *Antiquity* 68: 58–67.

Seitsonen, O. 2005 Stone Age sequence, lithic technology, and ancient lake level changes in the North Tanzanian Rift Valley area, M.Lic. thesis, University of Helsinki.

Sepulchre, P., Ramstein, G., Fluteau, F., Schuster, M., Tiercelin, J.-J., and Brunet, M. 2006 Tectonic uplift and eastern African aridification *Science* 313: 1419–1423.

Selvaggio, M. M. 1998 Evidence for a three-stage sequence of hominid and carnivore involvement with long bones at FLK *Zinjanthropus*, Olduvai Gorge, Tanzania, *Journal of Archaeological Science* 25: 191–202.

Semaw, S. 2000 The world's oldest stone artefacts from Gona, Ethiopia: Their implications for understanding stone technology and patterns of human evolution between 2.6–1.5 million years ago, *Journal of Archaeological Science* 27: 1197–1214.

Semaw S. Rogers M. J., Quade J., Renne P. R., Butler R. F., Dominguez-Rodrigo M., Stout D., Hart W. S., Pickering T., Simpson S. W. 2003 *Journal of Human Evolution* 45: 69–177.

Senut, B. 2006 Bipédie et climat, *Compte Rendus Palevol* 5: 89–98.

Sept, J. M. 1986 Plant foods and early hominids at site FxJj 50, Koobi Fora, Kenya, *Journal of Human Evolution* 15: 751–770.

1992 Was there no place like home? *Current Anthropology* 33: 187–207.

2001 Modelling the edible landscape, in C. B. Stanford and H. T. Bunn (eds.), *Meat-eating and human evolution*, Oxford: Oxford University Press, pp. 73–98.

Service, E. 1962 *Primitive social organization*, New York: Random House.

Shackleton, N. J. 1995 New data on the evolution of Pliocene climatic variability, in E. S. Vrba, G. H. Denton, T. C. Partridge and L. H. Burckle (eds.), *Paleoclimate and evolution with emphasis on human origins*, New Haven: Yale University Press, pp. 242–248.

Shackleton, N. J., Sánchez-Goni, M. F., Pailler, D. and Lancelot, Y. 2003 Marine isotope substage 5e and the Eemian interglacial, *Global and Planetary Change* 36: 151–155.

Shackley, M. 1980 An Acheulean industry with *Elephas recki* from Namib IV, South West Africa (Namibia), *Nature* 284: 340–341.

Sharon, G., and Beaumont, P. 2006 Victoria West – A highly standard-ised prepared core technology, in N. Goren-Inbar and G. Sharon (eds.), *Axe Age: Acheulian tool-making from quarry to discard*, London: Equinox, pp. 181–199.

Sharon, G. N. and Goren-Inbar, N. 1999 Soft percussor use at the Gesher Benot Ya'aqov Acheulian site? *Journal of the Israel Prehistoric Society* 28: 55–79.

Sharp, J. and Douglas, S. 1996 Prisoners of their reputation? The veterans of the 'Bushman' battalions in South Africa, in P. Skotnes (ed.), *Miscast: negotiating the presence of the Bushmen*, Cape Town: University of Cape Town Press, pp. 323–330.

Shaw, T. 1985 The prehistory of West Africa, in J. F. A. Ajayi and M. Crowder (eds.), *History of West Africa, Volume 1*, New York: Longman, pp. 48–86.

Shaw, T. and Daniels, S. G. H. 1984 Excavations at Iwo Eleru, Ondo State, Nigeria, *West African Journal of Archaeology*, 14: 1–269.

Shea, J. 1998 Neandertal and early modern human behavioural variability: a regional-scale approach to lithic evidence for hunting in the Levantine Mousterian, *Current Anthropology* 39: S45–S78.

Shennan, S. 2001 Demography and cultural innovation: a model and its impli-cations for the emergence of modern human culture, *Cambridge Archaeo-logical Journal* 11: 5–16.

Sheppard, P. J. 1987 *The Capsian of North Africa. Stylistic variation in stone tool assemblages*, Oxford: British Archaeological Reports.

1990 Soldiers and bureaucrats: the early history of prehistoric archaeology in the Maghreb, in P. T. Robertshaw (ed.), *A history of African archaeology*, London: James Currey, pp. 173–188.

Sheppard, P. J., and Kleindienst, M. 1996 Technological change in the Earlier and Middle Stone Age of Kalambo Falls (Zambia). *African Archaeological Review* 13: 171–196.

Shigerhiro, K., Nagaoka, S., WoldeGabriel, G., Renne, P., Snow, M. G., Beyene, Y. and Suwa, G. 2000 Chronostratigraphy and correlation of the Plio-Pleistocene tephra layers of the Konso Formation, southern Main Ethiopian Rift, Ethiopia, *Quaternary Science Reviews* 19: 1305–1317.

Shimada, M. K. and Hey, J. 2005 History of modern human population struc-ture inferred from the worldwide survey on Xp11.22 sequences, *American Journal of Physical Anthropology* S40: 190.

Shipman, P. 1989 Altered bones from Olduvai Gorge, Tanzania: techniques, problems, and implications for their recognition, in R. Bonnichsen and M. H. Sorg (eds.), *Bone modification*, Orono: University of Maine Centre for the Study of the First Americans, pp. 317–334.

Shipman, P., Bosler, W. and Davis, K. L. 1981 Butchering of giant geladas at an Acheulian site, *Current Anthropology* 22: 257–264.

Shott, M. J. 1992 On recent trends in the anthropology of foragers: Kalahari revisionism and its archaeological implications, *Man* 27: 843–871.

Siddall, M., Rohling, E. J., Almogi-Laban, A., Hemleben, C., Meischner, D., Schmelzer, I. and Smeed, D. A. 2003 Sea-level fluctuations during the last glacial cycle, *Nature* 423: 853–858.

Sikes, N. E., Potts, R. and Behrensmeyer, A. K. 1999 Early Pleistocene habitat in Member 1 Olorgesailie based on paleosol stable isotopes, *Journal of Human Evolution* 37: 721–746.

Sillen, A. 1992 Strontium-calcium ratios (Sr/Ca) and strontium isotopic ratios ($^{87}$Sr/$^{86}$Sr) of *Australopithecus robustus* and associated fauna from Swartkrans, *Journal of Human Evolution* 23: 495–516.

Sillen, A., Hall, G. and Armstrong, R. 1995 Strontium calcium ratios (Sr/Ca) and strontium isotopic ratios ($^{87}$Sr/$^{86}$Sr) of *Australopithecus robustus* and *Homo* sp. from Swartkrans, *Journal of Human Evolution* 28: 277–285.

Sinclair, P., Juma, A. and Chami, F. 2006 Excavations at Kumbi Cave on Zanzibar in 2005, in J. Kinahan and J. Kinahan (eds.), *The African archaeology network: research in progress*, Dar es Salaam: Dar es Salaam University Press, pp. 95–106.

Singer, R. and Wymer, J. 1982 *The Middle Stone Age at Klasies River Mouth in South Africa*, Chicago: University of Chicago Press.

Skinner, A. R., Hay, R. L., Masao, F. and Blackwell, A. B. 2003 Dating the Naisiusiu Beds, Olduvai Gorge, by electron spin resonance, *Quaternary Science Reviews* 22: 1361–1366.

Smith, A. B. 1975 Radiocarbon dates from Bosumpra Cave, Abetifi, Ghana, *Proceedings of the Prehistoric Society* 41: 179–182.

   1984 The origins of food-production in northeast Africa, *Palaeoecology of Africa* 16: 317–324.

   1986 Review article: cattle domestication in North Africa, *African Archaeological Review* 4: 197–204.

   1990 On becoming herders: Khoikhoi and San ethnicity in southern Africa, *African Studies* 49: 50–73.

   1992 *Pastoralism in Africa: origins and developmental ecology*, London: Hurst and Co.

   2005a *African herders: emergence of pastoral traditions*, Walnut Creek: AltaMira Press.

   2005b The concepts of 'Neolithic' and 'Neolithisation' for Africa? *Before Farming* [print version] 4: 29–34.

Smith, A. B. and Lee, R. B. 1997 Cho/ana: archaeological and ethnohistorical evidence for recent hunter-gatherer/agropastoralist contact in northern Bushmanland, Namibia, *South African Archaeological Bulletin* 52: 52–58.

Smith, A. B., Sadr, K., Gribble, J. and Yates, R. 1991 Excavations in the southwestern Cape, South Africa, and the archaeological identity of prehistoric hunter-gatherers within the last 2000 years, *South African Archaeological Bulletin* 46: 71–90.

Smith, B. W. 1997 *Zambia's ancient rock art: the paintings of Kasama*, Lusaka: National Heritage Conservation Commission of Zambia.

   2006a The rock arts of sub-Saharan Africa, in G. Blundell (ed.), *Origins: the story of the emergence of humans and humanity in Africa*, Johannesburg: Witwatersrand University Press, pp. 92–101.

2006b Reading rock art and writing genetic history: regionalism, ethnicity and the rock art of southern Africa, in H. Soodyall (ed.), *The prehistory of Africa: tracing the lineage of modern man*, Johannesburg: Jonathan Ball Publishers, pp. 76–96.

Smith, B. W. and Blundell, G. 2004 Dangerous ground: a critique of landscape in rock-art studies, in C. Chippindale and G. Nash (eds.), *The figured landscapes of rock-art: looking at pictures in place*, Cambridge: Cambridge University Press, pp. 239–262.

Smith, B. W., Lewis-Williams, J. D., Blundell, G. and Chippindale, C. 2000 Archaeology and symbolism in the new South African coat of arms, *Antiquity* 74: 467–468.

Smith, B. W., and Ouzman, S. 2004 Taking stock: identifying Khoekhoen herder rock art in southern Africa, *Current Anthropology* 45: 499–526.

Smith, J. M., Lee-Thorp, J. A. and Sealy, J. C. 2002 Stable carbon and oxygen isotopic evidence for late Pleistocene to middle Holocene climatic fluctuations in the interior of southern Africa, *Journal of Quaternary Science* 17: 683–695.

Smith, P. E. L. 1982 The Late Palaeolithic and Epi-Palaeolithic of northern Africa, in J. D. Clark (ed.), *Cambridge history of Africa, Volume I: from the earliest times to c. 500 B. C.*, Cambridge: Cambridge University Press, pp. 342–409.

Soffer, O. and Gamble, C. S. (eds.) 1990 *The World at 18,000 BP, Volume I, high latitudes*, London: Unwin Hyman.

Solomon, A. C. 1992 Gender, representation, and power in San ethnography and rock art, *Journal of Anthropological Archaeology* 11: 291–329.

1997a Landscape, form and process: some implications for San rock art research, *Natal Museum Journal of Humanities* 9: 57–73.

1997b The myth of ritual origins? Ethnography, mythology and interpretation of San rock art, *South African Archaeological Bulletin* 52: 3–13.

Solway, J. S. and Lee, R. B. 1990 Foragers, genuine or spurious? Situating the Kalahari San in history, *Current Anthropology* 31: 109–146.

Soodyall, H. (ed.) 2006 *The prehistory of Africa: tracing the lineage of modern man*, Johannesburg: Jonathan Ball Publishers.

Soriano, S., Villa, P. and Wadley, L. 2007 Blade technology and tool forms in the Middle Stone Age of South Africa: the Howiesons Poort and post-Howiesons Poort at Rose Cottage Cave, *Journal of Archaeological Science* 34: 681–703.

Sowers, T. and Bender, M. 1995 Climate records covering the last deglaciation, *Science* 269: 210–214.

Sowunmi, M. A. 1999 The significance of the oil palm (*Elaeis guineensis* Jacq.) in the late Holocene environments of West and West Central Africa: a further consideration, *Vegetation History and Archaeobotany* 8: 199–210.

Speth, J. D. 1987 Early hominid subsistence strategies in seasonal habitats, *Journal of Archaeological Science* 14: 13–29.

1989 Early hominid hunting and scavenging: the role of meat as an energy source, *Journal of Human Evolution* 18: 329–343.

Spielmann, K. A. and Eder, J. F. 1994 Hunters and farmers: then and now, *Annual Review of Anthropology* 23: 303–323.

Sponheimer, M. and Lee-Thorp, J. A. 1999a Isotopic evidence for the diet of an early hominid, *Australopithecus africanus, Science* 283: 368–370.

   1999b Oxygen isotope ratios in enamel carbonate and their ecological significance, *Journal of Archaeological Science* 26: 723–728.

Sponheimer, M., Lee-Thorp, J. A., de Ruiter, D. J., Codron, D., Codron, J., Baugh, A. T. and Thackeray, F. 2005 Hominins, sedges, and termites: new carbon isotope data from the Sterkfontein valley and Kruger National Park, *Journal of Human Evolution* 48: 301–312.

Sponheimer, M., Loudon, J. E., Codron, D., Howells, M. E., Pruetz, J. D., Codron, J., de Ruiter, D. J. and Lee-Thorp, J. A. 2006 Do "savanna" chimpanzees consume $C_4$ resources? *Journal of Human Evolution* 51: 128–133.

Sponheimer, M., Passey, B. H., de Ruiter, D. J., Guatelli-Steinberg, D., Cerling, T. E., and Lee-Thorp, J. 2006. Isotopic evidence for dietary variability in the early hominin *Paranthropus robustus, Science* 314: 980–981.

Spoor, F., Stringer, C., and Zonneveld, F. 1998 Rare temporal bone pathology of the Singa calvaria from Sudan, *American Journal of Physical Anthropology* 107: 41–50.

Spoor, F., Leakey, M. G., Gathogo, P. N., Brown, F. H., Antón, S. C., McDougall, I., Kiarie, C., Manthi, F. K., and Leakey, L. N. 2007 Implications of new early *Homo* fossils from Ileret, east of Lake Turkana, Kenya, *Nature* 448: 688–691.

Stager, J. C., Cumming, B. F. and Meeker, L. D. 2003 A 10 000-year high-resolution diatom record from Pilkington Bay, Lake Victoria, East Africa, *Quaternary Research* 59: 172–181.

Stager, J. C. and Mayewski, P. A. 1997 Abrupt early to mid-Holocene climatic transitions registered at the Equator and the Poles, *Science* 276: 1834–1836.

Stahl, A. B. 1984 Hominid dietary selection before fire, *Current Anthropology* 25: 151–168.

   1985 Reinvestigation of Kintampo 6 rock shelter, Ghana: implications for the nature of culture change, *African Archaeological Review* 3: 117–150.

   1994 Innovation, diffusion and culture contact: the Holocene archaeology of Ghana, *Journal of World Prehistory* 8: 51–112.

   1999 Perceiving variability in time and space: the evolutionary mapping of African societies, in S. K. McIntosh (ed.), *Beyond Chiefdoms: Pathways to Complexity in Africa*, Cambridge: Cambridge University Press, pp. 39–55.

   2001 *Making history in Banda: anthropological visions of Africa's past*, Cambridge: Cambridge University Press.

   2005a Introduction: changing perspectives on Africa's pasts, in A. B. Stahl (ed.), *African archaeology: a critical introduction*, Oxford: Blackwell Publishing, pp. 1–23.

   (ed.) 2005b *African archaeology: a critical introduction*, Oxford: Blackwell Publishing.

2005c Glass houses under the rocks: a reply to Watson, *Journal of African Archaeology* 3: 57–64.

Stanford, C. B. 1996 The hunting ecology of wild chimpanzees; implications for the behavioral ecology of Pliocene hominids, *American Anthropologist* 98: 96–113.

1998 The social behavior of chimpanzees and bonobos: empirical evidence and shifting assumptions, *Current Anthropology* 39: 399–420.

Stanford, C. B. and Bunn, H. T. (eds.) 2001 *Meat eating and human evolution*, Oxford: Oxford University Press.

Stedman, H. M., Kozyak, B. W., Nelson, A., Thesler, D. M., Su, L. T., Low, D. W., Bridges, C. R., Shrager, J. B., Minugh-Purvis, N. and Mitchell, M. A. 2004 Myosin gene mutation correlates with changes in the human lineage, *Nature* 428: 415–418.

Steele, J. and Uomini, N. 2005 Humans, tools and handedness, in V. Roux and B. Bril (eds.), *Stone knapping: the necessary conditions for a uniquely hominin behaviour*, Cambridge: McDonald Institute Monographs, pp. 217–239.

Steudel-Numbers, K. L. 2006 Energetics in *Homo erectus* and other early hominins: the consequences of increased lower-limb length, *Journal of Human Evolution* 51: 445–453.

Stewart, B. A. 2005 Charring patterns on reconstructed ceramics from Dunefield Midden: implications for Khoekhoe vessel form and function, *Before Farming* [print version] 4: 11–28.

2007 Refitting repasts: a spatial exploration of food processing, sharing and disposal at the Dunefield Midden campsite. DPhil thesis, University of Oxford.

Stewart, K. M. 1989 *Fishing sites of North and East Africa in the Late Pleistocene and Holocene: environmental change and human adaptation*, Oxford: British Archaeological Reports.

Stiles, D. 1991 Early hominid behaviour and culture tradition: raw material studies in Bed II, Olduvai Gorge, *African Archaeological Review* 9: 1–19.

Stiner, M. C. 2002 Carnivory, coevolution, and the geographic spread of the genus *Homo*, *Journal of Archaeological Research* 10: 1–63.

Stiner, M. C., Munro, N. D., Suravell, T., Tchernov, E. and Bar-Yosef, O. 1999 Palaeolithic population growth pulses evidenced by small animal exploitation, *Science* 283: 190–194.

Stock, J. and Pfeiffer, S. 2001 Linking structural variability in long bone diaphyses to habitual behaviors: foragers from the southern African Later Stone Age and the Andaman Islands, *American Journal of Physical Anthropology* 115: 337–348.

Stokes, S. and Bailey, R. 2002 OSL-dating of Nazlet Safaha and Nazlet Khater 4, in P. M. Vermeersch (ed.), *Palaeolithic quarrying sites in Upper and Middle Egypt*, Leuven: Leuven University Press, pp. 349–350.

Stokes, S., Haynes, G., Thomas, D. S. G., Horrocks, J. L., Higginson, M. and Malita, M. 1998 Punctuated aridity in southern Africa during the last glacial cycle: the chronology of linear dune construction in the northeast-ern Kalahari, *Palaeogeography, Palaeoclimatology, Palaeoecology* 137: 305–332.

Stokes, S., Thomas, D. S. G. and Washington, R. W. 1997 Multiple episodes of aridity in southern Africa since the last interglacial Period, *Nature* 388: 154–159.

Stout, D. 2002 Skill and cognition in stone tool production: an ethnographic case study from Irian Jaya, *Current Anthropology* 45: 693–722.

2005a Neural foundations of perception and action in stone knapping, in V. Roux and B. Bril (eds.), *Stone knapping: the necessary conditions for a uniquely hominin behaviour*, Cambridge: McDonald Institute Monographs, pp. 273–286.

2005b The social and cultural context of stone-knapping skill acquisition, in V. Roux and B. Bril (eds.), *Stone knapping: the necessary conditions for a uniquely hominin behaviour*, Cambridge: McDonald Institute Monographs, pp. 331–340.

Stout, D. and Chaminade, T. 2006 The evolutionary neuroscience of tool making, *Neuropsychologia* 44: 1999–2006.

Stout, D., Quade, J., Semaw, S., Rogers, M. J. and Levin, N. E. 2005 Raw material selectivity of the earliest stone toolmakers at Gona, Afar, Ethiopia, *Journal of Human Evolution* 48: 365–380.

Stout, D., Toth, N., Schick, K., Stout, J. and Hutchins, G. 2000 Stone tool-making and brain activation: position emission (PET) studies, *Journal of Archaeological Science* 27: 1215–1223.

Straus, L. G. 2001 Africa and Iberia in the Pleistocene, *Quaternary International* 75: 91–102.

Straus, L. G., Eriksen, B. V., Erlandson, J. M. and Yesner, D. R. (eds.). 1996 *Humans at the end of the Ice Age: the archaeology of the Pleistocene-Holocene transition*, New York: Plenum Press.

Street-Perrott, F. A., Holmes, J. A., Waller, M. P., Allen, M. J., Barber, N. G. H., Fothergill, P. A., Harkness, D. D., Ivanovitch, M., Kroon, D. and Perrott, R. A. 2000 Drought and dust deposition in the West African Sahel: a 5500 year old record from Kajemarum Oasis, northeastern Nigeria, *The Holocene* 10: 293–302.

Street-Perrott, F. A. and Perrott, R. A. 1994 Holocene vegetation, lake levels and climate of Africa, in H. E. Wright (ed.), *Global climates since the Last Glacial Maximum*, Minneapolis: University of Minnesota Press, pp. 322–356.

Stringer, C. 2002 Modern human origins: progress and prospects, *Philosophical Transactions of the Royal Society, London B* 357: 563–579.

Stringer, C. and Hublin, J.-J. 1999 New age estimates for the Swanscombe hominid, and their significance for human evolution, *Journal of Human Evolution* 37: 873–877.

Susman, R. L. 1991 Who made the Oldowan tools? Fossil evidence for tool behaviour in Plio-Pleistocene hominids, *Journal of Anthropological Research*. 47: 129–151.

Susman, R. L., de Ruiter, D. and Brain, C. K. 2001 Recently identified postcranial remains of *Paranthropus* and early *Homo* from Swartkrans Cave, South Africa, *Journal of Human Evolution* 41: 607–629.

Sutton, J. E. G. 1974 The aquatic civilization of Middle Africa, *Journal of African History* 15: 527–546.

1977 The African Aqualithic, *Antiquity* 51: 25–34.

1998 Hyrax Hill and the later archaeology of the Central Rift Valley of Kenya, *Azania* 33: 73–112.

Suwa, G., Asfaw, B., Beyene, Y., White, T. D., Katoh, K., Nagaoka, S., Nakaya, H., Uzawa, K., Renne, P. and WoldeGabriel, G. 1997 The first skull of *Australopithecus boisei*, *Nature* 389: 489–492.

Suwa, G., White, T. and Howell, F. C. 1996 Mandibular post-canine dentition from the Shungura Formation, Ethiopia: crown morphology, taxonomic allocation, and Plio-Pleistocene hominid evolution, *American Journal of Physical Anthropology* 101: 247–282.

Suzman, J. 2002 Kalahari conundrums: relocation, resistance and international support in the Central Kalahari, Botswana, *Before Farming* [print version] 1: 16–25.

2003 Hunting for histories: rethinking historicities in the western Kalahari, in A. Barnard (ed.), *Hunter-gatherers in history, archaeology and anthropology*, Oxford: Berg, pp. 201–216.

Swart, J. 2004 Rock art sequences in uKhahlamba-Drakensberg Park, South Africa, *Southern African Humanities* 16: 13–35.

Switsur, R., Otto, T. and Allsworth-Jones, P. 1994 New dating evidence and identification of wood charcoal from Kariya Wuro rock shelter, Bauchi State, *The Nigerian Field* 59: 135–145.

Szabo, B. J. and Butzer, K. W. 1979. Uranium-series dating of lacustrine limestones from pan deposits with Final Acheulean assemblages at Rooidam, Kimberley District, South Africa, *Quaternary Research* 11: 257–260.

Taçon, P. and Ouzman, S. 2004 Worlds within stone: the inner and outer rock-art landscapes of northern Australia and southern Africa, in C. Chippindale and G. Nash (eds.), *The figured landscapes of rock-art: looking at pictures in place*, Cambridge: Cambridge University Press, pp. 39–68

Tafuri, M. A., Bentley, R. A., Manzi, G. and di Lernia, S. 2006 Mobility and kinship in the prehistoric Sahara: strontium isotope analysis of Holocene human skeletons from the Acacus Mountains (southwestern Libya), *Journal of Anthropological Archaeology* 25: 390–402.

Takahata, N., Lee, S.-H. and Satta, Y. 2001 Testing multiregionality of modern human origins, *Molecular Biology and Evolution* 18: 172–183.

Talbot, M. R. 1983 Late Pleistocene rainfall and dune building in the Sahel, *Palaeoecology of Africa* 16: 203–213.

Talbot, M. R. and Johannessen, T. 1992 A high resolution palaeoclimatic record for the last 27,500 years in tropical West Africa from the carbon and nitrogen isotopic composition of lacustrine organic matter, *Earth and Planetary Science Letters* 110: 23–37.

Tanaka, J. and Sugawara, K. 1999 /Gui and //Gana, in R. B. Lee and R. Daly (eds.), *The Cambridge encyclopaedia of hunters and gatherers*, Cambridge: Cambridge University Press, pp. 195–199.

Tattersall, I. 2000 Once we were not alone, *Scientific American* 282: 56–62.

Taylor, A. B. 2002 Masticatory form and function in the African apes, *American Journal of Physical Anthropology* 117: 133–156.

Taylor, D. M. 1992 Pollen evidence from Muchoya Swamp, Rukiga Highlands (Uganda), for abrupt changes in vegetation during the last c.21,000 years, *Bulletin Société Géologique de France* 163: 77–82.

Taylor, D. M., Lane, P. J., Muiruri, V., Rutledge, A., Gaj McKeever, R., Nolan, T., Kenny, P. and Goodhue, R. 2005 Mid- to late-Holocene vegetation dynamics on the Laikipia Plateau, Kenya, *The Holocene* 15: 837–846.

Teaford, M. F. 1994 Dental microwear and dental function, *Evolutionary Anthropology* 3: 17–30.

Templeton, A. R. 2002 Out of Africa again and again, *Nature* 416: 45–51.

Ten Raa, E. 1969 Sandawe prehistory and the vernacular tradition, *Azania* 4: 91–103.

1971 Dead art and living society: a study of rock paintings in a social context, *Mankind* 8: 42–58.

Texier, P-J. 1996 Evolution and diversity in flaking techniques and methods in the Palaeolithic, in C. Andreoni, C. Giunchi, C. Petetto and I. Zavatti (eds.), *Proceedings of the XIIIth Congress of the International Union of Pre- and Proto-historic Sciences*, Forlì: A. B. A. C. O. Edizioni, pp. 297–325.

Texier, P.-J. and Roche, H. 1995 Polyèdre, sub-sphéroïde et bola: des segments plus ou moins longs d'une meme chaîne opératoire, *Cahier Noir* 7: 31–40.

Texier, J.-P., Lefrèvre, D., and Raynal, J. P. 1994 Contribution pour un nouveau cadre stratigraphique des formations littorals quaternaries de la region de Casablanca, *Comptes Rendus de l'Académie des Sciences* 318: 1247–1253.

Thackeray, A. I. 1989 Changing fashions in the Middle Stone Age: the stone artefact sequence from Klasies River Mouth main site, South Africa, *African Archaeological Review* 7: 33–57.

1992 The Middle Stone Age south of the Limpopo, *Journal of World Prehistory* 6: 385–440.

2000 Middle Stone Age artefacts from the 1993 and 1995 excavations of Die Kelders Cave, South Africa, *Journal of Human Evolution* 38: 147–168.

Thackeray, J. F. and Braga, J. 2005 Early *Homo*, 'robust' australopithecines and stone tools at Kromdraai, South Africa, in F. d'Errico and L. Backwell (eds.), *From tools to symbols. From early hominids to modern humans*, Johannesburg: Witwatersrand University Press, pp. 229–237.

Thackeray, J. F. 1984 Climatic change and mammalian fauna from Holocene deposits in Wonderwerk cave, northern Cape, in J. C. Vogel (ed.), *Late Cainozoic palaeoclimates of the Southern Hemisphere*, Rotterdam: A. A. Balkema, pp. 371–374.

1990 Temperature indices from Late Quaternary sequences in South Africa comparisons with the Vostok core, *South African Geographical Journal* 72: 47–49.

1995. Do strontium/calcium ratios in early Pleistocene hominids from Swartkrans reflect physiological differences in males and females? *Journal of Human Evolution* 29: 401–404.

Thangaraj, K., Chaubey, G., Kivisild, T., Reddy, A. G., Singh, V. K., Rasalkar, A. A. and Singh, L. 2005 Reconstructing the origin of Andaman Islanders, *Science* 308: 996.

Thiaw, I. 2003 Archaeology and the public in Senegal: reflections in doing fieldwork at home, *Journal of African Archaeology* 1: 215–226.

Thomas, D. S. G. and Goudie, A. S. 1984 Ancient ergs of the southern hemisphere, in J. C. Vogel (ed.), *Late Cainozoic palaeoclimates of the southern hemisphere*, Rotterdam: A. A. Balkema, pp. 407–418.

Thomas, M. F. 2000 Late Quaternary environmental changes and the alluvial record in humid tropical environments, *Quaternary International* 72: 23–36.

Thomas, M. F. and Thorp, M. B. 1996 The response of geomorphic systems to climatic and hydrological change during the Late Glacial and early Holocene in the humid and sub-humid tropics, in J. Branson, A. G. Brown and K. J. Gregory (eds.), *Global continental changes: the context of palaeohydrology*, London: Geological Society of London, pp. 139–153.

Thomsen, C. J. 1836 *Ledetraad til nordisk oldkyndighed*, Copenhagen: S. L. Møllers.

Thomson, L. G., Mosley-Thomson, E., Davis, M. E., Henderson, K. A., Brecher, H. H., Zagorodnov, V. S., Mashiotta, T. A., Lin, P. N., Mikhalenko, V. N., Hardy, D. R. and Beer, J. 2002 Kilimanjaro ice core records: evidence of Holocene climate change in tropical Africa, *Science* 298: 589–593.

Thorbahn, P. 1979 *Precolonial ivory trade of East Africa: reconstruction of a human-elephant ecosystem*, PhD thesis, University of Massachusetts, Amherst.

Thorp, C. R. 2000 *Hunter-gatherers and farmers – an enduring frontier in the Caledon Valley, South Africa*, Oxford: British Archaeological Reports.

2004 Archaeological research at Malilangwe Trust in the southeastern lowveld, Zimbabwe, 2002–2003, *Nyame Akuma* 62: 70–77.

Thorpe, S. K. S., Holder, R. L., and Crompton, R. H. 2007 Origin of human bipedalism as an adaptation for locomotion on flexible branches. *Science* 316:1328–1331.

Tillet, T. 1985 The Palaeolithic and its environment in the northern part of the Chad basin, *African Archaeological Review* 3: 163–178.

Tishkoff, S. A., Dietzch, E., Speed, W., Pakstis, A. J., Kidd, J. R., Cheung, K., Bonné-Tamir, B., Santachiara-Benerecetti, A. S., Moral, P., Krings, M., Pääbo, S., Watson, E., Risch, N., Jenkins, T. and Kidd, K. K. 1996 Global patterns of linkage disequilibrium at the CD4 locus and modern human origins, *Science* 271: 1380–1387.

Tishkoff, S. A., Gonder, M. K., Henn, B. M., Mortensen, H., Knight, A., Gignoux, C., Fernandopulle, N., Lema, G., Nyambo, T. B., Ramakrishnan, U., Reed, F. A. and Mountain, J. L. 2007b History of click-speaking populations of Africa inferred from mtDNA and Y chromosome genetic variation, *Molecular Biology and Evolution* 24: 2180–2195.

Tishkoff, S. A., Reed, F. A., Ranciaro, A., Voight, B. F., Babbitt, C. C., Silverman, J. S., Powell, K., Mortensen, H. M., Hirbo, J. B., Osman, M., Ibrahim, M., Omar, S. A., Lema, G., Nyambo, T. B., Ghori, J., Bumpstead, S., Pritchard, J. K., Wray, G. A. and Deloukas, P. 2007 Convergent adaptation of human lactase persistence in Africa and Europe, *Nature Genetics* 39: 31–40.

Tishkoff, S. A. and Williams, S. M. 2002 Genetic analysis of African populations: human evolution and complex disease, *Nature Reviews Genetics* 3: 611–621.

Tixier, J., Roe, D., Turq, A., Gibert, J., Martínez-Navarro, B., Arribas, A., Gibert, L., Maillo, L., and Iglesias, A. 1995 Présence d'industrie lithique dans le Pleistocène de la region d'Orce (Grenada, Espagne): quel est l'état de la question? *Comptes Rendus de l'Académie des Sciences de Paris* 321: 71–78.

Tobias, P. V. 1971 Human skeletal remains from the Cave of Hearths, Makapansgat, Northern Transvaal. *American Journal of Physical Anthropology* 34: 335–367.

1991 *Olduvai Gorge, vol. 4: The skulls, endocasts and teeth of Homo habilis.* Cambridge: Cambridge University Press.

Tocheri, M. W., Marzke, M. W., Liu, D., Bae, M., Jones, G. P., Williams, R. C. and Razdan, A. 2003 Functional capabilities of modern and fossil hominid hands: three-dimensional analysis of trapezia, *American Journal of Physical Anthropology* 122: 101–112.

Tomasello, M. 1999 The human adaptation for culture, *Annual Review of Anthropology* 28: 509–529.

Tonner, T. W. W. 2002 A spatial database for the Later Stone Age site "Dunefield Midden," Western Cape, South Africa, MA thesis, University of Cape Town.

Torrence, R. (2001) Hunter-gatherer technology: macro- and microscale approaches, in C. Panter-Brick, R. H. Layton and P. Rowley-Conwy (eds.), *Hunter-gatherers: an interdisciplinary perspective*, Cambridge: Cambridge University Press, pp. 73–98.

Toth, N. 1985 The Oldowan reassessed: a close look at early stone artifacts, *Journal of Archaeological Science* 12: 101–120.

Toth, N., Schick, K. D., Savage-Rumbaugh, S., Sevcik, R. A. and Rumbaugh, D. M. 1993 Pan the tool-maker: investigations into the stone toolmaking and tool-using capabilities of a bonobo (*Pan paniscus*), *Journal of Archaeological Science* 20: 81–91.

Tribolo, C. 2003 Apport des méthodes de la luminescence à la chronologie de technofaciès du Middle Stone Age associés aux premiers hommes modernes du sud de l'Afrique, PhD thesis, University of Bordeaux I.

Tribolo, C., Mercier, N. and Valladas, H. 2005 Chronology of the Howiesons Poort and Still Bay techno-complexes: assessment and new data from luminescence, in F. d'Errico and L. Backwell (eds.), *From tools to symbols. From early hominins to modern humans*, Johannesburg: Witwatersrand University Press, pp. 493–511.

Trigger, B. 1989 *The history of archaeological thought*, Cambridge: Cambridge University Press.

Trinkaus, E. 1993 A note on the KNM-ER 999 hominid femur, *Journal of Human Evolution* 24: 493–504.

2005 Early modern humans, *Annual Review of Anthropology* 34: 207–230.

Tryon, C. A. 2006 "Early" Middle Stone Age lithic technology of the Kapthurin Formation (Kenya), *Current Anthropology* 47: 367–375.

Tryon, C. A. and McBrearty, S. 2002 Tephrostratigraphy and the Acheulian to Middle Stone Age transition in the Kapthurin Formation, Kenya, *Journal of Human Evolution* 42: 211–235.

2006 Tephrostratigraphy of the Bedd Tuff Member (Kapthurin Formation, Kenya) and the nature of archaeological change in the later middle Pleistocene, *Quaternary Research* 65: 492–507.

Tryon, C. A. and Potts, R. 2006 Approaches for understanding flake production in the African Acheulian, Paper submitted to the Electronic Symposium "Core Reduction, Chaîne Opératoire, and Other Methods: The Epistemologies of Different Approaches to Lithic Analysis" at the 71st Annual Meeting of the Society for American Archaeology, San Juan, Puerto Rico, April 2006. (Accessed online November 3, 2006)

Turnbull, C. 1961 *The forest people*, London: Jonathan Cape.

Turner, A. 1999 Evolution in the African Plio-Pleistocene mammalian fauna, in T. G. Bromage and F. Schrenk (eds.), *African biogeography, climate change, and human evolution*, Oxford: Oxford University Press, pp. 76–90.

Tuross, N., Barnes, I., and Potts, R. 1996 Protein identification of blood residues on experimental stone tools, *Journal of Archaeological Science* 23: 289–296.

Tyson, P. D. 1999 Late-Quaternary and Holocene palaeoclimates of southern Africa: a synthesis, *South African Journal of Geology* 102: 335–349.

Tyson, P. D. and Partridge, T. C. 2000 Evolution of Cenozoic climates, in T. C. Partridge and R. R. Maud (eds.), *The Cenozoic of southern Africa*, Oxford: Oxford University Press, pp. 371–387.

Underhill, P. A. 2003 Inferring human history: clues from Y-chromosome haplotypes, Cold Spring Harbor Symposia on Quantitative Biology: Cold Spring Harbor Laboratory Press.

Underhill, P. A., Passarino, G., Lin, A. A., Shen, P., Mirazón Lahr, M., Foley, R. A., Oefner, P. J. and Cavalli-Sforza, L. L. 2001 The phylogeography of Y chromosome binary haplotypes and the origins of modern human populations, *Annals of Human Genetics* 65: 43–62.

Underhill, P. A., Shen, P., Lin, A. A., Passarino, G., Yang, W. H., Kauffman, E., Bonné-Tamir, B., Bertranpetit, J., Francalacci, P., Ibrahim, M., Jenkins, T., Kidd, K. R., Mehdi, Q., Seielstad, M. T., Wells, R. S., Piazza, A., Davis, R. W., Feldman, M. W., Cavalli-Sforza, L. L. and Oefner, P. 2000 Y chromosome sequence variation and the history of human populations, *Nature Genetics* 26: 358–361.

Ungar, P. 1998 Dental allometry, morphology, and wear as evidence for diet in fossil primates, *Evolutionary Anthropology* 6: 205–217.

2004 Dental topography and diets of *Australopithecus afarensis* and early *Homo*, *Journal of Human Evolution* 46: 605–622.

Ungar, P., Grine, F. E., Teaford, M. F. and El Zaatari, S. 2006 Dental microwear and diets of African early *Homo*, *Journal of Human Evolution* 50: 78–95.

/Useb, J. and Chennells, R. 2004 Indigenous knowledge systems and protection of San intellectual property: media and research contracts (with reactions from M. Biesele, P. Wiessner and R. K. Hitchcock), *Before Farming* [print version] 3: 95–104.

Vail, J. R. 1969 The southern extension of the East African Rift System and related igneous activity, *International Journal of Earth Sciences* 57: 601–614.

Vallois, H. V. 1971 Le crâne-trophée capsien de Faïd Souar II, Algérie (Fouilles Laplace, 1954), *L'Anthropologie* 75: 191–220, 397–414.

Van Andel, T. H. 1989 Late Pleistocene sea levels and the human exploitation of the shore and shelf of southern South Africa, *Journal of Field Archaeology* 16: 133–155.

Van Campo, E., Duplessy, J. C. and Rossignol-Strick, M. 1982 Climate conditions deduced from a 150 kyr oxygen isotope-pollen record from the Arabian Sea, *Nature* 296: 56–59.

van der Merwe, N. J., Thackeray, J. F., Lee-Thorp, J. A. and Luyt, J. 2003 The carbon isotope ecology and diet of *Australopithecus africanus* at Sterkfontein, South Africa, *Journal of Human Evolution* 44: 581–597.

van der Ryst, M. 2003 The so-called Vaalpense or Masele of the Waterberg: the origins and emergence of a subordinate class of mixed descent, *Anthropology Southern Africa* 26: 42–52.

van Noten, F. 1977 Excavations at Matupi Cave, *Antiquity* 51: 35–40.

1982 *The archaeology of central Africa*, Graz: Akademische Druck – u. Verlagsanstalt.

van Peer, P. 1998 The Nile Corridor and the Out-of-Africa model: an examination of the archaeological record, *Cultural Anthropology* 39: S115–S140.

2001a The Nubian Complex settlement system in Northeast Africa, in N. J. Conard (ed.), *Settlement dynamics of the Middle Paleolithic and Middle Stone Age*, Tübingen: Kerns Verlag, pp. 45–64.

2001b Observations on the Palaeolithic of the south-western Fezzan and thoughts on the origin of the Aterian, in E. A. A. Garcea (ed.), *Uan Tabu in the settlement history of the Libyan Sahara*, Firenze: All'Insegna del Giglio, pp. 251–262.

2004 Did Middle Stone Age moderns of sub-Saharan African descent trigger an Upper Paleolithic revolution in the Lower Nile Valley? *L'Anthropologie* 42: 215–225.

van Peer, P., Fullagar, R., Stokes, S., Bailey, R. M., Moeyersons, J., Steenhoudt, F., Geerts, A., Vanderbeken, T., De Dapper, M. and Geus, F. 2003 The Early to Middle Stone Age transition and the emergence of modern human behaviour at site 8-B-11, Sai Island, Sudan, *Journal of Human Evolution* 45: 187–193.

van Peer, P., Rots, V. and Vroomans, J.-M. 2004 A story of colourful diggers and grinders: the Sangoan and Lupemban at site 8-B-11, Sai Island, Northern Sudan, *Before Farming* [print version] 3: 139–166.

van Reenen, J. F. 1986 Tooth mutilating and extracting practices amongst the peoples of South West Africa (Namibia), in R. Singer and K. Lundy (eds.), *Variation, culture and evolution in African populations*, Johannesburg: Witwatersrand University Press, pp. 159–170.

van Schaik, C. P., Deaner, R. O. and Merrill, M. Y. 1999 The conditions for tool-use in primates: implications for the evolution of material culture, *Journal of Human Evolution* 36: 719–741.

van Schaik, C. P. and Pradham, G. R. 2003 A model for tool-use traditions in primates: implications for the coevolution of culture and cognition. *Journal of Human Evolution* 44: 645–664.

van Zwanenberg, R. M. 1976 Dorobo hunting and gathering: a way of life or a mode of production? *African Economic History* 2: 12–21.

Vanhaeren, M. 2005 Speaking with beads: the evolutionary significance of personal ornaments, in F. d'Errico and L. Backwell (eds.), *From tools to symbols: from early hominins to modern humans*, Johannesburg: Witwatersrand University Press, pp. 525–553.

Vanhaeren, M., d'Errico, F., Stringer, C., James, S. L., Todd, J. A. and Mienis, H. K. 2006 Middle Paleolithic shell beads in Israel and Algeria, *Science* 312: 1785–1788.

Vansina, J. 1990 *Paths in the rainforests: toward a history of political tradition in Equatorial Africa*, London: James Currey.

1995 New linguistic evidence and 'the Bantu expansion,' *Journal of African History* 36: 173–195.

1994/95 A slow revolution: farming in subequatorial Africa, *Azania* 29/30: 1–14.

2004 Bananas in Cameroon *c.* 500 BCE? Not proven, *Azania* 38: 174–176.

Vermeersch, P. M. 1990 Palaeolithic chert exploitation in the limestone stretch of the Egyptian Nile Valley, *African Archaeological Review* 8: 77–102.

1992 The Upper and late Palaeolithic of northern and eastern Africa, in F. Klees and R. Kuper (eds.), *New light on the Northeast African past*, Köln: Heinrich Barth Institut, pp. 99–154.

(ed.) 2002 *Palaeolithic quarrying sites in Upper and Middle Egypt*, Leuven: Leuven University Press.

2002 The Egyptian Nile Valley during the early Holocene, in Jennerstrasse 8, *Tides of the desert. Contributions to the archaeology and environmental history of Africa in honour of Rudolph Kuper*, Köln: Heinrich-Barth Institut, pp. 27–40.

Vermeersch, P. M., Gijselings, G. and Paulissen, E. 1984 Discovery of the Nazlet Khater man, Upper Egypt, *Journal of Human Evolution* 13: 281–286.

Vermeersch, P. M., Paulissen, E. and Huyge, D. 2000 Makhadma 4, a Late Palaeolithic fishing site, in P. M. Vermeersch (ed.), *Palaeolithic living sites in Middle and Upper Egypt*, Leuven: Leuven University Press, pp. 227–270.

Vermeersch, P. M., Paulissen, E., Stokes, S., Charlier, C., van Peer, P. Stringer, C. B. and Lindsay, W. 1998 A Middle Palaeolithic burial of a modern human at Taramsa Hill, Egypt, *Antiquity* 72: 475–482.

Vermeersch, P. M., Paulissen, E. and van Neer, W. 1989 The Late Palaeolithic Makhadma sites (Egypt): environment and subsistence, in L. Krzyzaniak and M. Kobusiewicz (eds.), *Late prehistory of the Nile Basin and the Sahara*, Poznán: Poznán Archaeological Museum, pp. 87–116.

Vermeersch, P. M., Paulissen, E. and van Peer, P. 2005a Palaeolithic chert exploitation in the limestone stretch of the Egyptian Nile Valley, *African Archaeological Review* 8: 77–102.

Vermeersch, P. M., van Peer, P., Moeyersons, J. and van Neer, W. 1994. Sodmein Cave site (Red Sea Mountains, Egypt), *Sahara* 6: 31–40.

Vermeersch, P. M., van Peer, P. and Rots, V. 2005b A Middle Palaeolithic site with blade technology at Al Tiwayrat, Qena, Upper Egypt, *Antiquity* 79: 1–7. Available online at http://www.antiquity.ac.uk/projgall/vermeersch/index.html. Accessed 1 October, 2006.

Vernet, R. 1998a *Le Sahara et le Sahel: paléoenvironnements et occupation humaine à la fin du Pléistocène et l'Holocène: inventaire des datations*, Nouakchott: Université de Nouakchott.

Vernet, R. 1998b Le littoral du Sahara atlantique mauritanien au Néolithique, *Sahara* 10: 21–30.

Vernet, R., Ott, M., Tarrou, L., Gallin, A. and Géoris-Creuseveau, J. 2007 Fouille de la butte de FA 10 (Banc d'Arguin) et son apport à la connaissance de la culture épipaléolithique de Foum Arguin, nord-ouest du Sahara, *Journal of African Archaeology* 5: 17–45.

Verschuren, D., Laird, K. R. and Cumming, B. F. 2000 Rainfall and drought in equatorial east Africa during the past 1,100 years, *Nature* 403: 410–414.

Veth, P., Smith, M. and Hiscock, P. (eds.) 2005 *Desert peoples archaeological perspectives*, Oxford: Blackwell Publishing.

Vierich, H. and Hitchcock, R. K. 1996 Kua: farmer/foragers of the eastern Kalahari, Botswana, in S. Kent (ed.), *Cultural diversity among Twentieth Century foragers: an African perspective*, Cambridge: Cambridge University Press, pp. 108–124.

Villa, P., Delagnes, A. and Wadley, L. 2005 A late Middle Stone Age artifact assemblage from Sibudu (KwaZulu-Natal): comparisons with the European Middle Paleolithic, *Journal of Archaeological Science* 32: 399–402.

Vincens, A., Tiercelin, J.-J. and Buchet, G. 2006 New Oligocene-early Miocene microflora from the southwestern Turkana Basin: palaeoenvironmental implications in the northern Kenya Rift, *Palaeogeography, Palaeoclimatology, Palaeoecology* 239: 470–486.

Vincent, A. 1984 Plant foods in savanna environments: a preliminary report of tubers eaten by the Hadza of northern Tanzania, *World Archaeology* 17: 132–142.

Vinnicombe, P. 1976 *People of the eland*, Pietermaritzburg: University of Natal Press.

Vogel, J. C. 1978 Isotopic assessment of the dietary habits of ungulates, *South African Journal of Science* 74: 298–301.

Vogelsang, R. 1996 The Middle Stone Age in south-western Namibia, in G. Pwiti and R. Soper (eds.), *Aspects of African archaeology*, Harare: University of Zimbabwe Press, pp. 207–212.

1998 *Middle-Stone-Age-Fundstellen in Südwest-Namibia*, Köln: Heinrich-Barth Institut.

Voight, B. F., Adams, A. M., Frisse, L. A., Qian, Y., Hudson, R. and di Rienzo, A. 2005 Interrogating multiple aspects of variation in a full resequencing data set to infer human population size changes, *Proceedings of the National Academy of Sciences (USA)* 102: 18508–18513.

Volman, T. P. 1981 *The Middle Stone Age in the Southern Cape*, PhD thesis, University of Chicago.

    1984 Early prehistory of southern Africa, in R. G. Klein (ed.), *Southern African prehistory and palaeoenvironments*, Rotterdam: A. A. Balkema, pp. 169–220.

Vrba, E. S. 1988 Late Pliocene climatic events and human evolution, in F. E. Grine (ed.), *Evolutionary history of the "robust" australopithecines*, New York: Aldine de Gruyter, pp. 405–426.

    1995 The fossil record of African antelopes (Mammalia, Bovidae) in relation to human evolution and paleoclimate, in E. S. Vrba, G. Denton, T. Partridge and L. Burckle (eds.), *Paleoclimate and Evolution*, New Haven: Yale University Press, pp. 385–424.

WAC 2006 World Archaeological Congress, http://www.worldarchaeologicalcongress.org/site/home.php. Site accessed 4 October 2006.

Wadley, L. 1987 *Later Stone Age hunters and gatherers of the southern Transvaal: social and ecological interpretations*, Oxford: British Archaeological Reports.

    1989 Gender relations in the Thukela Basin, *South African Archaeological Bulletin* 44: 122–126.

    1996 Changes in the social relations of precolonial hunter-gatherers after agropastoral contact: an example from the Magaliesberg, South Africa, *Journal of Anthropological Archaeology* 15: 205–217.

    1997a Where have all the dead men gone? Stone Age burial practices in South Africa, in L. Wadley (ed.), *Our gendered past: archaeological studies of gender in southern Africa*, Johannesburg: Witwatersrand University Press, pp. 107–134.

    (ed.) 1997b *Our gendered past: archaeological studies of gender in southern Africa*, Johannesburg: Witwatersrand University Press.

    1998 The invisible meat providers: women in the Stone Age of South Africa, in S. Kent (ed.), *Gender in African archaeology*, Walnut Creek: AltaMira Press, pp. 69–82.

    2000a The early Holocene layers of Rose Cottage Cave, eastern Free State: technology, spatial patterns and environment, *South African Archaeological Bulletin* 55: 18–31.

    2000b The Wilton and pre-ceramic post-classic Wilton industries at Rose Cottage Cave and their context in the South African sequence, *South African Archaeological Bulletin* 55: 90–106.

    2001a What is cultural modernity? A general view and south African perspective from Rose Cottage Cave, *Cambridge Archaeological Journal* 11: 201–221.

    2001b Preliminary report on excavations at Sibudu Cave, KwaZulu-Natal, *Southern African Humanities* 13: 1–17.

2005a A typological study of the final Middle Stone Age stone tools from Sibudu Cave, KwaZulu-Natal, *South African Archaeological Bulletin* 60: 51–63.

2005b Putting ochre to the test: replication studies of adhesives that may have been used for hafting tools in the Middle Stone Age, *Journal of Human Evolution* 49: 587–601.

2006 Partners in grime: results of multi-disciplinary archaeology at Sibudu Cave, *Southern African Humanities* 18: 315–341.

Wadley, L. and Harper, P. 1989 Rose Cottage Cave revisited: Malan's Middle Stone Age collection, *South African Archaeological Bulletin* 44: 23–32.

Wadley, L. and Jacobs, Z. 2004 Sibudu Cave, KwaZulu-Natal: background to the excavations of Middle Stone Age and Iron Age occupations, *South African Journal of Science* 100: 145–150.

Wadley, L. and McLaren, G. 1998 Tandjesberg Shelter, eastern Free State, South Africa, *Natal Museum Journal of Humanities* 10: 19–32.

Wadley, L., Williamson, B. and Lombard, M. 2004 Ochre in hafting in Middle Stone Age southern Africa: a practical role, *Antiquity* 78: 661–675.

Wadley, L. and Whitelaw, G. (eds.) 2006 Middle Stone Age research at Sibudu Cave, *Southern African Humanities* 18(1): 1–341.

Waehle, E. 1999 The Twa of Rwanda: survival and defence of human rights, in K. Biesbrouck, S. Elders and G. Rossel (eds.), *Central African hunter-gatherers in a multidisciplinary perspective: challenging elusiveness*, Leiden: University of Leiden Press, pp. 265–278.

Walker, A. and Leakey, R. E. (eds.) 1993 *The Nariokotome Homo erectus skeleton*, Cambridge: Harvard University Press.

Walker, A., Leakey, R. E., Harris, J. M. and Brown, F. H. 1986 2.5-Myr *Australopithecus boisei* from west of Lake Turkana, Kenya, *Nature* 322: 517–522.

Walker, J., Cliff, R. A., and Latham, A. G. 2006 U-Pb isotopic age of the Stw 573 hominid from Sterkfontein, South Africa, *Science* 314: 1592–1594.

Walker, N. J. 1990 Zimbabwe at 18,000 BP, in C. S. Gamble and O. Soffer (eds.), *The World at 18,000 BP, Volume 2, low latitudes*, London: Unwin Hyman, pp. 206–213.

1995a *Late Pleistocene and Holocene hunter-gatherers of the Matopos*, Uppsala: Societas Archaeologica Upsaliensis.

1995b The archaeology of the San: the Late Stone Age of Botswana, in A. J. G. M. Sanders (ed.), *Speaking for the Bushmen*, Gaborone: The Botswana Society, pp. 54–87.

Walker, N. J. and Thorp, C. 1997 Stone Age archaeology in Zimbabwe, in G. Pwiti (ed.), *Caves, monuments and texts: Zimbabwean archaeology today*, Uppsala: Societas Archaeologica Upsaliensis, pp. 9–32.

Walker, R., Burger, O., Wagner, J. and von Rueden, C. R. 2006 Evolution of brain size and juvenile periods in primates, *Journal of Human Evolution* 51: 480–489.

Wallace, I. J. and Shea, J. J. 2006 Mobility patterns and core technologies in the Middle Paleolithic of the Levant, *Journal of Archaeological Science* 33: 1293–1309.

Wallis, R. J. 2002 The *bwili* or 'flying tricksters' of Malakula: a critical discussion of recent debates on rock art, ethnography and shamanisms, *Journal of the Royal Anthropological Institute* 8: 735–760.

Ward, C. V. 2002 Interpreting the posture and locomotion of *Australopithecus afarensis*: where do we stand? *Yearbook of Physical Anthropology* 45: 185–215.

Washburn, S. L. and DeVore, I. 1961 Social behavior of baboons and early man, in S. L. Washburn (ed.), *Social life of early man*, Chicago: Aldine, pp. 91–105.

Washburn, S. L. and Lancaster, C. 1968 The evolution of hunting, in R. B. Lee and I. DeVore (eds.), *Man the hunter*, Chicago: Aldine, pp. 293–303.

Wasylikowa, K. 1993 Plant macrofossils from the archaeological sites of Uan Muhuggiag and Ti-n-Torha, Southwestern Libya, in L. Krzyzaniak, M. Kobusiewicz and J. Alexander (eds.), *Environmental change and human culture in the Nile Basin and northern Africa until the second millennium B.C.*, Poznán Archaeological Museum, Poznán, pp. 25–47.

Wasylikowa, K., Mitra, J., Wendorf, F. and Schild, R. 1997 Exploitation of wild plants by the early Neolithic hunter-gatherers of the western Desert, Egypt: Nabta Playa as a case study, *Antiquity* 71: 932–941.

Watkins, J. 2005. Representing and repatriating the past, in T. R. Pauketat and D. D. Loren (eds.), *North American archaeology*, Oxford: Blackwell Publishing, pp. 337–358.

Watson, D. 2005 Under the rocks: reconsidering the origin of the Kintampo Tradition and the development of food-production in the savanna-forest/forest of West Africa, *Journal of African Archaeology* 3: 3–56.

Watson, E., Forster, P., Richards, M. and Bandelt, H.-J. 1997 Mitochondrial footprints of human expansions in Africa, *American Journal of Human Genetics* 61: 691–704.

Waweru, V. 2002 New excavations at the Middle Stone Age Cartwright's site, Kenya, *Nyame Akuma* 58: 26–33.

Wayland, E. J. 1929 African pluvial periods, *Nature* 123: 31–33.

Wayland, E. J. and Smith, R. 1923 Some primitive stone tools from Uganda, *Geological Survey of Uganda, Entebbe, Occasional Paper No. 1*.

Webley, L. 1997 Jakkalsberg A and B: the cultural material from two pastoralist sites in the Richtersveld, Northern Cape, *Southern African Field Archaeology* 6: 3–19.

Weissner, P. 1985 Style or isochrestic variation? A reply to Sackett, *American Antiquity* 50: 160–166.

Weldeab, S., Lea, D. W., Schneider, R. R., and Andersen, N. 2007, 155,000 years of West African monsoon and ocean thermal evolution, *Science* 316: 1303–1307.

Wenban-Smith, F. F., Allen, P., Bates, M. R., Parfitt, S. A., Preece, R. C., Stewart, J. R., Turner, C. and Whittaker, J. E. 2006 The Clactonian elephant butchery site at Southfleet Road, Ebbsfleet, UK. *Journal of Quaternary Science* 5: 471–483.

Wendorf, F. 1968 Late Paleolithic sites in Egyptian Nubia, in F. Wendorf (ed.), *The Prehistory of Nubia*, Dallas: Southern Methodist Press, pp. 954–995.

Wendorf, F., Close, A. E. and Schild, R. 1994 Africa in the period of *Homo sapiens neanderthalensis*, in S. J. De Laet, A. H. Dani, J. L. Lorenzo and R. B. Nunoo (eds.), *History of humanity, Volume 1: prehistory and the beginnings of civilization*, New York: Routledge & UNESCO, pp. 117–135.

Wendorf, F., Said, R. and Schild, R. 1970 Egyptian prehistory: some new concepts, *Science* 169: 1161–1171.

Wendorf, F. and Schild, R. 1974 *A Middle Stone Age sequence from the Central Rift Valley, Ethiopia*, Wroclaw: Ossolineum.

1989 Report on Site E-81–5, in F. Wendorf, R. Schild and A. E. Close (eds.) *The prehistory of Wadi Kubbaniya III: Late Palaeolithic archaeology*, Dallas: Southern Methodist University Press, pp. 704–714.

1992 The Middle Paleolithic of North Africa: a status report, in F. Klees and R. Kuper (eds.), *New light on the Northeast African Past*, Köln: Heinrich-Barth Institut, pp. 42–78.

2002 The role of storage in the Neolithic of the Egyptian Sahara, in Jennerstrasse 8 (eds.), pp. 41–49.

2005 Le Paléolithique moyen en Afrique du Nord: un bref survol, in M. Sahnouni (ed.), *Le Paléolithique en Afrique: l'histoire la plus longue*, Paris: Artcom, pp. 157–204.

Wendorf, F. E., Schild, R., Baker, P., Gautier, A., Longo, L. and Mahamed, A. 1997 *A Late Paleolithic kill-butchery camp in Upper Egypt*, Warsaw: Polish Academy of Sciences.

Wendorf, F., Schild, R. and Close, A. E. (eds.) 1986 *The prehistory of Wadi Kubbaniya, Volume 1: the Wadi Kubbaniya skeleton a Late Palaeolithic burial from southern Egypt*, Dallas: Southern Methodist University Press.

(eds.) 1989 *The prehistory of Wadi Kubbaniya III: Late Palaeolithic archaeology*, Dallas: Southern Methodist University Press.

Wendorf, F., Schild, R., Close, A. E. and Associates (eds.) 1993 *Egypt during the Last Interglacial: the Middle Paleolithic of Bir Tarfawi and Bir Sahara East*, New York: Plenum.

Wendorf, F., Schild, R., Close, A. E., Donahue, D. J., Jull, A. J. T., Zabel, T. H., Więckowska, H., Kobusiewicz, M., Issawi, B. and el Hadidi, N. 1984 New radiocarbon dates on the cereals from Wadi Kubbaniya, *Science* 225: 645–646.

Wendt, W. E. 1972 Preliminary report on an archaeological research programme in South West Africa, *Cimbebasia B* 2: 1–61.

1976 'Art mobilier' from the Apollo 11 Cave, South West Africa: Africa's oldest dated works of art, *South African Archaeological Bulletin* 31: 5–11.

Wengler, L. 2001 Settlements during the Middle Paleolithic of the Maghreb, in N. J. Conard (ed.), *Settlement dynamics of the Middle Palaeolithic and Middle Stone Age*, Tübingen: Kerns Verlag, pp. 65–89.

Wenke, R. J. 1999 *Patterns in prehistory: humankind's first three million years*, Oxford: Oxford University Press.

Westbury, W. and Sampson, C. G. 1993 'To strike the necessary fire': acquisition of guns by Seacow Valley Bushmen, *South African Archaeological Bulletin* 48: 26–31.

Westphal, E. O. J. 1963 The linguistic prehistory of southern Africa: Bush, Kwadi, Hottentot and Bantu linguistic relationships, *Africa* 33: 237–265.

Wetterstrom, W. 1993 Foraging and farming in Egypt: the transition from hunting and gathering to horticulture in the Nile valley, in T. Shaw, P. Sinclair, B. Andah and A. Okpoko (eds.), *The archaeology of Africa: food, metals and towns*, London: Routledge, pp. 165–226.

Wheeler, P. E. 1993 The influence of stature and body form on hominid energy and water budgets: a comparison of *Australopithecus* and early *Homo* physiques, *Journal of Human Evolution* 24: 13–28.

White, H. 1995 *The Kagga Kamma Bushmen*, Cape Town: University of Cape Town Press.

White, M. D. and Ashton, N. 2003 Culture in bonobos? Between-species and within-species variation in behaviour, *Current Anthropology* 44: 598–609.

White, M. J. 1998 On the significance of Acheulian biface variability in southern Britain, *Proceedings of the Prehistoric Society* 64: 15–44.

White, M. J. and Plunkett, S. J. 2004 *Miss Layard excavates: a Palaeolithic site at Foxhall Road, Ipswich*, Liverpool: Western Academic & Specialist Press.

White, T. D. 1986 Cutmarks on the Bodo cranium: a case of prehistoric defleshing, *American Journal of Physical Anthropology* 69: 503–550.

    2000 Melka Kontoure, in E. Delson, I. Tattersall, J. Vancouvering and A. Brooks (eds.), *Encyclopedia of human evolution and prehistory*, New York: Garland, pp. 406.

    2002 Earliest hominids, in W. C. Hartwig (ed.), *The primate fossil record*, Cambridge: Cambridge University Press, pp. 403–417.

    2006 Early hominid femora: the inside story, *Compte Rendus Palevol* 5: 99–108.

White, T. D., Asfaw, B., DeGusta, D., Gilbert, H., Richards, G. D., Suwa, G. and Clark Howell, F. 2003 Pleistocene *Homo sapiens* from Middle Awash, Ethiopia, *Nature* 432: 742–747.

Whitley, D. S. 1992 Shamanism and rock art in far western North America, *Cambridge Archaeological Journal* 2: 89–113.

Whitley, D. S. 2000 *The art of the shaman: rock art of California*, Salt Lake City: University of Utah Press.

Whiten, A. 1997 *Machiavellian intelligence II: extensions and evaluations*, Cambridge: Cambridge University Press.

Whiten, A., Goodall, J., McGrew, W. C., Nishidas, T., Reynolds, V., Sugiyama, Y., Tutin, C. E. G., Wrangham, R. W. and Boesch, C. 1999 Cultures in chimpanzees, *Nature* 399: 682–685.

Wiessner, P. 1983 Style and social information in Kalahari San projectile points, *American Antiquity* 48: 253–276.

Wildebeest Kuil 2006 Wildebeest Kuil rock art centre, http://www.wildebeestkuil.itgo.com/. Site accessed 12 July 2006.

Wilkie, D. S. and Curran, B. 1993 Historical trends in forager and farmer exchange in the Ituri rain forest of northeastern Zaïre, *Human Ecology* 21: 389–417.

Williams, F. L., Ackermann, R. R., and Leigh, S. R. 2007 Inferring Plio-Pleistocene southern African biochronology from facial affinities in *Parapapio* and other fossil papionins, *American Journal of Physical Anthropology* 132: 163–174.

Williams, M. A. J. and Adamson, D. A. 1980 Late Quaternary depositional history of the Blue and White Nile Rivers in Central Sudan, in M. A. J. Williams and H. Faure (eds.) *The Sahara and the Nile*, Rotterdam: A. A. Balkema, pp. 281–304.

Williamson, B. S. 1997 Down the microscope and beyond: microscopy and molecular studies of stone tool residues and bone samples from Rose Cottage Cave, *South African Journal of Science* 93: 458–464.

2005 Subsistence strategies in the Middle Stone Age at Sibudu Cave: the microscopic evidence from stone tool residues, in F. d'Errico and L. Backwell (eds.), *From tools to symbols: from early hominins to modern humans*, Johannesburg: Witwatersrand University Press, pp. 512–524.

Williamson, D., Taieb, M., Damnati, B., Icole, M. and Thouveny, N. 1993 Equatorial extension of the Younger Dryas event: rock magnetic evidence from Lake Magadi (Kenya), *Global and Planetary Change* 7: 235–242.

Willoughby, P. R. 1987 *Spheroids and battered stones in the African Early Stone Age*, Oxford: British Archaeological Reports International Series.

2007 *The evolution of modern humans in Africa: a comprehensive guide*, Walnut Creek: AltaMira Press.

Willoughby, P. R. and Sipe, C. G. 2002 Stone Age prehistory of the Songwe River valley, Lake Rukwa basin, southwestern Tanzania, *African Archaeological Review* 19: 203–221.

Wilmsen, E. N. 1989 *Land filled with flies: a political economy of the Kalahari*, Chicago: University of Chicago Press.

Wilmsen, E. N. and Denbow, J. R. 1990 Paradigmatic history of San-speaking peoples and current attempts at revision, *Current Anthropology* 31: 489–524.

Wilson, M. L. 1996 The late Holocene occupants of Die Kelders: hunter-gatherers or herders? *Southern African Field Archaeology* 5: 79–83.

WIMSA 2004 Department review: Working Group of Indigenous Minorities in Southern Africa, *Before Farming* [print version] 3: 332–338.

2006 Working Group for Indigenous Minorities of Southern Africa, http://www.san.org.za/. Site accessed 12 July 2006.

Winterhalder B. 1990. Open field, common pot: harvest variability and risk avoidance in agricultural and foraging societies, E. Cashdan (ed.) *Risk and uncertainty in tribal and peasant economies*, Boulder: Westview Press, pp. 67–87.

2001 The behavioral ecology of hunter-gatherers, in C. Panter-Brick, R. H. Layton and P. Rowley-Conwy (eds.), *Hunter-Gatherers: an interdisciplinary perspective*, Cambridge: Cambridge University Press, pp. 12–38.

Winton, V. 2005 An investigation of knapping-skill development in the manufacture of Palaeolithic handaxes, in V. Roux and B. Bril (eds.), *Stone knapping: the necessary conditions for a uniquely hominin behaviour*, Cambridge: McDonald Institute Monographs, pp. 109–116.

Wiseman, M. F. 1999 Kharga Oasis, prehistoric sites, in K. A. Bard (ed.), *Encyclopaedia of the archaeology of Ancient Egypt*, London: Routledge, pp. 408–411.

Wobst, H. M. 1978 The archaeo-ethnology of hunter-gatherers or the tyranny of the ethnographic record in archaeology, *American Antiquity* 43: 303–309.

1990 Afterword: minitime and megaspace in the Palaeolithic at 18 K and otherwise, in C. Gamble and O. Soffer (eds.), *The World at 18,000 BP, Volume 2, low latitudes,* London: Unwin Hyman, pp. 332–334.

Wolf, E. 1982 *Europe and the people without history*, Berkeley: University of California Press.

Wood, B. 2002 Hominid revelations from Chad, *Nature* 418: 133–135.

Wood, B. and Collard, M. 1999 The human genus, *Science* 284: 65–71.

Wood, B. and Strait, D. 2004 Patterns of resource use in early *Homo* and *Paranthropus*, *Journal of Human Evolution* 46: 119–162.

Woodburn, J. 1982 Egalitarian Societies, *Man* 17: 431–451.

1988 African hunter-gatherer social organization: is it best understood as a product of encapsulation? in T. Ingold, D. Riches and J. Woodburn (eds.), *Hunters and gatherers, 1: history, evolution and social change*, Oxford: Berg, pp. 31–64.

Woodward, A. S. 1921 A new cave man from Rhodesia, South Africa, *Nature* 108: 371–372.

Wrangham, R. W., Hones, J. H., Laden, G., Pilbeam, D. and Conklin-Brittain, N. 1999 The raw and the stolen: cooking and the ecology of human origins, *Current Anthropology* 40: 567–594.

Wright, J. B. 1971 *Bushman raiders of the Drakensberg 1840–1870*, Pietermaritz-burg: University of Natal Press.

Wright, R. V. S. 1972 Imitative learning of a flaked-tool technology – The case of an orang-utan, *Mankind* 8: 296–306.

Wrinn, P. J. and Rink, W. J. 2003 ESR dating of tooth enamel from Aterian levels at Mugharet el 'Aliya (Tangier, Morocco), *Journal of Archaeological Science* 30: 123–133.

Wurz, S. 1999 The Howiesons Poort backed artefacts from Klasies River: an argument for symbolic behaviour, *South African Archaeological Bulletin* 54: 38–50.

2002 Variability in the Middle Stone Age lithic sequence, 115,000–60,000 years ago at Klasies River, South Africa, *Journal of Archaeological Science* 29: 1001–1015.

Wynn, J. G. 2004 Influence of Plio-Pleistocene aridification on human evolution: evidence from paleosols of the Turkana Bain, Kenya, *American Journal of Physical Anthropology* 123: 106–118.

Wynn, T. 1989 *The evolution of spatial competence*, Chicago: University of Illinois Press.

1993 Two developments in the mind of early *Homo*, *Journal of Anthropological Archaeology* 12: 299–322.

1995 Handaxe enigmas, *World Archaeology* 27: 10–24.

# INDEX